PATRICIA HIGHSMITH'S
DIARIES AND NOTEBOOKS

The New York Years

Also by Patricia Highsmith

*Nothing That Meets the Eye: The Uncollected Stories
of Patricia Highsmith*

Small g: A Summer Idyll

The Selected Stories of Patricia Highsmith

Ripley Under Water

The Black House (stories)

Mermaids on the Golf Course (stories)

Found in the Street

Tales of Natural and Unnatural Catastrophes (stories)

People Who Knock on the Door

The Animal-Lover's Guide to Beastly Murder (stories)

Little Tales of Misogyny (stories)

The Boy Who Followed Ripley

Edith's Diary

Slowly, Slowly in the Wind (stories)

Ripley's Game

A Dog's Ransom

Ripley Under Ground

The Snail-Watcher and Other Stories

The Tremor of Forgery

Those Who Walk Away

Plotting and Writing Suspense Fiction (nonfiction)

A Suspension of Mercy

The Glass Cell

The Two Faces of January

The Cry of the Owl

This Sweet Sickness

A Game for the Living

Miranda the Panda Is on the Veranda (children's literature)

Deep Water

The Talented Mr. Ripley

The Blunderer

The Price of Salt (as Claire Morgan)

Strangers on a Train

PATRICIA HIGHSMITH'S DIARIES AND NOTEBOOKS

The New York Years

1941–1950

EDITED BY
ANNA VON PLANTA

WITH A FOREWORD BY
JOAN SCHENKAR

Liveright Publishing Corporation

A Division of W. W. Norton & Company
Celebrating a Century of Independent Publishing

page 429: Facsimile Lovers Chart. Swiss Literary Archives, Patricia Highsmith Papers, Bern.
Diogenes Verlag, Zurich.
pages 614–15: Facsimile Entry from Patricia Highsmith's Notebook 19, 8/11/50. Swiss Literary
Archives, Patricia Highsmith Papers, Bern. Photo: Simon Schmid / NB.

For information about permission to reproduce selections from this book, write to
Permissions, Liveright Publishing Corporation, a division of W. W. Norton & Company, Inc.,
500 Fifth Avenue, New York, NY 10110

For information about special discounts for bulk purchases, please contact
W. W. Norton Special Sales at specialsales@wwnorton.com or 800-233-4830

Manufacturing by Lakeside Book Company
Production manager: Anna Oler

ISBN 978-1-324-09294-0 pbk.

Liveright Publishing Corporation, 500 Fifth Avenue, New York, N.Y. 10110
www.wwnorton.com

W. W. Norton & Company Ltd., 15 Carlisle Street, London W1D 3BS

1 2 3 4 5 6 7 8 9 0

For

GLORIA KATE KINGSLEY SKATTEBOL

and

DANIEL KEEL

Would I were greedy as now forever,
Not for fortune, nor yet knowledge, and not for love—never,
A muscled horse obedient to ruthless master, art,
Exultantly racing till he break his heart.

—NOTEBOOK 12,
6/20/45

So I want to write. I must write. Because I am a swimmer
struggling in a flood, and by my writing I seek a stone to rest on.
And if my feet escape it, I go under.

—NOTEBOOK 5,
6/21/41

CONTENTS

INTRODUCTION: Patricia Highsmith's New York Years   xi

FOREWORD by Joan Schenkar:
Pat Highsmith's After-School Education: The International
Daisy Chain   xix

1921–1940: The Early Years   1

1941: College, Politics, and Heavenly Kisses, or: "I have a
   great destiny before me."   4

1942: College Graduation, or: "I'm smoking too much and
   life is generally confusing."   121

1943: Living Alone, Working Full-Time, or: "I am a
   genius. I hear it from all sides."   250

1944: Winter in Mexico, or: "I am lonely for a thousand
   things."   354

1945: Writing and Dating, or: "The world and its
   martinis are mine!"   392

1946: Looking for Love, or: "I can never be moderate in
   anything."   430

1947: Drafting *Strangers on a Train*, or: "One does not live
   forever, and one is young even a much
   shorter time."   461

1948: Yaddo Artist Colony, or: "If only I'd known how to write a book before I started!"   499

1949: A Book Deal and a Broken Engagement, or: "I will not be imprisoned so."   530

1950–January 1951: Drafting *The Price of Salt*, or: "Writing, of course, is a substitute for the life I cannot live, am unable to live."   570

Outro: 1951–1995: A Life Abroad   609

ACKNOWLEDGMENTS   616

A TIME LINE of Highsmith's Life and Works   619

A SAMPLE of Highsmith's Foreign-Language Notes   621

BIBLIOGRAPHY   624

FILMOGRAPHY   630

INDEX of Names and Works   632

INTRODUCTION

Patricia Highsmith's New York Years

TWENTY-YEAR-OLD PATRICIA HIGHSMITH is certain that she is destined for greatness. But which path to choose? She wants to, no, *needs* to write. But does she dare to attempt writing for a living? Will she be able to subsist on an artist's unreliable income? In any case, she definitely feels she must plunge headlong into life, in order to garner material for her writing.

Reading Patricia Highsmith's vibrant early accounts of her life can leave the reader breathless. How does she handle the sheer pace of it? How does she reconcile college or (later) a job, a jam-packed social life—and still find time to write? She certainly does not waste any time on sleep. Early on in her twenties, a pattern of two contradictory impulses emerges. There's the urge to lunge herself into excess—"The world and its martinis are mine!" (1/24/45)—partying, smoking, drinking, constantly falling in and out of love. And then there's the urge to retreat into "the still point of the turning world" (as in the title of one of her first short stories), which is essential for reflection and writing.

In addition to writing fiction, young Pat also starts setting down an almost continuous commentary on her life in her diaries and notebooks—almost five thousand small-formatted, densely hand-written pages for the years 1941 to 1950, a captivating self-portrait of a young artist trying to find her path in life as well as in the bustling city she calls home.

If the young Texan felt like an outsider in New York when she first came to the city as a child, or felt guilty and singled out as a gay teenager, in her twenties she makes the city her own. She falls in with a tightly knit circle of older, successful, international, mainly lesbian artists and journalists, many of whom have recently returned from Europe and the frontlines of World War II.* Reveling in their company during martini-fueled lunchbreaks, at gallery openings and private soirées, Pat for the first time feels among her own. And she is provided with positive role models: women living lives they've chosen for themselves, and, more importantly, women making their lives with other women. Her "Madison Avenue gang" and the women she encounters roaming the Village's bars and gay haunts provide her with the safe space from which to grow into the person she longs to be.

Thus encouraged, she hones her craft in her spare time, collecting ideas and observations, writing short stories, and starting on her first novel in late 1942 (one she later discards). She seeks acceptance, a sense of belonging—but she also feels (and is also told she is) special—a person with a calling: "I am a writer . . . I am an angel, a devil, a genius. . . . My eyes are on the stars and beyond" (February 9, 1950).

The city opens doors for her that exist nowhere else in the world. Just out of Barnard College, Pat lands a job as one of the few female writers in the comics industry in its Golden Age, allowing her to move to her own apartment at just twenty-two. Yet she resents the time spent away from her true calling, her own writing: "How can one be a prostitute in the day and a good lover at night?" (4/17/43). She is keen to get herself noticed by people with influence in magazine publishing. When *Harper's Bazaar*'s fiction editor Mary Louise Aswell buys her first short story and, along with Truman Capote, recommends her to the prestigious Yaddo artist retreat, Pat rejoices. It's at Yaddo, far from the city's many distractions and her con-

---

* For more about Pat's network of women, see Joan Schenkar's foreword in this book.

stant pecuniary concerns that she will finish her first, breakthrough novel, *Strangers on a Train*.

Pat's ambivalent relationship with New York, which at once inspires and exhausts her, is paralleled in her relationships: aloof and desired, a magnet to both men and women, she loves as she pleases and as many as she pleases ("three nights, three people!"—July 23, 1948). She jumps from one affair into the next, forever failing to find in a partner both lasting comfort, *and* lasting inspiration. Within her circles she may be able to live out her sexuality relatively freely, but even in bohemian Greenwich Village she can get denied entry into a location for lack of a male escort, or for wearing pants, and of course risks getting shamed or even jailed, particularly toward the end of the 1940s with the rise of McCarthyism. The "lavender scare" persecution of homosexuals, along with her own conservative upbringing, drive her into psychotherapy, where she confronts her identity: "I want to change my sex—is that possible?" Considering the chartered "normal life" of most other women at the time—getting married, settling down, having children—both repellent and desirable, she finds solace only in her next novel, *The Price of Salt*, where she invents "a substitute for the life I cannot live, am unable to live" (5/7/50) and in which two women in love may live happily ever after.

How do I want to live and love? And how am I going to write about it? In Highsmith's case, these questions will remain inexorably intertwined. Even in a city full of people who seek to be unapologetically themselves, she still does not feel like she's found her place—it's a search that will continue for the rest of her life.

EDITORIAL NOTE

During her lifetime, very little was known about Patricia Highsmith's personal life, least of all the early years. So when a row of eighteen diaries and thirty-eight notebooks, dating back as far as 1938, was discovered tucked in the back of her linen closet after her death, it was a literary sensation.

It seems clear that Patricia Highsmith had long planned to have her notebooks published. The uniformity of the Columbia spiral notebooks she used throughout suggests it, even more so the fact that she kept editing them, making comments, cuts, and date changes whenever rereading. Most importantly, there are written instructions. A slip of paper in Notebook 19 shows that Pat's college friend Gloria Kate Kingsley Skattebol had at first been enlisted to publish a selection. Pasted to the April 2, 1950, entry, it reads: "A note after rereading all my notebooks—rather glancing through all of them, for who could possibly read them?—(and Kingsley, have some taste, have at least the taste I have in 1950 in weeding out what is already written, and recently written)." At other times, the author considered burning the notebooks or leaving them to the Lesbian Herstory Archives in Brooklyn. In the end, Pat appointed Daniel Keel, the founder of the Swiss publishing house Diogenes and her longtime worldwide representative, the literary executor of her estate, so it fell to him to decide what the author would have wanted to happen with her journals.

Keel had taken over as Pat's German-language publisher in 1967, and after a while became a friend and trusted adviser. In 1983, the uncertainty of her publishing situation in the United States finally prompted her to transfer the international rights to her complete works to Diogenes. When Keel and Highsmith reviewed her papers together before her death, the diaries and notebooks were expressly listed as part of her literary estate alongside her remaining unpublished novels and uncollected short stories. Keel recognized the collection as a literary treasure that should be presented as a unified whole, a task he passed on to me as Patricia Highsmith's longtime editor.

I first met Pat in 1984, when Daniel Keel placed the manuscript for *Found in the Street* on my desk and informed me that he had arranged a meeting with the author at a nearby hotel for a few days later—and with that, I was her editor. Pat greeted me coolly, disregarding my extended hand. She then ordered a beer and fell silent. It took me half an hour to get a conversation going about the manuscript, which was set in modern-day New York, but struck me as the New York of the 1950s. By the end of our conversation, she even laughed. Back at the office, I told my boss about the initial awkwardness of our encounter. To my amazement, Keel congratulated me effusively on my success, explaining that it had taken him years to coax more than a yes-or-no answer out of her.

To make Patricia Highsmith's original diary and notebook entries accessible to a broader public in one volume was an immense challenge. First, the handwritten pages had to be transcribed, itself the work of years. Gloria Kate Kingsley Skattebol checked the transcripts against the handwritten, often cryptic originals and added some helpful annotations. Then the sheer amount of material necessitated a culling, to carve out the essence of this "behind-the-scenes" work. As the author herself recognized, it would have been a mistake to reproduce the diaries and notebooks word-for-word, riddled as they are with redundancies, chitchat, indiscretions, and gossip—especially in her twenties, her notes from that period being so much more extensive than in later years, when her journaling had developed its cohesive style. Our selection is based on Pat's own focal points.

While earlier notebook entries exist, we chose to begin the book with her first diary entry, written in 1941. From this point onward, Pat essentially maintained a double account of her life: whereas she used the diary to detail her intense, at times painful personal experiences, she used the notebook to process these experiences intellectually and muse on her writing. Pat's notebooks were workbooks, and a playground for her imagination. They contain style exercises, insights into art, writing, and painting, and what Pat liked to call *Keime* (a German term meaning "germs"), ideas and whole passages for potential short stories and novels. Her diaries help us better understand the notebooks; they arrange the notebook entries within what seems to be a truthful time frame and personal context. In our edition, diary and notebook entries are interwoven and interlocked, the diary entries dated in long form (month, day, year), the notebook entries in numerical form (with slashes), as was Pat's style. While the two formats can be read independently of each other, when read in tandem they help to gain a holistic understanding—in Pat's own words—of an author who concealed the personal sources of her material for her entire life, and whose novels are more likely to distract us from who she was, than lead us to her.

In contrast to the notebooks, which are written almost entirely in English, Pat composed her diary entries in up to five languages, describing her diaries as "exercise books in languages I do not know." There seem to have been various reasons for this. Of course, a language enthusiast and autodidact like Pat would want to acquire new languages, particularly given her aspiration to travel the world and cultivate her more urbane sensibilities. She was an ambitious student, eager to apply and practice what she was learning in her diaries, enjoying the new means of expression and perspectives on the world each new language offered her. There's much to suggest that the exercise also served to encrypt some of the more intimate details, protecting them against unwelcome prying eyes.

Besides English, the languages she used the most were French and German, frequently switching to Spanish before and during her first trip to Mexico in 1943/44 (and to Italian in the early 1950s). We provide several examples of her original entries before translation at the end of the book. Pat was self-taught in Spanish and Italian, and her different level of proficiency in the various languages explains the differences in style and the more restricted vocabulary of some of her entries. Foreign-language passages in the diaries have been translated into English but tagged with superscript lettering to indicate the original language: G/GG for German, F/FF for French, and SP/SPSP for Spanish. Commonplace foreign phrases are left as is.

The reader must bear in mind that what is printed in this volume represents a mere fraction of Patricia Highsmith's entire diary and notebook entries, approximately 20 percent of all of her entries written between 1941 and 1951. For instance, we have not included ideas Pat began developing for certain pieces, those that later found their way into her published stories or novels as well as others that were ultimately discarded. Because of the at times chaotic and repetitive style of Highsmith's early notes, it was often necessary to also make cuts within single entries. We debated whether to indicate omissions and ultimately decided against it, to avoid bothering the reader with continual ellipses. Pat's own omissions and minor oversights have been corrected, while details needed for comprehension have been added in brackets. More .extensive explanations, including information on names mentioned, were added in footnotes where available; in those cases where we knew no more about someone than what Pat herself wrote, we refrained from adding footnotes that could do no more than repeat her information. Pat encounters and writes about a multitude of people; those with more of a relevance will soon become familiar to the reader, while others might be mentioned a few times only.

We have reduced all private individuals mentioned in the text to their first names, unless they were already fully named and described in extenso by Highsmith's biographers. And this regardless of the fact that almost all of them, being of Highsmith's age or older, are now deceased. Conversely, recognizable public figures Pat introduces, but calls by their initials, are referred to by their full names in brackets, as necessary.

As these are Patricia Highsmith's private diaries and notebooks, her views on people and facts are of course personal and tinted by her personal biases and the biases of the times in which she wrote them—especially so as diaries or notebooks are typically a platform where one expresses thoughts impulsively, on a whim, not necessarily thought out. Pat was inconsistent and rough around the edges, and some of her disparaging remarks readers will find offensive. In the earlier entries, there is also an issue of language, when Pat uses expressions that were common at the time but have since come to be considered derogatory and offensive. The author herself was aware of this, as proven by her request to change the word "negro" to "black" for the 1990 new edition of *The Price of Salt*, titled *Carol*.

Frequently, however, it is not just Pat's language but her views themselves that are offensive, rancorous, and misanthropic. We aim to represent them faithfully. Only in a handful of more extreme instances did we feel it our editorial duty to deny Patricia Highsmith a stage for them, in the same way we did while she was still alive.

We also felt it important to do justice to the fact that due to aspects such as her feeling of being ostracized, her homosexuality, expressions of guilt and resentment are inextricably and fatally interwoven throughout her diaries and notebooks. The sources of her resentment are difficult to pinpoint, notably in the case of her anti-Semitism, which becomes even more of a mystery embedded as it is in a volume in which we learn about the importance for the author of the many Jews she counts among her close friends, lovers, and favorite artists.

The compilation presented here is not meant to be read as an autobiography. As in any self-portrait, the person we encounter in the diaries and notebooks is of course not necessarily the "real" Pat, but instead the person she considered—or wanted—herself to be. The act of remembrance is also one of interpretation. Many people are familiar with the somber, caustic face of Pat she presented to the world in later years, and her early notes will be their first encounter with the author as a cheerful young woman with an optimistic, ambitious eye on her future.

Anna von Planta
in close collaboration with Kati Hertzsch,
Marion Hertle, Marie Hesse, and
Friederike Kohl
ZURICH, 2022

FOREWORD

Pat Highsmith's After-School Education: The International Daisy Chain

by Joan Schenkar

✣

HOW PATRICIA HIGHSMITH got herself from West Texas Cow Country to the "pot of gold" at the end of her American Dream had a great deal to do with a sophisticated international society of gifted, prominent, willful women who were making their lives with other women. In the 1940s and beyond, their tendrils of influence curled around every corner of Pat's life and work.

And Pat was ready to meet them: an attractive, intermittently forward, highly talented college junior with brains, a photographic memory for women's telephone numbers, and two fixed directions for success: Uptown and Europe. Until she could be famous, however, Pat was settling for seductive friendships. And many people were interested.

The prelude to Pat's initial Summer of Social Success began when she coolly dropped her first relationship with an older woman, a woman she'd met in a bar the month before: the "interesting" Irish émigré Mary Sullivan, who ran the bookshop in the Waldorf Astoria Hotel. It was Mary Sullivan who took Pat to gay parties in the Village, where Pat, precocious as ever, was already a young guest at the regular gatherings of (mostly) women hosted by the great American photographer (and inventor) Berenice Abbott (1898–1991) and her lover, the art critic and historian Elizabeth McCausland (1899–1965), in their two flats and a hallway on the fourth floor of 50 Commerce Street.

It was at one of Abbott's parties with Mary Sullivan that Pat first spotted the expatriate German photographer Ruth Bernhard (1905–2006).* Ruth emigrated to New York in 1927, and her career as a commercial photographer was already detouring into the kind of high art that would lead Berenice Abbott to describe her as "the best photographer of the female nude." Ruth developed an intense friendship with Pat, an *amitié amoureuse*, which, like so many of Pat's friendships, briefly broke into something like love before Pat triangulated it with another of her fascinations, the gay male German photographer Rolf Tietgens (1911–1984). Ruth knew very well that Pat "had a lot of connections," a lot of "love affairs." "Pat," she said, "was a very attractive person, a wonderful-looking woman, and people were drawn to her." Ruth made a classically aspirational photographic portrait of Pat in 1948—a "thoughtful," dignified, enduring image of the twenty-seven-year-old writer facing her future. And she was certain she'd photographed Pat in the nude.

Fifteen years older than Pat, Ruth Bernhard continued to meet Pat for coffee and conversation and mutual comfort: They went to gallery openings together, they took subways to Harlem, and they were equally enthralled by the female flamenco performer and singer Carmen Amaya, who dressed as a man and took the "male" part in legendary flamenco performances with her sister.†

Three years before her death, Pat telescoped her unlikely social successes as a twenty-year-old in Manhattan "trying her luck"—a phrase she used repeatedly—by attaching it to the string of high-

---

* Ruth Bernard was the daughter of Lucian Bernhard (birth name Emil Kahn), Germany's most inventive graphic designer and typographer.
† Pat was sufficiently taken by Amaya to send Gregory Bullick, the artistic teenage boy who spies upon and enters the life of another, far wealthier boy in her first unpublished novel, *The Click of the Shutting*, to a Carmen Amaya performance at Carnegie Hall.

style coincidences that began with her introduction to Janet Flanner (1892–1978) in the summer of 1941 and to some "20 [other] interesting people all in a fortnight, many of whom I still know . . ."*

This necklace of sinuously linked introductions ushered in an after-school education for Pat the year before she graduated, jobless and embarrassed about it, from Barnard College in 1942; an education that was a direct result of the war-driven exodus from Europe to New York of a phalanx of older, accomplished, expatriate mostly lesbian women: a great international daisy chain of intelligence, professional success, abundant talent, wealth, and/or privilege and freedom.

Among these women, recently arrived to New York from Paris, were Janet Flanner (*The New Yorker* magazine's Paris correspondent since 1925) and the painter Buffie Johnson (who had been studying painting with Francis Picabia in Paris and living in the famous soprano Mary Garden's Paris house). Like their muchtraveled women friends, they had been guests (and Flanner was a regular guest) at Natalie Clifford Barney's (1876–1972) fabled salon† of late Friday afternoon literary readings, theatrical performances, and amuse-bouches at 20 rue Jacob and at Gertrude Stein's (1874–1946) curated displays of modernist art, literature, and temperament on Saturday nights at 27 rue de Fleurus.

Pat took many of these older women to heart, and she took some of them to bed. And in her cramped and costive handwriting she also took relentless notes on what they said and did.

---

* Pat in a letter to Bettina Berch, December 22, 1991.

† The Barney salon, during its sixty years in Paris as the twentieth century's most subversive literary gathering (despite its *haut bourgeois* trappings and genteel mise-en-scène), entertained not only all the great male modernist writers, but also recruited, attracted, and showcased all the female subverters of the modernist style. Among them: the hostess Natalie Clifford Barney herself; Renée Vivien; Colette; Élisabeth de Gramont, duchesse de Clermont-Tonnerre; Romaine Brooks; Isadora Duncan; Ida Rubinstein; Gertrude Stein; Alice B. Toklas; Lucie Delarue-Mardrus; Mercedes de Acosta; Janet Scudder; Sybille Bedford; Esther Murphy; Radclyffe Hall; Una, Lady Troubridge; Bettina Bergery; Djuna Barnes; Marie Laurencin; Mina Loy; Marguerite Yourcenar; Janet Flanner; Elisabeth Eyre de Lanux; and Dorothy Ierne Wilde.

Janet Flanner, the incomparable purveyor of Paris's *air du temps* to *New Yorker* readers in the United States for five decades, filed nearly seven hundred witty and incisive "Letters from Paris" under her nom de plume of Genêt. Over the years, Flanner and her principal lover, the editor and broadcaster Natalia Danesi Murray (1901–1994), invited Pat to their summerhouse in Cherry Grove, admired her writing in letters to each other, touted her work, and were generous with introductions, translations, and help with book contracts in Italy and France. It was likely through Flanner in Paris that Pat met the critic and novelist Germaine Beaumont (1890–1983), Colette's protégée (and more) and, like Flanner herself, a regular at Natalie Barney's salon. Beaumont was one of the first (and most intelligent) French critics to write favorably about Pat's work. And Janet Flanner was probably Pat's Paris introduction to the flamboyant, wealthy Cuban-American poet and memoirist Mercedes de Acosta (1892–1968), another frequenter of the Barney salon, who accommodated Pat with social introductions, dinner invitations, and her flat on the Quai Voltaire in Paris.*

But it was the well-connected, generous, and very social artist Buffie Johnson† (1912–2006) who was responsible for introducing Pat to her most intense and enduringly "useful" friendship—and to the decades-long cascade of professional, artistic, and emotional consequences that followed. Buffie, who met Pat at a party in 1941, found her (as everyone did that year) "terrifically attractive and sparkly and energetic." Pat, Buffie said, was "bold in her approach," "far from sweet," but "sure of what she wanted," and they quickly became lovers. Buffie, who knew everyone and went everywhere, offered Pat the use of her town house on East Fifty-Eighth Street and

---

* De Acosta's chief claim to fame, was, as Alice B. Toklas put it, that she'd "slept with three of the most important women in the 20th Century." Marlene Dietrich and Greta Garbo were two of them; Eva Le Gallienne and Isadora Duncan were candidates for the third.

† Buffie Johnson was the painter of the largest abstract expressionist mural ever commissioned in New York, for the old Astor Theatre; also the close friend of Carl Jung, Tennessee Williams, et al. A world traveler, and a proponent of feminist goddess history. She had just come from Paris, where, irritated by being consigned to a corner with Miss Toklas and the "wives" in Gertrude Stein's salon (while Stein spoke of important matters with the husbands), Buffie reached over and pinched Stein's bottom on her way out. It had, said Buffie, "the consistency of a solid block of mahogany."

continued to provide her with introductions to New Yorkers like the cult lyricist and wit John La Touche (Pat was more interested in La Touche's wife, a lesbian from a prominent banking and investment family), the painter Fernand Léger ("Simply wonderful," Pat enthused), the architect Frederick Kiesler, the heiress, art philanthropist, and gallerist Peggy Guggenheim (who exhibited Buffie's work and introduced Pat to Somerset Maugham),* and many other pivotal people to whom Buffie had access and to whom Pat, still just a junior at Barnard College but circulating socially with astounding assurance, did not.

And then, two weeks after she met Pat, Buffie was invited to the party of a friend whose husband was the editor-in-chief of *Fortune* magazine. Knowing this occasion might prove "fortuitous" for her new college girl lover, Buffie took Pat with her—and Pat, said Buffie, immediately occupied herself among the partygoers. In Buffie's version of the evening's events, Buffie looked up from a deep conversation with her friend, the room had emptied, and Pat—"without even saying goodnight"—had left the party with a group of Henry Luce's magazine editors.†

Among that group was Rosalind Constable (1907–1995), the sophisticated English arts journalist who would haunt Pat's diaries, notebooks, and emotional life for the next ten years. Rosalind had light blond hair, light cold eyes, a serious intellectual background, and a pronounced ability to spot trends in all the arts. Long employed at *Fortune*, she was greatly influential in the magazine publishing world that Pat was finding so attractive. Sybille Bedford (1911–2006), who met Pat late in the 1940s in Rome "when she was a little bit wild" (Bedford was as much a part of the international daisy chain as Rosalind), knew Constable very well. In her beau-

---

* In 1943, Guggenheim included Buffie Johnson in the notorious 31 Women show at her just-opened avant-garde gallery Art of This Century on West Fifty-Seventh Street. Djuna Barnes, Elisabeth Eyre De Lanux, Elsa von Freytag-Loringhoven, Gypsy Rose Lee, Dorothea Tanning, Leonor Fini, Frida Kahlo, Meret Oppenheim, and Louise Nevelson were among the other exhibitors. The painting Buffie contributed, entitled *Déjeuner sur Mer*, was a seascape with two women clinging to a wrecked ship.

† Pat had a different memory of the evening. She describes a party at which only four people were present, with no mention of an early departure by her or anyone else.

tifully etched memoir *Quicksands*, Bedford wrote that Constable was "a bright light of the *Life/Time* establishment, hard-working, hard-playing." Rosalind was hard-drinking, too, and fourteen years older than Pat. She edited the Luce Corporation's in-house newsletter, *Rosie's Bugle*, whose sole purpose was to alert all the other Luce editors to the cultural subjects about which they should be writing.

Pat telephoned Rosalind the day after they met and, vigorously pursued by Pat and affectionately indulged by Rosalind, a long, complex friendship was launched. Done with sleeping on the current Highsmith living room couch, Pat spent nights in Rosalind's guest bedroom. (Pat was always spending nights in her older women friends' guest rooms—and then sometimes ending up in their beds—or, in the case of her longtime, hardworking agent Margot Johnson, in bed with their lovers.) And Rosalind, who brought Pat everywhere, was certainly responsible for Pat's introduction to Mary Louise Aswell (1902–1984), the literary editor at *Harper's Bazaar*, who, along with Rosalind, recommended Pat to the art colony Yaddo in 1948 and published her superb story "The Heroine" (rejected by the Barnard College literary magazine as "too upsetting") in *Harper's*.* Rosalind and Pat's relationship continued to be alimented by long hand-holding walks and long alcoholic lunches, with Pat sometimes ending up in Rosalind's lap. It was the kind of courtly love story Pat preferred when she was young: the sensual pursuit of an older woman lightly masked by an artistic and professional mentoring. This one had all the intoxications of a love affair that would never be physically consummated.

Rosalind introduced Pat to her own influential lover, the painter and revolutionary gallerist Betty Parsons† (1900–1982), and Pat took to spending time in the Wakefield Gallery where Parsons held sway. Parsons requested a copy of Pat's essay "Will the Lesbian's

---

* And when Mrs. Aswell retired to New Mexico with her lover Agnes Sims, she and Pat would keep up with each other through lesbian circles far and wide.

† Betty Parsons's eponymous gallery, opened in 1946 at 15 East Fifty-Seventh Street as a locus for abstract expressionism, was the only gallery willing to represent artists like Jackson Pollock after Peggy Guggenheim closed Art of This Century in 1947. Parsons ran her gallery until her death in 1982.

Soul Rest in Peace?"—Pat seemed to think hers might not—and Pat invited Parsons to dinner to look at her drawings. Betty Parsons (as Rosalind Constable's lover) gave Pat yet another opportunity to be the third arm of a triangle.

And it was through Rosalind that Pat met the Ziegfeld Follies performer turned influential Broadway producer Peggy Fears (1903–1994), a close friend of Louise Brooks's, and whose three marriages to the wealthy producer A. C. Blumenthal never interfered with her relationships with women. She built the first yacht-club-cum-hotel on Fire Island, and Pat, "looking for adventure," began visiting her every day, and then dropping in on her late at night, making Rosalind jealous.

Like Buffie Johnson, Rosalind Constable was responsible for Pat's introduction to both "quality" and opportunity in her life in art. So it is fitting that it was at one of Rosalind's parties in 1944 that Pat first met Virginia Kent Catherwood (1915–1966), the beautiful, witty Main Line Philadelphia socialite and heiress who would become Pat's Muse for Life, and her lover for a turbulent year in 1946—in not just one, but two triangular love affairs with two other women,* and then in an unusually long and focused relationship: the four-year union in which Pat Highsmith siphoned, as directly as a blood donation, the life history and styles of speech of Ginnie Catherwood† (as well as the very best version of her love affair with Ginnie) into a novel unlike any other she would ever write again.

This was the novel Pat released in 1952 as *The Price of Salt*. She published it under a pseudonym, dedicated it to three people

---

* Natica Waterbury, another daughter of the American Patriciate, who flew her own plane and assisted Sylvia Beach at Shakespeare and Co. in Paris, was Ginnie's lover when she got together with Pat—who then fell in love with Ginnie. Sheila Ward, an heiress from the West Coast (guano was the unlikely source of her fortune) was the photographer who eventually lived with Ginnie in the Southwest, but not before she and Pat got together briefly while Pat and Ginnie were still involved. The triangle was always Pat's favorite geometry in love.
† Ginnie Catherwood's alcoholism was advanced enough to make Pat's own youthful capacity for alcohol look almost reasonable. It was very far from reasonable, but in the 1940s, when everyone drank in quantity, it would have taken a keener eye than the casually admiring (or coldly curious) ones turned toward Pat during all her Manhattan nights to see that her seductive behavior, heavy imbibing, rapid advances, and acute withdrawals were signals through the flames burning in her psyche.

whose names she made up, left the United States before the book was released, and refused to acknowledge her authorship for nearly forty years. But the extended metaphors through which Pat associates *The Price of Salt*'s two accomplished women and their life-changing love affair with an ice-cold world of violence and danger and harm is the true language of Highsmith Country.

And the high-powered, communally driven engine of the group of women friends and lovers Pat met in New York in the 1940s continued to turn its wheels of influence in every hidden corner of *The Price of Salt*'s creation. The steady hum of their exits from their marriages, their love affairs, their families, and their other social martyrdoms idles in the background of Pat's least characteristic (and most true-to-self) novel like the getaway car at a bank robbery.

PATRICIA HIGHSMITH'S
DIARIES AND NOTEBOOKS

The New York Years

1921–1940

The Early Years

𝕹

BORN AN ONLY CHILD in Fort Worth, Texas, in 1921, Mary Patricia Plangman (known as Pat) grew up as something of a loner. Her parents, Mary Coates and Jay Bernard Plangman, had divorced before she was born, and since her mother, an illustrator, was working, Pat spent the first years of her life in the care of her loving but strictly Calvinist grandmother, who ran a boardinghouse. In 1924, Mary Coates married photographer and graphic artist Stanley Highsmith, an intruder in Pat's eyes.

At age three Pat could read, and by age nine her favorite authors included Dickens, Dostoyevsky, and Conan Doyle. She pored over the illustrated anatomy reference her mother used for work and Karl Menninger's *The Human Mind*, a compendium of popular scientific studies of abnormal human behavior: "I can't think of anything more apt to set the imagination stirring, drafting, creating, than the idea—the fact—that anyone you walk past on the pavement may be a sadist, a compulsive thief, or even a murderer."*

The family of three moved to New York in 1927, but financial, emotional, and marital crises forced Pat to travel back and forth between her new home and her grandmother's boardinghouse. At

---

* Patricia Highsmith in a letter to Karl Menninger on April 8, 1989.

one point, she lived with her grandmother for fifteen months; it was "the saddest year of my life."* Pat felt abandoned by her mother, something she would never forgive, especially considering Mary had promised her daughter she would divorce Stanley. The month Pat spent at a girls' summer camp near West Point, New York, in 1933 didn't fix things, either. Pat sent daily letters home from camp, and two years later this correspondence appeared as an article in *Woman's World* magazine—Pat's first publication, for which she received twenty-five dollars. This was also the year she met her biological father for the first time; a graphic artist of German descent, he was one of the reasons she decided to learn German.

Upon returning to New York from Texas, Pat was enrolled at Julia Richman High School, a girls' school with eight thousand students, most of whom were Catholic or Jewish. During this time, new literary preferences began to crystallize: Edgar Allan Poe (with whom she shared a birthday) and Joseph Conrad. With regard to her own writing, Pat felt drawn to the themes of guilt, sin, and transgression. By the time Pat was just fifteen, she was filling thick composition books with literary sketches as well as observations of the people around her. She also penned her first short stories, some of which appeared in her school's literary magazine *Bluebird*. Pat was an intelligent, ambitious, and imaginative teenager, but, saddled with shame because of her secret same-sex inclinations, she came across to others as serious and withdrawn. Patterns of behavior emerged that would prove characteristic of her later romantic life; for instance, she experimented with her first (platonic) love triangle with two other women, including Judy Tuvim, who later rose to fame as the Tony- and Academy Award–winning actress and comedian Judy Holliday.

She also proved herself an incredibly diligent student, and in 1938 was accepted to Barnard College. As an undergraduate, she studied zoology, English, composition, Latin, ancient Greek, German, and logic. During her first semester, Pat began to earnestly dedicate herself to journaling. She started her first notebook, which

---

* Patricia Highsmith in a letter to Nini Wells on March 9, 1972.

she called a "*cahier*," with the words: "A lazy phantom-white figure of a girl dancing to a Tchaikovsky waltz."

Those early entries are a colorful mishmash of observations, comments on the books she was reading, thoughts on what she was learning in college, and ideas about economy in writing. At times she used the notebooks to record homework assignments or write short stories for her English professor Ethel Sturtevant, whom she revered, or try her hand at limericks and even sonnets at various stages of her first few crushes. Almost half of the entries are undated, and we have chosen to omit them in this volume, as they provide readers with little more than passing insight into the life of the young Patricia Highsmith.

1941

College, Politics, and Heavenly Kisses, or:
"I have a great destiny before me."

✣

THIS COLLECTION OPENS in 1941, when Patricia Highsmith introduces the first of her diaries—Diary 1a—to be kept in tandem with her notebooks. On April 14, 1941, she writes, "*Je suis fait[e] de deux appétits: l'amour et la pensée* [My appetite is twofold: I hunger for love and for thought]." How much experience is needed, she wonders, in order to write about it? To what extent does one side of this equation feed off the other? The boundaries between Pat's diaries and notebooks are correspondingly porous, and each makes frequent reference to the other. Overall, she fills a total of 450 pages that year, writing in English, French, and German. Pat typically records the day's events late at night or in the early hours of the next morning, before going to bed.

Her workload at Barnard College is demanding, with assignments piling up on top of her own ambitious reading list. She becomes active in the Young Communist League and the American Student Union; when the endless meetings become burdensome to her quicksilver temperament, Pat's political engagement wanes. Much more important to her is her appointment as editor-in-chief of the student literary journal *Barnard Quarterly*, to which she contributes some of her own short stories, including "The Legend of the Convent of St. Fotheringay," a short story that reads like a personal manifesto on religion, gender, and her vocation as a writer. It is about an orphan boy discovered by nuns, who disguise and raise him as a girl. The boy is convinced he's a genius, and at age thirteen blows up the convent in order to live as a man, without religion, and pursue what he believes is his destined path to greatness.

Between her various commitments and her writing, it is not surprising that her grades begin to suffer. By far the primary culprit behind her poor performance, however, is Pat's social life. The Highsmiths live in a one-bedroom apartment—with Pat sleeping on a pull-out couch in the living room— at 48 Grove Street, in the heart of Greenwich Village, and after her school day ends, Pat goes out exploring. Long known as a bohemian hub, the Village is thriving with the arrival of such European émigrés as Claude Lévi-Strauss, Erich Fromm, and Hannah Arendt. (Illustrious as many of them are, U.S. society is not welcoming its new citizens with open arms. There are strict quotas, and anti-Semitism is widespread, upperclass society being no exception.) It also boasts a vibrant nightlife— and a relatively open gay and lesbian presence, bars and clubs where women in trousers can come and go as they please, free to flaunt their affections. Of course, homosexual love is legally still a crime, and police harassment of gays and raids on the—often Mafia- "protected"—bars are common. But Pat, impressively unfazed for a twenty-year-old, spends whole nights partying up and down Mac-Dougal Street.

Through Mary Sullivan, who runs the bookshop at the Waldorf Astoria, the twenty-year-old college student gets to hang out with the likes of photographer Berenice Abbott or painter Buffie Johnson, who in turn introduces her to British journalist Rosalind Constable (right-hand woman to magazine magnate Henry Luce, founder of *Time* and *Life* magazines), then lover of artist and art dealer Betty Parsons. Pat is at least ten years younger than her new friends, and the strong influence they supposedly have on her becomes a constant source of conflict between her and her mother, who disapproves strongly of Pat's drinking and rarely going to bed at a sensible hour. Her parents decry her new lifestyle as too extreme and even threaten to stop paying her college tuition if she continues.

🖎

"The painfullest feeling is that of your own feebleness; ever as the English Milton says, to be weak is the true misery. And yet of your strength there is and can be no clear feeling, save by what you have prospered in, by what you have done. Between vague wavering capability and indubitable performance, what a difference!"*

And here is my diary, containing the body—

JANUARY 6, 1941
^FFirst day of school. + Snyder:† a play about a woman in which I was a man. Helen‡ was my girlfriend. It was very good. +§ Letter from Roger [F.]¶ this morning. He says he loves me! A bit young, right?? + Meeting at Elwyn's** tonight. Only 5 girls were present. We will make something of it! + Am now financial secretary of the ASU. I hope to God no one will find out! Mother is very hostile. Particularly because I am not feminine enough.^{FF}

1/6/41
One brazen, conceited, decadent, despicable, retrogressive thought for today: I lost myself in a groundless dream, of life in suspension, and third dimension, of my friends and their types—of persons and faces, nameless, only filling spaces— and each one was quite to be expected, where he was—and the

---

* Quote from Thomas Carlyle, *Sartor Resartus* (1835).
† Another Barnard girl who attended drama class with Pat.
‡ One of Pat's closest friends at Barnard.
§ Throughout her first diary, Pat regularly uses the "+" sign as a separator between different topics within one entry, a practice that peters out in her second diary in 1942.
¶ One of Pat's admirers.
** A fellow communist. Pat was active both in the Young Communist League (YCL) and the American Student Union (ASU).

picture—which we call "life" or "experience"—was complete—
and I saw myself—filling in exactly where I was expected—with
no one looking or acting precisely like me. And I liked myself
best of all this little group (which was by no means all the world)
and I thought how something would be direfully wanting if I
were not there.

JANUARY 7, 1941

[F]I read [Stalin's] *Foundations of Leninism*. Very important,
including the tactics.[FF]

JANUARY 9, 1941

[F]Read *Taming of the Shrew* last night. Mrs. Bailey[*] very late
and very charming. I want to do each lesson in the grammar
book so that I can ace the exam. + The "Legend of St. Fothering-
gay" will be published in the next issue [of *Barnard Quarterly*].
Georgia S.[†] said today that it's the best we've had in years!
Sturtevant[‡] didn't like my "Movie Date"[§] story from last year,
and she'll be editing the *Quarterly* review this month! + With
Arthur[¶] tonight. We will have a Mannerheim Line.[**] Mother
doesn't even want to set eyes on him! Arthur told me that Keller
read my "House on Morton St."[††] and didn't find it convincing.
It's what I was afraid of. That Keller would know that a college
girl had written it. Isn't it terrible.[FF]

JANUARY 10, 1941

[F]Violet here at 9:30. Mother asked her what she thought of
Communism—Violet hesitated: "All the young people are inter-

---

* Helen Bailey, lecturer in French at Barnard College.
† Fellow student, also on the *Quarterly* staff.
‡ Ethel Sturtevant, assistant professor of English at Barnard and Pat's creative writing
instructor.
§ "Movie Date" was published in the Winter 1940 issue of the *Barnard Quarterly*.
¶ Arthur R., fellow communist and Pat's admirer.
** The "Mannerheim Line" was a defensive fortification line meant to impede the advance of
the Red Army at the start of the Soviet-Finnish war in 1939.
†† An unpublished story of Pat's.

ested in Communism—it's good—it gives them something to do." (!) Like throw bombs! Right? + Too funny! Volley Ball practice. I would like to write a story like the "Legend" about this. The people are marvelous! + Helped Fanny B. with logic. She's not very bothered about her work. She wants to get married. "Ted," who will be a professor. Her mother has no money, and Fanny won't go to school next year. But she's perfectly happy!^FF

JANUARY 11, 1941

^F I bought tickets for Lenin's memorial celebration at Madison Square Garden* Monday night. Two for Arthur and myself. The Workers' Bookshop† was fun yesterday. Mother Bloor‡ was there, signing her book for the regulars. There was a line for Lenin tickets, and everyone was smiling, as if they were in a propaganda photo. + Bailey at 9. She said that she liked my story and laughed about Sturtevant's critique. Perhaps I won't like this story in a year—but right now, I'm not ashamed of it. + Va. [Virginia]§ called me at 7:30. I was very happy. Met her at Rocco's¶ at 9 with Jack, a gay boy, and Curtis and Jean, two gay girls. Went to Jumble Shop,** etc. Beers and martinis, and now I'm drunk. But Va. kissed me!! I kissed her two—three—four—five times in the women's restroom at Jumble—and even on the sidewalk!! The sidewalk! Jack is very sweet, and Va. would like to sleep with him—but first she would like to take a trip with me

---

* The seventeenth annual Lenin Memorial Meeting was held at Madison Square Garden on January 13, 1941. Earl Russell Browder, then general secretary of the Communist Party USA (CPUSA), gave a speech, "The Way Out of the Imperialist War."
† The Workers' Bookshop of the Communist Party USA on Thirteenth Street near University Place.
‡ Ella Reeve Bloor (1862–1951), American socialist leader, writer, and trade union organizer.
§ An on-and-off crush Pat has known since high school, usually refered to as Va.
¶ Italian restaurant at 181 Thompson Street in Greenwich Village.
** The Jumble Shop, a place where women felt comfortable going with other women, was one of Pat's favorite hangouts. It was originally opened by Frances Russell and Winifred Tucker on Eighth Street as an antiques shop in 1922, then was turned into a restaurant and expanded to 176 MacDougal Street. The proprietors hung paintings of their famous and obscure clientele on the walls; some of the patrons were Ford Madox Ford, Thomas Wolfe, Martha Graham, Arshile Gorky, Willem de Kooning, and Lee Krasner.

some weekend. She loves me. She will always love me. She told me so, and her actions confirm it.[FF]

JANUARY 12, 1941

[F]Big surprise! Mother and S. [Stanley] persuaded John and Grace° to come to the Lenin memorial tomorrow evening! First Stanley didn't even want mother to go, because someone might see her there! Then, when they said they would go, John became curious! + I read *Work of the Seventh Congress*[†] which helped me a lot. Also *Much Ado About Nothing* which is very good. Started [James Joyce's] *Finnegans Wake*.[FF]

JANUARY 13, 1941

[F]Oh—the kisses last night—they were sweet, they were heavenly! Oh, the fine point of seldom pleasure.[‡] Shakespeare, you were right! + A discussion with Latham.[§] She doesn't like my solution to the Spanish situation (in my play): "You had a perfect dramatic situation—and you served up this communist tripe!" (And I only wrote that the revolutionaries conquered the aristocrats!) She advised me to work ("Step on the gas—hard!") and tasked me to write another play. On top of all my work! + Browder very brilliant and convincing tonight. We sang the Internationale.[FF]

JANUARY 14, 1941

[F]Oh—James Joyce is dead. I heard the news yesterday morning. The *Herald Tribune* ran a wonderful obituary! Browder received a 20-minute ovation. 20,000 present etc. David Elwyn says it's because they hate Roosevelt! + Worked on the play. Finished the second draft of the first act. B.B.[¶] likes my play and the stories

---

* Patricia Highsmith's uncle and aunt. John Coates was one of Mary Highsmith's brothers; Grace was his wife.
† The Seventh Comintern was held in Moscow in 1935.
‡ Quote from Shakespeare's Sonnet 52.
§ Professor Minor White Latham, associate professor of English.
¶ Babs B., high school friend of Pat's and fellow communist.

too, and her opinion's worth more than that of the whole school!
+ Ludwig Bemelmans* has a new book out: *A Donkey Inside*.
Brilliant, like all his books. I wonder whether he'll read my story
in *Quarterly*.[FF]

JANUARY 15, 1941
[F]I wanted to begin *Anna Karenina*, but a new book, *The Soviet
Power* [by Hewlett Johnson], is sitting on my table, nice and
neat: how can one read *Anna Karenina* in times like these?!—
Oh I'm dreaming! I'd like to travel to Russia with [Babs] B.
These days will never come again. I'm exactly like a person in
1917 in America. What should one have read? Nothing except
for stuff about the war. Everything else is an escape.[FF]

JANUARY 16, 1941
[F]I am happy—so happy! For many reasons! First of all, Sturtevant liked my story ("Alena").[†] And I finished my play tonight.
Mother likes it and says it's less cold than the other plays and
stories I've written. + Letter from Jeannot,[‡] November 24. He
had just received my letter from September 17! He was listening
to Artie Shaw[§] in Boston during the bombing!
    + My grandmother sent me two dollars for my birthday.[FF]

JANUARY 17, 1941
[F]There will be a party Saturday night when I was supposed to
see Ernst![¶] Poor Ernst! + [Marijann] K.[**] seems to like me a lot.
As well as the others in her class—to say the least. If only she
liked me more! My play is good. I won't be embarrassed to show

---

* Ludwig Bemelmans, Austrian-born American writer and illustrator of children's books.
† This story has been lost.
‡ Jean "Jeannot" David, young French cartoon artist from Marseille and Mary Highsmith's
pen pal.
§ Artie Shaw (1910–2004), American jazz clarinetist and prominent swing band leader in the
late 1930s.
¶ Ernst Hauser (later Ernest O. Hauser), photojournalist and postwar correspondent for the
Saturday Evening Post. Author of *Shanghai: City for Sale* and *Italy: A Cultural Guide*. Pat
first met him on a boat to Texas after she graduated from high school.
** Marijann K. is a fellow student.

it to anyone: B. or Judy* or Latham! + The book [*The Soviet Power*] by the Dean of Canterbury. Mostly a compilation of Russian growth statistics. Will be very influential—important. I would like grandmother to see the light before her death. + With John and Grace and parents at the Vanguard[†] at 10. Judy was there but I didn't bring her to our table, for which mother chastised me severely. I like Judy. (Eddy[‡] is a communist, and also a member of the police!)[FF]

JANUARY 18, 1941

[F]Mother and I went shopping. Finally a dress for me—very pretty—as well as a jacket and a gray skirt. + I made no progress on my work at all. This morning, John sent me a review of an anticommunist book. By a deserter, like all the deserters the newspapers like to feature. + Hilda's tonight. The regulars were there—but also Mary H. and Ruth. She is charming! A real person. Today was important because I met her. Mary H. told Ruth that I was the most intelligent person of the whole lot and I received many invitations from proper and polite people. I would like to tell mother about it, but I will only tell her about Mary H., and perhaps not everything.[FF]

JANUARY 19, 1941

[F]I'm twenty years old! It's terrific! Presents after breakfast. Just as many as Christmas. A polaroid lamp. And a triangular cushion for studying. + I was supposed to eat with Ernst tonight, but I had to study. Cocktails at the Fifth Ave H.[§] at 5 with John and Grace. Then champagne for Mother and myself. Very good.[FF]

---

* Judy Tuvim, Pat's classmate at Julia Richman High School. She will go on to become the celebrated movie star Judy Holliday.
† The Village Vanguard is a jazz club at 178 Seventh Avenue South in Greenwich Village. Beyond jazz performances by the likes of Thelonious Monk, Dizzy Gillespie, Miles Davis, and Art Blakey, the venue hosted poetry readings, stand-up routines, and concerts.
‡ From Pat's notes, Eddy seems to have been a lover of Judy's.
§ The Fifth Avenue Hotel, located at 24 Fifth Avenue on the corner of Ninth Street.

JANUARY 20, 1941

[F]David Jeannot sent me a radiogram yesterday. Happy Birthday![FF] + [G]It occurred to me yesterday that although England doesn't need more men now, if they start fighting in France, then they'll call for the U.S. Army.[GGF] Am exhausted by Shakespeare! There's so much I don't know! + Days without any creative work are lost days. An artist, a real artist, would work.[FF]

JANUARY 21, 1941

[F]Sweet are the moments in which I am not thinking of Shakespeare! I am thinking of Mary H., or of evenings in the wonderful future, or of the years ahead of me, of the people I will meet. + [William Saroyan's] *My Name Is Aram* and [Willa Cather's] *Sapphira [and] the Slave Girl*—articles—Shakespeare all day. Now I never want to read Shakespeare again![FF]

JANUARY 23, 1941

[F]A letter from R.R.[*] Haven't read it yet. He bores me. + I thought of the entire plot for an important, but simple short story that I would like to write soon. It's in my body like an unborn child. + Oh my God! The most important! I have the highest average in my Greek class! Hirst[†] announced it herself! It's a shame that I'm not writing in my journal enough. During the summer, I wrote in it every day. When one is at one's leisure, thoughts flow like beautiful water.[FF]

JANUARY 25, 1941

[F]Catastrophe! Latham gave me a C+! I don't understand. I would honestly have preferred an F to a C+! At least that's a distinction. It's terrible—worse than standing entirely naked in front of the school! Bad afternoon because of this grade. Virginia called me. Wanted to spend the evening with me and told me she loved

---

* Roger R., a longtime admirer of Pat's.
† Professor Gertrude Hirst, who taught classics at Barnard from 1903 to 1941.

me. We're going skiing next week. + With Peter° at Jumble at 7.
Three drinks for me. (Three too many.) Peter is very intelligent.
Knows everything about people quickly. And knows her Shake-
speare, dance, etc. But produces nothing. She's four years older
than me. I think I will be as mature as her in four years' time.
More mature, I hope.ᶠᶠ

JANUARY 27, 1941
ᶠThis was the first day I played piano with a certain amount of
confidence. It was encouraging. + I wonder whether I would
have done better if I hadn't read so much contemporary literature, if I'd read plays for Latham instead? Two reasons Latham
gave me a C: 1. Didn't like a play that portrayed the South unfa-
vorably. 2. Thinks I'm a communist. 3. Because I came with high
recommendations. Marijann K.—what will she say?! Oh my
God!ᶠᶠ

JANUARY 29, 1941
ᶠFrench exam this morning. It was difficult and I think I got all
the questions I guessed wrong. It's awful! I'm hoping for a B
now. I spoke to Latham, who was very friendly. Told me that
my play was very good and that it will take me a while, that it's
precisely because I have written so many stories that I'm having
trouble with the theater. Etc. But I'll keep going. + With Ernst
tonight. Champagne and dinner at the Jumble Shop. + Called
up M. H. (Ruth). She told me that Mary was observing us last
Saturday, and that she would like to paint us together. We'd
make a good contrast, she thinks. I'd be honored.ᶠᶠ

JANUARY 30, 1941
ᶠVery sick. It's the exams, no doubt. I worked very hard, and
today is my first day off. Every bone hurts. + My illness—today
and yesterday—gave me a bit of that unreal sensation that

* Another girl from her circle of Barnard friends, which also included Helen, Babs P., and
Deborah or Debbie B.

Proust was so familiar with. I wrote one or two paragraphs just as I liked. It's different—fluid, without any ambition, just for itself. One is happy when one looks at the time and two hours have gone by, as if there is an established time at which one will be in good health again. Did Proust say that already? Probably. But that's how I felt today.[FF]

1/30/41

From first acquaintance I had never liked my stepfather. I was about four when I met him, and I had already been reading for more than a year. I remember it was a book of fairy tales I had that day. "What's that word?" said my stepfather indicating with a long, crooked, hairy forefinger the most magical phrase I knew.

"Open See-same!" I cried.

"Sess-a-mi!" replied my stepfather with didactic peremptoriness.

"Sess-a-mi," I echoed weakly.

My stepfather smiled indulgently down upon me, his red heavy lips tight together and spread wide below his black moustache. And I knew he was right, and I hated him because he was right like grown-up people always were, always, right, and because he had forever destroyed my enchanting "Open See-same," and because now the new phrase would have no meaning to me, had destroyed my picture, had become strange, unfriendly and unknown.

JANUARY 31, 1941

[F]Much better but still sick. I read [George Bernard Shaw's] *Apple Cart*, [Paul Vincent Carroll's] *Shadow and Substance*, and a theater book. I'm diving into theater! I will be good, good, good!!! I will be feared! + I bought *Italian Concerto* with Wanda Landowska.[*] Mother is waiting to get it. She's somewhat annoyed. No

---

[*] A recording of J. S. Bach's *Italian Concerto* by famous Polish harpsichordist and pianist Wanda Landowska (1879–1959).

surprises why. She told me that S. sometimes says the most horrible things in an evening. Most of it is just moods, but so strange that she wonders if he isn't an entirely different species to us.[FF]

FEBRUARY 1, 1941

[F]Bought white socks (for men!), which are long enough—at last. Well, below my knees I am now dressed like a man. (It doesn't bother me.) + Grandfather is sick: a kidney disease. They have to get emptied with a tube, sometimes he can't do it by himself. It's difficult.[FF]

FEBRUARY 2, 1941

[F][Mary] H. at 11. They were still in bed and quickly got up when I rang the doorbell. Mary (I wish she was called something other than "Mary!") is charming to watch. She made a good beginning. In charcoal. Large canvas. We are life size, I with my hands in front of my body, Ruthie reading MSS. [manuscripts] to the left. We are seated. Mary is very intense when she works. She forgets about everything else. We will sit again Saturday or Sunday. Unfortunately, I'm in a jacket and shirt, and my posture is very masculine. What will mother say when she sees it? Something, I'm sure of it![FF]

FEBRUARY 3, 1941

[F]I got an A in French. And there were only two A's in the class. I'm very happy about the beginning of this new semester. Still full of hope for my writing. I have lots of ideas! At 20, I feel a bit guilty. So much time has gone by, and I've done so little.[FF]

FEBRUARY 5, 1941

[F]Sturtevant for French. Like the picture of a woman in a cookbook. Oh—Mrs. Bailey—! how inspiring she was! But this woman! She's just like my grandmother! *Quarterly* will be a lot of work. Rita R.[*] is in the infirmary. Georgia S. and I went

---

[*] Rita R. was also on the editorial board of the *Barnard Quarterly*.

to see her at 5. I brought her flowers. I like Georgia S. Would like her to invite me over. (She lives alone.) She told me that she writes homosexual stories only to get As from Sturtevant! I read [Eugene O'Neill's] *Emperor Jones.*[FF]

FEBRUARY 6, 1941

[F]Oh joy of joys! I can move to Mrs. Bailey's class! Miriam G. is in it, but at least we both got A's. I couldn't have sat in the same room as her if I'd gotten less than her! + I finished *Pointed Roofs* by [Dorothy Miller] Richardson. These books can only have been written by women. They bore me. They are very "cheery," active, like women when they visit one another. + [Katherine] Mansfield and [Virginia] Woolf are the same.[FF]

FEBRUARY 7, 1941

[F]What a surprise! Brewster gave me a B—in the exam! Mari-jann K. got a C and bought sodas at Tilson's for all her friends! Logic grades still in the pits. + I saw Helen walking in the rain. "Would you like to play in a love scene with me?" "I'd love to!"—but I wanted to say *for* me. I have often thought of H.M. recently. I wonder if I'm falling in love with her. It could be worse! She's a ravishing woman. I began [Pat Sloan's] *Russia without Illusions* and a biography of Samuel Butler. He was a homosexual, Ruth L. told me.[FF]

FEBRUARY 12, 1941

[F]Bailey published a letter in *Barnard Bulletin* which demands that girls who go to political conventions as delegates without official permission be called "observers." Doris B. probably reported us to the authorities! + I sent "The Heroine"* to *Diogenes*,† like Ruth suggested.[FF]

---

* "The Heroine" was published by *Harper's Bazaar* in 1945 and included in *O. Henry Prize Stories 1946.*
† American literary magazine.

2/12/41

When I start buying clothes with generous hems; when I can tell at a glance the defects of a (potential? no) apartment; when I stop eating something I like when I think I've eaten all I should; when I don't fall in love with someone because I don't think they're quite good enough; when I start going to bed at an hour when I can do my best work the next day; when I start saying the anti-liberals have a bit of a side too; when I can think of you without desire, without hope and without longing—then I shall know I am getting old. That I am old.

FEBRUARY 13, 1941

[F]I brought *Quarterly* to the printer's at 4. Marie T. helped me a little. She draws very badly—honestly! I could do better! Perhaps I will draw from now on. + Time is moving too fast for me. There are stories, my sculpture, my friends, my books, my dates, my thoughts, projects—projects! It would be no better if I were a Christian Scientist!* I'm sure of it. Otherwise I would be.[FF]

FEBRUARY 14, 1941

[F]Coryl's at 8 for League meeting. There was an extraordinary girl: Marcella, whom Babs B. told me about. She is marvelously beautiful when she speaks. I could fall in love with her just by looking at her! + I bought a small bottle of bath foam for mother's valentine.[FF]

FEBRUARY 15, 1941

[F]Mary has only painted my hand. But R.'s head was finished on Wednesday, very meager—the whole painting is meager—too much blue in the figures now.[FF]

FEBRUARY 17, 1941

[F]I should be more creative, more original at this age. I tremble to think that I am 20 years old. Nothing! Except for confused emo-

---

* Christian Science is a set of beliefs originating with founder Mary Baker Eddy (1821–1910), its most popular idea being that praying can cure diseases. Pat's mother was an adherent.

tions. I'm not even in love! I have to finish the ideas I've already had. Then the others will come like a rushing river.[FF]

2/17/41

I am no longer satisfied with mere "plot" and excitement stories either as I used to be. I've become more thoughtful about what I write, and the result is I'm writing less. Tending more towards the longer thing—the novel—too. I find it hard to see real "worth" in even the best short stories now. Don't know what I'm coming to.

FEBRUARY 19, 1941

[F]Things are improving. + Madeleine Bemelmans[*] spoke to me in class and seemed very friendly. Told me that Ludwig reads his books in bed, laughing loudly! She brought me home (by car). Madeleine told me she thinks her marriage was not the best idea—at least for her. But I think she's told this to a lot of people at school. She talks too much, really. Perhaps she'll invite me to have a drink at their place sometime.[FF]

FEBRUARY 20, 1941

[F]Went to school this evening to help Rita R. with *Quarterly*. Rita R. and I are both brimming with confidence. Rita R. told me that everyone thought I was independent and sure of myself when I was a freshman. It's funny to hear because I wasn't in the slightest. Then I completely changed, she said. Also that I'm the only person who can be editor-in-chief next year. + I read a bit of Thomas Wolfe[†] this morning. It changed my whole day.[FF]

FEBRUARY 21, 1941

[F]I saw Mrs. B. for a moment, without speaking to her, from a distance—I could easily fall in love with her, I think. (N.B.

---

[*] Madeleine Freund, Barnard '41 student. Married to Ludwig Bemelmans.
[†] Thomas Clayton Wolfe (1900–1938), American novelist considered one of the greatest voices of his generation. Pat will keep rereading him frequently over the years.

Mother said yesterday that Bernard P. [Plangman] once said that he had no need for a woman. I wonder if I'm like that? Time will tell.)[FF]

FEBRUARY 22, 1941

[F]Mary and Ruth came by to drink daiquiris. Mary looked at the whole apartment. Mother observed her carefully, but she told me that she would never have known she was gay. Mother liked Mary and Ruth. We drank a lot, played records, danced. Ruth is the better dancer. But at dinner, she said, out of the blue: "You don't like me, do you, Pat?" I have the unfortunate habit of letting people know too easily—must eliminate it.[FF]

2/22/41

I want to set down my choicest item in worldly revelations: The thrill, the unspeakably blissful sensation of being loved. To love unrequited is a privilege. To dream and to hope a joy that heaven could hardly match—but then—to know oneself loved, to hear it from another's lips—this is heaven indeed. (Or if it's not heaven, you say, go take your old heaven and be damned!)

FEBRUARY 24, 1941

[F]I canceled my date with Ernst. Went to Judy's at 9. Va. called me up beforehand and told me she was a bit sick—it was disappointing. I wanted to see her. Helen, Paula, Ruth, Mary and Ruth, Eddy, Saul B. Everyone a bit drunk. Judy was very attractive. Mary talks too much. We know it. And she's a bit of an old goose. But we love her anyway. + I desire Va. tremendously—there is no one as beautiful as she! I wrote her a short letter. We need to get along better.[FF]

2/24/41

What each of us mainly wants is flattery, appreciation—or at the very least—quick acceptance. But for whatever else we seek. We should listen to our own counsel. All we can depend on—all the wonder and value and beauty and love and faith and genius—

pleasure and sorrow, hope, passion, understanding—all these are within us, in our own hearts, and minds. And nowhere else.

2/24/41

We must think of ourselves as a fertile land on which to draw. And if we do not, we grow rotten, like an unmilked cow. And if we leave something unexploited it dies within us wasted. But to tax one's powers always at their maximum potentiality—this is the only way to live at all, in the proper sense of the word.

FEBRUARY 25, 1941

[F]Helen received a photograph of Jo Carstairs[*] from Enid F. How these girls beat about the bush! They are both as ripe as apples on a tree ready to be plucked—but not by me! + I spoke to Nina D.[†] about lowering my involvement. I have to do it. Even two nights a week are a big part of my life. + S. Butler's notebooks are charming. And quite stupid, just like mine sometimes.[FF]

2/26/41

The other night at J.'s, when I was very lonely and dull myself too, I was standing by the piano when P. & J. were playing. P. was doping out the base and she turned to me and said, "Is that right?—Is that right, Pat?" It was such a wonderful thing to hear her say my name. To have heard anyone say it at such a time. I cannot express in such short space all that this small thing held in warmth and *Menschlichkeit*[‡] for me.

FEBRUARY 27, 1941

[F]I heard Elmer Rice[§] speak at the theater. He criticized American theater mercilessly, as well as our spirit. He spoke as if he were at a Communist assembly! It was marvelous! + With Va. tonight.

---

* Marion Barbara ("Joe") Carstairs (1900–1993), a wealthy and openly lesbian British heiress and powerboat racer.
† Nina D. is one of the YCL girls.
‡ Humaneness.
§ Elmer Rice (1892–1967), Pulitzer Prize–winning American playwright.

We saw *Philadelphia Story.** The movies don't amuse me anymore. After that, beers at our favorite café. Now she's going to
Caravan† on MacDougal St. where the best gays go. She's looking for a woman older than me. But she loves me more than any
person she meets. I know it, and she told me: we'll go somewhere
by accident and discover each other again. Leave it to me!^{FF}

FEBRUARY 28, 1941
^FI sold a *Soviet Power* to Frances B. I can only bring them to
school when I'm certain someone will buy them.^{FF}

2/28/41
It's important to keep the serious side underlying all our course
of life: but it is equally important to temper this with the lighter
side. Without it we have sterility and a lack of imagination and
progress. On the other hand, completely serious people are so
ludicrous that I wonder is not this attitude, in the last analysis,
the lightest side. And accordingly, the lightest-minded people—
who have a good fundamental intelligence—are the most
serious, philosophic and thoughtful. It takes observation and
judgment and independence to laugh at things which should be
laughed at. However, I shall always keep the heavier side in the
more influential position, because basically that is how I am. I
do not have to think about it, and it would do me no good if I
did. This seems to me important and rather well-observed now.
Shall see later. I wonder if ever I shall edit and file all these notes,
as Samuel Butler did? And years hence, when I do, refer back to
these adolescent contributions.

MARCH 1, 1941
^FGood day! A good day! I spent the morning writing and fin-
ished the Morton St. story. It's completely different now. They

---

* A 1939 play by Philip Barry.
† Bar and nightclub in Greenwich Village.

like it at school. + I often think of Madeleine. I wonder whether I can invite her to go riding on Thursday. Dude Ranch on 98 St.

Began *Wolf Solent* by [John Cowper] Powys. The book belongs to Mary H. They have lots of books I'd like to borrow. + Oh, how I would like to go to the country with Madeleine [Bemelmans]! If she doesn't take me home on Monday, I'll be miserable! + Lots of projects in my head!FF

MARCH 2, 1941

FThis was my last day. My part of the painting is done. I don't like the skirt. Ruth came out of the bathroom in her négligée— only her panties!—and wanted to make cocktails, just like that. She got upset at Mary when she suggested putting some clothes on! Quite an interesting discussion alone with Ruth. If one should stay with someone one loves, if he (or she) has had, or is having, an affair with someone else. I would leave. Ruth would stay. A situation like this would destroy my love, I have no doubt. + I have lots of fun ideas—fragmentary ideas, but good ones. I am happy with this. + My play will be performed tomorrow. Oh, my poor heart! I'm full of energy. Would like to do something marvelous—physical or mental. + Good night! Good night, Madeleine! How beautiful you are!FF

MARCH 3, 1941

FA good day. But I received 89 on my Greek exam. That's bad! + Madeleine doesn't talk enough. I wonder what my next move should be. I always feel stronger in the spring—and full of energy, ambition. Love, without doubt, this spring. Who? Someone new. H.M. or—I don't know. Madeleine! Yes. + I wonder how this feeling of energy, hope will be as time passes—as life diminishes. The sensation is so strong and beautiful right now.FF

3/3/41

I can think of no great writers or thinkers or inventors who were notorious sots. Poe, of course. But the rosy haze of drunkenness is singularly unproductive—seemingly fertile at first—but

put your ideas into concrete practice and they vanish like a soap
bubble.

MARCH 4, 1941

ᶠThe girls in my play didn't want to stay on stage after 11:00.
They behaved very badly. I'd like to cut a few throats! I like
[Jean Sarment's] *Le pêcheur d'ombres* a lot. + My Morton story
is only 6 pages long. It's good. I'm proud of it. + Rose M. asked
me to come to the ASU office tonight. I simply don't have the
time. + Ernst called me at 10:30. He was opening a bottle of
Haig & Haig with Fauge and his girlfriend. I don't understand
his love of drink—or at least of scotch. Champagne, yes.ᶠᶠ

MARCH 5, 1941

ᶠSkipped French to rehearse my play. It was a flop! I don't mind.
The soldier was vague. The communist talked too much. I didn't
notice any of this when I saw it once in rehearsal. + I acted in a
play with Helen. How I could love her! And vice versa, perhaps.
I'll try. + Madeleine wasn't there. All the better! + Meeting
tonight at Flora's. Coryl criticized me because my report wasn't
detailed enough. She's right. She's very militaristic. It's for the
best. I was lazy. Will do better next time.ᶠᶠ

3/5/41

It has become a platitude that an artist's life should be hard,
should be blood and sweat, tears and disappointment, struggle
and exhaustion. This fight, I believe, should be in his attitude
towards the world: his difficulty lies always in keeping himself
apart, intellectually and creatively, maintaining his own identity at the same time he identifies himself with society. But in
his own work, there should be none of this pain. He creates a
thing because he has mastered it and is familiar with it. He produces it easily, having once taken his idea in his bosom. A great
struggle in composition is apparent in his work, and shows it
to be an artificial, foreign, and most of all, a feeble and unsure
thing. Great work has come easily: I do not mean fluently, but

easily, from this sense of mastery, and has been later if necessary polished and changed at leisure, and cheerfully.

3/5/41

I don't know whether I add more items to this notebook when I go out with people or when I stay home alone. Sometimes society is stimulating, sometimes it is stupefying. I'm very happy whenever I have something good on the nights when I've been with people, and I feel rotten on the nights when I've been alone and produce nothing. But I can't say on which nights I feel most fertile.

MARCH 6, 1941

[F]I bumped into Marijann K. while going to school and we sang Alouette[*] while running to Shakespeare. It's unimportant, but I'm writing it down because it won't happen again in a few years. Even when the proletarian revolution comes. I'm angry when I do nothing important in a day. I could at least sit in a chair and think. + Went to the Finnish Hall[†] tonight. YCL. We played "Mannerheim Line" in the stairwell. Such noise![FF]

MARCH 7, 1941

[F]What a day! First a Greek exam (went well!) in which I laughed a lot about nothing! + At the last minute, I wrote a paper for Le Duc.[‡] They say Mrs. Bailey's husband has gone mad. + I began my short story about the school.[§] Three judges tonight. Very good! + Then Peter and Helen, very drunk. Helen made a lot of passes at me. We went to Caravan. I danced with Helen and we held hands under the table. Curtis noticed us and made us come to her table. Very impressed with Helen: naturally, she thought

---

* "Alouette" is a French children's song.

† A meeting place for immigrants from Finland at 13 West 126th Street that the YCL sometimes used for their meetings.

‡ Alma LeDuc, assistant professor of French at Barnard College.

§ In reference to Pat's story "Miss Juste and the Green Rompers," published in the *Barnard Quarterly*, Spring 1941; also in *Nothing That Meets the Eye: The Uncollected Stories of Patricia Highsmith* (New York, 2002).

she was my girlfriend. Curtis told me that I'm "cute." "It's the company," I said. Curtis will tell Va. That'll be something! Debbie B. very severe, ended the night early. Helen's sleeping there. Oh my God, how she would like to be in my arms tonight. Curtis asked me if I get any studying done at school with Helen there! We'll see if I can.[FF]

MARCH 9, 1941

[F]I'm thinking of Helen. I'm happy. I'm thinking of evenings, sitting at a table—drinking, dancing. All kinds of things. + I finished my wooden head. I cut away too much. It doesn't matter. The wood wasn't good. + The parents and I discussed religion tonight, without coming to any realization, of course. Mother said that this world is a world of dreams, etc. It's impossible to talk with her when she says that I'm a person who hasn't yet carefully thought things through.[FF]

MARCH 10, 1941

[F]My first thought was to go see Helen. When I gave her my well-prepared apology, she said, "Oh, I liked it." "In that case," I said, "let's do it again sometime." + *Quarterly* is here.[FF]

MARCH 12, 1941

[F]Madeleine refused to accept a *Quarterly* yesterday: she doesn't want to see her story.[*] I'd like her to read mine! + Helen is cold. It hurts me. She doesn't call me "darling" anymore, the way she does Peter. I have no one to blame but myself. It will be difficult the next time because she'll be careful. Oh, I'd like to go with Cecilia E. once. An experienced woman. + We held the meeting here last night. Only 7 showed up. We are losing our enthusiasm. There will be a peace conference at Columbia this Saturday where I will speak.[FF]

---

[*] Madeleine Freund's short story "Genuine Harris Tweed" was also published in the spring 1941 issue of the *Barnard Quarterly*.

MARCH 13, 1941

^FI handed out pamphlets from 8:30–9. They called me "Red" to my face! And McGuire° came by (!) She saw me and smiled. Who cares? She'll tell the other professors. + A big piece in the papers (*World Tel.* [*Telegram*]) against the ASU. Red dominated, etc. Lists of our tactics, as if they were illegal! + Very tired tonight—too tired to write, really: smoking on the couch, thinking of a play.—Curtis called me up with an invitation to a party tomorrow night. From a girl called "Mary" who "admired" me at Caravan. I'll invite Helen to go with me tomorrow. I'm thinking about it all the time—I hope she doesn't have a date tomorrow. She can spend the night here!^{FF}

MARCH 14, 1941

^FHelen has a date tonight, but otherwise she would have gone with me, and she asked me if I'd receive more invitations! Of course! Well, Peter had a laugh! (I didn't do well on the Greek exam!) + The party was wonderful for two reasons: the hostess (Mary S.)[†] was very charming—a lot like Bailey. And there was a certain Billie B., much more attractive even than Streng![‡] My God! We sat on the divan together for a while, both drunk. We held hands, etc. Nothing else. She is very grown-up (35?), proper, beautiful—very beautiful, and dresses like Streng. Billie B. whispered that I should call her today. (Home at 5:30.) Oh! As if I wouldn't!^{FF}

MARCH 15, 1941

^FI can't think of anything else but Billie B. What a woman! Mary told me yesterday that she told her that she likes me. The two of us and Mary were the best of the bunch. + I slept for three hours. I did a bit of work but didn't go to the peace conference! I called up Billie B. at 1. She wasn't home. And then—!!!!!!! She

---

* Lorna McGuire, associate professor of English and freshman adviser at Barnard College.
† Mary Sullivan ran the bookshop at the Waldorf Astoria Hotel.
‡ Marion Streng, associate professor of physical education at Barnard College.

called me at 4. Called up Mary to ask for my name too! Oh, what a woman, to bother herself for my sake! No, no, that's not the right attitude! Oh, I am so happy I can only think of her!!—I wrote tonight, and then went to the Blue Bowl at 10. Billie was there in a black suit. We drank gin next to the restaurant. She is 30–31. Her husband (!) is a journalist. She lives with a Mary R. I drank too much. I don't know how I decided to go home with her. Perhaps she made the decision. In a taxi. Then I was sick. I got rid of a lot. A bit of coffee and then—bed. Mary's pajamas! My God!^FF

MARCH 16, 1941

^F[Billie] didn't do quite right by me. It was incomplete. She is tender, passionate, sweet, and feminine (!) The things one doesn't know until one sleeps with someone! She gave me what seemed like real love. But I've decided she's a bum. Tomorrow I'll tell Peter: "I met a beautiful bum." Home at 12:30. Studied a bit. Billie told me twice that she'll be home tonight at 9. She's expecting me to call her. I won't. I'll make her wait for me! All my excitement has petered out, like the air in a child's balloon: she didn't remain distant enough. Either she truly loves me, or she is easy and shallow—and a bit stupid. She's not as spiritual as I thought. Born in Germany. Height 5'8".^FF

MARCH 17, 1941

^FPeter very impressed by my weekend. + Lorna M. told me today that she liked my story*—well-written. But two girls came to her office and wanted to write a letter to the *Bulletin* because my story was against the educational system! + I didn't call Billie at 9, as she suggested. Not until 12. She's still charming. When can she see me? Friday, I said. She doesn't want to go to Caravan. But Curtis called me and told me that we'll go on Friday: Mary, Curtis, etc. Maybe Va. What will she think of Billie?!?!^FF

---

* "The Legend of the Convent of St. Fotheringay," which has just been published in the latest *Barnard Quartlery.*

MARCH 18, 1941

[F]I'm nervous. Couldn't study today. Helen invited me to have a cigarette—wanted to hear about Billie, etc. When I got home, there was a message from Billie. Mother had taken down her number. "I'm suspicious of your friendship with this woman" (my heart stopped beating) —"She's pursuing us." "Oh, my God, not at all." She simply wanted to know how I got home on Sunday, etc. Then I phoned B. when mother had left. She wanted to do something tonight (but Rita R. will come along). And I told her that she should stop calling me. She tried to remain calm. If only she were more subtle! More intelligent! Anyways—Rita R. came at 8.30. Good evening with my sherry. We danced. She dances very well. Lindy. Then I took her to Barnard. But first, I called Billie at 12:15. I told her that she's a bum—one of the best. She laughed. Nothing else.[FF]

MARCH 19, 1941

[F]Madeleine brought me home. She's sleeping with Arthur now. (A friend of Ludwig's, perhaps.) Madeleine is strikingly different from my distinguished friends. Ernst received a big piece in a Gramercy newspaper. I told him about Friday night. "Where do you find all these people?"[FF]

MARCH 20, 1941

[F]I studied well. Homer. I smoked cigarettes with Helen and Peter. How they frolic about all day! They would like me to come with them to lunch on Tuesday at the Gold Rail.[*] We drank at lunch. I wore my striped jacket which Va. doesn't like. Helen likes it! She called me "Darling" for the first time since Friday: yes—when I think of Helen, I'm happy. + ASU meeting. Didn't open my mouth. I washed my hair. And I finished the story about gym class![FF]

---

[*] The Gold Rail Bar, located at 2850 Broadway between 110th and 111th on the Upper West Side, was a casual hub for gay patrons.

MARCH 21, 1941

^F I met mother at L. & T. [Lord & Taylor] where we bought a red corduroy jacket. Marvelous. Mother likes it, which is unusual. + Met Billie at the World's Fair Café.* Drank a little. She was very pretty in a gray dress. Then back to her place for coffee. She kept drinking. We sat on the divan for several hours—until 2:30. It was very nice. She invited me—very politely—to stay the night. Mary wasn't there. ^FF

MARCH 23, 1941

^F I met an insufferable young woman from school on my way to Billie's. She was going to Temple Emanu-El† for a meeting of young gays. What a thing to do on Sunday! My good angel tells me that would be better—but my God! I'll take the devil! Billie very sweet—kisses, etc. She tells me that she likes me a lot. That she wants me. I feel very attracted to her. But I told her I was in love with Helen at school. Billie was very sad—I didn't allow her to touch me—anyways, we decided not to see each other for a month. She gave me a little gold chain for my wrist. I won't wear it—and I—I gave her nothing but one cent. ^FF

MARCH 24, 1941

^F I had a bad evening: in bed. Thinking, writing bad poetry. Accomplished nothing until 1:30 when I had to do my theater homework. I wrote a long letter to Billie. A good letter, but cautious. I'm not in love with her. Oh, if only she were unattainable—how I would love her then! ^FF

MARCH 26, 1941

^F Cecilia phoned me. We had a drink at the Jumble Shop. She told me that I'd changed since the evening when she first met me. That Mickey and she thought of me as "a real lady." Now I

---

* World's Fair Café was a restaurant and bar at 798 Third Avenue.

† Temple Emanu-El, a Jewish reform synagogue located at 840 Fifth Avenue on the northeast corner of East Sixty-Fifth Street.

seem like I could go to bed with someone: no shame, I suppose. Cecilia told me she liked my poems. Yes, they are good. It's exactly the kind of poetry I need right now. It makes me calm, thoughtful, introspective—sensitive—and tranquility allows me to write good poetry.[FF]

3/26/41

Love goes hurtling.

MARCH 28, 1941

[F]Felt very self-confident: it's filling my days. I don't think it's good. Georgia S. liked "Miss Juste and the Green Rompers." I bought papers for YCL at 3:30. Then I couldn't go to 126 tonight: something else more important came up: Jean was at Jumble at 9. Va. was a bit late, as usual. Curtis and Jack came later. Drinks (enough!) and on to MacDougal Tavern[*] and Caravan. Billie wasn't there. But I saw Frances B., Mary S. with Connie, and John with Mark, etc. Mary S. very charming. Connie told me that Mary has had a crush on me since her party. I'd like Mary to like me. She's clever. Connie said: "Mary likes you because you're intelligent—you have brains, she said." Then at the City Dump.[†] Va. and I went to the Vanguard and then to Judy's where we spent the night: 2:30–6:00 for me. I slept next to Va. naturally. A narrow and cold bed. Judy home at 5. Pretty, warm, charming coming up the stairs! I got home without parents noticing I was out all night.[FF]

3/28/41

Just now the world of experience seems more attractive than the world of books I have just stepped out of. I have not closed the door. I have merely left one room and gone into another. I have

---

* This may be in reference to Minetta Tavern, located at 113 MacDougal Street, an establishment frequented by E. E. Cummings, Ernest Hemingway, Eugene O'Neill, and Ezra Pound, among others.
† NYC City Dump Restaurant, located at 145 Bleecker Street in Greenwich Village, "where Park Avenue meets Bohemia."

found a new confidence in myself. I have become a person at last.

MARCH 30, 1941

^FI feel more relaxed—it's my love—my loves, no doubt. Then Graham R. at 4. Peter's. Daiquiris—don't know how many. Graham began to feel more and more at home—his compliments were lewd—so lewd. Enid F. with a young, sweet boy. Graham was so alive—alive—we danced. Then we kissed: on the divan. Don't know how, but one becomes stupid when drinking. We stayed for the soup. Graham and I left to drink Limericks at his hotel (I waited downstairs for him—it wasn't safe to go up to his room.) Taxi to a Romanian restaurant. I call out to him physically and intellectually, he says. He wanted to go to bed with me—after I told him about my love for a man—who is called Billie.^FF

MARCH 31, 1941

^FHelen sweet at school. Something's happening to her, she said. To me too, but I'm not as much of a dreamer. Our grades are going down. Hers the most. She's smoking, not eating, etc. It's me, I think. We very gently touched hands in Latham's class. It's so sweet, and incredibly timid and modest. I was appointed the new editor-in-chief of *Quarterly*. Rita sent me African daisies. Balakian was defeated.^°FF

APRIL 2, 1941

^FHelen came and joined me for a cup of coffee. I was writing my editorial statement—that the days of belles lettres are over, etc. Helen told me several interesting things. She's waiting for war because then, everyone will reject the shackles of life, etc. That she wants to have fun any way, with anyone. What the devil! I am having fun.^FF

---

* Pat defeated Nona Balakian (1918–1991), future literary critic and editor of the *New York Times Sunday Book Review*, who was also on the *Quarterly*'s editorial board, for the top job.

4/2/41

Lately I have been wasting time. I have been doing what I should have regarded with the utmost contempt at the age of sixteen. But it has done this for me: It has shown me that an unbookish life can be very useless. It has also shown me how what I have absorbed during my monastic adolescence can be used in a more normal life. And strangely it has made the books more important in one sense: that they are essential not for culture—or background—or scholarship—but to enrich the normal life. These sound like platitudes—at the most, truisms. But it has meant more to me than that, this discovery. I have seen and lived in the real world for the first time in my stupid life.

APRIL 4, 1941

^FHome until 11:45. Cralick* and Graham here. Good drinks, Cralick took a look at my writing. Flexible, developed in spirit but not in body—! We danced—Cralick and I. I was quite drunk when I left the house. I read *Best One Acts* of 1940— Percival Wilde (what a name!) on my way to Billie's. I have to accomplish something of value these days! Billie in her blue slacks. Generous with her liquor. It bothers me. I drank too much myself. Billie told me she didn't want me to stay—not when she was drunk.^{FF}

APRIL 7, 1941

^FAt Flora W.'s for ASU exec. [executive meeting]. They bore me. I wonder if I would have joined if I'd known? I do no more than sympathize. Graham came for breakfast yesterday. He stayed all day and this evening, too, working on his book. + A letter from Roger F. Wants me to come for Easter. We'll see! I have been spending too much money on drinks. I'd like to buy tickets—or one ticket a week—for the theater.^{FF}

---

* Jeva Cralick, a close friend of Pat's mother's.

APRIL 9, 1941

[F]Almost got sick because I was so tired. A letter from Dick,[*] who wants to start up our Thursday night meetings again. Communist reading circle. + Real hangover. Couldn't think straight today. It's not healthy. Went home at 9:30 and straight to bed! Slept until 10. Got up and felt much better. I'd like to write something tomorrow morning. My idea? I've had it for a while. I hope it's important. I feel as though my life in the South has given me an inexhaustible reservoir of stories—what riches![FF]

APRIL 10, 1941

[F]Good day! First day of break. I began my story about the girl from the South.[†] With the boy D.W.[‡] It will be good. + Went to Macy's—on foot—to buy pajamas. Nothing makes me happier than new pajamas![FF]

APRIL 11, 1941

[F]5 pages this morning. + Herbert L.[§] here at 7:30. Not in uniform. Quite experienced with women now. He's not the same boy anymore. But he still likes Bach. It's a pleasure to see him sitting at the piano. We drank two T. [Tom] Collins with quite some results. He wanted to go to bed together—in some hotel. It bears me down—I don't know—I should have seen Billie tonight. She invited me—but I was with Herb, and I wanted to go to the movies. Billie sent me a little pink rabbit: very cute and small. Herb wants to meet me tomorrow evening at Walgreen's to go to the hotel—I have no desire—otherwise I would do it—I have no scruples. That's not it at all.[FF]

APRIL 12, 1941

[F]Meeting at Coryl's. We accomplished nothing. It's disgusting. I continue to have no enthusiasm. Marcella was there. Gay? Don't

---

[*] President of the Young Communist League.
[†] This story has been lost.
[‡] Possibly a reference to her cousin Dan's son Dan Walton Coates.
[§] Herbert L., an old friend.

know. She doesn't mix business with pleasure. Then I bought a
box of cigarettes with a brown and blue hippopotamus on it for
mother. And a jar of jelly for Billie. Very pretty but not exciting.
+ I like [Elmer Rice's] *Flight to the West*. Wonderful. A play
that makes you think. Billie will come back to the city from the
country just to see me tomorrow.[FF]

4/12/41

I can work like a grub on an idea—on a story—realizing
something is of importance in it. Then after a few days
dissipating—with the job in the back of my mind, as such jobs
always are, I can come home with the truth of it exposed and
clear to me. I can sit down to write again with the true meaning finally in my mind. It's inevitable that a young person
spend more time living than working. He should. He must.
To begin work again is like starting with a new brain, washed
clean, yet wiser too.

4/12/41

I often wonder if it is love I want or the thrill of
domination—not thrill exactly but satisfaction. Because this
is often more enjoyable than the love itself; though I cannot
imagine a domination without love, nor a love without domination. False.*

APRIL 13, 1941

[F]I always feel happy when I'm on a walk with my mother. I wrote
a bit tonight. Then [at Billie's]. She'd just come from the country. We sat on the couch. Billie was speaking in platitudes, it was
like being with my family! She bores me so. I didn't even feel like
spending the night! Home at 2:30. And I forgot my key again! I
had to wake up Stanley. What a fuss! My mother was angry at

---

* Possibly added retrospectively.

3:00 AM. A rat in bed with them, etc. Made me sweep the living room.^{FF}

APRIL 14, 1941
^FI'm hungry for literature—for books, just the way my body was hungry one or two months ago. My appetite is twofold: I hunger for love and for thought. Together those two can take me anywhere, you know.* I wrote a poem about this.^{FF}

4/14/41
Note on the opposition of body and mind. My mind is now as greedy and as hungry as my body was four months ago—one month ago! It is amazing. They work at cross-purposes. Rather like two buckets on a well rope. One must be filled while the other is emptying!

4/14/41
Having just finished l'affaire B.—, is there any better proof that love disappears when the curiosity and the doubt and the struggle is ended? Mine might have been through forty-eight hours after I met B. I think it was.

APRIL 16, 1941
^FYesterday I met Carter in Wash. Sq Park. He's from Texas. He seemed pensive and told me that a friend had brought him sage—(I thought at first that he said "gays")—and this means marijuana: he's tried it perhaps 8 times in a dozen years. +
Felicia talked to me regarding my few sales of *Soviet Power*, that I haven't visited their meetings, etc. I am so bored with stuff. Political stuff in particular. + I finished [James Branch] Cabell's *Cream of the Jest*. Full of satire. One must get to know

* This entry was written in an imperfect French, leaving some room for interpretation: "*Je suis fait[e] de deux appétits: l'amour et la pensée. Entre ces deux, je suis dans chaque endroit, il faut savoir.*" It is also possible she could have meant to say: "Love and thought, wherever I go, I am always torn between those two," or "I am always looking for one of them."

both well-known authors and lesser-known ones: everyone has something.[FF]

APRIL 17, 1941

[F]Completely forgot to buy books for the League yesterday afternoon. A Freudian slip. I'd like to get out of it. I'd like some peace and quiet for a while. It's all my fault. I haven't behaved properly recently. But I'd like to get out of the fight until I've done something worth doing.

+ Reading [Pushkin's] *Eugene Onegin*. Bad (doggerel).[FF]

APRIL 18, 1941

[F]Had dinner with Billie. Fish. I wore my black dress, as she wished. Never-ending nightcaps at Delaney's.[*] Billie was sad and didn't say much. Difficult, wanted to stay at her place. Had 3–4 drinks I didn't want at Caravan. Then B. and I alone in the diner. 8 St. Billie—"Let's get things straightened out." She told me she's possessive, jealous, wants a lot. Asked me if I still love Va. There's a lot we can't say with words, she told me. Very tired. Sad. Didn't eat her burger. We left at 5. She took my last dollar. Could she have expressed herself more clearly?? I love her because she can't express herself.[FF]

APRIL 19, 1941

[F]Unfortunately Roger came—and I went out tonight. Fell asleep on the bus—he wanted to drink in nightclubs + I finished the story[†]—about the boys and the girl in the car. It isn't coherent enough—nor important—? It was written without much inspiration, like a lot of my stories. But I have two ideas that are important (I'm certain of it). One is the nucleus of a novel.[FF]

---

[*] Jack Delaney's was a popular Greenwich Village steak house at 72 Grove Street, near Sheridan Square.
[†] It is unclear which story she refers to here.

APRIL 20, 1941

ᶠBillie phoned me at 10:30. Mother answered. Then she said
with malice: "Does she want you? Tell her she can have you!"
I was cold, because my mother was listening. Watched *Great
Dictator* with Arthur. Then home for pie and cake. My mother
still likes him the most of all my male friends. He's a communist
too, which pleases me because of my mother. "You're not a communist. You've only got a pink toothbrush," she told me. Full of
ambition. I want to read the dictionary, all my books. I'll have to
keep a tight schedule until my exams.ᶠᶠ

4/21/41

People set such high value upon being loved—even greater—as
I've said somewhere before, than the joy of loving—they set
such high score by this that they will, without realizing what
they are doing, take the greatest pains to make themselves
loved, if they see another person interested in them: even if they
have no spark of love within them for the interested person. It
comes on one—this realization of our desire to be loved, and
the realization that one is actually encouraging the lover in
every way possible—It comes on one as a shock—of honesty—
such honesty—and with it a kind of guilt, a sense of hypocrisy, of shallowness and deception, of decadence and of an
unhealthy love of mockery.

APRIL 23, 1941

ᶠJ. B.˙ sent me a dollar (which will buy a present for Mary S.)
but not the slightest comment on "St. Fotheringay." Very tired.
Helen was charming in Latham's class. But I haven't touched
her since that lovely Monday a month ago. Oh well—I tried to
develop an interest in drama but it simply isn't there. Everyone
writes plays far more well-rounded than mine. But I don't care.

---

* Probably Jay Bernard Plangman, Pat's biological father.

It's not important! I'm thinking about my first novel*—about people my age. And about a woman like the one around whom the story will unfold—an intelligent woman forced to turn on them—so she can make a living. That will always be my topic.[FF]

APRIL 24, 1941

[F]We have to decide on our classes for 1942. I'll take Howard:[†] Advanced Comp. And another semester of Sturtevant. Those two classes will give me a lot of writing practice until I graduate.[FF]

APRIL 25, 1941

[F]Latham asked me why I take so long to write my plays. "You're too fussy," she said. + Called up [Billie]. She wanted to meet Curtis and Jean at Rocco's at 9. Then MacDougal for drinks, where I saw Connie and Mary S., Eddy, and Helen R., Billie and Curtis became more and more drunk at the bar. Then we went to Caravan. Billie sat down, singing along with the music in an effort, I suppose, to appear young and happy. I was disgusted. Then I lost my purse between Jungle Camp and Main Street. Bumped into Dorothy P. Drank 5, spent all my money except for a dollar. My keys, lipsticks and compacts were in the purse—luckily not my wallet. Parents didn't answer the bell. Then back to Main Street and finally home to Dorothy P.'s where I spent the night.[FF]

APRIL 26, 1941

[F]My parents didn't hear the bell. I was worried that they were angry. I didn't tell mother I'd lost my purse. Mother and I saw an exhibition: Rouault and Paul Klee.[‡] Went roller skating with Va. tonight: two boys—Lee M. and Frank B. They're in the army. So innocent! Lots of sailors at the rink. Such fresh and young

---

* Pat starts thinking about a novel. She will in fact start writing a "roman d'adolescents," inspired by her college friends, but only in 1943, and with a different story than the one she outlines here—*The Click of the Shutting*, a project she never completes.
† Dr. Clare Howard, associate professor of English.
‡ Probably "Understanding Modern Art" at the Museum of Modern Art, which also showed works by Picasso, Matisse, Braque, and Cézanne.

figures compared to last night. I studied well this morning. I feel
full of energy, though I know I'm not.[FF]

APRIL 27, 1941

[F]Went to Marjorie Thompson's[*] tonight. Larry M. was there
with his mother. Larry is definitely gay. It's amusing how one
can put the pieces together! His mother was interpreting what
Hitler said. She's confusing the sides—black and white—and
believes in Lindbergh[†] (who resigned today). Larry is more tactful. His mother is from the south and stupid.[FF]

APRIL 28, 1941

[F]At school, I'm told that it's awful I don't come to the meetings
anymore (there was one tonight). But for myself, as an individual, my studies are more important.[FF]

4/28/41

Having an automobile is like having your own woman. They're a
terrible expense and give you a lot of worry, but once you've had
one, you'll never want to be without one.

APRIL 30, 1941

[F]The plays we are putting on in class are almost professional.
Nonetheless, I have to write a better one. Judy at 6. Mother too
to see the apartment. Judy same as ever. Her imagination is at
work in everything she says. Sometimes that's amusing, sometimes boring or disgusting. But it's needed for her work. When I
was there, Va. called. Wanted me to go with them to a picnic on
Saturday. Even if I didn't have a play to write, I'd have books to
read—time flies and I haven't nearly read enough. Look at [Babs]
B.! Does she go on outings every week? Va. was still angry![FF]

---

* Marjorie Thompson, close friend of Pat's mother's.
† Charles Lindbergh Jr. (1902–1974), the first man to cross the Atlantic in a solo flight, was a
vigorous opponent of America's entry into World War II. When President Roosevelt decried
him as a "defeatist and appeaser," Lindbergh resigned his commission in the Air Force.

MAY 1, 1941

[F]Finally, I've done my schedule. I've become famous at the registrar's office for being absentminded. Sturtevant asked me if I was in love with someone. + I'd like to write my story about the woman who loves the fake count.[*] I'll do it well. + Phoned Billie. The days are going by, and I'm not thinking about her. We'll talk tomorrow, but I have no intention of spending a lot of money!![FF]

MAY 2, 1941

[F]With Billie tonight at 10. We were supposed to see [the film] *Pépé le Moko*—but it was already late. In any case, I wanted to talk with her. She said nothing about her conversation with M. Sullivan but I have no doubt M.S. told her what I said: that I feel young and stupid around her friends. So what.[FF]

MAY 3, 1941

[F]Billie invited me to go with her to Mero's tonight.[†] 10 St. + I could have done better on yesterday's exam. I knew everything. There's something that freezes in my brain and prevents me from using my knowledge. It's a bit of defeatism. + We took photographs in the garden. Me in slacks[‡]—my friends will be surprised when I tell them that my mother took the photographs! + I feel beaten down—discouraged from my work. I'm not developing enough, and I often think it's sexual. Don't know. What if these four years are lost! Wasted! I feel inca-

---

* Probably in reference to the short story "Silver Horn of Plenty," published in *Barnard Quarterly* (Winter 1941).
† Gean Harwood and Bruhs Mero organized the Nucleus Club, a small group of lesbian and gay male friends who regularly partied at their home in Greenwich Village in the late 1930s and early 1940s. They were careful to pull the blinds down and have women and men leave their apartment in mixed pairs.
‡ Pat often particularly points out wearing pants. To understand why, and its implications, it is crucial to keep in mind that pants for women were still considered innapropriate by many, and cross-dressing a telltale sign of homosexuality. There was a notorious "three-articles-of-clothing" rule—never actually a law, but still widely used by the authorities—that could get anyone arrested who got caught wearing fewer than three articles of gender-appropriate clothing.

pable of being truly courageous—the way I was when I was
16—14! That was terrific! I wonder whether true love creeps up
slowly—subtly—not in a fury! But I love fury!^{FF}

MAY 5, 1941
^FI began studying for my exams. Am happy. I should have gone
with [Billie] to the movies tonight. But I had to work on my
play. It's getting better (haven't I said so all semester?). I have
to study for each subject, and will start when I finish [T. H.
White's] *The Sword in the Stone*. Often I look at the books in
the library and think about my freshman days—how I wanted
to read each book over those four years. I'll do it. And I know
that, as soon as I have time, ideas and their realization will fall
like rain. With regularity, one produces something. I shouldn't
be afraid.^{FF}

MAY 8, 1941
^FThere will be a meeting tomorrow night, so I can't go to Bil-
lie's. She wanted me to spend the night. I would have liked to
stay a while, then go home. It's difficult to do otherwise as long
as I live at home. + Read *Hamlet* tonight! Memorized a few
things. Working now. And sleeping enough, which I haven't
done since I began university.^{FF}

MAY 9, Friday
^FHow I need peace and quiet. Tonight is the first Friday I've
spent at home since the evening with Peter and Helen.^{FF}

MAY 10, 1941
^FA whole day and I haven't opened a book. Looked for slacks this
morning. They don't fit me—those for women. + Then quickly
to Va. She actually gave me hers! Went to some place in the north
with Frank and Lee. It was amusing, but I'm wasting my time with
boys like that. Even Va. wouldn't pay them any mind if they didn't
have a car. They're too young, stupid, and ordinary for us.^{FF}

MAY 11, 1941—^GMother's Day^{GG}

^FMy slacks are wonderful! They're a bit short, just as they should be. I have to study a lot now. Also, [Paul] Claudel's play *L'annonce faite à Marie* is very lovely. + Cralick told me in earnest that I could get work at *Vogue* with my drawings. I believe it. I believe everything. Most of all, I believe in myself. I can do anything at all!^{FF}

MAY 15, 1941

^FHelen was very pretty today. I brought her books from the library. I like how much it disgusts Va. + I wrote to R. to invite them to spend Decoration Day* with Va. and myself. We would like to go north by car—their car. + Good game of tennis with Frances F. Then a shower—both of us naked—makes one feel good.—Then exhaustion. It's a good life. No worries. + I finished my play. "Kiss me Goodbye"—and the heroine is named Helen—of course.^{FF}

MAY 16, 1941

^FI got an A- on a paper for Bailey. + Lee phoned me this evening. I was reading *The Tempest*. Then Va. came by—they were taking a spin in the car. She came to my room alone. I kissed her—caressed her—without the slightest desire or pleasure. I don't know what I'm turning into. + Then [Janet] M. at 10:30. Mary was very (oh very!) sweet to me. Janet is blonde and tall, like Billie. Large apartment. Such opulence! But a bit cheap, just like her. Mary told me that Billie and [Janet] are together now. Janet has a car—and Billie told me last week that she'd sell her soul for a car.^{FF}

MAY 17, 1941

^FAlways working. Billie phoned me at 10. She was sorry about last night (but why!). Said that the girls are bitches—it's always the same with Billie—if she's under the impression she needs to

---

* Memorial Day used to be called Decoration Day.

handle me with kid gloves, she's wrong. We were never serious.
I studied hard. How much more naïve I was when I lived on
Morton St.* I was a cheery, happy child—and confident. Now
I've had too many nights drinking.[FF]

MAY 18, 1941

[F]Not enough time for studying. Ernst called me yesterday.
Wanted to hire me in two weeks.[†] Probably. + Oh, if only I could
feel love like a sixteen-year-old again! I was so happy! Now I'm
like an old woman![FF]

MAY 19, 1941

[F]Work! Work! I'm not even reading the papers. A ship sank. 190
Americans.[‡] Hitler, perhaps. Everyone is talking about Germany's victory. We've just entered the war.[§] + I read *Julius Caesar,
Measure for Measure*—etc. It's exciting to study like this: all
day! Other men's thoughts.[FF]

5/19/41

I am drunk now—in a house full of drunks, and everybody is so
damned busy expressing himself.

5/19/41

Possible basis for my weltanschauung. That the childishness
is never lost, but adulthood put like a veneer over it. We think
inside like children, react, and have their desires. The outside
manners are an absurd puff of conceit. Ponder this later.

---

* In 1940, Pat took a summer sublet at 35 Morton Street in order to get away from her family—
the address will later also feature as a setting in her novel *A Dog's Ransom* (New York, 1972).
† Ernst will employ her for some time to assist him in his writing.
‡ The reference here is not clear: Pat might be referring to the *Robin Moor*, a cargo ship
with forty-six people on board, which was intercepted by a German U-boat off the coast of
Brazil on May 21, an incident that prompted President Franklin D. Roosevelt to issue a May
27 proclamation that a state of unlimited national emergency exists. This would confirm yet
again that Pat often wrote diary entries retrospectively (and backdated them).
§ Not literally: The United States entered the war against Japan on December 8, 1941, one
day after the attack on Pearl Harbor.

MAY 22, 1941

ᶠI wasted two months on Billie. I don't regret them. But they were wasted, at least in terms of work. I only wrote the one story of "Miss Juste" and two plays. Now I'd like to spread out. Tomorrow we (Virginia and I) will go to Caravan, I think. She's young and sweet, compared to Billie. Oh Billie, you deceived me!! You're nothing but a drunk, nothing but a self-involved lover. A coward—a lazy bum—a passionate woman, but a good-for-nothing.ᶠᶠ

MAY 23, 1941

ᶠI don't care if I don't see V.S. [Virginia] for the next six months. There's lots to do. Each subject once more. + The trouble with Va. and I is that we don't have enough desire. We don't want each other.ᶠᶠ

MAY 23, 1941

ᶠWith Va. tonight, we fought. We won't go together on Decoration Day. I'm letting my feelings lead me, not my spirit. I've depended on it long enough. It's very boring. It's sterile. When I like someone, I'll do what I must without thinking.ᶠᶠ

MAY 24, 1941

ᶠA good day. The first of my new life. I finished my play *War and the Pettigrews* (now *the P's at War*), 21 pages. + With mother this morning. We strolled, then went to Orbach.* There are times I like being in a crowd. Today I hated it. Sometimes I touch a body and it disgusts me and makes me furious. + Spent the evening at the library. Wonderful books, and I'm still hungry for them. Ernst H. here for tea. Wants to pay me 20.00 a week. I'll do it. + I read *Bury the Dead* (Irwin Shaw) last night. It was good but too obviously communist, I think. It's surprising that he was popular for so long on Broadway. + Va. told me on Fri-

---

* Orbach's was a department store.

day that Schulberg* (or Thomas Wolfe) wrote that a man who is keeping a diary does so because he is afraid of saying what he writes. It's possible. It's true in my case. In any case, I like to follow my progress and regressions.[FF]

5/24/41

That night at the party, when I sat down beside you on the couch and we started talking, you might have been anyone else, any of the other people in the room I talked with that night. I can't say yet what it was exactly that made you suddenly different. But I loved you then, because you were strange. I loved you when you said good night to me. I loved you all the next day, though I couldn't sleep, or eat, or read, or even think coherently about you. Then when I did see you, I felt stupid, or I felt that you would think me stupid because I couldn't take my eyes off you. You were so very offhand and wonderful when I first came. We walked out onto the sidewalk down to a dive of a bar, and sat in a booth. And it was then that something fell away from you like a mantle slipped off the shoulders—perhaps I should say like a screen that conceals something not too attractive. I wish I could say what it was. Because if I knew—if it were simple enough to be discovered, I might be able to forget it. I should at least know what to fight, what it is keeping us apart. Perhaps I was shocked because you seemed to give me too much attention. Perhaps I was silly and didn't want anyone, after all, that I really might have. I don't know. But I know that after that wonderful evening before, when you hardly spoke to me, and after that sleepless night and that nerve-shaken day, and the counted hours before I finally saw you again—after all that, the change in you, (or in me) was like the sudden, unwelcome awakening from a glorious dream. An awakening on a Monday morning when, with one's castle and clouds and the silver sea dissolved into a sordid room, one real-

* Budd Schulberg (1914–2009), American writer and TV producer.

izes that one has to get up and dress in the cold night in a few minutes and plod through a weary day.

MAY 25, 1941

[F]A disgusting day. Not enough work, not enough pleasure. I spent too much time between the two. I tried to do a pastel drawing. It's difficult. Ink is my true medium. + We had dinner at Jumble Shop at 8 pm tonight. Mary S. came in with two men and a woman. Thankfully, they were straight. One was her husband. I introduced my parents, and she introduced her husband. Her hair didn't look good, but I didn't mind, except that I wanted her to make a good impression on my parents. She is pretty and sweet! Perhaps I could love her. Don't know. And why don't I do it if I can? Because I've become a Hamlet in every way. I'm a good-for-nothing. My heart has stopped beating.[FF]

5/25/41

It's so important that people—especially young people write some poetry during their lives. Even if it is bad poetry. Even if they think they do not like poetry or have no talent for writing it, they should write, and even badly, if it is sincere. And really sincere poetry is seldom bad even if the form is not perfect. But the poetry opens a new vista of the world. It is not so much that we see new things, but that we see old things differently. And this experience is invaluable. It is as soul-shaking as the experience of love. It is more ennobling. It makes philosophers and kings.

5/26/41

Every man and woman, in his or her life, makes decisions, knows emotions comparable to those felt by the characters in the greatest novels and plays. Yet such a small percentage of the world is articulate—the tiny handful of "writers" who, with few exceptions, gain their themes from observation of others, second hand. If we had the pieces in any form, the individual contributions through all the ages, what wouldn't we know now?

MAY 28, 1941

^FWrote this morning. Went to N.Y.U. at 12:30. Babs B. was there. There was also a man from the American Writers' Congress.[*] It's meeting in a week. I'll go. + Latham gave me a B. B in Greek too. C in gym. With Arthur tonight. He almost loves me. Wanted to dive into the world of love, passion, etc. + I saw Katherine Cornell[†] in *Doctor's Dilemma*. Very good. She isn't pretty. Voice slightly high-pitched. A white, clear complexion. The audience, which was largely composed of women, didn't clap when the curtain came down because they were getting dressed: hats and gloves. It was disgusting!^{FF}

5/28/41

We come into the world with a tabula rasa character on which the people about us write their messages. An admired character, we seek to imitate, a detested character, we seek to mold ourselves in the exact opposite. This is a more important factor than heredity or the physical environment.

Miscellania: How to get rid of persistent boy friends. Should I develop a healthy case of dandruff?

MAY 29, 1941

^FFirst day of work with Ernst. His dialogue could be better. I said as much as I could. His characters are speaking too formally. Home at 4:45. Not bad.^{FF}

MAY 30, 1941

^FDinner with Herb at the Jumble Shop. Sometimes he talks like an ass—especially when he drinks. It's a big flaw. He could easily be a fascist. (They called me yesterday to ask whether I'd

---

[*] The First American Writers Congress founded the League of American Writers, an association with close ties to the American Communist Party. Writers who joined until the League was disbanded in 1943 include Thomas Mann, Lilian Hellman, John Steinbeck, and Ernest Hemingway.

[†] Katharine Cornell (1898–1974), actress known as the "First Lady of the [American] Theater."

come to a communist assembly. Naturally I lied. Another evening with pseudo-pseudo people.) Herb and I tried to have an exciting time in bed. I could have been with my grandmother. + Would like to be alone now. Would like to write poetry about my last love—or what have you—[FF]

MAY 31, 1941

[F]The days go by quickly. I get tired in the afternoons—my posterior. No coffee either. Ernst is so comfortable in slacks and a white jacket. No tie. He walks about, smokes a bit, eats his coffee sweets. I've learned a lot from him. I'd like to write like him. I'm almost there: a final draft first, then corrections in pen later. I'd like to write my first long story on long, yellow paper. I don't think that there's a girl Ernst is in love with now. But one never knows with him. The things he does . . . I wonder what [Billie's] doing right now. She's in the country, I think, I hope. She doesn't drink when she's there. Oh, the Saturdays I've spent with her! She kissed me the last time we were together. Unfortunately she doesn't remember. Oh what does it matter! Once, I wrote in my diary that when I become careful—when I am not interested in a person because she is not "good" enough, I will have become old—and now it's happened. I would like to love someone without desiring to be loved.[FF]

JUNE 1, 1941

[F]A ghostly day—no ordinary people on the streets because everyone's out of the city. I wonder what Va.'s doing? + I learned a lot—Don't want to write stories about stupid, useless people. There are so many things crying out to be described. + Graham here 10:00. We talked quietly. The situations and circumstances at the camps are unbelievable.[*] A sentry shot two men obeying his orders! We listened to records. He was wearing my slippers. They look nice on his feet. I'm happy.[FF]

---

[*] The reference to camps here is unclear. Even the earliest rumors about the Holocaust would only begin to emerge later that year. The internment of Japanese Americans did not begin until 1942. She might have meant the United States' own training or "boot camps."

JUNE 2, 1941

ᶠBad day with Ernst. 3½ hours of sleep! Oh well! But he pays me for my work! + Began my story about the girl and the lost purse.* Will be good. + S.'s birthday. He's turning 40. Looks 35! + I'm afraid to see my grades. Even if I don't care what I did this semester, I like getting A's. It takes so little to get a B or a C. And then—you're a mediocre student! But next year I'll get excellent grades. I don't regret anything this year. I learned a lot.ᶠᶠ

JUNE 3, 1941

ᶠI got an A in French—and a C in Shakespeare. I don't get it! There were only 5 C's in the class! I hoped for an A! Logic hasn't posted yet. + I wrote 6 good long pages of my *Hangover*. Making progress. I want to read and write for the rest of summer. The past few months—in the past two months, I've done nothing but try to feel things. And didn't succeed, except for cigarettes and liquor.ᶠᶠ

JUNE 6, 1941

ᶠNervous because I'm going to the doctor. Dr. Jennings at 5:15. She's gay—45 years old. Wanted to check me for all kinds of things; examined me for half an hour! I weigh 107 lb. It was hard to endure—vagina, etc. completely normal except for the glands. Have to test my basal metabolism Wednesday. It will cost a lot of money. Probably ¾ of what I'll make this summer. It's too bad, but I can't avoid it. Am constantly disappointed because I'm not in love! One could kill oneself for that. + Saw *Pal Joey*† with Arthur tonight. Not as good as I'd hoped for. Songs were excellent. Arthur is falling in love with me, and getting serious. It's tricky. I can't tell him what I feel—because I feel nothing—for

---

* Unidentifiable or lost story.
† *Pal Joey* is a 1940 musical with music by Richard Rodgers and lyrics by Lorenz Hart. The original Broadway production, directed by George Abbott and starring Vivienne Segal and Gene Kelly, ran for ten months.

or against. How I would like to tell him—even tell myself—that I'm in love with—Helen, Billie, Babs, someone!!!!!!!!!![FF]

JUNE 7, 1941

[F]I have no summer clothes. It depresses me to walk through the streets when everyone is wearing light clothes. I am depressed so easily! And happy so easily! + Bought a necklace—pearls. 5 strands. Twisted. Billie will like it. Not a word from her. I'll call her on Monday probably. Commodore tonight.[*] We heard Millen Brand,[†] Joy Davidman.[‡] They say Steinbeck these days would no longer be allowed to publish his novel *Grapes of Wrath*. That's how close we are to war. + I'd like to write nonsense-verses—I'll do it.[FF]

JUNE 8, 1941

[F]Mother is unhappy at home. Perhaps it's her menopause—don't know—but when it comes, it will be much worse. She cried—said I was heartless. We took a walk at 9 pm tonight, close to the river. "I'm getting old, and there's nothing left for me here." In this house I see my mother and Stanley in a bad way—their work—not good enough—the house doesn't have enough dignity because we don't take enough care of it—my room is the prettiest and cleanest, though I work just as much as they do. Their time is mostly wasted—it all makes me sad—and I have no pity. (I wasn't born like that. A child is never cruel at birth. There it is, stated in brief.) I would like to leave home when I finish school. When my endocrinal glands begin to work, I don't know who I'll be, how I'll feel—who or what I'll love. What I'll want to become. I'll be a new person whom

---

[*] The Commodore was a hotel at Forty-Second Street and Lexington Avenue. It has since been replaced by the Grand Hyatt Hotel.

[†] American poet and novelist Millen Brand (1906–1980) was a member of the League of American Artists. During the McCarthy era, his books were banned from public libraries.

[‡] Helen Joy Davidman Gresham (1915–1960), American poet and writer who joined the American Communist Party in 1938 and later converted to Christianity. Her best-known work is *Smoke on the Mountain: An Interpretation of the Ten Commandments*.

I have to get to know. We'll see. It'll be the most interesting change in my life!ᶠᶠ

JUNE 9, 1941

ᶠMy story about grandmother* will need to be in the third person in the end. Otherwise there's too much time to cover. I hope that one day I'll re-read all of this—everything in this book [my diary]. My secrets—the secrets that everyone has—are here, in black and white.ᶠᶠ

JUNE 10, 1941

ᶠVery sad tonight because mother talked to me a lot. I really don't understand her sometimes. After that, Billie found me— could I come to the movies? I was afraid. But mother let me go. We had a drink at Shelton Corner's.† Very happy. Home very late, of course. My mother came when I was in the kitchen. Told me I had no respect. That Stanley is noble to do what he does— but Stanley is mostly afraid of getting worked up. That requires more courage than staying calm.ᶠᶠ

6/10/41

We love either to dominate or to be bolstered up ourselves. And there is no love without some element of hate in it: in everyone we love, there is some quality we hate intensely.

JUNE 11, 1941

ᶠAt 15 St. for my metab. test at 8:30. A young woman—very pretty. Don't have the results yet. Then an x-ray, where they almost gave me an enema! I escaped by 2 minutes!! + Mother serious. Almost crying, often. The decision about next year rests with Stanley (school or no school). + Billie sad last night. I told her a bit about my problems—that my glands need adjustment—

---

* This may be in reference to her third-person short story "Sundays at Grandma's," which Pat brainstormed in Notebook 1 during her pre-college visit to Fort Worth in 1938.
† Cocktail lounge and restaurant in Shelton Hotel, Lexington Avenue at Forty-Ninth Street, popular for its "unique Glass Dance Floor."

but nothing else. I told her that I don't trust any of my current emotions. She seemed interested. Naturally.[FF]

JUNE 12, 1941

[F]I told Ernst about what's happening at home. He got angry that I needed to spend all my money on clothes and doctors. He's never much liked mother. But he thinks they'll let me go to school next year anyway. Says my mother is completely childish. + *What Makes Sammy Run* by Budd Schulberg is very original. A lot of *joie de vivre*! It's a young book.[FF]

JUNE 13, 1941

[F]At the doctor's: I have a small pituitary—too small—the anterior node (the first one) is insufficient. Therefore, the thyroid is not strong enough. She gave me a small thyroid injection in the gluteus maximus. Otherwise I'll need to get my head x-rayed to fix it. + Mike Thomas tonight. Penthouse. 15 W. 95. Billie, Rita G, Rose M, Janet M., John M., Billy Livingston (army), Mary S., Curtis, Jean, Venetia (in a green suit—very striking—a bit butchy, but everyone was trying to pick her up). Mary talked to me—seemed to have told the men that I was almost perfect. I was supposed to go to Billie's after the party. But Billie got very drunk and left at 1:30 with Janet. Jean told me I have the most beautiful body she's ever seen. She is, in other words, on the rebound. Bernhard[*] was there too. Not attractive. + I spoke a lot with Mary S. who was flitting about here and there all night. The boys love her! But finally, Mary and I left to get a bite. Childs.[†] We spoke until 4:30. Then she invited me to spend the night. Her apartment's on 58 St. She slept for half an hour on the sofa under two blankets. I was in her bed without proper

---

* German-born American photographer Ruth Bernhard (1905–2006) moved to New York City in 1927 and soon got involved in the lesbian subculture of the artistic community in Manhattan. She became friends with photographer Berenice Abbott and her lover, art critic Elizabeth McCausland, and wrote about her "bisexual escapades" in her memoir. In 1934 Bernhard began photographing women in the nude—soon also photographing Pat.
† The Childs Restaurant near Times Square.

clothes. Finally, when I suggested that she could sleep next to me, since the bed was big enough, she accepted quickly! Very quickly! And then—well, we didn't sleep much, but what does it matter! She's marvelous![FF]

JUNE 14, 1941

[F]With Ernst at the Parkside,* two gardenias from Mary S. Ernst was curious, but I kept the card to myself. And lied to him. They are beautiful, fragrant. The card says only: "Mary."[FF]

JUNE 15, 1941

[F]With Billie last night. She phoned me, very apologetic that she'd left without thinking of me. Rita G. at World's Fair yesterday. Pretty, but not smart. With her Friday night in the bathroom. She kissed me twice. Drunk. I'll see Mary S. Tuesday night. She likes me. I hope I'll be able to like her too. We had breakfast at Schrafft's[†] at 8 on Saturday. Parents not angry. Why? Ernst nervous because the United States is confiscating money from foreigners: he might make 500.00 less. And he wants me to cure him of his nerves![FF]

JUNE 16, 1941

[F]Graham was here last night with Walter Marlowe. He's a Jew. Very intelligent. We danced, talked about everything, including Ernst's novel (which he forbade me from doing). + Tired but nervous because of Mary. I wanted a letter. Am still too sensitive! Finally I phoned her: "I'm a bit cross with you, Pat." (I didn't know what to say.) "I called your mother and broke our date Tuesday." I was gutted! Because she didn't hear from me about the flowers! I gave my apologies in my best bad fashion. She told me that she had heard I was with Billie Saturday evening. And not a

---

* Pat and Ernst are working from the Parkside Hotel.
† Schrafft's was a restaurant chain where women could lunch and dine alone. There was one in Greenwich Village on the corner of Thirteenth Street and Fifth Avenue.

word of thanks from me about the flowers—well, we said good-bye politely—and no doubt both had a more pleasant evening.[FF]

JUNE 17, 1941

[F]YCL kids here last night. Marcella too. Ann, who works at the Bookshop and who likes Mary Sullivan, didn't give her my message Saturday night. That's why Mary Sullivan was furious—not furious, but skeptical! Ann is jealous of me since last Friday. + Went to see Mary Sullivan at 11:30. She admires me like a painting, she said—she doesn't want to be Billie's rival: "I don't care to toss my hat in the ring." But most importantly: she would be just as happy if she could admire me but not possess me. She wanted to tell me her terms. She brought me home by taxi.[FF]

JUNE 17, 1941

[F]One is always ready to hear a good word about oneself. Mary S. is intelligent—infinitely more intelligent than Billie! She's come up with a fitting image: that B. wants me to be a pretty child, nice to show to others. That B.B. would be just as happy with a Maxwell Parrish[*] as a Degas. Billie, I've said for months, doesn't bring out the best in me. But it's different with M. She is the world—she has the whole world—and all the energy in the world within her. And she knows it.[FF]

JUNE 18, 1941

Wrote all morning with great difficulty—and little satisfaction. I am doing the tunnel story of Astoria[†]—with social viewpoint on the playgrounds. + Went to school this P.M. and got the shock of my life: D in Logic. My first D of course. Phi Beta Kappa forever goodbye! It upset me terribly. More than I had believed it

---

* A likely reference to Maxfield Parrish (1870–1966), an American painter best known for his painting *Daybreak*, a popular art print.
† Probably in reference to her (lost) story she'll soon try to publish under the title "Train to Astoria."

would. I just make eligibility for *Quarterly* touching the hurdle-bar as I go over.

JUNE 18, 1941

I shed one lone tear in the subway. Could not read for a while. But I suppose the correct way to look at it is that logic, being math, I could never quite touch it. And by the same token it can never quite touch me. I'm terribly sorry about it, though I can hardly say my social whirling of the past semester is responsible.

JUNE 18, 1941

Cralick here tonight. She fooled around with my hair—putting it up. Says my broad jaw is javanese. That I could get a job modeling or better easily. It's a matter of manner and *savoir vivre*, as I knew when I was fifteen. It requires a leisure that I find impossible to effect while going to school. Perhaps I—I will acquire it after school. My life will be a long one. Everything points to that. I'd like to look very nice Friday night at Abbott's* party.

JUNE 19, 1941

Miserable because I keep thinking of my D in Logic. In the catalogue this comes under "poor"—I wonder if I shall have to make it up in summer school? And if the *Quarterly* eligibility is made from this last semester or the whole year? Because I'm 1/10 short for this semester. What a loss of face that would be! + I felt like being very sad this evening and so I was. Wrote a poem which isn't bad called "Mamma Mia, what is mine on earth?" which came to me de profundis! Yes, the Mary S. affection has a strong element of the maternal. Hers too no doubt. It seems to me that perfectly normal women can take their pleasures so by some quirk in the past which has turned them from men: fear of childbirth, domination, love of independence (rare

---

* Berenice Abbott (1898–1991), American sculptor and photographer. She is best known for her black-and-white series *Changing New York*, which captured the architecture and shifting social landscape of the city during the Great Depression.

& generally only in butches). + The parents have, I suppose, stopped my allowance entirely. This makes two weeks now! + (They gave me the 5 bucks this morning.)

JUNE 20, 1941

Nice day at Ernst's, tho he had a stroke of the heat or something at 2:00. Entirely mental I'd say. Then home in all the heat and showered, wrote an hour—seems a pitiful little, but two of my best stories were written that way. Thomas Wolfe's book is making a great stamp in my mind. Mother says he was a colossal egotist & that I resemble him in that respect. Egotist, yes, and genius too. It takes a courage neither she nor Stanley can understand to say "For the first time I realized what a gulf separated the Artist from the Man!"*

+ Met Mary S. below Abbott's studio. The party was not too exciting. Mary & I alone in the bathroom. She's quite something. Several people kept interrupting us. Abbott pulled the shades down. And we were the absolute last.

6/21/41

We like to say it is love we search our whole life long, or we like to say it is Fame. But it is neither. It is understanding. We seek forever one other human heart we can touch and who can touch ours. We seek indefatigably like a hungry animal. For our heart is forever lonely. Forever alone. And wherever we feel this understanding may be, in a young girl, a young boy, a feeble old man, or a crone of a woman, in a drunkard, in a prostitute, in a madman, in a child, there we will go, and nothing in the world can hold us back.

6/21/41

I have never wanted to write as I do now. I have passed through such a hell of falsehood, tears, mockery, synthetic happiness,

---

* This exclamation of Pat's was probably inspired by Thomas Wolfe's 1929 novel *Look Homeward, Angel*, the coming-of-age story of an artist who assumed he was naturally superior to the mediocrity of the masses.

dreams, desires and disillusionment, of facades of beauty hiding
ugliness, of facades of ugliness hiding beauty, of kisses, and of mer-
etricious embraces, of dope and escape. So I want to write. I must
write. Because I am a swimmer struggling in a flood, and by my
writing I seek a stone to rest on. And if my feet escape it, I go under.

6/21/41

We don't know where creative ideas arise from. I find they
come when the conscious mind is occupied with something
else. Knitting, piano playing, reading a book so dull one's mind
wanders—these are excellent times. Even when we say we create consciously, is it not from some germ we received by these
means? Subconscious, or involuntary thinking, is the only and
inevitable means of creation.

JUNE 22, 1941

Russia and Germany at War!!! Extremely depressed & tired.
I still get a release from crying. I don't think it's weak if you
do it alone. What touches me most now is being loved. This
one wants more than Fame and Gold: to be loved, to be understood. And so I cry now, because happiness is so close and so
almost—realized.

6/22/41

There are some people we like instantly, before they have even
had a chance to flatter us (which is the greatest encouragement
to liking a person), because they have that quality of seeing in us
what we desire to be, what we are trying to be, and of not seeing
that which we are at the moment. We feel that they understand
us, we begin to feel that we have attained what we desire ourselves to be, and being made happy by this we inevitably are very
fond of the people who can make us feel this way.

JUNE 23, 1941

I feel myself filled with ideas. This summer I must get hold of
myself—get acquainted with myself, arrive once more at that

perfect equilibrium of discipline and nonsense which is my peculiar norm. I want to read a lot of long stuff like Quixote, Dante, Milton.

6/24/41

In my thesis on Christian Science: start with the origin of religion, its gradual clarification and growing specificness, ritualism: how the conception of God grew in men's own minds, how entirely religion is a product of men's minds. And especially, since man is endowed with the most esteemed of all gifts: intellect; especially how much more worthy he is of his kind if he rationalizes and reasons his own destiny! Like how much nobler for man to depend on man alone!

JUNE 25, 1941

Worked pretty well this AM. 5 pages done on tunnel story. I keep thinking all day at odd times about "straight" fiction I might do and especially about what medium I should use for my cartoons.

JUNE 26, 1941

Very serious & depressed and feeling that nothing I do is important—or ever will be—I have those moments too. I'm ashamed to say seeing a piece of crap in *The New Yorker* cheered me up—Someday I'll click there. Have a splendid idea I'll do next. [Pierre van Paassen's] *Days of Our Years*—beautiful reading. Mature, slow, and brilliant too. Stanley & I discussing the origins of war at dinner: he believes men's "inherent wickedness" responsible for war, and not the machinations of profiteers—(which is now the accepted fact, and is no longer even decried as Marxism!). + With [Billie] this evening. Saw *Citizen Kane*. Incredible maturity of [Orson] Welles!

JUNE 27, 1941

Had a wonderful evening alone before I went to Billie's. Read, wrote a really good first page to my story then went to see Mar-

jorie Wolf* a moment. She has spent a weekend with Babs B.
(who just lost a job at Altman's† because her school record was
more political than scholastic). Marjorie had a lovely girl named
Michael with her. How does she get them?! She paints. Then at
B.B.'s at 11:00. S., B., Ruth W. Mary R. came in later. Very nice
indeed. (I always thought so.) And to my surprise, M.S. was
won over to Mary R. and away from her darling Ruth W.—all
because Ruth, for some reason, rather snubbed M.R. on taking
leave. How very petty and female all this is! + Home with Mary
in taxi. Mary had not ironed her pajamas lest something go
wrong & I not stay!

JUNE 28, 1941

I need not record what happened last night. I'll never forget it.
+ And yet—why must I always stand aside and watch myself
and others as though we were on a stage? I shall never become a
part of life. I am not of it—yet. Flowers came at four this P.M.
I assured Ernst he would not be suspected, because who, with a
girl in a hotel room all day, would bother wooing her with gardenias? Ernst of course thinks Mike Thomas‡ sends them—as
my parents do too. Mary wrote "That such perfect moments
have a price, I know."

JUNE 29, 1941

Turned over my mystery plot in my head all day. Think I
have it airtight now. A plot grows from a single meager idea,
like a tall flowering from a scrubby little seed. You can't
tell where it comes from, but it comes inevitably like part of
nature's plan for the fertility of the earth: the brain is fertile
too. Smoking a trifle too much: maybe fifteen. Why should I
limit myself? I can at least not inhale. But limiting myself is

* Marjory Wolf was a high school friend of Pat's and Babs B.'s.
† B. Altman was a prominent New York City department store located on Fifth Avenue at Thirty-Fourth Street, no longer in existence.
‡ Mary is using her friend Mike Thomas's name as a cover when sending flowers so as not to get Pat into trouble.

part of that lousy system of checks that has made my last six years a form of imprisonment—that has ruined me really. +
I feel very affectionate to Roger lately. I think we'd get along.
+ Germans report successes, Russians report successes. The Russians, I think, will hold their own, though no one seems to think so.

JUNE 30, 1941

Another good day. Wonderful summer ahead—wonderful life ahead. I'm happy—that old seventh of March confidence returning despite scholastic setbacks.

JULY 2, 1941

So unbearably hot one loses all initiative. My writing and reading goes sliding by—all I do is shower & dress myself & comb my hair in the best 14 Street cutie manner. (Ernst prefers my hair up!) + I think often of how I'll burn up the town when I get out of school. Blitzkrieg on all sorts of things—cartoons, advertising possibly, & a great many lines of writing.

7/2/41

A novel about the twenty-year-olds. Just out of high school, just in college or just out of it. The bewilderment, the discouragement, the groping, the doubt, the hopes, the uncertainty of any permanence whatever. This could have great significance with respect to the times—economic, politic, the war and the knowledge—latent and unconscious, that we ourselves do not govern ourselves, and therefore are at other people's mercy, if any.

JULY 3, 1941

Cooler day. Came home at 4. Billie called me at 7:30. Would I have a drink. Beverly Bar 8:30–10:30. 3 or 4 there. Talking about nothing important. Mary's house packed, and Mary frigid upon my entree with Billie. But furious. Said [Billie] did it on purpose, etc. That everybody had gasped! When we came in. Girl painter named Buffie Johnson* last night. Rather cute & we got along. Buffie gave me her number. Tired.

JULY 4, 1941

Virginia called up at 6:30. Saw her at Jumble, then Tavern, home, Vanguard. She is a beautiful child, intelligent, smart, and very attractive what's more she loves me. Forever. Went to Judy's at 11:00. The show even better. New staff around. + Called Mary to tell her. Delighted. Also got Buffie out of bed at 1:00 AM. She asked me to cocktails tomorrow.

JULY 5, 1941

Worked with Hauser. And had a dreadful conversation about Eddy's & my conversation last night. He thinks I did him irreparable damage when I said he was sitting on the fence in his writing, while I thought this the most charitable thing I could say under the circumstances. Went to Buffie's at 5:30. Bijou of a place. 159 E. 46 St. She like a little oriental doll—Persia, I guess. And her work all over the walls. I was pleasantly surprised. Somewhat derivative—the Cézanne, Dalí, Chirico, Laurencin, Renoir School, but some portraits have something too. We sat about drinking Scotch & gin, at least twelve inches between us on the couch (how careful when alone!), and talking art. Buffie'd warned me first off that Bernhard was coming at 7:00. Started to go immediately because of [Mary] S. implications, but decided to make it a test case. Bernhard surprised of course. Said she'd have to tell S. because of her loyalty, etc. But later calmed down & agreed not to mention it. Buffie of course amused. She took my hand on coming in, and I had expected more, asked me soon after would I like to see her Monday night. So I went to the Waldorf [Astoria]. Had dinner with S. & Mike, Dean C., John at

---

* Buffie Johnson (1912–2006), American painter associated with surrealism and abstract expressionism. She studied at Académie Julian in Paris (where she also had private lessons with Camille Pissarro and Francis Picabia and met Natalie Barney, Gertrude Stein, and Alice B. Toklas) and at the Art Students League in New York.

Le Moal's.* Back to 98 exhausted. I told Mary I was going away with Virginia next weekend, and we still had a pleasant night. Then about 2:00 Mary lit a cigarette and told me she thought we'd better not see each other again. She mainly resented the fact I didn't want people to know how close we were—the fact is I was protecting her from shame as well as me.

JULY 6, 1941

I simply cannot say, at this time, that I care enough about Mary to say I shall see no one else in the world. She cried a lot tonight. She says it's like when she was a child and couldn't get the pony she wanted. So she cried. But only because she was mad. I hope, in the turmoil of all this Bernhard does not tell Mary I was at Buffie's Friday, that would be the *coup de grâce*. I can't say either that I have degenerated in the last few months. Everybody has his fling. Serious people get hurt in them. And the other person, myself, if they happen to be attractive, gets lots of flattering attentions from the serious (or not-serious people) and has a lot of fun. I've tried to do the things as gently as possible with Mary. She's been more than fair with me. What burns me is that she's ready to go off now with someone else. I should be jealous, yes. Because I want my cake & want to eat it too. I wish desperately that I could find it in myself to settle down, love someone steadily, not be greedy—but I cannot.

JULY 6, 1941

I finally understood Mary better. "Loving you less, I would accept you on those terms. But as it is I can't share you." I don't blame her. I'm not in love. But I know in the way of intelligence, fidelity, dependability, and intensity, Mary is superior to Virginia. Perhaps I shall live to regret it—breaking with her. I told Mary what I felt about her. "But it wasn't enough." And it wasn't. I'm still having a thing. When I get ready to pick up the pieces, maybe they won't make one complete person in the

---

* Le Moal was a French restaurant located at Fifty-Sixth Street and Third Avenue.

world. I'll take that chance. When I got home quite late, letter special delivery from Hauser. He says I needn't show up Monday. Since I've been spreading lies about him, we'd better not meet again. I wrote a nice answer. I must say it didn't faze me. My heart is completely torn up with other things now.

JULY 7, 1941

Spent the morning working. These are the days to fulfill "latent potentialities." + Read Van Paassen's *Time Is Now* today. Favors immediate entree [into war]. I do too. In spite of the communist angle that I've been fooling with. Now that Russia is engaged, we should enter immediately.

To Buffie's at 6:30. We had gin & whiskey. There was a cat. And the Rousseau garden. I told her all my troubles. With Mary and Ernst Hauser. Buffie is charmingly naive—after much delay I finally kissed her—on the couch. She makes love like a Frenchman, whispering passionate things in your ear. How she saw me first at the party. I must say she remembers well. I told her very soon though, that I was in no state of mind for a one-night stand. Buffie was awfully disappointed but she is going to call me afterwards. Going to be in the city indefinitely too! So, very drunk indeed, we went to Tony's for a lobster thermidor. By that time it was very late. Went to Spivy's* for night caps. Buffie, like her decadent fascist nobility, is the tail end of an era. A family in her case. She's merely added this *gaieté* to her list of bizarre accomplishments.

7/8/41

Nothing makes a woman, or a man either, watch her personal appearance so much as having enemies. She never knows when or where she will encounter them, but she must always be in top condition.

---

* Spivy (born Bertha Levine, 1906–1971), noted New York wit, entertainer, and actress, owned a nightclub on East Fifty-Seventh Street, Spivy's Roof, noted for its tolerance of gay performers and patrons. In the early 1940s, aged only twenty-one, Liberace was the club's pianist.

JULY 10, 1941

Buffie should send me a postcard. Hope she does. I keep thinking about her. I'm at loose ends and I might as well admit it. If
I only had one good recognizably lousy impulse to fight!!! But
no—not even that! At least I might prove myself decent. Was
with Arthur tonight. Took a Staten Island ferry & walked our
heads off out there. He says, when I refused to kiss him, that
I'm always psychologically unready but often physically ready.
What an observant lad—if he'd only go a bit further now!—

JULY 13, 1941

Entirely too beachy and housey to suit me but Virginia likes it.
There was a knocking at our door last night—Virginia nearly
hit the ceiling & clung to me like a wisteria vine. It turned out to
be a child. I thought it would be one of those things—"Why so-
an-so's been dead five years!" Took an enormous hike. Made a
sketch or two on a hillside where we ate lunch. Had a wonderful
day. I didn't make any passes at Virginia. Wouldn't have even
with liquor, I think, because, frankly, I can't even think of anyone but Buffie.

JULY 14, 1941

I'm so happy when I'm alone. I see all sorts of things and get wonderful ideas. I get to the bottom of myself. Don't know if it's the
extra sleep or Jenning's shots, but I feel full of energy & ideas.
Should like to do a novel. Something brilliant of course. Have two
possible ideas that need expansion & thought. Now [Thomas]
Mann's *Death in Venice* is considered brilliant. Anybody can be
so with a bizarre idea and a capacity for smooth writing. The
expansion of a novel is appealing to me. But in spite of my past
critical reading, I should think more about plot & action. + Came
home at nine. Looked for want-ad job. Frankly I want the money,
but I'd rather not work this summer, anymore. Could accomplish
more at home. + Virginia thinks I shall be famous. "Would you
keep me when you get famous, Pat?" I said perhaps, if she puts on
twenty pounds, and mends her nasty ways.

JULY 15, 1941

Called Mary S. for date this evening. Ate a lot & finally went home with her which I wanted to do anyway. I just felt like lying in bed, talking & doing nothing. But Bernhard, at Mary's gentle hint, came down & gave us her room. So the whole business. She keeps trying to wean me from my customary habits. Maddens me in a peculiar way. Says I might be as butch as she and just get pleasure making love. Mary can't stand to be touched herself. We spoke more frankly last night than ever before. Because it was the last time. After all my mind's on Buffie now. And that doesn't mean a great deal to me. I still have not felt the variety. There is still only "me" when it happens.

JULY 16, 1941

Sent "Vacant Lot" and "Train to Astoria"* to *Story* [magazine] also *New Yorker*. + Mary sent flowers. Had a dreadful time at Dr D.'s. He hurt like hell! I can't decide whether I'm in love with Buffie or her painting. I have a boundless admiration for anyone who can do what she does. + Started methodical reading. *War & Peace*. Mont Saint-Michel & Chartres. Survey of English Lit 1700. + Babs B. told me Monday night that Rose M. said she knew about my "women friends." That it seemed to be common knowledge.

JULY 17, 1941

Very happy indeed—and fighting pleasantly against that jag—those delirium tremens that attack me when I have a date on with people like Buffie. Tried to call Mary S. today. I want to tell her I am with Buffie tomorrow so she won't get heart failure as we walk into the Caravan. Also so she won't send flowers. + Saw some excellent exhibits with Mother this PM, Waldo Peirce's *Alzira & Anna*† is splendid! But much like Renoir. Also a good drawing by

---

* Neither of those stories has survived.
† Waldo Peirce (1884–1970), painter often called "the American Renoir."

Picasso which was worth all the rest. I wonder do we always not admire the kind of thing we come nearest doing ourselves?

7/17/41

Why do I always run to morbid subjects!

JULY 18, 1941

This day is momentous for one circumstance: Buffie is off my chest. We sat around till ten thirty. Very pleasant and warm indeed. But why do I lose interest having once got something? And what do I want? Somebody I think younger than I. But definitely someone when I can be respected for my work. I see now how that enters in. It's always present. Otherwise I might just as well be sleeping with a man. I must be head of the partnership. I think Buffie is quite serious. She must be about thirty-three. The damned cat stalks about constantly.

JULY 19, 1941

Decided yesterday at 4:30 that I am to go to California with John Coates before the 31st.* + Worked revising this morning. Not too enthusiastically about it tho I do take some pride in "How to write" for the "sleeks." Met Buffie at 1:00 Luncheon at [Hotel] Pierre's. Veddyveddy elegant. Then to Fanny M., girl my age who paints. Drinks. Then to Lola P.'s where I had one of the best evenings, or party evenings, of my life. Very quiet. Only Lola P., Buffie, Rosalind Constable & myself. Haphazard dinner followed by white wine, drunken in boredom at first and later with great enthusiasm. Had delightful conversation with Rosalind. She's on *Vogue* & *Fortune*. Long blond hair & English accent but looks Norwegian and she & Lola P. are falling all over themselves to introduce me to Editors, etc. Lola P. is—why describe them?—I shall be seeing them more often, I hope. Got Rosalind's phone number & shall call her before I leave. We got

---

* That summer, Pat drives across the country to California with her uncle John and aunt Grace.

on famously. A lot of bullshit, getting on a magazine. Pull and personality, she says. She got hers on her accent!

JULY 21, 1941

Read some in an unhappy disjointed sort of way. Got slicked up to go to Constable's at 6:30. I called her last night during the party 12:30 AM. She was delighted or seemed so. Lives 667 Madison. Her roommate Natasha [H.] is in New Mexico at Ruth W.'s ranch. We drank & played records. Finally went out to Sammy's.* + Thence to Au Petit Paris.† Nice meal & I got very high at one point. Rosalind has a wonderful mouth. Clean, young, and looks like she laughs a lot, which she does. So at 2:00 when I was about to leave, and could easily have done so, she said I should stay because of the hour. She felt like being a cautious mother that night. And indeed she was. She's so wonderfully well-hearted about it all. I slept in her room-mates bed & room. She joined me for a few minutes. We both were kidding around & laughing a lot. Then she left & we slept for a few hours. She has a good portrait of herself by Nelson‡ in her room. Somewhat like Modigliani.

JULY 22, 1941

We woke at quarter to eight & lay talking the rest of the time. Very very casual, superior about it all. Thinks I'm surely older, and considers me probably a somewhat precocious & blatant child. She's got the most intelligent looking face I've seen outside of Virginia Woolf. Had breakfast & I called Buffie & had an interminable conversation. Walked Rosalind down to Radio City. "You'll be leaving now—I shan't know ever where to find you again." I gave her reassurance. She's attracted and at the

---

* The New York institution Sammy's Bowery Follies was a notorious location at 267 Bowery that attracted a mixed and colorful crowd thanks to its cabaret license.
† Léon Gerber, a former pastry chef at the Ritz Hotel in Paris, purchased the old Madison Tavern in 1939 and reopened it as Le Petit Paris in 1945.
‡ Probably the abstract expressionst painter Leonard Nelson (1912–1993), whose art was exhibited among others at Betty Parsons's gallery and at Peggy Guggenheim's Art of This Century.

same time has her tongue in her cheek. I think she's tied up with a painter who's "coming to live there in September."

JULY 23, 1941

Spent this night with Buffie as I knew I would. Arrived about five—she gave me a gorgeous pair of cufflinks—gold with a brown stone. Rather large. Then we picked up Irving D. & Billy Somebody & went to Spivy's anniversary party. Then home. I'm not in love. Can't even say I wish I were. Buffie is so damned "bandbox," as Constable so aptly put it.

JULY 24, 1941

Home & restless. Walked a lot. Walter Marlowe came at six. We couldn't swim where we wanted to. Upstate a ways. Dinner at Fleur de Lis. His place is really charming. He's done so much with it. A remarkable man. Somewhat of an inferiority complex with women because of his height & hair. But he's the kind of man I'd marry. + Called Rosalind at dinner. She thought I'd gone & was pleasantly surprised. She says it's a good thing I'm leaving because she's too "enthusiastic." I'm sincerely fond of her. Not like I was about Billie. Constable is an admirable person. And honorable. And intelligent. I wonder if she's the next step towards a man?

JULY 24, 1941

Enjoyed this last evening with Walter Marlowe so much. He's so wonderfully thoughtful—he makes me feel quite sluggish and careless intellectually. Because his thinking is so rich. It is the most amusing task in the world—the unraveling of an idea—or the pursuit of an answer. He is what I demand most—an inspiration: because my whole preferences in people are based upon—subconsciously and consciously—a furtherance of my terrific ambitions.

JULY 24, 1941

I should feel so much today that I don't. What will it take & when will it come? I feel a transitory state—because I'm not working regularly & smoking too much. Buffie says she adores me. And I believe her. And how terrible it will be if I suddenly discover my heart is definitely someplace else!? She is so good to me—so thoughtful. And I am absolutely tongue-tied around her. The nice things I think of—that I could say—I can't. I feel shy. Don't know why—perhaps they don't burst out of me. And they really should.

JULY 25, 1941

To Constable's at 5:30. Called for her Reception room on 30th floor. She on the 26. She was very nice to me. We taxied to her place & had two quick drinks. There is so much laughter & so much brains. I believe I'm in love—I didn't need to say believe, but I know it will have to come this way—because now I'm no longer carried off by a stupid pretty face. Kissed me several times. I hate to think of myself as a clever little monkey showing off for her benefit. There's been too much of that.

JULY 26, 1941

Caught the bus at 10:50 last evening. Graham along to see me off. Hot tiresome trip. I feel blue. Thinking constantly of Rosalind & not at all of Buffie. I am an ungrateful fickle little bastard. It's so much fun to ride along, letting one's mind build things like an Erector Set, and being quite alone as the miles go past, enjoying cigarettes & coffee, and thinking of possible stories, and of Rosalind, and of the busy, active, amusing, and wild life before me—not only next semester, when I shall work like hell, but for all time. I have a great destiny before me—a world of pleasures and accomplishments, beauty and love.

JULY 27, 1941

Saw Chicago this morning. A splendid exhibit at the Chicago Museum of Art. Carl Milles* & International Water Color Show. Still got my mind on Rosalind. Buffie is too young for me—not

---

* Carl Milles, a Swedish sculptor best known for his fountains.

young enough to dominate as I did Virginia, but too giddy and feminine to dominate me. So I lay on my stomach in the park, waiting for the Museum to open, & wrote to Rosalind. Told her I thought I was in love with her, but that I soon blew over, & not to bother. (the hell she won't!) And would she please write to me at Sioux Falls. She'd better!

JULY 28, 1941

We keep stopping at tiny towns—the people all eating heartily. Some sick. And more interesting. After seeing some of the sections I wonder why anyone lives anywhere but N.Y.C. After seeing some of the people, I'm very glad they do.

In Sioux City for five hours. Went to the library & read Powys' *Meaning of Culture*. Very good & calming. Finally got to Sioux Falls at 3:45, just about at the end of my rope physically. Filthy, dirty. John is preoccupied with his school & Grace is her same stupid self. I'm in a tiny room with one window & no breeze. Temp. nearly 100°. This town is incredibly small. + Don't feel in the least like writing to Buffie. Wonder how I shall go about breaking off—and if she will ever guess it is Rosalind? And if she does, will I lose her friendship entirely? But Rosalind, I gather, is inextricably obligated. I shan't mind—I worship her anyway. God if she only writes me & doesn't worry that my uncle will open them! + S. sent me gardenias the day I left. They were more beautiful than ever.

7/29/41

What I admire most in an individual is a kind of activity—a liveliness either of mind or body or both—which alone can assure the development of the character I prefer. I believe liveliness and animal energy are the sine qua nons.

JULY 30, 1941

Wonderful how reading good prose all day stimulates one's imagination. One even thinks in good English. Had a stupid conversation with Grace on Socialism. She has read nothing,

and would not have the mind to assimilate if she had. After
a hamburger & a walk returned & found an airmail from
Rosalind. I flew up the stairs. One slender page—but what
a kiss from her lips. "Darling" but no acknowledgments. A
superficial, intellectual style of brilliant writing. Much like
her conversation. Plethora of peculiar words. I had written her
modestly—4 pages an hour before—and I wrote her again. I
think I'm in love, the kind of intellectual, unpassionate love that
I shall, I suppose, always give.

7/30/41

The perversity in human nature reaches a peak in the sexual
compartments. If one's love affair is running smoothly and
a new face appears, which will necessitate an unreasonable
amount of trouble and disruption, and delay and unhappiness
to attain, one will make for this new face like a man wandering
on a desert will make for a distant sign of habitation he has just
spied.

JULY 31, 1941

A final pleasant day in the library. No letter from Rosalind
though she might have. In my excitement (at leaving tonight) I
wrote her again—this time—that I worshipped her—which I do
goddamn it. I speculate about what course I might have taken—
to be aloof—to have gone without telephoning her, to have disappeared for a summer and to return and find her in love with
me. The game would decidedly have been worth the candle. But
I, I'm afraid, am not up to the game. I must blurt out all that I
feel, with the consolation that, whatever the results, I have been
I, and I am that I am. Rosalind, bless her heart, seems to like me
as I am. Bought some wonderful blue sneakers this PM. And in
those and my gray flannels, we embarked from Sioux Falls.

AUGUST 1, 1941

Tonight at ten thirty-five. A glorious, wild, and fast ride forty
miles due west without a turn in the road. Through the black-

ness, under a half moon. With only the radio playing poor jazz to spoil the romance of it. It was a wonderful experience. Full of promise, expectation, happiness. And—love—to come, ecstasy and success, reward and affection. And my own dreams of no one and nothing except Rosalind.

AUGUST 1, 1941

John and I get up in the mornings, go down and have a good breakfast and then start out. Saw the Rushmore (Borglum) monument* this afternoon. As art it is beyond consideration—as a monument it is an insult to the majesty of the mountains. Stopped rather early at Gillette, Wyoming, and I walked way out in the prairie, only afraid, not of being raped but being robbed, since I had my wallet with me.

AUGUST 2, 1941

Crossed the badlands yesterday, and the Rockies today—ending up at Cody, Wyoming, at 5 o'clock, since there is nothing around the Yellowstone Park. Saw the nightly rodeo here. Local talent—one lad was stomped on in the bareback riding. Rope tricks by Pat Henry, and good showmanship. I spent a lovely hour choosing meticulously one tan cowboy belt I bought from Dave Jones $1.95. The thing, however, came from Ft. Worth Texas. The day was wonderful. Cody is 5,000 feet high. The night cool, I walked into the hills, supper alone at Cowhand café after John & Grace had gone to bed. Cowboys all around. $7.50 shirts and $7.50 Stetsons, and in my happiness I had to write to Rosalind. We shall be in Frisco Tuesday.

AUGUST 3, 1941

Tough day driving. Not enough sleep. Beautiful scenery, canyons and mountains. "Laughing Pig" and "Elephant Head." The more I see of the country, the more faces I see, the more I

---

* The Mount Rushmore National Memorial in South Dakota was created between 1927 and 1941 by Gutzon Borglum.

know there is one home and one face. No home, really, because home is your lover's heart, nowhere on the earth. This evening after a dinner we had a memorable conversation from ten to one when we got to Elko, Nevada. About Socialism first. John doesn't scruple to call Browder an S.O.B., which I should not do to F.D.R. But Grace on one of her tangents told me off about my Communist manners, etc. How I put my foot on the dash, and vote where I want to go, and don't carry out responsibilities about the thermos, etc. I find it hard to argue with them. Each is adamant and unread. And each seems to attack me personally which can make things unpleasant as hell.

AUGUST 4, 1941

Grace last night mentioned that John was giving up business because he didn't want to disappoint me about the trip. Just why this should be so, I don't know because I felt him out most tactfully before deciding. John was quite uncomfortable when that conversation was taking place last night. They were right, of course. I have an arrogance that I shall never lose—that I really don't want to entirely. I should try to be more polite but the hard "knocks" accruing from my native rudeness, I take as the husk around the kernel.

Drove some today; over 100 miles. I don't jerk the wheel as most women do. John was very pleased. Got into Nevada (Reno) in no time at all. Wide-open town. Business booming because of raised prices on cattle and minerals. Everybody's gambling. Got quite merry, on two gin rickeys. I think of Rosalind—I can see her smile in the dark. Lost $1.00 at roulette.

AUGUST 5, 1941

I drove today part way from Reno to Sacramento. Made excellent time and landed in San Francisco at 2:30. The city is all sprawled out & very hilly—the way cities in the west sprawl when they grow instead of growing upward as New York had to—so you have these suburbs practically that take 5 miles and a horse to get to. We established ourselves in Geary St. and I called Rita. I went out on the 6:00 bus. They live in a lovely home 25 rooms. Rented partly. We had dinner & then tramped around. She's a smart kid, with that New York tenseness which is the blessed heritage of the place—that won't let its children rest.

AUGUST 6, 1941

Rita handicapped because of being Jewish in getting a magazine job. Perhaps if I looked like [her] or like Babs B., I should be a martyr to the cause, too. But life is too pleasant now. + All the gay people, it seems, are in L.A.—S.F. is extremely conservative. Must get there. Rita and her sister both expressed their belief that I shall "become a writer." Mainly on account of my "drive."

AUGUST 7, 1941

No letter, no letter, no letter! Is there anything in the world more desolate—Tomorrow surely! What is she thinking about, I wonder. And how often does she think of me, and with what sudden consciousness, I wonder.

8/7/41

Sex, to me, should be a religion. I have no other. I feel no other urge, to devotion, to something, and we all need a devotion to something besides ourselves, besides even our noblest ambitions. I could be content without fulfillment. Perhaps I should be better off in such an arrangement.

8/7/41

A woman is never, or very seldom, hopelessly in love with one man. She can make a calm choice between the man with the money and the man without, the better father and the bad father, who may be handsomer. The woman, because, chiefly because, she has less imagination, has less passion. She brings less, and she takes less.

AUGUST 8, 1941

Decided to go *tout de suite* to Los Angeles as John may be leaving Tuesday for Denver. Was to go tonight but called Rita and there was a letter—from Rosalind of course—and wild horses could not have torn me away without it. Went out, a bit ginny, after dinner. I read it. Non-committal until the last page. "What can I ever give you to keep you in my life? You will go in so many directions. The most I can hope for is that you will come to me when you are tired. Perhaps." And of course, I sat up till two writing to her. What can she give me? Everything. What will she? Everything in one way. Nothing in another. I shan't mind.

AUGUST 9, 1941

Boarded the train at 8:00 AM. Borrowed $15.00 from John. Not such a fast train, but we got to Los Angeles at 5:30. Established myself at the Hotel Bertha & sent a letter to mother immediately saying please don't make me go to Denver, Colorado. I want a verificatory wire by Monday night. I saw the Moon Festival in Chinatown.

AUGUST 10, 1941

Lonely last night. But it's wonderful just to think of Rosalind. Dressed nicely for the Countess. She was glad to see a friend of Constable's, but she was moving. Tomorrow at 6:00 AM. The Countess (Marta) is about 45, blonde-gray, enormous, hard living & drinking. We had a hasty dinner at Brown Derby* which the Countess paid for. Afterwards I wrote Rosalind which is becoming a daily ritual with me. Marta said Rosalind had her first book published when she was sixteen and that she wished she'd find a man to marry because she thinks that's what she wants—(I don't). The Countess asked me point blank if I was in love with Rosalind and treated it with amused tolerance, which I think she really feels. Little interest in the boudoir—well, she's had her day, I suspect. Bought [D. H. Lawrence's] *Lady Chatterley's Lover* .75.

---

* The Brown Derby was a famous Hollywood restaurant with a clientele composed largely of celebrities.

AUGUST 11, 1941

Walked around Chinatown & had some wonderful tortillas & milk (6$!) + caught the noon Daylight out of L.A. 40 minutes late. I can think wonderful thoughts while traveling—not concentrating on it, but just as they emerge from the under-consciousness which is how they must always come anyway. Arrived at 10:45. Letters from Mother. One surprised no end that I need money & with $10.00. Wait till they have read my letter of yesterday morning asking for $30.00! I'm still $5.00 in the hole with John & broke stony, too. John intends to leave Wed. God if I have to go!

AUGUST 12, 1941

We made a day of it and went to Twin Peaks, where I was the highest person in San Francisco for a while. Then to a redwood forest and to San Rafael for an enormous 3 o'clock fish dinner. I didn't want to go to Denver. I shall have to, because there's no excuse. I'm restless over something.—Would I be more satisfied in N.Y.? I doubt it. I should see Rosalind, but that would only remind me more vividly of what I can't have. And I should have my all-soothing routine. Yes, I should be happier.

AUGUST 13, 1941

Eureka, Nevada.

Left S.F. at eight. I wonder under what circumstances I shall next see it. And with whom. + John let me drive some 70 miles today. Great fun. Long stretches without towns. All mining around here. The stars were lovely tonight. What I think of constantly is of making something of myself—a good job and good living on the side. Something to make [Rosalind] respect me and take notice of me as something besides an attractive and precocious child. As a matter of fact, compared to her, I'm not. Thus women have been, and will always be, the inspiration of all the best in the world. A man goes to his soul and to the universe, creating and building, inventing and discovering, only to lay it, or its rewards, at the feet of some woman.

AUGUST 15, 1941

It's an odd thing, I can't remember Buffie's telephone number, but I can both of Rosalind's. One up for Herr Freud. Little library where I read for an hour or so. [Sir James] Jeans, [Irwin] Edman, criticism. Then back down the lovely mile outside of town.Very, very happy and full of thwarted ambition—I want to sit down at a typewriter in a room all alone. I want long days to mull over what I've seen, silent hours to dream out stories that are as delicate, in the first plot germs, as smoke rings. And long evenings, which will be fewer now, I imagine, with Rosalind. Sometimes it's better, however, with a group of people. I've often found it so. We like each other better then. + Played with the animals this morning. Two bouncing dogs with a deer's foot, horses standing in a stream, a black kitten, and two calves. + Wrote Countess Marquiset. A rather conceited letter, saying if she mentioned that about the waitresses in the B. Derby, I'd mail her a time bomb.

AUGUST 16, 1941

Got into Denver, Colorado, at 11. Very pretty town. T.B. cases all over because of the altitude. Read T. S. Eliot this afternoon. He's a splendid poet and a good critic too.

8/16/41

Denver, Colorado.

The few hours I have spent with you—that I have ever spent with you—I can at least amuse myself reliving, over and over again, like a favorite book that one reads a dozen times, each rereading yielding a new emotion, a different thrill. The words of a book are always the same, just as the things we did are always the same. But in the formless, wordless land of imagination, where our short hours are, I can embellish and recolor and project. Outside my window, someplace, they are singing the "Lorelei." *"Ich weiss nicht, was soll es bedeuten, dass ich so traurig bin—"**

---

* "I don't know what it can mean / that I am so sad . . ." The opening lines of one of Heinrich Heine's most famous poems and which has been set to music by different composers.

AUGUST 17, 1941

A rare day. Breakfasted with John. He's one of those men who govern their womenfolks about when to sit down and when to leave. Bad manners. + Roamed about the city visiting museums, etc. Some good stuff from Mesa Verde. Fossils and mummies and skulls. Read first volume of Stendhal's *Le Rouge et le Noir*. Hearty breakfast, hamburger for lunch and dinner at the Blue Parrot Inn. Apparently, I'm burning it up. Go to bed hungry every night wake up ravenous. I wish it were tomorrow already. I want my mail.

AUGUST 18, 1941

Raced down to the post-office before breakfast. But no mail. How alone and neglected it makes one feel! Want to read the *Divine Comedy* while here. However most important is browsing. At the P.O. at 3:30. Letters from mother, with 30 dollars, J. B., Roger, etc. + If it is wonderful to love a woman (the parts of her sweet, irresponsible ways) how much more wonderful to love a woman with a power and will like Rosalind's. How much more challenging she is.

AUGUST 19, 1941

A stinking lousy day. I am up to the neck in scenery! Insupportably boring! Especially when we had to wait 1½ hrs. at the near top of Mt. Evans. A sillier, less pleasant way to ruin a car I can't imagine. How I wished I could have been in the library, finishing [Malcolm Cowley's] *After the Genteel Tradition*.

AUGUST 20, 1941

Somewhat better because we came home early. Saw the Garden of the Gods and such rot. Mushroom rocks the best. Some snaps. Seeing all these peaks and "gorgeous gorges" is a mild form of insanity. John and Grace have to get at least ½ way up every hill they see. The most "gorgeous gorges" are those they do in restaurants.

AUGUST 21, 1941

We shall leave Saturday morning. I'm happy! Chicago—then home! Breakfasted with John & Grace. Library at 10:30. A typical Denver day. Went for mail at one. A letter from Buffie. A dread of opening it and seeing her writing. Whether she still cared. Hoping she did for my ego's sake, for the desire one has always—to be loved—but mainly hoping she did not. Bought Buffie the lucite and gold leaf stone. $5.50. Useless like so many things she likes.

8/21/41

This summer I have climbed, like a struggling Junebug on a fluted lamppost, to a higher ledge. A kind of higher standard, but above all a new hope and confidence. I intend to stay here. Right here and beyond.

8/22/41

It's strange the older I get, the less respect I have for so-called logical thinking. Thinking is creative, and we create subconsciously—in flashes. When one has a problem to work out—a problem of one's own relations with others, one can seldom arrive at anything by an "assembly of facts." Perhaps after one has dropped the matter—minutes later, there will be a sudden insight, often in a projected imaginary situation which will come or might come—and one will never get closer to the truth than this one flash. We cannot even push the flash further.

AUGUST 23, 1941

Packed this AM. Caught the 1:00 Rocket from Denver. I thought about R. during the train ride and while I was reading [Émile Zola's] Nana inattentively. And also about Buffie. Dante had his unrequited love for Beatrice and he had a wife, too. I simply prefer my Beatrice. She is beauty, goodness and intelligence. She is man's striving on the earth. She is a bit of heaven I've been lucky enough to find. How could I ever leave her? And what would I not give up for her! I am leaving the bad for the good. The evil for the pure. And if I ever think this an extravagance, God damn me!

8/23/41

A very small number of people are conscious of their individuality and live always to develop it and to excel. The vast majority try desperately hard to show, in everyway, that they are exactly like everyone else. This gives them a kind of security and self-assurance and contentment.

AUGUST 26, 1941

Very eager to get home. Tired, of course very tired, but happy too. *Wie schön ist die Heimat!*[*] *"Und kennst du das Land, wo die Citrönen bluhn? (auf Säulen rüht sein Dach!)"*[†] Sat about talking. I told almost all, I think. Good to see a couple of intelligent faces. Then I called R. around eleven. She was in bed, knitting, having just flown in from Washington. She knew my voice. Her laugh was the same—only so much more wonderful than I could imagine. Shan't tell Buffie I'm in town until after I see R. Should be sober when I speak to B., I suppose. Though it's not the easiest way. + I want to do so much. The one moment of discouragement and doubt comes before all one's things are put away again, when one sees all the old books and thinks that one has read them all and how little one knows anyway, when one sees unfinished manuscripts and thinks of the labors ahead. I am aiming higher than ever before. God or something give me courage, and power!

AUGUST 27, 1941

R. has been (and is) a wonderful influence on me. I have no desire to mix with [Buffie] or Mary S. or [Billie] the way I

---

[*] How beautiful is home!
[†] Excerpts from Goethe's poem "Mignon": "Do you know the land where the lemon-trees bloom . . ."

was doing. I prefer to stay at home nights. I wonder how long this will last? Yet I am not so coldblooded as I was. Not since Virginia.

8/27/41

I wish I might write music from twenty to thirty, books from thirty to forty, and paint from fifty to sixty, and perhaps, while I could still wield a mallet, sculpt from forty to fifty.

8/27/41

We live in flashes, like as we think and create in flashes. Possibly the only other times we live is in anticipation. By living here I mean any enjoyment. In my trip to California, I enjoyed very little in the anticipation except the passive excitement. But the moments I shall always treasure were the ride west in the night from Sioux Falls, South Dakota, and the walk in Chamberlain the same night, and hearing Beethoven's Fifth in the middle of the desert in the hours before midnight, and the wonderful letter from Rosalind in South Dakota—reading it, and thinking of it that night as I fell asleep, and the instant when I felt all at once the spirit of the circus in Denver as I watched the percheron horses pulling against their collars (big black heavy leather studded with gold). There was no enjoyment in the keener sense in seeing canyons or mountains too long approached, or seeing the "pièce de resistance," San Francisco from the Twin Peaks. The less happy moments, too, somehow one would not exchange. Whether for curiosity or simple love of emotion, I don't know. There is the deepest sadness in the world in not receiving a letter from someone we love. I felt this. And I have felt, too, the peculiar discomfort and fear when I have received a letter from a person whom one no longer wants. But being in love, unlike all other experiences, visual, physical or mental, is a constant pleasure. Alone or together two people in love are happy. In a sense they are always together, and alone, too. Love is a thing you can have in your pocket.

AUGUST 28, 1941

Worked this AM. Letters from Buffie, against my 31st arrival. My mother likes her handwriting. She is steady. But I simply don't care for her. + Sold some books & went shopping, rather nervously with Mother. + Chez Rosalind's at 7:07, after a drink on myself. Billie A. was there. Gave R. the ice freezers and the record, which she hardly attended because she's tense about her deadline tomorrow night. I wonder shall I grow tired of this arrangement, or have I become so ascetic that I shall find the restraint exhilarating and inspirational? It had better be so. I saw a picture of Betty Parsons,* the painter, who is coming to live with R. Very cute, young, nice forehead. "I chose," says R. She had nothing forced upon her. I didn't kiss her. We lay—or sat—on the couch before driving down to Nino & Nella's for dinner. Then to Jumble Shop. Drove home with R. against her protestations. I merely enjoy breathing the same air for a while. As I say. I can't imagine changing from her. Not her!

AUGUST 29, 1941

Wrote the *Quarterly* booklet. Not bad. And cracky, I hope. It seems everybody is out of town. + Read [Carson McCullers's] *Reflections in a Golden Eye*. Not good at all. + Saw Rogers (Ginger) picture which stank. + Called Rosalind who was out at 11:05 and abed at 11:45. Natasha had to hang up from her room. Rosalind very nice to me. She's giving me a lot of time. Such things as this can be very flattering, I know—and not boring unless one becomes dog-like, which I shall never do. What shall I do? Make myself as amusing as possible, and work like mad to be something.

---

* Betty Parsons studied painting in Paris, where her circle of friends included Man Ray and Alexander Calder as well as Gertrude Stein and Sylvia Beach. One of her fellow students was Alberto Giacometti. In 1948 she would open her own gallery on Fifty-Seventh Street. She is considered the "mother of abstract expressionism," having represented artists including Jackson Pollock, Mark Rothko, Clyfford Still, Barnett Newman, Hans Hofmann, and Ad Reinhardt.

8/30/41

Sex and alcohol I refute thus: alcohol is not worth its price—as a habitual source of pleasure and inspiration. And sex is a hoax. As big a hoax as a Coney Island sideshow. And as overrated as a trip to Pike's Peak. Marriage is like going back to the same sideshow twice, a moronic thing to do certainly. For women, it is even worse, because they come out on the short end.

SEPTEMBER 1, 1941

Sent folder to Comet Press.* A good morning's work rewriting first draft. Three mornings on a 10-page job is not too bad. I thought of my poor Rosalind working perhaps all day. I wonder if her husband is still in love with her. Or if he ever was? Probably not. Damned if he isn't gay. Shall call Buffie tomorrow. I don't like to remember those times when calling her—even the anticipation of it—was a delight. Now I've become so skeptical, I try to choose the faults of anyone I am in love with—with Rosalind it could only be her cynicism. At least this is not a thing like B. [Billie] B.'s stupidity or B. [Buffie]'s fussiness—a thing that could make one wince upon recollection. No I think I have my gimlet eyes open. + Proust is a delight and an inspiration. Perhaps one should reread him every three years.

SEPTEMBER 2, 1941

Rosalind called me Darling today, so there is little more I have to say about this Tuesday. I finished my story, called Buffie (it preyed on my mind horribly) at 10. Called Mary S. and saw her tonight. We had drinks at Rochambeau's.† I told M. how I felt about R. Also that Janet Flanner‡ & Betty P. & the whole bunch are gay, and that they've had their fling and so can now be quite "honorable" because they are tired out physically. If I had more room I'd say it more beautifully.

---

* Comet Press in Brooklyn, where the *Barnard Quarterly* is printed.
† Rochambeau's, a restaurant located at 28 West Eleventh Street.
‡ Janet Flanner, noted freelance writer and journalist based in Paris, who for many years contributed to *The New Yorker* under the pseudonym Genet.

SEPTEMBER 4, 1941

When mornings begin with rejection slips and end with lectures on four-year-old diets, life begins to be a burden. At least around here. There comes a time, I always say, and all these times seem to come at twenty, when one no longer wants to live at home. Real independence seems attractive. At the same time mother says I never was so young. It's rather confusing. I never was so tense and restless about the house. Now Dr. S.L. is giving new trouble about my Ca [calcium] deficiency. It will necessitate an inlay, which is expensive. + Am working on my gray flannels thing now. Seven pages. Should be fine. I filed all my manuscripts today. What's the trouble with my stuff is no action. My best stories have the most action and are the least labored. Here is my clear lesson.

SEPTEMBER 5, 1941

Mother very depressed, and calling me a bastard practically, and contemplating my removal from school. + Date with Virginia & lovely evening. Rode the bus down. Jumble Shop drinks, where I told her in cold sobriety, all about Rosalind, and even showed her the letter, after deliberation. Then to the Caravan. + Then I called Rosalind, my business call about the French men's shop Hermès in Rue de Rivoli, she said. And said she loved my letter & thought the sketch "enchanting" though not flattering, and that she would be seeing a lot more of me, and what about some night next week to meet Betty & Natasha?

SEPTEMBER 6, 1941

Spoke with Dr. S.L. this A.M. with Mother. $15.00 per inlay and 3 of those. Every time I think of [Rosalind] I feel happy. Stanley and mother however tie up my present friends with my past and present extremist conduct. That I have not come down to earth etc. It is a matter of touching something else. Perhaps in their sense I shall never touch earth. This is not I. Nor my genius of person. We are different. + Started the autobiography of Alice B. Toklas [by Gertrude Stein] this eve. Superb writing. I have turned a new leaf in writing. Only stories with real peo-

ple & plot & action from now on. I thought out a real plot for
amusement while out taking a walk. And afterwards even the
people looked different on the streets. I felt more of them. Too
much of my stuff is cynical and sarcastic.

SEPTEMBER 8, 1941

In a way I do not feel so sad about B. & R. Living with someone you love is so disillusioning. And the element of change—
restlessness—in all of us—is on my side at least. + *The New
Yorker* would take the slacks story from Hellman.* Wish there
were another similar market; but no. Played the piano loud
& rather well. + A meeting this evening of the League. I feel
uncomfortable with them and useless, because now we are all
supposed to be collecting money. I wonder if I should tell them
I am a degenerate & be expelled? Called Buffie afterwards at
12:00 sharp. Very short & sweet & would I see her tomorrow?
Yes. I shan't tell her, I think, about the other one. But how do I
know what I'll say?

SEPTEMBER 9, 1941

The Russians & British alternate nights bombing Berlin. The
people are going mad, because Göring told them it was impregnable! + Buffie called twice. We arranged a date. Drank three
gin rickeys before our rendezvous at [Grand] Ticino's.† (Before
that I had been to Dr. S.L.—with Novocaine and read a delightful Bemelmans [book] in the Jumble Shop alone. He's a genius
of his own type.) Buffie was late. I was high. She wouldn't eat or
drink or smoke at Ticino's. Thence to the Brevoort,‡ & stinking,
expensive dinner, at the end of which I told her. She was quiet,
quite unshocked, the way I suppose any properly controlled person would be. No names mentioned, tho I did tell her I was in
love. Then in a cab to her house where I put her to bed and filled

---

* Lillian Hellman (1905–1984), American playwright and memoirist.
† Grand Ticino, a West Village restaurant later used as a setting in the movie *Moonstruck*.
‡ The Hotel Brevoort, located at Fifth Avenue and Eighth Street, was a fabled gathering spot
for years until 1956, when it gave way to an apartment building also named the Brevoort.

her hot water bottle. She's doing a silkscreen thing now that I don't like. She was the same as ever. Wants me to call her soon.

SEPTEMBER 10, 1941

A dreadful day because Mother fussing. She is so bitter & so vague—and I am so self-righteous & so vague—she has brought on herself all that I am—I as an individual contribute little. Children's and adolescents' emotions are, I believe, constructive and optimistic. Any deviation is conditioned. + My story is progressing & at Rosalind's at seven. Mrs. Betty Parsons there & another of whom I was terrified until I found her talking of art and saw she knew nothing. Betty is older than Rosalind. Charming, intense, serious & thin. Is managing an art gallery now. Her watercolors are bold and rather good. We danced some and drank a lot. I suppose Rosalind could be very happy with Betty without much trouble. Saw Rosalind Webster's book: "Paddle"* clever. Quick. For 1927 I suppose quite daring. But the writing shows great immaturity. British upper class taken off rather wittily.

SEPTEMBER 11, 1941

I can see no one but Rosalind. As I have said before, I shall go with many others, just to keep myself from stagnating—so keep her amused when I am 30 and she 44. But I adore her. And I shall take the rest holding my nose, like a dose of castor oil. Too much reading at once. I should stick to one or two but never do. + Up at Harlem at 7:30. With Richou going door-to-door. The youngest are the most cooperative. F.D.R. spoke on the sea atrocities. And the need for real shooting all over the place. Mother won't take coffee with me in the mornings, and won't let me give her a birthday present. We are in a vicious circle, of which each of us forms one half. Each the cause and the result. And we can't change our course. The solutions that occur to me are nothing more than little tangents that fly off and die like sparks.

---

* Webster was Rosalind Constable's maiden name. The full title of her book is *They Who Paddle*.

SEPTEMBER 12, 1941

First day of tranquility in a week. + Looked over that *Vogue*
Prix thing. First entree Nov. 20. 1st quiz.* I think I could write
decent articles all night. I do know things about art, & possibly
literature. + Watercolor this evening. Not like I intended but did
a gay thing of Harlem. How much pleasanter it is to love and not
be loved, than to be loved and not love. Thank God, the delight
of giving and the happiness of devotion are greater than the
always momentary pleasure in flattery.

SEPTEMBER 13, 1941

A rather good day. Autumn is definitely creeping into the bones.
Letter from Jeannot with sketches. What a good fellow he is.
Guileless and fun-loving. He is pondering a book, but whether
the bitter struggles of the bewildered Français or the gay café life
of Paris, he does not know! Very very happy, with drinks galore,
Jeva & Marjorie tonight. Walter had business engagement.
Managed to get R. in at 12:40. She said I made a big hit the other
night. I felt that I didn't. She said sometimes one does better
when not performing.

SEPTEMBER 14, 1941

Things are coming to a crisis, Stanley says. Mother is nervous,
again talks of removing me from school. I shall be lost. All the
jobs I want require a B.A. She is jealous of my friends. Constantly making comparisons between herself & them and jealous
too of my courtesy to Jeva & Marjorie when they come over.
And could I possibly be in love with my own mother? Perhaps in
some incredible way I am. And it is the recalcitrance in all of us
that shows in my ingratitude for my mother's over-zealous effort
to please me, and to do things for me. It is the old story of things
being too simple—and of our refusal to throw our love to the
easiest and most deserving and most logical object.

---

* The "*Vogue* Prix thing" is likely an initiative for finding new writing talent. Pat works on
her submission well into 1942.

SEPTEMBER 16, 1941

Finished *Pendennis*. What a moral little thing! How smug, the eternal, complaisant, equanimous, and so intelligent Mr. Thackeray! + Called Rosalind and had a wonderful time. She must have called me darling at least twice. She was suffering a hangover, martinis and benzedrine both in her at 2:30. She said that if she couldn't make it this week she'd hate not seeing me for so long! I couldn't say anything for at least 30 seconds. But painting, when I stood still a moment, whistling the second Brandenburg [concerto by J. S. Bach], I think, I felt an overwhelming love for R., a security of it and a happiness in it. I have waited so long, and this is it.

9/16/41

I thought, eating the last meal of the day, so balanced and attractive, of all the people in the world who'd have given a day's labor, if they had it in them, for a piece of decent meat; and I thought, sending back my butter practically untouched, of all the people in Germany and Italy and occupied France, and in so many places in Europe and Asia that I cannot even begin to name, who have not seen butter or even dirty grease in months. Here I sit in America, sending back my meat unfinished to be dumped into the garbage, brushing the crumbs off my lap, using half my allotted cream measure, declining delicately the cream of mushroom soup in favor of the vegetable vitamin cocktail. What right have I? And what are we to do? How much are we to think, to let ourselves think, to dare to think without losing our minds at the absurdity and inhumanness!

SEPTEMBER 17, 1941

Mother doesn't think I can do the Negro* story.† Cheery love. + Worked a short morning then went to Jeva's for lunch, with

---

* From the eighteenth century to the late 1960s, Negro—much as it is offensive now in both British and U.S. English—was commonly used to describe people of Black African origin.
† It is unclear which story Pat is referring to.

Mother, Marjorie, Nelson, Jeva, (who paid) to Alice Foote's.*
Enormous martinis, Jeva looked elegant. Cheveux straight
up. Smoking like hell, but I loved her even for that. It was
part of her great enthusiasm for the occasion. We told all
kinds of jokes.

SEPTEMBER 18, 1941

With Walter [Marlowe] last night. He says Mother and Stanley are deep conservatives, that I am a strange product & that I
should make every effort towards conciliation. I wonder why all
the nicest men (Walter & Arthur) are the sexy type? The propo-
sitioning type? It is a kind of generosity. An appreciation of pleasures. We almost did it last night.

A lovely day with new books. [Thomas Carlyle's] *Sartor
Resartus*, highly recommended by Walter & [Stephen] Spender's
The Destructive Element.

SEPTEMBER 19, 1941

Friday a rather wonderful day. Paid my bill at school. *Quarterly*
bulletin looks nice. Saw Helen. What a tan! What a girl! Made
my surrealist thing this afternoon. The writing of course. I
think I'll redo "The Heroine" before anything else. But it would
be good to have the Fascist thing for the first issue. There is so
much to show Rosalind tomorrow! So much reason to be happy!
I called her from Barnard—historic Barnard Hall. Shall meet her
tomorrow at 6:00!!!! Damn it I've always had what I wanted and
shall have it still.

SEPTEMBER 20, 1941

Saturday: Bought *Decision* [by Kay Boyle] yesterday. Very inspirational, poetic. Also the English magazine *Horizon* [by Cyril]
Connolly, S. [Stephen] Spender. Worked some and read a bit,
but mainly working around preparing for Rosalind like the

---

* Alice Foote MacDougall ran several restaurants named after her, e. g. one in the Hotel Peter
Stuyvesant, located at 2 West Eighty-Sixth Street.

b. for the b. Had a drink & went up to her office at 6:00. She wasn't there. Waited till 6:30 & phoned. I was supposed to meet her at home! We connected finally at the Shelton & met Mary S. In a dither as usual. Jane doesn't know about her & Helen but is sitting on H.'s doorstep & can't be removed even by the gendarmes. Later to Nino & Nella's. And a good glass of wine that put the finishing touches. We went to the Hotel Albert.[*] (I kissed her in the ladies' room! and said—I never thought that would happen again.) We met Merino, Floy, Butch from Key West. Went with them to Mrs. Kuniyoshi[†] & thence to the Vanguard. What fun to go thru the Village streets with Rosalind, holding her hand and feeling very drunk and proud. Before her friends she calls me Baby. "I've got to take Baby home." (In a taxi where I sat on her lap.) Native gin plus wine is an excellent boilermaker.

SEPTEMBER 21, 1941

Buffie wanted me to brunch with her. But mother & I went to Brooklyn Museum instead. Also called Rosalind. (She says I have telephonitis.) [Ernst] Hauser also called. Dinner date Tuesday. I suppose in a few more years I shan't mind going out 5 times a week either.

SEPTEMBER 23, 1941

Sent "The Heroine" to *Accent*[‡] and *New Horizons*[§] with letters. Went to school to make program changes. Saw Alice G. & Rita R.'s gal with British accent. They think the *Quarterly* folder is

---

[*] The Hotel Albert, located at 65 University Place in Greenwich Village, has since been converted into an apartment building.

[†] Even though the painters Katherine Schmidt and Yasuo Kuniyoshi divorced in 1932, she was still sometimes refered to as Katherine Schmidt Kuniyoshi. So this could be a reference either to her, or to Yasuo Kuniyoshi's second wife, Sara Mazo Kuniyoshi, a dancer, actress, and art curator.

[‡] *Accent*, a quarterly of new literature.

[§] Perhaps in reference to *New Horizons*, a magazine published by Pan American World Airways.

just the thing, etc. Had dinner with Hauser at Ticino's. Much
white wine. Called Rosalind at 8:30. Betty in the same room,
God! There will come a time, but we shall both be drunk when
it happens, unfortunately.

SEPTEMBER 25, 1941

Splendid day! Program difficulties all settled. I'm taking Ameri-
can Literature & dropping Howard, etc. + Worked on totem pole
which I might give to Marjorie. + This marks the first year that
I have tried to think. Perhaps the first half year. Finished [Julien
Green's] *The Dreamer.* Very Proustian. An excellent novel. I think
Escapism, but it's now becoming the fashion to condone escape.

SEPTEMBER 26, 1941

Met Arthur on the street. He's thinking of getting an apartment so we can carry on our non-existent affair. + At [Emily]
Gunning's for Political Council discussion. Painful and short.
No special purpose either except collective masturbation of our
dormant political consciousness. + Worked on story. Preferred
whittling but I must get in a couple of hours writing every day.
One is not sufficient anymore. Should like sometime to read
thru all my diaries and notebooks. Would take as long as reading the Bible and is more important to me at this moment.

SEPTEMBER 27, 1941

With Ernst from nine to six. Went to Fire Island.* It is wrong
to say I am never bored. Beaches bore me beyond words.
Travel annoys me, too. Too much time idle, with a person
beside you so that you can neither read, nor converse amusingly all the time. We made snapshots. He has a funny little

---

* Fire Island, just south of Long Island, has been a magnet for gay New Yorkers at least since
the 1930s. Legend has it that at Duffy's Hotel in Cherry Grove, Christopher Isherwood and
W. H. Auden celebrated gay culture, dressed as Dionysus and Ganymede and carried aloft by
a group of singing worshippers. Throughout the years, Pat knew many people who had taken
houses there, and she visited regularly.

bathing suit with legs. + With Billie B. tonight at Mero's. She drank tea and we danced like a couple of floating sea buoys. Congaed with Bruhs. He and Gean are quite willing I become a member.

SEPTEMBER 28, 1941

Finished my story and Stanley read it, and to my great delight, liked it enormously! Only it needs climax at the end. Too much of the "quiet incident." Still. Such work! And I do want something special for the first issue of *Quarterly*. I felt a peculiar friendliness to Stanley today. His reading my story helped us both. It will be a slow, and painfully self-conscious process for us both. But he didn't think I could write a story like that, probably. So much as has passed, I should like this union feeling with Stanley.

SEPTEMBER 29, 1941

Read [Thomas] More's *Utopia*, first and second books. Worked on little woodman. It takes so little to make me happy. A book, and thou—and not even thou in the flesh, worse luck. I dream of her sometimes, day dreams, when I see her across a restaurant, or in a room with other people, and we look at each other and know, and know that others know, too, that we are ours and nobody else's. That's what I want!

SEPTEMBER 30, 1941

A real wintry day—autumnal and coming. Kingsley, who sent me the phantasia, is the girl with the British accent, raised by English parents. She was in *Quarterly*, Babs P. told me, to see her "comments" and said, "of course they'll print it!" Work—work—work! Mountains of reading! And I'm unhappy because of my hair! I was going to wear it up and I still have that clipped part to contend with. Roger sent me a necklace, rather nice, of tropical fruits. I want to see Rosalind! I want to see Rosalind wherever I turn and wherever I look!

OCTOBER 1, 1941

A good day. Philosophy is with Montague,* but I suppose he's forgotten about the D. Hope so. Read history this afternoon. Reading it like a story and to hell with notes till a later date. Helen damn sweet & asked me for coffee, but I had to study. There'll be plenty of time, if I get started. + Kingsley, when asked by [Minor] Latham what was her stake in life, replied, "Immortality." She interests me because of her self-confidence. Wonder would Rosalind like to meet her? + Finished "Mr. Scott Is Not on Board."† 8,750 words almost. It is graceful! Shall send it to the *Post*‡ for a once-over, then cut it down for something else. Quite an ordeal to type. Should like to do the Fascist kid story of the auto this weekend. Am not writing enough in my notebook. That comes of long slow evenings, reading and musing on my couch.

OCTOBER 3, 1941

I was en route to Chock Full O'Nuts§ for an innocent cup of coffee when Helen dragged me into Tilson's. Peter was there & Tony. Peter: "Your friend Rosalind's name wouldn't be Constable, would it?" Seems she met her at a British Motor unit at 68 St. this summer. We talked quite freely, exchanging friends. Helen: "What is this?" So she went to study & Peter & I got soused at the Gold Rail. I called Rosalind & made a lunch date for the three of us next Friday. "That gives you a whole week of freedom," I said. "Do you think I want freedom from you?"(?) Peter seems very eager to meet R. (Why the hell

---

* William P. Montague, Johnsonian professor of philosophy at Barnard College. He also taught logic.
† A lost mystery story.
‡ The *Saturday Evening Post*, where Ernst Hauser works. The *Post*'s covers were designed by Norman Rockwell in the 1940s. It reported on political and national news, but also published short stories by young authors such as F. Scott Fitzgerald, John Steinbeck, William Saroyan, and Ray Bradbury.
§ Popular chain of coffee and sandwich counters.

wouldn't she be?!) Everybody in town, unfortunately is nuts about Rosalind!

OCTOBER 4, 1941

Cut my "Mr. Scott" down some 13 pages. Wonderful! Billie B. [and I] dropped in on Mary S. Mary says Buffie's dull, but God, her antics are same, too. Drinks constantly and the same old exclamations about their results. All of us are boring if we go out all the time and build no individuality within.

OCTOBER 7, 1941

I wish Helen could stay in the city Friday night and make an evening of it. + Walter phoned. Had been in Washington. Wants a date this weekend—and I don't. + Read some layouts for *Quarterly*. Terribly discouraging. You wonder what sort of introversion and conceit led some of these kids to write!

OCTOBER 11, 1941

Much better day. Even with a hangover. Worked on play this AM. Talked with mother some. There is so little we talk about. Our intellectual conversations reach impasses very soon. She is simply not interested in the abstract, tho there's nothing intrinsically the matter with her brain at all. Read [Edmund Wilson's] *Wound and the Bow*.

OCTOBER 12, 1941

Roger called so I broke the date with Buffie (!) & drove with him upstate. I try to understand the fury in him. What I say to such young people who cannot accept the world that they're in: "What have you done—and what can you do?" and usually it is nothing. Nevertheless, I feel a great affection for Roger. More physical than Arthur—Arthur's is more intellectual.

OCTOBER 13, 1941

Helen M., when asked by Miss Latham to have me as gov't official, said "Miss H. is my hero!" Latham, "Oh is she!" + My clothes depressed me today. Lousy shoes & hair & sweater. Can ruin me physically and mentally. How lucky men are with their very regular clothing! Sent "Mr. Scott" to *This Week*. Mother wrote some housemaid's verse, part one stinks. Second fine.

OCTOBER 14, 1941

Still haven't called Rosalind and I think it's slowly driving me mad. She's never home at night. Does she even think of me? God what a sad life! I think of her when I hear nice music. I think of her every time I have a moment of tranquility, which fortunately for my nerves, is seldom. + I have a psychosis about work. I work till I nearly drop at 9:30—writing my play and then rest 5 minutes & start again. Read [Richard Brinsley Sheridan's] *School for Scandal*.

OCTOBER 15, 1941

Date with Walter. He hums at dinner, and holds my hand when he plays the Brandenburg [concertos] and "Liebestod" [in Richard Wagner's *Tristan and Isolde*] when I had much rather be thinking of Rosalind—that's all I have against him. Also that someday he would like to put the "Liebestod" to the purpose for which it was written! Likes his cake with ice cream, I'd say! To me, it would sacrilege the music—The music was written as an approximation, a synthesis and a sublimation—an artistic condensation of the act. It would be a sensual greed—Ossa on Pelion* and all that. I should merely like to lie with my head in Rosalind's lap—or vice versa.

OCTOBER 16, 1941

Read [C. G. Jung's] *Modern Man [in Search of a Soul]* again. Stanley comes out rather more clearly: toxic condition because of repressed impulses. And he cannot take pleasure in any exterior thing in New York. Even [in] his camera work—an inner

---

* In Greek mythology, the giants attempted to reach heaven by piling Mount Olympus and Mount Ossa onto Mount Pelion.

private hobby—he is unable to relate to the outside economic world. Lives in movies and books.

OCTOBER 17, 1941

Lunch with Rosalind and Babs. Rosalind had to go at 2:30 but Peter & Helen phoned & came at 2:45. Del Pezzo's.* I had more to drink than was good for me. Helen, too, and I kissed her in the bathroom. She wanted it badly.

OCTOBER 18, 1941

Worked like hell. Six hours at the typewriter. Finished play this AM. Sent Babs P. a note, commending her mariners, etc. I remember in '38 when I used to write to Judy Tuvim. Saw Museum of Modern Art furniture exhibit, and some fine things by George Grosz[†] of Germany. Came home, wrote my editorial and discovered with some dismay that Rita R. said almost the same thing in '40, only less amusingly. Besides I have announced a policy of "less cynicism and more poetry," which absolves me. + Worked very well on "White Monkey"[‡] this evening. + Letter from Babs P. this AM saying Rosalind was worthy of me (!). Unable to contact Buffie. I find the contemplation dreary.

OCTOBER 19, 1941

Graham R. is being shipped to the Philippines. Worked like hell again. Did first act for performance Wednesday & shall do second. Stanley thinks I am "over my head" in my materials, but one can't go writing about school days just because that's what one knows best. I'm quite proud of my editorial. Fun with Graham this evening. He's quite concerned over the scarcity of books where he's going!

---

* Del Pezzo Restaurant, frequented by *Life* magazine staff and singers from the Metropolitan Opera, including Enrico Caruso.
† George Grosz (1893–1959), German painter who immigrated to the United States in 1933. He later taught at the Art Students League of New York, where Pat will also attend classes.
‡ "White Monkey," a (lost) story in progress.

OCTOBER 20, 1941

Palma came across with her poems. I want to print the one about love on the bed in the blackness, but she's got cold feet. Babs is considering them tonight. Palma asked me to lunch tomorrow. "I love your profile, frowning," she said—joking of course!

OCTOBER 21, 1941

Rehearsed play 1–2 haphazardly. Helen & I sit together, touching our arms while we watch the drahmah—and finally touching fingers surreptitiously between us. No mention later. No glances—no regrets—only whets the appetite and rattles me, and excites me, I am very nervous and shall be, I suppose, till the magazine is sent off. *Quarterly* is really coming into its own, my summer dreams come true. It depends, as usual, on money.

OCTOBER 23, 1941

Thursday: Rewrote my editorial & met Babs in Time & Life* at 7:00. Rosalind up to her ears in Art & the Everyday Life. Ate at Del Pezzo's. I gave her my editorial to read. Liked it a lot & suggested one little change. Saw the Rodeo afterwards with Babs. Judy called me earlier to check on our date & since R. had to work, went with Babs. The child was rather nervous, inevitably, but Judy nice. Rum drinks, then Eddy arrived, looking like hell. We had more drinks at St. Moritz, where Judy had to have spaghetti too. Home & bed at 5:10!

OCTOBER 25, 1941

Grand day. Worked on play. Saw the Metropolitan Exhibit of watercolors. I think as I told mother over coffee this afternoon, that the time of social significance (i.e. working class) novel passed with Sinclair's & Norris'† youth. [T. S.] Eliot knows the

---

* The Time & Life Building, located at 1271 Avenue of the Americas, headquarters of *Time, Life,* and *Fortune* magazines.

† Upton Sinclair (1878–1968) was an American writer known for his socialist views and attention to social and political issues in the United States. Frank Norris (1870–1902) was an American novelist known for his naturalistic depiction of life in the United States.

real tragedy—the spiritual tragedy. The tragedy of the man that
has some money and can develop the perversions and contor-
tions of the twentieth century mind. A spiritual wasteland, yes.
Furthermore the downfall, or at least the most serious fault of
the Communist youth is their stereotyping. They do not allow
for spiritual growth (if they have any left) and for emotional
changes that only bring maturity.

OCTOBER 26, 1941

Wrote Friday night my poem on the immortality of dental fillings. Might go for *Quarterly*. Worked on play. All but done now.
Phoned Babs P. She asked me for a drink at 5:30 & I interrupted
studying history and went. We played [Eddy] Duchin records.
How nice to sit with Babs and hear good music. Tho I know
there could never be anything twixt her & me on my part. Babs
said I had a spiritual richness that Peter lacked. That she wished
she'd known me sooner, that she had known all along about me.

OCTOBER 28, 1941

Babs asked me yesterday to come for weekend Friday. Shall go.
Should be very important. Also says she's not always a decent
little girl. Cold as hell. Saw a wonderful suit at A. Constable's*
and bought it. $29 reduced from $45! I'll wear it Thursday—for
Rosalind—and buy a conga record—for Rosalind—and look
my very very best—for Rosalind.

OCTOBER 29, 1941

Ecstatically happy—Walked into a History quiz but must have
got a B. Rehearsed Helen, Willey, Roma (swell kid!) and McCor-
mick & Leighton on my play. Went on finally at 3–4 with great
success. No applause, but the thing was too shocking. Marijann
K. was sitting in. Everybody hanging on their chairs on the third
act. Even Latham said it was good professional line. Helen & I
can scarcely keep apart at the right times. We hand each other

---

* Arnold Constable was a department store.

fake guns and our hands cling. Disgraceful! Things are getting across. Kingsley flunkeying all around for me. She's lived with her mother (that woman!) for 12 years in one room. Hence her dallying around school.

OCTOBER 31, 1941

Met Babs & her father: at Grand Central & rode up—(4.00—Cape Cod. Providence). Babs quite reserved & serious. She's very slow and thoughtful. Long drive with Newt to their house—a gorgeous place—old & well-established—20–15 rooms! Wonderful food + Babs & I ran around, walked, sat by the fire & drank. The night is peculiar—each talking—twin beds. Each claiming to be cold, doing nothing about it but put on sweaters & socks—how much are people shy these days! I told her if she wanted she could share her own bed—I didn't kick & my bed was hers to begin with. But nothing came of that.

NOVEMBER 1, 1941

We played poker this evening where I won like mad. I got high just before the steak fry came on. We made pumpkins and I distinguished myself by tearing a beer can in two with my bare hands. + Babs & I talked from 1:30–4:00 in bed. Babs has almost the same menstrual difficulties. I wonder if it decreases the sexual desire? I still am most attracted physically by someone like Helen—like all the straights I was so violently in love with when I was younger. Babs P. says she is attracted to Helen, too—she wants to get far far away, etc. I'm afraid I want to get closer! + I feel restless & can't stop smoking as I had intended. Now I do not resent the talking chitchat, but only grow weary that it is all a facet of me which is not at all sincere, that I am wasting my time and everybody else's.

NOVEMBER 2, 1941

Read [Alexander Pope's] *Essay on Man.* Babs told me her mother says I was so nice to have around, so attractive! Very nice all right. Drove with Babs from Providence to N.Y. 4–11:30.

Hamburgers en route. We talked. She's happy to have someone she can talk to now she says—before she had no one. She says she doesn't like the idea of being physically "unused." I think she'd sooner trust me to have an affair with her than anyone else. She still thinks I'm sincere and very well reputed.

NOVEMBER 3, 1941

I believe my real study days are over. S. [Samuel] Johnson said the same thing. Thank God I was once a grind, a drudge, a thirster after knowledge, and a martinet of myself!!! On that I coast now, and bank forever! + Helen delightful! Winks at me when we meet, and holds my hand in Latham's class, rubs my sleeve surreptitiously with her fingers and generally makes herself very dangerous. + Dined with Mespoulet* (like Voltaire) and Alice K. (like an old mummy) at Nino & Nella's at 7:30. Drank too much. Mespoulet talked exclusively to me, but my conversation was not too brilliant and hers not too entertaining. It is so futile to discuss the war! Really! Everyone has a different opinion—which is just as conclusive as religion! Whether by revolt or by military defeat will Hitler meet his doom, etc.

NOVEMBER 4, 1941

Slept, studied, wrote—resigned from the [Young Communist] League in a well-worded epistle. + Roger sent me 10 bucks to come to Boston. Also pictures of him carrying one Hollywood cutie. + Bought Rosalind a boogie-woogie record—"The Stomp" [by Albert Ammons] and went up there at 8:10. Natasha, Betty, Rosalind eating dinner. My face swollen from my bad eye, etc. and I feel more than ever like a kid! We listened to election votes returns. They are all for La Guardia† of course. Talked of books and men. Very delightful and charming—with

---

* Marguerite Mespoulet, associate professor of French at Barnard College.
† Fiorello La Guardia, mayor of New York City from 1934 to 1945.

Rosalind knitting Del P.* a pair of green socks for Xmas—all
evening.

NOVEMBER 5, 1941

Fine day. Wore my suit to school with great success. Got A- in
History quiz of a week ago. One of very very few, I'm sure. Buffie's [for] tea. Howard, Mrs Hughes,† Miss Green (awful & I
suppose a patron) and Florence Codman, publisher who spoke
to B. Parsons last night while I was there. Buffie presented me &
heard Codman say "are you the Miss Highsmith Rosalind Constable's been telling me about? I've been wanting, etc." I made
a fine impression. + Babs called with the "chance of my life"—
tickets to *Macbeth* with Helen Tuesday night! Very nice of her.
We did make hash of her play today, too. She's so sweet—never
unkind, never impatient. Asked her to come with us Monday
night—the Madison Avenue gang.‡

NOVEMBER 6, 1941

Got a card from *Accent* saying they are fighting over my story,
etc. We go to press in an alarmingly short time! I phoned Rosalind & got Betty. We talked full quota about the tea yesterday.
Unfortunately and very Noël Cowardishly§ I'm quite fond of
her!

NOVEMBER 7, 1941

Thank God for a little work again. First night at home in over a
week. Wrote eleven papers (satire story) of the "Horn of Plenty."¶

---

* Rosalind's friend Lola P.'s husband.
† Toni Hughes (1907–?), American sculptress whose work was shown several times at the
Museum of Modern Art in the 1940s and '50s.
‡ The Madison Avenue gang most likely consisted of Rosalind Constable, Natasha H., and
Betty Parsons.
§ Noël Coward (1899–1973) was an English playwright, composer, director, actor, and
singer. During World War II, he worked for the Secret Service as well as entertaining the
troops across Europe, Asia, and Africa.
¶ "The Silver Horn of Plenty," published in the *Barnard Quarterly*, Winter 1941.

Kingsley returned [André Gide's] *The Counterfeiters*,* with the question, why did I lend it her? And she told me she gets violent attachments. Wonder if she knows I'm gay and has a crush on me? + Saw Helen—God, that name is my nemesis. How simple it would be to fall for Helen! And how adolescent. Like preferring a chocolate soda to frogs-legs Provençale!

11/7/41

Kingsley loves my handwriting! Soon she'll be picking up my cigarette butts. She may suspect me and Helen. I wonder if she has a crush on Helen, too?

NOVEMBER 7, 1941

Shall enjoy talking to Babs Monday next. How strange it must seem to her to be presented to a room full of people—all gay— all wonderful—all bewildering, frightening perhaps—and somehow full of foreboding and intimations of the great future. I was thoroughly disgusted last night at Rose M.'s. [She and Billie] are sex machines—as overbalanced as Freud in his theory— God give me people like Rosalind & Betty and Natasha (who would never mention Sylvia at all!). And give me strength to be like them!

NOVEMBER 8, 1941

Slept late & needed it badly. Odds and ends I did this AM. which felt very good, a rare comfortable feeling. What a genius I should be with leisure! + Went to see Wakefield Gallery.† Presented my mother to Betty Parsons. Buffie had been in a moment before, she said. I think of Helen & holding her hand, in my odd moments—very odd moments.

---

* *The Counterfeiters* is a novel by André Gide that prominently features adolescent homosexuality. Pat reads it several times before starting to brainstorm her first novel, *The Click of the Shutting*.

† The small art gallery in the Wakefield Bookshop at 64 East Fifty-Fifth Street run by Betty Parsons until 1944.

NOVEMBER 10, 1941

Helen said she smoked a lot over the weekend too. I wonder if from same reason. She looks at me with an admiring & come-hither eye. Home at 4:30 for the dreadful message that Rosalind has the grippe. Nevertheless met Babs at Buffie's. + Short dinner & to Barnard to see Helen sleeping over. She was delighted so see us. And Babs, ever tactful, left for the John & we fell in each other's arms. I kissed her on the bed. God what goings on! Helen's marvelous!

NOVEMBER 11, 1941

Three hours' sleep & studied this morning early & wrote a fine examination I think. Read *Pride & Prejudice* ½ this PM. & wrote 6 pages final draft on "Silver Horn of Plenty." Kingsley spoke to Babs yesterday. Babs told her she knew of her affection for me—"Is it that obvious? Thinks I'm sincere—the soul of sincerity." I often feel inferior to Babs and Debbie B.'s devotion to ideal. I wonder if I have lost too much in promiscuity? I am ruled too much by physical desire—the moment's prompting. Feel myself more masculine lately, with growing self-confidence. Had a long talk with Muret.* She talked of creative thinkers & career women & the enduring delights of the intellectual life. Asked me to call again.

NOVEMBER 12, 1941

Wrote Helen a note Tuesday that last night was rather nice but Public Opinion would improve if we sat apart in Latham's. Signed verse of experience. She wrote me back (nearly late for 5 o'clock getting it, because I knew she would) To Pat the Prudent. "I think your note was heaven and it really is a shame that we two must be cloven to preserve the Public Name." Oh the delights of the primal stages! I feel gayer every day and must take

---

* Dr. Charlotte T. Muret, History Department associate at Barnard College and a renowned expert on modern European history.

steps to remedy matters. I suffer from a Puritanical background: it is having the usual effects.

NOVEMBER 14, 1941

Melancholy—never like this—morning. Gym was torture. Kingsley showed up at one, and confessed her fine attachment to me. (Also [Babs] P. & Helen.) Then Peter. We had a few, I about 4 martinis. Bought a blue & red muffler at Lord & Taylor's (drunk) and came home where Jeva & Mother & I had more drinks. I was high. And not too cheerful. I wanted a date with Helen & Babs tonight, and as it happened they called at 10:30. If I'd known, I shouldn't have got so drunk. They came by & we went to the Tavern, Caravan and met Leslie S., unfortunately, who was with us the rest of the time. More gays at Casino. But Helen was lovely—wonderful. She looks at me with her heart in her eyes. I'm a lucky son of a gun. She says I'm cute. Got lipstick all over Helen's collar in the L.R. [Ladies' Room], but it was worth it—to her I mean. And certainly to me. We make love all over the place, in fact that's all we do.

NOVEMBER 15, 1941

Slight hangover but gone suddenly at 12. No cigarettes. Read most of [James Fenimore Cooper's] *Last of the Mohicans.* Went to Brooklyn to see Comet [Press]. The proofs look good. Shall have to write a couple of gratis ads to fill spaces [in *Quarterly*]. I keep thinking of Helen—she keeps intruding. I have a violent physical longing—I don't suppose I've ever felt such attraction from a straight.

NOVEMBER 16, 1941

Read proofs, wrote ads. Studied English lit. Helen not so seriously on my mind today—my heart still starts beating but she's just a pleasant thought—someone to look nice for in school. + Did some work on "Silver Horn of Plenty." Damn it, it should sell somewhere, that's just the story I should like to sell first—Is great showing even though really my heart is not in it.

NOVEMBER 17, 1941

Unfortunate day. Rehearsals all the day—*Accent* returned
"The Heroine" with marginalia and a long letter: Good but not
good enough. A good yarn—not a document. And send them
more. Then Mme Muret said she liked my stories immensely as
she returned my C+ paper on Machiavelli! Kingsley stalks me
around, thinking I go to *Quarterly* when I get coffee, etc. Pete &
Helen amused. Helen looks at me with hungry eyes. God! What
sex appeal that little thing has!

NOVEMBER 19, 1941

Splendid day. My hair up & a white shirt, the button-down
Helen loves. Peculiarly tranquil so I read philosophy "with great
delectation." Helen & Babs were delirious—esp. Babs. Helen has
her worried tho. Seems they talked long last night, mainly about
how inadvisable things were & how Earl would satisfy her on
his heralded return. Evidently Helen agreed with Babs but today
found her as magnetic as ever. Boy what a figger she's acquiring,
too! She said she'd love it if I came up to the dorms Friday. + My
mother said some curious things: that I was like a chameleon
with my favorites (girls) while very strong of character in other
things. Also that New York social life breeds Lesbians, that I'm
always happy when I go out with girls & bored stiff with men.
That my girlfriends all live with each other & don't take interest
in men, etc. There's the pieces, Bacon,* put them together!

NOVEMBER 21, 1941

Read Shaftesbury tonight. Didn't go to the Caravan but to Helen
at Barnard instead at 10:35. No one knows, or shall know. She
kisses like a thousand dreams, and her cheek is as soft as nothing I've ever felt. Strangely enough I was *en-bas* most of the
time—being quite tired anyway—She's afraid to go further. I
think—afraid when I say I might fall in love, because of people

---

* Francis Bacon (1561–1626), English philosopher, essayist, and statesman, also known for
his method of message encoding, Bacon's cipher.

involved. Otherwise as far as action is concerned I think she
would. I shall never forget this night—It was like some dream
when we kissed—when I felt her cheek on mine—so long and
hard pressing. I felt no part of my body—it was all sensation—
and not in my head, but floating where out in a sea of perfume
and white flowers, without time and beyond time.

NOVEMBER 22, 1941

Saturday: Ran into Rosalind & Natasha on 57th. Was with M.
& S. & didn't introduce them. Rosalind grinning like mad &
both gawking. It would have been disastrous—Natasha!

NOVEMBER 24, 1941

Quarterly's out and looks magnificent! Peter liked the poem
& Helen the editorial. Everything elegant! Shall get McGuire
to review it. I find it hard—and unpleasant, too—to recall the
pinched Freshman years—the pinched belly, the pinched soul,
and heart. (And mind.) I've come a long way! I find so much pleasure in the passage of the weeks—idle pleasures but so new to
me I am excited—almost contented but not quite and therein lies
my salvation. I need to write more & read more. Helen thinks it
remarkable that I'm able to keep the friendship of the women I've
broken with. I think it's because there is of necessity more an element of Platonism than in the male-female relationship.

NOVEMBER 25, 1941

Went with Helen to lunch at Del Pezzo's. Rosalind & Natasha
at 12:50. Was glad N. came. I like her very much. She's least
affected of all. Rosalind in wonderful spirits. + Later unwisely
had coffee with Helen, and she suffering wounded pride from
being left out rather in the presence of Rosalind, told me off
about philandering. We saw [Ruth] Bernhard's exhibit at Lord
& Taylor's. Helen said she expected something to happen Friday night. That I was the only girl she'd ever been attracted to,
& that it's going to be hell the rest of the year. I think she rather
enjoys the hell.

NOVEMBER 28, 1941

Pleasant day. So much of the history is fascinating—you want to
go on reading biographies & detailed histories—which is what
the course is for. Helen absent because of heart flutter. Cigarettes probably. Read [Edmond Rostand's] *Cyrano de Bergerac*
12:00–3:00. Shopped for a blouse & then to Constable's at 6:30.
Betty asked me to party Thursday afternoon. I suppose Buffie
will be there. Rather exclusive nonetheless. + Rosalind liked my
story "Silver Horn of Plenty." "Damned good" she said. Only
two phrases on correction. + I am exhausted. It was a week ago
this very moment, that I was with Helen—amid the purple lilies
at the bottom of the sea—this moment. + There's still no one
like Rosalind, however, not even me.

NOVEMBER 30, 1941

This sterile period is indicative really of some progress. Ideas are
not bursting on me as they used to—good and bad and mainly
bad. Now when I write a story I like to think it will definitely be
printed somewhere. It is no longer an exercise in sublimation. It
is all the better for it.

DECEMBER 2, 1941

Helen doesn't mention Earl per se anymore. Says anything she
does doesn't concern me much. She almost cried. Let's say she
did cry. She still would recommence. We attract each other. I
see no reason to fool around. No one attracts me beyond reason
except Rosalind. Why should I lower myself? It's very flattering the way Helen is about me. The bathroom kisses, miserable
as they seemed to me, meant more to her. A kiss is a kiss—a
moment made immortal with the rush of wings unseen. Be it in a
bathroom or a pastoral arbor. I know that, too. I underestimated
her. I thought she was playing. I see in her eyes a devotion that
shames me. And yet I don't see that I'm to blame. It was merely a
misunderstanding all around. I could take her now—and I could
not do it with my soul touched—so I shall not do it at all. I feel a
pain at my heart—how many times have I loved unloved.

DECEMBER 3, 1941

Fatigued and slow and sad. Met Gordon [Smith] for lunch—where we discussed morals. He believes in free love—is a pessimist and delighted to find I am, too. I am only a pessimist generally and an optimist specifically. Rehearsed with Helen. Some of those triangles sound like they were written to order. Helen very energetic and impersonal—very fine of her. Nevertheless I miss her horribly. I love her gray skirt. It reminds me of that night in the dorms—warm and fuzzy. Why could I not love her? I would. Only Rosalind stands like a Titan between. Helen is not so high—yet. Wrote her a long letter (5 pages). Read the *Alhambra* of [Washington] Irving.

DECEMBER 4, 1941

All very miserable at school. Gave Helen my note. She looks very tired. And she read it by the river & answered me between 11 & 12. Darling, too, and how she "cries at the oddest moments and always because of you—because I love you so much—" + At Betty's show at 5—thence to Wakefield (Ossorio)* and with her to Midtown. Hope Williams† there, Buffie, Harper, Arden, Hughes, Natasha, Lola, Rosalind (in too tight black suit), but very nice to me. Plenty of drinks. Buffie left right away (6:00) and Lola asked me to cocktails tomorrow. Some fun tomorrow night!

DECEMBER 4, 1941

Had a beer with Helen at 3:50. We both know things are impossible now. She said she'd been wanting something like this to happen to her for a long while. And she's glad it did happen. Only people don't get mixed up with me & forget it in a hurry. Just as *malheureusement*, I shan't forget it in a hurry.

---

* Alfonso Ossorio, American-Filipino artist best known for his abstract expressionist paintings and unique sculptural *Congregations* series.
† Hope Williams (1897–1990), American actress most noted for her roles in Noël Coward and Oscar Wilde plays.

DECEMBER 5, 1941

Friday: Gloomy day. Short school. Went to Lola's at 6:00. Gillespie, [Toni] Hughes, Buffie (whom I scarcely spoke to), Jimmie Stern & many Frenchmen. Also Melcarth.* Thence to Barnard. Mary S. (also there) said Helen was the cutest thing she'd seen in years. That my taste was in my mouth. I didn't know what she meant. Helen has all the warmth—and she wore her gray suit tight because she knows I love it—and we could not keep our eyes or our hands off each other all evening and it was all very beautiful. She loves me—she said so—in the cold air outdoors. And she means it. Why should I lie? I miss her so when I'm away an hour I can't see straight. The first time I've been in love—the terrific physical appeal plus my love of her—God what a perilous combination!

DECEMBER 6, 1941

Called Helen at 8 at Latham's. She was right there. I hope she had been waiting. We had a terrible time talking. But I managed to tell her that I spent 2 hours reading 20 pages of [Bernard] de Mandeville during which I realized that I should have been the same last night no matter who had been present. "Anybody?" she said. Yes, anybody. Then she said something, but she was crying I know. That's the way it hits you. And she said, "God, I like you!" Which was quite good enough for me in Latham's office. I'm in love with her. I can't imagine what I shall do with myself if she doesn't come through to me. She's wonderful—all the rest seem shams beside her. I love her. But I haven't said the words yet. I practically told her—(I shouldn't have been able to go on, I know) Later—I don't know why I cried—the sweetest tears I've ever known. If I might wash away all my shame!

DECEMBER 6, 1941

This was such a bittersweet day—to use Helen's word. How beautiful her letter was. And how beautifully sad this uncer-

---

* Edward Melcarth (1914–1973), American social realist painter whose patrons included Peggy Guggenheim—he designed her iconic bat-shaped sunglasses for her.

tainty! She can't give me up! I'm sure of that. God help me I'm a lucky bastard. I watched the moon passing in and out of the black wisps of clouds tonight—a full moon but very small and high. They were playing the "Good Friday Music."* And the tears came, tight and exquisite—and I passed in two minutes from the awfullest possibilities to the best—and back again. Still I don't know, I don't know. But I believe, I am sure, this is too rare and too wonderful.

DECEMBER 8, 1941

Japan declares war on United States.†

Miserable at school until I talked with Helen at 1:30. We walked by the river, then to West End‡ for a beer. I told her then what she meant to me and God keep me I cried tho I didn't mean her to see it. And she said "What do you want me to do, Pat?" And that she couldn't send [Earl] off to war telling him. And I said she must do what she felt she should. That I loved her for her honesty. She asked me twice "What do you want me to do, Pat?" God, it was like something terrific shaking me! She said it was Friday (that Friday) that she realized—that all the melancholia in her had risen in this last hectic month. I adore her. I don't deserve her. She's beautiful through & through—and don't I know how rare this is! I spoke from my heart today. She made me do it—nothing good in me. Good lord, this is it! this is it!

1800 men killed at Pearl Harbor. Perhaps Graham—

DECEMBER 9, 1941

Rode with Jo P.§ She paid for it. Mausoleum of a house. 5 stories, & two maids. She rode back to school & had coffee with Helen,

---

* From Richard Wagner's opera *Parsifal*.
† Japan attacked Pearl Harbor on December 7, 1941.
‡ The West End was located at 2911 Broadway. Jack Kerouac was one of the patrons.
§ A new friend of Pat's she has recently met through Va. when the two made plans to go horseriding together.

Babs, Pete. They all like her. Lunch with Rosalind. She is *dis-traite** with the war. She talked like an adult to me.

DECEMBER 9, 1941

Rosalind talked a long while about parents and about hers. Her mother is a well-known anti-Semite (Nazi) and the split came over Rosalind's Jewish friends. Also her mother told her off—while Rosalind stood by the window. Then she said "What would you say if I told you it were all true?" And her mother said, "I'd rather see you dead at my feet."

DECEMBER 11, 1941

I gave Helen my letter—my beautiful letter. And she wrote me one back, telling me as she gave it, "You're going to hate me—" And when I read it, it was all might-have-beens and how she must do what she must do, hating it. And how she wants to keep me, and she'll follow along. Contradictions. It was a hasty letter, born of sudden fear. So I cried all afternoon—with Kingsley & then with Helen. And she didn't quite see [that the] over-whelming questions are: What was she struggling with these last weeks? And what did she want with me? (Besides a female joy of conquest—that's all.)

DECEMBER 12, 1941

Coffee with Helen. How perfectly she has recovered, and how well she misunderstands me. I asked her why she had been upset—because she didn't think I cared—What she wanted of me?—for me to love her. Voilà! Such craziness. Yes, I could soon hate her perhaps. She tore through the fine fabric of my sweet life like a meteor. Coquet—with its classic definition. So I lunched with Alice T. & Peter, and afterwards escaped with Pete to New Canaan. Phoned Rosalind from Cortile. "You're in a state." I was crying. And I said "I was being shanghaied & did she want to look in a minute?" I wonder if she gave it ten min-

---

* Pat most likely means "distraught" (not "distracted").

utes' thought? Cried with Debbie B. in the kitchen & in general behaved like a cloud of gloom having some bitter fun with Peter by telling her Helen loved her. That accounts for so much, said Peter, swelling with masculine pride. *Cyrano de Bergerac* stuff. Home again at 1:30, mother gone & more gloom. I should be writing now—will I be able to recapture all that I've felt the last few days? One comes to question the value of human emotion: just what is it worth when after exerting the maximum control, something still tears one up?

DECEMBER 13, 1941

Thursday afternoon Kingsley probed all around to find out. Once she asked if it were Rosalind, and then "You haven't fallen in love with Helen, have you?" I think she hates her now, tho of course I covered well about the question. Kingsley told me she's only loved one—me, that if I were a man it would be all she wanted. And Helen said to me at West End she'd never care for another man (besides Earl). And the juke box played "You Made Me Love You" and it was all very sad.

DECEMBER 14, 1941

All things changed. Read [Henry Fielding's] *Tom Thumb the Great* and *Christ*.* Played the piano and took a walk. This day memorable because I laid out my two plays & can hardly wait to get started on them. This day also memorable for my contrition: I love Rosalind. I have really not been away from her. The last week was like an opium dream—I rather hope to see Helen tomorrow with circles under her eyes. She needs a rest. I associate last week too, with that peculiar phenomenon rare in myself—the menstrual period. God knows women are batty, and God knows why! + Kingsley here at 5:00. Did the proofs together. She told me what a god I am. How all those at school who know me treat me as something out of another world, fearfully—even Babs, Helen & Peter. Did me a lot of good. K.

---

* Possibly Ernest Renan's *The Life of Jesus*.

said she hoped I'd never love a man, that she wouldn't like to see me so much in the physical. Sweet child. Billie phoned to drink champagne. No go. Working. Altogether a splendid day. Arthur here—told him gently I loved another—God, the appalling conceit of the man! + How I shall look at Rosalind tomorrow! Like I had never seen her before!

DECEMBER 15, 1941

Lovely evening with Rosalind. Came up in elevator with Betty & Mr. Eastman. Rosalind drunk, and told me she was handicapped "obligated" but too many beautiful dark-haired people around. God, she was lovely to me. Ate at Sammy's. Just what she told me to. She's marvelous—Shall try to get her tickets to *Macbeth*. She said Betty has 89 friends to her 13. That she likes one per year (& I'm it) while Betty picks up six per evening.

DECEMBER 16, 1941

I am smoking too much—pack a day often, but getting the greatest relish out of it. Getting the greatest relish out of everything. Helen & Peter hungover with 13 Scotches apiece yesterday. Look like two pieces of fragile old china. She didn't speak to me today. No doubt she's worse off than ever now—because she was in such close reach—and scored something of a victory and has all my letters to reread—and yet—I'm gone. I feel quite brilliant these days. Home at 1:00. Shopped. Did 8 pages in Philosophy paper. Read D. H. Lawrence's *Assorted Articles* which is lousy. Phoned Rosalind at 3:10. She was wonderful & stinking from three martinis. I asked her if she felt funny (because I felt funny—like a cloud—like old china) and she said—"Ye-ss"—always yes—but like a piece of old cheese. So I asked her to go to *Macbeth* with me Saturday. $3.30 apiece it'll cost—but who else is there glamorous in my life!!!

12/17/41

No man really likes a woman. He is either in love with her or she annoys him.

12/17/41

God knows love, in this room with us now, is not kisses or embraces or touches. Not even a glance or a feeling. Love is a monster between us, each of us caught in a fist.

12/17/41

Passed my first suicide moment this evening. It comes when one stands confronted with work, empty sheets of paper all about, and inside one's head, shame and confusion, inside a maelstrom that will not subside, fragments that will not hang together. Showing essentially how trite and universal and eternal is every great human emotion. This was a great human emotion. When I wonder now that I have passed it, if I shall ever commit suicide, the question is, shall I ever fail myself and others in an equally important crisis in my life? Life is a matter of self-denial at the right moments. Looking ahead won't do. We can make out a too rosy future. Successful living is self-denial without asking why.

DECEMBER 18, 1941

Up early. Wrote Helen last (?) note with the foul word— coquet—and why I told Peter what I did. Also told Babs about it, and Pete's remark on being told. Babs might as well know it all. Very interesting from novelist's point of view. December 18, 1941: Our finances are at their nadir; $100.00 in the bank. Incredible! S. is really worried. Another Maundy Thursday. Peter scarcely speaking, as Babs informed me Helen & she had compared notes Monday night during the 13 Scotches. Peter told Helen I said she was in love with her—So Peter is in a huff—and permanently, if I know Peter. I feel the natural regret at losing a friend. Helen is icy. If this has severed her it has served its purpose. But she says I still haven't made her hate me. I should never have said that. Babs maintains usual neutrality. I can understand Helen's resentment but Peter's no. I don't know why yet I said it. I didn't think it would reverberate. I shouldn't put it past [Helen] to have shown Pete my letters. People who meet crises drunk!—I defy her to find one fake word in my

letters—I defy her to find one gay gal who would have behaved
as well as I did. I defy her.

DECEMBER 19, 1941

A month ago was the night—two weeks ago another night—one
week ago another night. Tonight nothing but me. + Up early &
studied for History. Think I did well. Muret especially wished me
a good Xmas. Babs making it a point to speak. Also Helen said
"Hello, Patricia!" God, I couldn't look at her that way now unless
she apologized. + Bought Roger sox, mother a fine compact and
some garters. Wrote a good poem. "I am too much master of
myself." (at 6:00 P.M.) Read Rilke & finished the book. Trivial
sometimes, and sometimes wonderfully queer and delicate as in
"Girl in Love." Translation sometimes better than the German.

12/19/41

One is never lonely with ideas, but alone or no, how lonely I am
without them!

12/20/41

Perhaps I have said this before, but it should be in each notebook: a short story (or a novel-germ) must come from an inspiration which, on first acquaintance, seems better suited for a
poem. Action germs are usually successful only when the element of oddity or excitement or queerness is developed. And
the writer, like a man in the beginning of his love, should be
passive to the inspiration of the world and the earth, who is his
seducer. She plays with him, forces herself upon him until he
becomes conscious of her. He never seeks deliberately. Inspiration comes many ways at many times, but I like best inspiration
with a smile on one's face and a relaxation in the body. Such
inspiration is healthy and strong.

DECEMBER 21, 1941

Terribly cold. Hard to walk any distance. Heard [Handel's]
Messiah at First-Episc. Tonight with Virginia. Little done today

except some solid reading. I hate to feel like a sponge, however. Jumble Shop for martinis. Called R. as usual. Got Natasha in merrie mood—Sylvia M. is here. Rosalind asked me to pick her up Tuesday at 8 at Crillon's* Party. Eating later also Spivy's thank God. + Virginia quite gorgeous in a beaver coat—! She propositioned me. My moral code is becoming quite as narrow as my bed. Rosalind or nothing.

12/21/41

The sex act should be done either in a white heat or with the best sense of humor. Technique is a matter of imagination, and consideration only of the other person; a talent never found in men.

DECEMBER 22, 1941

Fine day. Finished play. Finished [Thomas Hardy's] *Dynasts*. Finished staining Marj's figger & delivered that & T. S. Eliot back to Jeva. She was simply overcome with joy & emotion & bought me two martinis at the Mansfield.† I asked Jeva was she ever violent, [she] said no.—While drinking I had the thought women are not hard enough—and are too ready to speak their weaknesses which a man would keep, more wisely, to himself. I feel very blunt and slow and honest with Jeva lately. She cautioned me about going entirely with girls—they disappeared finally— you need some young man to share and in short to foot the bills. Kingsley here at 6. We did errands & decorated Xmas tree. Got tight & called Rosalind (who asked me to brunch Xmas day). Read Virginia Woolf's *Between the Acts*. Jack Berger of Comet Press asked me to dinner (!). Knew it was coming.

12/22/41

When this fine maturity comes, what do people like V.W. & J.S.‡ do for the violence and the unrestraint they must have

---

* Crillon was a restaurant located at 277 Park Avenue.
† The Mansfield Hotel was located at 12 West Forty-Fourth Street.
‡ V.W. could stand for Virginia Woolf, whom she's just read; J.S. possibly for John Steinbeck.

known in their youth? Without which the tranquility (afterwards) is nothing but stagnation (but during which, strangely,
nothing comes but shards brittle and small, fragments and ker-
nels of something great). How do they keep their production so
fine and so powerful, too? What is the secret excitement behind?

12/22/41
Babs has something fuzzy standing two feet out around her,
touching gently in anticipation and warning something warm
and comfortable. But I run into people like a steel needle.

12/22/41
Do you remember short days ago we laughed and said how lucky we
were that we were the best-looking people we knew, that we were
the smartest (almost) and certainly had the best sense of humor. And
now that the magic potion that was in our veins has been assim-
ilated, diluted (one might almost say excreted), we see only each
other's faults, when we look, and more than that we hate each other
because we remember the beautiful bondage and are afraid.

DECEMBER 23, 1941
Another day—generally speaking—delightful. But filled with emotional ups and downs that are becoming common now, they are so
much more perceptive when one is alone. Wrote seven pages longhand of "Passing of Alphonse T. Browne."* Will have to be revised
no end. Painted a couple of watercolors in which I got something.
Someday I shall be good. In everything. Goodness—excellence is
my goal. + Jack B. sent me lineo-type New Year's Greeting & a
babushka. We ate at Ricoto's on Vandam St. He's only 24 & looks
34. Picked up Rosalind at Crillon's at 8. Quite drunk. Fortune
party. Went to *Macbeth* where she nodded frequently during first
act. After she was too sick to go to Spivy's. Not drunk, just a sore
throat. I ministered to her like an angel, she said.

---

* A (lost) story in progress.

DECEMBER 24, 1941

Worked on story. Wrote Babs & gave family bottle of Crème de
Cacao. Delivered it myself. Bought Rosalind Eric Coates' "London Again Suite." Perhaps she can understand English music. I
can't think much of it. Buffie called last night about dinner party
tonight. I went with her. Drunk & exhausted, phoned Helen
secretly after martinis & champagne. She was glad to hear
me—I loved her & told her so—and she said to get over it. Buffie
knew. At least she knows it isn't Rosalind now.

DECEMBER 25, 1941

Most peculiar Xmas. Eyes like golf balls this morning. Breakfast then presents, some eggnog. Got pajamas—Mozart's 23 in
A major. K. 488! My dream of three years. To Rosalind's at 2:15.
All merry, and presents by the dozen. Del P. very handsome.
Lola there, Natasha, Niko,* Betty, Sylvia, Simeon & Guy M.
Great success, the whiskey sours & bean soup. Natasha kissed
me thrice on entering. Rosalind didn't open my present yet. They
all adjourned to Natasha's. Asked me to come, but Stanley was
home getting dinner alone so I didn't. Lovely dinner—this barrier
between us is too great perhaps. There is now not the desire to
break it. I've changed my mind, about money. I once believed it
blunted appreciation, but it really heightens it, it lets you get what
you need and gives the leisure and security to taste it.

DECEMBER 26, 1941

The seventh morning of work—not bad. + Mary S., Marjorie
T. here this evening. Putting her maternal finger on the trouble
immediately, Mary [S.] suggests playing along with Rosalind &
Helen will come running again. Deception of the most innocent
and strategic kind however, is unpleasant. Virginia was to come
but she got wind of Mary [S.]. I don't like anyway that she asks

---

* Probably Nicolas Calas (born Nikos Kalamaris), a Greek-American critic and poet who
came to New York as one of the first émigré surrealists in 1940.

me who's coming. Quite rude & childish. She hasn't grown up &
I'm not waiting.

DECEMBER 27, 1941

Rosalind called! Very nice & we talked a long while. She wants
to see Cocteau's Surrealist film at 5th Avenue. She was on her
5th whiskey sour, & en route to Del's country place. It occurred
to me today Betty Parsons is tense & too on the alert. I wonder how confident she is really? And how much Rosalind sees
through her? How much she loves her & why?

DECEMBER 28, 1941

Jack B. came at 1:30. Saw *Chapaev*!* Museum of Modern Art.
All the Russian things drag finally. Left him there & met Roger
who just came in. We drank martinis here. Got a telegram at 7
from mother that Grampa died this morning. I didn't feel any
better for that. Roger polite, but kissed me goodnight, which
was distasteful under the circumstances.

DECEMBER 29, 1941

Finished "Passing," but Roger said tonight [that it] doesn't get
started soon enough. Too subtle. He wrote a story in the evening, right off, and got an A on it. Well he and I are different.
He isn't confident. Tonight he wanted to eat at a French place,
so we did (Au Petit Paris) & afterwards to take a horse &
buggy thru the park. But he doesn't like T. S. Eliot. I'm at the
age where I cease to reform my tastes: I accept what I find—
within—without shame. + Phoned Rosalind miserably at 12
and delightfully at 4! (After doing errands around the house.
Stanley doesn't lift a hand.) Del P. asked for me to come to his
country place New Year's if they go. Read [Stephen Crane's]
Red Badge of Courage. Splendid writing + Saw Dumbo with

---

* *Chapaev*, a Soviet war film, based on a fictionalized biography of a Red Army commander
and Russian Civil War hero.

Roger. Not so good, but excellent of its kind. Movies stink. I have been to six this year.

DECEMBER 30, 1941

Sent the "Passing" to *New Yorker, Matrix* & *Accent*. Read *Don Juan*. How much more fun to produce than to absorb sometimes—and sometimes the other way. Mary H. phoned, wanted me to come over at 4 so I did. Smaller apt. She's quite depressed, having sold only one sketch at her show. Photographs of our painting: frankly not good. She says she's beginning to feel her age—the lack of spirit to combat difficulties. + No news from mother. I begin to think my letter not lugubrious enough & Stanley didn't like my telegram. We both think, however, flowers out of place for us. Started my story of John and the Jewish Boy.

1942

College Graduation, or: "I'm smoking too much and life is generally confusing."

❧

PATRICIA HIGHSMITH PASSES two major milestones in 1942: she turns twenty-one and graduates college, and although employment proves elusive, Pat is certain she wants to make a living as a writer. She certainly fulfills her desire to write, if only for herself initially. Between the diaries and notebooks, she fills an astounding 750 pages this year with details of her life and ideas for writing, the entries written in a combination of English, Spanish, French, and German.

Pat takes one lover after the next. Very rarely is there someone she is deeply attracted to both physically and emotionally. Her circle of successful older women soon includes exiled German photographer Ruth Bernhard, who introduces her to another German photographer, Rolf Tietgens, and Pat quickly forms an intense bond with both.

The United States joined the Allied Forces in December 1941, but World War II seems to mostly pass Pat by. She does learn first aid, and the Navy recruits her for a course in decoding and plane spotting. Whereas her male lovers and friends are drafted, as a woman Pat is free to quit the service, which she does for lack of patriotism and satisfactory pay.

In May, the Highsmiths finally move to a larger apartment in midtown Manhattan, a step upward on the New York social ladder Pat has long been hoping for—but by that time she is desperate for her own place. Their relationship worsens: Pat's parents despise her so-called snobbish friends. Mary watches in horror as her daughter grows increasingly "masculine" and estranged from her.

Pat receives her B.A. in English in June. Despite letters of recommendation from her friend Rosalind Constable, Pat is not hired by any of the reputable magazines she had hoped, such as *The New Yorker*. Determined to write for a living, she is forced to temp, first at F.F.F. Publications—a house that generates articles on current affairs for the national Jewish press—then as typist for *Modern Baby* magazine, and as a street promoter for a deodorant manufacturer. In mid-December, Pat's luck finally changes when she successfully tries out for a writing job in the comics industry. With a fixed income in sight, the year ends on an optimistic note with Pat's confidence in her talent and potential firmly intact.

PROLOGUE
Look before and look behind,
There's still time to change your mind;
Perfidy no time assuages;
Curst be he that moves these pages
5/2/42

1/1/42

Chestnut for the new Year: our pleasures, preferences, delights, vices, and passions are our vulnerable spots. They are cracks in our dikes, and flaws in our armor, holes in our masks, termites in our wooden legs. And the whole world sad, and all the sadder because the sun is shining, and because the air and the light is the same as at the best, but only man's own sadness oppresses him. It is within him and he makes it around him. Is each of us born with a measured number of tears? Or are they number-less? I wonder often whence comes the sheer energy that keeps us moving? But it would be of no use to ask "why?" We are not able to stop.

JANUARY 1, 1942

First real hangover on New Year's that I can recall. This year I really come of age. Took down the Xmas tree in an orgy of melancholia, and went for a walk (on eggshells) along 8th St. Bumped into a man who said he met me at Billie's last night. Tibor Koeves.* I don't remember a damn thing. He told me about his novel he's starting today. Rosalind phoned at 6:30 PM. I went up. Del, Lola. Betty & Billie there. All solicitous of my health. We had drinks. I feel quite dull, which is mainly [due to] living alone with no routine. This year I shall not only do schoolwork but write in the evenings. I work better and more brilliantly under pressure. Home quite late. Rather low, but prospects in petto. Down but not out—quite.

JANUARY 2, 1942

Went to Billie A.'s. My clothes there but not my lipstick. Lovely place really. She was just having it cleaned. Cigarette stubs, sand-wiches in flowerpots . . . With Walter Marlowe. Dinner at Artist & Writers.† Wonderful talking really. Should put some down.

1/2/42

Why are creative people melancholy? Because they have not the hard frame of behavior all the others wear. They are grass in the wind, to be whipped this way and that, flattened at times on the ground. The creative person would, intellectually, first believe

---

* Tibor Köves, or Koeves (1903–1953), Hungarian Jewish journalist and author.
† Artist and Writers was a popular hangout for journalists especially from the nearby *Herald Tribune*, but also from *The New Yorker* and the *Times*, who gathered at 215 West Fortieth Street in the afternoon. Women were no longer banned as they had been during the place's speakeasy past, but the atmosphere was rowdy and men dominated the crowd.

the price too great. Worst of all, the horrible knowledge, that this fighting (the story of it) is invalid for literary purposes.

JANUARY 3, 1942

Mother starts for home tomorrow morning. Her letter said gramps passed very tranquilly, cracking jokes with the boys only the day before. Gramma is living on at the house. They put her to bed with a mild sedative. Will be so unspeakably glad to see mother. Although I can't tell her all my problems she symbolizes all the stability, the femininity, the comfort and warmth of my life. Shall have to take her to the Amen corner* for champagne cocktails and a long talk Friday. + Dinner with Tibor. Told him of family difficulties, and we decided, together, that that restraint was the cause of my emotional knot, which is the cause of this turmoil. He keeps the homosexuality out of it. This thing with H. was the first time I gave my soul—saw my soul or could have given my soul, that is. What I shall want all my life is to give and receive warmth. I suffer from cold physically and psychologically all the time.

JANUARY 4, 1942

Up at terribly late hour: 11:00! Worse than New Years. Finished story—my first which "wrote itself." Perhaps good writing, but needs the climaxes played up. I consistently muff climaxes: literary and factual. Read [Walt] Whitman, for whom I have a two-day penchant. Walked in the street and nearly killed myself. What for? Unlike Nietzsche, my best thoughts do not come in the fresh air. More and more I crave change. By God if we don't move in April I shall be sad. We need a couple or three good sized rooms where we can stretch our legs and live with dignity—Shall use my invincible powers of persuasion on mother when she comes.

---

* One of the downstairs sitting rooms of the Fifth Avenue Hotel on the northwest corner of Fifth Avenue and Twenty-Third Street.

JANUARY 6, 1942

And the mountain came to Mahomet tonight: Rosalind phoned at 8:20. Reprimanded me for being tight at Billie's. "Rather rude, with people you hardly know—" In general left me uncomfortable the rest of the evening. But she asked when she could see me (for further chastisement) & we have a date for Friday lunch.

JANUARY 7, 1942

Play went over with the greatest success. Latham asked me was it "seemly." She was shocked at first, then laughed loudly, with the rest. Helen still acting dopey. I feel very vague about her. The physical feeling has left like a passing tornado.

JANUARY 8, 1942

Good day. Thornbury* said no novel is great without violent action. Home at 4:30 for tea with mother. She still is in a flurry and I can't talk very much. Says I'm very businesslike to make a date to talk. I was called up by Ladue of math. dept., selected for intelligence work—decoding. Right up my alley. Only 15–20 from seniors chosen. Shall perhaps go to Washington when school is out. I should be good at it.

JANUARY 10, 1942

Marjorie's [Thompson] at seven. I feel the old hostility with mother. It works this way: I'm happy if I can be the boss. Lighting her cigarettes and dominating as I did yesterday. I think I'm disgusted with her conversation—lightheaded, impulsive, trivial and proud, in a crowd—with Marjorie. I don't see myself living with them. Their pettiness begins to annoy me—their triviality—(Perhaps mine in seeing it.)

---

* Ethel M. Thornbury, English professor at Barnard from 1940 to 1943. Pat wrote "Tradition in American Literature" for her course and kept it in her files.

JANUARY 11, 1942

Breakfast with mother. Told her then how I felt about Stanley: that we alone could be amiable together, but his presence is alien. I told her too of the fixation element and that I must try and correct it, not they thru discussion. Purely emotional. I hope she doesn't tell this to Stanley.

JANUARY 12, 1942

Only travelers & lovers live somewhat in the present: there's a possible Thursday night for me & R. & K. this week. And a certain Friday lunch!

1/12/42

I wonder is the measure of emotion budgeted either to be used over a long period of time, or to be shot all at once like a double barrel Winchester?

1/12/42

When I write a novel: D.P. says one can't write a novel about dull people. Even Tolstoi's social significance is shown thru superior-minded people. And Steinbeck won't last, everyone says. No. I should take just my own class, speculate on Texas—New York or New York. And why the desperate heroic themes I often ponder? Why the wild young man, not the person like myself, curious, energetic, seeking, suffering and believing, weeding out and seeking in, finding and losing, failing and succeeding. The bogus people and the few honest people. But irrevocably New York. In fact, perhaps, New York could be the hero, working like a many faceted, powerful, fertile character, upon other worthy characters. (Worthy to be written about.)

JANUARY 13, 1942

All papers back from Thornbury. About 3 A's and four B's. Nice lunch with Babs [P.]. Simply ideal—martinis, omelets, string beans & spinach—and a good talk. She said she hated the secrecy with her family—some day she would have to conceal so much. I asked her what. She said someday, she hoped, she would fall in love with a woman. Spoke with Sturtevant. Said she read my "Silver Horn" twice & thought it was excellent.

1/15/42

I am not interested in people, knowing them. But I am intensely interested in a woman in the dark doorway on Eleventh Street, reading with difficulty the name plates, by the light of a match. Such a scene sets me thinking of all-time, all-place, all–past and present and future happenings. Is this real? Our only reality is in books: the purely fictional distillation from the impurity of reality. This woman in the doorway, I felt, was reality poised for an instant in the impure waters. This scene was perfect as it was. I do not care for humanity in individuals. I do not care to smell their breaths.

JANUARY 20, 1942

Kingsley annoys me. Saw her today & she phoned afterwards, just to tell me how sad I looked. So what? She's so damn unattractive looking! Why the hell doesn't she lose weight? + Rosalind didn't know it was my birthday yesterday—: I didn't expect her to, but it would have been so nice if she had. Perhaps she doesn't give a damn after all.

1/20/42

I love to be in love. It fastens me to the earth, and releases me to play in the clouds. I feel like a tree, taking root with my feet and stretching terribly high with my arms, and bursting all over into little buds.

JANUARY 21, 1942

Up early in the 18th century manner. At school at 9:00. The exam was beautiful and I think I did a good job if I catch Thornbury in a good mood. I should have been very tired, but I was elated over having lunch with Rosalind. Thought about it as much as possible during the exam, and afterwards smiled at everyone and took my leave. + Rosalind hung over, which is getting to be quite a habit. Showed my Naval Dept. paper quiz. She laughed at my answers. Very interested. "No days absent from school." "Physical defects: none." Why don't you put: "I'm perfectly beautiful"? + Then she said out of the blue that Betty's going to be gone over the weekend & she'll be rather free— Odd's Blood and all that!

JANUARY 22, 1942

Read Willa Cather's *Not Under Forty* and [Franz] Boas's *Mind of Primitive Man* & Napoleon's Letters to Marie Louise. + Shall start a story tomorrow I'm quite excited about.+ Did [Renoir's] *La Baigneuse* in water color. Could be better, but rather fits what I wanted it to. I feel wonderful—very confident and happy—about the future. About R. I don't know. Many things are possible. I think she'll not resign a lease with Betty. I shall probably marry Ernst. I like no one better. It will be purely an intellectual decision. I look for no further awakenings. I've been around, and the sexual world (whether completely explored or not) I have glimpsed its pearly gates.

1/22/42

Able to think only when I have a background, of music, of voices, of lecturing, able to think creatively only in the unconcious, losing the thread when I realize I am following a thread, much addicted to cigarettes and alcohol; shy about emotions of any kind and disturbed at their display; caricaturing my own talents as they lie now, writing facetious (and rather good) doggerel, sketches and perhaps whole books, specializing in takeoffs and pure whimsy and fantasy; highly critical of people, but with a circle of friends as wide as the Tropic of Cancer; subsisting mainly on fruit of citrus nature: rarely going in a church door except to hear Bach or Händel; fond of 18th century literature and music; dabbling in water color and stabbing at sculpture; aiming high and believing myself capable of great things. Falling in love more and more easily and "irrevocably." Happier still when most alone.

JANUARY 25, 1942

Mother will doubtless move. She talks about it. While I walked
I thought happily of my story of the executive girl.* It all seemed
possible, logical, "true" as Koeves would say. The task is writing
it. I must do it. It's an important thing to me to express. + Heard
Bach's B minor mass with mother. Kyrie Eleison the most beautiful. The rest remains cold to me except for a few lines, except
where I close my eyes. Bach is rich. + Mother & I had a beer. I
talked of marriage, which is politic as well as being some concern right now. Mother said she thought of grampa during the
music, that it was almost like having him there.

1/28/42

I believe in inspiration, mad, unreasoned inspiration from the never
never land. I must have the idea, leaping to the surface from the
subconscious as a sparkling, cavorting fish leaps an instant above
the surface of the sea. In that instant I must remember; to record
and develop is later duller work perhaps—the only work I will
admit. My characters are purely imaginary, because I seldom am
able to go on from one that I know. I have a strong trend to the evil,
like many young people. But not evil hidden behind a mask, and
not evil that is oral generally. I hate complicated relations, which
really worries me a great deal, (this hate) as a writer because human
relations are always, complicated. I am annoyed when real human
relations have tangled me, or when even I see them tangling others.
And hearing the situations, I forget them easily. Being unintuitive
I must meet many people, many kinds of people, worthless people
and petty people. Sometimes my friends find it hard to understand.

JANUARY 30, 1942

My notebook grows apace with such stimulation. I keep putting down tripe here. I want to tell Rosalind all about myself—
not for impression—but because she is wise, and young at the
same time & can understand as I do. Rosalind has a "yes-

---

* It is unclear which story she refers to here.

complex"—a positive, healthy, optimistic complex. She says the word more beautifully than she says any other perhaps, except "darling" which I haven't heard lately. And certainly, she says "yes" more beautifully than anyone else in the world.

FEBRUARY 1, 1942

Pleasant day but not exciting in any way. Too many evenings at home in succession are as bad as too many going out. Mother said [Stanley's] love for her was utterly without inspiration—that he deliberately stifled all creativeness in her. This is partially true, partially alibi—but at any rate what I used two and four years ago on their separation. I wish something would come of it, for mother's sake, soon, even at the risk of changing my own precious plans about an apartment.

FEBRUARY 3, 1942

Kingsley called with wonderful message: She'd been to the Wakefield [Gallery] where B. [Betty] Parsons asked her to sign the register, and asked who'd sent her and said, "Oh Pat! Yes, Rosalind talks about her constantly! About how brilliant she is. In fact I'm rather tired of hearing about her, etc."—(No doubt Betty knew well this conversation would be relayed precisely to me.) Kingsley introduced it thus: "I have it on reliable authority that Rosalind Constable is your slave!"

2/5/42

If people would only leave me to mellow. Like old wine they might trust to age of itself. But they plunge their alien fingers to the bottom. And I am cloudy with the sediment and best left alone.

FEBRUARY 6, 1942

Dinner with Hauser, we cooked, haphazardly, and started from scratch. Plenty of liquor. But no magic—no thrill, no beauty—no imagination, no ecstatic present, now perfect in the lift of a glass or a cigarette as I felt with Rosalind! I merely sit there, thinking of what to say next, stuffing my face and pondering on the per-

sonal spiel of certain people. He is all very well. I understand him
and really like him—but he is as common to me as my bathmat.

FEBRUARY 9, 1942

Kingsley & I called on Rosalind, bringing her raisins & collecting my books, but she & Natasha were at the Normandie
burning* at 49th St. We went over. Didn't see them. The ship's a
wreck. Saboteurs. Gave me an idea for a one-acter on the war.
The Saboteurs—Shall probably even write it, too. Happy evening, once more alive.

2/9/42

If I were a boy now, being in the army, I should be writing action
stories probably with new settings—writing with authority I can
never acquire through pure imagination. Thus men are thrust
into exotic surroundings (foreign) which they are less able to
handle than women. While women are left at home, to watch the
human relations of long standing, which, while they understand
them, and indeed contribute too much to them to understand
circumspectly, they are less qualified to handle in the subtleties
than their men.

2/9/42

My darling, darling. Darling—no I won't go skiing with you,
with a smile of desperate pleasure stretched across my face—
because I get so god-damned cold! But yes, my darling, if you'd
ask me to swim across the Hudson River in this sub-freezing
weather, then I would. Provided of course it's only a whim: if
you're certain it's only a whim.

FEBRUARY 10, 1942

The lunch date [with Rosalind] was not wonderful because 1) I
was dressed chi-chi, which she doesn't feel comfortable in any-

---

* The SS *Normandie* was undergoing conversion to a troopship when she caught fire and
capsized at a dock in New York City. Although sabotage was suspected, it was never proved.

more than I 2) she had work to do & could not drink much 3) we both had colds 4) I'd seen her too recently anyway. She questioned me about working & writing: I said I could do both and needed to do both simultaneously. She said people never do write while working. It remains to be seen. With Buffie at [Fernand] Léger's* madhouse cocktail party. Hughes there first—spoke to her. She'd read my story & liked it ("Silver Horn"). Met Stewart Chaney,† [Arthur] Koestler‡ (very nice). [Buffie] gave me a Valentine rose. Now I feel quite socialized once more. I want to be alone now. Much to read & do. This socialization is necessary like a shot of dope in the arm that hurts going in, but which will make me run a while longer.

2/11/42

Mozart concertos! Aged sixteen in my room at One Bank Street, with the door closed. The piano sings alone, and I lay down my books and close my eyes. One phrase in the slow second movement, with gentle fingertips, touches me like a kiss—I had not noticed the double notes, the dancing phrase in thirds, and it is a revelation—just as a kiss is a revelation from one we have known before, but whose kiss is the new unknown. At sixteen, I lay and asked myself could there be anything ever in the world so wonderfully beautiful, so perfect, as this Mozart concerto? And the answer was, no, not really—only someone might somehow be a concerto.

2/14/42

I had a strong feeling tonight, sitting talking with R. that I was many-faceted like a ball of glass, or like the eye of a fly.

---

* The French painter, sculptor, and film director Joseph Fernand Léger (1881–1955) lived in the United States during World War II before returning to France, where in his later years he developed a style that would greatly influence pop art.

† Stewart Chaney (1910–1969), American stage, set, and costume designer.

‡ Arthur Koestler (1905–1983), Hungarian-born British author, journalist, and political activist. After joining the Communist Party in 1931, he resigned in 1938 after becoming disillusioned with Stalin. In 1940, he wrote the anti-totalitarian novel *Darkness at Noon*, which brought him international fame.

One facet is the true one that lets light in without refraction. The others refract and are false. I have to try them all before the proper one is discovered. I have not found the true one yet, which should release my energy in a true stream. I see the right one is in me. It is what people see when they talk to me, when they set me apart for some reason, and say, I have a life ahead. I shall be something. I shall do something. They are all quite sure of that. Surer, sometimes, than I, but not really surer than I. Someday I shall find the facet. It is not so difficult and it will not take forever.

FEBRUARY 17, 1942

I think much about writing. I have written so many beautiful, fresh paragraphs. The problem is synthesis around one idea. As Sturtevant said years ago, I can write if I had something to write about. Mother fears a complete blot out of commercial art. Stands to reason—all art-work except war commodities becomes inessential.

FEBRUARY 18, 1942

Kingsley said first she thought my *cahier* (I brought her yesterday) was wonderful. [Then] disappointed in the book's lack of originality. (What the hell did she expect.) And that the cloud of greatness is forever lifted from me. Tut! Tut! Just as well for both of us. We've heard of another place 4½ rooms on 57 St. Tomorrow the inspection. Stanley is scared silly of the rent! Says our income will be taxed beyond belief next year. Still mother wants a larger living room, I want a decent house. And never underestimate the power of a woman.

FEBRUARY 19, 1942

Saw our future apartment: 345 E. 57 St. today with mother. Only drawback is the view: more yards to house backs, ending at level of our ceiling. Not bad. The fireplace isn't real either, but the neighborhood! And the house! Worked my last afternoon on the crypt course. Latham is against as a waste of time. I do think the scant chances of remuneration makes the thing unfair. Patriotic motives are another matter. But I can't afford the time. I have to prepare for things not yet begun!

FEBRUARY 21, 1942

Roger F. here. Brought me a gardenia. We had martinis, & dinner at Jumble. He bores me. Said I was too self centered to fall in love. I told him I was, however, more disgusting double standard talk, and over rating of sex. A lot he knows about the real Pat!

FEBRUARY 22, 1942

Worked on play. Slow business. But sinking my teeth in more. Kingsley here & we did the magazine. She made me nervous. Besides I'm never happy when I see the nakedness of print and my own story there! Naked in the marketplace, as Hawthorne said.* Were I to write a novel now, choosing my deepest sentiment it would be that human beings could make a paradise with their own love if they but knew how—if they but realized what they had. But this theme is of course by my past, too—and present. I don't care to start first on a lesbian novel. There's no need. It comes out well enough in other themes as well. One can't help it. Should like to do something great soon. I feel enough and the expansion, growth and strength emotionally and spiritually. I should write of devotion, and it would be the least cynical, most idealistic piece I'd ever do.

2/23/42

Leviathan! I should like to call my first book. It should be long and deep and wide and high. Thick and rich, too, like America. None of the thinner, twenty-four-hours-in-a-bedroom stuff for me. I should have elaboration with conciseness. Slow reading and fast, fast writing and slow, because a novel needs no standard tempo.

---

* Hawthorne was almost pathologically shy. The quote "The lovers are naked on the marketplace and perform for the benefit of society" is by another of Pat's favorite authors, though: Henry James, commenting on how George Sand incorporated her affair with Alfred de Musset into her writing.

2/23/42

Insincerity: Artists are logically the most insincere people. They must be for a while whatever they work at. A murderer, a poet, a philanderer, a traitor, an explorer, a child, a savant. They are all these in turn, and none of them and nothing themselves. They are their own canvas, a palimpsest of all their creations, and if when not working, they are a dirty smudge of coarse cloth, that is no fault of theirs.

3/2/42

My very first story was "Crime Begins."* I tend to that and do suspense well. The morbid, the cruel, the abnormal fascinates me.

MARCH 3, 1942

The Japanese are making great headway in Java and have really got Rangoon, Burma. Not so good, not so good at lunch.I get depressed in dark clothes, when my hair isn't right. Rosalind looked gorgeous in her gray flannel pinstripe, beige blouse and pearls—just the things for a blonde. We ate at Golden Horn.†
How wonderful when Rosalind breaks out in a laugh and says, "I'll have a martini, but I'll go to hell for it!" She said, "My spies tell me your *Vogue* papers are pretty good." But they've found a dream girl. I don't think I advanced myself any. But Rosalind continually says "You're a career woman" or "You're going to be just like us."

MARCH 7, 1942

Pretty nice day—tho still not perfect and it should have been, being entirely in my hands. Where do I fail? A certain discouragement in the morning, starting my one-act *The Saboteurs*— Not bad, but a definite feeling I should have done better. Nevertheless, I have to put something down to start. I can't

---

* This story of Pat's has not survived.
† Located on Broadway near Times Square, the Golden Horn was considered the most elegant of Manhattan's Armenian restaurants and attracted theater and sports personalities.

think very long in the air. Afterwards I'm tolerably willing to
revise. Women's uniforms are getting commonplace. I don't see
any need for ties.

MARCH 9, 1942
Signed up for Airplane Spotting. A mild young man teaching.
Important enough and very interesting.

MARCH 12, 1942
Mother's income is now less than Stanley's. Odd how both
are not successes—not failures. One thing—I shall never try
to combine work with marriage & a child. One or the other,
not both—unless I'm so rich I can take the child & house off
my hands. Ran into Berger at Fifth Ave. Playhouse.* ᶠ*Crime et
Châtiment*† and *The Brothers Karamazov*. The first is excellent!
Harry Baur. Every scene is a masterpiece! A novel like that is a
real work of art. A murder—a killing in a novel fascinates me.ᶠᶠ

MARCH 14, 1942
Berger sent flowers, which were here when we came home.
Drinks here at six. He's wonderfully outspoken and gets on with
the family in an unusually adult fashion—says his mind & that's
that. He's getting very fond of me unfortunately. Dined at Cafe
Royale,‡ then saw *Café Crown*. Pretty fair. He wants to teach
me the Hebrew alphabet since I'm interested. He came home at
twelve and never wanted to leave. Nice fellow. And did a swell
job on *Quarterly* which I saw Friday. Don't know whether I shall
show it to Rosalind or not. Berger mentioned dearth of love stories in my writing. No work of any kind done of course.

---

* Arguably the first art movie house in the United States, it opened on December 16, 1925, and
was noted for showing French movies in French.
† A 1935 French film based on the eponymous novel (*Crime and Punishment*) by Fyodor
Dostoyevsky.
‡ Restaurant at Second Avenue and Twelfth Street, where the Jewish intellectuals and the
stars of the Yiddish theater gathered.

MARCH 17, 1942

Lunch with Rosalind. A gentleman from the Navy called on her about my "applied for job" and questioned especially re the ASU. Rosalind had the British genius of combining honesty with discretion. She's delighted to come to Greek Games*—In fact Betty too and a Mrs. Sikilianos, of Grecian lore from somewhere. Shall get at least four tickets! Rosalind gave me Djuna Barnes' *Nightwood*,† which I shall reserve for some precious day in the Easter holidays.

Read *Democracy at the Crossroads* of [William Pepperell] Montague. Writes better than he speaks. Started [Edward] Gibbon's *Decline & Fall* [*of the Roman Empire*]. Simply superb! Another great book like [James] Boswell's *J.* [*The Life of Samuel Johnson*] and I approach it with the same subdued & cautious enthusiasm—an ecstasy of a sort.

3/18/43

The most salient feature of this century is the insignificance of the individual, the consciousness of it in us all, the absence of our rightful dream of greatness, nobility and destiny.

MARCH 19, 1942

MacArthur's‡ in Australia, and got there by motorboat, then flying. The Americans are doing things fast. I'd like to be there! Rosalind & Betty very interested in Jeannot's latest letter. Eight pages about the Grand Prix§ and cartoons. Rosalind said *Life* [magazine] might use it, but I think it's German propaganda.

---

* Greek Games: Contest at Barnard. In 1942, the fortieth annual Greek Games were held in its gymnasium.
† *Nightwood* (1936) is considered a pioneering work in American lesbian literature and the most important work of writer Djuna Barnes (1892–1982), whom Pat would later also get to know personally.
‡ General Douglas MacArthur, an American five-star general, chief of staff of the United States Army during the 1930s. He played a key role in the Pacific theater in World War II.
§ Possibly the Prix d'Amérique, a harness race, held at the Hippodrome de Vincennes in Paris on the last Sunday of January every year.

I must get more sleep. I'm dead all the time. One doesn't enjoy things so much. Let this be my motive.

MARCH 21, 1942

Now of course, being twenty-one, I feel a great responsibility to do something good in everything creative. No more reasons for imperfection due to immaturity. Mother in a stew all day about Jack Berger's coming tonight. I wished I hadn't had him to dinner, but I wish more mother'd take things easier. She has a masochistic complex of bearing an impossible burden which prevents her working at art, she says. I did a little reading, and got her quite tight at dinner. Her opinions on the Negro question,* which we discussed tonight, were vague & unprincipled and emotional. She refuses to think or reason. Berger said he was in love with me. I rather pity him. We all go around chasing each one another's tails and never making it, don't we? He read my play in oddly fifteen minutes, as it should be read. Liked it quite a lot, the dialogue, the idea. The Ghosts. Means more to me than the praise of the whole class!

MARCH 23, 1942

Have discovered this instant why writing this diary is necessary to me. It's been the only time, a few minutes, when I was still today. It makes me quiet a few moments, besides clarifying items that would otherwise drift in my head.

MARCH 24, 1942

Started working again at 9:30 & Rosalind phoned. She asked me was I coming Thurs. night, and what had I been doing? Then out of the blue: "How would you like to be an office girl

---

* We have no information on what exactly Pat's own opinion was at the time on "the Negro question." From later entries we know that she had strong objections to the treatment of Black Americans in her home state of Texas. Certainly, the fact that thousands of Black troops served in World War II while racism and segregation prevailed added fuel to the public debate over equal rights for all.

for Time, Inc.?" I told her yes. Natasha had recommended me
to the personnel, and possibly I'd be interviewed. Damn nice of
her. Mother says it's ideal. Not too high a salary. Rosalind said
they don't keep one on as office girl there very long. The boys are
being drafted away, and they're now fooling around with female
high school morons.

3/25/42
Probably the most serious handicap to a woman's becoming
President is her clothes. Just imagine trying to please every sec-
tion of the country!

MARCH 26, 1942
Rosalind quite grim. Telling me what not to do—namely not to
have my friends up or to make conversational calls on phone—
which is equivalent to telling me not to throw cocktail parties in
the main foyer! She must think I'm indiscreet! She said she and
Natasha think I'm a menace!

MARCH 28, 1942
Read [Henry James] *The Ambassadors* this A.M. very happy.
Want to work—want to write—express somehow what I feel
about the thrilling and wonderful impracticability of being in
love with R.

3/28/42
On drinking and the time question. (Forever lost to posterity—
forgotten in inebriation.)

MARCH 29, 1942
Fair day. I'm still an old pearl in a new oyster. This house
must get mellowed before I can write in it. I feel much better
tonight—this minute perhaps—than ever before here. Mother
is miserable just now. I'm surprised (pleasantly) to see that
Stanley supports me greatly. Mother he says "exaggerates"
the situation—that I'm not hopeless. Mother of course says

I'm inhuman, I treat her like a dog, I don't do a thing around
the house —every whit of which is (a) jealousy (b) inferiority (c) retribution for her not getting sex and consequently
looking for guys to go down in the elevator with all night.
Met [Florence] Palma at church where we heard the St Mat-
thew Passion. The music did wonders for me. It made me still
inside, made me think independently of the two inches before
my nose—made me think of myself too however, and sent me
home optimistic, having shed a few Xtian tears, but having
wandered up and down mentally into the most sordid corners,
too. Such is the human mind with no hand on the steering
wheel.

MARCH 30, 1942
Mother getting harder to live with. The advertising business
will jolly well fold flat if the war goes on. As Berger said last
night, many men talk of 5–10 years. Seems to me the art game,
unless one strikes the top and stays there, is the most under-
paid of all. The war brings at least temporary good wages,
so why not avail oneself of them? I see Stanley in a couple of
months doing something entirely different, and being a lot happier, too.

MARCH 31, 1942
Berger called, and I'd forgot about Fri. and dated Mary Sullivan.
He had tickets. Does him good for a change.

3/31/42
Reading love letters when one is not in love is humiliating. It is
being outside looking in.

APRIL 1, 1942
I wonder if I should go out tomorrow? I can't relax, God damn
it. I need a good love affair. All I do is keep myself in perfect
shape—for what? For whom?

APRIL 2, 1942

Slight progress. Worked on story and had lunch with Rosalind—
We had a martini and a half, which she allowed me I suppose
because I told her of the sad situation at home. She's quite eager
to meet my mother. With Hauser tonight. Very very hospitable.
We had martinis and ate at Pete's.* He still wants to get married,
wants to meet Rosalind, wants to write a good non-fiction, and
go to China first. Feel like an adult today—like a more adjusted
person—good for writing? Not always.

APRIL 3, 1942

Woolsey Teller[†] here at one. Free for the day, he was, sadly. But
such an unbearable cliché expert! He got quite nervous and sentimental. Kissed me on parting. The least I could give him in lieu
of time and in return for Chateaubriand lunching. Walked to 36
St. to give blood. Terribly nice down there. I damn near fainted
however. I feel lonely now. Discouraged at my progress, and
my only joy in life. The only comfortable arms I can hide in are
Rosalind's.

4/3/42

The world needs an injection of naivete. Try to get a job, and
you find this out. The arteries are hard, and people think they
know, too well, what they want. Nothing else will do. Even the
escapists, the detective story readers, the movie-goers, have set
standards that would put a Greek aesthete to shame. Variations
will not do. The frame must be there, and within the frame novelty at any cost. The world is too easily bored by the very things
it seeks to escape boredom, because the novelty which speciously
attracts is soon discovered resting in the old frame, without

---

* Pete's Tavern, located at 129 East Eighteenth Street, claims to be the oldest operated tavern
in New York, immortalized by O. Henry in his short story "The Lost Blend."
† Woolsey Teller (1890–1954), an openly anti-Semitic and white supremacist writer and
editor who dedicated his career to the promotion of atheism.

which the novelty never would have gained entry into the great presence: the consuming employing, escaping public.

APRIL 4, 1942

Shall write a Royal Hash of Queerness for *Quarterly*'s next issue. Something out of this world for bizarrity. Phoned Rosalind at 2:10. Called me darling—I always nearly drop the phone.

APRIL 7, 1942

Splendid day. Judy [Tuvim] & I had a fine time. She said I never looked so pretty, etc. that I'd absorbed a lot of glamour in the last few months. I could mention one reason. She's very eager to meet Rosalind.

APRIL 8, 1942

My play (the *Saboteurs*). The audience actually gave a patter of applause. I am the kind of person whose novel (or book) among a dozen others of my classmates, the future alumnae of Barnard would choose to read first. Regardless of actual merit, I should enjoy this privilege.

APRIL 9, 1942

Rosalind agreed with me on the *Daring Young Man* argument* with M &. S. [Mother & Stanley] this AM. Of course, they thought he was not a sensible young man not to work at something else besides writing. The argument was further continued this evening, and elaborated into a harangue by Stanley on all my short-comings. He says I choose friends who'll compliment me. That I behave too dramatically and act a fool all the time. It's the old argument. I could list his vices, too, and his sins of commission and omission. They feel inferior to me. Billie invited me to a cocktail party Saturday afternoon. 5–8. Goodbye Mr. Berger!

---

* Likely refers to William Saroyan's story of a young writer dying of starvation, "The Daring Young Man on the Flying Trapeze."

4/10/42
A clever brain in sobriety will serve you even better when you
are drunk.

APRIL 11, 1942
Berger here at one. I feel uncomfortable with him. Just as, really,
I feel uncomfortable and vaguely annoyed when I am with any
one person besides Rosalind—or perhaps Helen. I am not yet
adjusted—to pure sociability. Even with Judy or Virginia, or
Babs, or Wolf I should feel this annoyance. Wrote Helen a letter,
still somewhat under the effects of two ½ martinis. Told her I'd
split with Kingsley and that I still love her as an eighteen-year-
old. I feel distraught. (Berger says I am like the allied army—too
thinly deployed on too many fronts.)

APRIL 12, 1942
[Ruth] Bernhard called at 12:30 & we walked on the bridge &
Welfare Island.* She's O.K. But we talk (even me!) about nothing
in particular. Corregidor† is now getting hell. And I'm smoking
too much and life is generally confusing.

APRIL 13, 1942
Bought Ballet Tickets for Rosalind & me Thursday. I was
ecstatic she could go! She's coming Thursday quarter to seven,
meeting les parents, and having a drink. Highly eventful evening
with Bernhard. M. & S. fairly hung around. She was in a gay
suit of brown. But so was I and so was Jeva. Otherwise nothing.
Bernhard showed some new work and S. was speechless with the
thrill of being in the same room with her.

---

* Originally Blackwell Island, renamed (in 1921) Welfare Island after the eponymous city
hospital there. It hosted a penitentiary (later moved to Rikers Island) and (from 1939) a
chronic care hospital. Renamed Roosevelt Island in 1923.
† The Japanese bombarded the Filipino island of Corregidor, which served as U.S. Navy
Headquarters in the battle of the Philippines, for five months until finally forcing the
surrender of U.S. and Filipino troops in May 1942.

APRIL 14, 1942

Very good day. I think—I think—if it were any one before R. it should be Bernhard. I appreciate her, and I appreciate myself for appreciating her.

APRIL 15, 1942

My feet are killin' me these days, I fancy it hampers my thinking as an otherwise perfect physical specimen. Oh happy tomorrow!

APRIL 16, 1942

Rosalind here at 7:10. Could have been worse on my parents' part, and could have been better on mine. They talked of ballet in that careful way people have of exercising their own voices on first meeting. M. & S. left us soon. Rosalind then said they couldn't have been more friendly. I almost kissed her when we left but not quite—those moments come when we are about to put on our coats standing in living-rooms. Taxied there. *Magic Swan** stank, and Shostakovich's choreography little better. We drank Courvoisier between the acts in a vain (rather) attempt to get even with an insolent waiter. Rosalind dropped a great black cloud with the short sentence: "Betty & I are going up to spend a couple of weeks on Papa's estate." Five miles to the house from the gate and all that. Which makes me money crazy all the more. I find shoestring living so distasteful—without even the compensation of artistic satisfaction—that I shall surely remedy my situation.

APRIL 17, 1942

Terrible—simply terrible buying liquor for a party. Bought all kinds of things and answered telephones & read away—strategy of World War one (very interesting)—till Babs came at nine ten. In fact all my guests came—more out of curiosity than because of me I suppose. Babs told me in strictest confidence that my

---

* One-act ballet choreographed by Alexandra Fedorovna after Marius Petipa's third act of *Swan Lake*, composed by Pyotr Ilyich Tchaikovsky.

name was on Phi Beta [Kappa] list. Virginia looked wonderful!
And I was right proud of her. Fresh as a daisy. In fact it was her
birthday. The liquor went like water & food too. Va. & I necked
in the hall. I don't bother scrupling about Rosalind. She's enough
man of the world to blame me if I don't get a little healthy excitation elsewhere. Eddy & Judy asked me next weekend to their
country place. Should like to go but shall be broke and busy.

APRIL 18, 1942

Fine day. Dashed off the 10-page English Literature paper this
morning. Went with mother to Matta's* show at the Matisse.†
Mother was crabby all morning—by God! when a Xtian Scientist is crabby what the hell good is it!? It's proof of failure right
there. Pessimism and doubt is supposed to block the channels of
love or something. The Matta business is interesting, carefully
done, gaudy colors.

APRIL 19, 1942

Very stimulating day though I did little work. Bernhard very
glad I phoned & we dressed elaborately in sweaters, went to the
tavern & breakfasted. Berenice Abbott there, we didn't speak
tho. One over-eager young man fawning over B. She takes her
reputation very lightly. Agfa,‡ for instance overawed by her
request for menial job writes that she would please think of a
job she might do. Wonderful evening with Walter Marlowe. He
does me good, like an outboard motor given a spin with a string.
We had much to talk about. Marlowe on me: that I treat my parents as people rather than parents, and they don't like it. And
that they (mother) are jealous of me—not being able to stand
competition.

---

* Chilean painter and architect Roberto Sebastian Antonio Matta Echaurren (1911–2002).
† French art dealer Pierre Matisse opened his own gallery in the Fuller Building at 41 East
Fifty-Seventh Street, which existed till his death in 1989 and exhibited Joan Miró, Marc
Chagall, Alberto Giacometti, Jean Dubuffet, André Derain, Leonora Carrington, Balthus,
and Henri Matisse, whose youngest child he was.
‡ For decades, Agfa was one of Europe's major manufacturers of photographic film and
equipment, second only to Kodak and Fujifilm.

APRIL 20, 1942

Latham said in conference I should point up my *Saboteurs* & she'd try and sell it. Terribly absent minded today. Amounts almost to a disease! Lost lipstick & keys. Mother & I got on to more arguments. We approach each other with dissent already in our minds. Things are so bad at home now I'm distracted—I must admit. But the fact is one of us is crazy, and it isn't I.

APRIL 21, 1942

I really hope for some money to do things with. It's been so long since I've had a new something to wear, I shall have to warn my friends when I get something.

APRIL 22, 1942

I should love to see Rosalind, only I've been working so hard I'm not beautiful. These are no days for creative effort. I mean exams not the war.

4/22/42

I know I shall never write—never thoroughly understand— the broader channels, deep mother love, love of soil, family ties. I shall know thoroughly, however, the isolated pleasures of falling in love, of jealousies, of waiting, of watching, of planning, the delirious mad joy of reward, the isolated pleasures of good shoes on a dirt road, of clean socks in the morning, of clean sheets at night, of water going down the parched throat like a metal stream of mercury, the delight of coming into New York from the far West, from the sea, from merely upstate when the lights are strung out across the bridges, twinkling on the river, dotting the shore like a necklace of diamonds, when the beacons play at random on the pylons like wasteful children with a hose, catching an airplane occasionally as a dog catches a ball, and then dropping it, the streams of cars eager to get into the city, each thinking only of himself, coming into New York! With a good band on

the radio in the car, and young peoples' voices around me—
coming home! What a home!

APRIL 23, 1942

I sigh for the wonderful five days in December. I gave Helen two
months, she gave me five days—but at least we both knew living
at the crest of the wave, with the inevitable break on the sands
we refused to anticipate.

APRIL 24, 1942

A splendid poem of [Judith] Paige's which we'll use—late copy.
Wonderful ideas and real power in it. Wish I'd done it. Bernhard here at 4:30. Taxied to Pete's. I don't think she'd think
twice about having an affair. We both talked about it, and we
are sensitive intelligent people—we should know it was neither
a one-night stand, nor the real thing. Went to splendid recital at
Weidman's* studio. Shakers the best! Saw Nina D., worse luck.
Afterwards hunted up a party. Found something at Fern's (228
W. 13 St.). She's nice—but just misses, the way all of them just
miss—a certain spark of mind, a certain discipline and activity
of thinking. I made a great hit, as I can sell only one thing in the
world: myself, when I want to.

4/24/42

I get stimulation out of even the dullest people. Being amusing
for them is like practicing the piano when you are sure no one
is listening. You can be freer, attempt bolder things, and often
succeed.

APRIL 27, 1942

Phi Beta Kappa ceremony: A wonderful address by Nicholson on
noblesse oblige. didn't Babs didn't make it either. Tho she was

---

* American choreographer and dancer Charles Weidman was considered one of the pioneers
of modern dance in America. Together with Doris Humphrey, he started the Humphrey-
Weidman Company in 1927. He created the choreography of *Shakers*, about the eighteenth-
century American religious group in 1931.

on the list, too, I feel that she is one of the intellectual nobility of the school: they don't always hit it right. We both have D's.

APRIL 29, 1942

Very tired. Insomnia last night—probably because I was happy thinking & talking about my paper to Stanley. Mother read it to him in two evenings, in her remarkably uninspired & uninspiring delivery. He thinks it's my best writing. Yes, in the critical way. Should love for Rosalind to read it. Mother never has any disagreement. She yawns, puts it down, goes to bed. She suffers not only now from her habitual lack of interest in any impersonal matter (feminine) but from sheer lack of energy. I see Rosalind Friday. Fifteen days it's been. I have so much to tell her. I shall want to make everything as elegant as possible that day! Wrote a funny little poem about her choice, which she will have to make sometime. The time is coming: whether she wants money, appearance, or the real McCoy. Made sketches. Read Shakespeare. I ponder the Phi Betas lovingly. I should have had it, were there justice in the world. And if there were ever an examination in general knowledge I should top them all. Helen sent me a note saying couldn't I speak to Kingsley because she worries her. I said "Darling—I speak to her twice a day." And Helen held it in her hands the rest of the hour, & the word "darling" was in both our minds. I can't forget her. I won't forget her. She's a slice of heaven walking around on earth. Should like to call Pete & date her Fri. at 11.

APRIL 30, 1942

Lovely day. Letter from Mrs. Fraser (Miss) [of Time, Inc.] saying no in 190 words. Lunched with Rosalind, who kept me waiting pleasantly for an hour & then brought Natasha.

Spoke to Babs today. I looked very nice in hair up & snood, white shirt, gray flannel & red corduroy. Pete turned around & said, "did you call me up last night?" I said, "yes, I did." She was very friendly, & probably is glad as all hell I called, I dare say. Well, I'm glad, too. Very good indeed to be talking again.

5/1/42

Crossing a street is one of the few things one should do by halves in New York. It's no good waiting for the all clear. The safest thing to do, positively, is to charge as soon as you see the white of the center line, providing you can stop yourself when you get there. Standing in this three inch wide margin of safety, all you stand to lose is a couple of great toes or a slice of posterior. Thus people have been known to survive the passing of two streetcars, but this is not advisable for everyone to attempt. When you see two streetcars approaching, jump on the nearest cowcatcher. No faith in human law approaches that of the New Yorker in his center line. Making one, even if it is half a job done, is half a job done. It's a real thrill when you can join the swaying, teetering row of pedestrians on the white line, see their comradely smiles as they all collect themselves for the rest of the charge.

MAY 2, 1942

Wrote 4-page stream of consciousness story à la Sherwood Anderson, in longhand on the young man drunk being kissed at a party, which should get an erection out of Rockefeller. Little else to report except great confidence & happiness, which is odd because:

a) have no money particularly & Rosalind's birthday is three weeks
b) didn't make *Time*
c) didn't make φβκ [Phi Beta Kappa]
d) haven't seen Buffie lately & should, to regain social status if for no other reason.

I'm going to need stimulants (alcoholic, nicotinic or sartorial) in order to work properly. My age or character? I don't care. I don't think I'm intemperate generally speaking. Most people overdo it regularly if they do it at all. I don't. Never have hangovers. Life is much more interesting without them. Mother said Berenice Abbott looked like a "les" (her favorite term) so I said there were men at the party last night. Changed

Vogue idea. Am doing more difficult but proportionally more interesting article on Art. Chagall, Breton, Miró, [Walter] Quirt, Owens. Ozenfant, Ernst, Tchelitchew, all the ones I like! Went to Marcus Blechman's to see Bernhard. Who should walk in but Judy! She knew him thru the show or something. He looks like he could never dance a step (arthritic) but maybe he can.

MAY 4, 1942

Simple exam in plane spotting. Wonder should we take in Fern's party? The fact is only Buffie, Rosalind, Billie A. are decent gay people—I get so disgusted with these half-baked, dirty, stupid, gay girls, who merely didn't make the normal social grade. This protracted and assiduous reading is excellent right now. An emotional relief from writing, and much more needed background plus ivory towerism, which I know how to take and leave now. Growing into maturity is a matter of knowing how to take one's condiments as needed, resulting in a chef-d'oeuvre, in the kitchen or the study.

MAY 5, 1942

Spoke to Thornbury. Should like much to have a drink with her. She is art to me and has so much of Henry James. Wonderful and strange ideas tonight. I feel myself hastening to maturity. I have unsteady progress—some days like yesterday with inordinate and disturbing physical desire, followed by days of unusual tranquility & satisfaction. It's more than spring. Tonight I read "Tyger Tyger" [William Blake's "The Tyger"] again, the only poem in English perhaps which moves me to tears. It is like all art is in those few lines, all painting, all literature, all poetry, all love and all frustration all fulfilment.

MAY 6, 1942

A drink with Helen & Babs, which led to Pete, which led to two drinks & three, & home & money, & dinner, at Nino's

& crazy postcards to people I can't even remember. But the beauty of it all was Helen. God I love her! She told me when Pete was away a moment that she, if she had it all to do again, would be a free woman, meaning the absence of Earl of course. That I was the only woman she'd ever loved before or since. I said did you love me even for a moment? She said she adored me and she still loved me. And we held hands in the car & I wanted to kiss her and it was almost like December! I feel about Helen as I said before and before. She touches something so deep in me that I cannot talk alone with her or look at her without crying. She is the one I could love, eschewing all others, forever and ever.

MAY 7, 1942

Slight hangover. And rainy day. Me despondent, with remorseful thoughts about last night. Only $3.00 but I could have lived on it & had $10 by this week towards the 21st. I rationalize ever thus: that temperance in youth is not a commendable virtue, for it leads to utter constriction in maturity; while intemperance in youth might lead to temperance, tho I shan't be too sorry if it doesn't. Pete & Helen looked very fine in clean clothes and rods. What different worlds they live in—with time and freedom, money and happy homes, food and drink. I'm really sorry to see Babs turning so masculine. She walks every step like a man, wears shirts often, sloppier than ever with her hair, and seems to be getting down on her chin.

[My] teeth look as good as the old days. Great relief.

5/7/42

There may be the girl waiting, the kiss in the dark, the whispered word of promise, the sun in the park on the swans on the lake, the job for me and the job for him and for him, the flag waving bold and free forever, and over and over again the handsome boy meeting lovely girl and all the lovely love pursued and captured. It might all be for the best, God's will might be done to him who helps himself and there might be a friend in need lined with silver standing in a pot of gold but I don't see it that way. I never will. I just don't see it that way.

MAY 8, 1842

Saw [George Bernard Shaw's] *Candida* which I loved with all my heart. What a fine piece of what theater ought to be. Met Mary Sullivan & Henry Streicher (Jesse [Gregg] and Jane O. there too), they were nice, but horrified at the coming of Bernhard. They loathe her for a "bore" and Mary Sullivan says she has done her some nasty tricks. I'm bored, too, with her stories, but there is something true in her which I love, too. We shall never have any kind of an affair for any reason, I know.

MAY 10, 1942

Read some history but terribly restless like all these days: the most restless, undoubtedly of all my life. I am so untried, and now untrying. I cannot loaf and invite my soul. Inside is a maelstrom of love & hate for one person or the other, and my artistic endeavors are either abortive or interrupted, at any rate completely unsatisfactory. Jack called. I envy his peace of mind. Said to M. if she were sick S. might treat her right, but he didn't know about me! I often think my only friend is my little pack of cigarettes.

MAY 11, 1942

Returned to school dressed to the hilt in black. I'd like to do something terrific Friday night. A healthy habit one night a week I call it. Read Blake with pleasure—and thought of D. H. Lawrence in concern with the detachment of sex experience from the flesh—and of course thought of Helen and me. Sex should be the furthest removed from the body, because the essential beauty of sex I knew as we lay there in her room—we both knew. God what work I have ahead. It's such fun to race forward like a steam engine, and see it be crushed before me, leaving a smooth hard packed trail.

MAY 13, 1942

Today—with very little emotion, I had turned it over in words so long—I told Helen to take it for what it was worth, I was in love with her. She said that only made it worse. I said I didn't expect her to give it much credence or credit for enduring, but that I was and that was all. That neither Rosalind nor Va. had I really loved. Maybe she believes me. (She took my *Quarterly* picture lighting the cigarette today. I thought K. had stolen it.) She bitterly, and more bitterly every day regrets committing herself to Earl—I wonder would she stay with me were she to be free?

5/13/42

Yes, maybe sex is my theme in literature—being the most profound influence on me—manifesting itself in repressions and negatives, perhaps, but the most profound influence, because even my failures are results of repressions in body & mind, which are repressions of sex.

MAY 14, 1942

Went to Betty's & Rosalind's tonight, Rosalind getting ready for bed in yellow pajamas at 10! I brought beer, & she was polite enough to take some. Asked me about *Vogue*, etc. Seems to like *Harper's Bazaar* or *Mlle** to get on first. Came home full of love for Helen—and beautiful phrases—not mushy ones—but going deeper perhaps almost touching the right answer. I was born the way I am. I am of good character, I love many things and I am interested in many things. The fact is, however, immediately I am not old enough for Rosalind. Perhaps in six months, perhaps three, if enough happens to me, but now, no. That is all. There is nothing to be ashamed of, and a person of my age & upbringing could hardly have been otherwise.

---

* The women's magazine *Mademoiselle* was founded in 1935. It published writing by the likes of Truman Capote and Flannery O'Connor and ran a prestigious internship program, hiring a number of promising college students each summer—referred to as "the Millies"—some of whom, like Joan Didion and Sylvia Plath, went on to become well-known writers themselves.

5/14/42

I am no babbling brook of rebellion,
But a great smooth sea, of varied but honest character
And if I am green, while other seas are blue,
I was born green and born a sea.

MAY 15, 1942

And I asked her [Rosalind] what she wanted for her birthday—
a wallet? She said no, at first, and started talking about phonograph records—but I put my foot down. Finally she said the
black wallet was an old one of Betty's & didn't hold money very
well, and if I did get one she'd probably use it, which amounted
to a green light. I was terribly happy! So we had a delightful
lunch. Afterwards, I looked at Dunhill's & Lord & Taylor's
for wallets, but nothing can compare with an $18.50 job at
Mark Cross which I'm holding. Wonderful ostrich, with ostrich
inside, two compartments (no change section because that looks
sissy!). I shall try & get it before the lunch Thursday—with initials R.C. in gold like the gold corners. It couldn't be better in
all of New York!!! I should like very much to go on vacation in
New Hampshire after school with Bernhard—but completely
with the understanding that nothing happen between us—I
couldn't not for Helen & Constable—or myself. But such a
thing would be all over town. Not a chance! M. & S. think
she'd be wonderful to go away with(!)

MAY 16, 1942

Lunch with Berger very nice. *Tales of Hoffmann*＊ stank! We had
loads of fun giggling like school kids. Later he sent me a dozen
poppies, which are lovely! Intense, nervous, excited, not happy,
in spite of my best intentions.

＊ *The Tales of Hoffmann* (*Les contes d'Hoffmann*) is an opéra fantastique by French
composer Jacques Offenbach based on three stories by German writer E. T. A. Hoffmann.

MAY 17, 1942

It will be twenty-five years from now until I shall have the fortitude to decipher all these pages. We had Bible reading this evening. Then I met Bernhard & Ethel, Fern, Hazel, etc. at Carnegie
[Hall] & saw Carmen Amaya!* She's really passionate—ugly,
crude, awful bore, but passionate and that is all one thinks of. She
is very slender, gives all she has in every dance.

5/18/42 .

Creation of the best order comes from the greatest need. Who
never has sat on the edge of his bed weeping through the night,
conscious of the tongueless voice within him, thirsting after the
beautiful tone, the exquisite line of verse, the perfect stroke,
the flavor in his mouth that would tell him perfection, does
not know what I suffer now, and will never create. Let me be,
says my own voice. Let this first painful child deliver itself.
Then come, if you will, probe and test and kill me, but I shall
never die then. In the air-pockets, in the mountain tops, in the
clothes of all mankind, in the rock of the earth and the cement
of the pavements, in the waters of the seas I shall be then! But
I that am heavy laden now, leave me be. I shall fashion my
own tongue out of the dross of the fire, I shall find it buried in
the twisted ashes. It will be there for me, it will be like no one
else's. Then I shall speak not greatness, not life, not growth
perhaps, not family nor brotherly love, but speak the need of
others like me who have not found their tongues, or for whom
perhaps there will never be a tongue but mine. The duty is
great and the burden is heavy on me, but the work will be the
deepest joy on earth. Not life shall I create, not life, but truth
above all, as no one has seen it before.

---

* Carmen Amaya (1913–1963), world-famous Spanish Romani flamenco dancer, singer, and
actress. She was the first woman to dance the flamenco in trousers. Fred Astaire admired her
talent and President Roosevelt invited her to perform in the White House.

MAY 20, 1942

Happy, happy day! The comprehensive wasn't so hard. I wrote on Shakespeare's audience & the physical stage effects on him. It was so boring I couldn't even reread it, so it must be quite good. With Bernhard at 9:00 in the Modern Art, Steichen* show. M. & S. left too early. The show was good American. Later Bernhard & I saw [Berenice] Abbott, Georgia O'Keeffe,† Carl Sandburg,‡ etc.

MAY 21, 1942

Wonderful wonderful happy day again! Philosophy exam a dreadful bore at 11:30. Came home & got money & met Rosalind, Betty & Natasha at Tony's. Del there, and his brother Phil who's nothing like him, but good Bostonian. Peggy Guggenheim,§ Buffie with a Bella, Mrs. Briton, Billie A., etc. We all had a lovely, packed time & moved on together to Chez Paris for dinner. Del P. spoke a long while to Rosalind & me about a job. He thinks *Fortune* is bad if I want to write. Rosalind upholds me embarrassingly well. Chez Paris full of us. Drinking more, etc. and somehow Natasha got perfectly stinking! She was wonderful though. Very passionate about Sylvia. Kissed me, pulled my chair and behaved like a good Russian, said Sylvia was heaven & she'd fight for her till she died! Asked me was I in love with Rosalind & I said no. We had a terrific time—Natasha & I ate at the bar with the men. Rosalind said "where's my present?"

* Reference to the 1942 exhibit The Road to Victory, co-curated by Luxemburg-born artist Edward Steichen (1879–1973).
† Georgia Totto O'Keeffe (1887–1986), dubbed the "mother of American modernism," was an American artist known for her paintings of enlarged flowers, New York skyscrapers, New Mexico landscapes, and images of animal skulls. During the 1940s, she had two one-woman retrospectives, the first at the Art Institute of Chicago (1943), her second as the first woman artist to have a retrospective at the Museum of Modern Art in New York (1946).
‡ Carl August Sandburg (1878–1967) was an American poet and biographer. His biography of President Lincoln won him a Pulitzer for history in 1940.
§ Marguerite "Peggy" Guggenheim (1898–1979) was an American heiress known as "the mistress of modern art." A passionate collector and major patron, she amassed one of the most important collections of early and mid–twentieth century, mostly European and American cubism, surrealism and abstract expressionism. In 1938, she opened her first gallery of modern art in London, followed in 1942 by the Art of This Century gallery in New York. After a brief marriage to Max Ernst, she moved to and settled in Venice in 1949, where she lived and exhibited her collection for the rest of her life.

at Lola's and she opened it in the bedroom. She seemed very
pleased & said she'd surely use it.

MAY 22, 1942

Hangover naturally. I wonder how Rosalind felt and Natasha!?
Studied from 10–12. In school late enough & Helen waved at me
a moment, and good luck. I was in the same clothes I wore last
night, for luck my flannel suit. The exam was dreadfully hard—
second & hardest part of Comprehensive. Later discovered thru
2 kids that Latham gave me an A (minus) in playwrighting—one
of my prize possessions this year!

5/22/42

Most important facts discovered to date: That if life is a tragedy
to those who feel and a comedy to those who think, most people
do neither.

MAY 23, 1942

Read [John Millington Synge's] *Riders to the Sea.* Some good
speeches—but still a mystery to me how some plays become
immortal and others are forgotten. Evening with Berger. Saw
The Strings, My Lord,* etc. which stank to heaven. Berger says
he's in love with me, which is likely true. He says eventually
he'll marry me. I feel no less or more attraction to anything
male. Kissing them is like kissing the side of a baked flounder, and one mouth might be another. There is something in
me independent of mind—pure physical reaction that works
slowly and sexually as tho under the influence of a regular dose
of dope. But I get no great pleasure—and consequently can
give not enough in return—from men.

MAY 24, 1942

Another fine day,—tho tired from Berger the night before. He
called twice—second time telling me to write in on the male ads

---

* *The Strings, My Lord, Are False* was a 1942 Broadway play directed by Elia Kazan.

for office & editorial work. Good idea. Anyway I'd written to *Mademoiselle*—a good letter—today. Read [Pavel] Biryukov's *Tolstoy* which made great impressions. I flatter myself I resemble him—in temperament, in activities in youth—but do I have the religious pilgrimage to find salvation & happiness? All my life work will be an undedicated monument to a woman. As part of my training now I'm making a plot every night under the shower. Much fun.

MAY 26, 1942

Unfortunately, I got C+ on the Comprehensive. Ignominious enough. I drank too much the night before & was in no way psychologically prepared.

MAY 28, 1942

Sunned on Sutton playground. Very interesting brats there. A nice letter from *Mademoiselle* saying they liked my references & accomplishments. I was in an "active file" and would I come for interview. I should be happy now if I had the A in the comprehensive, if I had a good job with Time, Inc., a promise from Helen and money in my pockets! Utopia! Now I am subdued, depressed, tho still optimistic about getting a job in general. Made sketches, some good, in a furious attempt at self-justification, artistic satisfaction. My energy, fortunately, is irresistible, psychically & mentally. Went to town tonight on my story. A fresh sweep. Pretty good. Also hammered on torso, getting the real meaning out better. The trouble with me is I become absorbed in the manner of presentation rather than the idea. Cashed my 20.00 check from grandma, for graduation, at Jimmy Daniels'.* With it I shall 1) take Rosalind to dinner & shall 2) buy a piece of wood for a figure 3) take Buffie to dinner 4) go out on a binge with Helen & Peter & Babs. Debbie B. I hope. 5) should also do something with mother 6) with Bern-

---

* Jimmy Daniels restaurant, located at 114 West 116th Street at Lenox Avenue, owned by the popular café singer of the Harlem Renaissance, James Lesley Daniels.

hard. Then to a Chinese place where I danced with Henry Langston & Sgt. Greene, soldiers—some rough dancing, too. Home awfully late & to bed at 5:30 by daylight.

MAY 29, 1942

Had the pleasure of paying a Constable bill this P.M. to get her electricity turned on again. They were using candles. Wrote in my stride this evening—or at least I know now how to approach the story. Wonderful feeling. Walked with Bernhard & Lucien* this evening late and had coffee & chocolate. Lucien is suppressed, but powerful too. Later Bernhard & I returned & had stuff here. I think she would consider living with me. I should be able to get along with her well.

MAY 30, 1942

I can't fail to think of how it would be with an A. Congratulations, and confirmation of every one's high estimation of me. Which will still survive, however, oddly enough. A depressing day. Mother & Stanley disclosed at dinner that we are in the hole—more money owed than possessed actually. They speculate on going home [to Texas] soon, begging Grandma until the war's over. That's what has knocked us out, of course, the income taxes, the reduced income. I want any kind of job therefore, and fast. These dull, frustrated harassed days are artistically productive: I am so dissatisfied, I must create something, & I work passionately at everything.

MAY 31, 1942

Doubtfully pleasant day. Jack B. here at 9:00 AM but we missed the boat to Rye, & took one around Manhattan instead. Very educational, and nice surroundings. We bummed around in the Syrian markets, in Chinatown from 3 till 8:30. Tea & dinner

---

* Ruth Bernhard's father, Lucian (Lucien) Bernhard (born Emil Kahn, 1883–1972) was a German graphic designer and professor.

at Port Arthur,* then a Chinese theater which was quite boring & apparently unsubtle. He constricts me so, however, that
I can't even go to the bathroom. I called Bernhard. She came
here at 10:30 & met Berger; I got rid of him at 11:00. There
comes a time on these excursions when I can't stand to be with
anyone—I am miserable with people consistently—for ten or
more hours. Talked with Bernhard about this—I can always
talk very freely with her. Bernhard thinks I'm very bright,
should be a model, or work for *New Yorker*. I wrote a letter in
answer to an ad, under Berger's supervision, lying like mad.

JUNE 1, 1942

Sent my *Saboteurs* to Cedar Rapids Play Co., exhausted the last
ounce of my patience, fortitude and general energy yesterday.
Waking up on a cold gray Monday, sans job, sans everything is
not a pleasant thing. I worked with a headache on my Barney
story which is growing threadbare from active and constant
polishing. At school I discovered to my mild disgust I had only
B+ on the Government exam. Raided *Quarterly* bringing home
my weight in manila envelopes, stationery, etc. Saw no one, tho
today was Sr. picnics & tomorrow graduation!

   Read a wacky story of Djuna Barnes in the *Harvard Advocate*, which was certainly written in drunkenness, even if conceived in sobriety. I have appointment with *New Yorker* and
[*New York*] *Times* now.

JUNE 2, 1942

Diogenes' [magazine] Arthur Blair sent me "Silver Horn" yesterday with inane comment. I'm launching Blitzkrieg on publications now. Even ideas for sleeks, female stuff! Helen phoned
at 1:20. She's going to graduation as Babs and Peter too. I said
grad. was like getting married. Helen said she'd surely have
drinks before that (yes, seven or eight). The call was depressing

---

* Founded in 1897 by Chu Gan Fai and located at 7–9 Mott Street, the Port Arthur was the
first Chinese restaurant in New York to obtain a liquor license.

& I had to convince myself again I didn't want to go. Caroline
Abbott [from *Vogue*] wants to see me at 10 AM. Rosalind also
had called, saying not to tell me, lest I get my hopes up. She evidently pushed the interview. I don't think my papers would. I
feel optimistic however, and definitely confident I can do what
they ask. For Rosalind—for Helen—for me—what incentives do
I lack?

JUNE 3, 1942

[Interview with] Mrs. Daves [at *Vogue*],* about ideas I might
contribute to the magazine—in which I definitely did not dis-
tinguish myself. Rosalind called at 8. Wanted to see me at home
at 9:00 P.M, where I was. Showed me her scrapbook of *Vogue*
writing, which is horrible and horribly wonderful of its awful,
terrifying type—well—nothing I can muster in adjectives can
express my complex dislike and mistrust of this hopeless literature. Read part of *Tentation de Saint Antoine* par Flaubert.
Wrote Helen a good letter.

6/3/42

I am too familiar to myself—too old—and rather boring. The
avenues of varied goals are closing up. And wherever, even, I
commence the long pull anew, I shall have with me the same
teeth with the same fillings, the same aches on rainy days, the
same wrinkles in my forehead. Is this some chance unfortunate combination of elements in me? In my body? In my brain?
This scar upon my finger, this birthmark on my arm—should
they have been elsewhere, perhaps half an inch? How would
another carry them, and how notice them or how forget them? I
feel my grave about my shoulders, the light grows dim never to
rise again, my breath is feeble and disinterested. Oh, but I shall
live so much longer! And there will be moments, whole weeks,
whole years when there will be no grave and no mold-smell. But
intervals there will be, too, when I, regaining energy meted by

---

* Mrs. Daves may be Jessica Daves, future editor-in-chief of *Vogue*.

the dry crabbed hand of sleep, of food, of intercourse, will see as though my eyes turned inward to reality, the hollow-orbed face of death, the flaking skin like medieval painted saints, and know then that life is one long business of dying.

JUNE 4, 1942

Went shopping. Buffie phoned & I went & sat with her 5–6. She told me she worried about me—sexually, and in a neat catchy presentation like a lawyer's two-edged sword, told me she worried if I had ever had an orgasm. I made no reply. Any being commitment, and nothing being her business, anyway. Lots of nice dates looming around the corner—and loads of details in these many days unwritten.

JUNE 6, 1942

I'm horribly worried about *Vogue*. Rosalind told me not to write. Mad enough today to bite a corkscrew. Bernhard [and I went to see] a wonderful Paul Klee show. His persons, as abstract pattern, are as exciting as Blake somehow. Coffee at the [Central Park] zoo. Rather pleasant, but I feel she is gripping on to me, & I don't like her personally, because she's not my type, & neither would she be good for me, which is worth considering, though I seldom do, correctly.

[Goethe's] *Wilhelm Meisters Lehrjahre* is intolerably dull, even with my patience with classics.

JUNE 8, 1942

Rosalind's heard nothing & neither have I. God I hope so. Read [E. M. Forster's] *Passage to India*. Wonderful feeling today. Painted & sketched. But not very successful. Only mildly so.

JUNE 9, 1942

Jo told me she'd four times been in love, the third with a girl. She's wrestling, she said, with the problem of mores & homosexuality, though she rationalizes herself out of it. Says I overcompensate in hard work, generally implying the truth, and getting nothing out of me to mention.

JUNE 10, 1942

Wonderful, glorious, beautiful, memorable day! Riding with Jo at 7:00 A.M. Very instructive ride, but I wasn't bored with her as expected. Nor last night either. She's an extraordinarily sensitive child—even with horses.

JUNE 11, 1942

Fine day. Worked fairly well on new story—the Sutton Park man.* Mother gives me brief but devastatingly discouraging lecture on how I'm different from other people as a result of behavior in the house, & consequently won't get a job or succeed anyway. I tell her it is sex primarily and my maladjustment to it almost from babyhood as a result of suppressed relations in the family—which is all a child's world for many years. I talked of a psychiatrist, & she talked of M. B. [Mary Baker] Eddy!

Phoned Rosalind at 5 but she'd gone off [for] the weekend (!) Vogue had sent me at 4:30 a telegram saying I'd won honorable mention (one of 20) and wishing me luck. Understand they contact me on the interviews promised, however.

JUNE 12, 1942

Worked like a grub this morning. Quite unsatisfied. I should have a theme so great the demands & logical expectations of parents & myself should not intrude. But I haven't. Settling down to some kind of work will really be equivalent to a year's vacation and a private morocco-lined study. That's how I feel about the New Life to come. I also feel it is just around the corner. Made New Yorker appointment again with Shawn.†

---

* A story that has not survived.

† May refer to William Shawn, assistant editor of The New Yorker, who oversaw the magazine's coverage of World War II and was later promoted to editor.

JUNE 13, 1942

Worked this morning. I contemplate another stream of consciousness about the independent girl yielding to the ordinary man. Her bitter and pitiful true estimation of him, her flinging his faults, his disgustingness, in his face, and her inevitable yielding, as a purely intellectual yielding, from the desire partially to maintain herself "normal," to win her ration of thrills from youth & from what meager fare N.Y.C. has to offer. Her desire really to maintain Freddie as a friend. Her desire to show herself absent from home for a night, her desire to feel of some importance emotionally in an emotionally starved life. Read Mushroom book in which recondite & eerie subject I delighted! Went with W. Marlowe to see Norma Ringer at 4:30, who was in the middle stages of induced menopause and behaving like a frustrated tabby. Walter is lonely & unappreciated. He thinks I appreciate him, which I do, I might come to sleep with him even.

JUNE 14, 1942

Saw Ernst at 8. We had coffee and a good chat like Goethe & Schiller about affairs of life & the world, politics & society. He's writing to [Edward] Weeks of the *Atlantic Monthly* for me. The drawback is he's in Boston. How nice would an interview summons and a trip there be! Perhaps I should even look up Roger! Pleasant evening. Some good ideas. On mushrooms, on things in general, which makes me feel alive regardless of the other situations & conditions. Oh Rosalind—

JUNE 15, 1942

And this is the day—the *dies irae, dies illa* I said would never come. This day should have a sunrise edged in black and a horizon rimmed in black, and a sunset without sun. It was going to be my lucky day. I worked well in the morning. Met Buffie at seven, after a drink with M. & S, whose wedding anniversary it was. Buffie very free with her liquor & drinking herself. We went

to Famous Door* after many drinks at the restaurant. Well the
upshot was I lost my wallet. It was not the wallet, not the four
dollars. It was Rosalind's letter—the one thing I have, besides
memory, that belongs to those wonderful first days, when I was a
child of magic (and when I was!) and when Rosalind was heaven
with a golden head. It tore something out of me—something
I can never possibly recapture! It was that it happened in the
cheapest nightclub, when I was disgustingly befuddled, that it
happened with Buffie Johnson—I went home with her and the
whole damn business happened again. Buffie was ravenous for
female companionship and I?—I was at the lowest point of my
brief career. But there is little remorse now, and when I decided
to study last night I had calculated all the whys & why nots in
my head. We woke with mouths & bodies like furnaces & I very
soon got up & had a bath. Buffie was affectionate, and I made
her lemon juice & fixed coffee & she lent me 4 dollars. No luck
at Famous Door.

JUNE 16, 1942
Saw Mr. Shawn of *New Yorker* at 5:00. A wonderfully honest,
sincere, modest fellow. Wants to see my stuff, & considering
me as "cub reporter" for them now instead of men. Life is interesting, but is like a maze of varying trials and punishments.
The one and only reward must lie in the end. Death? Rank
symbolism—!

JUNE 17, 1942
Perhaps I should read some poetry. Another black day. They
come like the waves I saw on the Pacific—especially shocking,
because I trusted so in the Pacific being beautiful and smooth.
I phoned Rosalind at seven thirty. She said "you didn't get the

---

* The Famous Door was a jazz and later bebop club in Manhattan made well known by
radio bandleaders and musicians like Jimmy Dorsey, Glenn Miller, Billie Holiday, and Count
Basie.

job," "I know it," "you could have got that job. [You looked like] just out of bed. The jacket was very nice, but a white blouse that was not too clean, etc." I was mortified, of course, not for myself, but that Rosalind knew me at all, & that the stuff came thru her friend Marcelle. Well, I was stupid in the first place to come without a hat, she said, and stupid not to split a gut, the way she did, to get dressed to the hilt for *Vogue*. Rosalind gave it to me plenty, but said perhaps *Vogue* isn't the place—perhaps—I'd get a job on the *New Yorker* which is infinitely better. But the second prize was anybody's meat & some dame with a neat hair-do got it, that's the bitter truth. It doesn't hurt me that they looked down their lorgnettes, that they said my shirt was dirty when I know it was clean. But only that Rosalind had troubled to recommend me. Well, I did comb my hair first before going in—there are a hundred things I remember, that I'll never forget, but why set them down here. There'll come a time when I shall be bigger than *Vogue* and I can thank my Star I escaped their corrupting influences.

JUNE 18, 1942

Wrote this P.M. & studied Spanish *Si, yo estudio el español y el inglés.* Oh for money in my pocket, for my wallet in my pocket, for Rosalind in my pocket, for a telegram from *Vogue* in my pocket. Jo here for dinner. Made a modest pass at me, which succeeded as well as it could under the domestic circumstances. No ideas. I am depressed, I couldn't, perhaps, sink any lower. The British have lost Tobruk* now, & things look lousy in China. The Japs† are already invading Manchu Siberia, & the papers are playing down our misfortunes.

---

* Tobruk is a Libyan port city on the Mediterranean. In 1941 and 1942, it became the scene of several big battles during the African Campaign in World War II.
† While this terminology has since come to be seen as offensive, it would have been considered quite common wartime rhetoric at the time of Pat's writing.

JUNE 19, 1942

Rosalind couldn't have been nicer to me. We ate shrimps at
Crespi's. And in the course of time I told her all about the interview, how frightened I was, how I never should have succeeded
at all in the contest if it weren't for her influence, and she told
more about her getting on, how some friend was turned down
because she was too stylish. I get the impression that R. &
Natasha consider *Vogue* a corrupting influence. Life is a series
of attacks. On how good one's military strategy is depends
one's success. Ernst Hauser here for a very pleasant dinner,
which I cooked. Read Havana book. My Spanish doing nicely.
I have many ideas. Some bound to pay out. The old habit of
getting my brain too much into working gear must still be overcome. Should like to see Madeleine, but really should not like to
see anyone until I get a job.

JUNE 20, 1942

Wonder what Jo's next move is? How seriously does she feel
about anything, & how much is she afraid of? It wasn't the first
time Thursday night, that's the interesting thing. Saw a couple of mediocre exhibits with mother, & on the way home met
Buffie & a man(?) coming out of Maison Marie. She deliberately avoided us, which is well enough. Read Santayana's *Life
of Reason*, which overall philosophy is full of platitudes but
heartening. Jack B. here ^Fwithout a tie. I could have killed him!
Oh well—I like him for other reasons.^{FF} He said I should be
awarded an award for platitudinous remarks! He should know
that I'd really rather be alone sometimes, when I must walk
beside him, listening to didactic conversation & attempting
only occasionally to vary my "hmm-s" with an actual phrase.
He should know what goes on in my mind, he would not think
it platitudinous! We saw *Iolanthe*,* which stank, but was funny
because of the lines by the fairy who was a fairy in the play from

---

* *Iolanthe* is an 1882 comic opera written by W. S. Gilbert and Arthur Sullivan.

the waist up, but in reality that and the waist down, too. Went into Grotto,* where Berger encountered several remote relatives, very pleased, no doubt, that he was seen with a Shiksa.

JUNE 21, 1942

Worked this morning. Again, unsatisfied with Sutton Place story (the businessman & the girl), which will be, like the Boston story, an exercise in flowery writing. Walked with Bernhard to Blechman's. The pictures of me nude were not exciting, because I did not contribute, mentally, to the subject. Next time I shall know, because I am sure I can do it. So is she. I seem to live on next times, which makes me desperate & furious. Bernhard wants me, but in what capacity I hesitate to think, I am not the excitement she plainly considers a requisite, to love. And yet she paid me the compliment of saying I was the only woman in N.Y.C she felt completely at ease with, with whom she could be all the time. Came home & found flowers (great long gladiolas) from Berger. Cleaned up the old ones badly (I hadn't had time to finish) & mother slapped my face for what she called "back talk" & what I called trite conversation. She was sorry afterwards, & split a gut being nice at the table. Stanley & she talked about difficulties. Stanley has the least intellectual approach, of course, & formulates the most stupid & naïve theories & solutions. Mother sits considering & frowning but does little better. What do they know of my fury, impatience, frustration, ambition, energy, desperation, loves & hates and of my ecstasies!? Nothing! & they never can! Worked well on sculpturing in my anger. Saw Va. tonight. Her home is dirty & sloppy. I have outgrown her, and I find her dull, depressing. Phoned Bernhard at 10:10, saying I had an overwhelming question to ask her. I had intended earlier (in sobriety) asking her if I was in love with her, but wisely postponed this until Friday, at least when she'll meet Rosalind. So

---

* May refer to Grotta Azzurra, a restaurant in Little Italy founded in 1908, frequented by notables such as Enrico Caruso and Frank Sinatra.

we had a most pleasant and unforgettable hour at Hapsburg House,* which Ludwig [Bemelmans] decorated when he lived there, ate cherries & drank martinis, & talked of the wonderful things that only we can talk of. I need her, & she needs me. There is no one afire for her now, I know. She doubtless will protect herself against future hurting. Hence all this circumspect behavior & conversation from both of us. We are shy. We know each other so well already.

6/21/42

Shower bath at two in the morning. For unadulterated opium dreaming, pipe dreaming, for the most ecstatic time of plans-to-come, creations, ideas, campaigns, rosy futures, or even sheer animal happiness of the present, try the shower bath at 2 AM, before going into the kitchen to absorb the martinis (one or two only) in some good Italian bread and milk.

JUNE 23, 1942

My hair gives me hell. Got some laquer today. [SP]I saw Jo P. and had dinner with her.[SPSP] Again the same thing, Jo very slow & shy, but says kissing me gives her a kind of peace few things can. She said she'd never kissed a girl before. Odd & she does it so well! I read *De Profundis* of [Oscar] Wilde. Studied Spanish.

6/23/42

The remnants of the past, for me, are tattered enough. There is still the charm, however, of the Wednesday afternoon trips to town, when I wore button shoes & walked, holding my Grandmother's hand, over the viaduct which spanned the wonderfully interesting Mexican settlement, with its stray dogs and half clothed children, with the colorful and mysterious activities of

---

* The original Austrian owners of the Hapsburg House created the restaurant as a private club for their friends. Ludwig Bemelmans became co-owner when they commissioned him with the wall paintings in the dining room. Hapsburg House was used as a location in the Hollywood movie *The Scoundrel* (1935).

the men, who would either be lounging about the shanties, or bringing home (white figures in their clothes) great parcels of groceries, push wagons of vegetables, junk, and newspapers to a grateful family. I remember the movie shows (they were slightly cheaper on Wednesdays) where we saw Clive Brook* in Mounted Canadian Police serials and where I could smell the clove my grandmother always laid on her tongue before going out, to sweeten her breath. She carried her packet full of them, and though I would always be given one, if I wanted it, I never really liked it. I always had a Hershey bar, which I made last throughout the entire show, biting almonds in half and peeling down the tinfoil as the chocolate melted in my hands, licking the scraps of tinfoil before I dropped them on the floor. I remember the colorful visits to the five and ten [store]. (Kresses, a name which to my ears, was the auditory epitome of cheapness—to be used some times in its place, for paper napkins, for safety pins, to be used at others for utter monetary and social contempt.) I remember walking around the backyard in my button shoes, just come from town, when Willie Mae sat in speechless but unenthusiastic admiration of my adventures and pleasures, when I showed her my jumping frog from Kresses that you worked with a pressure of the two handles. I remember Billie Mae in her shapeless denim overalls, the sweat dirt-streaking her freckled forehead, barefooted and dirty toe-nailed, sitting with knees higher than her head in the cement spattered wheelbarrow, and though she envied me the half-finished bag of popcorn, the memory of the serial, the feature and the vaudeville show which would last me until next Wednesday, I envied her more at those times.

This was America—Texas—in 1929.

---

* Serials were short ongoing stories often shown before the main movie. There are several that feature the Royal Canadian Mounted Police, the so-called Mounties having long been a popular subject of novels, serials, and movies. Pat connects them in her memory with English actor Clive Brook (1887–1974), a major Hollywood star in her youth.

JUNE 24, 1942

Very pleasant evening ^{SP}at home alone.^{SPSP} Odd news. A Mr.
Goldberg* phoned at 11 P.M. asking could I come tomorrow for
an interview on the editorial assistant's job for which I wrote
long ago. Have an idea I'll get it. He'll probably want to jew me
down to eighteen a week, which I shall not take.

JUNE 25, 1942

I guess I got the job. Only 20 per week. I didn't haggle, being
poor at haggling. Goldberg seems to be of some repute—
somewhere. F.F.F. [Publishers], a Jewish House, giving most of
their stuff to Jewish papers. We'll work on a F.D.R. magazine
to appear in the newspaper & then possibly in book form (if
I'm interested, he said) & I'm to get my royalties, and also to do
magazine work if necessary, to make more money. Hours will be
hard & irregular. Everyone thinks it's better than I do.

6/25/42

Second reactions: boredom, and wondering, as one walks along
the street, what motivates these people who move at top speed,
yet with the inevitability of wound-up dolls. And the eternal
answer comes: not to keep body & soul together, not primarily
to make money, certainly in most cases not from special ambition
and desire to create, but from a sense and habit of imitation, from
the ties of birth, which are most difficult to break, and perhaps,
among the most "thinking" few, to milk the cow of New York
while they are young enough to try and catch her flying udders.

JUNE 26, 1942

It's a lousy, journalistic, unscholarly job, and I'm frankly bored
& ashamed of it. Why couldn't it be on the scarabs of Tutankha-

* Ben-Zion Goldberg (born in Vilnius named Benjamin Waife, 1895–1972) was an
influential—and, because of his pro-Soviet views, controversial—Yiddish journalist and
editor. His books include *Sacred Fire: The Story of Sex in Religion* and *The Jewish Problem
in the Soviet Union.*

mun? Why not the history of the Dalai lamas? Why not the paleontology of the ancient Cretans? Why not the story of the Philosopher's stone?!

JUNE 27, 1942

^SPFirst day of work. I went to the library (42nd Street) at ten thirty. Read magazines all day long. Mr. Goldberg (!) arrived at three, and said I have to write more fully (also more clearly!). He is not wrong.^SPSP The work is tedious, slow, & boring, until I see what we are getting on paper. I'm terribly tired. My greatest fear today—this first day, without much sleep the night before—is that I shall not have enough energy to do all I wish. Read Dante tonight. Studied Spanish, worked on a story. I have several worthy ideas to play with. This now is unimportant. Is [this not] really the most frightening sensation of our time, the fear of loss of energy, exhaustion for a machine we care nothing for, the spending of all that is "us"—the consumption of life fluid as though it were gasoline? What is more terrifying than this?—not Purgatory or Hell!

6/29/42

The sensation of failing always, leads to this in the still active person: a desire to be "someone else," the feeling that even with a new and propitious idea, the executor is the same, the executor and artist is "I," bringing inevitably the old train of faults the old plan of stumble-blocks, makes one want a new inside, a whole new inside.

JUNE 29, 1942

Came pretty late to the library. I phoned unavailingly Rosalind & Bernhard, feeling very lost, in spite of myself, and wanting like crazy to have a lunch date or a date tonight. Went to see R. at 12:10. She had just made a date. Looked up a file on Goldberg, who was arrested in 41 for shouting "Scab!" Not a bad record. Came home to eat. Saw Alice T. when I returned. We had a cigarette. Obviously likes me better than Va. Well, why not? Va. incidentally has a big picture of me (on the piano) in her room. Also a sketch. So she still lives with me. Jo sent me a beautiful (rather) alligator billfold, gold tips four. Western Union. With a card: "A compromise. Jo P." How sweet of her to do that. I thought of it, & wanted it, but dropped no hints, of course, which I found too embarrassing.

JUNE 30, 1942

[SP]Saw Betty on the way to Del Pezzo's. She didn't see me. Then she and Rosalind arrived together.[SPSP] R. finally waved at me. She saw Bernhard pretty well. I didn't mind in the least, of course, I only hope she didn't think I was checking up on her. I've written thousands of words today. Didn't see Goldberg but dropped off my notes. The three other girls seemed to be loafing. One is gay by the way. Someone made a pass at Bernhard, which boosted her ego 100%. I don't do that enough to suit her. Lovely drinking martinis again at lunch.

With R. tomorrow. Want to buy a suit at Saks. Worked on "Russula,"[*] almost done & have real ambitions. Wonderful how one's energy never wanes. Egypt looks lousy. The British falling back to Alexandria, tho more allied reinforcements are coming.

JULY 1, 1942

Rosalind told me I was too vague about what I wanted to do with myself when I asked for a job. Very likely, only now, with this month's experience, I feel I could do worlds' better. I shall try once more with Fraser after a few weeks' experience here or elsewhere. Goldberg I find very boring & he wants me to put the whole article down on paper first! Buffie phoned for party tomorrow night. Mad costume.

JULY 2, 1942

Very dull day looking up S.D.R. [Sara Delano Roosevelt], whose sister I don't know the married name of, and who pos-

---

* Unclear which short story she is referring to here.

sessed the dubious distinction of having had an obituary written on her concerning her '62 trip to China. There is nothing
left to find on this trip to China except the knot speed. Goldberg sent me on a job at 5:30! Louse! Nevertheless, I shall
work cheerfully. N.B. We aim to please. Went to Buffie's party
later. Buffie was even better than I imagined—better looking
in pink corset, tights affair—no sleeves—stopping roughly
& abruptly at the crotch. Black net stockings. Also there De
la Noux.* Toni Hughes with a fine young man named Keith
who knows Ernst Hauser & [Marjorie] Wolf & likes Wolf
(!), Julian Levi, Mr. & Mrs. Watts (the husband has beautiful
bare feet & knows it) & Teddy & Touche.† Touche is horribly,
sickeningly flippant. Teddie I like—tho I never saw such masculine gestures outside of a butch. She was in cream colored
tights. Coachman livery or 18th century gallant style, with
black boots—may have contributed. Anyway, we talked a long
while. Touche puts his beefy arms around every woman eventually, with a flip answer for everything. Said I must come to
his place. De la Noux looked lovely as usual. White blouse,
prevented from rivaling her teeth by a lavender scarf. Should
like to see Teddie & Toni again.

JULY 3, 1942

Easy pleasant day. Went to 25 St. on a job, then back to Goldberg who sat talking with me in the Shanty [restaurant] for an
hour about the Venture.‡ It would involve giving all my spare
time (even evenings) to reading, if I went into this book. Still
Goldberg's methods are sound. I like him, personally, furthermore, & he must like me. I haven't talked salary yet, & I
shouldn't write for less than $30. He's looking at my writing this

---

* It is likely this is a misspelling and she means the bisexual writer and designer Eyre de
Lanux (1894–1996), also an acquaintance of Rosalind's.
† Cult lyricist and wit La Touche (born John Treville Latouche, 1914–1956) wrote the lyrics
for more than twenty musicals, most famously *Cabin in the Sky* with the song "Taking a
Chance on Love." He also wrote the "Ballad for Americans" that both Paul Robeson and
Bing Crosby performed regularly. He was homosexual, as was probably his wife, Teddie.
‡ "The Venture" refers to one of Goldberg's book projects.

weekend & will probably give me whole chapters to write if he does the outline. That'd be fun.

7/3/42

One's most stubborn addictions, one's deepest loves, such as smoking, drinking, writing—are first unpleasant, almost unnatural things to do. Proving the death instinct at least "present" in the man on the streets, in the ecstatic results of smoking & drinking; proving the arts are born of strangeness, fascination, pain & slow acquaintanceship. Like writing, like painting, like composing music. Still, now, when the writer says, I hate to write, it is the physical effort of the brain which prompts this. He might hate drinking water when he does not want it, but he will for his health, and the inevitable condition of the body prompts it.

JULY 5, 1942

SPA pleasant day because mother was with Marjorie, doing prints. One of my wooden women which I should show to Mr. Crowninshield from *Vogue*.* He buys similar things.

Russia says that the Germans have crossed the lines. The war is going worse for them than before . . . I took a walk with Mother and we had a very serious talk about things at home. She will be more agreeable now, I think. S. is always the same. Didn't speak a word today.SPSP

JULY 7, 1942

I suffer these days not only from diffusion of ideas in writing, but from diffusion of my whole energy. I should love Helen! Perhaps I do. I certainly do whenever I think of her. I certainly found in her & with her what no one else has ever or perhaps

---

* The cultivated and elegant Francis Welch Crowninshield (1872–1947) was best known for his twenty-one years at the top of *Vanity Fair* during which time he turned it from a mere fashion magazine to one of America's most prominent literary magazines, publishing Aldous Huxley, T. S. Eliot, Gertrude Stein, and Djuna Barnes—all in a single issue. He later also served as an editor for *Vogue*.

can ever give me. Why do I fret about Rosalind? Even about
Bernhard?! If Helen is a losing fight what matters that to me! I
of the losing fights! I of the ideals in love! [SP]Things are better.[SPSP]
Pleasant evening sewing on slipcover, reading Dante. I remember
Mrs. Lordner's advice: "If you don't make it these days, you're
just dumb." Goldberg asked if I wanted to do the household section of *The Jewish Family Year Book.*[*] I said yes!

JULY 7, 1942

[SP]I want to take all my notebooks and read through them for
important phrases—use them.[SPSP] It would be wonderful to do it
on a weekend. Alone, in the quiet.

JULY 8, 1942

[F]I received my diploma! In real vellum[FF]—[SP]it's in Latin, so I
couldn't read it! I used a dictionary! But it's beautiful, and I
want Grandma to have it. I ate with Rosalind and gave her
my magazines from Jeannot. We saw the Malvina Hoffman[†]
exhibit. It wasn't good. It occurred to me that Rosalind might
easily get tired of me. I tried to tell her what I thought about
my life with—her—with me. That there might not be a reason for me to always stay with her, like—what? Like some
nobody![SPSP]

7/8/42

Each person carries around in himself a terrible other world
of hell and the unknown. He may rarely see it if he turns his
mind to it, but in the course of life he may perhaps see it once
or twice, when he is near death or when he is much in love, or
when he is deeply stirred by music, by God or by sudden fear.
It is an enormous pit reaching below the deepest crater of the

---

* Presumably a reference to *The Jewish Family Almanac 1943*, which was edited
by B. Z. Goldberg and Dr. Emil Flesch and published by F.F.F. Publications.
† Malvina Hoffman (1885–1966), noted American sculptor.

earth, or it is the thinnest air far beyond the moon. But it is frightening and essentially "unlike" man as he knows himself familiarly, so we spend all our days living at the other antipodes of ourself.

7/8/42
I'd be very content if I could take a story of two perfectly normal newlyweds, bursting with good health and sexual energy, and make a good story out of it.

JULY 9, 1942
[SP]Mr. Goldberg raised my salary, I don't know how much, maybe $23–24. I want to buy a Spanish dictionary. Jack enters the Army on July 29. But he'll be here until August 14. He's serious and sad now.[SPSP] Good ideas & pretty happy. Mother cheerful as a cricket!

JULY 12, 1942
Sewed some—very frantically—on the slipcover. Makes me furious because sewing embodies, in a particularly violent and overwhelming form, all the vigors—all the familiar sensations of failure!

JULY 13, 1942
[SP]Yesterday was the worst day the Russians have had to date. The Germans have advanced very far into the country. The two armies are almost divided now, N. & S. [North and South], and the Germans are headed for the oilfields. The English have stopped Rommel.
    A day full of work. I looked for facts for the article about the budget and I wrote it in the afternoon. A card from Jo P.[SPSP] "Your letter was an oasis in a desert of Southern belles, etc." And that she misses me. [SP]Also, a card from Jeannot. Only "*Espoir*" [hope]. Walter Marlowe here at 7. Some books. He spoke about how all goes according to the wishes of the rich.

Wow! A marvelous meal at the Salle du Bois* and some good conversation. Later we went to Spivy's.[SPSP]

JULY 14, 1942

[SP]Goldberg had a lot of corrections for my article. It's much better now. I did research again for tomorrow's article. Very tired. I told Bernhard that I couldn't do our date tonight. Instead of the theater I read Dante and worked on my story. It's very good, too.[SPSP]

7/14/42

What we call "hell" is an earth-imagined state born of the physical sensations of shame, which are always those of inner "burning."

JULY 16, 1942

[SP]I wanted to see Rosalind the 19th. It's our anniversary. But she won't remember. Never—never—never! *Mademoiselle* called me at eleven. They wanted me to come tomorrow at ten for an interview. There's an opening but they want a stenographer. [SPSP] I should so like to get on *Mademoiselle*—mainly because I would thus redeem myself with Rosalind. If I could only tell her, when I lunch with her Monday that I'm actually working there! I would even go there for less money.

JULY 17, 1942

[SP]I worked the whole day and wasn't able to read or study at all. Paddy Finucane[†] died over the Atlantic in his airplane. The Germans hit his radiator and he wasn't high up enough to get to England. When his plane touched the sea it was probably in pieces! And only twenty-one years old. With Billie B. last night. Drank at the Cape Cod Room. Later we went to her house where I spent the night! Nothing to tell. Billie is bad in bed. I had

---

* La Salle du Bois at 30 East Sixtieth Street.
† Brendan Eamonn Fergus ("Paddy") Finucane (1920–1942), distinguished Irish fighter pilot.

known about it before. Her bed is also narrow. I woke up early
and was at home by eight. The parents will never know.[SPSP]

JULY 18, 1942

[SP]I saw Mr. Goldberg, who told me not to go to *Mlle.* That he is
interested in me, which is true. I don't know whether I'll go or
stay.[SPSP]

JULY 19, 1942

[SP]Today is the day I met Rosalind Constable. I would have been
with her tonight. I could have gone deeper or at least drunk a
drink to our souls. But she is far away now and never thinks
of me. It's also the hottest it has been all year. I worked on my
story and will show it to Mr. Goldberg tomorrow. I still want to
move, I think that is how I will mature! I read Dante and Heraldry* again with great pleasure. I'd like to write a piece for the
theater. Some piece about a soldier—who leaves.[SPSP]

JULY 20, 1942

[SP]The days pass happily, but progress is slow. I worked today
with the same tranquility I had in my youth at Morton Street.
I wrote a good article about "Trends in Fashion" this morning,
and ate lunch with Berger who drank a Tom Collins and read
the paper. I felt that he was thinking of me from across the table.
He would do anything to please me.

I studied and also wrote two pages of a wonderful story
about "Manuel."† It will truly be marvelous! The English are
thinking about what might happen if the Germans manage to
take Alexandria. Meanwhile the Russians are fighting valiantly.
And they're losing. I'm happy—I'm happy and why is that? I
don't have anybody. Nobody![SPSP]

---

* Possibly Pat refers to Henry Wall Pereira's book *On Dante's Knowledge of Heraldry* (1898).
† Pat commences a new short story that she will continue to work on for the next few months.
This story does not survive.

JULY 22, 1942

[SP]I wrote this morning, and later Mr. Goldberg asked me for my notebook. I said yes but later decided no. It's not possible to give him anything that isn't good! Bernhard has a studio now with a photographer. She wants me to come with her tomorrow evening to get the room ready but I need to work. I really don't give Mr. Goldberg enough work. I won't receive a larger salary this way! I was thinking too much about myself.[SPSP]

JULY 23, 1942

[SP]Goldberg is good. We talked about work, then later about my story. I have to rewrite eight pages. Bernhard called me. But I don't have enough time to play every night.[SPSP]

JULY 24, 1942

B.Z. [Goldberg] in nasty temper [F]this evening.[FF] How much nicer if I worked elsewhere—no wishful thinking allowed, however. I'll spring that place soon enough. Phoned Jack. He was so overjoyed he later sent me a telegram. Studied Spanish—but hereafter my evenings shall commence writing.

7/26/42

Wagner's music—almost any of it good to make love by.
    (What horror!—1950)

JULY 27, 1942

[SP]Mother and I went to Winslow. Excellent dinner. She asked me about Jack and Marlowe. Who do you prefer? Etc. In truth I don't know. She told me Jack adores me. It's true. A bourgeois night for once—we saw *Mrs. Miniver* at [Radio City] Music Hall. Mother ate so much—or drank so much that she kept falling asleep the entire time. The film was marvelous. I phoned Bernhard, and now I regret it because I'll spend the whole night wanting it to be tomorrow.[SPSP]

JULY 30, 1942

Last night and a year ago, Rosalind wrote me the beautiful letter that made me love her—the letter I got in Sioux Falls, S. Da.—the letter I read till it wore out, the letter I never betrayed, the letter I knew by heart, the letter she believed and I believed in—the letter I would have given a front tooth to keep—the letter I lost. Most of the phrases linger in my mind, I shall hate to see them fade out of memory but it seems silly trying (and failing) to recapture even part of it. ^{SP}Miss Weick* is writing articles now, but none of them are as interesting as mine. Totally without ideas at the moment, but at least writing went well tonight after First Aid class on my story "Manuel." Tonight we looked at the arteries, etc. My girl (the one I'm working with) is pretty, but so big that I couldn't find the vessels. We examined the body, even the toes, the chest, the breast, throat, and back. I want to see Rosalind. I want to go home with her.^{SPSP}

JULY 31, 1942

^{SP}A typical day, smoking far too much, working too much. I went to Fornos Restaurant, where I ordered rice and chicken. ^{SPSP} Goldberg said: "There's something in your writing that intrigues me—rhythm & an occasional new turn of phrase. But it's inclined to be poetry. Uneven." ^{SP}I got another raise: $25 per week. Jack told me he spoke with Goldberg. About business. He called me tonight during the blackout.† Jack told me that Gold-

---

* A work colleague of Pat's at F.F.F. Publications.
† There was no continuous nightly blackout in wartime New York. But blackout drills were held mostly in the early years of the war, when there were fears that German bombers might appear overhead. In spring 1942, the Army considered that the glow from Manhattan's city lights was silhouetting ships offshore, making them easy targets for Germans that had sunk scores of oil tankers and freighters bound for Britain. So under an Army-ordered dim-out, the neon advertising on Times Square went dark, stores and bars dimmed their exterior lighting, just as streetlights and traffic signals had their wattage reduced, car headlights were hooded, and the Statue of Liberty's torch didn't glow.

berg paid me a lot of compliments which he will tell me about on Monday.[SPSP]

AUGUST 2, 1942

Sent Rosalind a letter with the "Welcome, soldier!" sex hygiene brochure. I think she's on vacation which is why I haven't seen her in 24 days & 12 hours & 25 minutes.

8/2/42

Why can't I write of apple-blossom faces, of valentines and bedsteads, kitchen fires? Because there's too much wrong with the world, and the old ways are not the way out.

AUGUST 3, 1942

Berger came tonight. Lovely evening. He gave me an unpolished Mexican silver bracelet. Dinner at Proust's which is a sad hashery. I still want time alone tho Jack's fun to be with.

AUGUST 4, 1942

[SP]Met Bernhard near the library. She's still sad—she can't work with Tietgens[*] and d'Arazien[†] around. Later on I wrote the article about Lasting Peace at the office but Goldberg didn't like the style. He wants to go to Poughkeepsie tomorrow, but by boat, to plan the book about American nationalities.[SPSP]

AUGUST 5, 1942

I miss Rosalind, hundreds—yes, hundreds of people call me up— and I sigh for one of her chilly yeses. Being with G., telling all day

---

* Rolf Tietgens (1911–1984), the "Poet with a Camera," had already published two extraordinary photo books by the time he was forced to leave his native Germany and emigrate to the United States in 1939. He soon succeeded in working for important magazines, getting his photos published in *Popular Photography*, *U.S. Camera*, and in the special issue of *Fortune* for the 1939 New York World's Fair. He also published essays, on topics such as "What Is Surrealism?" In 1941 the Museum of Modern Art acquired two of his pictures for its permanent collection. Pat's book *The Two Faces of January* (1964) is dedicated to him.
† Arthur d'Arazien (1914–2004), renowned Turkish-American industrial and commercial photographer.

of plot, character, possible plots does make me happy. By the way, Goldberg said he'd get me a commission from a newspaper (?) to go to USSR after the war!

AUGUST 6, 1942

Worked on this Lasting Peace job this P.M. (I find it difficult and damned awkward to write on such a pleasant & equivocal matter as "democracy." What can one say that isn't worn out, and isn't too Communistic for the paper?) Turned out something that might just as well have been titled: "How to Build a Lasting Henhouse." I shall ask Goldberg to get off Saturday—Bernhard wants to go away. Wrote fairly well after First Aid. Once more an "excellent," like my partner Margaret Zavada. (Czecho gal from Peru.) She's very warm, holds my head lovingly and rests it against her lap as she gropes for my temporal artery.

AUGUST 7, 1942

Berger phoned early, because I wouldn't make a date this week-end. Matter of fact [I have one] with Bernhard. Wrote on Lasting Peace. (Done.) Hauser must be gone, snatched away, because we had a date tonight & I didn't hear from him. Perhaps he left on the same clipper tonight as Queen Wilhelmina,* who went to London. Worked on "Manuel" two hours tonight—more in fact—and did well. I love it. Hope to make something rather good. I'm no good at concluding phrases.

8/7/42

Virginia Woolf committed suicide because she could not reconcile art with human slaughter. Individually (as Virginia Woolf always thought), one cannot reconcile them, because the individual does not go to war of his own will. But collectively, wars are an expression of humans just like murder is. Wars are mass mur-

---

* Queen Wilhelmina (1880–1962), queen of the Netherlands from 1890 to 1948. Her radio broadcasts from London during World War II made her a symbol of Dutch resistance to German occupation.

ders, and wars are manifestations of one facet of human character, a very ancient one. If they are not "inevitable" long, if the common man may oppose his will to peace, then they have been heretofore "inevitable" in the sense that intelligent nations have let themselves be driven into wars by their leaders. If man is anti-war, then he is merely the corpse in the hands of the murderers, who are performing a human action, or one, that is characteristic of humans occasionally, those of us who have the desire of committing murder.

AUGUST 8, 1942

[Bernhard and I] caught the train to Valley Stream. J.J. was swimming, so we bought lunch & ate in the forest, building a minute fire for no reason at all except to smoke up our hair deliciously. J. J. Augustin* is a rather undistinguished German in that indefinite age of 37–38. Two-story house, rather secluded, with Police dog (Silver) and cat (Pussie). He told us of his troubles with the neighbors and FBI. The neighbors are cranks, and accuse him of everything from espionage & homosexuality to wireless operating and procto-phantasm. He made us wonderfully at home, served us Wiener Schnitzel and potato salad, & buzzed about the house like an *echte Hausfrau* [housewife]. But in the afternoon, he told us all about his family in Germany, his mornings, his activities at the house, and of the telephone tapping of the FBI.

His little living room centers about the fireplace, flanked with phonograph albums, wood storage, etc. And on the opposite wall is a huge bookcase of German style, one of 5—the only one he was able to get out of Germany. Many first editions, and all expensive editions, particularly those of his own printing or of his father's. They love books on philology and native painting, weaving, etc., and J.J. printed, in conjunction with Gladys

---

* Johannes Jakob Augustin, son of Heinrich Wilhelm Augustin, then owner of the J. J. Augustin printing company in Germany.

Reichard* of Barnard, the only authoritative book on Hopi &
Navajo sign painting. He knows about six Indian languages, to
read & write. All about are evidences of this Thos. Mannish
existence in Hamburg and München, the days of second breakfasts and long hours with linen-bound volumes of Goethe &
Swedenborg. Rolf evidently explained things very well, because
he put us into one room, one bed, & probably would have been
surprised had we asked for separate ones. The inevitable happened, with B. withdrawing (in confusion or impotence or lack
of confidence) at the crucial point.

AUGUST 9, 1942

Since I hate beds I am late to them and early from them.

J.J. is an artist. He has done much in his life. It is a pity the
line will die with him. There is a French Jewess en route from
Cannes, whom he will marry, but she is a Lesbian, & they will
not even live together. J.J. is a person I love, like Bernhard, like
Rosalind, Betty, Natasha, like Bach and Mozart. Rolf Tietgens
arrived around 12:00. We had another lavish dinner, tho J.J.
always remarks how low he is in funds, what with lawyers' fees
and the American lack of appreciation of his books, he manages
to cook with scads of butter, and to have plenty of liquor & cigarettes on hand.

Bernhard & I took a walk in the swampy forests and I was
bitten by a police dog in the rear end on the way home. Broke
the skin, too. The funniest thing is that Bernhard was trembling
and crying as soon as it happened, embraced me all the way
home & practically had to be treated for shock. Bernhard very
happy all day. Last night was the first time in a year & a half
[for] her she said. (A year & a half ago, I was a virgin.) I feel
new desire to learn more Bach, & to live as J.J. does, with my
books, my tobacco, liquor, music & dogs. I wonder is Bernhard
in love with me? Not in the real way I must be, however, & she,
too: somewhat madly & unwisely & illogically and definitely

---

* Gladys Reichard, associate professor of anthropology at Barnard College.

suddenly. Unless in all this rest period, her mores erotica have changed. She is so unfortunately feminine inside.

AUGUST 10, 1942

Goldberg asked for me at 10:30 to layout the new book. I made the title: *The People Made America.* And Weick, G. & I compiled the chapters the rest of the day. G. asked me to lunch. Del Pezzo's—all but empty. And really empty without Rosalind or Natasha. Why doesn't she even write me a card? I still feel lonely without her, no matter whom I see, no matter what I do. I feel lonely, very lonely. Jack B. here when I came home. Fried chicken dinner in Mother's finest style. Jack B. & I went up on Empire State, 102 stories. Wrote card to Jeannot. We had Tom Collins & earnest conversation, me being quite reserved, consequently fatigued, bored & boring. I cramp myself so I go to sleep. But one cannot expand in such company. He counsels me against celibacy, etc. Then tonight, horrible bear hugs which I endured as duty, sending a man off to war, etc.

AUGUST 11, 1942

Dropped back on Bernhard at 1:45 but she'd had lunch. Rolf eyes me like a wolf, looking around the studio, always dreaming of something. B. & I went to drugstore where I had a lunch under physical conditions I could hardly bear. Neither can I bear the price of salads, coffee, cigarettes, when I pay all the checks. Bernhard is no check grabber, while I am a check grabber from way back. B. was in a troublesome time of month, and add to that the fact that she is wild that Rolf take me away from her, and you have the unholy spectacle of the female fighting for the young. She wants to tell Rolf he hasn't the chance of a snowball in hell, and wants my sanction to it. She said Rolf thinks it's a terrible thing to do to her, so obviously she has let him think we are together, which is not true by any means. Rolf should know we are not together, then if he wants to do anything about it, he should come to me. However, he wants to talk to B. I warned her against being dependent on me. From my own state of mind this

noon, I know she might wonder whether I'm in love with Rolf
or not, too. Matter of fact, Rolf I should love easier than anyone
I know. I shall someday marry just such a man as he. Though I
think his affair with me will go as easily as it came.

Saw Buffie for dinner. Martinis & serious discussion before
8:30 when we went out to Chateaubriand's. C.—that louse, that
sheep in clown's clothing—is Lola's lover & has been for over a
year. Where Del gets off I can't see. Why does he tolerate it? Has
he someone?

Buffie was adorable tonight. Lovely shaped head, lovely hair,
and the most exciting perfumes from head to toe. She moves
like a strong Indian about the house, amid china closets and
lace antimacassars, but her own strength dominates the scene. I
love to look at her so. She had me pose for a portrait of someone
(Nina Jacobsen) and half naked, too. Meanwhile she kissed me
and said her magic words and wanted me to stay. I was tired—
too tired—that is all. Otherwise I would have. I find her most
attractive physically. Damn, so many people aren't! Buffie would
make a night of love of every date I made. Come for tea & stay
for breakfast. "It's nice to look at you all evening and then kiss
you goodnight," I said. And she called me naughty & laughed at
my naiveté. I admire and envy her energy. She doesn't drink or
smoke at all now. I must say she looks better for it.

8/11/42

This notebook should see a change, a very important change
from all the others. I am no longer fascinated by the decadent,
much less captivated by its color, variety and sensational possibilities in literature. And oddly enough, it has been the war
that made the change. The war makes a writer, perhaps makes
everyone, think of what he loves best. With myself, I had to ask
a long while what I loved best, what sort of life I wanted, what
rate of speed, what environs, what goal, what amusements and
what labors. I like a room of my own, with long evenings in
summer, in snowy winter, in the exciting fall and the spring. I
like to read my books when the radio is playing Gilbert & Sul-

livan operettas, or Bach sonatas or Boccherini concertos. Yes
and I like the lives of the people I don't know: of the rich old
gentleman whose daughter brings his hot chocolate up the stairs
to him at four on the dot, when he is finishing his after-lunch
pasting in stamp collections. I like the lives of the mechanics of
Detroit, who read Dickens on Sunday afternoons because they
love him, and because, too, they think they are absorbing culture. I like the farm boys who come to town once a month to
see movies and sleep with a girl and buy themselves ten-a-shot
drinks. I like the artists, the painters, photographers, window
designers, copywriters, playwrights, novelists and short story
writers who live with a mildness in their eyes and a calmness
in their hands, who do not remember what they had for breakfast, and who do not know what they will have for dinner. I
like the poor Jewish family who sits next to me at the Lewisohn Stadium,* the sailor in glasses who reads beside me in the
Public Library, the good Chinaman who washes my shirts. I
like my Sunday mornings with marmalade from England, the
paper at my door, the symphonies in the afternoon, and the
toasted marshmallows in the evening. Best of all I like the artists, professed & unprofessed, who of all people, live closest
by the belief that man is the most wonderful creation in the
world, most wonderful of animals and more wonderful than
all creatures of his own brain. That is why I like artists best,
because their eyes are open and their brains stirring, because
they see and hear and feel suddenly man in new form, and, having captured it, have contributed so much to the great mosaic
of wonderful man, which will never be done, and yet never be
destroyed. And what do I hate? There is so much to hate, that I
cannot tolerate people who say: "I have nothing to say." There
is so much to say about the ugliness of line and color, the simple
cruelty of leading men to buy what they do not want or need,
the sin of publishers who sell inferior literature by advertising

---

* For more than fifty years, through 1966, Lewisohn Stadium was a staple of New York City
cultural life, drawing hundreds of thousands of spectators to summer symphony concerts.

campaigns, sell it to those who can afford to buy and who can't afford to buy, who buy it for culture, for escape, for keeping up with the Joneses, to those who buy because someone is having a birthday, and because so-and-so is top of the list, through the purchasing of others like them. I hate the speed, the noise, the absence of prized possessions, the absence of leisure to visit rarely and long, to study long and often, to become familiar with the beautiful lines of one's handmade furniture in one's own home, the failure of machine made shoes to compare with those made by feeling the foot with the hands of a master, the absence of discrimination in art, advertising, printing, ribbons, clothes, and the absence of joy in life due to all of these: haste, economic pressure, fear of want, days without leisure. It is very late. I have said only half the things I love and hate, and said them very badly.

AUGUST 13, 1942

Much better feeling today: mother put my hair up. *Mademoiselle* sent me a letter, would I be interested in being *Charm*'s "feature editor." (i.e. writing captions & goosing refractory writers) Stopped by Bernhard's at 1:30, but she was in Scarsdale. I'd forgotten Rolf was there with my photos. Two of which are good. One very serious I liked. Rolf said: "I knew you'd like that one. Because you look very boyish. You are a boy. You know." Very attentive, & walked me finally up to 57 St. I told him B. & I were not together. Rolf wants to go for a walk Sunday—Van Cortlandt Park but he's afraid Bernhard will be jealous. She shouldn't know. Should like to ask Rolf for dinner Sunday. I know he would find los padres *Spiessbürger* [bourgeois]. Yesterday when I was upset, I could not really think why. The fact was, as I later discovered through intuition alone, that I didn't want B.'s grip on me at all. I want no commitments. I wonder could I be in love with Rolf. Neither of us will admit it can be the opposite sex, and both of us can excuse ourselves by saying it is not, of course, the opposite sex. Buffie showed me photos last night of the "writer" she will probably marry after the war. He's in the army. How lovely she was last night. How nice to be married (both of us) and go on as before, in perfect confidence and harmony.

AUGUST 14, 1942

I guess I feel down. Finished "Manuel" tonight & started another better draft, in the style I know it must be. Went down to S. & S. [Street & Smith] to see some nobody about that feature editor job. A young girl spoke to me, whom I impressed unmercifully. She'll call me later.

Goldberg, however, is very happy about *The People Made America*, the advance folder for which came out today. Should be impossible to leave at such a time, when deadlines must be met. He even wants me to work on the weekend. Finished Dante's *Divine Comedy* this evening, remembering a few good passages. But the inner life is hard to return to after a day of trivia. My notebooks go two & three days untouched. The magic paragraphs don't come without solitude & free quiet hours. Can't be helped.

AUGUST 15, 1942

Dinner with [Walter] Marlowe. Another gorgeous gardenia. We went to Café Society Uptown.* The evening uneventful except for revelatory conversation in his room on my sexual reactions. Finally I got around to telling him a) I didn't enjoy attentions of any kind from him or anyone b) I should not until I had found myself, something to be proud of, something substantial. He was most sympathetic, but I don't like his joking about the sexual act, which he considers just as lightly (with his fine adjustment) as ordinary friendship with a girl. "Don't you think sex is here to stay?" etc. No thanks. Boy, could I show him a thing or two or could I?! Shall speak to Rolf tomorrow on it—the problem of

---

* Café Society at 1 Sheridan Square in Greenwich Village was the first racially integrated nightclub in the United States. A second branch, Café Society Uptown, opened in 1940 on Fifty-Eighth Street between Lexington and Park Avenues.

not trusting rough trade men, and the problem, too, of mistrusting women's genius & drive. He should be versed in the subject.

AUGUST 16, 1942

I think this is the strangest day of my life. At any rate I am nearest to falling in love with—Rolf Tietgens. Met Rolf at 2:00 at Lexington & 59. We rode up to Van Cortlandt Park. He gave me a tiny Mexican (Indian) doll out of wood, which a little Indian boy made. I told him first what Walter & I had talked about last night—my inherent dislike & mistrust of men. So he was downcast. It rained like mad, & we got soaked. We came home after much delaying and *Pilz* [mushroom] picking, & ate eggs on toast & cake & coffee. He was determined not to be hungry but ate everything. Then we sat in my room & talked. He looked over all my books. Especially liking Blake & Donne, whom he knows thoroughly. We walked down 57th to the river, the only place he seemed to be happy today. It was actually fun standing there with him, & very strange because it was fun— the simple reason is, he is the only man who ever knew all about me. God what a difference between him and Walter!—and Jack! So we watched the boats & the lights & he told me all about Hamburg, Lübeck, the marshlands. Then we walked to the cobblestoned street that was deserted & stood there over an hour. He kissed me a few times—rather a mutual thing for a change. It was quite wonderful & perfect, and for several moments I could see happiness and read it in the sky like a strange new word written. He said he was so happy he couldn't eat & sleep for months. And we mustn't tell Bernhard.

So tonight—I am new. I am a new person—and who knows what will come of it? I should like very much to sleep with him. And I know he wants it. So I guess we shall. Where? At his place? At J.J.'s sometime when Bernhard doesn't come? Being with him is like reading a wonderful poem—by Whitman, Wolfe, or the First Voice himself. He reads such things into me, but I am mute beside him. He is quite impracticable & wild. Wants to wipe everyone out by war & start over—but with him wiped out, too. And his brain is tenanted with all the sad Indians he met in the Texas jails. Wild good men, imprisoned on white men's laws.

Would like to go to J.J.'s soon.

AUGUST 17, 1942

^{SP}I worked particularly well this morning. I wrote "Best Movies of the Year," *Mrs. Miniver*, etc^{SPSP} [for Goldberg]. Very amusing to write & read. Took it down to the office at 2:30, stopping by Bernhard's en route: Tietgens there of course. We behaved very well. Bernhard very busy, & studiedly cheerful in spite of fortune's reverses. Rolf came down & walked me to 67th. He told me he'd told J.J. all about it—last night—when he talked with him all this AM. That J.J. was delighted, & said we must come out just the two of us, but that Rolf should be careful with Bernhard. Read Ecclesiastes tonight, & it's splendid. Rolf once shouted it into the desert. My parents think he's an inveterate panhandler—a bum— a vagabond. But they know nothing of things of the spirit. He's as improvident as the wise man in the Bible.

AUGUST 19, 1942

"Statues are building themselves in me, which I should eternalize in monumental paragraphs," I wrote tonight. It centers around Rolf. Bernhard told me tonight, when we had drinks here, that she cannot understand me if I like Rolf (tho I think I assured her I did not love him!) and that were it Rosalind I had succeeded in interesting in me, she could understand & would not mind—Rolf upsets her—tho she says she has no claim on me & told him so. He exaggerates everything either of us says. So it is wisest to say nothing henceforth. We ate at Fleur de Lis, a rotten place really. Then we saw *Moscow Strikes Back,*[*] a fine film. We walked home wonderfully happy, & sat before the river of an hour, talking magic.

---

[*] *Moscow Strikes Back* (1942), a feature-length Soviet documentary film that won a 1943 Oscar for Best Documentary.

AUGUST 20, 1942

ᴳYes, I'm happier than ever before. Don't understand it, and besides, Rolf. I looked out the window at 8:30 and there Rolf came skulking without a hat, as always, and no jacket. We were so happy to see one another. Walked along 1st Ave. And drank a beer. (Rolf two.) He was suffering terribly from the heat. He was crushed to learn I hadn't told [Bernhard] the truth yet. We stood on our street, the quiet little street by the river, where grass grows between the stones, green and soft and waving in the wind, where nearly no one passes, save the occasional policeman. It was the most wonderful evening. He wants to live with me and plans to earn money right away to that end. He wants me to come home with him and talk the whole night through. Yes, and that's what I want too. But I fear I will become like a regular girl, that a man will keep me from my work. But on the contrary, he calls me a little boy and makes me a better writer. What will Rosalind and Natasha & Betty & Babs, Peter & Helen say? What will the world say?ᴳᴳ

AUGUST 21, 1942

ᴳRolf sat by the window, and Bernhard wasn't there.ᴳᴳ He was very happy & said the gods are with us. Yes, he fancies me a boy, and his homosexuality before came from a Grecian pride in men's superiority and a mistrust of women's wiles and weaknesses. He likes me because my body is lean & hard & straight, and because I speak bluntly. He talked of Germany & his family, while the sun brought out the urine of the monuments like a yellow rainbow around us. What a city, with no place to be alone! Berger phoned at 6:30, very disappointed I was "going away" for the weekend, and in a rage that I am dated all next week.

AUGUST 22, 1942

Woke up sick in the night—ravenously hungry & all food sickening. Made a stab at working. Got my check, Miss Weick told me to go home. Very concerned, though she said one true thing: every one who gets anywhere abuses every law of physical health and 8 hrs. sleep is a myth. [Rolf] came at 7. We sat in my darkened room & talked, shyly at first, because sickness takes all the spirits out of me. He brought me Hamsun's *Mysteries*. He was embarrassed that the lights were out, lest my parents should come home. He has his hair cut short as a convict, still sweats, & wears a denim shirt. The elevator boys look him up & down, but I don't mind.

What a lot has happened in the last seven days! No wonder I became ill.

AUGUST 23, 1942

A pleasant Sunday. A rarity. I finished (wrote an end to) "Manuel" this morning when the family was at church. Reveled in not going out of the house all day except at 6:30 a moment to purchase some C & B marmalade, which was pure whim. I read W. H. Auden's *Double Man*. Rather good. But not so brilliant or concise as [T. S.] Eliot, whom he imitates occasionally. How good to have a day without telephone calls! I read "Manuel" aloud to M. & S. and they liked it—possibly the first time this has happened. I consider them pretty fair critics of a sort. What a pleasant feeling—a story that I'm not ashamed of—one that I'm almost proud of—one that many people would consider better than "Silver Horn of Plenty," though "Manuel"'s not so brilliant. And I am not so pleased with it. But the emotions, etc. were much more difficult to handle, than the simple one of hate, which comes easily to me. I feel gradually very capable of handling complex situations, simple emotions which were heretofore foreign to me. I feel that I'm growing & shall grow, and these growth periods come only on such long, private Sundays.

Tonight I commenced [Franz] Werfel's *Forty Days of Musa Dagh*. The writing is superb! Better than I had dared hope.

8/24/42

Examine any work of art as a scientist would, and it appears a distorted product of a madman. An artist's contribution is the sum of many small madnesses, anomalies, embellished to a beautiful power, trifles which a saner mind would have wisely discarded.

AUGUST 25, 1942

Rosalind phoned me at 9:35 this morning. I was so happy I couldn't talk straight. She told me to come to lunch with her. I spent a hell of a long time choosing my clothes, did about one hour's work this morning. Lunched for an hour & a half. She looks swell—tan hands & back, and the old gin flush face, with upper lip slightly peeling from sunburn.

Goldberg read "Manuel." He liked it. Said he'd recognize my writing in a pile of stories. I feel such a deep happiness now, such a confidence in my own ability, that Rolf must be a major part of it. Well, say I'm in love with Rolf & Rosalind, too. That's the simple truth, and what's one to do about it?

AUGUST 26, 1942

And I live on the knife edge of my emotions these days anyway—much as Helen did last December. Called for Rolf & we went loping off to lunch. I was starved. How nice to eat with him when the sunlight falls on the table, and I feel I can never get enough of him, or the food. Then we spent an hour getting shoes (F. Simon's 9.00). Red ones, too. I have decided to go so far as to tell B. She was shortsighted in limiting me to liking only girls. Really most unbecoming in her—& obviously self-motivated.

AUGUST 27, 1942

The Duke of Kent was killed Tuesday in a plane crash over England. Called for Rolf, whom I saw in the window. & made the awful bust of addressing him before seeing Bernhard there. She was a small piece of ice thereafter. ^GSo Rolf whispered to me to tell her everything—and B. and I went across the street to get drinks.^{GG} One—two—three martinis—explanations, tears from her—^Gand everything fell to pieces.^{GG} My class in First Aid seemed insignificant besides Bernhard there pouring her heart

out. She loves me. She can't take this. We kicked the traces &
went to Hoboken to a clam joint, with sawdust floors and oyster
shells. She says the trouble is that she has exactly to offer what
Rolf has—only in less exciting & intense form. That is true.
However, I feel this is the end. She is wonderful to me, but I love
Rolf more. I am not so patient or so wise that I can choose tenderness over fierceness. Got home after 12:00, Rolf of course
waited for me, & mother said he came over, much disturbed,
and alarming them.

AUGUST 29, 1942

I can make no contact with anything but myself—and that with
difficulty. The stricture of the atmosphere stops the beautiful
osmosis of the city. Dulls my brain, clogs my very bowels. The
decadence before mine eyes! As Rolf puts it: this fantastic continent they ruined in a hundred years!

8/30/42

The Wonderful Day in California! The promise—the delight in the
half-revealed, half-known. It was a time that can never be reduplicated again—because I was twenty and one half then, and now I
am twenty-one and one half—My love was so young that day—
two or three encounters old. How can a poem reproduce it adequately? For the words I should use would be, at best, those with
the associations of that day, and would, at best, evoke only for me
that afternoon. How can I possibly communicate the feeling?

There was rain and I didn't care. I had an awful cold and I
didn't care. I was a rocket ready to be touched off, and aimed
straight for you.

What does one do with these experiences that shake one's
roots? Does one wait?—Then it's hopeless! Moods pass and cannot be revoked either by imagination or deliberate reassembling
of circumstances. What remains is not even a particle of the
mood, the aura, the intangible emotion, but only the memory of
the entire period of time, which even the recalling of whole sentences of dialogue, whole panoramas seen cannot bring back per-

fectly. Here I write mechanically what I must write to remember what I must remember, inferior, incomplete, impotent compared to the actuality, but nevertheless absorbing me and bewildering me. I loved you so then. I believed so then. I was on top of a mountain breathing thin air. You were all around me, all those two months. I take delight in being impractical about you. An impractical love is the most beautiful and the most fitting. If love should be the deepest touching experience, the most divorced from all other experience, as it surely is, then let it be the most inadvisable. Curse me if I ever spend a moment thinking what I should do, tactics, or what even you would want or expect me to do. Let me be forever that rocket waiting for the match.

AUGUST 31, 1942

This morning mother & I filled the bookcase—rather well, too, even if the spaces are more numerous than I like. Buffie came over at 7:15. Drank a bit of Sherry. She's getting married this week! To some gay soldier named John Latham. After several martinis I took her out to dinner at the Hapsburg House in 55. Charming dinner, but I was so damn tight I ate only ½ of it. Buffie offered to share the bill, but I was feeling much too elegant. We went back to her house, bought beautiful grapes. Two people came over, which annoyed me, because we were listening to records. I slept at Buffie's house. It might have been great, but I was so ridiculously tired from the liquor—next time I shan't take the third or fourth martini.

SEPTEMBER 1, 1942

Mr. Latham called at precisely the wrong moment last night around one, from California. Buffie has to go there for the wedding, afterwards coming home, to resume the old life unchanged. She talked very offhandedly of it even to my mother. Tried to phone Buffie—one just doesn't say goodbye after that— she called me, too, when I was out. Called on [Rolf at] the studio. Looked at his books printed in Germany. He wanted the shades drawn for no particular reason. So B. passing saw them, called him down later about "cheap behavior." So neither Rolf nor I want to or can go there again. Anyway he's taken the 50th St. furnished room beginning Saturday. Took first aid final orally. Rolf there afterwards. Lovely walk home & mother fixed coffee while I gave him a few stories. Including the Subway one* which I think he'll like. I hope so. Wish he could get money & dress a bit better. Just a bit!

SEPTEMBER 2, 1942

I am almost overwhelmed, crushed, defeated—by all the wonderful things I have yet to do, make, think, create, plan, taste, love, hate, enjoy, live. I should never have thought my worst enemy would be fatigue, the brother of my best virtue, industry. But the fatigue is always physical, and remediable, never mental or psychic. Lunched wonderfully with Rosalinds. She's on the wagon to get rid of the gin flush, if it is a gin flush. Personally I like it. And I don't like R on the wagon. She isn't herself. She has a nice, adequately pleasing veneer. She can display sober, but it has no mystery. I should like to see her quite drunk—as I have. We discussed fully the Rolf-Bernhard crisis. She defends me & Rolf. Rosalind said if she goes asking for hard luck, she'll get it. And tho I said B. had had 6 months of happiness with the right person, Rosalind said she was lucky to get that, and all our lives we never have the person we want. I wonder whom she wants? And why can't I—and why can't I? No I am not ready for Rolf, because I should run to Rosalind's arms the moment they looked like they were opening to me.

SEPTEMBER 4, 1942

Lunched with Rolf in the Automat.† I feel occasionally endangered of my power of detachment that I loved so well before I

---

* Pat mentions a story about people "writing in the subway" in her diary in July. It's possible that this is the same one. It could also be the one she will sell to *Home & Food* under the title "Friends" in 1943.
† Automats were cafeterias in which individual portions of food were dispensed from small glass-doored compartments.

was working. One must guard it, though I believe undoubtedly it is ever there. It is merely a firm piece of metal to keep polished. There was a terrific explosion in 48 St. at 9:30 this AM. Suicide touched off by the maid's ringing the bell. And Mary Sullivan, says the paper, was blown out of bed!

SEPTEMBER 5, 1942

With Rolf tonight. We walked to Buffie's first. Her mother was there, discouraged the idea of my watering the flowers—and Buffie, who is never to be circumvented, sent Rolf like a flunky out to make a duplicate key. I am the only one in N.Y., besides her mother, who has a key. Very nice of her. ("You too can have a honeymoon—" Buffie whispered.) But the hell with that. I should like much to go there occasionally, look well at all the pictures, browse among her books. She was sending invites to that crazy wedding. At least 500 of them, Cartier Stationery, inside & outside envelopes. And I must send ½ of them on to Mr. John Latham, whose name Buffie has only yesterday learned to spell.

Rolf & I took a walk in the park, where I was compelled to tell him of Helen, and of how we both felt about each other. Men are not magic to me that is all. Perhaps I must have magic instead of bread and meat, as I had rather have a cigarette than a hamburger. Rolf worried lest I run off again with a girl. Let him worry. It will let him down easier if I ever do. But I like Rolf very much, and see no leaving him soon.

SEPTEMBER 6, 1942

ᴳNice day. Got up early to go to J.J.'s with Rolf. Took a long walk along a brook. Rolf is really beautiful. He fell asleep on the sofa by the fire. But eventually came to my room—(he was nervous at first, handling all manner of things in the room). Then he was pleasantly shy, wanted to do everything, but also didn't want it. Am happy he didn't do anything, though, otherwise I'd be disgusted in the morning. He came to me maybe three times. I was shy myself.

Nice breakfast in the kitchen. Rolf tired. He didn't say anything about how I behaved (last night)—as always, I don't know what I want. He really likes me—truly—so gently, so deeply. Rolf wanted to hear all my concerns, and I told him about everything I felt for Rosalind—everything. He understands me. He just wants me to be happy and do good work. He wants to help me. Wants to meet Rosalind, too, because "she has such a huge influence on you!" Yes, if I have the money—Friday lunch. We read all sorts of German books, Hölderlin, Goethe, Morgenstern as well as Saroyan, whom it turns out Rolf knows. Love Rolf a lot, but am not yet in love with him.[GG]

SEPTEMBER 7, 1942

Strange day. Worked hard. I wanted to see Rolf, only I was so busy I almost forgot him, then he was walking up & down on 44th St. opposite the studio. He said, if I phoned him in the middle of the night to "go west" he'd pack up & go in 5 minutes. Only his overalls he'd need. Rosalind asked me to come to dinner with her. Betty was not coming until Thursday. She said—letting herself open more to me than almost ever before: "If I were your age, I should find myself dull company." So like her. And my heart bursts with wonderful unspeakable words. She is so strange, unique, wonderful, wunderbar, like nothing on the earth or in heaven, and what do I say? I cannot even say with my eyes—we were both sad. We talked vaguely of the war. I am always vague, because I am neither communist nor reactionary. I had to touch her once & kiss her—in the air—on the right side of her blond hair. She said "Bless you!" & I was gone down the hall, in a burst of tears. Why I don't know.

SEPTEMBER 8, 1942

[G]Rolf came by at 5 to get me. We saw [Frank Wysbar's] *Fährmann Maria*, a very good film from Nazi Germany. Later we walked to his house. Two little garret rooms full of pictures, books. I couldn't settle down, though. I have so much to do. We lay in bed for a minute. Then we came to 57. Very sad. He wanted to lie down in the gutter and die. I felt so sorry I couldn't spend more time with him. Wrote two letters. Had nice thoughts. And read [H. G. Wells's] *World Set Free*, not long, not great, not especially thrilling. But solid.GG

SEPTEMBER 10, 1942

I receive wild compliments from the elevator boys—probably duplicated to every girl in the building who isn't a walking mummy. Saw Rolf at 12:20. And again at 5:30. He spends about .20 a day on calls, as he shouldn't. Jo P. came for dinner. She stays unconscionably late. The same thing happened again. I feel sorry for her because she is lonely. That's all. Afterwards I regretted most bitterly & I see no reason why it should happen again. I am old enough to want to live my own life. I have done experimenting, wasting precious time that is ever running shorter. I should gladly give up—ridiculous phrase—my drinking, dinner going, cocktails, absurdities!

SEPTEMBER 13, 1942

Stalingrad is all but taken. The Russians with incredible courage, have destroyed all retreating bridges & roads, determined to die. Yesterday I sent "These Sad Pillars" to *The New Yorker* care of Mr. Shawn. Even if he doesn't remember me, the thing'll go to the fiction dept. With his note. Also "Manuel" at *Story*. Anxious as ever—as in the rather hopeless days of 1938—because now my powers are coming. I spent several hours turning thru my notebooks, pondering my next thing—certainly no definite story, merely trying to distill the murk of emotions inside me.

9/13/42

The most spiritual and "beautiful" literature has already been written—in the Bible, in the Greek dramas, in their philosophies. What we have to attain is at best the material representation, a poor substitute for the eternities we cannot logically hope to emulate. Spirituality in our day is as difficult to attain as a pair of wings and a halo.

SEPTEMBER 14, 1942

Wrote 3 pages (^{G}very difficult^{GG}) on new story of the virgin mother.* Also pleasant evening because I was alone, those delicate ideas coming, which generally are better literary material (for character) than the physical activities that might occur to one in more disturbing surroundings. Read *Mysterier*.

SEPTEMBER 18, 1942

Saw Rolf tonight after dinner. I should have worked & stayed home, but he was in such good spirits from having money. We went to Buffie's to look at books. We took our clothes off finally & lay a while on the bed. Neither of us feel any physical excitement and neither want nor cause anything to happen. I was terribly restless because of the house, the bed, & memories, and this Rolf couldn't understand. I have decided, at last, that I have a definite psychosis in being with people. I cannot bear it very long. Perhaps in all the world there is only Rosalind with whom I can feel calm for hours on end. With others, I am obsessed by the sense of time passing, by the [amount] of work that remains for me to do. Even tonight with Rolf, things were rather bad. We ate later, after I could stand it no longer. He told me he had never gone to a prostitute, never slept with a girl.

9/18/42

[Listened to Frederick Delius] "The walk in the Paradise Gardens"—and I am obsessed by the wonder of what can be done with words, oppressed by the fear that I can never get at it, never create it with words.

SEPTEMBER 19, 1942

A very fine day. I thought of Rosalind about fifty million times. Worked this A.M. Lerner† said he will put me on seeking adver-

---

* Likely refers to the story titled "Miscellaneous" in her archives, published as "The Hollow Oracle" in *Nothing That Meets the Eye: The Uncollected Stories of Patricia Highsmith* (New York, 2002).
† Another employee at F.F.F.

tising (should get a raise if I'm good!) and that the year-book
will have a second edition in January—in which time I hope to
be at Time, Inc. Even if it's pushing a broom.

Me & mother for lunch at Del Pezzo's very pleasant. Man-
icotti. She bought me a blouse ($1 left over) & we saw some
exhibits. Oddly it was [Yves] Tanguy who interested me most.
He's a prophet of what will come, a precursor of decadence. The
small tightly-locked objects in nimbus are mechanico-organic in
shapes suggesting frozen power & movement.

Worked happily on my Christ story.* I have faith in it.

SEPTEMBER 20, 1942

Insufficient reading. I must change my habits or remain a dolt
as to world literature. Rolf came at 2:00. Half sick with la
grippe. Fixed him a hot rum & then we saw the Met's Toulouse-
Lautrec† exhibit of posters. Really exciting, and depressing when
one compares our present magazine covers and cigarette ads.
We went to his place, lay on the bed, where for a half hour all
was fine—perhaps (no doubt) I absorb vicariously some of his
sudden tranquility & happiness. Afterwards—well, I grow self-
conscious or else want something physical to happen (a normal
& purely instinctive half-excitement from proximity) and nothing does happen with Rolf. He is miserable over the fact that he
does not grow excited. One could hardly expect him to function
as an ordinary man after years of opposite habits. He, however,
curses himself, & says he will only make us part unless he can
correct it. Really it is unimportant to me, because I love Rosalind, & want nothing else in the physical sense—really I don't
want her, because I love her in such a beautiful way. The fact is,
I worship her! Home late and dissatisfied. One glimpse of Whitman tonight at Rolf's. Very beautiful.

---

* Probably again "The Hollow Oracle," the story she refers to as her "story of the virgin
mother" above.
† Henri Marie de Toulouse-Lautrec-Monfa (1864–1901), French postimpressionist most
famous for his poster series for the French nightclub Le Moulin Rouge.

SEPTEMBER 21, 1942

Wonderful day. I loafed all morning, writing a good letter to Miss Williams of Time, Inc. Rolf called at 12:00. I do hope he comes around with his little difficulty. Otherwise he will just say goodbye to me. How dreadful it would be to give up Rosalind because of some imaginary or real physical defect when I love her only in an idealistic way. I think almost all the other times I was in love (perhaps indeed all—except for Helen) it was so physical it depresses me to think of it. All the intensity & vanity of Romeo & Juliet. But Rosalind goes on and on. How nice I chose the right words to tell her last year. "I worship you—" nothing else would have done. Called her this afternoon & tho she was busy she made a date with Rolf & me for tomorrow. Read Colette's *Indulgent Husband* which is the rottenest thing I have seen in years! (Saw K. Kingsley in the library 58 St tonight with her mother. We weren't close enough to speak. She looked the same, hair shorter, all a-fluster, red coat. She would have liked to speak to me I know.)

SEPTEMBER 23, 1942

Worked this AM. at the office & picked up Rolf. Del Pezzo's at 12:25 but Rosalind didn't come until one. How proud I was of her today! She's wonderful to look at, wonderful to hear, to touch! And she was exhilarated with the blood-letting and funny as hell. I think she liked Rolf—tho I wish he'd improve his English. He shall, under my tutelage, & I my German.

Very nicely chilly tonight. And [an] air-raid alarm for unidentified plane. Very disobedient people in N.Y. Disgraceful discipline. Read nothing & suffered the ravages of the world. I work & think much better when I am pure from a day of peace alone. One's brain otherwise grows too fast & superficial.

SEPTEMBER 24, 1942

$30.00 in the bank—all saved since my job began. That means also $30 in defense stamps. The war should mean drastic living

changes within a year. Perhaps a better salary will only about
lever it to present standards.

The time has come for me to leave Rolf Tietgens. With effort,
I might think myself in five minutes into the same positive
emotions of a month ago, but of what use is thinking in such
things? The truth comes with uncontrollable emotions, which
I already feel for someone else. With the frightening sagacity of
the "unrelated bystander" Rolf asked me pertinent questions
about Rosalind. He said there was "no chance for me" because
she's superior in age, attainments, thoughts on Weltanschauung,
etc., ᴳall kinds of things that are necessary.ᴳᴳ What do I give her,
when she can get more from older women?—nothing but adoration which always flatters older people, Rolf says. I adore her—
but how bad she is for my frustration complex! It is more simple
to say what living would be without her, perhaps, than to say
what it is now in positives.

Bernard* writes that Mr. Plangman is in a sanatorium & Mrs.
P. is having a "nervous breakdown."

SEPTEMBER 25, 1942

The Russians, who alone are fighting the war, are holding Stalingrad in the thirty-second day of siege. They fight even for possession of the floors of houses!

I have a dreadful cold & can barely breathe or talk. Rolf's
cold. Rolf sold his car to J.J. for $100—He gets $50 & cancella-
tion of 48.00 debt. So we ate royally at lunch at some Hungarian
place that served the now phenomenal six-course meal for .50$!
Later we saw the *Song of Ceylon* at Museum of M.A. Wonderful
memorable stuff. Rolf still wants to see me every day, tho God
knows Rosalind should discourage him!

Read almost nothing, because I feel so lousy. Constructive
revision of my Christ-story however. By the way the Subway
story & "Manuel" bounced today which doesn't discourage me

* Jay Bernard Plangman, Pat's biological father.

at all. Also Mrs. Williams of Time, Inc. sent me a letter, saying she was interested in what I'd been doing, would like to see me & some research, tho they're not enlarging their training staff at present. Shall ask Rosalind does she mean typewritten notes, I suppose so. I feel happy. A long long happiness.

SEPTEMBER 26, 1942

Nice day, after all. Met Rolf at 9:30 at the subway. I read *Mysteries* after we got to J.J.'s, so he thought me very impolite & told me so while we walked. The fact is he is just as difficult as I to get along with & even worse about making concessions to the social graces. We walked in the woods, amazing conversation dealing with *Unterleib* [nether regions]. Nice lunch, & then we tried going to the beach in Rolf's car (now owned by J.J.). The gas ran out in 5 minutes, & after some pushing Dr. Hoffmann brought us home. Rolf & J.J. talked in German in the kitchen, R. told me, & J.J. said what else could you have expected but that she wouldn't love you? It's impossible. So we ate a silent dinner—(Rolf was so isolated he could barely be dragged to the table) & we left in the rain.

9/27/42

Sometimes I feel so much wiser than my body: then I begin to feel wiser than my head, and finally wonder what it is that feels wiser, that is wiser, which brings me once more to the insolvable problem of what am I? I do not believe in happiness or the so-called normalcy as the ideal of human life. People who are "ideally happy" are ideally stupid. Consequently I do not believe in the remedial work of modern psychiatrists. The greatest contribution they could make to the world and to all its posterity would be to leave abnormal people alone to follow their own noses, stars, lodestones, divining rods, phantasies or what have you.

The world is filled with the peas that have rolled down the center of the board into the most full partition. Psychiatrists spend their time trying to push the odd peas over the barrier into the already crowded mean, in order to make mere regular peas to which they sincerely intend to point with pride. I believe that people should be allowed to go the whole hog with their perversions, abnormalities, unhappinesses and construction or destruction. Mad people are the only active people. They have built the world. Mad people, constructive geniuses, should have only enough normal intelligence to enable them to escape the forces that would normalize them.

9/27/42

I have poked so many books into me that I am like an over-stoked oven without a match.

SEPTEMBER 28, 1942

GMy German grandfather died Friday. He was in a sanatorium. Don't know what was wrong. Took a taxi with Rolf to his house with his things. He embraced me, which I don't like one bit. "Is it so repellant?" he asked. Yes, unfortunately!GG

OCTOBER 3, 1942

FA strange day. I worked a lot—not in the morning, but the afternoon! We went to India Shop, where I spotted my next hat—9.75—the price of which mother and I will split. A little hat, like that of a bellboy. Nothing I did today took more than three hours to accomplish. Only Goldberg's poor planning required me to stay at the office.

Rolf phoned me at 5. I didn't want to see him. He got angry at me—was really upset. He called again to tell me that he wanted to see me. At 7. When I got home, tired and sad, I had to lie down for half an hour. Afterwards, he told me what was bothering him: that I've changed, that I've stopped caring about my friends, that nothing will come of this business with R.C. (tho nothing will not come of it!), and that he never wants to see me again if things don't change between us. A long conversation, in which, for some reason, I told him a lot about my physical life, my insecurities and my hopes. He understands. Even though it seems as tho we will never see each other again—at last he understands. I want to accomplish a lot—and though Rolf tells me that I must first become a good person—a great spirit, I want to accomplish a lot, and do so alone, without a man and perhaps without a woman at my side. In the next few years, I will have no need for anyone.[FF]

OCTOBER 4, 1942

[F]A good day. But not my day. Went to the office at 2 pm. A large Polish parade this afternoon, but few spectators. Goldberg and I went to the printer's to look at the proofs. I found mistakes that Goldberg hadn't noticed. Then we ate at the Balkan restaurant. Shish kebab. Goldberg knows how to eat! He told me that he wanted me to write a novel—a large *oeuvre*. I also read the Bible. It's a very good book, the greatest, really. My mother has been thinking a lot about my difficulties since I told her last night that I needed to improve my psyche. And my σῶμα [soma, body] too.[FF]

OCTOBER 5, 1942

[F]Good day. At the office. So many little things I have to get done. At 6 pm I met Rolf outside the building, bought him a cup of coffee, and we went to Wakefield [Gallery]. Rosalind, Natasha, Nickola, Lola P., Mrs. McKeen, Betty (hair like a broom— exhibition was called "The Ballet in Art"). Jane O, whose pictures Rolf likes, was there too. I was largely filled with confusion and very anxious, tho I knew most of the crowd. Howard Putzl there too. Irving Prutman. Rolf didn't like the group. Needless to say: a multitude of homosexuals who were looking at each other more than the artworks. It's true. Betty fills me with dread and discomfort. Rosalind pure and pretty, blonde, clean! How I love her! Jo here, [G]dammit![GG] And we couldn't avoid going back to her place, where we listened to records.[FF]

10/5/42

I walked through a street of brownstones one misty drizzling morning. All the windows black holes except one. There stood a woman, slender, in sweater & belt & skirt, pinning up her short curly hair. I stopped where I was and leaned against a step post. I could not take my eyes from the square of yellow light. I wanted almost uncontrollably to go to her. I wanted to embrace her, feel her heat, smell the fragrance of her body, her hair and her clothing, press the yielding flesh of her arms, I wanted to feel the warm breath of her in my ear and to hear her voice saying affectionate things to me. I could not tear myself away, and to go off to work as I surely had to do, seemed not only painful physically but the most utter insanity. Why? Why must I go? So I stood, and people passed, though very few, and I did not care what they thought of me, I was seized with a paralysis, a nostalgia, a delight, a melancholy, a bewilderment, a fear, a confidence, a certainty, a hope & a despair. I watched her move about the window and I was racked with apprehension lest she go away. And rather than this, to leave me frantic with disappointment and frustration, I turned away my eyes and lifted my feet.

OCTOBER 6, 1942

[F]Worked on unpleasant things. Met up with Rolf at 12:30. After a ten-minute lunch at the Automat I wanted to go by the cobbler's briefly and then to the library to read *Brave N.W.* [*Brave New World*]. "Well, goodbye," he said in parting. "I'll see you when you have some time!" Well, even mother told me that I should be tougher on him. I've never been this severe to a man! But I don't care! A good evening. Finished my story of the madwoman*—the first draft. Life alone is so wonderful! Now, at 21, I know what I need. I want to be alone as often as possible.[FF]

10/6/42

The autobiographical novel is out for me: my childhood & adolescence is a tale told backwards, lighted with will o' the wisps, revealing sporadically decaying corpses and wracked,

---

* Probably still "The Hollow Oracle" she refers to first as the "story of the virgin mother," then as the "Christ story."

impassioned faces hurrying through the night on the way to Somewhere which exists only in their own minds. It is what would be called uneventful, but by no means uninteresting psychologically.

OCTOBER 7, 1942

ᶠWent to see Mrs. Williams at Time, Inc. at 3:30. Shouting at the top of my lungs that I needed to get a job at Time. "Let's stay in touch!" she said, sweeping me out of her office.ᶠᶠ

OCTOBER 9, 1942

ᶠHappy but so tired I can't think about anything important. I met Rosalind in her office, hair pulled back with a barrette. Very pretty, sweet like a girl, and it makes her look slimmer, too. I wanted to have lunch at the Golden Horn and—yes. Rosalind wore her checked suit, I was glad, we're doing better now. She thinks that the letter from Shawn (which I received this morning) is very good. He invited me to write something for Talk of the Town in October. Mr. Shawn runs *The New Yorker*, Rosalind said. So happy at lunch. I wanted to spend all day, all night with her. All my life! Back at the office, where Goldberg told me that I had to work tomorrow. ("Can you work—") When I told him I wanted more money, he told me that Flesch* would give me a raise in two weeks as long as I kept up the work.

Rolf phoned me. Need to kiss him tomorrow. I registered for the primaries at Public School 57. Parents too. Very amusing. I wrote. I worked. But I didn't think one bit.ᶠᶠ

10/9/42

You have pressed upon me your standards: spiritual love, sweetness, poetry, beauty, anarchy besides, however, and irresponsibility, bitterness, some mockery, much arrogance & stubbornness, above all contempt for every man who does not see eye to eye

---

* Dr. Emil Flesch, also at F.F.F. Publications.

with you. You are so painfully right in most cases. It is difficult to deny you. It is difficult not to follow, until one realizes that the following swallows one up like a dust mote in a tornado.

But the fact is, my standards of "love"—(even physical love, yes—which you of all people, were so quick to incorporate into general love) my standards of love, beauty and truth are simply not yours. I do not want the lover who refreshes me with the harmony of his voice, the tones in his throat as he reads me Blake, nor do I want the lover who cleaves unto me, whose heart is my heart, whose soul is ever in communion with mine tho we are apart. Give me rather the lover (or the loved) who drives me mad with the antithesis of all your peace, who is not spiritual except in his most ruthlessly physical moods, who never heard of Blake and doesn't want to—Give me only the beloved with a question and a mystery to solve, who changes faster than I can follow, whose every gesture, breath, movement is an intense delight to me, who leaves me no peace when she is gone. And I defy you to tell me that my beloved is any less spiritual (to me, which is what matters) than yours. And your Jeremiads I grow tired of, and your eternal masculine conceit. Because I do not hate the scientific progress, the shameful mess of 1942 and even the men who now extricate us, you make me feel a compromiser, I am no compromiser. I am not compromising with you now, as I might.

OCTOBER 10, 1942

Exhausted—after thirteen days (& a few evenings) steady labor. Kingsley accosted me on the street. We had coffee & cigarettes in a drugstore, she was quite as usual—asked me no embarrassing questions, told me all about School. Rolf phoned as I came in & after debate (with myself) decided to meet him at 10. I haven't yet read the letter (delivered) which he wanted back again. Disgustingly adolescent writing—which I'd kept to show to Rosalind, and bad would-be Wolfe Lyric (He said he didn't love me tho every fiber, etc—)

OCTOBER 11, 1942

^FWhat a wonderful day! I grew today! A good breakfast. I
worked more calmly than I have in the past three months. I
read my story about the madwoman to M. & S. Mother understands it. But S. said that stories like this are "beyond him!"
Pretty good writing M. thinks. How sweet life is! I finished
Jean Cocteau—*Les Enfants* [*Terribles*]. What a memorable
book! Viva!^{FF}

OCTOBER 12, 1942

^FA letter from Rolf—that he still wants me, and what would he
do without me? He'll yet learn that I don't want to be "owned."
An ordinary day at the office. The world is intruding—and
during the night, I lost yesterday's sense of tranquility. Looked
for ads in magazines. There are some for radios, etc. Gave blood
at 5:30. Very pleasant. Then read Kafka's *The Castle* (from
Rosalind).^{FF} Very good—and imaginative—very tired. The flesh
is weak.

OCTOBER 13, 1942

^FNever before have I been so enraptured with my life! It's quite
an impersonal sensation. It comes when I am alone or with
someone, when I am reading a splendid book, looking at an
imaginative image, or listening to good music. It came today,
with fantastic and sustained force, when I was listening to
"Sheep May Safely Graze" by J. S. Bach in a music shop during
my lunch hour. It came on even more strongly when I read a
page in *Mysticism* by [Evelyn] Underhill. It's my faith—it's my
life. There is nothing but art.

Another ordinary day at the office. Miss Weick was moved
to the other office. I'm with Goldberg, around whom I can't
smoke as much as I'd like. I am filled with inexpressible happiness. Yet it is sadness too. It is much greater than I. I do not
concern myself with my own person: only with my aspirations, my desires, my work. I concern myself with the things
I love.^{FF}

OCTOBER 14, 1942

Very happy indeed. Had a hamburger at the old White Tower on
Greenwich, & went for a stroll down Eighth Street looking with
new ideas (since Rolf, since my job, since finding out more truths
this past month) & then to the Music Shop. No [Bach cantata]
"Wer mir behagt," but did meet a ᶠyoung Jewish man,ᶠᶠ who
was very helpful. Offered to give me his superior record now
unobtainable. We saw the Whitney [exhibit] together. A marvelous painting of Philip Evergood's called *Lily & the Sparrows*.
Then to gramophone shop with my friend whose name is Louis
Weber, 9 W. 97 St. He wants to bring over records to play Monday night. Shall ask Marjorie. I love all things—I received happy
thoughts. In some way I am walking with God these days.

OCTOBER 15, 1942

Very tough day. Goldberg talks—anecdotes—so much we never
get any work done & consequently had to work tonight. Herr
Goldberg came home with me—afoot—at 12 midnight, carrying my books.

OCTOBER 16, 1942

ᶠAn alcoholic day. Alice T. at 1:00. We ate at Castille—very
crowded and full, very hot. They are not serving martinis by
the carafe yet. She was astounded that I knew so many "important" people who are older than me. Drank two martinis with
Valerie Adams at the Hôtel Pierre. She knows Kay Boyle—
P. Guggenheim—le Paris. Wanted to bring me with her to the
Guggenheims. Also, a matter which disgusts me—Kingsley told
her that I was (now) obsessed with a woman—"a woman older
than me." It's the most recent mistake—it's the sin which cannot be forgiven, and though there are many things we have forgiven each other for—this is impossible. What can silence her?
Do I have to shoot her? With Billie B. at W. Fair tonight. Drank
quite a bit. Didn't see a single person, man or woman, who
seemed to me intelligent, spiritual, perfect—no one. I have had
my fill of drinks and parties for a year.ᶠᶠ

OCTOBER 17, 1942

[F]Bad day. Worked hard all day, didn't go to see any exhibitions with mother, didn't even manage to brush my teeth because of the booze last night, couldn't do any good work because I'm not being paid what I'm owed—I should have received 1½ for my overtime. I'm angry, furious! But I was a schoolgirl and did nothing—

Jeva phoned me at 8:30. Very sweet—would like to stay with her—no matter where. Bought shoes—which cost all my money—have only $4.00 to get through next week. It torments Flesch so when one asks him for money!

I bought a philodendron—green, tranquil, patient. Unlike me. I'm miserable.[FF]

OCTOBER 18, 1942

Worked comparatively little on my story but ended second draft. The next I may show to Goldberg. It should be good. Then I'll make over what few things I've done since school, & then perhaps start the novel.

The injustice of my employers oppresses me. I shall leave as soon as possible but first I'll write a letter saying Mr. Flesch had better employ only those unacquainted with the Wagner Act.[*] I should also like to tell Kingsley just what I think of her soon.

There is so much beauty—and I shall see it tomorrow—standing waiting for a light, reading a snatched page in the library tomorrow—and today it was so hard to open my work-benighted eyes.

OCTOBER 19, 1942

[F]Very nervous and very awake. Spoke to Goldberg about my assignments. I was so confident and so calm that he couldn't help but acquiesce—I will receive my overtime instead of a raise.

Saw Rolf Tietgens at 2. Coffee at Caruso's, like the first

---

[*] The National Labor Relations Act of 1935, also known as the Wagner Act, affirmed workers' rights to organize and engage in collective bargaining, or to refrain from such activities.

time. The idiot told Bernhard that "we are no longer as close as before."

A wonderful evening! Louis Weber came by early, we played his "Sheep May Safely Graze" which he gave me. Louis asked for some of my stories. I gave them to him. He particularly liked the "Silver Horn" which he read here. He observed me closely tonight, saying that I was very complicated, important—that I've got "the stuff." But he's very strange. He must live quite alone, of that I'm sure.

P.S. Bernhard phoned me at 9:00. Wants to see me—Thursday night. I'm very nervous about seeing her again—I was just regaining my sanity.[FF]

OCTOBER 20, 1942

Spoke to Rosalind this A.M. Told her I'm broke for lunch. She said make it Fri.—she wouldn't be broke. Bad precedent, I say—

My tooth—the one that gave trouble last summer in California—is hurting again. Consequently I can't receive any communications from the misty lands or see pictures reflected in the mountain lakes of warm water. I am here—with my lousy tooth. I wish it were out—I see the drench of blood and pus, and feel the terrible blessed relief, the bitter hole in my face, and the relaxation of my brows that have been taut for weeks.

OCTOBER 21, 1942

[F]With mother at Pete's for dinner—how I dreamed of taking mother out in the evenings once I had some money. Saw a very good dance performance. Oh—my God! What a woman Jean Erdman is!![*] Tall, slender (but not too slender!), an intelligent and smiling mouth. What legs, what a waist! We sat in the first row—only a few feet away. I would have loved to go backstage and tell her how I felt about her art! It was dangerous tho, mother might have noticed something.[FF]

---

* Jean Erdman (1916–2020), American modern dancer and choreographer.

OCTOBER 22, 1942

Very late. Read in Library & got caught in first daylight air-raid drill.

Dentist at 3:15—one Ralph Miller, of third rate intelligence, who did "spot-drilling" on this damned upper right & told me the wisdom tooth was pushing the others out of line. $1.00 it still hurts. Worked some this evening, though I go slowly & need much tranquil times. Went to see Bernhard at 9:30 at 155 E. 56—her new address. Rather monkish, one room. She in bed drinking Rock 'n' Rye. Pajamas. She is filled with this "stinko affair" of Rolf's & mine—how we "fled" very indecently—etc. that killed—10–11 o'clock came & still the same subject. So I said if she asked me to come to criticize me she didn't need to because the story had preceded me wherever I've been the last four months. So she grew more friendly. I had shattered her unwise, uncalled for trust, but we might begin from beginning. So—she has a show next Wednesday—and I'm to go—& the evening, too. Not much time in sight & I have a great project in mind.

OCTOBER 23, 1942

[F]A wonderful day! Lunch with Rosalind at 12:30. She gave me advice on my hair—I've got to cut it. Yes, it's done now. We discussed art. Then went to Petit Français to see the Surrealist exhibit. It was marvelous! Tanguy, Chagall, Ernst, Berlioz, Lamy, Matta all well-represented. Also a woman, Leonora Carrington,[*] in whom R. is very interested. Rosalind put a safety pin on one of the nails of Picasso's guitar. We laughed! How I love her! She's always this happy on Fridays because she goes away with Betty on the weekends. It's sad—I suppose. But I'm happy when she is. This is how much I love her.[FF]

OCTOBER 24, 1942

I am happy. Put 45.00 in bank. Goldberg there, Flesch & Lerner worried at my working, lest I request more money! Saw Rolf.

---

* Leonora Carrington (1917–2011), British-Mexican surrealist painter and novelist.

Disgusting behavior, more psychopathic, more neurotic because he has been living alone now. [Dr.] Dobrow's for a filling. He talked more intelligently—I favor the young dentists if they already know enough.

Jack here at 7:45. Rather nice after all. He is so terribly in love with me, and furthermore knows what to do about it, which is more than I can say of Rolf. We saw a Spanish theater vaudeville at 116. Bus ride. Then home for Bach, coffee & cake. He kissed me most passionately—I shouldn't mind sleeping with him. I might enjoy it—knowing he would so. He's been "rolling around" with all manner of femmes in Manhattan in the last months.

I am filled with confidence & ideas!

10/24/42

And Sunday afternoons I shall go alone and take a golden chariot ride through Central Park. The people will be amorphous subaqueous organisms, suspended in gelatinous depths, or swaying gently upon their pedicles. I shall be able to see their entrails working and pulsing and changing color from red to green to chartreuse. The museums, the zoos will be as castles in a goldfish bowl, and though I do not swim through them, I shall pass through them in my chariot at the same time viewing them from the outside. The park itself will be sunken deep, and only the gray Sunday sky will border its furthest treetops. I shall converse with whom I will, with Phaeton first for courtesy, with the molecules of air I shall exchange pleasantries, with the trees I will hum cantatas, with the rocks of the hillocks I will argue and contest the probability of immortality and the proving of emancipation. I shall make colors, and no colors, sounds and no sounds, at my will, for I shall have the power, being able to imagine these things.

OCTOBER 25, 1942

ᶠRe-read my story of the madwoman. It's very good, but needs another 24h—straight.

With Rolf 2–6:30. He took 12 photographs—several nudes.
He gave me books, and we ate at Fish Place—3rd Ave. It's more
pleasant now, when he expects nothing of me.[FF]

OCTOBER 27, 1942

[G]I'm so tired, so melancholy, so dissatisfied. Saw Rolf at 5:45.
The photographs are good. We sat over coffee and looked at
the pictures. Later went to the Guggenheim Museum, which
beyond doubt houses the city's best pictures. All sorts of Surrealist artists, but especially Paul Klee, Ernst, Miró, de Chirico.
Then Jack B. came over, just to pick up a book he'd left behind.
(He stayed for several hours, though!) We listened to Bach,
Mozart, Beethoven. He leant me *Jesu, der du meine Seele*. But
I want to work. Always, and in order to fall asleep tonight, I
vowed in writing to go out just once a week now. That alone
will hold things together—make me healthy and happy. Otherwise I'm most terribly beat down, oppressed, and neglectful
of my own soul. How I need Rosalind! Where in the world do
I find beauty but in Rosalind! Whom do I truly and actually
love but Rosalind! Who wishes not to see me but Rosalind! I'm
a fool not to spend more time with her. She is my heart, my
spiritual bread and water—and sometimes, though only in my
mind, she is my sin, my escape, but in my soul my one love and
lover forever and ever![GG]

OCTOBER 28, 1942

[G]I'm driven quite mad by these nights without rest and solitude
upon which the sheep of my soul graze. My heart is so full, it
breaks in two, and the pretty jewels and fantasies are like poison in my veins.[GG] Went to Laboratory Institute at 6:00 & was
offered all tea, coffee & whiskey—I took the latter as any man
of spirit. When B. came I'd had 2 & had 3 before leaving. Bernhard's pictures looked better than ever. We had a drink—me
one too many. So Bernhard said let's go to her place a while.
(Why I can't imagine!) And I soon got sick. Had to stay. Bernhard wonderful to me, fetching this & that. She must love me

so passionately—well with a certain passion that is not entirely physical, & yet which hasn't let itself go yet either.

OCTOBER 29, 1942

Woke up with slight headache. Should have liked to have breakfast with B. but I scrammed at 8:10. The worst thing is facing the elevator boys, who've learned not to bat an eye. Showered & went to work. I think about the adolescent novel. I am neurotic & young enough to write from memory & autobiography and most of all love! *Liebe! Amor! Amore—amour!* ἀγάπη.

Saw Mr. Shawn of the *New Yorker* who very courteously gave me two assignments to prepare for Talk of the Town rewrite man—good stuff—& the secretary took my jobs on the list. Real McCoy. Perhaps no duplicates. Read Sir Thos. Browne—who said tonight: "All things are artificial, for nature is the Art of God."*

OCTOBER 30, 1942

FA good day. Not a lot of work at the office—Goldberg even told me I could work on my stories, but warned me not to read any books, because Flesch noticed that once. Went to see Rosalind in a red shirt, straight hair. She saw Lola P. last night, who's separated from Del. Mutual agreement. Lola is writing surreal stories now. Rosalind and I discussed stream of consciousness in [Dorothy] Richardson,† whom she doesn't know, Kafka, lots of things. I asked her what she thought about a novel about teenagers—15–18 years old? "Well, it's like saying what about a novel on marriage?—Sure—Sure fire stuff." But then I told her what I want to do with my characters—it will be better than Daly‡—of course.FF "There should be something said on what the younger generation is thinking—" That's not what I'd write

* Quotation from *Religio Medici* (London, 1643).
† The English author Dorothy Richardson (1873–1957) is credited with having written one of the first stream-of-consciousness novels.
‡ Maureen Daly (1921–2006), Irish-born American writer best known for her 1942 novel *Seventeenth Summer*, which she wrote while still in her teens.

on though & she knows it. I watched her in the bank, where she goes always on Fridays—and she looked very masculine, very gay. Something in the lie of her hair, the squint of her eye. And gosh she can flash a gay smile occasionally! I wonder why she doesn't ask me to their place sometime? I wonder xmas? I wonder my birthday? I wonder ever?

OCTOBER 31, 1942

[F]I am happy, but not very happy—it's as if I'd fallen asleep under an open sky. I am filled with my novel—the teenagers, but there is nothing to write in my notebook—I haven't thought it through yet. It's funny.

I'd like to have time and more time.

I'd like to do everything, lots of things both in my head and out of it.

I'm walking on tiptoes through a world full of traps.[FF]

10/31/42

Sometimes she would see only women friends for weeks at a time. She would say: "I am happy. This is my world," or she would grow disgusted with the recognition of their shortcomings and say: "I have nothing to do with this." Then she would have weeks of masculine company—when she would be the only girl in a house full of homosexual men & boys, each more intelligent, more attractive and beautiful really than the women, and certainly more honest with each other. "This is my world. Here people are square with no vanities," she would say (for indeed the homosexuals she knew were not of the vainer type). But both these conditions palling, switching, palling, she had only to conclude that neither world was "hers" but that hers was a separate world. In short, she could never find her social milieu, and knew even at twenty that she never could. She was quite right, unfortunately.

11/1/42

Night writing—Certainly all younger writers should write at night, when the conscious brain (the critical faculty) is tired.

Then the subconscious has its way and the writing is uninhibited. Even older writers feel some of this—those who either are not good enough to escape self-criticism (of the hyper sort) or who have found no release in their conscious minds, or perhaps those who have pleasant memories of explorative days when they were learning to write.

NOVEMBER 2, 1942

[F]What an excitement! Miss Weick quit today! She couldn't get her typewriter to work, and Lerner was calling her "stupid." Well—she got everything off her chest that had been bothering her for two months—and quit—simply marched out of the office! I addressed envelopes all morning. Goldberg invited me to lunch. I gave him my story about the madwoman, and he told me that I was trying to write in the most difficult fashion—the analytic kind—that the great writers use. That's what interests me; what am I supposed to do about it? This story is really very tricky, because I don't want to write more simply, make it easier. I will move on to other things—as usual.[FF]

NOVEMBER 3, 1942

[F]With [Dr.] Dobrow who was very rude. Because I asked him questions, he accused me of wanting to lecture him about his job! It's ridiculous! I can't go back again. I left, smoking a cigarette. Voted for the first time this morning at 10. Israel Amter made the primary, Flynn, Davis, Poletti, etc. Most are ALP.[*]

I began the story about the hotel to which people who are about to die go.[FF]

NOVEMBER 4, 1942

[F]A good day. I did much more of my own work than that of F.F.F. Went to Brentano's [bookstore] at 10:30. They'll add the

---

[*] American Labor Party. Both federal and New York State elections were held on November 3, 1942. Israel Amter, Elizabeth Gurley Flynn, and Benjamin Davis Jr. were candidates for the Communist Party.

J.F.A. [*Jewish Family Almanac*] to their stock. If they consider it a periodical. Then back to the office, where I addressed envelopes—but not for too long. No letters. I wrote my piece on undergarments for *The New Yorker*. Not finished yet.[FF]

11/4/42

Preface to *The Book of Pleasant Things*.

I am writing a book of pleasant things because I am so long and so deeply convinced that all things, and by this I mean everything, in the world is not pleasant. If it is pleasant for a time, it is unpleasant eventually by our having to leave it soon, or by invidious comparison which all humans make with something better. Melancholy and pessimism, coupled with a kind and generous heart and a broad mind, are the noblest virtues of man. They let him sink to the depths of himself, no less interesting or splendid than the heights, and they let him taste heavenly delights when he finds their shadows in matters here on earth.

NOVEMBER 5, 1942

[F]A good day—spent all day thinking of the evening with Rosalind. She came at 7:10. We drank—martinis for me, tomato juice for her, prepared by mother. She was so beautiful. She didn't like the pictures on my walls, or my bathroom. And didn't care for Rolf's photographs.[FF] She scarcely listened to my Bach, which I had so anticipated—both her not listening, and my listening with her. [F]I drank too much, which I don't want to do again. We ate at Petit Paris. I paid too much for everything.[FF] "You shouldn't drink so much. Betty & I both think you drink too much—it's slightly sordid—a good-looking kid like you—" We said good night—and I dared kiss her on the cheek—God knows if she minded. I don't know.

NOVEMBER 7, 1942

Splendid day. Tho I'm going to bed disastrously late, I got fired at 11:25 today. No notice—Flesch never heard of it. I must say I'm glad. Goldberg is sympathetic. Flesch told me no more writ-

ing is necessary, etc. Bought Marjorie Thompson a drink at the
Mansfield [Hotel], and we saw Bacon's show* with mother. Simply wonderful and with the energy & concentration of a man—
some of it. Then tea & the Guggenheim once more, where sat
Peggy & the dog, too. Talked to Kiesler.† Very nice.

NOVEMBER 8, 1942
Fine day. I worked hard on *New Yorker* & will be able to show
it tomorrow. Saw Rolf at 5. We talked—he says he doesn't love
me anymore, would like to kiss me however. I am very cold, and
do not trouble sufficiently to analyze him. As always, he said the
crucial thing of me—that I must write what I have experienced,
and leave imaginary stories be until I am strong enough to inject
life into them. After indecisions (which are characteristic of both
of us German, stubborn, egocentric and undersexed people) we
went to Petit Paris & had tenderloin steaks, & white wine.

NOVEMBER 9, 1942
Lunched with Bernhard, which she unfortunately couldn't pay
for as scheduled. I have $6.00 & shall have to go into my bank
account, which hurts like I can't say. Also applied for unemployment insurance.
    I shall be once more the person I was at fourteen & fifteen
& partially sixteen—alive & capable of loving and losing, too.
Imaginative and full of lyricism, the intellect only awakening,
& in no danger of exerting its throttling control. This question
of "What do I feel?" is at the root of all: It affects my writing,
my expression, my happiness, and depends on my food intake,
physical habits, etc. I should a) correct menstruation b) think
about normal things instead of morbid, even impersonal intro-
spections c) never think of myself except in regard to finding my
emotional responses, and expressing them d) get over the Rosa-

---

* Francis Bacon (1909–1992) would become Pat's favorite painter.
† Frederick John Kiesler (1890–1965), Austrian-American architect, theater and exhibition
designer, artist, and sculptor.

lind crush, and not regard it as an established course which must be followed e) say to Bernhard freely all the affection I feel for her so often f) write only lyrical stuff for a long while g) examine my journals at 14–20 and see what and why—above all I must believe, as I surely do, that sexual experience at my age is not absolutely necessary, and that many normal people, even geniuses, had not had it at my age, that I can come to the Golden age once more with faith in myself. I carry always this feeling that some day the cloud will lift, as it does when one studies uncomprehendingly mathematics for a long while, and then one day comes the revelation. So it will—or perhaps already has come to me. Then Rosalind and Bernhard will take their proper places, dependent on their characters—both excellent—and not upon me, unless I am truly in love with one of them.

NOVEMBER 10, 1942

^{F}I worked on my *N.Y.* [*New Yorker*] assignment and finally sent it off. Sent the *Jewish Family Almanac* to grandmother. Pretty funny. I sang today while I was walking in the rain—I was singing Bach. And it was as if I was in love. The rain, wet shoes, the cold, the effort of walking didn't matter to me at all. Am happy. Have lots of wonderful things to do.^{FF}

NOVEMBER 11, 1942

^{F}Rosalind said she'd have lunch with me on Friday. That's good, because I must see her before leaving the city that night. I don't want to sleep with R.B. Naturally, however, they will put us in the same bedroom. Oh! If only Rosalind would take me! If only she would change her mind! How much longer can she stay with someone like Betty? I did nothing much today except write a long story in my notebook about my confused and confusing life for an indifferent posterity. Mr. Shawn received my work today. No one can know how much trepidation I feel— did I say enough, etc.? Mother is worried because she thinks

that the letters I write to Gramma are not "warm" enough.
Gramma gives me 5.00 a week. I need it badly. It would be
good if the *New Yorker* were also to pay me, but it makes no
difference. The Germans are marching through France. Marseille has been occupied tonight. The Americans took Africa—
without fighting, and the French flotilla coming from Toulon
just joined the allies. Everything is all right. Also, the people to
whom I wrote the letter on Sunday phoned me to schedule an
interview.

I read *Christian Morals* and *Letter to a Friend* by Sir Thos.
Browne.^{FF}

11/11/42

I feel the multitudinous conceivings of my brain clamoring, from
time to time, like molecules of steam under a pot lid. They make
a steady din. I do not hope for one so big as to blow the lid off. I
must do that myself. I wish I knew the engineering.

NOVEMBER 12, 1942

^FLunch with Goldberg at Café Raffier. After I hinted at drinks
once or twice, he asked for a martini and an Old Fashioned—
then another round halfway through the meal. Not bad! He said
my novel is a good idea, it could be sold (!) after or during the
war. Am happy. Except that I want to work. I continued working on my story at home. I'll show it to *The New Yorker*. It will
be good. My story of the year—my best story since "Heroine"
and "Silver Horn." The idea's not so great or different, but it's
better written. Tonight at home—I thought in my darkened
room about my teenage novel, and I began a notebook especially
on this subject.[*]

I've written enough for today. My head keeps working when I
am alone here, with nothing "to do" in the world outside.^{FF}

---

* This specific notebook was lost.

NOVEMBER 14, 1942

[F]Bernhard [and I] left at 11:15. The house in Westport, Conn. belongs to Ms. Beecroft, who lives all alone except for an aunt who may die at any moment. The aunt lives in the room upstairs and lies in bed in a coma. Ms. Beecroft never smiles. We are being fed a lot, and Bernhard's appetite is astounding!

Terribly cold! It's impossible to take a walk on the beach. The water is not far from the house. There is a dog here, Toby, and death, the person upstairs. I am growing sick of Bernhard's egotism. One puts up with it because she is an artist, but after 24 hours it becomes unbearable! I was cold despite myself when we went to bed and I had no desire to kiss her. It's too bad, because she paid for me—and I gave her nothing in return. Anyway, it was really too cold to make love—we slept in all our clothes![FF]

NOVEMBER 15, 1942

[F]I was hungry all day. An egg, toast, and ersatz coffee this morning. One night, then back home. Am very happy, even though I have nothing to do in the city, no means to make a living! I wrote a long letter to R. Constable. Drawings—of the house with the apple tree, of our hostess, of the dying aunt, of our tour on the beach, and ten small scenes of our non-amorous night. I hope they will amuse her.[FF]

NOVEMBER 16, 1942

[F]Woke up very anxious—nothing to do—except find a job. With Rolf 3–6. Several photographs, no clothes, and my face. A letter (note) from M. Clark at *Bow*, to whom I sent my "Silver Horn." Recommended I send it to *Parade*,[*] which I did. She's interested in my work, etc. A ray of sunshine which made me happy— writers work so hard![FF]

---

* *Parade*, a weekly Sunday supplement to more than seven hundred American newspapers starting in 1941.

NOVEMBER 17, 1942

^FStill have nothing to do: for money. Called up Shawn—his secretary told me that he'll doubtlessly call me soon. Successfully repaired two mirrors at home. When one has nothing to do, one works like a farmer. Went for a stroll 2–4. I'm not eligible for unemployment—I didn't work long enough. Saw J. Stern* on 57 St. around the Ferargil Galleries. Spoke to me. Didn't read enough this week.^{FF}

NOVEMBER 18, 1942

^FBig day! Worked and finished another draft of "Manuel." Then went out for a stroll. Bernhard called me to say that she was let go from [Norman] Bel Geddes.^{†FF} Goldberg has a part time job for me. $15 a week, possibly tomorrow. Very nice half evening at home. I read much in Blake, which stimulates me to do wonderful things, generally unrelated to Blake.

11/18/42

The homosexual man seeks his equal or seeks a young man whom he may educate to his equal of intellect and appreciation. This is the ideal, spiritual homosexual. The Lesbian, the classic Lesbian, never seeks her equal. She is Vala,[‡] the corporeal understanding, the *soi-disant* male, who does not expect his match in his mate, who would rather use her as the base-on-the-earth which he can never be.

NOVEMBER 19, 1942

Excitement. At 42 St. at 10:45. The office is that overtaxed building, 55 W. on the 7th floor. In room 724 five people hover frantically around one desk, one English typewriter & one Yiddish typewriter. I had to see one Rudko, or Miss Milanov, etc.

---

* James Stern (1904–1993), Anglo-Irish writer of short stories and nonfiction.
† Norman Bel Geddes (1893–1958), American stage and industrial designer.
‡ A term from Germanic mythology for a female shaman and seeress.

program for Nov. 29 in Carnegie. Nuts! Anyhow—I couldn't keep the lunch date with R.C. But a Miss Todd of Time, Inc. phoned—Mrs. Williams wants to see me tomorrow at 11:00. A job? Who knows?

Unger, who haunts the office gratuitously, is frantic to have me stay on & do English publicity. I am definitely no longer unemployed.

NOVEMBER 20, 1942

[F]A good day—but very tiring. Time, Inc at 11:30. Mrs. Williams doesn't have a job for me—but she and Mrs. Fraser are very interested in the young women who haven't yet come to work at Time, Inc. I told her that I'm also working for the *New Yorker*. Then I phoned Rosalind. She said there was a job at *Harper's Bazaar*. They offered it to her, but she didn't want it. They're looking for two inexperienced girls or a genius—Rosalind.[FF]

11/20/42

Guilty sensations on first drinking alone are easily overcome. The second sensations are those of quiet conviviality—with one's self. All the joys of society, says the introvert, with none of its hideous faces! How can one be happy in New York when all the bad people are merely evil, and all the good people merely compromisers?

NOVEMBER 22, 1942

[F]Good day. Am tired after 5 hours of sleep, but I wrote the best draft of "Manuel" so far. Then I read a bit of *Varouna*. He makes me happy—[Julien] Green writes about things I like, and which make me feel lofty! M. [Marjorie] Wolf came at 3. Went with her to St. Bartholomew's to hear [Bach's] "Brich dem Hungrigen sein Brot," but the words were in English, singers timid & few. An up and down in the service—Episcopalian. We drank 2 martinis at Mario's, then went home for dinner. M.

talked civilly with the parents at the table, discussed the Negro question, the people of the South, etc. One listens to her—she has real warmth, a truly human heart, I like her a lot. All alone in the room, we listened, in the shadows, to [two Bach cantatas] "Jesu, der du meine Seele," and "Schafe können sicher [weiden"]," holding hands, perhaps desiring to do more. It was very strange! She'd like to live with me—would like to leave her mother—slip out if she doesn't let her. In truth, I imagine she might be a better companion than Bernhard. But I can't do anything else unless we come to an agreement.[FF]

NOVEMBER 24, 1942

[F]I am very happy today because I spoke to Rosalind on the phone. She almost smiled at me. The women from *Harper's* would like to see me—I can use her name. "You don't have to look too fancy. But look your best." She would also like to go to the swing concerts at Town Hall. (I wanted to take her to Cherry Lane[*] Friday night.) Worked a lot and well this evening, then made a small card for Virginia on the occasion of our anniversary—Thanksgiving—four years! Four years since I laid eyes on her for the first time!

I do not spend enough time thinking when I write. I have a surfeit of ideas and good ideas, but it takes so long to get from them to their actualization. I must change my life.[FF]

NOVEMBER 25, 1942

[F]A marvelous time with Bernhard at Del Pezzo, where Christopher Morley[†] was eating a few tables from us. Then we went to see the men who make puppets—marionettes. They are interesting, and like all men who make their livings in New York's nocturnal establishments, they have turned their work into an art

---

[*] Cherry Lane Theatre, located in Greenwich Village, is the longest-running off-Broadway theater.

[†] Christopher Morley (1890–1957), American writer, editor, and cofounder of the *Saturday Review*.

par excellence. Now at Sons of Fun* and the Rainbow Room. They're both gay, of course.

It's still raining gently, and I walked through the streets after having read a few pages of Kay Boyle in the library. How she writes! So light, but so heavy with meaning! Intelligent and simple people, in old English houses, women who dress like men, who eat eggs while standing in front of the fireplace. Orgies full of sex!

I'd like to write with more lyricism, but I find this quite difficult—the way I find telling my thoughts to Rosalind, or to anyone, difficult. I am constrained. Back at home with Jo P. at 11. We drank coffee and listened to "Schafe können sicher weiden." And "Jesu." She appreciates them, just as I appreciate her records. It's true friendship.[FF]

NOVEMBER 26, 1942

[F]Very anxious. Sometimes I wait all day for those rare moments in which I feel at peace. I'm destroying myself, I know. I'd like to have a corner of my room that's peaceful, where I can write very slowly, and I have one! But whenever I possess something—it loses its value. Office at 10. No one on the streets except for countless British marines, strolling, looking for Times Square, wondering what to do on this peaceful day. Took several letters to the offices in Canal St. in the dirty buildings where the Jewish newspapers have their headquarters. It's disgusting.

Jo P. at 7:45 for dinner with us at the Jumble Shop. Was happy tonight. Gave small presents to the family. Dinner was good. Afterwards, Jo came back home with us. I wanted to kiss her. I am at peace with her, because she makes me live in the moment: neither ahead of time, nor behind. More importantly: lots of notes on my novel after 12.[FF]

---

* The musical revue *Sons o' Fun* ran from 1941 to 1943 and starred comedy duo Olsen & Johnson.

NOVEMBER 27, 1942

^FA sparkling day—a marvelous lunch with Rosalind. We ate at the Golden Horn, both of us starving, and laughed at everything. She's expecting great things of me.—Are you working on your novel? (Yes.) The photographs Rolf took of me are good. I was at 8 St with him until 10, because every appointment with Rolf takes the whole evening! Bernhard here at 11:30 when I told her I had photographs by Rolf. She likes them. But she thinks she could do better. I kissed her with pleasure at my door at 1:30. I would have preferred to kiss Rosalind! How I loved Rosalind today!^{FF}

NOVEMBER 28, 1942

^FRead a bit more of my journals. I have to read a lot before writing. In any case, I'm almost certain that one must write good stories first. I saw a piece of luggage left behind on the subway platform. I wrote a story about it.[*] Am happy. Bernhard gave me one of her pictures. A less sexual photograph, for my room.^{FF}

NOVEMBER 29, 1942

^FWrote on my new story about the paralytic and the man who looks like Paley.[†] It will be good—an action-packed story—they find a piece of luggage together—and tonight I wrote half of it by hand, lying on my bed. One must always allow the blood of a story, its muscles, to come naturally into one's mind, without thinking about it. Then it will be good.

The family confronted me about all of my current and former faults, with S. saying that I hadn't improved much since 1935. And "You are not being honest or natural to yourself." Exactly what I told myself three years ago! If only they knew! How different I had to appear from what I wanted! It's no wonder I'm repressed.

I'm smoking too much on Sundays. I'm smoking now. What does it matter? I can't think of one good reason why not.^{FF}

---

[*] She begins work on the short story that will be published as "Uncertain Treasure" in 1943.
[†] One of her colleagues at F.F.F. who inspired her in the writing of "Uncertain Treasure."

11/30/42

Shall I give her the Romantic Symphony for Christmas?—or will she, English like, think it sentimental, hearing an occasional phrase as she lights a cigarette, pours another's drink—shall she miss all that I love, even with her intelligent eyes, her polite ears? I could not stand that. And yet here I sit, listening at this second, and hearing all the deep reds, the rich purples, the autumnal yellows, and burnt oranges, the crisp winds, the warm bricks of the fireplace that we shall never share, that I can never give her except in a piece of music, which she may fail really to hear.

DECEMBER 1, 1942

FStrange. Many ideas yesterday. Today: nothing! Went to the library this morning to read *Harper's Bazaar*. It's been around since 1867! Then *Harper's* at 3:30. McFadden made me wait. She's quick, not very chic, but intelligent of course. She'd like to see several of my stories. It makes me happy, because they're the most significant ones—"Heroine," "Mighty Nice Man," "Silver Horn," etc. Mr. Alford at *Modern Baby* offered me work this week (typist stuff) while his daughter is getting married. How much will he pay me? Don't know. At least $20.00, so I could take Rosalind out Friday night.FF

12/2/42

What to do with homosexuality? The transformation of the material is utterly impossible—unless one changes the characters to be abnormally inhibited, so that such things hold all the excitement, the forbidden piquancy of the true first feelings. This makes, generally, a sexual weakling, a schizophrene, an inhibited suppressed person of a vigorous one.

DECEMBER 3, 1942

FAnother sleepy day after 8 hours' sleep—for the third day in a row! Don't know what to do! I'm fortified against the wind, can resist the cold, and I'm never hungry. I'm so busy that ideas aren't coming easily, quickly, the way they do when I am calmer

during the day, like a true artist. But they're still there. Phoned
Rosalind. She laughed when I told her I was working for *Modern Baby*. "It's good training for you?" (Yes, but what isn't?)[FF]

12/3/42
The effect of sleeping—logginess, mediocrity, absence of excitement & pleasure of hunger, absence of dreams, ideas, greater
reality unpleasant. Effects of not sleeping—unreality. Mañana
complex, dreams and fancies, hunger, always physical consciousness of some kind pleasant to the ego-centered.

DECEMBER 4, 1942
[F]Last day at *Modern Baby*, thank God! They only paid me 10.00,
which is $3 less than what the union stipulates. Paid my dentist,
and I have two dollars left after three days' work. My Christmas
present would be a job at *Harper's Bazaar*. I'd like a steady job.
    I worked well tonight, which made me happy as usual.
Ecstatic! And how!
    Big discussion tonight after the parents came home from
the movies. They don't like Tietgens' pictures. Janie found one
today—and mother was embarrassed—frightfully embarrassed!
"It's awful. Neither man nor woman! I don't want them on my
walls! Not even on yours!" And that her life is terrible because
I'm at home, and that she'd be better off if I were gone. Well, as
soon as I find a steady job, I'm gone![FF]

DECEMBER 5, 1942
[F]Saw the Alajalov[*] exhibition with mother at 5. Greta Garbo[†]
was there, wearing brown suede shoes, with her shopping bags

---

* Constantin Alajálov (1900–1987), Armenian-American illustrator and painter best known
for designing the covers of publications such as the *Saturday Evening Post*, *Vanity Fair*,
Fortune, *Life*, *Harper's Bazaar*, and *Vogue*.
† Pat was a lifelong admirer of Swedish-American actress Greta Garbo (1905–1990). In a
tribute published after the actress's death, "My Life with Greta Garbo," published in the
Oldie on April 3, 1992, Pat remembers stalking Garbo on the streets of Manhattan, once
almost colliding with her on a corner. Garbo was part of the Sewing Circle, a clandestine
association of lesbian and bisexual women in Hollywood.

and a big hat to hide her face. But she was still so frightfully beautiful!

I made a big decision tonight: I will buy Rosalind a music box for Christmas. I must give her something that no one else will give her. Buffie came by at 7:30, looking very pretty. Went with her to Nino & Nella, Peter and Helen weren't there. Neither was Bing Crosby, thank God. There were two drunk women, one had lost her son in Africa. Very sad, really. What can I do with this story? On 6th Ave. we browsed through the bookshops, bought books, records, etc! What a music shop! where boys and girls listen to great, exciting swing shift records after midnight. At Tony's 52 St (who sings Italian songs while standing on his head)* we saw several of Buffie's friends, the kind who come up to you saying loudly "the last time I saw you was in Paris." It disgusts me. I wasted far too much money frolicking about with her tonight—$5 and I don't have a job right now. And the music box for Rosalind will cost $35.00. Oh, I'll be a miser for the next few weeks!!

Kingsley called me—very calm and quiet. Would like to have lunch Tues. at 12:30. The traitor! Would like to write Jeannot[†] but I might endanger him because the Germans are there now and looking for Allied sympathizers.

Quarter to four![FF]

DECEMBER 6, 1942

[F]Ate a lot and worked a lot and wrote perhaps the best story of my life. It doesn't have a name yet, but I'll find an excellent one for it. I really must sell this story—even the parents like it. I read it to them tonight after church and mother said it was my best. It's the one about the paralytic. Thinking of Rosalind. I wonder

---

* Singing Italian songs while doing a headstand was Tony Soma's signature trick. In the 1920s, when Tony's was Dorothy Parker's favorite speakeasy, it was apparently there that she answered a bartender's question of "What are you having?" with her famous line: "Not much fun."

† Jeannot lived in Marseille. When the Allied forces landed in North Africa in the fall of 1942, the Germans and Italians retaliated by invading Vichy France.

what she was doing today while I was working. W. Marlowe and
Jack B. also phoned, but I won't speak with them.[FF]

12/6/42

You look in a cluttered top drawer and you expect to see either
a man or a woman reflected in it, and it is very disturbing when
you see neither, or when you see both.

DECEMBER 7, 1942

[F]Happy, happy (but only because my future is nearing). That's
for sure! I want nothing in the world but money! Went to the
bank this morning—I have only $63.00—and my ego will force
me to buy the $35.00 present for Rosalind. Worked on the good
story again this afternoon. Am happy—because the writing is
coming along—finally, I am writing like K. Boyle with many
adjectives, many strong, sensuous words that one feels in the
body.

[Goldberg's] mother-in-law died. Mrs. Sholem Aleichem, the
wife of the great writer.[*]

Read another year of my journal (which I found very boring).
Bernhard came over at 8. Then Virginia, then Jo. We had dinner at the Chinese restaurant on Lexington. Virginia very pretty
(a glass-blown face, Bernhard said). Then to R.B.'s where she
showed us all of her photographs. Jo lay down on the bed, saying nothing, eating nuts, making her observations. Even Virginia
found Bernhard charming and "passable."[FF]

DECEMBER 8, 1942

[F]Not so happy because I am tormented by the thought of
money—which I do not have. Spoke to Lewis at Amer. Inst.
Elec. Engineers at 10 this morning. He would like to hire me
but would pay me no more than $25.00 a week. I told him it's
hard to live on $25.00 a week. We'll see on Thursday. I would

---

[*] Goldberg was married to the daughter of famous Yiddish playwright Sholem Aleichem
(1859–1916), one of whose stories was adapted as the musical *Fiddler on the Roof.*

like very much to work for Willard Co. at Paterson, who wants 20,000 women immediately. I definitely need to earn money.

With Kingsley at 12:30. Very pleasant until I brought up Val Adams, and what she had said regarding Rosalind and me. She denied everything, of course. Told me she had only mentioned our names, but she's lying.

Worked well on my story today, which is improving day by day. My prayers have been answered: I will have something to show Rosalind. I wonder whether she'll give me a photograph of herself.[FF]

DECEMBER 9, 1942

[F]Will write my father for money. I've never done that before. Will have work on Monday, thank God! The city was bright and beautiful this morning. I went to Carnegie via 57th St. to buy tickets for Sunday. Snow was falling softly, and though there was a changeable wind, everyone was smiling. Christmas trees are in front of every flower shop, and the snow was dusting them with white flecks, which looked like cotton. I was so happy, not thinking of the past or the future, but only of the present (what a rarity).

Interview with Jacobson at Park Ave. He wants a young girl straight out of college who will edit his new magazine—which is for ordinary women, unlike *Vogue*. Unfortunately, I was dressed like a young girl at *Vogue*, but he may have liked me. I would prefer a job at *Vogue*. Perhaps I'll still get one. Then I saw an excellent exhibition of twentieth century portraits. Buffie was invited to show, but she was in Calif[ornia]. There were lots of photographs by Berenice Abbott—Joyce, Rulin, Laurencin, and also one by Leonora Carrington. What a woman! 25 years old.[FF]

DECEMBER 10, 1942

[F]Good day—a bit of work when I went to *Modern Baby* to do some typing like a slave—form letters. They offered me only 4 dollars—which won't cover my expenses for tomorrow night— if at all! It's absurd, and completely against union regulations!

I'm ungrateful, mother says. Bernhard has good nudes of Buffie.
I'd like to have one. Miserable walking through the streets this
afternoon because I have so little money. Sent another letter asking for money to father, who has never given me anything, really.
Read a lot of my notebook. 1937. When I began to live a little,
with Jones and Peggy, and not with Janet, whom I should have
kissed.[FF]

DECEMBER 11, 1942

[F]I wouldn't have thought it possible that a day could be so boring, deadening. One can easily understand how one goes mad
doing such work, drinking, smoking, dancing, doing destructive things. Bought a coat. Money is gone, gone, as usual. Have
nothing but 13.00 in the bank. But the coat is lovely. Light and
warm, soft to the touch.[FF]

12/11/42

Sometimes I have the strange belief that there is a remedy for
every sensation of discomfort, physical or mental. When I drink
water after long thirst, eat food after hungering, or once every
five years take bicarbonate of soda for a digestive ailment (nervous indigestion) and when the pain passes in two or three minutes, the dull ache inside of me lifting and disappearing, keep on
at my books with the fathomless ingratitude of a young person
who has always been healthy, when such things occur then I
think one may always make arrangements to stay comfortable all
one's life. And yet this is the very opposite of what I have always
believed (since I began believing anything, around the age of
fourteen) and what is in my blood to believe. I believe in constant
discomfort, varied equally like the ups and downs of a business
chart about its line of normalcy, as the natural state of mankind.
Therefore these happy, blind, animallike "insights" disturb me.

DECEMBER 12, 1942

This morning I performed the ignominious task of taking three
coats to the thrift shop: my polo coat, which has seen so many

faire & foul days at Barnard—and Morton Street! My little green Harris Tweed riding jacket, in which I spent the proudest, happiest hours of my life perhaps—and another little blue reefer. I was offered $1.50 for the lot at the first place, and the woman howled with horror when I proposed $4.00 at the second. I came off with $2.00, and bought a bird book and some exquisite doilies at the dime store.

Ended the semi-final draft of Archie, the paralytic. Tonight when mother read it, she found inconsistencies in style, too high a social scale where he lives, etc. And my restless brain jumps even as she speaks, wondering what I shall do next! Oh god the ripeness that is growing in my face, the maturity that is progressing in my heart, my soul, all these are ready to speak. They speak briefly in moments of brief tranquility. Two months earlier, when I had steady work I could have begun the great opus, had the other conditions been present as they are now.

DECEMBER 13, 1942

ᶠTonight, Carmen Amaya! Who always blows me away! For real! I can [almost] touch her body, taste her on my lips, on my tongue! She fills my blood, burns me! She was terribly, dangerously close to me. I could see her eyes, her lips. Mother was observing me closely, and focused particularly on Bernhard, who was wearing a silk suit and looked like a zombie. Carmen appeared in black stockings in the second act, clapping her hands, directing her sisters, who danced around her, framing her. I wonder how Antonio Triano could restrain himself while dancing with her! Terrific! I wanted to rise up like a balloon, I wanted to embrace her! At B.'s afterwards for sherry. And to look at photographs. Mother was speechless, which pleased me greatly. Perhaps I could truly love Bernhard—when I work hard, when I am calm. Otherwise, women like Carmen Amaya trouble me—and disturb me even more because one can only look at them, but not touch them. It's absurd! When B. and I were alone for a moment, we held hands, kissed on the lips, etc.

It's late. I'm full of sensations and don't want to sleep. Important ideas for my novel tonight—oddly intellectual.^{FF}

DECEMBER 14, 1942

^FArthur told me yesterday that he sold a story to *True Romances*. Or at least the idea. It was written by a woman who writes for the female readers of the magazine, but he made $75.00, which is good. Played piano for a while. It's been wonderful lately, when I'm deeply troubled. Then finished my subway story, though I have to keep working on it. Lou Weber here tonight, who said (and he's right) that I'd put too many insignificant details in it. ("The F. Train" etc.) Was so taken I worked until 3:00 tonight.

With Bernhard at Wakefield [Gallery]. Bemelmans, Gergely, Queenberry show. I can't speak to B. Parsons. She gives me the shivers. I would have liked to tell her how much I liked the show, but her eyes, her lips were observing me!

Bernhard's at 11:00. She asked me what I wanted in a lover. First, I must have the inspiration to work—and then always be happy, full of energy—a vigorous sex life. Bernhard told me that she could live with me forever without a sexual experience, even though she was dying for it! And she kissed me several times. She's afraid that I've suffered too much already because I've been frightened—by Buffie, Mary, Billie. But she knows I'm not like that. I can feel sensations in my head, like last night with C.A., but not in my body.

It's cold. 24°.^{FF}

12/14/42

Security on the brink: writing and exulting in a comfortable traditionalism, fatally attracted to the exotic at the same time.

DECEMBER 15, 1942

^FAt Madeleine's [Madeleine Bemelmans's] where I made martinis. She's reading Goethe right now, from the same book we

had at school. Ludwig is working with [Mary] MacArthur* on a piece based on his old book, *My War with the U.S.* It won't be good. Madeleine spoke about the biological inconvenience of being a woman when she wants to go to greasy spoons, bars, etc. She mentioned once that she seriously considered taking up women, but I told her it wasn't a good idea. After lunch, she stared at me steadily for a minute. Very troubling.

I looked very good today—even though my teeth are tormenting me. It's only in my head: they aren't in bad shape, but I keep getting more and more brown stains, even on the front teeth. Don't know what to do.[FF]

DECEMBER 16, 1942

[F]Went to Michel Publishers[†]—comic monthlies—this morning at 11:30. A man explained the job to me. I'd be a researcher for illustrated stories. Adventure stories in particular. And I'd get to write! I'm happy about it. I was assigned a story on Barney Ross.[‡] I'll finish Friday. Then to Betty Parsons', but only Sylvia was there. We ate and drank at the Winslow. Mother doesn't like it when I come home smelling of gin and having spent too much money. Bernhard & Buffie called. Bernhard and I will go to see the Amayas Dec. 29!!! What a glorious day!

Goldberg came by at 9. Very agreeable. He spoke to my parents about my writing, that there's something there, etc., that I don't say enough, and that there are still some rough spots in my stories. But he read the story about the paralytic and said, to my great pleasure, that there were no rough spots, that it was perhaps (no, truly!) my best story! Perhaps I'll need an agent to sell them. Work will start next week, or perhaps next month. At 3 F [F.F.F.]. But I would rather slit my throat than go back![FF]

---

* Drawings of this project survive as part of the actress Helen Hayes's estate—her daughter Mary MacArthur (1930–1949) died of polio at the age of nineteen. Bemelmans's book *My War with the United States* was first published in 1937.
† Michel Publications is the name of an imprint of the American Comics Group founded in 1939.
‡ Barney Ross (1909–1967), boxing champion and war hero.

DECEMBER 17, 1942

ᶠOh! Sylvia told me yesterday that Rosalind was not full of
"self-chastisement" but that she does exactly what she wants!
That's a lie, because Rosalind is English. I had to go to Cooper
Union to research Barney Ross. Very interesting, but it took 3
hours. I worked almost 9–10 hours today, without getting much
done at all! I wrote the story, but I'll have to reorganize it. I'm
still pondering what to get Rosalind. The music box is really
too expensive. Am I growing old? I'm working so hard that I
can't keep my eyes open at night—but I stay awake at the typewriter. I haven't had any peace and quiet for a week—not even
opened a book! In short, one needs work to be happy!

Things are getting worse and worse at home. Mother will be
happy to see me go when I find a job. I could be gentle, ask her
to let me stay here, but for what? It's not anger or pride: I swal-
lowed them a long time ago—what a luxury. It's my friends—
who keep coming. And everyone loves me! (Except those who
could give me a job!) But I find it impossible to believe that
someone might not like me. She doesn't. But it's not true.

Oh hell! I'd like to have fun, write, love, live, drink, laugh,
read, and—worse!ᶠᶠ

DECEMBER 18, 1942

ᶠGood day! Work, work, work! The Barney Ross story is going
well. Almost done now, but it's very late. Called up Mr. Sangor,*
who told me that tomorrow was fine. "I won't be able to tell you
anything until the end of next week." (Too bad—nobody hires
anyone until after the first!) Then at Carter's (Little Liver Pills)
where they need researchers. They want me to ask people on the

---

* Entrepreneur and publisher Benjamin William Sangor (1899–1953) founded what would
come to be known as the "Sangor Shop," a studio of comic writers and artists at 45 West
Forty-Fifth Street producing artwork for different comic imprints, mostly Sangor's son-
in-law Ned Pines's Standard Comics with its subsidiaries Better and Nedor Comics; and
National Comics, which would eventually evolve into DC Comics. The 1940s are known as
the Golden Age of American comic books.

street about their experience with Little Liver Pills and Arrid.* Who cares!

This week maybe the most peculiar of my life—but then I say this almost every week. Mother said she'd like me to "escape" from Bernhard's clutches! But she's been invited on Christmas to drink eggnog and open presents with us![FF]

DECEMBER 19, 1942

[F](Would like to be a child of 12.) Another day in my own inner chaos. And I'm getting a cold!

Mother is becoming worse and worse. It might be her menopause. She's always got "too much to do—not enough time" and I've been given all the privileges without anything left over for the parents! etc. Today she came into my room (at 2:35 AM) and told me "You must love these interviews! You're becoming such a great artist!" In short, I have to get the hell out.

Surprise! Carter's little liver pills wants me Monday 9 AM for their silly work![FF]

DECEMBER 20, 1942

[F]Rolf came here yesterday afternoon, very lively, because mother offered him everything in the house to eat, etc. She treats him like an over-sensitive boy, which he is. I don't feel much. I love him because he is sensitive. Everyone sensitive should love one another. I finished the story which I titled "Uncertain Treasure." It's a true uncertain treasure for me. Buffie [and I] ate out with Simon, where Simon went around kissing everyone (female) and Buffie picked up the bill. She told me the story of her family. Lots of money and hysteria. Then back to hers, where we stayed in bed, read a bit, etc. Then the rest. I did my best. But she did me at least four times. It was sweet; easy and relaxed, luckily.[FF]

---

* Her "filler" job at Arrid Deodorant Company is the only post-college job Pat mentions in an article commissioned by the *Oldie* magazine in 1993, omitting her six months as an editorial assistant to Ben-Zion Goldberg at F.F.F. Publications and her seven years in the comic book industry.

DECEMBER 21, 1942

^GLate to work because Mother didn't wake me till 8:10. On purpose, I'm sure. I had to ask 45 women between the age of 20 and 60: "Do you prefer this or this"—two sentences about Arrid, they're actually both the same. At 12, after we had stood for maybe an hour and a half at Stern's, I phoned Mr. Sangor about my story. He said: "I think you have the makings. I have to look at some others & I'll tell you in 2 days." So I came home at 2, even though I'd surveyed only fifteen women. Last night I felt the scent of Buffie's breath on me for hours. I'm so free with her and wonder what kind of love I feel. Phoned her at 3:00, and she wants to see me Wednesday! Good heavens! Just three days! Arthur here at 8:00. A very nice evening, he told me all his stories, his loves, etc. He has wonderful ideas. He'll be a [Joseph] Conrad someday. Visits! We listened to Schubert's *Die schöne Müllerin*, which is why I'm writing in German. Didn't read anything. Sent my story "Uncertain Treasure" to *Harper's Bazaar.* McFadden sent back my other stories. The letter read: "Thank you for your story. I'm so sorry there isn't any space for it in *Harper's* just now, but we'll keep you in mind." Crap. ^FBut what does it matter. Sangor loves me!^{FF} Seeing Rosalind tomorrow! Want to read Goethe. Want to settle down a little. And don't know where. Made two sketches. One for Buffie that she'll like a lot: an octopus—not I, not she, but—only with fountain pen [*Feder*] and ink [*Tinte*]. *Feder* and *Tinte*, what beautiful words! They remind me of my wonderful first schooldays when I first started learning German, the books with little pictures of children, rucksacks, etc. How wonderful, how peaceful those days were!^{GG}

DECEMBER 22, 1942

^FThings are getting worse and worse: I accosted no one today! My quota was 50, and I pretended to have reached 40 or 41! I parted from the two other girls at Grand Central, took money out of the bank, and went to look for a cup and saucer for Bernhard. I found them: the cup is gray and black—smoked, by

the Chinese—they only cost 3.00. Then a martini at Savarin, and then to Del Pezzo to meet Rosalind. I cannot understand the cosmic meaning of this romance: Her eyes never gaze softly upon me, and if they do, only for a second. She wants to see me for Christmas. And she will give me something special for my birthday.

At Raphael Mahler's[*] for three hours. Typing for him. A charming wife. $2.00. Gramma sent me a dollar. Have $12 now, $20 from the bank today, and still only $30.00 left. Absolutely must find work. Bernhard "admitted" tonight that she might be a bad influence on me, when I can "go" to men the way I "went" to Rolf. But she's wrong.

I have to get a new job, because this job will morally corrupt me.[FF]

DECEMBER 23, 1942

[F]Wonderful day but terribly tired. Mr. Sangor called me: I got the job. Will start Monday at 9. 9–5:30 and till one on Saturdays. I'll make at least $30.00 a week. I'm very happy.

Buffie met me downstairs. Very pretty, very perfumed, we went to her place. She treats me like a king or queen or princess. In any case, it pleases me greatly. She told me everything about the terrible treatment Peggy Guggenheim received from Max Ernst.[†] It was somewhat dull, but I wasn't much better. Then we made love. We turned off the lights, and we were together. I was tired, so only once. But oh so sweet! And I spent the night. "I've never had a lover who took so much time," she told me. And that I'll learn to appreciate men one day. It seems impossible. "You're so much nicer than when I met you for the first time." Of course. Buffie's skin is like exquisite liquid, sliding over mine

---

* Presumably Jewish historian Raphael Mahler (1899–1977). He cofounded the Jewish Young Historians Circle, which later affiliated with the YIVO Institute for Jewish Research, where he was a researcher and editor.
† While helping his then-wife Peggy Guggenheim prepare her Exhibition by 31 Women at her newly opened Art of This Century Gallery, Max Ernst fell in love with the painter Dorothea Tanning, whose work was part of the exhibit.

like a piece of satin. We talked about the past like we never have, and I wanted to stay up all night. Buffie would happily have me as her only lover instead of her husband. Perhaps we'll keep our Wednesdays.^{FF}

DECEMBER 24, 1942

^FThe girls are very excited about my new job. I'm free on Monday. I almost became hysterical because the music boxes hadn't yet arrived at Brass Town. So, I went to this wonderful boutique where they still sell English hairbrushes. I bought R. one for $12.50—the back is made of golden oak, stiff, slightly yellowish bristles, which are the most expensive kind. I hope she likes it! I will be mortified if she doesn't. I hope that she realizes that it's a pretty good present. I wrapped it carefully, wrote an ordinary card, and brought it to her at 11:00. Also a letter inviting her to the house tomorrow morning, telling her that I have a new job. I'm proud, of course.

Heard a terrible mass at church with [Marjorie] Thompson and the parents—would have made God and his son's hairs stand on end! I have $20.55 in the bank. I should be able to put $10.00 a week into the account thanks to my job, pay off my coat, buy theater tickets from time to time, etc. I bought dogs made of bronze and iron for mother. Small, discreet, exactly what she wanted. They only cost five dollars. Am happy, and there's so much to think about that I'm not thinking at all.^{FF}

DECEMBER 25, 1942

^FA good day—a Christmas where I felt very grown-up, because I gave just as many presents as I received, perhaps more. I received oil paints from Stanley, a cup and a saucer, etc. Large ashtray. Drinks (brandy) from Marjorie. A bottle of gin. Then Jo P. (she gave me the Fauré Requiem) and M. Wolf here. No Rosalind, of course. We drank eggnog and ate fruitcake. Bernhard gave photographs to everyone in the family—a small silver pin for me—a lover's knot. She didn't seem pleased with her gift. She thinks of herself all the time, and recently

I find myself daydreaming about the sweetest moments with Rosalind and Buffie. Speaking of which, Buffie called me at 10:20 when she was leaving for the country: "Well Sweetie, I wish you a Merry Christmas & success and happiness & a lot of love goes with it—" Goodbye before I could respond. She is sweet, and I thought about her a lot today. Mother kept looking at Bernhard, and sometimes tears came into her eyes. It makes me horribly sad, but I have the right to choose my friends. I have to stop seeing Bernhard this often. That will be one of my New Year's resolutions. Oh! Rosalind phoned me at 7:00. She spent the day brushing her hair. I hope it's true. She wanted to see me tonight—also tomorrow night, when we'll have dinner. "It's a beautiful brush!" Exactly what I knew she'd say.

Now, so late, I feel as if I am beginning to live like a human. There is so much to do—and a firm path to follow—like a powerful train on a railroad track.[FF]

DECEMBER 26, 1942

[F]Another holiday—another day of eating. I spent the whole day writing my Barney Ross story. It took so long—so long that I'm embarrassed. Finally—nothing at all, except I phoned Buffie at 5:30. She had guests. But she said: "Call me tomorrow or call me very soon so I can see you!" Mother canceled the 51 dollars I owed her for my coat. That was one of my Christmas gifts, the biggest of them!

Tonight at Rosalind's; a wonderful evening. She was by herself. We spoke about Dalí, Calas, Tanguy, then music. Good intellectual evening. She gave me *Roman Portraits*, a big book, which Betty recommended. But no photograph of her. It's a shame, though the book is good. We dined at her place—she made bouillabaisse. Afterwards, Scuola di Ballo, Debussy, Petroushka, Sitwell, Penny Candy. And more discussions of music. She wanted to kiss me as I left. She was tired—otherwise I would have tried something. She'd like it. She leaned towards me—and I kissed her on the cheek. It was far too intellectual. Does she prefer me this way? Only in her brain—and yet what does it matter?[FF]

DECEMBER 27, 1942

[F]Bernhard's at 3. She bought presents for the [Amaya] family. For Carmen, a pin, blue with diamonds. Carmen didn't show up for an hour. Then appeared in a white and red jacket, very small, very intense! Bernhard was in a state of the most abject idolization! The house was full of family, friends, neighbors. It was absolutely necessary to speak Spanish, which I had completely forgotten! Bernhard held Carmen's hand for at least ten minutes.

With Buffie tonight. She immediately bowled me over—wanted to make love and nothing else. I was shy—(why the hell?) and couldn't do much. She said some very true things. But she adores me—I drive her crazy, etc. She likes making love to me, etc. I'm full of useless energy—I will accomplish so much this year. I hope that in a year, I will still have this job. Most of all, I'd like something constant and reliable.[FF]

DECEMBER 28, 1942

[F]A good day. Hughes[*] couldn't be nicer. I'm busy right now with the details—then I'll start writing. Met everyone in the office. And I was happy that it rained all day. I had to go home at 12 because even hamburgers cost .15.

No invitations for Dec. 31. Who cares! I want to be home, alone.

With Bernhard at 8:30. We went to the Rainbow Room.[†] When I hear White Xmas I dream about Helen and myself—when we danced together, and she gazed into my eyes, and I into hers. I am absolutely, hopelessly sentimental. Bernhard was

---

[*] Richard E. Hughes (born Leo Rosenbaum, 1909–1974), American writer and comic book creator who conceived and scripted stories for Black Terror, Fighting Yank, Pyroman, the Commando Clubs, and Super Mouse. He became an editor at the Sangor Shop in 1943.
[†] Glamorous rooftop bar sixty-five stories above Rockefeller Plaza, one of the highest bars in New York City.

crying—because she saw her first love today—whom she never had. It's sad. And she plumbs it to its depths. That disgusts me. It's neither German nor Austrian—but simply Jewish. Arthur came to the R. Room because we had a date! Terrible! I wanted to give him something, but there are better things to do with my money.[FF]

DECEMBER 29, 1942

[F]A good day but so tired it felt like an ordeal. R. E. Hughes even nicer. I clipped stories from periodicals, magazines, and then put together one frame of "Phyllis the Impregnable Fortress." I have to write it from start to finish: he wants to teach me slowly. And now, after all the insults, after this long period of unemployment, there's a job at *Vogue*: Miss Campbell phoned my mother today, very politely. I'm on their list. Couldn't yet speak to Rosalind about it. I'm happy—that's important to note. Would like to start my novel in the new year.[FF]

12/29/42

You and I were born so far beyond the others, in time, in thought, in pleasures. Where are there two to equal us? There will be never one to equal us together. What does our genius mean to you, beloved?! What does this gift mean for you?

12/29/42

And why does she give me Saturday night
And why does she give me Saturday night
And why does she give me Saturday night—
Except to sleep with her!?

DECEMBER 30, 1942

[F]Hughes made me write another four pages. On the SBD[*] in Guadalcanal. "If it's of any interest to you, I have no doubt you'll be a good writer." (Who had any doubts?)[FF]

---

* Marine aircraft bomber.

DECEMBER 31, 1942

I was at *Vogue* at 12:00. Miss Campbell says I am "the kind of person they'd like to have on their staff"(!) tho the $35.00 job she offered is dull—letters to the editor, etc.

Went to John Mifflin's party with Bernhard at 11:30. The gorgeous blonde there, at whom I used to stare on Grove St. when she rode her bike. She lives with Cornell, a girl who paints extremely well says Bernhard. The blonde gave me her number etc. She knows Alex Goldfarb.* She is "Texas" something.†
Bernhard never looked better. Silver in her hair & very smooth indeed. We later taxied to Village with Bill Simmons and Becky & Marjorie. Welcome fun etc.

---

* Alex Goldfarb, alias Josef Peters, notorious communist agitator and spy.
† "The gorgeous blonde" Maggie E., also called "Texas" or "Tex," is lover and roommate to painter Allela Cornell. Cornell studied under Kuniyoshi, Zorach, and Alexander Brook. She was primarily a portraitist, equally skilled in watercolor and oil, She went unrecognized commercially, however, and was forced to do pen-and-ink portraits on the sidewalks of New York for a dollar apiece. Texas, Allela, and Pat will soon form a complicated love triangle.

1943

Living Alone, Working Full-Time, or:
"I am a genius. I hear it from all sides."

WORKING FULL-TIME as a comic book scriptwriter at the Sangor Shop certainly does not help Pat in her attempt to reconcile her many passions. For most of the year, she is torn between her desire for independence, her artistic calling, and an energy-sapping social life.

One of very few women in the industry, Pat creates superheroes with alter egos and meets the likes of Stan Lee and Mickey Spillane. Although she earns her keep in comics, her literary ambitions never waver, which might explain why she later keeps mum about this income stream (which ultimately will support her a good six years). For the time being, her day job enables her to secure her own apartment at 356 East Fifty-Sixth Street. Small as the distance to her parents' may be, it's enough to make Pat's heart grow temporarily fonder for her mother.

Pat still paints, draws (with her left hand), and writes (with her right—a reformed left-hander) obsessively. Her burgeoning multilingual diaries and notebooks reach seven hundred pages this year. Prodigious a reader as ever, she has now added Julien Green to her list of favorite authors, alongside Kafka and Freud. Pat also sells her first story to a magazine, "Uncertain Treasure." It features two men in reciprocal pursuit, a hallmark of many Highsmith stories to come.

In April, Pat meets and falls in love with painter Allela Cornell, whom she has to share with another young woman, Maggie E. (aka Tex). More soul mate than flame, Allela seems to fuel Pat's fantasy of having a life partner and moving to a house in the country—a fantasy that wildly contradicts her desire for freedom and unrestrained Manhattan party life. Allela paints a prophetic, somber oil portrait of Pat, which will hang in every one of Pat's future homes.

Pat's swinging nightlife continues to take precedence, and her literary writing suffers as a result. Her impulse is to escape. Toward the end of the year, Pat travels abroad for the first time; she crosses the border to Mexico with Chloe, a blond fashion model from Texas. In the early 1940s, Mexico had replaced Nazi-occupied Paris as the bohemian hot spot of the day, with its promise of long sultry nights and cheap tequila. Pat plans to stay until her savings run dry.

Away from her busy city life, Pat aims to finally make headway on *The Click of the Shutting*, an "adolescent novel" she began in 1942, but that had been germinating in her notebooks for much longer. The book is about a young man who—not unlike her future character Tom Ripley—wonders how it would feel to shed his identity and slip into that of his infinitely more captivating, handsome, and wealthy friend.

❧

JANUARY 1, 1943

ᶠJo stayed after the guests left. We listened to the Fauré, which makes Jo melancholy. Me too, but as Jo and E. A. Poe say, there is sadness in all beauty. Jo very stimulating tonight. When I'm with her, I feel alive, like a writer.ᶠᶠ

1/1/43

Very few people we hate in our life, mostly those with whom we have once been in love. Why? Because we still feel (fear) the vulnerability of our love period.

JANUARY 2, 1943

FWent to Buffie's at 12:30 AM with great difficulty. Parents hadn't a clue. I only went because I was bored—I have enough to do at home, but I'm always in search of pleasure and wisdom. Buffie has both, yet we did nothing but lightly touch on the pleasure of which I was capable—it was not at all sufficient—and did nothing but destroy the somewhat fatal resolutions I made long ago. And in the middle of it all, her husband phoned her from Cal. at 3:00 A.M. and talked for an hour! The whole time I was kissing her and doing what I pleased. What a marriage! I'd love to see Rosalind! I am stupid like that—she doesn't make me happy—but I'll be sad if I don't see her.FF

JANUARY 3, 1943

FVery disturbed, troubled, and can't write anything until I'm out of the house & elsewhere. It's in me, I have no doubt. Rosalind somewhat reserved and sad. She told me that she was also troubled—in a difficult mood, thinking she hasn't done enough for the war. I told her everything about Bernhard, how she doesn't behave the way I'd like. Rosalind said it was a Jewish thing. Then a beer at Jumble Shop. When we were alone for a moment I touched her hand, holding it in mine. And she kissed my hand in leaving.FF

JANUARY 4, 1943

FI re-read my notebooks. It will take a lot of time to read them all—and I will have to read them before writing the great novel that is growing inside me. ($30.55 in the bank—sad.)FF

JANUARY 5, 1943

FGood day. All day I wrote short paragraphs which say what we have to get across in our stories—if there is anything at all.

Galileo Galilei. Livingstone, Themistocles, Einstein, Cromwell, Newton, etc. Ate a poor man's lunch in Bryant Park and the birds seemed so cold I gave them half. Good evening with Buffie. Instead of the theater, we went to La Conga, where Carmen Amaya was dancing. I wrote her a nice little note (Quien no ha vista Carmen no ha vista nada,* etc.), inviting her to drink some *puerto* with us. No answer. Then I went backstage myself, and said I was Bernhard so she'd see me. She was with a sister, dressed in a lace dress, white, frightfully small in the waist. Then back to Buffie's. We slept a bit with great success. Am happy. Buffie is now exhibiting at the "31 women" exhibit at the Guggenheim.[†FF]

JANUARY 6, 1943

[F]Hughes wrote a synopsis for the Rickenbacker story[‡]—a brilliant synopsis, and I'll write the story now. I wrote another story—for Fighting Yank,[§] etc. Now we're playing Bach—"Bist Du bei mir." It's very sweet, tender, and it reminds me of the days in which I studied every night, and when there was always something to write. Now I'm always on the go, and ideas (only) come rarely. I was home alone—reading the last year of my diaries 1935–9. All about Virginia. I wonder why we don't love each other anymore! I wonder what ended this strange love that never began! Rosalind was sweet over the phone, asked me about work, etc. I'd like to touch her hair now.[FF]

JANUARY 7, 1943

[F]Roosevelt gave a good [State of the Union] address, saying that the Nazis have asked for it—& they are going to get it. And that

---

* Whoever hasn't seen Carmen has not seen anything.
† The Exhibition by 31 Women was one of the first shows at Peggy Guggenheim's Art of This Century Gallery in New York City. It ran from January 5 through February 6, 1943. Among the the artists exhibited were Buffie Johnson, Djuna Barnes, Frida Kahlo, Leonora Carrington, and Meret Oppenheim.
‡ Eddie Rickenbacker was a celebrated World War I pilot.
§ In 1943, alongside *Black Terror*, *Fighting Yank* was the best-known and most important superhero comic produced by Cinema Comics.

this congress will have much to do in making of the whole world safe. I retrieved my pullover from La Conga, and for a moment saw Carmen Amaya walking towards me (without seeing me) with her two sisters, like stars in the Pleiades.[FF]

JANUARY 8, 1943

[F]I'm getting more used to the boys at the office. I finished the Rickenbacker story—good work, said Hughes. He's a good writer, and takes his work very seriously. *Harper's Bazaar* sent back my story "Uncertain Treasure" but with a letter from [Mary Louise] Aswell,[*] lit. ed. "Your writing has considerable quality, & while this story is not for us, would you let me see some more of your work?" It's my best story. This job is good for me after all, because it's made me write faster. Lots of action, yet sincerity of a certain fashion—that is necessary. Now I'm ready to write my novel—yes—it's the natural thing to start now. It's at the forefront of my mind. [FF]

JANUARY 9, 1943

[F]A good morning—I still have to write the script for Catherine the Great of Russia.[†] $40.55 in the bank. It's growing slowly. Rosalind's at two. I feel as though we are a bit bored—that we need a big explosion—something![FF]

JANUARY 10, 1943

[F]Read [Julien Green's] *Varouna* and almost finished. Without fail it makes me think of the problem of human identity, the secret of human life. I am at once child and man, girl and woman. Sometimes a grandfather.[FF]

1/10/43

The girl who is about to leave home for the first time—at the age say of twenty or twenty-one. How she feels as she gets a

---

[*] Mary Louise Aswell, fiction editor at *Harper's Bazaar*. Under her editorship, *Harper's Bazaar* published early pieces by such writers as Truman Capote, Jean Cocteau, Carson McCullers, and W. H. Auden.
[†] This was another script for *Real Life Comics*.

cup of coffee on the way home to her parents' house, the night before she is to leave, thinking as she goes out the door of Riker's how depressing would it be if her meals alone were to be such brief respite, in the days when she will have only too much time for herself, eating tensely on a stool, without conversation, seeing only her own face opposite her, a bit yellowish in the mirror under the fluorescent lights.

JANUARY 11, 1943

^FAt home, they're always discussing the friends I take out to restaurants, the theater, etc. Other young ladies go out with young men. And this costs them nothing, while I spend too much—at least 5.00 every evening. It's true, but as ever, I prefer putting my own hands up my skirt. At the office—sent off the Rickenbacker story. "This is really good writing. Inspirational captions and well hung together." Etc. Most of it is Hughes' work and I told him so.^{FF}

1/20/43

I have the odd feeling these days that I become more substantial mentally—as far as soundness of character & personality are concerned—and more insubstantial, more decadent physically. The span of my rotting and transparent body put against the normal measure of cosmic hardships is a despair to contemplate. The lineaments of my face establish themselves in handsome sanity and complacency: inside is labefaction and imminent death.

1/27/43

I came home one night towards midnight, so drunk with alcohol and cigarette and sleepiness that I weaved from one side of the pavement to the other. Out of a Third Avenue bar came a boy and girl about sixteen. "Take care of that cold!" the girl said with all the love, warmth, sacrificial, miraculous power of women throughout the ages! "You take care of it for me!" said the boy. "I will!" as they parted. I followed the girl to her home two blocks away, half trotting over the snow and slush to keep up with her. I almost spoke to her. I loved the sense of fiction in the scene. I should not have remembered very well if I had heard this in soberness. My sodden brain supplied the mood, the style, the atmosphere and the tones unplayed above and below, the multitudinous sketch lines which a writer might have put in before and after, some of which he would have left unsaid, like those I imagined I was seeing and experiencing. Drinking is a fine imitation of the artistic process. The brain jumps directly to that which it seeks always: truth, and the answer to the question, what are we, and what caverns of thought and passion and sensation can we not attain? There is therefore something of the artist in every drunkard and I say God bless them all. The proportion of men drunks to the smaller number of women drunks is parallel to that of the men artists to the women. And perhaps there is something homosexual about the women drunks too: they care not for their appearance, and they have definitely learned to play.

1/30/43
  Things I wish yet to learn about:
    1) Geology—composition past and future of earth
    2) Various countries—Poland, Czechoslovakia, Lithuania, Finland, etc. to know the real personality of each—the ur-personality as I come nearest to knowing of England
    3) Mathematics—(persistent curiosity, at same time a begrudging of time spent on this branch of knowledge for which I haven't the least aptitude)
    4) The Russian language
    5) Hebrew language
    6) Various scripts of all languages

2/3/43
      Writing—"I want to be"
      Painting—"I want to possess"—all creation is to change oneself psychologically. Not to create for pleasure or art's sake.

2/6/43

It's all but impossible for two artists to be close friends. One will phone demanding to see the other, who may be at the stage where he must be alone. The artists, when together, will be at different rates of speed. In general it is a constant effort to pull each into the other's orbit. They will not merge. It is as simple as two cogged wheels moving at different speeds. They cannot merge.

2/12/43

With you* I am so happy I wish all the world were closed up from us. Near you, I feel such sweet contentment that I would like to whisper to you, this is my journey's end. Let only the stars gaze upon us, let only the sun warm our feet from the other side of the earth, and seal this room and this moment forever!—How sad that I cannot speak such words to you, and that I cannot write them without a pain in the throat like something that wishes to kill me!

2/17/43

Living alone is an experience dominated by small experiences.† One is soon accustomed, logically, to not having an icebox to raid at midnight, to having to do one's own laundry or at least see to it. The real experience of living alone is the water tap always running icy or seething hot, sending prickles of displeasure up one's spine, the running up and down stairs to fetch little pans of water for one's painting, most of all the encountering of strangers in the house to whom one must speak to be civil—whereas in one's own home one could eat, work, live, without disturbing the precarious tide of creative thought in one's subconscious.

The first apparent joy of living alone is the privilege of keeping silent a whole evening when one is in belligerently unsocial spirits.

---

* It is unclear who the "you" is here.

† Thanks to her job, Pat can finally move out. In February she finds a temporary rental, then in early May moves into her first own apartment, a studio at 353 East Fifty-Sixth Street, a stone's throw from her parents' home on East Fifty-Seventh Street. She'll keep returning there and hold on to the lease until the 1950s.

2/22/43

In my generation (and perhaps for two or three others to come) women are busy attaching themselves to the man's world. Men have been so long attached that they can afford occasional detachment. Therein lies the reason for the woman's characteristic lack of humor in business, characteristic unimaginative, unsympathetic, disciplinary management of her own business and private life, and of the lives of the others who may be under her.

3/5/43

Most people are not what anyone could call passionate. Passion requires one of two factors: complete tranquility as the idle rich Greeks had—or actual suffering and misery, either being endured or remembered vividly with compassion and horror, too.

3/20/43

There is a quality, detectable throughout all ages of literature, which can come only when the writer is in love himself. It is the unutterable sweetness Shakespeare wrote into the Romeo and Juliet scenes, the inspiration of the young Jewish poet of our time who wrote simply and literally of the embraces of his sweetheart. It is a masculine quality for it springs from the male desire in love, physical, but mentally sublimated to a fountain of unselfconscious utterance. When one reads such lines unloving, they seem nonsense and sentimentality, certainly indicative of feebleness in the writer. Read them over when we too are in love and each word has its proper, subjective meaning and effect.

MARCH 30, 1943

ᶠWith Goldberg at Anthony's tonight. The first page is hard, he's right. He's looking for an apartment for me. It's funny. He's truly affectionate.ᶠᶠ

MARCH 31, 1943

[F]Very tired at work. I think I should quit this job and find something at *Vogue*. I could write stories at the same time. Sent my two scripts to Fawcett.[*][FF]

APRIL 1, 1943

[F]Bad, uninspired day until I phoned Helen. I'll see her tomorrow. "All right, darling. Goodbye." Oh, I'll remember that "darling"! Sent MSS to Kapeau at Parents' True Comics.[†] I'll have something soon. Am happily thinking of Helen who is doubtlessly in bed at the moment and will look very pretty tomorrow.[FF]

APRIL 2, 1943

[F]Good day but didn't work—had lunch with Helen at the Golden Horn. Drank two vodka martinis. Too much, really. She told me that Kingsley had shown my sketchbook (or some drawing!) to Mespoulet, and Mespoulet said it was vile—horrible and disgusting (!) And that even though my diaries are strangely devoid of sensuality—even when I was obsessed with Rosalind! It makes me sick! Helen wanted to come with me tomorrow evening, anywhere, but I don't have a free room for her here. It's a shame!

Work at the office is very boring. I'm jealous of how happy Everett[‡] is. His world is full of light—women—meat, sweets, liquor of all kinds! Instead of working, I saw Virginia at the 52nd St. bistro. Later, Kingsley phoned and came by at 11:35. She emphatically denied showing anything to Mespoulet. Someone's lying—or exaggerating.[FF]

---

* Fawcett Comics is best known for introducing Captain Marvel.
† True Comics was an educational comic book series published by the Parents' Institute from 1941 to 1950.
‡ Everett Raymond Kinstler (1926–2019) dropped out of the School of Industrial Art in Manhattan just before his sixteenth birthday to accept a full-time position at Cinema Comics. He later went on to become a renowned portrait artist who painted hundreds of celebrities, including eight U.S. presidents.

APRIL 3, 1943

^FI wrote five pages before going to Jo P.'s. Stayed late at Jo's, and she invited me to stay the night. I said yes. Two beds, clean and beautiful pajamas. I told Jo that I love her, it's strange, but I love her. She loves when I hold her head in my arms. It's very peaceful with music. But at night—nothing.^{FF}

APRIL 4, 1943

^FSaw Bernhard at 8 o'clock. A drink at Jumble Shop. Then I felt like calling Rosalind. She was with some other women, relaxing a bit, etc. I love Jo P. almost as much as her, perhaps. Not in the same way.^{FF}

APRIL 5, 1943

^FStanley Kauffmann* from Fawcett Pub phoned me this morning and wants to see me. That means work, which means money. The woman from the apartment on 34th St. says I can have it for $40.00 a month with a one-and-a-half-year lease. That's a long time! Almost a twentieth of my life! A tenth! But I think I'll still take it. I'll never be ashamed of this apartment and I can invite all of my friends there. I also asked for a raise and got it! Hughes will talk to Sangor.

Spent tonight at home, where I wrote what may be the beginning of the novel.^{†FF}

APRIL 6, 1943

^FNervous last night. I must write lyrically without getting terribly lost. It's so easy to say, but when I write, I write with my whole heart, my entire self, great effort, blood, and lastly, with my head. It will be better to start things differently.

First—Fawcett at 12:30. Kauffmann told me that my stories had excellent dialogue but that my plots were boring! All the

---

* Stanley Kauffmann (1916–2013), American author, editor, and film and theater critic.
† Her first novel, *The Click of the Shutting*, which she will abandon later.

same, he gave me two Lance O'Caseys* for which I'll write two episodes.

Worked badly, because I'm always tired lately. Rosalind's at 7:10. We ate dinner at her place. Soup and cheese, coffee—and her—it's heaven, it's paradise! It's all I can ask for, even if it doesn't last. Afterwards, beer and sandwiches at Sammy's. "Comb your hair. You look like Byron with a hangover." She told me many wonderful, private, secretive things—lots of little, unimportant things, but they made me happy. She gives me quick pecks on the cheek, like an old aunt. I want her lips, her intelligent, soft, loving lips! I'll have them one day. Tonight made me certain of it. One can learn so much from the little things.[FF]

APRIL 7, 1943

[F]An ordinary day. Actually, I forgot to call Rosalind—to tell her that last night was wonderful—perhaps the most wonderful night of my life. Hughes only gave me a $4.00 raise. I'll make $36.00. I was a bit sad when he told me. Sy Krim[†] hopped up on benzedrine at 9:40. He disgusts me sometimes. Not his way of living, but his violence. I'm starting to think that Del P. was right: I need a job that doesn't demand any creative effort.[FF]

APRIL 8, 1943

[F]Very, very happy! Worked well tonight. Del Pezzo's at 12:30 with Helen. She told me she wants nothing but good meat, a fullfilled sex-life, a husband who loves everything she loves, books, a job. But she's carefree, she said, not like me—naïve and melancholy. It was almost a perfect day—even found inspiration for a sculpture. But mother's angry at me, and said that I don't listen to the doctor, and that I'll have to pay all my bills in the future myself.[FF]

---

* *Lance O'Casey* was a Fawcett comic book title.
† Seymour Krim (1922–1989), American journalist, author, editor, and educator.

APRIL 9, 1943

ᶠAn ordinary day—I didn't sign the lease because they were asking for $50.00 a month including an oven and refrigerator. It's absurd. I'll have to keep looking.ᶠᶠ

APRIL 10, 1943

ᶠFor two and a half hours, I was in the dentist's terrible chair. I cried, I trembled—but he took his time. He's stupid! But cheap. Then I had a cup of coffee and went to the Perls museum to see the Darrel Austin* exhibit. It was wonderful! Buffie was there and a bit cold towards me. I have to buy her something and take her out to dinner. My mother—for whom I bought a pen that doesn't work—gave me milk with egg and put me to bed.ᶠᶠ

APRIL 11, 1943

ᶠParents very cold and unsympathetic. I've got to get out of here immediately. Rosalind's at 9:45. For some reason she was preoccupied, serious. Cornell's after eating at Grand Ticino. Rosalind has old friends there. She likes the restaurant. I told her my idea for the story on "Laval" and the paranoiac.† Texas was very agreeable, both of us at her place, beers, paintings, etc. Texas made a few passes at me. She knows I'm looking for a woman to live with. Rosalind seems serious sometimes, but she looked very pretty tonight, almost beautiful. And she likes Cornell, who was fiercer than ever! We got lost on the subway and walked to Sammy's for a beer, but Spivy came in, purple suit, big hair, just another boozer. I felt very ordinary that night, my brain wasn't working any better than that of the other drunks! Not amusing in the slightest. Home at 2:35 AM.ᶠᶠ

---

* Darrel Austin (1907–1994), American commercial artist and painter.
† According to Pat's notebook, this lost story is about a man who is persecuted because of his resemblance to Pierre Laval, a French politician who collaborated with the Germans and was subsequently convicted of treason.

APRIL 13, 1943

ᶠGood day. Worked slowly at the office. I haven't been going to bed at a reasonable hour lately. I imagine that will change when I find an apartment. *Atlantic Monthly* sent "Mountain Treasure" back to me, and I showed it to Cammarata* who liked it a lot. "Rough spots occasionally." But I never want to change anything. I'll take the parents to the circus. At Mr. Steiner's to deliver books, I noticed that I had left behind three volumes of personal journals! He must have had a good laugh! It's awful. Everything—absolutely everything— about Buffie, Rosalind, Betty, etc. In short, the last three years! I have no doubt that he read all the notebooks—at least, as much as he wanted to. Texas phoned me at 5:00. I met her at *Vogue*, 46 & Lex. She doesn't want a roommate. But she wants an affair.ᶠᶠ

APRIL 14, 1943

ᶠA pleasant day but completely disgusted with myself. I have to write for a set time, study for another, eat for another, sleep for another. Right now, I have no discipline whatsoever. I'm half-way satisfied, because I'm doing what I want, but I'm not happy! Ate at 1:30 with Texas at Del Pezzo. She listens and listens to me and tells me that all my ideas are good. She wants it, no doubt, but when? Where? I wonder if I'll do it—for my health. Joseph Hammer phoned. He wants to see me Saturday and Sunday, but it's impossible because I've been hired by a friend of Goldberg's who is writing a dissertation. 200 pages. I should make enough for a gabardine suit.ᶠᶠ

APRIL 15, 1943

ᶠFeeling very happy, my novel is growing sound. I will write it with lots of people at first—then slower-paced. I must

---

* The artist Alfredo Francesco Cammarata (1905–1993), or "Al Camy'," worked on comics such as *Spectro*, *Crime Crushers*, and *Phantom Detective*; he was the first to draw Airboy, an aviator hero who debuted in 1942.

describe the various things that occur in a single day. I wrote a Ghost.*

I'm smoking too much now. Bored at lunch. Thought of Texas and decided I'd do it. Called her around 5:00 and saw her at 5:30. I am in great need of strange lips that don't mean anything to me. Am living now in curious excitement.[FF]

APRIL 17, 1943

[F]Am so tired it's a sin! I really am just like my Gregory[†]— full of potential with no clue as to how to begin. Saw Rolf at 1:30. He was almost rude this afternoon, didn't say more than a dozen words, etc. Saw *Skin of Our Teeth* by Thornton Wilder. Bernhard was marvelous, the play too. It's a real piece of theater.

Joseph H. came by at 7:00, laden with gifts—records, books, candy. Stainer's *Crucifixion*, [Franz Schubert's] *Der Tod und das Mädchen*, [Bach's] "Little Fugue in G minor." *Omnibooks of Humor* and *New Yorker* stories. I need books like this. It's funny how one always wants to play their favorite records for friends, and they never listen properly, never understand them. Even [Joseph] H. He was torpedoed between Cuba and Puerto Rico, was on a raft for two days and made $500.00 a month for his pains. He doesn't want to see me again because I'm in love with "Richard"—my pseudonym for Rosalind. It's funny, and sad. Because he loves me, probably— as well as he can.[FF]

4/17/43

Then said the writer to himself in privacy: "I may starve, but I will not work for another man and burn out the oil of my days. How can one be a prostitute in the day and a good lover at night?"

---

* Probably a reference to the comic superhero the Ghost, who first appeared in 1940.
† Gregory is a protagonist of her current work-in-progress.

APRIL 18, 1943

[F]A day just like the days I dreamed of when I was fifteen! Slept until 11. Sent proposals off to Fawcett. At 5:30 PM we found my new home—373 E. 56 St., right next to Piet Mondrian,[*] who uses the same door. Lights, paintings, and for $40.00 a month. One room, kitchen, bath. Small, but it will do until October, when God knows what will happen! I signed a five-month lease. Texas phoned at 6:30. I was so excited, I sang in the streets. Went to Nick's[†] for a drink. I called Rosalind who told me to watch my step with Texas. She's my guardian angel, I told her. Ate at El Charro where we caressed almost the whole night—an excellent dinner, but our hands were always together, lips almost, but not entirely. How lovely Texas is up close! How happy she makes me when she smiles, when she speaks of nothing. How I'd like to see Texas, I told her, in a vast bed, with white sheets, all alone with me. It's so sweet and simple because she wants nothing more than this, and neither do I. At her place, in the hallway, she turned off the lights and kissed me, a long, terribly tender kiss, which she loved just as much as I did. We left one another wanting more. In bed at 5.[FF]

APRIL 20, 1943

[F]While I was working tonight, alone at home, Texas phoned. She told me twice that she loved me, in that joking tone that Southerners have. "Whisper sweet within's—" It's sweet, and I'm light as air when I heard her voice. Today was remarkable. I began to menstruate for the first time in a year and a half—if the little in December 1941 counts. Wrote 5 pages, but I'd like to write the Laval story first. Am very happy.[FF]

---

* The famous Dutch abstract painter Piet Mondrian (1872–1944) moved to Manhattan in 1940 and lived there until his death in 1944.
† Nick's was a tavern and jazz club in Greenwich Village, which had its golden days in the 1940s and 1950s, when musicians such as Bill Saxton, Pee Wee Russell, Muggsy Spanier, Miff Mole, and Joe Grauso performed there.

APRIL 21, 1943

[F]Good day. Work was easy. Joseph H. came by because he was
going to see Ralph Kirkpatrick[*] and wanted to bring me along.
He had a drink with Rosalind yesterday afternoon, during which
they talked about me. Joseph said: "She thinks the world of you!
She thinks you're a genius." Ralph Kirkpatrick very polite, young
(36), lives on 62 & Lex. Two good rooms, lots of books and a
harpsichord. He gave us a drink. They wanted to come back here
at 9:30, and how can one say no to Ralph Kirkpatrick?[FF]

APRIL 22, 1943

[F]Lunch with Rosalind at Del Pezzo. She's very interested in
Joseph H. If he makes a single move on her, I'll slit his throat!
She didn't know he was Jewish. He told her I'm a musical genius.
(I want to call Allela tomorrow, spend the evening at hers.) My
head is always full of music, and I hear each note [G]clear and
bright.[GG] My novel—it's a heavy, weighty opus now, and it
would be better to leave it for several days so as to retrieve the
strong emotions which made me want to write it. I am full of
energy, and so they (everyone) think I am a genius. I hear it from
all sides.[FF]

APRIL 24, 1943

[F]Good day, but I haven't done anything yet and am becoming
more and more disorganized. Started drinking at 2:00 P.M.—
saw the excellent Wakefield [exhibition by] Steinberg[†] who is
funnier than Bemelmans. Betty Parsons very nice. Then exhibits
by Dalí ([G]Horror of horrors![GG]) and Mondrian—which I didn't
like. Then Tex and I walked through the streets until we arrived

---

* Ralph Leonard Kirkpatrick (1911–1984), world-renowned American harpsichordist who
taught at the Mozarteum in Salzburg and at Yale University. Kirkpatrick wrote a biography
of Domenico Scarlatti, one of Pat's favorite composers, something she and Tom Ripley—an
amateur harpsichordist himself—have in common.

† Saul Steinberg (1914–1999), Romanian-born American cartoonist and illustrator who
worked as a freelance artist, primarily for *The New Yorker*.

at Stonewall* where I drank two beers. I told Texas frankly that I wanted to sleep with her and nothing else. She swears I'm the only woman she's been with since Cornell. Can I believe her? I called up Rosalind—and Cornell—to whom (Cornell) I said that I love Texas simply because she loves me, and I probably won't see her again. Cornell always seems very calm towards me, very light. Perhaps what Texas says isn't true—but she told me that Cornell and she often fight about me. I told Rosalind at 7:10 that I love her very much. "I love you too," Rosalind said. That was the first time she's ever said those words. They make me frightfully nervous. "I'm your guardian angel," she said. Yet tonight, I kissed three girls.

I had a drink at Cornell's. Texas lay down on the bed, and I jumped on her, wrestled, etc. She pulled me down but didn't let me go further. It's funny too. But she's stupid, and just as stupid in bed. I went out at 10:00 to Judy's for Mickey's party. I was the only Christian there. On the balcony I kissed Cecilia, who likes me a lot—and can't wait until I have my apartment where she'll visit me, alone. Danced a lot and with J. Tuvim who was very pretty in black. Home at 5.[FF]

APRIL 26, 1943

[F]Saw Dr. Borak, he'll give me two treatments before my next period in May. I'll finish before Rosalind's birthday. I want a new suit, but I also want to buy something big for her birthday. I don't have to pay rent until June. Months are going by and I'm not working on my novel, but I'm thinking about it, and when I'm alone, it will be like on the tropical ocean. I will write faster, better, and more. Joseph phoned me at 4:00 to tell me that Ralph [Kirkpatrick] is in love with me. I don't believe it. He hasn't even phoned me yet. I'll take Cornell to Bach's St John Passion May

---

* The Stonewall Inn, located at 57 Christopher Street, in the heart of Greenwich Village, was the scene of New York's first gay rights demonstrations in July 1969. It has since been considered the flash point of the gay liberation movement.

4. Kirkpatrick will be playing harpsichord. I worked on Lance tonight. I need money.[FF]

[F]Bumped into Herbert L., now a lieutenant in the Marines, who spent the winter in Russia! He's handsome. Truly handsome, and smokes a pipe. Seemed happy to see me, but he was very shy, probably because of our last date at my place, when we went to bed together.

Phoned Allela—a great conversation in which she was very amusing. She has a great sense of humor and is intelligent enough to display it even when she doesn't feel like it.[FF]

[F]Made a call (finally) to Ralph Kirkpatrick at 5:30. He was a bit shy but: "Let's get together & do something some evening." And "Swell"—that I'm coming to St John's Passion Tuesday.

Had a date with Peter and Helen at Jumble Shop at 6:30. They were an hour late and already drunk. A woman at the restaurant read our palms and gave me the best reading, that I won't get married, that I have a big imagination, etc. It made Helen and Peter jealous.

There's so much I want to develop in myself. I spent last night with girls I've already left far behind.[FF]

[F]Am thinking with disgust of last night with Helen, who means less and less to me—Peter too. I told a lot to my mother. I want to buy a suit right away and wear my hair up. I phoned up Rosalind tonight to tell her that I will move Saturday afternoon. Wants to see me later this afternoon, and my apartment. I hope she won't think it too small. It's enough, really. Kingsley and Jo came by. Kingsley didn't talk enough for her own liking, so she became boring and intolerable whenever she did! Jo pretended that she had to leave in her car, and K. left too. 11:00. Then at 11:20, Jo came back. "Did you say something about coffee?" I kissed her

immediately. We were both in heaven, in paradise. We did almost
everything on the sofa—it was our first time, and couldn't have
been better if we had planned it. I like her a lot. She seemed to
have done all of this before. Finally, she stayed overnight—in the
living room. She is sweet, and understands everything, and has all
my heart—whatever's left after Rosalind.[FF]

APRIL 30, 1943
[F]Good day, am thinking sweetly of Jo. She came into my room
at 8 o'clock, dressed, ready to leave. She spoke to mother over
breakfast. She seemed happy, though we didn't mention last
night, of course. It was good. But she must have done it before!
She couldn't really tell when I came. And she—I don't think
she did. Texas came to see me at 5:30—she was smiling, pretty,
warm, and wanted to read what I had written. Oh me! Oh
Texas! How sweet it is to stroll through the streets with her! We
drank beer at the Boar's Head [Tavern], and held hands, and she
told me out loud that she wanted to kiss me! Oh paradise! She
will sleep with me! Worked on Lance. Almost done.[FF]

MAY 1, 1943
[F]Not a word from Jo P. What's she up to? Perhaps taking a spin
in her car somewhere, thinking and wondering whether what
happened really happened. I am too. Spent the afternoon settling in here. Now the pictures (paintings) are on the walls,
and I'm awaiting the furniture, which will come when the
money does.[FF]

MAY 4, 1943
This day might be terribly important. It is now 5:20 A.M. [F]I was
very nervous at the office. Met Texas E. and Cornell on 55th St.
at 6:45 P.M. Then Cornell and I went to Carnegie Hall, a bit late,
where we heard the St John's Passion. Then drinks at the Faisan
d'Or. She invited me to come upstairs to her place. Then a glass
of milk, then conversation, etc. in which I hope I won her over—I
hope so because I adore her, and I told her so already. She said to

me: "I could love you very much." She's still on guard. How do I
win her? Through modesty, patience, the natural superiority to
all her other friends. Finally, I kissed her, and though the first kiss
wasn't good, the others—I'll never forget them! I love her, I love
her, and I am so happy right now I don't at all care what time it is.
I want the morning to come so I can talk to her![FF]

MAY 5, 1943

[G]Last night Cornell made all the first moves, which makes
me happy today. I know she loves me, at least a little. Today I
couldn't work till I'd called her (at 10:30). All day I felt her lips
on mine, and in short, I'm completely in love with her. Nothing like this since Rosalind. Today I also thought that we're too
alike and therefore won't love each other long. I won't look at
any other "beauties" as long as I've got her.[GG]

[F]Dinner with the parents. Wrote a synopsis for Fawcett's
Golden Arrow,* though I didn't get more than three hours of
sleep last night. Oh happy day!

Am reading German poetry tonight.[FF]

5/5/43

Compared to the artists, all the rest of us lead very ugly lives.
It is only merciful that the overwhelming majority can never be
aware of this appalling and depressing discrepancy between the
ideal and the merely adequate. So we have the tiny group who
are aware of it, melancholy unto death itself, or content to be
passive observers, appreciators, sybaritic, hedonistic, infertile
save in the spring of their own reflected derivative enthusiasms.

Enthusiasm. This is the God in the artist which makes him a
god. The artist says, "*Fiat lux!*" and there is light.

MAY 6, 1943

[F]Cornell has many work projects outside of the city this summer, perhaps beyond. That would be awful! But she does only

* Golden Arrow was a Fawcett comic book series about a western hero.

have four dollars in the bank and lives on 15.00 a month. Texas E. has no suspicions right now, and it will stay like this. I think of long, tranquil evenings in which we'll work together, read together, lie in bed together listening to music. That's worth more than anything in the world! I adore her. I love her—her soul—and what else? I am certain tonight that I can finish my novel. It's the first time I feel like this in this apartment, and I'm very happy!FF

MAY 7, 1943*

FI met Stan,* who told me that they were expecting great things of me at Fawcett. "We have bigger stuff than Lance and Golden Arrow." Perhaps, if I write good scripts, they'll offer me a job. I'd like to earn more money. For my friends. Not for myself.FF I think of meeting every other kind of person in the world— in brains and appearance and degrees of human warmth, and I cannot imagine any superior to [Cornell]. She is goodness, godliness, and I compared am a longshoreman who has seen the sights of Singapore and Hong Kong, Nagasaki, and Calcutta. I feel we could be healthy and happy and creative together, finding peace at last—something I've never found. I am lonely, something I thought I never would be—and lonely for Cornell—I was never lonely for Rosalind, because I could not envisage the sort of life we might make together. It was a fantastic dream, of no substance. [Cornell and I] are perfect together! And Tuesday night she kissed me like she meant it.

"Were you drunk?" I asked.

"Yes."

"Do you think I was drunk?"

"Yes. Do you think I was drunk?"

"No. I wasn't."

"Then I wasn't either."

---

* Stan Lee (1922–2018), American comic book author and editor, actor, and film producer. While still a teen, Lee was hired as an assistant at Timely Comics—which would later become Marvel Comics. He was a cocreator of Spider-Man, among many other characters.

"Shall I forget Tuesday night?"
"No."

MAY 9, 1943

^{F}Cornell and Texas came to my very clean apartment at 6:45.
We drank a pint of gin. Cornell told me that Texas is a bit sad—
because she thought I was in love with her; I'll have to be nice
and gentle. We went to their place by bus at 9:30. We put Texas
to bed and took a walk to get milk. Finally back at her place,
downstairs, I dropped the bottle of milk! I cried and cried—I
couldn't help myself. She kissed me all over, and I wanted so
badly to spend the night there—with her—in the hallway. It was
almost impossible to leave! Texas E. and Cornell are good people. They are honest and sweet.^{FF}

MAY 10, 1943

^{F}Very hungover today until 6:30, when I drank a beer with Sy
Krim and Knight—a boy who wants to work in the movies.
Cornell phoned me at 10:40 as I was writing a poem, and had
just been reading Kafka's *The Castle*. I felt like white, powdery
snow—light and clean and thin. She spoke very sweetly, but she
knew that I was working. I love her and she loves me; I'm sure of
it. But tonight I thought of the problems we'll have with Texas.
Texas is sweet and simple like a little girl. I could show her some
affection, and it would be safe because she would never do anything to hurt Cornell. I've never met two better women. I read
over my novel for a bit, and I think it's good. I want to work
hard, and I'm afraid of nothing.^{FF}

MAY 11, 1943

^{F}My darling—Texas—called at 8:40 while I was still asleep! Very
sweet. I wonder if she truly loves me—if she loves me enough
to tell me so—I'm still vain, after all. Met Cornell at 5:30 at M.
[Metropolitan] Museum. 3 martinis (together) at Anthony's. I
was shy—she was talking about her friends far from here, and I
was jealous, very jealous of these brilliant men and women she's

known for such a long time. I was a chicken tonight, a coward—
because I wanted to ask her if she would ever love me. Because
I felt as if I couldn't have another hopeless love, like Rosalind.
But a question like that wouldn't be fair to Cornell. Worked on
my novel tonight—a Herculean task. Sometimes I wish I were a
painter. But as Rosalind said: "One does what one can."FF

5/11/43

I suffer from emotional constipation—even emotional condem-
nation. When I am in love, it is a miracle the other person knows
it except by my tortured expression. I think eloquently, and see
her across a table and can say nothing. I dream beautifully. I
want to love and be loved with no shadow of a doubt, I want
the two peaks of the mountain breeze blowing either side of my
face and disturbing my hair on top. I want the flux and outflux
and influx free and light, and I want to give it no thought. I want
to live by unconscious thinking. I want only the inspirations,
thoughts, desires, that have come from I know not where. I want
the clear face, the smooth forehead and the tranquil mouth of
the Buddha, the Light.

MAY 12, 1943

FA marvelous day! Cornell, Tina, and Marg. were all home.
Texas prepared dinner for us all. They were very happy, and
Cornell, then Texas, brought me to the bathroom to embrace
and kiss me. It was fantastic. But kissing Cornell was better, and
brought me the most pleasure. Finally, I went to sleep in Cornell's room, in the corner.FF

MAY 13, 1943

FVery important day because I have decided to be an ARTIST
instead of a writer! Slept perhaps 4–5 hours, and saw the sun
rise in the white room—and fall on the painting of a spiritual
man. It was a new world—a world that I understood, that I had
understood before, but! Gthat I'd so far rejected, because I always
wanted to write. It is the world beyond consciousness, the best

of all worlds! I saw Vaslav Nijinsky*and Ellis† and Goethe, and then Texas woke up, very happy. Then Cornell—who kissed me—how sweet she is! To me! She almost loves me, but her life is so mixed up! She will have to live alone, I'm afraid!

Coffee and rhubarb compote on the bed—the three of us. Then, when Texas left, Cornell came to my bed and we talked for almost an hour—I spoke most of the time. Nonetheless, last night her friends liked me much more than Texas—they liked my face and hands. We lay down together and listened to Bach Toccata & Adagio in C, Boccherini Cello Concerto and Mozart Paris Overture. It was unforgettable! Then I began to menstruate, which disgusted me. She read me a letter from one of her friends and I left. She was looking at me from the window as the bus was leaving. Texas told me that morning that *Vogue* very much likes my ᴳ"Letter to One's Darling"ᴳᴳ—and that they may run it! It's fantastic.ᶠᶠ

MAY 14, 1943

ᶠA marvelous day. I spent two hours at lunch! Saw Jack Schiff from Detective Comics‡ on Lexington Ave. He wants me to give him ideas—not synopses—for any character whatsoever. Met Tex and Cornell for drinks. Met a lot of their friends. Tamiris,§ etc. Had dinner at Eddie's Aurora.¶ Very nice. I wanted to kiss Cornell all evening and we tried to hold hands as much as possible. Though Texas tried to stay up, she fell asleep at 11:00. And Cornell was truly troubled. It was sad. The world is beautiful!ᶠᶠ

---

* Vaslav Nijinsky (1889/1890–1950) was a Polish ballet dancer and choreographer.
† Possibly a reference to Henry Havelock Ellis (1859–1939), an English physician, progressive intellectual, and social reformer who (co-)wrote the first medical textbook in English on homosexuality in 1879 and later published on transgender psychology.
‡ Jack Schiff (1909–1999), American comic book writer and editor, wrote various comics about Detective Comics' (later shortened to DC) best-known superhero, Batman.
§ Helen Tamiris (1905–1966), American pioneer of modern dance, choreographer, and teacher. Her works address issues of racism and war. She is best known for her suite of dances called *Negro Spirituals*.
¶ Eddie's Aurora was a small Italian restaurant in Greenwich Village that attracted an "arty" crowd.

MAY 15, 1943

[F]"I've never been as happy as I was today! A quick morning then—with $210 in my pocket ($4.00 now)—went for a beer with Camy—(he pockets money each week which his wife knows nothing about—it disgusts me!) and to buy a pizza for Rosalind who came by at 2:20, while I was on the phone with Cornell. Then we went to Chinatown to get my tattoo. I was a bit ill at ease—but after two bourbons, just fine. It's green—the tattoo*—and almost as small as I wanted. I'm happy about it— not proud but happy. Rosalind enjoyed the afternoon and spoke to several soldiers and sailors. Even went to those bistros where you never usually see a woman.[FF]

MAY 16, 1943

[F]Cornell phoned me at 11:30—still very happy too. "God, I love you," I said. And then Texas called a moment later. "Who were you talking to?" I told her Rosalind had called me. "You must be very happy." Phoned Rosalind. She wanted to see me on the early side, and I went over at 1:30 very happy. Hungover. Rosalind. What a surprise! Texas phoned me again at 5:30, and I phoned Cornell at 4:30. It was a disaster, because Cornell was serious, even sad.[FF] "Take care of your cough," I said, "I don't want you to die." She laughed. "Wish I could say the same." Oh God preserve her. When I die I want my tombstone to say that I was born in 1943—on New Years Day—and on May 4, 1943.

MAY 17, 1943

[F]A good day. Worked hard, but Camy bought me a cup of coffee at 11:00. I showed him my tattoo, and Jeannette too. Texas phoned at 5:20, but I didn't want to go to theirs and then go out with her after dinner to see her friends while Cornell is giving drawing lessons. Phoned Cornell when Tex was leaving. She

---

* There is no description of her tattoo in Pat's diary, only that she's considering getting one on her wrist. In 1946, she will mention another visit to a Chinatown tattoo parlor, again with no comment as to the design. According to Kingsley, Pat had a tattoo of her initials in Greek letters on her wrist.

wanted me to come and draw with them. I said no—but as I was going home, I couldn't resist—I had to go! I was so embarrassed when I entered the room! But I wasn't as uncomfortable as another young lady—a Negro woman who posed very well—and it amused me so I forgot the time. I stayed when the others left. We kissed maybe twice—when we heard Texas coming up the stairs! She came back early—and I didn't want her to know I was there! But nevertheless—when Cornell got into bed we kissed wildly—like a dream! She told me that she loves Tex, too. I said, yes, so do I. "But I love you and in a different way." I hope it's sexual!^{FF}

MAY 18, 1943
^FGood day—as I was dreaming of Cornell almost all day. Saw [Rolf] at his house for lunch. There's a magazine, *Home & Food** where the editor may like my stories. That would be a miracle. I'm thinking of Cornell, of her tongue in my mouth, of our moist lips—wet—together, of her hands on my body! There's so much to discover and explore that I will die of heat next time we are alone together.

Lots of fun with Rolf. He took nine of my stories—to show them to this woman. Perhaps I will sell one. I feel as though I can do anything at all. I think I will never again write a single word that isn't good. I'll make all the money I want, work in peace, and be very happy with Cornell, who will feel all the things I feel.

I'm full of great confidence!^{FF}

5/18/43
The first days of love are sweet, when one must dream long minutes after minutes, when the eyes cloud over like with blindness. (Why is it when one does not concentrate too hard, the sensations of the body are pleasurable and intense in these love

---

* Rolf Tietgens was *Home & Food*'s art director. The magazine not only bought two of Pat's stories, but also some of her drawings.

dreams? Nature bestows the highest delight, perhaps, upon
the more bestial, simple people who do not confuse their love-
making with intellectual processes, which may be successful in
heightening the pleasure, but which generally creates fiasco.) I
move around like a glass vial filled to the brim with ecstasy. I am
suffused with love, and all my pulses throb when I dream these
things. We are gentleness and honesty.

MAY 19, 1943
^FWorked all day on Black Terror*—and saved Hughes about
$12.00—he would have paid $37.00 for the job—"piece-work."
Rolf phoned me to tell me that the editor likes my stories and
that they'll buy "Friends"—the one about two people who communicate through the subway doors! I'll make $50.00. Perhaps
they'll buy a story a month. It's the day I've been waiting for
for six years, and I am so tired right now that it doesn't matter.
I'm happy and proud—why—for myself? No! Because Cornell
will be proud of me. She will read it, and perhaps she will love
me more. I wonder what she's doing right now. Sleeping, I hope.
In fact, Texas is in my bed right now. She forgot her keys at
home—she says. And she fell asleep—it's already 1:10 A.M. "I
don't want Cornell to know," I told her. But Cornell will know,
Tex said. There'll be nothing else to say other than she spent the
night at my place.

I envy Cornell slightly less today—and I still think that I am
emotionally unstable—and perhaps that I won't love her in a
week. At the parents' house for dinner. I told them the story
about the party at Hoyningen-Huene's and Horst B.† with Rolf.
It's astonishing how much I can tell them! The next step is to tell
them that Rolf is gay, and that I am too, I suppose.

I'm happy. Am reading *Les pensées* by [Charles] Péguy. Very
good.^{FF}

---

* Black Terror was a comic book superhero created by Richard E. Hughes. The character first
appeared in January 1941.
† Georg Freiherr von Hoyningen-Huene (1900–1968) and his lover Horst Bohrmann were
two of the most noted fashion photographers of their time.

5/19/43

Two hours before the dawn, with the rain speaking in staccato slowly from the sleeping eaves, the sleepy drip-drip-drip to the moist black ground, to the wet leaves of the hedges, and the coal dark cement. The air is not air but a distillate of the night and of what has happened or might have happened or yet will happen, or of what will be said—by whom? By the poet with his lover in his heart, pregnant figure soft and incorporeal as the delicately gray shadows. Man—this is the hour. Search now whatever you seek vainly in the day and in the night. Search between the two thin edges of the knives! That together will destroy you!

Lover, go forth!

MAY 22, 1943

[F]Met mother at Winslow at 1:30 for a drink. I have now realized that she possesses all the joie de vivre I feel right now. She has always possessed it. We often discuss homosexuality, and perhaps it won't be long before I tell her the truth. My love for Cornell seems to me so great, beautiful, and pure that it should not be kept secret—and yet when I'm with her and imagine I've already told her, I feel confused, unhappy, and don't know what to do. I'm so tired that I've almost lost the happiness—the wild joy—I've had all week. I would be too tired to make love to Cornell—and that would be a disaster![FF]

5/22/43

Surely there are times when the most ardent and devoted lovers have no desire—even in the beloved's arms, when the moisture of her lips is something unpleasant, to be wiped away. Then it seems the kisses and embraces are the candy one has eaten enough of—and the work one must do is the bread and meat. This is frightening to experience the first time. I think it is all the more indicative of the true love, which varies with the variations of the mind and moods, and is not dependent upon physical stimulation, but on mental and psychic needs and demands.

MAY 23, 1943

[F]Good day, but I hate Sundays—I never get anything done. I only had two minutes alone with Cornell. I won't deny it—the desire—the powerful desire is gone. I am not crazy, and I wasn't crazy last week. The kisses are, as I said, like candy. Now I am in need of bread and meat, and I have found them within her—solid and plentiful.[FF]

MAY 25, 1943

[F]Had a long talk with Camy over two beers. "If I weren't already hitched, I'd lead you a merry chase!" Cornell's at 8:15. There was a small but shapely young woman there. Like a good Degas. And lots of other people. I drew better than last week. Cornell sat close to me, but I didn't show her my drawing. Afterwards—we were on the sofa—and I told her slowly—everything I've wanted to say for a long time. Texas made a comment about my breasts, and Cornell wanted to know how she knew? And surprisingly enough—Cornell said she thought we were making fun of her—that Texas and I were in love, etc. It's incredible—I don't think she truly believed it. "I think you both want to be nice to me." Cornell prefers to be loved, passive. And she prefers women because she doesn't have to give as much to them as men. But she can love both. I've kissed her a thousand times—but not like Sunday night—I've been smoking too much, and my tongue is bothering me. Peace—we found it for a few moments, when we were together, head to head, lips to lips, fingers running through each other's hair. And we will find it again when we live together.

Bought T. S. Eliot: 4 *Quartets*. $2.00 for 37 pages![FF]

MAY 25, 1943

[F]Fawcett sent me four synopses: they took one Spy Smasher.[*]
Three rejected: two Ibis[†] and one S.S. I'm happy. 10 pages means

---

[*] Spy Smasher was a superhero who first appeared in *Whiz Comics* #2 (February 1940), published by Fawcett.
[†] Ibis the Invincible was a comic book superhero who first appeared in February 1940.

$30.00. Tired at the office—I exerted myself too much last week.
Allela came by at 5:30. Incredibly enough, she looked at the
pictures with a serious eye, and said it would be fun to be an
"inker."* It's awful—!FF

MAY 27, 1943
GWonderful day, although it would have been better to spend
the evening at home. I don't make enough money. Wish I could
bring work home to make more.GG

MAY 29, 1943
GSaw Cornell at 8:15. Bought her 6 bottles of Coke and brought
her a frog—which she liked very much. I wanted Texas to go
to bed, but she came along to the movies at 42nd Street. Saw
Bucket of Blood, very "nice"! I wanted to go home with them
after, but have work tomorrow. Love Cornell—her mind,
though, because I don't like her body. Her hands, her lips—yes,
but not her body.GG

MAY 30, 1943
GAllela—very loving—called me at 7:00. She wanted to see *Desert Victory*, but not without me. Found her and Tex and Peto on
8th St. Held her hand with such passion during *Desert Victory*, I
really am in love! Oh, God! When she pulled my hand—twice—
into her lap!—I shot straight up to heaven! Five years ago, such
little things (?!) would have aroused me terribly, made me happy.
Now I just want more and more, like I always want more money
in the bank. They wanted me to spend the night at theirs, but
tonight I wanted her too much. It would have been torture. The
body wouldn't understand.

I sometimes feel inadequate, compared to Texas. I wonder if
Cornell thinks the same? I want to be everything to her. If Bernhard knew, wouldn't she say I was playing the same game as
with her and Rolf?GG

---

* In comic book production, an "inker" is an artist who retraces pencil line drawings in ink.

JUNE 1, 1943

ᴳA day of importance—of utmost importance. At 7:30, Tex called. She brought me a glass of brandy. Naturally I drank the entire glass and then we kissed, like lovers, almost like how I kiss Cornell, but without the dreaminess and without the tenderness. And in tears, Tex said how she wanted to make love to me and had even started to, when Cornell phoned. In flagrante delicto—truly, because I couldn't talk straight. She knew everything when she came at ten o'clock. I was completely crushed and couldn't speak. I truly hated Texas. I told them they wanted to make each other jealous. It's true, and that means they still love each other.

"Right now I think you are a bitch," Cornell told me, "I hate this!" And I felt as I did in Dec. 1941, and January. I wanted to jump out a window. Lastly—"I wish I could give you what Texas gives you." "I think you could give me much more." My heart skipped a beat—"Then I won't go jumping out of any windows!" It was wonderful, and her cheeks were as soft as ever. I don't deserve her, but I have her. Everything I've worked for, thought, felt—everything was for her, I know it. It was never for Rosalind, she doesn't understand me any more than I understand her. Cornell wants a lot from me. She already takes a lot from Texas, but "I think you could give me much more." I will never forget that. Our three lives are tightly interwoven. We love each other. What happens now?ᴳᴳ

JUNE 3, 1943

ᴳGood day—although it started out sad with Allela. She fought with Texas last night, and Texas threw the clock at the wall. Allela said Tex doesn't want us talking behind her back, etc.

I talked to Camy today, and he said: "If you go out with the other fellow—do it good. His friend doesn't want it any more'n you do." Yes—I could make her so jealous, but that doesn't interest me. I always want to be upright. Can't do it. This all proves that Cornell loved me, I'm sure of it. She wants to hurt herself, torture herself, and may even want me to love Tex for a while so she can feel sorry for herself. It's embarrassing to me, and what a waste of precious time!!!! We won't live forever! (Worked on Bill King.)[*][GG]

JUNE 6, 1943

[G]Sunday—how boring! How useless! I have so much time, I can't settle down enough to work! Looked for milk and cursed the housewives of the Bronx—who had already bought it all up! I hope the useless, unnecessary bottles spoil in their coolers! And they will! Painted a window in the kitchen.[†] Adam and Eve— Adam hanging from a branch, eating an apple.[GG]

JUNE 7, 1943

[G]Went to Eddie's Aurora with Fij and Dolly.[GG] [F]Lots of coffee. I saw the black-haired woman who lives on Grove St.—the one I fell in love with and who made me feel shy and scared, all when I was 20! She came in with her husband, Crockett Johnson, who writes "Barnaby" for PM.[‡] She saw me and smiled at me. Am tired, but happy.[FF]

JUNE 8, 1943

[G]Fantastic day! Hard work at the office. Dan[§] phoned at 12 and we ate together at Del Pezzo. I was terribly bored, though, so I ate like a sailor. Nice to be alone at home this evening. Painted the wall—white fireplace,[¶] but didn't finish. Washed up, read ([Freud's] *Moses and Monotheism*).[GG] [F]I was so happy I asked

---

[*] Bill King was an *Exciting Comics* character. The heroic soldier who fought in the Pacific during World War II made his first appearance in April 1940.
[†] Pat decorates her apartment with trompe l'oeil paintings.
[‡] In 1941 Pat had a crush on a beautiful woman she regularly bumped into in her neighborhood. This was Ruth Krauss (1901–1993), an American children's book author who wrote such classic titles as *The Carrot Seed*, still in print today. In 1943, Krauss married Crockett Johnson (1906–1975), an American writer and children's book illustrator who created some of the twentieth century's most beloved comic-strip characters, including Barnaby.
[§] Her cousin Dan Coates, who is visiting New York.
[¶] Another trompe l'oeil painting, this one of a fireplace.

myself whether I should actually go away this summer? I could manage to have fun in the city.^{FF}

JUNE 9, 1943

^GPhoned—no—Cornell phoned me at 8:45, and I phoned her at 12 and 12:30. "Will you miss me?" "A little." "You bitch!" My head is full of work, though, and I'm sure several days will pass before I fully comprehend that she's gone. Worked on Spy Smasher tonight, then Sy Krim stopped by, and later Texas! Pleasant evening, as I finished my work. Feel happy—sold the story about the cripple.[*] That means $100.00, so now I can buy the radio at Lino's.^{GG}

JUNE 10, 1943

^GNo letter from Allela, but a card from Bernhard. Mother here to paint my bookcases. And she said I mustn't become like Cornell, crying every night, wanting to be "pretty," but not doing anything about it. She also used the word lesbian. Wrote to Allela, although I was far too tired. Am still happy and full of hope.^{GG}

JUNE 11, 1943

^GWhat distresses me at the office is the confusion all day long! Worked on Pyroman[†] synopsis today, and every word was torture! But three stories came back for revisions. Must work more slowly without worrying about how many stories I am able to write. At home, at my parents'. Stanley just got a new job! Industrial Press layout, type orange—art Director. Very nice, and the change will be good for him.

I am full of power, strength, and^{GG} I "shall go in so many directions."[‡]

---

* "Uncertain Treasure."
† Pyroman was a superhero who first appeared in December 1942.
‡ Quote from Rosalind in her letter Pat received in San Francisco on August 8, 1941.

JUNE 12, 1943

^GMet Tex at 2:00, and we went to Leighton's. We found some beautiful silk shirts, marked down from 5.98 to 1.29 (!). We bought five, two striped for me, along with collars and cravats.^GG

6/13/43

Strange, unearthly perfection of the week after one has fallen in love, when the ringing of a doorbell in one's court seems part of a prearranged and beautiful plan, when the pattern of the people on the street is inevitable and pleasing, when all shadows and substances are distinct, with individual qualities, that one can, with a magic omniscience, understand and feel in detail. What becomes of the evil at such times? We smile at it, if we happen to see it or think of it, and so this proves we are drunken, temporarily, drunken.

JUNE 15, 1943

^GMade the acquaintance of Fenton* at 12:30. Rolf there. Pretty girl. And she wants more writing. At my parents', but I can't stand Dan any longer! Wrote Golden Arrow and sent it to Fawcett. Perhaps the last, because it's time I started living. That means writing, thinking, loving.^GG

JUNE 16, 1943

^GGot enough sleep, and work went better. Read Kafka in the sun at 12:30. Now *Home & Food* is using my story about the cripple. Went by Rolf's at 5:45, and he took several photographs. Then we translated a poem by Hölderlin, which sounds very nice. He wanted to eat with me, which is why I didn't do any work. Anyway, how—how could anyone work after discussing ancient Greece and art? We talked about everything beautiful and ugly in the world. We were joined in mind and heart and body. I loved Rolf very much tonight. We paged through *Hellas*, which J.J. [Augustin] made, and he stayed till 2:30 a.m.!^GG

---

* Possibly Fleur Fenton, managing editor at *Home & Food*.

6/16/43

The terrifying, bestial ugliness of a scolding voice in the darkness, somewhere. When I lie in bed and hear this, I am seized
with fear, shame, and simple pain. Why is it? It is something
akin to pity—because we can imagine the same sensations if we
watched a murder, when there was no danger of harm to us.

JUNE 18, 1943

GDan left yesterday—thank God! I am full of love—and desire
Allela as I desire endless peace—as I desire answers to all the
questions in the world. No letter, and I'm bored talking to
myself. Phoned Rolf tonight, yet I'm still lonely! Took great pleasure in reading the *Encyclopedia Britannica* this morning, since
Hughes was out. Egyptology. Then to the dentist at 2:00. The
[laughing] gas was sweet, and I wanted it! Hungered for it! Had
all kinds of dreams. There were countless circles containing natural phenomena, and I sought with the discovery and bestowal
of knowledge that I was God! That I, of all people on earth,
lived before the earth's creation, created the earth, and would
live to see it end. In short, that I knew the philosophers' secret!
Would that it were true!—I wouldn't be happy, in that case, but
miserable! Have the tooth.GG

JUNE 20, 1943

GHome at 11:00 and cleaned everything—Mother came, and
alone again afterward I painted the fireplace and mantel-
piece. And a golden clock, which looks wonderful. Proud of
it. But I did absolutely nothing to make money. I painted 4
hours and read Kafka this evening. My dear soul, today was
your day!GG

JUNE 21, 1943

GFantastic day. Hot. Worked quickly at the office, wrote a little
to A.C. Texas was very attentive this evening and read some of
her letter from Allela out loud—that she loved her—loved her
very much—and that A.C. wanted her to be with her on vaca-

tion. I was so disgusted by Allela's indecision that I soon left the house.^{GG}

JUNE 22, 1943

^GI wrote Allela that I have to set out on my own and probably can't see her anymore. That I have no patience for weakness and indecision. And after posting the letter, I wondered why I didn't feel sad and downtrodden about this girl who's become downright indispensable to me and with whom I am inextricably bound. Now—when I recall the many times she said "I love you" to me, I feel neither sad nor hopeless nor ashamed of what I wrote. I don't want to write her again. She'll miss my letters and without a doubt later find some resolve. It—love—is as indispensable to her as she is to me. Got good work done, which surprised me, especially in this heat! I felt good about Cornell—this is the tooth extraction that will "make it all good" again.^{GG}

JUNE 23, 1943

^GI had no right to write such things to Allela. It's all true, but I shouldn't have written it. I spent all day thinking about this evening, when I was supposed to call her. Ate at my parents', who seem so common to me—particularly now that I'm in heaven with Allela. At 8 o'clock I called Allela in Wash. D.C. She's coming back Friday, and I'll be at the train station. Her voice sounded beautiful to me, gentle and quiet, and as full of affection and love as she can sometimes make it. Yes, I love her unconditionally. Rewrote S.S. synopsis.^{GG}

JUNE 24, 1943

^GO happy, happy day! No letter this morning as I ate peaches and cream, but there was one this evening when I got home. Airmail!!! It was pale red—the stamp—and I laid it on the carpet till I had taken a shower and dusted the house, poured some rum, lit a cigarette—and finally—four yellow pages—all about the cat painting, and on the last page—last line, she wrote: My

love Pat really—Allela. And my heart soared once more! I'll keep
the letters—(four) of course. Forever.^{GG}
 ^FI cut my hair.^{FF}

JUNE 25, 1943
 ^GToo hot to work or sleep. 96, I think. Cornell comes back
today!
 Fawcett taking second S.S. and second Lance. That means
$54.00. Got good work done, and the longer stories come to me
more easily—you can take them further. Read lots of Freud,
which brings my heart joy! Psychoanalysis of religion. Wonderfully interesting! Dentist at 1:30. I've recently come to endure all
kinds of pain! Nothing is too awful or alien! Home at 6:00 for
a shower, then at Penn [Station] at 7:30. Texas E. there too, but
I saw Cornell first. Black dress and smiling. We had 2 drinks at
Savarin, and there were a few wonderful moments, seeing her—
so close to me. She loves us both equally. What will come of it
all? What?—I have to hold myself together, without becoming
sad or hopeless or hopeful. Must work, because that—working—
is the purpose of the life I want to have with Cornell.^{GG}

JUNE 26, 1943
 ^FSaw "Globalism"* at Wildenstein—nothing that Klee, Miró, or
Dalí haven't already done. Feininger, etc. and a painter named
Sewan (I think) [Schewe]. His work is considered "poetic," and
we both were in this hot room, spoke a lot.
 Lots to do at home. It's important for me to live alone because
I want to plumb all of my moods, and I don't want a woman to
come over to me with a mug of hot chocolate! No! In times like
these, I consume myself, and I love it. Then, when I wake up, I
am still myself, and am happy for it. Energy is a gift of the gods.
 Good night! ($280.04 in the bank.)^{FF}

---

* The Wildenstein Gallery held its third annual exhibit of work by the Federation of Modern
Painters and Sculptors.

JUNE 27, 1943

[F]Not a good day—accomplished nothing of importance. Went to the Metropolitan Museum at 3:30 with mother to see the Bache collection.[*] Magnificent objects, not paintings. The Michelangelo sculptures pleased me greatly, and "*The Young Sophocles*" by (who?).

At home, Krim phoned me. Against my better judgment, went with him to the Hymans'[†] who work for the *New Yorker*. Disgusting Jews.[‡] But the wife, Shirley Jackson,[§] was alright. We drank a cup of coffee together (two) and I told her about several of my stories. She writes for all the magazines, and suggested I find an agent. Yes.[FF]

JUNE 29, 1943

[G]Normal day at the office, but too much to do—always too much. The maid didn't come, so I had to clean the entire house for Rosalind. She came over, so I put on my new slip and made a wonderful drink of rum, water, orange, etc. Sugar. "Heaven!—It's heaven!" she said, as she lay on my bed. Rosalind was genuine, laughing, pretty. She drank slowly, looked at my fireplace, which she likes very much. It was raining when she left—but it was a wonderful, rare evening.[GG]

JUNE 30, 1943

[G]Today Mr. Hughes reprimanded me for missing two mistakes in a story. Said that I get to work late, take too long to eat, and

---

[*] Jules Semon Bache (1861–1944), American banker, art collector, and philanthropist.

[†] Stanley Edgar Hyman (1919–1970), American literary critic and staff writer for *The New Yorker*.

[‡] Patricia Highsmith's anti-Semitic abuse of the Hymans was mistakenly omitted from this entry in the 2021 edition of *Her Diaries and Notebooks, 1941–1995*.

[§] Shirley Hardie Jackson (1916–1965), American writer of horror and mystery novels (e.g., *The Haunting of Hill House*, *We Have Always Lived in the Castle*) and more than two hundred short stories.

that I take the job for granted. "There was a nice spirit when you started—you have to hold on to that, etc." Yes, I was sad, because it was all true and I am so hopelessly bored. Rosalind said: "You shouldn't stay there too long!" Yes, of course. I'm not going away this summer vacation—I don't have the money and there's too much to do here—not in the city, but in my heart and in my soul. I have to look for a new job.

Cornell came at 6:00. We sat a long time, nipping at our drinks, and could finally have a nice conversation. We looked through *Hellas*. And I saw heaven as I kissed her, as I lay with her on the bed, our kisses so wonderful I almost made love to her. But as my hand was about to touch her, the telephone rang—doesn't it just figure?! She almost cried—it would have been so nice. Taxi to hers, and she kissed me for what might be the last time for the next two months! I came home as if on a cloud. Have no money, but no matter—have so much else!GG

JULY 1, 1943

FI feel like the high period—the mania—is here now. 3½ hours of sleep and I feel wonderful! Full of energy! And this morning, I thought of Allela so much I had to go to the bathroom to relieve myself of a large erection. Is that disgusting? Am I a psychopath? Sure—why not? I almost had an orgasm just thinking of her! It can happen! The stories continue to bore me. Two synopses today. Phoned Rosalind at 8:00. Looked at apartments for her. There's a large one above me—that's the apartment Rosalind will probably take. This development gives me a lot to think about. I'm thinking of breakfasts together in the winter when it will be cold, when we will work hard and I will bring her soup, or something else. I love her, and this would suit us better than actually living together.

Camy came from 9:00–10:20. He talks too much about himself. Did nothing.FF

JULY 4, 1943

ᶠBuffie came at 8:30. She likes my apartment—somewhat—my fireplace, yes, but no comment on my drawings. Would like to get a lot done tomorrow. Buffie very stupid tonight. She gave me a pretty red jacket. With the parents—mother and I had another disgusting conversation about Negroes—we haven't done so in two years, and it's just as pointless as mother's remarks on Marjorie Thompson's corpulence. I should stop coming over. She makes me terribly nervous, and that's why I moved out in the first place!ᶠᶠ

JULY 5, 1943

ᶠCornell woke me up with a phone call. She wanted me to come to the train station at 4:00. But I didn't go. Cornell was sad, like a little girl, and mumbled, "Well I want to see you—I want you to see me off." She called me again from the street—(secretly) and—still I said no. She told me that she doesn't think I love her because I'm making her suffer. But she understands that it's because I love her that I can't be content with half-measures. She left very melancholy—and that's what she needs! She must love me passionately or forget me completely. No reading—no writing—a real day off.ᶠᶠ

JULY 6, 1943

ᶠSpent a miserable day in my heart, in which I experienced all the sadness which I feel now, just like before I met Allela. To give her up would be madness. My body is closed up, my wings are on the ground. And my spirit, my brain, body, and soul revolt against this refusal. Bored at the office. At Fawcett, Magill is going to quit in order to write popular stories for magazines. It's disgusting. All these small minds!

Lola and Rosalind here at 8:20. Rosalind very kind and affectionate tonight. Lola liked my drawings too. I can imagine what R. said about me at dinner—that I have a lot of talent—more than anyone else she knows. Isn't that so? Happy. Headache—but:

1) Cornell will no doubt write me—

2) Rosalind will come live here.

3) Rosalind will come eat here this week.

4) Began the Laval story.

5) A good hour with Péguy.

Yes—my blessings.^{FF}

JULY 7, 1943

^FNo letter yet, and I—I asked myself all day whether I should write her—yes or no. But it isn't pride. It's only that I want us to be together. Well—I didn't write and I won't. She's behaving like a woman and waiting for me.^{FF}

JULY 8, 1943

^FToothache last night, perhaps I'll have to get another one pulled!

At last—a letter from Allela—I opened it with some trepidation! Written in pencil—four pages. She wrote it on the train to Hampton. Her words are so beautiful, her feelings delicate and strong at once! She still loves me, like one spirit loves another, and she will never cease loving me—and though I gain nothing from it—she thinks that love—this love—is worth the suffering and anxiety of waiting. Oh, how true! I know it well! And her letter gave me much hope. I wrote her almost all morning. It's food for my soul!

I may have sold two of my drawings to *Home & Food*. Nitsche[*] has to see them.

Bored at the office, and desperate for my vacation. Wrote 7 pages of the Laval story. They're good, I think. Had dinner with the parents tonight. When I told them that I'd received an eight-page letter from Cornell, mother said: You're saying that like a lover! What does it matter? I don't care!^{FF}

---

* Possibly Erik Nitsche (1908–1998), Swiss-born graphic designer and artist who contributed to the magazine *Simplicissimus* before moving to New York and working for *Life*, *Vanity Fair*, and *Harper's Bazaar*.

JULY 10, 1943

ᶠNo one—almost no one—in the office, and even Hughes didn't dare ask me what I was working on! Didn't have a single idea and didn't do a single thing.ᶠᶠ

JULY 11, 1943

ᶠI know I will get a letter tomorrow morning, and so I've gone mad! I've gone as violently mad as I've ever been—when I was 6—12—15—17—20—and now I am mad with greater reason. I am reading good books—the Bible—[Charles] Péguy, [Julien] Green, old books that are the best—and all my love joins with theirs. They are one. In the world, there is one image, one virtue, one work—the truth within man's soul—and I am this man. Only Cornell is compatible with this—the truth of the flesh and the spirit. I felt that this day was full of truths. It is because of days like these that I hope this diary will be re-read one day! I made Virginia pose until one. Not bad, but my drawings could be better. She was ungrateful as usual, but what do I care? I am happy, and rich in the treasures of the spirit!ᶠᶠ

7/11/43

What gentle madness in me. It comes when twilight comes. It is hardly worth mentioning. But it is as strange as the stirring of one leaf on a tree, when there is no wind.

JULY 12, 1943

ᶠMiserable this morning—not like a young girl, but like an old philosopher. I thought quickly and well about lots of things. There was no letter from Cornell. I couldn't work at all this morning, and the next few weeks until August and my vacation will be hell! No rest for body or spirit, yet I took a (troubled) walk home at 12:45—and incredibly, still no letter! Oh, I can bear everything except this silence! This solitude! Misery—misery at the office!

Marjorie W. and D. Lawrence tonight. They're a bit strange—the kind of people who don't drink or smoke enough.

I made drawings of Marj and D.L. They think I am or will become a good artist.[FF]

7/12/43

The making peace with myself is the hardest, and perhaps will be the greatest accomplishment to my credit when I die.

JULY 13, 1943

[F]I'm ecstatic—a letter arrived—a white, slender letter in the mailbox. I worked well. Now, everything is bearable. Bought two tickets (for R. and myself) for July 15, which is our anniversary, but I won't remind her of this fact. She phoned me. She almost always calls me "darling" now, and I thought tonight that she must love me a lot—because she knows I am faithful—in the only manner she requires—I am always by her side to help. When she moves, for instance! Read Péguy and wrote Cornell a long letter—modest but truthful, in which I told her I'd sold these small drawings—and a message from Péguy—that the body is joined to the soul like two hands in prayer. It's beautiful. Made five new drawings tonight—very pleased—and two are good enough to send to the *New Yorker*.

My love grows and grows for my other soul: Allela Cornell.[FF]

JULY 15, 1943

[F]Texas E. will go to Texas in August—and we'll be left alone together.

Drew tonight, too, without much luck. I have to let go and allow the expressions within my soul to arise.[FF]

JULY 16, 1943

[F]Am largely happy, would very much like to spend some time with R. [Rosalind] C. and speak with her. She has decided against the apartment. (It's an ugly apartment for the money, I think.) Near midnight, I took a short walk around the neighborhood. The moon is big and round, an immense circle in the sky![FF]

7/16/43

To be creative is the only excuse, the only mitigating factor, for being homosexual.

7/16/43

To pass by an open garage, to catch the dynamic aroma of rubber, gasoline and compressed air, to see the rows of shining, black, powerful cars, is physically the most exciting experience I know. It is movement, freedom, leisure, and the absence of all fettering of daily routine.

Yet how selfish to think of such things, when even tonight I read a stirring account of the American landing in Sicily, and for a moment actually saw the body of the young American soldier, his fists clenched, charred to death on a landing barge. How prosaic to relate this experience, these importunate, irrevocable, ineluctable facts!

JULY 18, 1943

FOh God—there's a good life to be had, single, working, making beautiful, lasting things—but I cannot bear this life! It's suicide, it's a sin! I must change it! Made drawings of R., because I would like to make a wooden head,* and I'm getting sick. Being sick is very enticing—tomorrow—mother could take care of me—bring me my letters, my books, and I could write the Laval story, for which I now have a good outline.FF

JULY 19, 1943

FOn this day two years ago, I met R.C. at Lola P.'s. A bad day— a day that should have been so happy! Mostly, it was because of money—which disgusts me, but it's always a problem. Wednesday, I think, I'll go to Sangor and ask for a raise. I deserve at

---

* Pat did indeed make this wooden head. Rosalind returned it to her in 1992: "In case you wonder why I am parting with it [. . .], it is because I am putting my house in order. I expect one day soon, if not already, somebody is going to write a life of you, and these evidences of what you do with your left hand might come in handy" (letter from Rosalind, June 30, 1992, Swiss Literary Archives).

least $125 a week. I'll ask for $75.00(!) Rosalind was late, first
at Edward Melcarth's, who will give her a painting for *Fortune*.
His figures are beautiful. Rosalind very quiet, almost indifferent
towards me. Naturally, she didn't know that today was our anniversary. We are shy together, almost boring and bored, would
like to say something to each other—but aren't brave enough to
say it.

I'm moving in circles now. Nothing certain except that I must
change my life—more money or another job. In any case—talk
is cheap! I want to paint. I want to create all sorts of things, and
I will. On my walk tonight with Rosalind—I felt once again that
we have no one except each other. I believe it.[FF]

JULY 20, 1943

Reading Julien Green today. I thought how foolish of me to go
on writing this diary in foreign languages*—and so badly that I
don't exercise the speech forms that would come in English—so
badly that the words shouldn't appear anywhere but in a grammar notebook—I am so ambitious, that I must telescope 2 separate activities—writing a diary and learning a language.

7/21/43

We can make things alone for pleasure—and the moment they're
sold and bring in money, we're ashamed of them! Why? Because
too much is expected of the thing that is "sold"? or more likely
because we have betrayed this innocent, docile, unsuspecting
little living thing.

7/21/43

The ideal life—the activities of a perfect fortnight. Two such
fortnights per month, twelve such months per year. Work in the
daytime, read and dream and perhaps work at night, thirteen
out of the fourteen days. On the fourteenth night, be with a
number of congenial people, some with brains and some with-

---

* Pat writes this, then promptly reverts to French in her very next diary entry.

out. The evening must begin with good conversation, and end
in utter drunkenness, carousing, incoherent speech to show the
potentialities of the language, incoherent pictures in the eye, to
show the miracles of visions and visionaries!

JULY 22, 1943
[F]Still no letter from Allela—and though I'm not miserable, I'm
a bit sad. Lately, I can't imagine her face. In a certain sense, I
killed that unerring happiness I knew in May! But it will come
back when she does. In truth, I don't have enough time to imagine my kisses—as slowly as they should be. Spent some time
with mother tonight. I haven't written my grandmother in six
months! I didn't even notice! I read some Christian Science,
which will do me a lot of good.[FF]

JULY 23, 1943
[F]I was at the station at 5:45. After having chased down a dozen
trains, my eyes almost brimming with tears!—I found Lela,
standing all alone, smoking, in front of the big gates of the station! She was wearing her red dress and took my hand. Oh, she
looked beautiful! We waited for Texas—then Breevort, where
we drank 10 drinks between us. Cornell has obtained an invitation for me to her parents' tomorrow night. Come to dinner! It
will be very important. And I'm thrilled about it![FF]

7/23/43
At the dentist's—I turn the knob of the door, and with the resistance of the knob—the visit has definitely begun. But I have not
composed myself enough. If I had only five more minutes outside the door how much better I could face it! I think about gas.
Would Julien Green's and Picasso's gaseous hallucinations not
be more interesting than mine? Than other peoples'? But why
should they be until their artistic minds have altered them? They
would be the same as the next person's until this occurred. Or is
there such a thing as an educated subconscious? Is there an intelligent or an artistic subconscious? Especially I reflect that when

death comes, I shall be no better prepared. I shall still wish, with
all my dwindling strength, for five more minutes in which to for-
mulate some idea of what I am about to experience, two more
minutes to make my peace with God, one more minute to kiss
her goodbye and to swear that she will join me finally in that
realm where there is only perfection.

JULY 24, 1943

FDid nothing today—except what I wanted. Went to see the
parents, saw two exhibitions, then went with mother to the
Bowery to buy two shirts, one for me, beige, silk, $2.50. I'd
like to get my monogram on the shirt. I read a bit—then to the
Cornells' for dinner. Mr. Cornell is tall, somewhat handsome,
a bit like Claude Coates. And finally, Allela—the life and
blood of the family! She's very brown from the sun. Tex looked
very beautiful in her black dress. The grandmother is old, very
thin, and smokes and drinks! A bit stiff, dignified, but has a
sense of humor. Very good for a grandmother, and knows a
bit of German. A weak drink prepared by Mr. Cornell, then a
big dinner, very lovely—though I was shy. Cornell very sweet.
She took me upstairs, where she kissed me—I kissed her very
slowly, very tenderly, both of us standing in her room. How I
adore her lips! Oh, we were alone for five minutes! She is still a
bit shy, just like me, but she gave me as much as she could! And
I did too!FF

JULY 25, 1943

FA bad day, the saddest of my life so far. Breakfast at 11:00,
too many cigarettes and too much coffee, then drew, none of
the drawings any good. Wrote 7½ pages of my story but it was
done too fast. At parents' house at 5:30 for Allela and Texas.
Then Three Crowns for dinner. I drank too much and my throat
hurt—smoked too much—maybe three packs today. In any case
I was miserable and sad, because I didn't manage to say any of
the things I wanted to. At Nick's together, where we stood at
the bar, listening to music. Then at Figi's for a moment, then her

apartment on Grove St. My throat hurt badly—and then got worse—I almost wanted to die! And I wrote one or two pages about this when I came home. Tex said that we have Cornell "in common"—she knows about everything, I'm sure. (And at the parents', the conversation was about homosexuality.) And with Allela—when Tex went upstairs—I couldn't speak, so quickly went home. I couldn't kiss her. I touched the most profound depths tonight.[FF]

7/25/43

My own work is unfinished, and I owe a great debt to all those who have fed and clothed me all these years. I owe a different debt to the one I love best. All the tears I should have shed in a long lifetime are coming now and mean nothing to me. There is no life nor truth without the one I love. There is no optimism and no accomplishment. There is no health and no future.

I have wanted long labors, of detail, and perfection, affection and great care, worthy of past artists. Inspiration is a great arc of momentum, and the momentum is love, and love requited. I cannot speak humbly enough of all the humble things I have to speak of. The absence of you has torn my insides out! I am sick with tears, and sick with the stoppage of my love. My love is greater than I, and dammed up has risen and drowned me! What does this night foretell? A quiet house, a peaceful fire-placed room, with a woman in a long brown velvet dress. What does this foretell?—Good work and healthful days? I don't believe it, because God has made this moment too poignant, and actually too perfect of its kind. My mouth is bitter and I don't want to kiss you. No, I am not in command of myself, but love is in command of me, and this love is destructive, though meant to be creative. Never more than at this minute, was I ready to meet the Omnipotent One. Never more fearless, never more proud of myself and never more humbled before this power infinitely greater than I.

JULY 26, 1943

^{F}Sick this morning—couldn't speak—but Cornell phoned me
at 8:30. Met her at Penn Station at 9:25. We didn't have much to
say to each other—just that we had a good time and that there
will be more good times to come. Finally, she kissed me on the
train. Yes—during these months, I've forgotten to be grateful
for her—grateful for the future itself! She is the future—I am the
present. I am here, and without her. And now I must work.^{FF}

JULY 28, 1943

^{F}I've done nothing over the past months except love Allela—but
isn't this my entire life? No letter this morning, though I went
down to look three times! How sad it is to come home and look
at this empty box! If she knew, she'd write, I think. She has to
do something without my control. I wrote 6 pages of the Laval
story, and I think they're good. I must always stay confident.
Was happy and phoned Rolf. He has 16 pages in the next *Coronet!** Raphael Mahler gave me a call, and will come Sunday night
to speak our two languages.^{FF}

JULY 29, 1943

^{F}I can't work with J. [Jerry] Albert.† It's better in the factory
in front of the office. It made me think that I wouldn't want to
write if I didn't live in New York! One must have something to
fight against before one can produce. Joseph H. phoned me,
but I wanted to write tonight—and I wrote six pages. The story
is coming along well, I think. Julien Green is giving me a lot
of inspiration, and I'd like to write him. He's here now, in the
army. (!)‡ Italy is almost defeated. The Germans continue to

---

* *Coronet* was a pocket-sized general interest magazine owned by *Esquire* and published
from 1936 to 1971.
† Gerald "Jerry" Albert, fellow scriptwriter and also editor at the Sangor Shop.
‡ During the Nazi German occupation of France in World War II, Julien Green supported the
French Resistance from the United States.

fight the allies, with more strength than the Italians. I'm hoping for—a letter tomorrow.[FF]

JULY 31, 1943

[G]Pleasant morning and got my money at the bank. $250.00 and $250.00 in bonds, nearly.

Rolf was horrible when I went to visit. He was reading Dalí's autobiography [*The Secret Life of Salvador Dalí*], and as always thinks that no one understands the stuff but him, and I got the distinct sense he wanted to fight with me. He's like a woman. When God puts us two together, I'll be the better man! Tex phoned at 8:15. She said she and Allela decided to put a bit more money into the house so that they'll be able to spend their winter evenings more agreeably at home. So sad, so deeply sad, I've rarely felt like this in my life. When October comes, will I be alone? Worked hard, though, and finished my Laval story. 25½ pages of yellow legal pad paper. And I felt better after.[GG]

AUGUST 2, 1943

[G]Letter from Allela. She worked hard last week—and loved it. Nervous at the office. Short conversation at 6:00 about my requested raise. They're offering $42.50, which almost made me laugh! We need to speak with Sangor again. He wanted me, Hughes said, because I was the "healthy type." I think there are other reasons—little money and no office. (Aren't I mean!) Painted the cabinet this evening and wrote the necessary letter to Alice Williams at Time Inc. I want to find another job right away. It would be nice to say—"if you don't give me $75.00 a week, I'm leaving—" and then leave! (FEEL VERY ADULT AND REASONABLE!!) Wrote a good letter to Allela as well. She's coming August 13th! She must come. It is of cosmic consequence![GG]

8/2/43

Almost everybody in the world lives because he believes it is more pleasant than to die. I see for the majority no ambitions

---

and no goals. Love and work are the two enduring possessions here and hereafter, and how little do most of us make of them! We make them commonplace, silly and degraded. And yet all religions teach that to die is to be reborn, that the afterlife for one who has kept God and love and righteousness intact is more desirable than this!

AUGUST 3, 1943

ᶠI can't work in the office any longer! It's completely impossible! Sometimes I think I can't even write another page! And I tell myself that in three weeks, I'll be gone! Ken [Battlefield] understands, and Marty Smith does too. But not the others. Met Tex at *Vogue* at 5:30. Also met Mallison* who liked my drawing of the Hungarian soldier. She said: "For the love of God, make some other drawings and bring them to Lieberman at *Vogue*.† You can draw!" Declarations like this make me very sad! Tex and I had drinks at Shelton Corners. I made her dinner. We were happy, we were hungry, and there was love in the kitchen— not physical, but in the air! But my damned tooth ached badly. Couldn't sleep until 4:30.ᶠᶠ

AUGUST 4, 1943

ᶠHorrible day. My tooth hurt like hell again at 12:30. It has to be pulled. I can't take it any longer! I long for those beautiful days when I worked like a man—at home, for myself, and—

Last night, Tex said that Allela belongs to the whole world. It was very profound! With the parents for a moment by the river. Then at home, mother helped me paint my cabinet. And I'm just as happy now as I was miserable all day long. Wrote Allela of course, but no letter from her since Monday. Tex is leaving for Texas on Friday and I'll have to give her something very nice.ᶠᶠ

---

* Possibly Clare Mallison, Vogue Studios.
† Alexander Lieberman, at the time art director at *Vogue*.

AUGUST 5, 1943

^FThe office is much better now. I like Everett, as well as everyone else, really. *Partisan Review*^* arrived, and I'm very proud to have it.^FF

AUGUST 6, 1943

^GNothing at Time, Inc., where I met with Mrs. Williams again. She always looks at me with some kind of sympathy, but shakes her head. She doesn't have a job for me. Am (almost) certain there are no jobs where one can put oneself on display and speak one's mind. Feel so happy about my clean bed, my newspaper, and my milk in the evenings, but am concerned I might be turning bourgeois?^GG

AUGUST 7, 1943

^GI couldn't work until I'd asked Mr. Hughes about my raise. Spoke first with Sangor, who's a bigger man than Hughes. A bigger personality. I felt sick by the time they finally called me into the room, and then Sangor said, I'll give you (!) $50.00 a week. And that was that. Drank whiskey with Hughes and he told all sorts of dumb stories and shared a few platitudes about Eliot, Wolfe, Steinbeck, etc. And then I went home. My parents are very impressed by my raise, I think. I make $5.00 more than Stanley!^GG

AUGUST 10, 1943

^FI'm happy beyond all reason! Is it Allela? My new salary? The calm at the office? Whatever the case, I'm happy with work for the moment and will try to remain content for as long as possible, because when I no longer am, I'll quit. Painted the apartment today, movies tonight with mother. We talked about a thousand things, but too quickly and superficially. It will always

---

* *Partisan Review* was a left-wing political and literary journal founded in 1934 and which, despite the small 1934 edition, had quite some bearing on the literary scene, thanks to the support of authors such as Hannah Arendt, Saul Bellow, James Baldwin, and Susan Sontag, several of whose short stories and essays it first published.

be like that with mother, and even more so as she grows old. She has never thought seriously or at length about issues that do not involve her. I am full of life, and wonder what will happen this weekend? Will I sleep with—her?[FF]

AUGUST 11, 1943
[G]A nice letter from Allela—oh, I knew what it would say! That she's coming on Friday at 5:51, and true enough! We'll be together Saturday evening, and I bought tickets for *Skin of Our Teeth*. And later, Spivy's. Happy at work. Wrote a funny story about Squeak, practically Disney! Went to the dentist, and he drilled my front tooth. Very necessary. Worked with Mother here this evening. The walls are beautiful. Paged through Dickens a little, which made me very happy, as it recalled my childhood.[GG]

AUGUST 12, 1943
[G]Am terribly happy but still got good work done. A new hero. The Champion. Who cares?! Looked for clothing fabric with Mother. Mother has known for a long time that I spend most of my money on women, which is why she's encouraging me to spend a bit more on myself. S. and M. here, and the house looks gorgeous! The wall, blue-green, with Bernhard's photograph, is the very best! Oh God—I am happy—and pensive, and should always think of these days! They're the very best![GG]

AUGUST 13, 1943
[F]I felt happy and complete all day, worked well even though I was thinking of Allela—of the moment I'd see her. Well—with 20.00 in my pocket I met her at 6. We were strangely relaxed. There was no one at her apartment. We were like old friends. I lathered her back in the bath, and we sailed the little ship I gave her. It was lovely. Then—in bed together, naked, the light sheets on our two bodies—our soft skin rubbing together over and over again—she whispered "yes" to me and it was sweeter than anything I've ever known! I fell asleep while she was touching my lips with her marvelously light fingers.—And in the morn-

ing, we woke up and discovered each other again. Finally, she touched me first—and I don't know why—but it happened under her fingers. It is paradise to be in bed with her. It's beautiful and complete![FF]

AUGUST 14, 1943

[F]After breakfast—I bought her peaches, a banana—she wrote postcards. I am noting down details because this day I'll want to re-read. Went to the Museum of Modern Art. There was an exhibition on Bali. Allela came at 4, an hour late! Rum. It was strange after last night. It was calm, tranquil, and we felt peaceful. I began to think that maybe I don't love her. But it's just that I've never had a woman I've loved. I love her. But tonight, after a walk down Broadway, when we said almost nothing to each other—I was really too tired, too sad, and my new shoes were hurting me. (What kinds of things transpire because of a pair of too-small shoes!) I spoke cruelly to her, told her that she doesn't love me enough. I accused her of being selfish, of taking what she could and giving nothing. At home by 4:45 A.M. very sad, and thinking for the fifth time that I'd given her up.[FF]

AUGUST 15, 1943

[F]Last night, I said what should have been said a long time ago—that she doesn't want to change her life. That she lives with Texas because no one better has come along. She didn't deny it. And it made me furious! Can I share her under such circumstances? Today, I think I can. I will be happy and work hard, and derive most of my happiness from work—as I always have.[FF]

[G]We've concluded that we—both—love ourselves better than anyone else, and that therefore, the chain that connects us is stronger than if we were living together. I feel tremendous relief! As does she. I really think we are much closer to one another this way. She called me again at 12:10, after I had worked around the house with pleasure—with great pleasure—and our conversation was full of laughter, full of love, and I am very happy about it. Reading [John William Dunne's] *Experiment With Time*.^{GG}

AUGUST 16, 1943

^GYesterday I forgot to say that I've got a woman, or even better, what I've got is an artist. I've got Allela as much as I will ever have any woman, and she's got me the same way. And we've both got as much as we want from each other. We don't want our whole selves taken.^{GG}

AUGUST 18, 1943

^FIt's strange what I think of Allela. Will I be searching for something better my entire life? Oh, there's no one better than she! She is the best—the best soul I could find! Dan at the parents', very boring. He lives entirely in the present, and the present is petty and insignificant.^{FF}

8/18/43

Looked into a parked car this evening and saw two people kissing, very tenderly, oblivious of the noisy street (57) around them. It was good to see, and I wished then everyone would live at all times as tenderly as they (everyone) surely have been at one moment in their life.

AUGUST 20, 1943

^FAt Rolf's at 1:30. He still loves me a little. But he hates my story (Laval), and he's right. I'll rewrite it.^{FF}

AUGUST 21, 1943

^FFriday—one week ago I was peacefully sleeping next to Allela. ^{FF G}I want to see Allela, kiss her, hug her. Want to live with her. Want to love with her, see the world. Want to work with her. Read [George Frederick Young's] *The Medici* again.^{GG}

AUGUST 22, 1943

^GRolf came by at 11:45. He loved my fireplace, very impressed, also by my artworks around the house. We went to Central Park and rowed on the lake. Rolf was nice. He went home at 3:00, and I went to see *Forgotten Village* at the museum. Really learned a lot this week. About myself, about work, about Allela.^{GG}

AUGUST 23, 1943

^GNo letter from her. One from Rosalind, who got back today. My check from *H. & F.* From her, though—nothing. Am at work with Dan Gordon.* Clever artist. Can think of nothing but Allela—she's torturing me. Still, I was somehow happy tonight, because I was alone and working. Trying to master an entirely new style. Very, very simple, almost sweet, not like when I used to need so much.^{GG}

AUGUST 24, 1943

^GOh—fantastic day. The postman woke me at 7:30 with a package from Roger R. (A small glass horse, already broken.) And a letter from Allela! I was so happy—I washed and ran back to bed to read it. "Oh Pat let's try to keep this goodness! I feel that I can with your help." I will always help her.

Gordon drinks. You can tell from his face. He has a strange effect on me: I'm like a sixteen-year-old around Clark Gable. Was being very foolish this afternoon. Bumped into Camy on 56th St. We went to a bar. 3 Tom Collinses, and when I left him alone for a few moments, I think he read my letter to Allela. Doesn't bother me.^{GG}

AUGUST 25, 1943

^GAnd when I got home, in high-heeled shoes that tortured my feet, tired from working for someone else—I thought how nice

---

* Dan Gordon (1902–1970), an American comic book and storyboard artist and film director. Gordon was one of Famous Studios' first directors, and wrote and directed several Popeye the Sailor and Superman cartoons. Later, at Hanna-Barbera, Gordon worked on several cartoons featuring Yogi Bear, Huckleberry Hound, and others.

it would be to wander the streets in comfortable shoes, the time my own, my work just making beautiful images with words and lines—that would be wonderful and shouldn't be impossible. I shouldn't consider it a dream, but rather something coming soon that requires just a few years or months of work. Tex returns Sunday, and we'll soon be together again, we three. Why? What will happen? What won't?

Preparing the house for Rosalind.^{GG}

AUGUST 27, 1943
^GAm very thin and very happy. Letter from Allela. Went into Dan Gordon's office to see him. When we were alone, he said I should "join him for a walk at Paramount"; it doesn't matter, but—but he has a strange effect on me. Want to drink with him.

24 pages this week. Rosalind had a hangover that sent her to bed at 4! I went over at 7, and we drank and ate. She was tender and nice, but "I smell like old cigarettes" and couldn't kiss her. Saw her to bed with her cat Natashas (Siamese) around her neck. She was dog-tired.

I enjoyed paging through a book on Chirico.^{*GG}

AUGUST 29, 1943
^G$285 in the bank. $260 in bonds. Bought all sorts of things this afternoon and felt very independent. My parents came at 9:00 with beer. They're like good friends. And later, after calling first, Rolf Tietgens came with a bottle of rum. We almost emptied the bottle, and he spoke on and on with his wonderful eloquence about the nostalgia we all feel. He stayed overnight. He was not aroused, of course, but he did feel me with his hands, and I— yes—it was strange.

The rest is just poetry.^{GG}

---

* Giorgio de Chirico (1888–1978), Italian painter and graphic artist. With Carlo Carrà, he outlined the theoretical tenets of metaphysical painting, one of the most important antecedents to surrealism.

AUGUST 29, 1943

ᴳHappy but restless. We ate together at Rosalind's. She said:
"You're a sloppy Joe, I've decided, but I also think you're an artist!" "That's fair," I replied. And we drank! After that, went to
row on the lake in the park. Rosalind attracts a lot of attention.
Her clothes, etc. We were speaking a bit slowly, and not very
intelligently. Alcohol doesn't improve the mind. It disgusts me.

Went to my parents'. Mother and I took a walk, where she told
me I should go out more often with young men! That if I looked
for men as I do for women, I could get them. Handsome men,
too, who are worthy of me! And that I should live outside this
city at some point. Yes—that is true. But she knows about the
unpleasant experiences I've had with various men, which have
been enough to convince me men aren't as good as women.ᴳᴳ

AUGUST 30, 1943

ᴳDid nothing and did nothing and did nothing, except for painting. Giorgione—La Venus Masturbataire.* Behind her stand the
buildings of New York. Tired at the office, and now I don't want
to sleep. Why? I want to read and maybe study something. Am
an artist and my head is full of ideas. I want to make a painting
every night.

Went to Shelton's at 6:00 with Tex, who had all sorts of experiences in Texas—and she slept with at least one girl! Tex said
she felt "so far from N.Y.—and that everything was so nice and
easy." Yes—but it's not physically necessary for her, so it is a
sin. Right? I couldn't do it. Especially if Cornell were so clearly
mine.ᴳᴳ

AUGUST 31, 1943

ᴳGoldberg came over at 8:40. He brought a bottle of champagne (domestic) and we talked for hours. He wants to write
a book about the history of Jews throughout the world. I'm to
do the research for $30 a week, 8 hours a day. That would get

---

* Giorgione's *Sleeping Venus*, also known as the Dresden Venus.

me out of this job, but I'd still be working freelance. A pleasant evening, though, as I return to egotism. I'm going to be a big hit or a big flop. There's no in-between. I am an extraordinary girl. Around Goldberg I felt light, needed, strong, creative, a genius—I am, too!^{GG}

SEPTEMBER 1, 1943

^GHappy day. Worked slowly—sad and tired. Saw Posada* exhibit at the library. Mexican artist who influenced Orozco† and Rivera. Wrote a story for Cinema [Comics] for the first time. Dreadfully moralistic stuff. Jerry says I'm too serious. Boohoo! Cornell says I have what she never will: A creative imagination. I see so many who are much worse than I am! I am good.^{GG}

SEPTEMBER 3, 1943

^GBeautiful, dark day, but how happy I am! Wrote 10 pages at work, despite Jerry's endless interruptions. Met Allela at 53rd and 5th at 5:40. I could see she was sad before I reached her. She's lost her momentum and feels useless as a result. I tried to urge her to leave Tex and live by herself for a while. Cornell: "We could never—never live together! You know that, don't you?" "Sure!" I said, and I meant it!^{GG}

SEPTEMBER 4, 1943

^GAllela invited two girls over and wanted to leave them with Tex, but Tex refused to be left alone, so Allela had to stay there. So I drank and wrote like an artist who doesn't need any friends! Natasha called me at 9:30 P.M. to invite me to a social tomorrow evening at Angelica de Monocol's. Rosalind doesn't know about it, but I hope she'll be there tomorrow. Am—what—happy? Yes, I think so.^{GG}

---

* José Guadalupe Posada (1852–1913), Mexican engraver, illustrator, and caricaturist.
† José Clemente Orozco (1883–1949), Mexican painter widely considered one of the founding fathers of contemporary Mexican painting alongside Diego Rivera, one of the main representatives of Mexican muralism.

SEPTEMBER 5, 1943

^GSketched a little. Got ready for the big night at Angelica de Monocol's. Her husband is an artist—and just 24 years old. Made the acquaintance of Chloe—a model for H[attie] Carnegie,* who was very beautiful, and also a lady. All that I remember is that I was sitting with her, my nose in her hair, which was very clean and soft. That I felt her lips with my fingers, and that she said—"I'm really quite straight, but you do something to me." Got home at 4:30! Rosalind very serious and sober, I think.^{GG}

SEPTEMBER 5, 1943

^FI was adrift this morning—walked all the way to 72nd and York. I felt dirty and sordid. The first thing I thought of this morning was Chloe's hair, and her innocent lips. She suggested that she come over at 5 this evening. The apartment looked perfect when she came. I had a new bottle of rum out. She looked ravishing, and she knew it. She sat in the chair, looking at me, sipping on her drink and smiling. I made her sit on the bed and finally I just had to embrace her—to which she reacted with sighs. She doesn't know what she wants, she said. That's nothing if not encouragement. Rolf came at 7:00. Dinner with Chianti. ^GAnd my story, which I will finish tomorrow.^{GG} Chloe gave me her number with pleasure—went to an evening at J. Levy's.† She doesn't know Buffie, but she knows that she's a little phony! Am happy, but it was a lost day—and I have lost doubly if I have lost Cornell.^{FF}

SEPTEMBER 6, 1943

^FChloe on my mind all day.

Tonight was very serious, finished the Laval story. With Rolf's

---

* Hattie Carnegie (born Henrietta Kanengeiser, 1886–1956), Austrian-born American fashion designer and entrepreneur.

† Julien Levy (1906–1981), American art dealer whose gallery was located at Fifty-Seventh Street and Madison Avenue and specialized in surrealists, avant-garde artists, and American photography of the 1930s and 1940s.

suggestions. Chloe gave me a ring at 7:30—a lovely conversation. She feigns innocence, but is very amused when I make unseemly suggestions. She came at 0:00—more charming than ever. I was full of thoughts on my work and my books, and showed her my photographs. Finally, I embraced her and kissed her, and it was so sweet—so sweet—I was extremely tender with her because she is like a river—not because she is pretty—no—she is sick too. She was trembling inside. I could feel it when I held her hand. She said that she doesn't want to go to bed with anyone. That she wants a friend who will talk to her and go on long walks. But—finally—after five kisses, after a lot of light touching, we went to the banks of the river and she told me that she had gone on a voyage when I'd kissed her. I hope it gave her pleasure, because it was a dream for me. When I wake up tomorrow, I may think it didn't happen. I'm thinking of Allela, of course—will I never manage to be faithful to anyone but myself? Tonight was real life, with which I have nothing to do.[FF]

SEPTEMBER 8, 1943

[G]Thought of nothing but Chloe.[GG] [F]Had lunch with Cornell at 1:00.[FF] [G]Poor child—and great artist[GG]—[F]Someone had cut her hair back to her scalp![FF] [G]She didn't look good enough to take to Del Pezzo.[GG] [F]I told her that nobody is faithful to anyone except themselves. She has no doubt I have another woman on my mind. It's a bit sad—I'm so like a man in that beauty affects me so much. Truly, like the monster I am, Cornell disgusted me today. No stockings—no refinement—and when I read these words again in a year, my heart will weep. Chloe phoned me at 8:30. She speaks slowly, smilingly, and calls me "darling" often. Rosalind phoned me at 9:00. She was surprised, naturally, that I'd seen Chloe. She had "seen" Natica (the 22-year-old girl) and wanted to bring her to the party on Friday, when I'll invite Chloe. I phoned Chloe at 10:00 with the message that "I'm crazy in love with you." Which was true at 10 o'clock, nonetheless.[FF]

[F]I will probably have less money—with the T.S.F.[*] and the parties, I hope—with Chloe—but I'll get used to it. I'm above that,
and can do what I want. In every area of my life.[FF G]Could barely
work at the office. Am so nervous! Prepared myself for Rosalind,
who was meant to come first—but it was Chloe who climbed the
stairs so lightly. Rosalind—Chloe shone in her eyes, and she had
to spend the whole evening at her side. We took a taxi to Sammy's. Rosalind was on the edge of her seat, looking at Chloe all
the while, but was jealous of me, because Chloe preferred me.
Then Chloe wanted to go to Cerruti's, but Mary S. was there.
Ultimately Rosalind shoved Chloe and me into a cab. Chloe
wanted to go for a walk, so we got out at 2nd Ave. I spoke quietly to her, "What do you want?" "I want to go home with you,"
she answered. She pulled off her dress; and was in my bed when
I came from the shower. It was wonderful! Terrible! And I lay
in bed, and she wanted nothing but that I hold her tight. She's
not thin, nearly fat! But how firm her body is! Naturally didn't
go to the office Saturday morning. We lay in bed till 1:30 P.M.!
Mornings are the most beautiful! But she didn't allow me to
touch her. I gave her a ripe black olive. We read what I had written to her—"as Oberon parted the pendant mass of his trees in
search of Titania, I will part the melancholy forest of your hair
and drink from the secret spring of your mouth"—I wrote that
Thursday evening with Goldberg (!) in the room. And she likes
it a lot. Went by hers at 6:00 for a drink. Lexy has no character
and is not an ideal roommate for Chloe. She wanted me to spend
the evening with her, but I had to see Bernhard. When I called
Chloe [later], she said she had taken 6 sleeping pills, but Tony
was there. Frightened, I went by myself to 56th and 2nd Ave.
Drank a beer with a worker who told me a sad story about his
girl, then Chloe called back. Tony invited me over. Chloe was on
her bed, half asleep. I didn't see her till Tony had gone. Then she
asked me incessantly to get into bed with her. At 1:30 I took off

---

* TSF (*télégraphie/transmission sans fil*), a wireless radio device Pat wants to buy.

my clothes—just as Lexy got back! I was naked! Lexy smiled—
she's always smiling, like a fool, and watched over us all night.
But there was nothing to see.[GG]

SEPTEMBER 12, 1943
[G]Woke in her arms—and she is always so beautiful in bed, so
beautiful in the early morning! I said that (and her husband says
the same). How nice it was to kiss her when Lexy went to the
bathroom. There was a letter from Götz van Eyck* on the bedside table, scribbled in pencil. When I held her close to me, she
said: "Don't—you make me want you—so terribly." Naturally
I felt like a king—who has spent a second night with a queen!
"My God—I've spent almost all weekend with you in bed!"
Chloe: "It could be worse!"—
    Saw Bernhard at 5:00. Think she likes me as ever. Didn't
mention Chloe. Didn't phone Cornell—have no interest in doing
so, and I'm disgusted by the thought of kissing her again. Yes, I
am fickle when it comes to physical love, but I loved an idea in
Cornell—that of art—I still love that in her and will forever and
ever—but physically—not anymore![GG]

9/12/43
Why this secret fear that I have lost my roots? Because I have
given up my love, my physical love, of one who was never more
than the embodiment of an idea that I shall always love, and
turned it, the physical and the imagined (forever imagined!)
mental, to one who will surely go away more quickly even than
my cigarette smoke. But the remembrance of her never. Will
I ever tell her, I wonder, these unpoetic, unbeautiful words—
which are the top froth of the too-full vessel. My heart is heavy
with confusing emotions, beclouded.

---

* Götz van Eyck (1913–1969), German-born film actor who gained international recognition
with leading roles in Henri-Georges Clouzot's *The Wages of Fear* (1953), Fritz Lang's *The
Thousand Eyes of Dr. Mabuse* (1960), and Martin Ritt's *The Spy Who Came in from the
Cold* (1965).

SEPTEMBER 13, 1943

ᴳWonderful day! I don't love Chloe—but she has severed me from Allela. That's no cause for joy, but it had to happen, and not a moment too soon. And when I ultimately leave Chloe (when she ultimately leaves me), I won't shed any tears. She's beautiful, and I visit her as I will someday go to heaven to stay.

Pleasant in the office, and compliments on several stories. Purchased *The Early Chirico* for my mother's birthday and made a down payment for the radio, $75.00, which will arrive this week. Cornell phoned and I found her at the Winslow at 6:00. She's very downcast and looks at me as if she already knows everything. It's a mistake, without a doubt, but I can't look at her, can't take her hand.

Went to my parents' with a box of sweets and my book. We were very happy and content, drank lots of claret, and opened the presents like children. Fell asleep at 10:30—for one hour!—doubtless the wine—and imagined, as I woke, that Cornell had killed herself. It was alien, strange, as if I had taken anesthetics so she could die alone. Read Donne. And sketched.ᴳᴳ

9/13/43

What called me so powerfully and strangely to sleep tonight? I have never slept at such a time before, and this was more frightening than sleep. This was nature's anesthesia. And seeing you today, when nothing more was between us, except the thin and inorganic air, seeing so clearly that you understood, I wonder if as I slept, you died? How? By your own will or God's? Or with the winding down of this outlandish, unproductive machinery? Now at five minutes to midnight, I am afraid to call you. Perhaps I have dreamed, and forgotten, that you died.

SEPTEMBER 14, 1943

ᴳSaw Camy twice, and at 5:30, I was feeling so nervous, we bought a drink at Cocktail's. And I said, "I'm going to see the prettiest woman in New York!" And he started to say something—but stopped. He knows, maybe. I think? Chloe was expecting me.

Like every pretty woman, she loves to talk about herself. As we approached 57th, I invited her up for some hot milk. I prepared her milk with love. A little rum found its way in, although she's not drinking this week. And after she finished half the cup, she said "I'm drunk—" and in saying so—or better put, in not saying anything, she pulled me toward her—and it was like heaven itself to feel her hand on my neck! My God, how wonderful! And I kissed her—but deeper than before. Then she went home and I sketched—without much success—but aren't I pretty wealthy?GG

SEPTEMBER 15, 1943

GConversation with Leo Isaacs,* who really is a poet. Writes lots of poems and hates this ugly world of commercialism. Now, that's a man! Mother was here tonight, and we sketched each other—she made a large gouache of me that didn't turn out too badly. Oh, I am happy—because I have Chloe and because I can now start to work again. Cornell is coming tomorrow evening, something I'm not looking forward to.GG

SEPTEMBER 16, 1943

GCamy bought two drinks at 6:00. He's considerate, a rare quality in any man. Prepared the house for Cornell. I expected the worst this evening, but I tried, and she tried, and we amused ourselves quite well. Cornell understands how I feel about her. I want nothing more to do with her physically. And that means the end of our love, and she knows that. How smart and understanding nature is, always leading us to the most beautiful! A.C. went home early, and I got to [Chloe and Lexy's] at 11:00. Chloe looked very beautiful and was happy to see me. Without a doubt. Lexy fell asleep. Then we kissed softly, and Chloe whispered my name, which always winds me up. And whenever I tried to leave, she pulled me back. It was heaven. Then I turned out the light and we lay together for a while, our heads alone touching. Our lips barely touched, our teeth barely touched. I kissed her eyes, her lips, her hair, her neck,

---

* Leo Isaacs, freelance writer at the Sangor Shop.

her breast, her hands. I wanted to kiss her body, her thighs! Came
home as happy and high as only a poet could be!GG

9/16/43

The perfumes of the women will finally drive me mad. My heart
beats wild at high noon at the scent of the stenographer with her
coffee cup opposite me at the cafeteria table. My head turns reels
on the streets and a terrible force draws me after the prancing filly,
the lumbering dowager, the smooth, straight-limbed Negroes.
Anything! Anyone! Let me bury my nose in their clothed bosoms.
Perfume! Dream of the nighttime, the promise and the memory of
love, proof of the lover and badge of the beloved. Perfume! Sweet
and lewd in the bright sunlight, tempter of all the senses.

9/16/43

Idle thought: that the many divorces in America are due to the
national ambition. We are always striving, attaining, and not
wanting. It is not that we do not know how to dramatize, glorify
and romanticize her once we have her, not merely this, but also
that we see someone better (physically better, for that is all we
take time to explore) just as we see always a job that is better.

SEPTEMBER 17, 1943

GOne week ago Chloe and I first went to bed together! And how
wonderful, how godly it was! Could be—certainly am—bored
by her mind already, but never by her beauty. She inspires me
with wonderful, lively ideas, she excites me with love and life.
I'm not in love with her, though, which I told her this evening.GG

SEPTEMBER 17, 1943

G[Mother and I] visited the Ferargil Galleries to see Constant*
and Takis†—very interesting. Felt lonely and had to go to my

---

* George Constant (born George Konstantopoulos, 1892–1978), Greek-American modernist
painter, etcher, and printmaker.
† Probably Nicholas Takis (1903–1965), an American expressionist painter.

parents'. Ate heartily, and they came over to my house to see my radio. It's magnificent! Then as I was writing, the phone rang loudly—and it was Chloe, who said: "I'm at home. I thought maybe you'd like to have a drink with me." She was quite drunk and wanted to stay up all night. It was past 2:30 A.M. when I finally managed to put her to bed. How fine a duty! ^{GG}

SEPTEMBER 18, 1943

^GChloe busied herself with preparing my breakfast. We had some ham, lots of beautiful fruit, and every time we passed each other, we had to hug and kiss. It was heaven! "Pat, I adore you! I think I'll fall in love with you." Chloe: "Don't you want to get married sometime?" "Yes—sometime." "Why don't you marry me?" "Now you're talking." The Levys—Muriel in particular—have convinced Chloe she should live with them! They live above the galleries on 57th Street—but Chloe wouldn't have enough privacy. I know that our friendship probably won't last long and that our nights together, at least, are already numbered! Chloe is a sprite, a married woman (first of all) whom I must treat like a queen.

Went to Cornell's social at 5:00. Lots of people. Charles Miller, whom I'll see again soon, and Alex Goldfarb, who didn't look so great. More later—it's already 1:30—and I've slept so little.^{GG}

SEPTEMBER 19, 1943

^GStrange day. Leo Isaacs confessed that he tried to reach me on the phone from 4–8 yesterday. He was drunk. And had a hangover. We went to Raffier's on 51st St. and had 3 drinks (!) and ate. "You are beautiful," he said. And the first "new person he's met this year." Another drink at Cocktail at 4:00, which made for a very short and drunk afternoon. Jerry and Martin doubtless sensed something, but I don't care. Invited Chloe over for martinis at 6:15. She left too soon—and Leo Isaacs came a short time after. We played the radio. Nothing to say here but that we had a nice evening and drank far too much. He kissed me many times, something I maybe shouldn't have allowed.^{GG}

SEPTEMBER 20, 1943

^GNice day—but rather conscious of Leo Isaacs. When I went for coffee at 3:00, he came out of the elevator, and we went down together. Without a doubt, in these two days the entire office already knows about our afternoon. And Marty and Jerry, the two old women, want to know if we spent the evening together. Leo's fallen in love with me (or so I believe, without pride—but with a certain happiness). He won't clean his shoes, because I left a little scuff on them! [He's behaving] like a child—just like I do when I'm in love with a girl, and I like that a lot. "God you're gorgeous!" he said as we drank our coffee. And with that, it's like a nice secret, a private state of being when we're together, even if the whole world is standing around looking at us.

Thought a lot about Chloe, but decided not to call her today. Roger came over at 7:00. We drank, ate at Café Society (the bill was 11.50!), and now he's lying on my bed, snoring. What will happen, I don't know, but I won't have anything to do with him. I belong to Chloe, and no one else. Leo gave me all of his poems and published writing. I want just one evening to myself!^{GG}

SEPTEMBER 22, 1943

^GNice day, but got little work done and walked around the city at midday, since I figured Dan and Leo would be drinking. When Chloe turned up with a white necklet under her black suit, when she said my martinis were better than the ones Muriel Levy makes, my heart soared. Went to my parents' for dinner at 8:00, only Mother noticed I had the mark of a woman's lips on my cheek! "Whose been kissing you?" and smiled, as if I were a boy.^{GG}

9/24/43

Sexual love is the only emotion which has ever really touched me. Hatred, jealousy, even abstract devotion, never—except devotion to myself. But love touched me willy-nilly.

SEPTEMBER 25, 1943

GViewed several exhibits with Mother after a nice martini at
the Winslow Bar. She always looks so pretty. And Chloe didn't
phone. I lay restless in bed. Ultimately—I called her at the Levys'
at 6:00. And she had broken her appointment with Gifford
Pinchot*—had already had several drinks and wanted to eat at
my place. I was immediately charmed! I ran and jumped in the
air, sang along to the radio—and bought lots of things to eat, far
more than we'd be able to. I got ready like a husband, and phoned
Rosalind at 7:00, my first martini in hand. Regarding Chloe,
she said: "This must be the first time you've been involved with
someone who isn't very sensible." And that Chloe could be good
for me, because she's so well-dressed. And so Chloe came at 7:50
with a hug and a kiss for me. We drank—and listened to records,
and then I prepared this great dinner, which Chloe loved—corn,
two lamb chops. And cheese and fruit. How nice, how warm,
how lovely to watch Chloe gnaw on the bones! By 1:00 she was
already tired. I easily convinced her to stay over. Then she took
off her dress, and it was done! Chloe in my bed again. Have
known Chloe twenty days and slept with her four times. Went
further with her tonight than ever before, but not far enough.GG

SEPTEMBER 26, 1943

GWhat a nice day to finish this book!† In bed with Chloe. I got
up at 8:30 to go to the bakery and pick up some brioche and
croissants. How patient I was with the French customers in line,
who took so long. I ran home to jump back in bed!GG

SEPTEMBER 26, 1943

GAt 6:20—Chloe invited me to the Levys' for a drink. I don't
like them. Julien is like a snake, Muriel like a piglet. And her

---

* Gifford Pinchot (1865–1946), early American advocate for environmental conservation and
twice governor of Pennsylvania.
† "This book" refers to "this diary." Pat ends Diary 4b by listing her income and expenses,
e.g. "Outgoing: 40.00 rent" or "Incoming 21—Bill King, 27—Spy Smasher."

paintings are even worse. I felt very nervous, very dumb. Hurried home to find Leo. Drank martinis, and he was practically violent in his pronouncements of love. My days are wonderfully rapturous, wonderfully colored, after these nights with Chloe. Went to Nick's, where I saw Charley Miller. And went to Cornell's. Cornell was friendly—at least to me—though I'm not the same as I used to be. How could I be, when my body still smells of Chloe? Got home around 2:00–3:00, where I made coffee for Leo, because he wanted to stay all night. And I was happy as I went to bed at 4:45.[GG]

SEPTEMBER 27, 1943

[G]Sad letter from Cornell. She said she doesn't want to see me again, that I might be giving someone else what I once gave her. Leo very curious about my friends. 3½ hours of sleep yesterday, but feel just fine. Most ordinary evening I've had in a long time. Made good progress on a gouache. Went to my parents', too, who love me more and more as a person.[GG]

SEPTEMBER 28, 1943

[G]Gave my story "The Barber Raoul" and five spots to *Home & Food*. This morning Mother completely surprised me: she would like to see me go to Mexico, but with Leo! (I'm reminded of the weekends with Ernst Hauser!) I phoned Chloe later—nothing special—but this evening, when I said I might go to Mexico, she said—"Are you going? I'll come with you!" Fun at the dentist at 6:00 with Mother, who also had a tooth pulled. I had the same terrible, wonderful dream that I was God, that everything began in me and would end in me, that I alone understand the mysterious plan. "Book—book—book!" said the running, punching figure circling the cosmos.[GG]

9/29/43

Basically, the reason I don't like male homosexuals is because we basically disagree. Women, not men, are the most exciting and wonderful creations on the earth—and masculine homosexuals are mistaken and wrong!

OCTOBER 1, 1943

GI had nervous indigestion all day and felt uncontrollably verbose. That means it's time to begin a long, ongoing project. My book. Yes.

Charley Miller didn't phone, which makes me very happy. He's nice, but I have too many.GG

OCTOBER 2, 1943

GCocktails with Mother at my place following a few exhibitions, with Camy, Cornell, and finally Leo Isaacs. Camy and Mother amused themselves well, and Cornell too, but she grew serious when we were alone and had to kiss me. I'm not happy about it. Leo stayed, drinking my Calvert's, which was likely the very reason he came. But I can't spend much time with him without feeling bored and like I'm wasting my time. Want to see Rolf tomorrow.GG

OCTOBER 3, 1943

GToday was miserable. Chloe didn't call all day. Short walk with [Marjorie] W., who's in love with David Randolph.* Oh, how wonderful to be straight.—Yes? No! Finally, at 4 o'clock—four o'clock on the dot, Ann T.† came over, who had been riding with Ellen B. We had some tea with baba au rhum. Finally had to call [Chloe]. Did she want to see me again?—"Whatever's best for you," she said, suggesting that it didn't matter to her one way or the other. I was just sick over it. Wanted to get drunk, and we went to Sutton [restaurant]. 3½ martinis. Could barely stand up straight and called Chloe. And I said she wasn't my type, etc. and was just nasty! Don't remember much of the conversation. Ann

---

* David Randolph (1914–2010), American choral conductor (the Cecilia Chorus of New York) and music educator.
† A twenty-five-year-old Pat has recently met, who works at Scribner's.

and I ate a little something, listening to music around midnight. Don't know how it started, but we finally ended up in bed, and Ann said that Virginia asked: "You know what I think of Pat?— You know how long it would take for me to fall for her? Approximately five mintues." "Highsmith, you're terrific!" She stayed till 5:30 AM, and it was very gentle and nice. We both needed it.ᴳᴳ

OCTOBER 4, 1943
ᴳTwo hours of sleep and a good idea for a story.* Chloe promised to call me. She doubtless wants an apology from me. I'm happy to give it to her. Don't regret what happened last night, but these love affairs move so fast! Phoned Ann and she had written a poem about me. She has a brain, which is very refreshing. Reading Wolfe and want to write a good story. It's such a good feeling—and so strong, I could barely sleep from 6 to 8 [this morning].ᴳᴳ

10/4/43
A novel about a man who believes himself to be God. What a theme, and what presumption, because the writer would have to believe himself God, too, as I, in fact do. Yes, more than the extent to which God is in me and in all of us.

10/4/43
Your lips have drunk from all my glasses,
Tumblers, beermugs and demi-tasses.
And I can imagine in every chair
The bland impress of your derrière.
We have christened every sheet
With lipstick, love and smudgy feet.
And you have used in this short while
Every telephone number on my dial.

---

* Pat will work on this (lost) story she will later call "The Three" for the following two weeks.

Your green toothbrush in the cabinet
I know will never more be wet.
My tomato juice in the morning, dear,
Will now be drunk without Worcestershire.
Forget all this, and me, if you will.
But I'll remember (and with lover's a thrill)
When others have come, when others have gone,
How beautiful, always, you were at dawn.

OCTOBER 5, 1943

GThought of Chloe from the moment I got up. And had to call
her. "Oh, I'm so torn up! I'm drinking day and night, etc."
Chloe wants to see me again, and finding her in this state, I
wanted to help her again. "Let's go to Mexico!" "Yes, let's,"
Chloe said. Lunch appointment with Ann T., who was waiting for me in dark glasses at Scribner. At Del Pezzo's, which
I loved, because first Maria turned up, then Natasha H., and
finally Bachu. But not Rosalind. We spoke a little too loudly
about various love affairs. Ann said, "When can I see you
again?" as though I were some grande dame. She was briefly
involved with Buffie's friend Peter, and I don't at all like that
she's discussing such short affairs. I'm next in line. Did great
work this evening. On my story, the theme of which is worthy of Julien Green. Mystical and symbolic, I hope, of the soul
itself. Happy—but mostly because Chloe's not upset with me.
Yes—I don't like Ann enough.GG

OCTOBER 6, 1943

GWorked well at the office, which is extraordinary right now. But
I am using up too many nerves there. Went to Chloe's. She made
strong martinis and we discussed her men. She doesn't want to
write Chandler S.* anymore! She doesn't want a divorce! But
she also wants to marry Götz [van Eyck]! For God's sake, what

* Chandler S., Chloe's husband.

does she want? Told her about Sunday night. "You betrayed me!" she said. "You never were mine to betray," I said. "Now we can be good friends." "Yes," she answered. My God! She's a beautiful woman, but I can see right through her because I'm just a bit smarter. Came home at 8:30 and phoned Ann T. She read out four lines from her poem about me, and they were wonderful. "What are you doing Saturday night?"—I want to ask Chloe what she's doing. Finished my story about the boy on the street—myself—I think there's something to it—something I haven't written before.[GG]

10/7/43

How delicate is the scale in which an artist weighs his worth. It must be delicate. There must be no overconfidence in the sustaining of his creative period: there must be confidence only in his honesty, and in nothing else. The reprimand of some slight fault, the polishing of a piece of work, in an evening, instead of the satisfying act of creation, is easily enough to destroy all that gives him joy, courage, pleasure and reward. A wastebasket out of place can do it. A cut in the finger can do it. And only the making of new life can reconstruct the shambles.

OCTOBER 8, 1943

[G]Got sick today, which is the pits, because I want to sleep with Chloe tomorrow. Two Manhattans with Leo. He's going to Guatemala in three months. Ann called me. Ellen B. threw a whiskey sour in her face when Ann told her she'd slept with a girl! "You whore!" Ellen B. said! Ann can never see her again and had to take the elevator all wet! Didn't get much work done.[GG]

OCTOBER 9, 1943

[G]Happy, happy day. Worked, then met my parents and Claude [Coates]* at Del Pezzo. Hurried home. And then finally, she came. She was so very beautiful—black suit, little black hat,

---

* One of Pat's maternal uncles.

and furs. We listened to the music she likes, "The Last Time I Saw Paris," "Why Do I Love You," and "Make Believe." Later we took a taxi to 8th St. and 5th Ave. And she held my arm and looked so beautiful and smelled so wonderful! I felt too much— and against my wishes—like a man—in a suit, etc. We went to Nick's at 11:30, where I finally found Leo, introduced him to Chloe, and we drank for a few minutes. Chloe was very tired, though, and Leo was asking me all sorts of questions. Chloe eventually said she was going home and left alone. I hurried after her, though, very worried, because she and I were both so drunk. Took a taxi—first to 353 E. 56th, where Chloe—and I— had warm milk with rum. And I took her clothes off. The night was nice—more later.[GG]

10/9/43
You can never touch me, my dearest, my beloved. Never.

OCTOBER 10, 1943
[G]We got up at 11:15. Unfortunately, Chloe then called Julien, who demanded she come home and prepare his breakfast. "Pat, I'm so sorry—" she said. I was terribly despondent and hated Julien Levy for twenty minutes, going so far as to call and tell him how angry I was with him. And he hung up on me. It would have been an insult, if he were a stronger character. And I had gotten rolls from the French pâtisserie for Chloe and me! Oh, I was disappointed as a child!

Read *Confessions* of St. Augustine and felt more like a— what?—a man—without sexuality. Phoned Leo at Nick's. He came over, pretty drunk, asking all sorts of questions! He had a big epiphany last night. I had to explain things slowly and carefully. Eventually Chloe called. She was drunk, and I said I was bored of hearing about hangovers. "If you're bored, you know what you can do," she replied. "Goodbye!" Leo told me not to call her back. Of course, he would say that—and throughout the entire conversation, he kept trying to kiss me, etc. And I allowed him. It has to stop. Didn't go to bed till 3:30.[GG]

OCTOBER 11, 1943

^GI wrote a good poem for [Chloe] and posted it. Got good work done on my story. And read Green. Today I was a poet. And that makes the whole world beautiful.^{GG}

OCTOBER 12, 1943

^GWent to my parents' for dinner at 6:00, but we had to wait for Dan, and having to wait for an hour and a quarter disgusted me terribly. Hurried home, washed my hair, and Ann T. called. She came over in a cold sweat, nervous. Gave her rum. Then Chloe called. She was in the neighborhood and asked first if I was alone. "Yes," I said, not knowing she wanted to come over. But as Ann was reading my poem about Chloe, she entered the room. Walked several blocks with [her], thinking she had something to say, but nothing. Nothing about Ann, about my poem, or about Leo. Nothing—! Ruined my whole evening because I did nothing but entertain my friends. Now I can work.^{GG}

OCTOBER 13, 1943

^GTerrible day. The type of day I always have to fight against. Monday was the only day this week that I was really living and creating. Camy drunk, and we had two at 4 o'clock, one at 6:00, before I found Dan. Funny, how a couple of cowboys in a bar can turn the whole place western! They're all so nice and pure. Especially one "Slugger" Sloan. The rodeo was very fine. Roy Rogers*—oh God!

Chloe is moving to Kay French's tomorrow. (N.B. Leo had to make the announcement that "A Chloe called." It made me smile, but he showed no outward emotion.) I told Chloe that I can't express my love out loud—only in poetry. And she— responded that the poem gets better each time she reads it. It

---

* Roy Rogers (1911–1998), popular American country singer and actor, known as the "Singing Cowboy" in numerous western movies from 1938 to 1953.

makes me happy that she won't throw away these poems for many years—maybe ever. Ann, who received my poem today, said it was wonderful. But she's probably biased.^{GG}

OCTOBER 14, 1943

^GGot very good work done, even though my hair was flat and the day was gloomy and strange. Cornell came over at 5—and that bothered me a little. First I told the story about Saturday evening. About Leo too, and my parents. ("They know, without a doubt," Cornell said.) Cornell has seven paintings at the Pinacotheca* and is going to the country on Wednesday. Camy bought me an eggnog at 3:00. Then he came over here at 7:00 to bring me a book of Chinese love stories. He talked too much, but there's less and less I have to say about him. Worked on my story, which is coming along, but slowly. What will happen Saturday? I want to spend it with Chloe. And if not, I won't see anyone.^{GG}

OCTOBER 15, 1943

^GExcellent day. Went to the Wakefield at 12:45 to see the Theater in Art exhibit. Mother was nervous and strange. Said I don't have any time for my relatives, but plenty of time for that bitch Chloe! If she hadn't been so ridiculous about it, I'd have left immediately. I will mention it again at some point and tell her that this kind of behavior is not appropriate. Of course it's always the same—with Va., with Rosalind, and probably, don't remember, with Cornell.

   Ann T. called at 8:15. Told her all about Chloe. Then she asked me—which really threw me for a loop—if I'm fickle? Maybe it's true. I've loved three since New Year's Day: Rosalind, Cornell, Chloe. But Rosalind lasted a good two years. Cornell was an idea, and I still love them both, love them for the same things I first loved in them. And Chloe—it's all nice and phys-

---

* The Pinacotheca, also known as the Rose Fried Gallery and located at 40 East Sixty-Eighth Street, is now part of the Tate Gallery.

ical, but physical like a schoolchild, admiring, pure, fair and beautiful, and precocious, far beyond its years!

Got good work done on my story, which is almost ready to type up. Am as proud of it as I was of my "Uncertain Treasure." In this story I show some of my own ignorance and some of the knowledge of being.[GG]

OCTOBER 16, 1943

[G]Today should have been such a nice day. Drank with Leo— too much—before visiting the van Gogh exhibit. Phoned Chloe twice, and somehow Kay French ended up inviting herself along. They got here at 7:30. At 11:30, when we were alone [for a moment], Chloe said softly to me: "I want to stay here. I want you to undress me." My heart leapt, but for what? Kay took her home at 11:30. I was terribly disappointed, because if Chloe loved me, if she had any character, she'd have spent the night here. Leo called at 12:00. He's coming over, he said. So depressed—and thought, these are the times that prove men's souls. I wanted to call Ann—all those who truly love me. Was still crying when Leo got here. We took a walk till 3:00. Went to bed, decided not to drink so much next week. Certain I'll never get any sort of satisfaction from Chloe. I want a quiet life, don't need this level of excitement, need to work like a man. I need a woman—but one who loves me deeply and quietly.[GG]

10/16/43

Every artist possesses a core—and this core remains forever untouched. Untouched by the lover and the beloved. However much you may love a woman, she can never enter.

OCTOBER 17, 1943

[G]I finished the story: "The Three." Wrote well. Ann came over at 9:00 and she loved it. She can probably sell it somewhere. Yes, I am strong. Don't need anyone. Certainly not Chloe. I have my art, and my art alone is true.[GG]

OCTOBER 18, 1943

^GA nice, strange day. Ran into Rosalind and Angelica when I went to 52nd St. to pick up my [phonograph] records. They had hangovers and invited me for a drink. Went to Billy The Oysterman.* I was terribly serious. Told them a lot about Chloe. I ultimately recited a few lines of the poem I wrote for Chloe. "So, you're doing great, then," she said. "What better use can you make of a person?" I had just said I didn't need anyone at all.

Couldn't get any work done this afternoon. I wanted to visit [Chloe]. Went to see her at 4 o'clock. God, yes! I remember the days when the chance touch of a girl's hand was heaven to me! And there she lay this afternoon on her bed, and allowed me to kiss her long and hard! And she finally opened her mouth and moved under me and caressed my cheeks! My God, how wonderful!

Swung by *Home & Food*, who want me to illustrate a story. And they've bought my last five spots. Very happy. Just this evening I typed up my story, "The Three." *Harper's Bazaar* first, I think. Ann called to tell me I'm a genius. She's read "Silver Horn of Plenty" five hundred times. And Tex—jubilant about a six-pound beefsteak she had. And finally—Chloe, the loveliest, at 12:30. She had spent the evening at Betty Parsons' and ate with her. First she bumped into Rosalind at the Wakefield, because there was an opening. And of course R. invited Chloe for a drink! At Giovanni [restaurant]. How envious would she be to learn that I—I—have slept with Chloe six times!^{GG}

OCTOBER 19, 1943

^GYet another strange day. Becoming increasingly serious and increasingly happy without becoming overly self-satisfied. Getting older too. I simply must write something good soon, and although it's all just words, the ideas, the intentions are more than that. Work proceeded as usual, i.e. not very well. Chloe

---

* Billy the Oysterman was one of the best-known seafood restaurants in New York in the 1930s and 1940s.

wanted to see me, and I found her at Tony's at 5:40. She had three daiquiris with me. We talked about Rosalind, how I loved—and love—her, and how I have never felt closer to her than I do now, but that I am no longer in love with her. That's all true, but when Chloe said R. bores her, and that she's a big phony (!), I was outraged. Today I thought that the day will soon come when R. and I are together, because I am always waiting, really, for her virtues, her mind, and her wisdom—as these values of mine remain undiminished. Have much to learn, but I'm a fast learner.[GG]

OCTOBER 20, 1943

[F]I gave Chloe a call. I'd like to see her Saturday night, but if it doesn't happen, I won't eat my heart out. I'm thinking about my illustrations and my story, and my days are full of work. Phoned Rosalind at 8:30. I told her what Chloe said about her when she was drunk, and Rosalind said: "A magnificent shell! But she bores me terribly. Chloe doesn't understand that the two people she loves—you and Betty—are my two closest friends." I shouldn't be so nervous.[FF]

OCTOBER 21, 1943

[F]Tired at the office, and when I'm tired everything seems hopeless. Coffee with Leo, and Chloe called at 5:30. Saturday night?—We'll see! she said. 4½ martinis with Leo, though I wanted to work. I don't know why I want to drink but—anyway—I was very happy because Chloe phoned me. With Rosalind—who wanted to see me—at 9:40—although Leo wanted to make an evening of it. He understands everything, but what does it matter? "Is Chloe in love with you?" Rosalind asked. "Not at all," I answered. "That's absurd." And so on and so forth. I really loved tonight a lot.[FF]

OCTOBER 22, 1943

[G]Very good, productive day, because I got nearly enough sleep. Wrote 7 pages this morning. It rained all day. And Chloe has influenza. Two martinis with Leo at 6:00 and dinner at Raffier's.

Cleaned the whole house because Chloe is probably coming over
tomorrow evening. She had a home visit from the doctor and is
feeling a little better.[GG]

10/22/43

There will come a time, oh Methuselah, when you will want
to declare your independence of drink and of women. And be
alone.

OCTOBER 23, 1943

[G]Terribly depressed to find out Chloe couldn't spend the night.
She's feeling worse. So instead—a drink with Leo—two—and
lunch at Hamburger Mary. I've been talking about Rosalind so
much (lately) that he's completely forgotten about Chloe. Didn't
get anything done in the afternoon—this drinking really has got
to stop! Two martinis with R.C. at the Winslow. Had my notebook with me, and she paged through, commenting on several
passages written to Chloe, about Chloe—about sleeping with
women. She eventually said: "Is this your diary?" "No—it's just
literary." Very drunk later and disgusted with myself. Swear I
won't drink next week! I swear it![GG]

OCTOBER 24, 1943

[G]Sad, restless day. Felt hopeless at one o'clock—and went to
Cocktail with Leo. Two martinis. Hamburger, and I confessed
to him that I don't want to go to Mexico because he thinks he's
in love with me. He threatened to break the neck of whomever
else I might go with. Two martinis—one brandy, and I felt like
a character out of Kay Boyle's *Monday Night*. I have to do a
lot of thinking about my life. There's a lot I have to find myself
and give myself. And what that ultimately means is—writing.
Went to my parents', who neither influence nor inspire me. Leo
brought me a magnificent big pumpkin. And only stayed a minute, like a gentleman. Chloe called at 11:00 and my heart soared!
My God, must I always drink so much that I make a fool of
myself? Smoking too much. Chloe wants to meet Rolf. Probably

Tuesday evening. And she wants to [carve] the pumpkin with me some night.^{GG}

OCTOBER 25, 1943

^GGramma arriving at 8:30 AM Thursday. Would go to the station, but prefer to see her first at Mother's house. That will be a happy moment! Chloe came over at 11:20 and stayed till 2:00, during which time we had the longest, most wonderful, most unbelievable kisses! Afterward she said she was crazy, that we were crazy, and that she worshipped me. Made plans to see Rosalind. She said "Yes" and called me "Patsy." They loved my illustrations (at *H & F*) and will probably give me a Christmas story to illustrate.^{GG}

OCTOBER 27, 1943

^GHappy day, but still very tired. Must run an experiment: 1) to get enough sleep 2) to find enough inner peace to dream 3) to write a book 4) to see the world as it truly is for the first time. Does that sound simple? ridiculous? childish? The greatest artists are always childish. I will start the experiment immediately. First and foremost is quieting my soul. Lunch with Rosalind. Told her what Chloe wants and doesn't want, etc. Finally admitted I'm governed by a perverse force, namely that I will stop loving a girl if she starts to love me more than I love her. "We all experience that," she responded sadly. Interesting. Wayne Lonergan, Patricia Lonergan's husband who probably killed her, is gay.[*] That's what Mother said this morning. Very interesting legal case, because they're both wealthy, etc. Maria and Angelica knew Patricia. Rosalind knows of many "boys" [and] "men" who are very scared, because they don't want their names to be made public.^{GG}

---

* New York socialite and heiress Patricia Burton Lonergan was found strangled in her bed on October 24, 1943. The murder trial, which ended with the conviction of her husband, Wayne Lonergan, galvanized the press and public. Interestingly, Dominick Dunne compares Lonergan to Patricia Highsmith's Tom Ripley in his article "The Talented Mr. Lonergan" for *Vanity Fair* in July 2000.

OCTOBER 28, 1943
GGood day. Got good work done, because something like
Gramma's arrival doesn't throw me off at all. Spoke at length
with Jerry [Albert], whom I like more and more. Grandmother
doesn't look as weak as I'd feared. She showed us lots of family
photographs—which will finally be passed on to me. The prettiest one: that of my mother at age thirteen or fourteen. She was
an angel! Goldberg called. He'll be in Mexico in January and is
working on two books. Called me "Pat" (!) and I, awkward (as
an ass), called him B.Z. for the first time. Joseph H. here. He's
being court-martialed for disobeying some command or other at
sea. Not at all interested in seeing him. Texas said Wayne Lonergan (who just confessed to the murder) was at Mifflin's 1942–43
social. That means I met him, but I don't remember it.GG

OCTOBER 29, 1943
GSpoke with Hughes about Mexico. He doesn't want to let me
go, because he says when a writer leaves the company, he never
comes back. Too big a time difference between N.Y. and Mexico, etc. Today he dropped all sorts of hints to Camy and Leo,
which means: if I go to Mexico, he'll fire me. Talked about it
for too long (with Leo) and broke my nice weekly average. My
thoughts always return to Chloe. I called her at 10:30 and was
invited to spend the night. Of course I went, quick as a thun-
derbolt. First touched her as she pretended to be asleep, but did
not try to arouse her. She was completely dry—really, while I
was like a spring. Is that why she's barren? Frostie? Who knows.
Götz called from [California] at 3:00 AM, and [they] talked for
an hour while I sat in the other room. When I came back in, she
kissed me as warmly as ever, but was all scattered.GG

OCTOBER 31, 1943
GChloe called me at 1:30—she wanted to see me right away: [she
was expecting] a telegram—from Götz, and she couldn't open it.
She claimed to have left him at 5:00 AM. Didn't know if I should

believe her. Broke my engagements with [Raphael] Mahler, Mother and Ann T.—and went to bed with her. The telegram interrupted us—"Donnie was right and I will never not feel it. And maybe we'll live again I do not know. I have struggled with my arcangel and I have lost. I'll write you one more letter." Götz. She showed no emotion—for ten minutes. Then she began to shake, and drank whatever was in the house. She wanted more to drink, and finally, after we put together an answer, we went (she in a skirt with nothing on underneath) to Longchamps. 1½ martinis. Then we came back and went to bed. I made love to her—her first time with a woman—and the earth didn't shake— but I did it well enough—and nothing matters but that I made her happy for a minute. My God, when all of her was on my lips, I knew I would find no peace if I could not express what I had to—love. So I did. Have so much to think about. But one thing is certain: [the time has come to] write something important. Something necessary. Something big. A major dream of my being, from deep within. The poems will come later. My heart, though, is full—far too full tonight. It won't allow itself to be poured out.[GG]

NOVEMBER 1, 1943

[G]I was swimming in confusion all day: how long will Chloe last? What should I do now, since I never finished my last story? And what about Mexico—up until this evening, I thought I had to know happiness and peace (yes, peace). Otherwise there's no making art or writing. Got good work done. It feels strange, after yesterday, to see my mouth as always, my fingers at work as always, my eyes as always. And I made a woman happy! Today or yesterday evening Chandler suffered through an appendectomy. Chloe is of course very concerned, and I'm happy about that. Reading [Julien Green's] *Closed Garden* with great pleasure.[GG]

NOVEMBER 2, 1943

[G]Uneasy all day, and smoked [a lot], despite getting good work done. Spoke to Chloe at 2:30; Chandler's condition is worsening, and Chloe's leaving for California right away. "You'll be happier if I go." "My God! What kind of perversion do you think I have?" I screamed, almost in tears. How sad. How sick and how hopeless! Had the strange and rare pleasure of drinking my own rum by myself. Like a gentleman, like a wise man, and went by Chloe's with a nice, small salad. Kissed her masterfully as she lay on her bed. "You drive me crazy!" she kept whispering. Quiet—heavy—her kisses are heaven!^{GG}

NOVEMBER 3, 1943

^GHappy day—because Mexico is set! Spoke to Hughes about it, and although he can't guarantee my pay, I think he'll try. I.e., I can send stories back to him. News received quietly at my parents', [they're] convinced I'll achieve success in Mexico. Goldberg at 8:30. He gives me so much! Encouragement, etc. and always convinces me I'm a writer. I have got to write a novel in Mexico. Chloe or no Chloe—I'm going!^{GG}

NOVEMBER 4, 1943

^GTold Chloe that I want to leave for Mexico as soon as possible. "Then I'll come with you," she responded. My heart soared! Chloe has an engagement tomorrow evening with Kiki Preston*—a decadent, depraved woman she met a long time ago. Had to go to the theater drunk, *Petrouchka*. Impatient. Then went straight to Rosalind's. Cutty Sark with Rosalind till two.^{GG}

11/6/43

Necessary to be alone to realize how sad one is. And just as necessary to be alone to realize how happy. The last sensation is the rarer and more amazing. But for the happy one the blessings are without end.

---

* Kiki Preston, née Alice Gwynne (1898–1946), American socialite, distantly related to the Vanderbilt and Whitney families, and a member of the hedonistic Happy Valley set in Kenya. Known for her beauty, her drug addiction, and her many lovers, she allegedly had an illegitimate child with Prince George, Duke of Kent, son of King George V.

11/6/43

An artist cannot live with himself and with a woman, too. How this has ever been arranged I cannot understand.

NOVEMBER 7, 1943

^GChloe brought me a bouquet—one rose—several chrysanthemums—which I will keep for the rest of my life. She wants to spend "one month—maybe three" in Palm Springs. And doesn't want to see her husband now. Kiki invited her to stay with her. That's the latest. And it's plenty.^{GG}

NOVEMBER 8, 1943

^GAlmost sick all day. Didn't hear from Chloe. She's doubtless shifted her plans again. She shifts faster than the Russian front. Learning Spanish—studying hard.^{GG}

NOVEMBER 8, 1943

^GNice day. Wore moccasins to work with great success. Stopped by Missouri Pacific [Railroad]. 190.00 roundtrip, and I could have left the 28th. After a conversation with my parents, though, I've decided not to leave before the tenth of December. Worked hard and felt very excited, satisfied, and happy.—But I still want to leave this city. Chloe is staying in Palm Springs for a week. Reading poems.^{GG}

11/10/43

Sentiment comes suddenly, in the juice of love, sympathy, sexual emotion desire. It turns on at the turn of your companion's phrase, as a faucet turns. And consciousness can shut it off as soon.

NOVEMBER 11, 1943

^GHappy day. I'm entering a manic period where I need little sleep or food. Chloe moved to Kiki Preston's this afternoon. For nine days—officially. Keep getting thinner, although I'm eating a lot. Gramma and Mother very curious about my feelings for Chloe,

"Why?" and "What does she have [to offer]?" and "I'd like to learn what strange power this girl has!"^{GG}

NOVEMBER 12, 1943

^GCan't get a seat on the train before December 12. That's fine. A secret was revealed at home: We don't like Grandma. She's jealous, talks too much, wants to spend lots of money, and doesn't show any thoughtfulness [toward] Mother. It concerns me to see Mother still trying to understand Grandma, change her, show her where she's wrong. And that Mother's always searching for something that was never there.

A letter tonight from Allela—it was very nice, saying she still loves me, etc. I had to respond right away. Tonight, without the least effort, I began to dream up my novel. That's healthy. The work comes much later.^{GG}

11/12/43

More than most writers realize, or admit, inspiration, whole story places, come from visual objects: a house, a suitcase, a glove in a gutter. Why say indirectly? If indirectly, it is so simple to trace the development, that it becomes directly responsible.

NOVEMBER 13, 1943

^G2 martinis with Leo. We're growing apart and awkward and are not happy together. He's living fast, doing lots of little things, but probably lacks the virtue for any bigger dream. That's the dream that makes a great artist.

Went to the Martin Beck Theatre* at 2:45 with Mother and Grandma. K. Dunham† very thrilling, but not like Carmen

---

* The Martin Beck Theatre in midtown Manhattan opened on November 11, 1924, and was renamed the Al Hirschfeld Theater in 2003.
† Katherine Dunham (1909–2006), American dancer, choreographer, anthropologist, and activist. In 1937, she founded the all-Black Negro Dance Group, using their performances to protest against segregation. She was one of the first African American choreographers at the Metropolitan Opera in New York. Her dance students included James Dean and Marlon Brando.

Amaya. Hurried home. Needed lots of things, which cost me a lot. More gin. It's always the alcohol that makes me poor. Chloe came over at 6:30. I wanted to get her drunk this evening, but without success. She had to go to Kiki's, who's very sick. Chloe said that if she were to fall in love with a woman, it would be me. But that she prefers men. It's wonderful—how much drive one has when one's woman leaves in the night. That's how I feel this minute. It was extremely maddening, because I wanted her badly.

Want to get so much done before I leave. And thinking about my book.^{GG}

NOVEMBER 14, 1943

^GWasted so much time again, but that's how every Sunday goes. Breakfast at my parents', because I'm so lonely when I don't have Chloe. That probably makes me a coward. Then I had to take a walk with Mother, and we hurried to the nearest bar. We [spoke] frankly about my grandmother. Something must be done, because she has the intention of coming here every summer. Mother will grow old, because she drives us all to drinking.

Chloe called. She's worried she could ruin me if we spend time together. I have the strength, the ability, the power, or the indifference to shrug that off. Happy, and unhappy, definitely very busy.^{GG}

NOVEMBER 15, 1943

^GOrdered two seats on the train. Dec. 11 and 12. Chloe is coming with me, I say, because she doesn't have any big plans for herself. I, at least, am decisive, and she's coming with me, if only as a result of my orneriness. Called her at 2:00, told her what I'd done, and she replied: "Good!" Went to the Wakefield Gallery—no Bernhard, but Rosalind, Natasha, and the Calkins, all very friendly toward me. Feel happy.

Jerry is doubtless going to war November 26.

$340.26 in the bank.^{GG}

NOVEMBER 18, 1943

^GRosalind and Betty came over at 9:30. They were very formal at first, but eventually Chloe called: she and Kiki wanted to stop by for a visit. Kiki is slim,^{GG} an old bag from way back. ^GChloe very drunk when she arrived. Rosalind enjoyed herself immensely. Cheese and Scotch, and long pauses, full of meaning. Kiki was determined not to leave without Chloe, but Betty Parsons somehow managed to throw her out of the house. Betty likes my sketches and paintings. And she wants to include several of them in her next show! Betty liked me very much this evening, and I liked her. Happy about nothing—but especially about my work and my wonderful life! I want to do lots of things. I want to be a giant!^{GG}

NOVEMBER 19, 1943

^GI'm tremendously happy that Chloe has finally decided to come with me. We spoke for a long time today. She has an income of 81.50 per month. She'll be rich in Mexico, but has little cash at the moment. I'll buy her one-way ticket. Not concerned about it, except maybe about not being concerned.^{GG}

NOVEMBER 20, 1943

^FHappy but terribly nervous. In this instant, after an evening with Chloe, I am completely free of her. Now—with 7 hours of sleep in 48 hours, I want to write, read, do all of the calm and spiritual things which have always occupied me. I am full of strength. Worked with great difficulty of course. I have only $165 in the bank, and after I bought Chloe's ticket, $64.00. A brandy with Camy, who is dearer and dearer to me. The Chagall exhibition—marvelous! He's my old favorite. Also Tamayo*— not good. Camy here at 6:45 to get my table, and no doubt to meet Chloe. He was extremely attentive, cleaned my kitchen,

---

* Rufino Tamayo (1899–1991), Mexican painter who painted figurative abstraction with surrealist influences.

etc. and gave me a massage because I was completely spent. Then Chloe at 7:30. A bit drunk, but she likes Camy and he likes her. Finally alone at 9:00. Chloe very sweet, told me that Kiki tried to give her dope. Kiki rushed into the bathroom on Thursday night, Betty said, to take five big pills. Chloe still wants to go to Mexico. But Kiki, who's worried about Chloe leaving, will do anything to keep her here. And Chloe?—It would hardly make any difference if she didn't come.[FF]

NOVEMBER 21, 1943

[F]Good day—slept until 11:30 when I went to have lunch with my parents. I told them all about Chloe. My mother didn't say much, but was certainly interested. Chloe spoke seriously of our trip for the first time. I gave her instructions on how to obtain her visa. The little darling—she should have a man to do all of this, and I'll do it with pleasure. My parents will probably give me $100. And as a Christmas gift, I'll accept it. At the Museum of Modern Art. Very inspiring. Romantic painting. Oh, I want to paint in Mexico! And made some progress on this long road which will return me to myself. Tranquility is of the essence. But it's difficult—when Kiki could be, at this very moment, in Chloe's bed, giving her dope pills. It deeply troubles me. But in three weeks—less than three weeks—she can't form a habit.[FF]

NOVEMBER 22, 1943

[G]Lunch with Parsons at Del Pezzo. Of course Betty and I spoke mostly about Chloe. She told the sad story of her divorce from her husband.[*] Chloe called me at 3:15. Very despondent and sad. Wanted to leave for Mexico tonight.

Sketched very poorly in class, and don't know why. I have to write to rediscover my self-esteem. God give Chloe the strength to endure these two and a half weeks![GG]

---

[*] In 1919, Betty married Schuyler Livingston Parsons, a New York socialite ten years her senior, who her family hoped would inspire her to embrace a more conventional lifestyle. They divorced in 1922.

NOVEMBER 24, 1943

^FArrived at the office at 11:30 because I had to get some sleep this morning. My tooth hurt so much I couldn't fall asleep until 6:00 AM. Hughes very cold when I came into the office. Jerry said that Hughes always comes into my office when I'm not there. He thinks I spend a lot of time out of the office. At the dentist's at 2:30. The tooth has an abscess and I'll have to get two pulled. The wisdom tooth too. Chloe phoned me at 1:00. Very serious, and not at all drunk. "I'll lose my reputation, but what's the good of a reputation anyway?" I didn't know what to say. "And for whose sake if not yours, my love?" I'll lose mine too—no—but what a great, beautiful loss!^{FF}

NOVEMBER 25, 1943

^GChloe very sweet. I feel more warmly toward her, but still feel shy kissing her. For instance, when I do make the first move, she reponds to me as a lover would. She's concerned I'll fall in love with a Mexican girl. "And where will that leave me?" she asked sadly, smiling.^{GG}

NOVEMBER 26, 1943

^FI'm happy when I think about our departure. We will be together at my parents' house, and it will likely be the closest experience to a honeymoon I will ever know. And the parents will know. The day will come when Chloe, upon waking, will look at me pensively and ask herself, "Who are you?" And I will know then that she is cured and no longer needs me. I will try not to be sad. Leo continues to make outrageous remarks about Chloe, and if I had more respect for my Chloe, I'd punch him!^{FF}

NOVEMBER 27, 1943

^FA miserable day. I haven't done any work in three months, and I'm not lying. I can't seem to collect myself. But my desire to work grows every day. And right now, I am incomplete. I brought all my records to Rosalind in a suitcase. Rum at her

place at 4:15, then the Berman* exhibition at J. Levy. Julien not very friendly, but Muriel smiling, very sweet. Then Wakefield, where R., Betty and I were like old friends. 2 martinis, while I was thinking of Chloe. Dinner with Camy, and I was rather drunk. He likely knows everything there is to know about Chloe and myself.[FF]

NOVEMBER 28, 1943

[G]Worked hard and feel happier. Mother had the audacity to call at 9:15 AM, while I was still sleeping. Yes, I want to live like a professor—my quiet hours, my tea, my books, different projects, different studies. The only tumult should be internal. Life is tumultuous as is, but inner tumult is the only kind compatible with work.

Cocktails at my parents' with Bernhard. She looked at my grandmother's photographs. I love Bernhard very much. Nervous dinner with the family. I'm not talking much to Gramma, and although she notices, there's not much I can do to help. Menstruating—a week early. Am very aroused, though, and want Chloe like a husband wants his wife.

Thinking about my novel.[GG]

NOVEMBER 29, 1943

[G]My grandmother leaves by train tomorrow. Oh! How happy, how excited I was when she arrived. But the terrible feeling grew stronger and stronger—I don't love her. I can't love her. I want these remaining ten days to be quiet. We'll see. I want it with all my heart. I want it more than I want a woman. Thinking about my novel.[GG]

NOVEMBER 30, 1943

[G]Hardest, most furious day of my life. Had tooth pulled from 7–8. Perlman gave me 3 Scotches. Hadn't gone under when he

---

* Eugene Berman (1899–1972), Russian-born American neoromantic-turned-surrealist painter.

pulled the tooth. The same horrific dreams in which Chloe was the only woman in the world, in the entire cosmos, and I knew everything about everything, and that the whole world, and history, was a performance for my pleasure! Yes—I felt guilty and weak by comparison—but I was utterly dependent.^{GG}

DECEMBER 2, 1943

^GTerrible day. Saw Dr. B. at 1:00. Vaccine against typhus. Very quick. About a half teaspoon. Afterward I went to Lechay's* exhibit. Good watercolors. Big, fine-tasting cup of coffee at Hamburger Heaven. Maybe that's why I got sick so quickly. Nauseous and faint, and I thought without a doubt I'd die. Am certain the doctor gave me a bad vaccine and I could have died. A small child can endure all manner of vaccines, because he doesn't know what he's enduring. But I—with an all too active imagination for bodily pain—cannot endure it. Fever and headache. Typhus.^{GG}

DECEMBER 3, 1943

^GGot my "PASE" to México. Very easy at the consulate-general. I want to plan my entire life. I want the peace of "Come, sweet death!" Quiet days, and a woman?—there I'm not so sure.^{GG}

DECEMBER 4, 1943

^GDoctor Mahler stopped by with three gifts for the Rosenbergs. Two pairs of nylons, [Pearl S. Buck's novel] *Dragon Seed*, and a box of almonds for me. And an oil painting—luckily small. Met Rosalind at 5:00. She paid me the highest compliment, that she only counts Natasha, Betty, and me as friends. That it will be a lonely Christmas, because I won't be here. Went to Chloe's at 8:00. Fever of 103.4. Tony Werner said that the Span-

---

* James Lechay (1907–2001), American painter, leader of the Artists Union (an organization of artists employed by the Works Progress Administration), organizer of exhibits of works by Milton Avery, Max Weber, and other WPA artists. In both 1942 and 1943 he was exhibited at the Ferargil Galleries.

ish influenza was highly contagious and an epidemic. I took no precautions against it. Odd—that I want Chloe and don't want her, that I'm convinced I can do everything I want to do with or without her. Restless again. Have much to do, and wasted most of the day.[GG]

12/4/43

God showed a ribald sense of humor when he created the physical body. When I die, I'll think of the sweating, the shivering, the headaches, the unsuccessful love making, the effort of getting up in the morning, and laugh so hard that I'll split my sides, if I have any. Then I will live in the realm of pure thought and artistic perception and perfection. But I shall not be so surprised as most, because I expected it all along. Nevertheless, I shall be among the most grateful.

DECEMBER 5, 1943

[G]Chloe's getting better. Her fever is gone and she took a bath. Wanted to go out! Prepared all sorts of books, boxes, etc. (with Mother). Have nothing more to do. I'm taking very few books. Thinking a lot about Rosalind—who made me so happy yesterday. Surely I must truly love her—now that the fire has gone—now that love remains. Now—but first I must make something of myself.[GG]

12/5/43

I met you by accident. I loved you by accident, and immediately. My love grows more beautiful each year as a good piano grows more rich. As in the first days when my dreams were all future with you, now my thoughts are of us together, the future being much sooner. Now I am solid, without the drunkenness and the unreal excitement and the uncertainty of the trials and tests of each new encounter in each evening. Surely what exists now is love, and surely I have never known it before.

DECEMBER 7, 1943

GSpoke to Ann T. Ellen B. killed herself three weeks ago in West-port. Suicide, with a pistol. It really all goes back to the night when Chloe didn't call me. It's why I got drunk the next night—and Ann stayed [over] and told Ellen all of it, and she wasn't the same after that. Chloe—you really are Helen III of Troy! Spoke to Rosalind, who will always be dear to me. My parents are very concerned because I mentioned I might live with Rosalind someday. "I'd much rather see you with a husband and family," Mother said. Naturally, but I'm not exactly one with nature. Got ready. For my destiny.GG

DECEMBER 8, 1943

GTerribly nervous. I don't know if I can do anything to improve my nerves, or if they'll grow perpetually worse till I'm dead and buried. Met Perlman at 6:00. Ate at Palm Restaurant, 49th St. Fantastic steaks, $3.00 apiece. I didn't want to eat much, though. I want to think, live slowly, compare and taste everything—as one must always live. Radio City—where the movies were so boring I had to get up and call Chloe. Bored to tears is an every-day condition of mine. Perlman guilty of various devilries—he kissed me, to my utter disgust!GG

DECEMBER 9, 1943

GWorked as always. Mother came by at 12:30 and met Jerry—he thinks I'm "prettier" than my mother. Something dumb as that must mean he's fallen in love with me. Bought shoes, bags, and gifts for the Plangmans. And best of all—Chloe got her visa. The men in the office were of course very polite! Why wouldn't they be? Has Mexico ever seen such a woman?

Jerry gave me Burns Mantle's [Best] Plays* —with an

---

* Robert Burns Mantle (1873–1948) was an American theater critic who founded the annual publication Best Plays.

inscription—very kind. I love him very much—and what a
strange start (nothing physical until only two weeks ago!).^{GG}

DECEMBER 11, 1943

^GYOU FAITHFULLY SEEK THE ILL AND ERRING
AND WE HASTEN WITH WEAK YET EAGER STEPS—
TO YOU—TO YOU*—We are sick—but together, thank
God—^{GG}

DECEMBER 14, 1943

^GSan Antonio at 7:00 AM. Had to find a dentist immediately
and saw one at 9:00. Later—finally, peace. Eons later.^{GG}

DECEMBER 14, 1943

^GStill quiet. Still scared. Tooth is worse. Breakfast next door to
our terrible, bleak hotel, and later looked for a dentist. Doctor
Durbeck, who was supposed to X-ray me. "Abscess, no doubt,"
he said. A big incision, lots of blood. My fears remain, but I am
fighting them with all my might. Finally together with Chloe—
who had a headache, who can think of nothing else, we came
back to our hotel, still pretty quiet. Chloe thinks I've abandoned
her, that I'm a Jekyll-Hyde person.

On the train at 7:30. Much happier, because I thought my
suffering was over, my tooth better. In Laredo tonight. We
rode [past] the Grand Canyon very late, 1:30 in the morning.
Covered wagons, the people quiet, looking at each other mean-
ingfully. Presented our visas. Mexican officers. The censor
read our letters, all from G. v. E. [Götz van Eyck] to Chloe.
And he wouldn't let mine in, because there were too many.
I should have stayed overnight in Laredo, but C. was afraid
of arriving in Mexico alone. She was also afraid of spending
the night with me in Laredo. Had to send my luggage back to

---

* Fragments from Johann Sebastian Bach's cantata *Jesu, der du meine Seele.*

N.Y., and Ch. promised to pay. She was almost hysterically happy tonight.

But in the morning—^{GG}

DECEMBER 15, 1943

^G—in the morning always so much worse. And the doctors can't do a thing. Read X Science all day, although it doesn't work with Chloe. She isn't happy with anything—I keep leaving her alone, and it's always my fault.^{GG}

DECEMBER 16, 1943

^GThe long journey through Mexico, Laredo to Mexico—D.F.* Poor children, poor women selling all sorts of things in the villages. They beg and are very clever. C. wants to give away her money, and I must control her. I prefer to learn the language and customs.^{GG}

DECEMBER 17, 1943

^GReached the Hotel Montejo. Chloe found it. Very charming. Very cheap for gringos. $20.00 a day. I can't write here, the way I want to—this city is wonderful—and not very alien. Chloe very sad, and I keep saying that I'm really quite sick, and that's all. I'm scared, and I can't be myself. Visited the Rosenbergs. Very nice. Rosenberg sold two tickets for a conert at the Palacio de Bellas Artes this evening. It's very inconvenient not to have any of my clothes. If I'd done that to C., she'd never have forgiven me! The books and sketch paper too.^{GG}

DECEMBER 18, 1943

^GFor the first time—I heard C. really cuss me out! Two tequila cocktails at 6:00. She said she's better than me, that I'm neurotic, that she wants to leave for Cal. [California] immediately. That

---

* De Efe/Distrito Federal, or Mexico City.

I'm a liar. "Why did you invite me to come to Mexico?" Yes—
that was tough—!^GG

12/20/43

It is difficult. Yes, yes, it is difficult. So difficult—all the way to
the grave.

DECEMBER 21, 1943

^GTerrible evening with Gene Rossi and his friend Lew Miller,
who picked us up as we sat drinking at the restaurant. 2 daiquiris here, plenty, but then another at Tony's. Then Ciro's,* a
wonderfully sleek nightclub run by Blumenthal,† Peggy Fears's‡
husband. Very very nice, and Chloe very, very pretty. I was
wearing my gray suit, which always depresses me. But what does
it matter, when Chloe is so beautiful? Lew very serious, because
he recently returned from war. Went to Casanova's later. Chloe
drank much too much. A certain "Teddy Stauffer"§ runs the
Casanova. Chloe ran into several friends from California and
Hollywood. But I didn't drink a thing and was almost bored to
tears.^GG

DECEMBER 22, 1943

^GWant to buy Chloe a chihuahua for Christmas. It will be like
having a child. I'll be very happy once we leave this city. But I'm
well aware that it's the best part of the trip for Chloe. Or maybe
not. I can't know that for certain. But this city disgusts me, and

---

* Ciro's was a flashy cabaret in the Hotel Reforma decorated with murals by Diego Rivera.
Until it closed in 1948, it was one of Mexico City's most luxurious venues, attracting a crowd
of rich expats, royals, diplomats, and artists.
† Theatrical promoter Alfred Cleveland Blumenthal (1885–1957) made his fortune in real
estate before he left the United States for Mexico to escape the U.S. tax authorities. Ciro's
presented him with a useful front in his next business venture, drug trafficking.
‡ Peggy Fears (1903–1994), a former Ziegfeld Follies showgirl, appeared in Broadway musical
comedies before becoming a Broadway producer with her husband, Alfred Blumenthal. They
were responsible for productions such as the 1932–1933 show *Music in the Air.*
§ Teddy Stauffer (1909–1991), Swiss jazz musician, swing band leader, and hotel and club
owner, helped transform Acapulco from a small fishing village into a vacation destination for
Hollywood film stars such as Hedy Lamarr, whom he would later marry.

it's not even Mexico! Saw a wonderful market. They sell all types of figures, animals, people and birds for Christmas decorations. Gene came over, very persistent, very rude, but I have to say, Chloe encourages him. He wants to take her to the horse races Thursday. And to a social Christmas Eve. The twenty-fourth. Lots of Chloe's friends will be there, and I expect she'll go. But not me.[GG]

DECEMBER 23, 1943

[F]Our days are becoming more and more disorganized. We don't get up early, of course, but 9—10—11—whenever. I went to the hospital, where Barrera was. He's about forty, very friendly, and devoted to Betty Parsons. He doesn't like socializing. He suggested we take a house—one week in San Miguel Allende, perhaps. The town Tamayo works in.

Watched Chloe as she dressed herself for an hour and a half. For Teddy Stauffer. She changed her mind again and again—but I was having fun, and she left very happy. Thought of my novel all evening. Work is going well—even though I'm here. And yet I'm happy. It's past midnight, and Chloe's not back yet. I'm reading Blake and Donne with great pleasure.[FF]

DECEMBER 24, 1943

[F]Last night Chloe got home at 5:35 AM. Naturally we didn't get up before 11. We took a five-hour walk, until I was exhausted! Branches for a manger. I made it myself from 6–8, it's splendid. Jesus is larger than his mother and father. I also made a white, innocent sheep, and an angel, who watches the scene in supplication. Green, with lots of flowers I bought at the market. It made me very happy.

Chloe was supposed to come home to have dinner with me, but she was with Gene Rossi. She doesn't like him, but he creates an interesting situation in which Teddy is jealous of Gene, and vice versa. Teddy Stauffer sent an orchid. It all provides me with innocent amusement, because I always want Chloe to do what she wants. It's 2:00 A.M. now. She said she'd be home early! I ate alone, thinking of the good music that they are playing now in New York, thinking of my family, of Rosalind, to whom I wrote 8 pages tonight—telling her all about my teeth, my troubles, etc. I am filled with satisfaction—thanks to God. The manger is standing by my bed. The angels will fly all night. Their wings will caress me. God bless Chloe tonight, and give her peace. Show her that the truth is within and not without, that the joys of the spirit are the only joys. Teach her selflessness, and the meaning of love. And send her a shining new year.[FF]

DECEMBER 25, 1943

[G]The saddest, most wonderful day. It wasn't Christmas. Like any other depressing day, we slept till 11 o'clock. Big breakfast ($8.00), which I paid, but no presents—I just gave Chloe a nice, big bar of chocolate. She didn't give me anything. At 4:30 we took a walk to Chapultepec Bosque,* where the museum was closed, but where I met a group of friendly soldiers. One talked to me for nearly two hours. It was cold and damp, and we laughed to keep warm. It was the one thing that felt most like Christmas. Teddy invited me over with Chloe. We three had nothing to say. Chloe never has anything to say—she just drinks. Finally dinner came, but Chloe didn't like it: everything could have been so much nicer. Everything. But it's utterly impossible, as is always impossible with Chloe.

Chloe got into a taxi with Teddy for several minutes. I didn't know if she would spend the night with him, but it was unlikely. She encourages the men, but doesn't give them anything, just like she's never given me anything. But I was in tears as I wrote her a letter [about] how she never would, or could, share anything with me, how I wanted nothing from her but soil for my searching roots. She got back at 3:00. Read my letter—as I blushed in shame. But where to?—Where to—and why? We are done—there's nothing left. I fell asleep with a piece of the chocolate I had given her in my mouth.[GG]

---

* Bosque de Chapultepec is a large park in central Mexico City.

DECEMBER 26, 1943

GChloe and I went to Chapultepec Bosque, but we got there at 2:30 and the museum was closed. And Chloe, exhausted through and through, had to take a taxi back to the hotel. That's right! God! I shouldn't record such trifles! I should be occupying myself with work! Why do I still mention Chloe? It's ridiculous, and the sooner I'm free of her, the better for me and for everything I hope to accomplish!GG

DECEMBER 27, 1943

GTried to find my luggage from N.Y. Had to go to the Palacio Nacional, etc., and ultimately—it hasn't arrived. I went for a walk at midnight. A man, Hernando Camacho, followed me, and I went with him and his friend to Casanova, where Chloe was with Teddy. I like Camacho very much—although Del P. is the only man I love. We danced (!)—me in huaraches and a black shirt, and we drank tequilas. He kissed me when we got home. He has a brain, and it isn't bad. Regarding Chloe, he said— "Beautiful, but phrenologically speaking nonentity." Wants to ride horses with me tomorrow. Yes—like him very much!GG

DECEMBER 28, 1943

GBarrera is—as Chloe says—without a doubt homosexual. I— yes, I would have sensed it now too. All Proust, *Well of Lone-liness*,* in his books; and *su amigo* Augusto was at his house again. Decided what I'm going to give Allela for her birthday: a silver bracelet with her name on it. I'll buy one for myself too. And I so hope she'll love it.GG

DECEMBER 29, 1943

GMy novel needs so much work, and I've been thinking about it, of course, all day. Although much of the story remains to be con-

---

* *Well of Loneliness*, a lesbian romance by British author Radclyffe Hall, portrays homosexuality as a natural, God-given state and makes an explicit plea: "Give us also the right to our existence."

structed, I think I can get good work done with my notebooks. Yes—God—what a terrible life Chloe creates for herself! It's sad that she can never forget it, and that she'll be bored and alone in some small town, in real life. Spent the evening with my friends Camacho and España again. Went to a Mexican cinema. I am rich in spirit—and I want to move on. Am happiest when imagining my new life on my own. We moved into a smaller room. Chloe only has about ten pesos left till January 4th. I can't always pay two bills.^{GG}

DECEMBER 30, 1943

^GWent to El Horreo,* but there was no letter. Feel sad about it, and glum. Talked to Barrera, who kindly invited me over tomorrow evening. Mass at church followed by a buffet. I'm very happy about it—I'd love nothing better.^{GG}

12/30/43

Mexico, D.F.—it is so beautiful and the Americans have made it so stinking.

DECEMBER 31, 1943

^GJalapa—Jalapa—Jalapa—I love your name! What have you got for me? Two weeks here already! Spent so much money that I'd be concerned, were it not for the knowledge that I can soon leave for the village. Bernhard said I should be very industrious— and that's why—and for the benefit of my soul—I want to start working now! Rode the second-class omnibus today. Lots of fun, and the people are good and friendly. It's simple, and I like that. I know what disgusts me about this city. It's that I'm not spending enough time by myself. I can't work—i.e., dream without being alone, no more than one can sleep and dream together.

Didn't eat enough today, and one tequila with Chloe at 9:30 nearly wrecked me. Chloe and Teddy left at 10:45. I went to the tavern, where I found España. Another tequila. Then finally

---

* Unclear, possibly the name of a restaurant Pat had her mail delivered to.

Barrera and Augusto. We went to a church—San Filipe—for midnight. Afterward—in the street, we embraced and wished each other a *feliz año nuevo*. Barrera's house—my God, how beautiful! A big table—*ponche caliente con rhum*—*queso y jamón*—*tambien caliente*—*sopa de jitomate*—*vino*. Barrera couldn't have been more lovely and kind. Barrera and Augusto were wearing ties and shirts with the same pattern, but different colors. After coffee we drove to Chapultepec Heights in Augusto's car—till 4 in the morning. This was the best New Year's Eve I've ever had! Yes—a home! A house—a house for living in! That's what I want! Chloe got back at 4:15. She was drunk, ugly, and dog-tired.[GG]

12/31/43

I hope I sometime pass a new year when my heart is not somewhere where I am not.

1944

Winter in Mexico, or:
"I am lonely for a thousand things."

※

PATRICIA HIGHSMITH'S FIRST trip abroad is so important to her that she dedicates a separate diary to it—the aptly named "Mexico Diary," composed in German, French, and rudimentary Spanish. After the tumultuous beginning of her journey, and hoping to finally find the peace and quiet she feels she needs to write, Pat is soon ready to leave not only Mexico City, but also Chloe behind.

Continuing on her travels solo, Pat moves on to Taxco, a picturesque colonial town famed for its silver mining and jewelry production. She spends most of her time there in the highlands, where she withdraws into the cottage she's rented—Casa Chiquita—to work on *The Click of the Shutting*. The novel centers around Gregory, an artistically talented teenager who cannot yet stand on his own two feet. Prone to feelings of inferiority and bouts of infatuation with other boys, he ultimately weasels his way into the life of a rich, spoiled young man—much like Tom Ripley will later insinuate himself into Dickie Greenleaf's. Indeed, Pat herself later comes to see Gregory as a prototype for Tom Ripley; this earlier character is her first literary foray into the great wide world of alter egos, which have otherwise been relegated to her comic book scripts.

Pat remains torn between becoming a painter or writer and imposes a strict work regimen on herself: she paints in the morning, before the light grows harsh, and writes in the evening. She pens yearning missives to her mother and friends back in New York, hundreds of pages of diary and notebook entries, and pointed character descriptions, which she will later transpose into tragic short stories about expats who succumb to alcohol and the exotic in Mexico.

In early May, Pat sets out for home, destitute and exhausted from the Mexican heat, the countless benders, and the futile search for a female lover who really inspires her. On the way back, however, she stops off in Fort Worth to visit her grandmother Willie Mae. She does not write in her diary from May 12 through November 14, a lapse she attributes to her days simply being too full and happy for journaling.

Back in New York, Pat worries again that her work in comics—a more lucrative endeavor, now that she is pursuing it freelance—could be detrimental to her writing. Still, by the end of the year, she manages to secure the help of a literary agent named Jacques Chambrun to sell her stories and her novel-in-progress.

During this time, Pat dates various women concurrently, as is her wont. By late September, though, her relationship with a wealthy heiress from Philadelphia named Natica Waterbury emerges as the most important and lasting thus far. Pat is taken with Natica's daredevil feats (she flies planes) and literary interests (she was Sylvia Beach's assistant at Shakespeare & Company in Paris), but is forced to share her with another well-heeled scion from Philadelphia: Virginia Kent Catherwood, daughter of inventor and manufacturer Arthur Atwater Kent. Both women will profoundly inspire her in life and work for years to come.

JANUARY 1, 1944

SPBoarded the bus at six. Chloe kissed me several times. Jalapa at 12:30. Walked through the town all morning. Very pretty.SPSP

JANUARY 3, 1944

^FA marvelous day—some of the streets of this town make me feel almost sick with happiness. It makes something break in my heart—that these people live as God intends them to. For example, at eleven o'clock I heard music coming from a house—Mozart—and when I stopped close to the window to listen, an old man observed me, smiling. Finally, he stopped too, and wished me a happy new year—"*Feliz año, señorita!*"

But my room is cold.^{FF}

1/4/44

Languages—are like games, trying on the brain, competitive between yourself and the native. You and he play by the same rules, as everyone else in the country, and your successes are mildly exhilarating, like points won in sports.

JANUARY 4, 1944

^FA horrible day in a horrible room. Sent Chloe two telegrams. The first to ask if she'll come, the second to tell her that I'll come—will leave here tomorrow night. "Vamos a Acapulco," I wrote. She'll be happy, and so will I—it's hot there.^{FF}

JANUARY 6, 1944

^FRather cold en route. Chloe wasn't there. I took our old room. Hungry, freezing in the morning. Rang Teddy S. who knew her whereabouts. An apartment in Tabasco 130. Joined her at 1:00. She didn't ask me to move in with her.^{FF} "You must admit that we didn't really get along great." ^FNo letter from New York. Why, with people who truly understand me—why am I always so reserved? Tonight I love Cornell—I have always loved her soul, but tonight I love her—and not because I have finally separated from Chloe, or because I am alone. It's because I am now beginning to see the truth, and beginning to live—and because I am beginning to write out of love for writing.^{FF}

1/6/44

A new year's wish—to live with as much dignity as the servant, Pedro, whom I met in Jalapa. He is an a man of fifty or sixty, with grizzled hair close-cut on a round head. He stands upright with a sturdy chest bulging under his shirt, and he smiles easily. He loves to talk, small talk, friendly talk, lit with a personal imagination. His hands are rough and knobby with work, but he says proudly as he greets you, "I bring in my hand the warmth of my master's hand."

JANUARY 7, 1944

FMade a new friend, "Larry" H. I think we'll grow very fond of each other in Taxco. Exciting to get there. The road winding up through mountainous landscape, and the stretch before the town is breathtaking. Thought of Chloe—with no tenderness in my heart. Felt the urge of writing her that I don't want to see her when she comes to Taxco. That she's never been my friend. Arrived at destination at 1:00. Very lonely, but don't care. I want to be alone.FF

JANUARY 8, 1944

GFinally—a room, terrace, laundry, and maid (cook) for $45.00 US a month—it's not great—you could live off $5.00 US a week in México, but it's good for Taxco. This evening I started to think and feel. And write, in [my] notebook. The maid prepared my bath. One must make a fire to heat the water. It makes me uncomfortable, uneasy, ordering a girl around. Bought a bottle of wine to bless my future and my arrival. Bought slacks, stockings, and *cinturón* at the market—$11 pesos—not bad. There's always music in this city. At night, in the morning, in the afternoon. And in some mysterious way, one ends up spending a lot of money.GG

JANUARY 9, 1944

GA good day—but no mail—am used to it by now. There's too much to eat here, and I'll get fat if I don't stop. Impatiently await-

ing my typewriter.* Am happy—and ready to work. But I want
a fire at night. After all that's happened, I finally want a house
to myself. That would be heaven. At least you can wear slacks
here—something you can't do in just any little Mexican city.†GG

JANUARY 10, 1944

I have many fleas, Gand crimson blotches on my legs. I'm
miserable!GG

JANUARY 11, 1944

GHave found and rented the most beautiful house in Taxco—
and written three pages of notes for the novel. Wash basin made
of blue stones, lots of sunlight, interesting windows, etc. Everything so pretty and bright and pure! Going up the stars, you can
smell the flowers. Am happy—I can have whatever I wish. Even
a maid. And peace and quiet—without Chloe whom I don't even
like anymore.GG

JANUARY 14, 1944

GAnd when the rain fell last night, I started working on my
novel. Nothing good—I started over this evening. I am so happy.
I plan to paint and sketch in the morning when there's light. In
the evening, when it's dark, I plan to write. I have to write for
at least five hours a day. Drink seven cups of coffee a day. I can
work—but only when I'm alone—then the ideas rise like water
from the ground! Like gold from the ground. Like oil from the
ground.GG

1/15/44

How can painters work here in so much light? The light is difficult to work with. Light is not particularly beautiful or interest-

---

* Because of the problems with her luggage at the border, Pat is still without her typewriter.
† The expat community was substantial enough in Taxco that Mexican locals were
accustomed to seeing women in pants.

ing. It reveals too much and makes a painting thin. It is the end, while painting should show the means. The particular specialty of this country is color. The colors should be clear and exaggerated. One cannot do this with an excess of light.

JANUARY 17, 1944

ᴳWhat a strange way to spend my winter! I can easily imagine spending my life here—if I became "famous"—and had enough money and were happy—but—I would always have the feeling that this country is foreign. That's inescapable. Two letters! One from Roger F., the other from Leo Isaacs—a beautiful, "wise" letter. So happy that I had to buy a bottle of wine.ᴳᴳ

JANUARY 20, 1944

ᴳWrote a long letter yesterday to Leo Isaacs, air mail. It is curious—or maybe not so—that I wish he were here. And this letter shall bring him here, especially since he wants it himself. He doesn't know yet that I'm in Taxco, without Chloe, and alone. He'll come. I'll get a telegram soon that he's on his way. Good day. Wrote for a long time: an "introduction" to the novel. Wrote quickly, but it's better I write that way. Otherwise I'm lost in a number of details! Expected Larry* this evening, but she didn't come. Her husband probably arrived. Hoping for a letter from Mother. Why not? Why?ᴳᴳ

JANUARY 21, 1944

ᴳLetter from my mother! And from G. Albert. Sat in a corner at Paco's, drinking 2 tequilas *con limas*, reading and studying the delightful letters. The one from my mother was terribly preachy, but there were also nice words in it—*my darling*, and *darling*— that I would never hear in New York. Can't always sleep well, but the coffee is worth it!ᴳᴳ

---

* Larry, an occasional lover of Pat's.

JANUARY 25, 1944

^GToday at 5—seven letters! Strange—that my mother's letters bother me so much—bothered me to the point that I couldn't work this evening. She preaches to me, because she knows so much—that I drink too much, that I need to clean my house before I can start living in it, that my life is founded on alcohol and duplicity. All lies!

(3 tequilas—and no mirth!)^{GG}

1/26/44

The size of paper one writes a letter or a book on is vitally important. The length of the page, the width, even the space between the lines, influences the rhythm of the sentences. Today spent thirty minutes choosing a *cuaderno* into which I would copy my book. Having got a block from the ^{SP}printers,^{SPSP} I went back and asked to see a longer, larger book. He had one—one like Proust might have written *Remembrance of Things Past* in. Still I debated whether the dialogue would not be influenced by the 10-inch-long lines? Whereas the prose would be to my liking—long and rolling and detailed. I am still debating, although I came off with the smaller notebook.

1/26/44

I never before saw a Mexican village where the natives drank—until I saw Taxco. Strange to think, during the weekdays, that these faces and figures one sees on the streets, working, doing commonplace things, hold also that virus of city life, that hidden cancer that drives one to alcohol! Strange that their uncomplex minds would crave alcohol. On Sundays the streets are full of reeling men, old men, too, cracking their brittle knees on Taxco's cobblestones.

JANUARY 26, 1944

^GMy luggage arrived at 4. Quickly wrote an 8 page story.^{GG}

JANUARY 27, 1944

^GQuickly wrote another 8 pages till 3:30. 16 pages in 24 hours! Fervently hope—no I'm certain that Hughes will buy them. They're two of the best concepts.^GG

2/2/44

Mexico! It has to be seen from a bus window going at maximum speed, just so the luggage on top doesn't pull the bus over. You have to feel the clean wind in your face as you coast down from Mexico, down, down, and the road markers saying, three miles, too late, "*camino sinuoso*."* Sometimes the hills look like the backs of stampeding elephants, sometimes like deep napped rugs thrown carelessly in a heap. They are always so tremendous that the imagination cannot match them. The road is cut into the sides of hills, and as the crow flies would be four-fifths shorter. Far away two Mexicans in white pants, their shirts and sombreros covered with loads of corn-shucks, walk together far below the road. The petty, noisy, overpopulated peninsula of twentieth century Europe is vulgar and insane compared to this. These two are so wise that they do not know their wisdom, wise enough to be so proud of themselves that they are humble in the landscape and count their lives as two lives in millions. In the air from some house above the road now comes guitar music and soft voices, these musicians who seldom drink or smoke because they can make poetry in the thin daylight. Mexico with her feet in the earth and her crown in the sky.

FEBRUARY 5, 1944

^GWrote a tricky scene this afternoon, had a mind filled with difficulties and lively ideas, yet I [search for] answers with Larry. My God! Why am I going with her? I can't bear it any longer! No poetry—no thoughts—no soul! And I really hate drinking, particularly if I fail to get drunk!^GG

---

* Winding road.

FEBRUARY 7, 1944

[G]Letter from Chloe today. She was here, but "circumstances" prevented her from coming to see me. Circumstances in pants![GG]

2/10/44

Julien Green was right: one can have but one language for one's every day clothes and one's best hours. There are words, blunt seeming when written, and grating on the ear, which appeal to the emotions and make, unbeknownst to the author, good literature.

2/10/44

A person with an imaginative, complex, and complicating mind needs often the effects of alcohol to let him see the truth, the simplicity, and the primitive emotions once more.

FEBRUARY 12, 1944

[G]Worked slowly. And seriously. But I don't know if I'm telling my story as well as I could. With Larry—*biftec*, beer—and we saw three kittens at the Chino's. I can take one of them tomorrow! Am very happy! One—two tequilas at Paco's, where we saw Bill Spratling* drinking with several other gays. What a man! Interesting chin, and highly sensible.[GG]

FEBRUARY 15, 1944

[G]Wonderful day because I received a letter from Cornell. And two from Mother. I sat in the square, reading. Cornell spent a sad vacation (Christmas Day) with Texas. How wonderful to read her words! "My love—Pat—truly—my love is forever yours—" etc. My heart was full of hope (for what, I don't know) and I responded as soon as I got home.[GG]

---

* William Spratling, an American architect, produced jewelry inspired by pre-Columbian designs in his silver workshop in Taxco. He is still known as the "Father of Mexican Silver." His friends included William Faulkner and Diego Rivera.

2/17/44

It takes a hell of a lot of time to be in love.

FEBRUARY 18, 1944

GTelegram from B.Z.G. He's in Mexico and will call me tomorrow.GG

FEBRUARY 23, 1944

[Mexico City.] GSaw many buildings around the city. Lots of Orozcos at the preparatory school* that were far better than Rivera. Orozco shows people, Rivera [shows] nothing but things. And B.Z.G. [Ben-Zion Goldberg] (who's been holding my hand for days) finally told me he only came to Mexico to see me, etc. I was utterly disgusted. Phoned Chloe—tried to see her later—but by 1:30 AM she wasn't home (although we'd made plans). Goldberg has found great success (he said), but he has not achieved what he came here for: namely, to grow closer. He said that I am impersonal through and through, that I am asexual—but also, that that kind of person doesn't exist.GG

2/27/44

Man without a god is worth nothing at all. The god may be a woman, an inspiration, an ambition, a fetish, an indulgence tempered with ceremony and self-denial, but unless he lives by something which he serves as being greater, consciously, or unconsciously to him, than himself, he is less noble than his own dog.

MARCH 2, 1944

GPrepared myself. And worked. And how unfortunate—that I have an inferiority complex! I don't know why, as it's an accumulation of my falling out with Rosalind, misfortune with Cornell,

---

* The Colegio de San Ildefonso, a Jesuit seminary turned museum famous for its murals by José Clemente Orozco, Diego Rivera, and other artists. At the time of Pat's visit and until 1978 the building housed the prestigious National Preparatory School, "El Prepo."

misfortune with Buffie, Chloe, etc. And I'm ashamed of my teeth, a shame I must dispel, and will.[GG]

MARCH 5, 1944

[G]Wrote to mother. Lately, her letters have been very agreeable, full of love, says she misses me.[GG]

MARCH 7, 1944

[G]Left tonight, Goldberg and me. The journey was long. Goldberg observed me all night with concern, and—I hated that. "Should we have our honeymoon in Acapulco?" But I was utterly disgusted. Especially by the hubris of these fifty-year-old men.[GG]

MARCH 8, 1944

[G]Got to Acapulco at 5:30 AM.[GG]

MARCH 9, 1944

[G]Swam twice. Impossible for me to work by the sea. Have to be alone first, at least in my own room. Goldberg writes columns, and that's much different. Wrote to Chloe. Have to write an article about Acapulco.[GG]

3/9/44

What a desolate, despairing, exquisite thought, that one cannot live without loving someone. What a more desperate thought, that one cannot create anything without this inspiration!

3/10/44

In whatever milieu the artist first felt himself to be an artist, he should live and do his work. The desires of an artist, should they be freedom of scene, social behavior, or the imagined confines of his own mind, should never be attained in reality, but only in imagination through his work.

MARCH 11, 1944

^{SP}I worked very hard this morning and afternoon, and at night spoke about my novel. Goldberg says I'm incapable of loving, that I am in love with myself. It's not true. Writing this novel is really what troubles me, which means I have to free myself from the ties holding me back. The food here is always the same. Fish, beans. Pastries at two. Chicken. If only I had a carrot, a banana, a piece of celery without salt! I'd be content! I'm really enjoying reading *History of Mexico.*^{SPSP}

MARCH 13, 1944

^{SP}I think about Allela all the time, no doubt there's a letter from her waiting for me in Taxco. Goldberg pretends to be very lonely and comes to visit every evening around 11 or 12. Tonight he stayed for two hours. We spoke about my story—about the love between Gregory and Margaret, which could be very potent. In fact, I could be in love with Margaret myself, even before writing her. I find his conversation inspiring, and he is very patient in trying to make me fall in love with him, but it's impossible. Was very happy and relaxed, because I made progress on the novel.^{SPSP}

MARCH 18, 1944

^{SP}I was really tired tonight and wasn't able to work much. B.Z.G. either. I wish I had more of my novel for him to read before he leaves, but it's not possible. I have the sense that I'll never finish it because there will always be a chapter I want to rewrite.

I have some six freckles!^{SPSP}

MARCH 22, 1944

[Taxco.] ^{SP}Letter from B.Z.G., more about our friendship. Got ready to take the bus to El Naranjo* this morning, very happy

---

* A small village twenty miles from Taxco.

there. [Before,] met Paul Cook* in a bar—with no money. Then
with a certain "Carlos" to Minas Viejas, where they are mining
coal. Later met Paul again in the door of a bar—with money.
Two tequilas and then dinner together at the Victoria. Very
agreeable. Oh, if only I could live with Paul, I really like him.
How annoying, that "the public" assumes—always assumes—
that a woman and a man must then also spend the night
together.[SPSP]

3/25/44

Night-time! Six o'clock, the hour for forgetting. Seven o'clock,
the hour of the phantasy-at-the-bar. Eight o'clock, the hour for
the aerial romance with the lady in the dark corner who seems to
be thinking the same thing, but is she? Nine o'clock, ten o'clock,
twelve midnight. The moon is like a tired wheel of chance rolling across the sky, and I am to be found in a bar. Hours and
hours I sit watching the business man from Chicago paw a lady
who is not his wife, listening to the jaded mariachis grinding out
"Jalisco," absorbing greedily a thousand monotonous details
that I have seen a thousand times before, absorbing alcohol to
feel things I have felt a thousand times before. This morning, this
afternoon, I was complete, replete, and my work was bread in
the mouth and why am I incomplete now? Why forever incomplete? The answer means nothing. The question is a vacuum, the
answer is less than a vacuum. The vital question, the only question, is why do I guard so vigilantly my incompleteness?

MARCH 29, 1944

[SP]I wrote letters to Allela and my mother. Both are very beautiful, but maybe they weren't worth spending the entire morning
on. I'm very sad. But I always am, even when I work well. I think

---

* A character inspired by the painter and writer Paul Cook will later resurface in Pat's
short story "In the Plaza," published posthumously in *Nothing That Meets the Eye: The
Uncollected Stories of Patrriciua Highsmith* (New York, 2002).

about Allela. I think about Rosalind, and I want them both! It's terrible! I don't have anybody, except my cat.[SPSP]

MARCH 30, 1944

[SP]It's very pleasant to think that I'm turning a new page in my life. There is no end to the pages. I have fleas again. I worked very hard, I wrote a lot. I have to make up for last night, I drank too much and wrote a very sad letter to Rosalind. Working late into the the night, I felt absolutely desperate. I'm constantly sad and hopeless: I think about my life and work, and the thought occurs that I will never accomplish anything. There's no remedy. There are no miracles—neither in my head, nor from the mouth of God.[SPSP]

3/30/44

I want to write the saddest story ever written, a story that compresses the heart and brings tears to the eyes of every man from the lowest peasant to the highest genius. I will write it weeping such tears as were never wept at Troy or Carthage or at the Wailing Wall. The sadness will be a purge of my brain and heart, a hot iron to level and clean me, salt of my tears to purify my blood. My body will wring itself and writhe in pity. What story? Maybe mine.

APRIL 1, 1944

I worked this morning until I went to Mrs. Luzi's by appointment. She wasn't ready, & we didn't get off to the Victoria until after two, during which time she had overturned an ink bottle and a quart of milk on her sarape* in pursuit of an imaginary scorpion. The mail man beckoned in the post office & gave me a letter from Ann T.—"Why I love you Patricia Highsmith, will forever remain a Freudian enigma." The rest is probably witty, but seems full of non-sequiturs. She amuses me. She flatters me. She has intelligence of high and rare quality, but can she ever

---

* Traditional Mexican cloth, usually worn as a cape.

put it to use? I don't know. I wrote her a grateful letter—and late tonight a Purple Paragraph, because for ten minutes, at least I was in love with her. In general, if I had some of her and she some of me, we should both be better writers.

4/2/44

I am lonely in the evenings, when the dusk invades my room, so politely, so subtly inviting me to do the things one cannot do alone. Sometimes the desire is in my arms only, and they are hungry like the stomach is hungry, for the solid embrace. Sometimes the desire is in my lips only and I bite it out of them. Sometimes the desire is a ghostly counter part of me, and stands beside me sadly. In the nights I lie and watch the moon on [its] hopeless quest, and learn anew the inexorable equation, my loneliness of one is the loneliness of one plus one and one times one and two.

APRIL 3, 1944

"April the saddest month—"* T. S. Eliot, where are you? And why the hell don't these goddamn Mexican censors spend a little more time at their jobs and a little less at their meals? I want my books. I can't live without them.

4/3/44

I am lonely for a thousand things. Mainly certain people and certain conversation. Today, this morning, I struggled up almost perpendicular hills, carrying for the tenth time my three valises containing typewriting paper, notebooks, books, behind me an old Mexican carrying the heaviest valise by a strap on his forehead. I don't like the house. I sit in the littered room, and ask myself, why am I here after all? Oh drinking is the logical thing, the normal thing, the only thing in this particular night. The other nights will be work, but not this one. I want talk with peo-

* Correctly cited, the opening line of T. S. Eliot's poem "The Waste Land" (1922) would have to be "April is the cruellest month."

ple, who understand how one can work, and not work and drink, and work again. I want to see Paul Cook, my artist friend, in the Victoria Hotel. I come home to wash and dress for him. Oh we will sit hours in a corner of the hotel bar and perhaps, he will drink tequila with me, though he is not supposed to be drinking now. And the world will be right again, because two minds in the corner of a bar are very strong. But while dressing I suddenly feel tired, and stop with my blouse on and skirt off. I put out my cigarette. I will not go. (The audience applauds.) Besides there is no water to get clean with. I throw down a dinner I do not want, and much coffee. I start to work with "Smiles" on my neighbor's radio. I work until long after midnight, until I am too exhausted to feel lonely, or desirous, or melancholy.

APRIL 4, 1944
Paid my rent, unfortunately, and the turkeys are right outside my window. They are as close as they can possibly be to my ear, without being in my room—all of which prompted me to write a fictitious story of it this afternoon. Terminating in blood revenge. Worked very hard all today, making also what I call the "commercial gesture"—the story—which I should do in the form of writing or drawing each day now, if I expect to exist. Don't know when to expect reimbursements from Chloe. After all this time I consider her behavior skunky. Invited Margot C. for a drink at Paco's; ran into Paul Cook, who crashed with Margot immediately. Then Tony, exuding warmth and friendliness, came over + wanted to contract Paul to do a portrait of Margot. Paul asks 200 dollars. Presently, M.C., Paul & I joined the Peter M.'s, later going to supper at the Victoria. Pleasant, smart people they are. Paul walked me home, stopped at Paco's, met the Newtons, thence ensemble to Chachalaca—a typical Tasqueñan night. Was boosted over this 10 ft. wall at 1:30 by Paul Cook.

APRIL 6, 1944
A typical Tasqueñan day. Something had to be wrong, because the water was flowing and had to go in to the Chino's for café.

Coming back met José Barrego, who invited me to lunch. We had a beer at Paco's first. Worked this afternoon on my book. It is terribly slow, and often I am faced with such questions: how am I going to end the story, have I anything to say, and is it worth the trouble? But at the same time, fortunately, I do not believe I could stop now and leave Gregory's story untold. It is a heightening and romanticizing of my own aspirations, found-delights, and material disillusionment coupled with, I believe sincerely, a spiritual awakening.

4/6/44

If I had been born into the home of musicians, I should have died of happiness at the age of four.

APRIL 8, 1944

The rats are playing tag in my roof. Yesterday they ate a tile through and dropped it on the bathroom floor. Today a most melancholy feeling that I am exhausted and that Mexico has done it, and will continue to do it. It will take something more than willpower to keep me here another five months— something approaching the passions of a flagellant.

APRIL 9, 1944

Another day of escapism—very slight drinking, much sociability. Productive of one thing: I am leaving Taxco for San Miguel [de] Allende come May. I dare not—I do not hope for the great renais- sance of 1943 there—but at least I'll be away from the drinkers here—getting to be too many, from the corrupt atmosphere, from the hostile natives (somewhat) and from this war of attrition (imagined or real) of Taxco versus the human will. Shall, I fear, have to ask Chloe for some money, & if she does not come across, shall have to go home. Shame! But my own fault for putting it up.

APRIL 10, 1944

Letter from Mother. Ernst pays visits, claims he is still in love with me, as though he ever was; that he thinks Goldberg is in love with me [too]. Unfortunately all leave me cold. I must work out my own mess for myself. Always Paul puts his finger on the trouble. "An artist is licked, when he sets limitations for himself," says Paul, of my saying I can't think of love at the moment. He is right. The excellent critique of short story of mine of Mexican rooster. Not enough emotion. Not enough passion. What have I? Something. Something as honest as the world has ever seen, but whether I can combine this with the all-essential passion or not I don't know. At the same time, I have no doubt but that I have felt equal to the most impassioned of our writers.

APRIL 11, 1944

After eating at Chino's, Paul & I came home ere, & he read my MS—liking it very much, I'm happy to say. In fact almost raving. Then after rums it was much too late for him to go home, so he slept here, first on the porch, then with me—I didn't like the idea, but he kept his side of the bed and seemed to want to sleep in the same bed just for camaraderie, which might sound corny to anyone else but not to someone who knows Paul.

APRIL 12, 1944

Got a $50.00 check from my parents for Easter. What a nice present! And I felt rather ashamed I did not send them even a card. I get frequent letters from B.Z.G. and mother now, asking me would I like canned food, would I like more money, a maid, a pension? And would I want to come home and work in New Hampshire, from my mother. Stay on from B.Z.G. Lonely, and homesick, and beginning to hate & fear Mexico. Don't know if I want to stay much longer. I wrote Chloe for money. Would feel much better with that. Everyone here seems so substantially placed, tho no more content than I am. Met Mrs. Luzi in the Plaza. She and her husband have had an amusing quarrel, that I've written up in my notebook,* and

----

* The anecdote about the Luzis finds its way into Highsmith's short story "The Car," first published in English in *Nothing That Meets the Eye: The Uncollected Short Stories of Patricia Highsmith* (New York, 2002). While the story ends tragically, in reality Marguerite and her Swiss husband continued to live in Mexico.

may put into a second book I have in mind doing, about Taxco—
what happens when Americans go to pot—and why they do. Came
home at 12:30 to find my house invaded, my kitten up a tree yowl-
ing, and Paul in my bed! I was so mad I felt like kicking him out,
but made my bed on the porch instead.

APRIL 14, 1944

There is something evil in me that leads me to believe all I touch
will be corrupted or be a failure—I mean all in the creative field.
No production ever is smooth, with sufficient joy. I mean to
correct this by "playing" as much as I can with the work itself.
Sketching foolish things helps mostly. Didn't see Paul all day.
Rather unusual. Went to El Naranjo at 1:30. Got my book box,
went to Iguala and came back to Taxco via the most wretched,
foul, disgusting Flecha Roja [bus] that ever crept along the
road. My right foot was on somebody else's, my left foot out
a window, and my rear end dipping into a vat of greasy lamb
stew at every rift in the road. 1 hour-and-a-half for a 20 minute trip. Also got my typewriter. My books fill me with joy! La!
La! Tonight, so happy I chose Hölderlin to read. There is also
Proust! Fragments of my first book, too, some of it excellent
writing which will have to be interpolated. I have my work cut
out, and will do no dissipating the rest of this month.

4/14/44

Paul Cook—who talks better than he writes or paints. He
knows the dramatic and artistic essentials of a creative work.
He was a football player, married at thirty-two, to a Texas
woman of good and wealthy family. Divorced last year after
14 years because of jealousy on her part, demands, criticism
of his drinking. He has always drunk quite a little and now in
Taxco drinks quite a lot. Wanted to commit suicide last year
and dove a plane into the Atlantic, being rescued immediately.
He is the son of a Welsh doctor and an Italian woman. He is
6'3", lanky, blue eyed, and distinguished looking no matter

what he does or how he dresses. A good and interesting set of false teeth he has had since twenty-seven, because of some brain or nervous disease. The cantina proprietors adore him, for sincere reasons. He is paid $150 dollars per month by the U.S. Government to catch dope peddlers. Sometimes he makes a catch. Ostensibly, he is the washed-up American painter going to hell in Taxco. He has done what no other American I know had done, made the Mexicans like him, I mean inspired their friendship. Despite his height, despite his blue eyes, they love him.

4/16/44

In Taxco people do not drink to fill social intervals, or as a ritual between four and six, and do not drink for a mild lift, but for total oblivion. In Taxco one has not had a satisfactory drink until one staggers, until one doesn't care that tomorrow is *mañana*, and the whole future is *mañana*, and when that comes—*mañana*. And the present is already just past.

APRIL 17, 1944

Paul has been preaching asexuality, and impersonality, is the most sentimental person, next to myself, whom I know. He is also sub-sexed, as I am. Left him in quite a temper, and it'll be just as well if I don't see him again—for a long, long while.

APRIL 18, 1944

Worked 8 hours today. The first chapter's style is easy and good reading if a certain momentum is kept. Something like Carson McCullers. I heard from the Selas, Paul Cook was in awfully drunk at 5, and about to start a fight. He was placed in a taxi by Dr. Newton this PM, but was not at the hotel at eight. I wonder if he's in jail already? The Selas said he was trying to send me a note, but couldn't write well enough to do it. He is sentimental and lonely, disastrous combination. Fleas, ants, cats, dogs, the Mexicans—all prey upon me. Some want money, some food, some flesh, but all want something, and as this is their country they get it.

Reading Oriental Philosophy—very pleasant.

APRIL 22, 1944

We'll leave Monday. I know too many people in Mexico—in Taxco—and for all one's good intentions—even willpower, it is impossible to maintain one's independence, and one's stability— while seeing them, drinking with them—the social system being as vague & informal as it is. I am running away—yes, but not from myself—from the Tasqueños.

APRIL 23, 1944

I decided not to leave now. It costs less, & things are about to break here. The Duchess (Mrs. Nina Engelhardt), over many beers, invited me to stay 3 days at the Sierra Madre next week. She has sacks of money.

APRIL 24, 1944

Much thinking about my book & little writing—& just as well. Paul thinks it drops after the very first section after Gregory's walking to the house. I'll never get it published, I think, or want it published, unless all of it is up to the standard of the first section. Therefore a complete rewriting is necessary. Spoke long with Paul—my God, what a brilliant, understanding fellow, & how much he has helped me on my work! My problem now is not liquor, not homesickness, not laziness certainly, but strictly physical living conditions. Saw *Casablanca* tonight with Tom G., whom I let kiss me at 1:00 AM—why I don't know.

Paul gave me the most charming earrings.

APRIL 25, 1944

Moved into the Sierra Madre at 11:30, & found the Duchess and Del Gato drinking beer. Life is one long beer & cigarette, not good for the nerves, the conscience, or that organ producing human happiness, wherever it lies.

APRIL 26, 1944

Shall be glad to see Grandma—very much, and I want to leave. The end of the month. The reason is that due to over-drinking, lack of a house, I have lost myself, with whom I am never bored or lonely.

APRIL 27, 1944

Wrote my mother that I should start home the 4 of May. Conversation gets duller, on everyone else's part and certainly on mine. Americans cruise like hungry sharks over the town, seeking for few moments' companionship with anyone.

Once they spot you, it is impossible, even a little cruel, to shake them off. Paco's is the habitat of the corpses. My cat is the liveliest, most normal creature in Taxco.

APRIL 28, 1944

Dreadfully tight, the tightest, came home & Paul arrived at 2—AM—until 3:30. Said he loved me more than anything else in the world, wanted to stay of course, but absolutely impossible. I wrote 11 beginnings to Rosalind & wrote the 12th letter passably. I love her more than anything else in the world, so help me God! I wonder—I wish—I wonder—I should write more, somehow. I should express myself more & better. I should write stories perhaps instead of a novel. But were I writing stories, I should say I should write a novel!

4/29/44

Art is a stone-faced mountain that we attack again and again, always to be thrown back. We sit long minutes on a rock and look at the mountain with chin in hand, rally ourselves, and attack once more. We break first our noses, then our heads and then our hearts, but our way is in this direction and we cannot turn back. Finally we lie below, prostrate on the ground, and the mountain gives no shade for the flesh or the bones in the hot sun of exposure. And if we are worthy at the last, posterity points to the dents.

MAY 1, 1944

The Duchess, under the effects of three potent drinks, invited me once more! We leave for Mexico Saturday, after Cinco de Mayo, which is another damned thing.

MAY 5, 1944

FLASH! Fragonard catches her first mouse! Am so eager to be off! But my wallet is certainly getting flatter since I met the Duchess, & hers no doubt since she met me.

MAY 6, 1944

Drinks were flowing like tequila (not like water because there is none).

5/8/44

The Monte Carlo Hotel in Mexico City is a stamp of authenticity. Because the place holds them all—those with a sense of humor, those with the individuality and the courage of it. In the Monte Carlo, there is always the feeling that something is about to happen. That it never does, does not matter. Every corner, every wall, every floor, holds a history we do not question out of sheer respect for it, as we do not question a venerable fighter, be he ever so disreputable and feeble, on his own history, out of respect for him.

MAY 11, 1944

Nina had turkey sandwiches for me, & with Tom & Paul, invited, we all got into one taxi & drove to the station. "The stars set in heaven when you go away, Pat," Nina said, almost crying, as she kissed me goodbye. I suspect she did cry, for when the bus pulled out, they were all gone. Oh the wonderful night rides on the bus, when I think, I believe, I know, all things are possible, when the mind, untrammeled, unanchored, moves like a primeval, omniscient, omnipotent thing, from abstraction to concretion, to fantasy to fact, and strings them all together in a wondrous necklace. Then, I believe, I saw my book as different from Joyce's *Portrait*, in no way derivative, in no way, really, necessarily, secondary. I ate a turkey sandwich and smoked some of the Camel cigarettes and for a few hours was in heaven, at least mentally.

MAY 12, 1944

[Monterrey.] A lot of facts written tonight—but there is more in my heart—poetry, hopes, sadness, loneliness, love, inspiration, frustration, and no fear—

5/12/44

I touched the horns of a young buck today, felt the moss-like fuzz on its short horns, slid my palm down its soft neck while it gazed calmly into space. Free, free, it was. Severe in mind and unquestionably, unquestioningly true in heart. But man, and Patricia Highsmith, were born to trouble, as the sparks fly upward.

6/7/44

Weeping, weeping, weeping tonight inexplicably. Inexplicably, except, perhaps, for the possible futility of life. Tonight I am, I hope, Santayana's* young man, who will not be a savage because he has wept. Perhaps some day I shall be his old man who is not a fool because he can laugh. But I do not think so. Long before I am old in a physical sense, I shall have killed myself, and left behind me this note: "I am sick to death of compromise in all its hideous guises."

6/10/44

[Texas.] The couple who discover someone has written a foul 4-letter word on their new cement sidewalk, directly in front of the house. The husband is for leaving it to mellow out of its conspicuousness, but the wife first insists it must be filled in, then when it is, and spread wider, and cracked deeply, almost dies of

---

* George Santayana (1863–1952), Spanish writer, literary critic, and philosopher.

anguish. The husband's indifference hides a certain satisfaction: his wife who has been indifferent to his own desires, indifferent to this his own shocking, hideous, foul, exciting command in Anglo-Saxon is beside herself when she sees it written by an anonymous hand.

6/18/44

Note here: Happy days lead to stagnation of the mind. Happy days even in my opinion, reading, writing, drawing. Nothing has come in the way of ideas in the last two happy days. I used to think such days produced ideas. Now I wonder if frequent disturbance isn't necessary.

6/22/44

Raging mad this afternoon when a small cousin refused to sit properly for a portrait on which I had spent many hours already and had come near losing. I was too nervous to eat dinner, & walked west, west, west, until I found myself suddenly at the edge of town, viewing a broad sweep of the low horizon, bomber plants, oil fields, farms, distant houses, each of which held many souls. And the voice from the clouds said, "Behold all this greater-than-you. And think how small is that ruined picture!" But, alas, the panorama with all the souls was not greater than this one picture. This is the fact of it. This is what will make me happy or miserable.

(At such raging times, "suicide" flashes to my mind, as inevitably as lightning produces thunder.)

7/3/44

Love is no stranger here. He is in the slouch of the soldier on the counter-stool, in the rolling eye and the gum-chewing jaw of the waitress, in the flies that copulate on the rims of greasy plates, in the unsubtle music of the jukebox brought by loudspeakers into every booth, in the baggy back of the cattleman leaning against the slot machine as he drinks his lukewarm Jax beer and

talks to a blond hussy in slacks. Love is there, too, warm and red
and smiling. Love is only a stranger though in the formal eating
places of big cities, where two people face each other like brick
walls across a table, and Love grows in one only, like a tender
shy vine between two bricks.

7/6/44

Sexual intercourse, while the most perfect thing, is not ever
quite perfect. There is always some one-sided amusement about
your or the other person's limitations, and a terrible sadness
like defeat in the last ditch. (This note taken in drunkenness, Ft.
Worth, Texas, mid-afternoon.)

7/15/44

[New York.] You have to enjoy the weather always. Walking
home from Sixty-First Street on Second Avenue, eleven beautiful black blocks. (The moon is not, the lights are, you are,
your feet with the spring in them, this is youth, now!) You
inhale the soft cool night, you gaze on the lighted bar door-
ways fondly. Your shoes, for once, are comfortable. Your head
is filled with a number of things, among which undoubtedly
are the remnants of your last words with her, the problem of
whether one can be in love with two or three, with the youth's
grudging appreciation of the splendid night, and with the consciousness of health, future, potency. Breathe deep! Your lungs
are still functioning perfectly, your thighs do not shake too
much, your calves are resilient, your toes eager. Every muscle
is obedient (taut for an instant, then couchantly relaxed), every
dream will come true.

7/29/44

The aftersmell of summer rain, through a city window, up
from lightly moistened tar, cement and red brick, is dusty, dry,
organic, containing the sickeningly organic smell of beheaded
chickens, their feathers dark-bloody and drying.

8/5/44

What can match in dismalness and melancholy the aria of *Madame Butterfly* drifting from a brownstone window across the street on a Sunday afternoon in summer?

8/6/44

What is so accursed about this century that an artist can do his best work only when his lungs are stabbed with tobacco smoke, when his brain is frenzied with coffee, liquor or benzedrine? A shameful fact, as this is a shameful age!

9/11/44

"Of course I work late at night," the writer said gloweringly. "I have to keep body & soul apart, don't I?"

9/13/44

The day we say goodbye forever to each other,* let us go to some quiet café for a stirrup cup and a Strauss waltz. (Strauss waltzes are so much nicer than you think, darling.) Not that a Strauss waltz is in any way like either of us, but for some strange reason I always think of meeting you, of having met you, to one. And I was so horribly drunk that evening it may have been so. I shall summon the waiter with my grandest flourish and call for a double brandy for myself, and probably a stinger for you, and, oh yes, would you have the string quartet (it will probably be a tired Viennese ensemble) play the Emperor Waltz, or if they do not feel up to it then the An Artist's Life, and after a quarter of an hour please, the halting, but so determined Motor Waltz, which will be our finale. Its halting but so determined phrases are fitting now. We can dream about the straight spines, the rigid arms, the adoring looks we would impale each other with, as we whirled about the ballroom amid the envious company, the couples and couples, who would gyrate in lesser orbits

---

* It is unclear what woman inspired this and the following entry.

about us like the host of minor planets about Saturn. (Are you saturnine, darling?) So I should leave you, with the money for the check, of course, perhaps before the last strains died away, so on the final chord, you could look across the table and see no one, except that ideal you might imagine, that you always did imagine so easily, and with your next stinger coming up, you might drink the one you hold to the dregs, yes, all the powdered ice, and still, still before the evening is over, before you drink half the next stinger, that chair across from you may be filled with someone more charming by far than I, for you, who could never be alone.

10/20/44

Tonight the rain comes down slimily and eternally on my court, making a high-pitched spanking sound with occasional drops, a too sharp sound that plays on the nerves, and when one walks in the rain makes one grimace and shrink as though from a repulsive, chill thing. Tonight I have nothing to do with the rain. Tonight I am in love, for the sixteenth, seventeenth or eighteenth time in my life (I never can remember, nor remember which times should be eliminated) and I have promised it will last until Sunday morning (tonight is Friday), and have been promised it will last until then. Tonight I am as happy, and with as much reason, as an egg in a refrigerator of a big household, rejoicing that so much has happened and still its shell is not cracked. After tonight, after tomorrow night—what? Isn't it a beautiful life? Isn't it beautiful?

10/31/44

Jews—why do I consistently find some fault in them? I dislike them for their mere consciousness of being Jews (none can possibly be without this consciousness), and dislike all the multitudinous, multitudinous, contradictory manifestations of this consciousness. The Christians have made them conscious of being Jews. Therefore, in a sense, being a Christian, I must hate myself.

11/1/44

The first days of being in love—there is no use in struggling against daydreaming. Daydream we must, for every object, everything around us, inside us, is new. All the things we took for granted and were familiar with are no longer familiar. The chair, the wastebasket, the desk, one's own fountainpen, the music we knew and (and thought we knew) and loved are no longer familiar, but quite new things to be re-observed and judged. It is a new world, and we view it like children.

11/6/44

Homosexuals—what is the specific virus that results in the eternal impermanence? Some say it is the ego of the active part-ner, who after six months must make one more new conquest. This implies, doubtless, that she has tired of the other. Why? Because homosexuals are not often enough romantic. The cart before the horse, this is leading to, though I do not know which is cart and which is horse. Some prescience of impermanence must poison the mind (the heart) from the outset, and result in a holding back in order to escape the affair with as little pain as possible.

As for myself, I prefer to be romantic. I want the strand of hair, the desperately opened, desperately guarded letter, the scuff on my shoes I will not shine off, the telephone call that means life or death, the sweet pain that comes when the one you love has done you the simplest kind of favor. Two peo-ple dancing together, knowing someone will come up soon, within moments, within a minute, within three seconds, tap you on the shoulder and take her away forever. I want the summit to be so high in the clouds my nose bleeds, my ears crackle, my lungs cry for oxygen. I want the end to be a fall deeper than from Mount Everest so that it will terrify me, as I watch the whole world fall with me, that will land me, a heap of rubble, on some lifeless desert, on some unnamed, uncharted planet.

11/13/44

Love, and the expression of it, acts like oil on the machinery of one's whole life.

NOVEMBER 14, 1944

^GN.[*] called at 4:30 AM—lots of questions—and came over at 4:45. These early mornings with her . . . We cooked potatoes (fried, the only way I know) the way she loves them—fried! And later, after several difficulties, which I was probably imagining—it was morning by the time we went to sleep. And then—calls—Mary H., Rosalind (who banged on about buying me a cat for Christmas in order to find out if Natica was here and what happened overnight). Natica [here] till— 6! Another day wasted—but Rosalind says there's no such thing as a waste of time! It's just so sweet being with her, and we're just—sad when we have to say goodbye. The old line by Shakespeare—"Parting is such—" finally has meaning. Terribly tired, as we usually are, after one night and one day!—two days and one night, or two nights and one day! But wanted to see Bernhard and Cornell for dinner at Romany's.[†] Natica is moody, doesn't want to say much, but that interests me. She needs something to do, but this is heaven for my starved heart: that she has nothing to do but kiss me again and again. Walked her home at 12:00 midnight. I want to find an unfurnished apartment for her. Then she'll be happy. I'm happy now, but this day was crazy!^{GG}

---

* Natica Waterbury, Pat's new lover. Natica was, however, already involved with another woman, Virginia Kent Catherwood, like her a product of Philadelphia high society. The two had presumably been acquainted—at the very latest—since their respective debutante balls, events so significant as to receive coverage in the *New York Times*.

† Marie Marchand (1885–1961) was a key figure of Greenwich Village bohemia. Whenever her restaurant moved to yet another of many locations, a crowd of devotees was sure to follow. Romany Marie's, as it was invariably called, was especially popular with artists— not least because those who needed it could always get a free meal. Marchand's portrait by Romany regular John Sloan is today housed in the Whitney Museum of American Art.

11/14/44

Shall I say I can work when I am most unhappy? Perhaps this is the only way I can dupe myself, the only way that will let me produce any work. Anything, you know, to get one's mind off oneself.

NOVEMBER 15, 1944

GNatica didn't call me all day. And this evening took the train to Philadelphia. I had the biggest news to tell her—I sold "The Heroine" to *Harper's Bazaar*—and would have been so happy if she were the first to know. But tomorrow at the social, I'll tell Rosalind and Natica with great pride. Am convinced that *Harper's* has a better reputation with regard to literature than any other magazine in the country. How can I express how much Natica means to me?! She's my succor, life itself, and joy. God!—do not forsake me—that she might stay with me! Happy—so happy I can only see my beautiful world, the way I am ascending—as I am doing now, as I have been for three weeks! Tomorrow—makes it three weeks! Natica—it feels much longer. She's counting the weeks too.GG

NOVEMBER 19, 1944

GWorked alone all day—10 pages of comics. And N. still hasn't called! Her landlady said she spent the night elsewhere, with a friend (as long as it's only a friend!). I was very nervous today, delivered her typewriter to her house, and went for a walk (a cold walk) by myself, trying to believe that I'm very happy, very trusting, that I will always be with her, and always be happy.GG

NOVEMBER 20, 1944

GAnother day without her! No word! I'm still living with the strength she gave me, but I have to see her—have her—again soon! What does she want? Is she thinking of me? I believe so.GG

NOVEMBER 21, 1944

ᴳConversation with Mrs. Aswell at *Harper's*, who was very surprised to learn that I haven't studied psychology. Wants to read
more of my stories. Very content with the conversation, happy
upon coming home to wait for Natica. But she didn't call—until
6:00! Wanted to meet me at a friend's. Went there. Her name
is Virginia Catherwood, "an old friend from school." Spoke
at length with her in her room. I felt that she knew everything
about N. and myself and didn't object, as she likes me. When
we joined the others, Natica was jealous—Ginnie mentioned it
first. I smiled, it was so unnecessary. Ginnie made me some coffee once the others had left, asked me to stay, but I wanted to see
N.! Ginnie called at 2:00—just when Natica came in. Maybe she
heard it, but I don't know.ᴳᴳ

NOVEMBER 22, 1944

ᴳShe came at 12 midnight, brought me this book, and even better, herself. She stayed, and thus passed the most wonderful
night we have known! Everything was wonderful—she slept
in my arms, and whispered in her sleep, "How can two people
have so much?" I was so happy, proud, content, and satisfied,
though, that I couldn't fall asleep. Peace, quiet, and the two of us
together! This day—Thanksgiving.* I have a lot this year.ᴳᴳ

11/24/44

Perils of a first novel: Every character is one's self, resulting in an
oversoft or overhard treatment, neither of which results in the
objective, which is essentially what has made good so much of
the writing one has done before.

11/26/44

Thank God for work—the only balm in this world. Work,
blessed murderer of the monster Time. Work makes the night

---

* Thanksgiving is on November 23, and Pat is as usual writing well past midnight.

come, makes hunger, fatigue, and sleep come. And when Time is dying, even makes the telephone ring. Work balms the flayed nerves, washes the eyes so one may see, mends the heart so one may love. Do you wish on me, beloved, the hell of this morning? Do you know what this morning was like? I hope you do not, and I will spare you a description. I wish only happiness for you, and all joy and good I can give you.

11/26/44

What shall I cry for, mercy or the moon? I do not know which is easier attained.

NOVEMBER 27, 1944

ᴳRained all day. No letter in the letter box, no calls. Had to call Rosalind at 5:10, couldn't stay alone tonight. We read the dictionary, but Kirk was there, so I couldn't stay. At home, worked—had to.ᴳᴳ

NOVEMBER 28, 1944

ᴳCatherwood is in love with Natica. Says Rosalind, and it must be true. At 4:15—as I finally—for the first time in three days, was lying happily, peacefully in bed with a fountain pen, wanting to work, Natica called! Later, nice dinner at the pizzeria. And—bed. It's getting better, nicer, more enjoyable. I am so happy with her, and she with me. But she denied having received my letters. I don't know. Only that I love her, that she is nothing but destruction for me, but that I love her nonetheless.ᴳᴳ

DECEMBER 1, 1944

ᴳOh—thank God it isn't this month one year ago! Excellent day—but without having done much work. Only I read for nearly two hours, a luxury I rarely allow myself. Went to Macy's with Mother for Christmas gifts etc. As usual, the day isn't interesting until I get to Natica. She called at 1:30 AM. Went to the psychiatrist, told him that all her friends are homosexual. "That isn't the cause of your homosexuality," he responded. Of course not, but what else? Looking forward to her coming tomorrow evening.[GG]

12/1/44

Pulps versus fine writing: One simply cannot concern oneself eight or even five hours a day with nonsense-taken-seriously and not be corrupted by it. The corruption lies in the very habits of thought rather than the habits of expression: the latter could be overcome, but the former concerns the individual's self or soul. I have read recently of "the young men who write movie scenarios and comic strips. They are generally college graduates, people who read the classics in their spare time." Men who know what they are doing, in other words. Perhaps they do. But after a few years, it will be of no use to have dreamed of afternoons browsing in Brentano's Bookshop, to have snatched an hour before bedtime to read a bit of Sir Thomas Browne, to have congratulated oneself on the immunizing power of a college background. The habits of thought, the power to dream without critical influence, the functioning of an artist, will have been riddled as though by termites—and must collapse!

DECEMBER 2, 1944

[G]Too much satisfaction—that's my fear as I write this Sunday evening. Two months ago it was the opposite. Natica taught me to relax. Now I'm afraid. Natica at 8:00. She was full of things her psychologist had said. He'll see her again Wednesday, [but] she hasn't made any "decision." What kind of decision? She doesn't know, as one never knows, if he's "good" or "bad." At Jane Bowles's at 8:30. Dinner. Too much whiskey and too little coffee. Betty friendly, but N. and I bored. Bowles steadily better the more drunk she gets. Depressing conversation about the war. Bowles explaining she can no longer write etc. Finally, at 3:00, N. and I left. It was freezing, and my house was closer. Only fell asleep at 8:50. But the nights keep getting better, and we're growing in our understanding. When I'm with her, I have something that neither time nor money can buy. Love. Happiness. Don't know how long it will last, but now that I have it, I feel proud, happy, high as a king.[GG]

DECEMBER 3, 1944

[G]I'm saying too little about these hours with Natica, hours as I've never had them before! They are Elysium! Heaven! Another human! A woman! My God! The conversations as we lie in bed. The windows, the cigarettes, the glasses of milk or water, the apples, the figs! And the indescribable pleasures, in particular, that we can give each other![GG]

DECEMBER 6, 1944

[G]Friday. I don't know why I recently haven't been writing my diary. These days are (as I am well aware) the best of my life. Yes, for even if I should find something even better, I am young now—and those days won't last. At times they are most happy, at times most sad, but always important, even if they are neither happy nor sad. Am often with Natica, here. And too many hours go by.[GG]

DECEMBER 12, 1944

[G]Worked on the book, and brought what I have to Chambrun[*] at 4:30. He was very pleased. Loved the synopsis, etc. "I wouldn't be surprised if we sold this book," he said. He likes the title— "The Click of the Shutting"—too.[GG]

DECEMBER 13, 1944

[G]At 3:30—I was downright sick with cramps worse than I've had in 7 years. Couldn't sleep, and had to call my parents at 5:30

---

[*] Probably Jacques Chambrun (1906–1976), whom Pat will mention repeatedly in 1945 and who seems to have been her agent for a while. Other clients of his included Mavis Gallant, Stefan Zweig, Franz Werfel, Alma Mahler, Lion Feuchtwanger, and W. Somerset Maugham.

AM. They came over but were useless, helpless, till the doctor came at 8:00 AM. I almost died in the meantime. Totally exhausted with terrible pain in my belly! It was the kind of sickness that makes a person consider his last will and testament. I thought of my own and realized I am prepared to give Rosalind all of my diaries, letters, and notebooks. Natica came over at 3:30. She was an angel! Kissed me many times, although I looked like a potato. Felt better immediately!GG

DECEMBER 16, 1944

GHappy all day—so often happy these days that I wish there were another word.GG

DECEMBER 18, 1944

GI wish to write all of Natica's comments, but they're so personal, so soft, so sweet, so memorable, incomparable. One thing: she can't bear leaving me in order to go to Burma or Paris with the Red Cross. I'm clumsy and always say the wrong things. It's difficult and uncomfortable and dangerous to be a woman.GG

DECEMBER 20, 1944

GBought a beautiful chain for Stanley's pocket watch—pure gold! $30. From mother and myself. He doesn't expect it at all, and it will be so lovely when he sees it. An old French chain.GG

DECEMBER 21, 1944

GComics till N. called [to say] she was coming over this afternoon, but she didn't show up. Ate with Mother—we're growing closer, and there's no doubt she knows all about my life, loves me, and understands me. Bought a Christmas tree that's rather too big for my little crowns. (Made lots of crowns this afternoon, along with stars, icicles out of scrap paper from Hughes's office last year!) Snowflakes out of white napkins (paper). Natica called just as I was getting home, came over, helped me with the Christmas tree. But after three days of not seeing each other, we first had to embrace, as if it had been weeks.GG

DECEMBER 23, 1944

  ^GHung stockings on my mantel with Natica's and Rosalind's gifts. Busy all day, especially this evening, when Rosalind came for dinner. Bought a doll's head for Natica that looks a lot like Rosalind's ex-husband. The house was ready when R. arrived— The gifts looked magnificent around the fireplace. Natica didn't arrive till 10:00 o'clock—and the first thing I saw as she entered was the shiny gold bracelet that [Virginia Kent] C. had given her. Next I saw the cat she held in her skirt. A real Siamese cat that's mostly brown. I couldn't love it more!^{GG}

DECEMBER 25, 1944

  ^GA year ago I was miserable. This morning I got up to the "Hallelujah Choral" and went over to my parents' with my cat, Mrs. Cathay. Everything lovely, breakfast, eggnogg, presents. But N. didn't call from Phil. Forgot the number? Probably.^{GG}

DECEMBER 26, 1944

  ^GA normal person would say that this time is just what one hopes for, and that I now lead a happy, normal life. But I know better. I'm replete with a bliss that will seldom return. No, this remaining life of mine will scarcely be as pleasant! Slow and steady with the book. I always feel artistically excited, happy in December and January. [It's when] I write and sketch best. Why? The weather or my horoscope?^{GG}

DECEMBER 28, 1944

  ^GWhen I work (write), I must have the very best—the best cigarettes, a clean shirt, because I'm like a soldier in battle, but in this case the enemy is terrible and brave, and I sometimes fail to prevail.^{GG}

DECEMBER 29, 1944

  ^GWhy do I start every night with "am happy" or "unhappy"? So far, happiness hasn't been my goal, or even a particular pleasure. Natica called at 2:00. She's back—but at Ginnie C.'s? Promised

to maybe come by, but didn't. I didn't mind. Worked. What—
what if she spends New Year's Eve with C.? That would be a
blow from which I shouldn't recover.^{GG}

DECEMBER 30, 1944

^GWork. And this morning I phoned Rosalind several times,
because she had invited Natica and me to dinner. She said that
[Virginia Kent] Catherwood would doubtless drive me crazy,
that N. has to choose, etc. And I thought [about it] later, writing
a page to Natica, in which I broke everything off. Thanked her
for everything, too. I knew she spent last night with C., that she
prefers other things to seeing me. Figure it's pride, but I can't
stand it any longer. The game is not worth the candle. I held
onto the letter, though, till this evening.^{GG}

DECEMBER 31, 1944

^GThis day requires more time to describe than I presently have.
When I awoke with Natica beside me, I regretted inviting her
last night. Today was pleasant enough—things like breakfast,
sketching after breakfast, etc. But she was ultimately very cold,
she has no intention of breaking things off with Catherwood. So,
between two and four this afternoon, I said every horrible thing
to her I wanted. That she's only seeing C. because of her money,
that she doesn't have the guts to make a real decision. She finally
left the house with me at 4:30, saying that she would spend
tonight, midnight, alone. The strange thing is, I'm not sad. Even
though I naturally wanted to spend this evening with N. She
knew that, but she was depressed and couldn't give me anything. At Lola's and Niko's with flowers at 7:30. Rosalind there,
too. Later at Marya Mannes', a polite gathering of straight people, who bore me terribly. Not always, but most of the time.^{GG}

1945

Writing and Dating, or:
"The world and its martinis are mine!"

✣

ON HER TWENTY-FOURTH BIRTHDAY, Pat takes stock of *The Click of the Shutting* and decides to abandon the 300-page manuscript. Increasingly, Pat turns to drawing to express herself creatively. In the summer, she enrolls in the renowned Art Students League of New York.

Even when not working on a novel, Pat writes tirelessly. She continues to make a living as a comic book scriptwriter, even as many contracts dry up after the war. Over the course of 1945, she also writes more than a dozen psychological short stories that she tries to sell with the help of her agent, but that remain unpublished for many years.

It is not uncommon during this time for Pat to compose long notebook entries and journal twice daily, a practice resulting in diaries upwards of three hundred pages long, largely written in German. Whereas the notebooks contain thoughts on literature, religion, history, sexuality, politics, and current writing projects, Pat attempts to keep up with her complicated (love) life in her diaries. By now the initial thrill of her affair with Natica Waterbury has subsided, and their trysts grow increasingly brief and sporadic. Pat tries to find comfort in other little affairs, though without much success.

Allela Cornell, her former lover, attempts suicide toward the end of the year. Pat feels responsible, despite Allela's insistence that Pat had nothing to do with it.

This emotional free-for-all is understandably damaging to Pat's psychological state. She's gripped by depression, weltschmerz, and frequently overcome with curious fears. The stress causes her to lose her period for months on end, which leads to a further fear of pregnancy, as she does sleep with men occasionally. In her double work life, she also pushes herself to the point of physical and mental exhaustion.

As is so often the case, literature provides Pat a way out. In mid-December, while strolling along the Hudson with her mother and stepfather in upstate New York, where the couple has recently moved, Pat comes up with the idea for a story about "two soulmates" who swap murders. She thus begins crafting the plot for her first (finished and published) novel, the international bestseller *Strangers on a Train*.

❦

JANUARY 2, 1945
ᴳStill alive, working, and happy. I do not know whether I am free from [Natica] already. I am not too proud, I don't know if I am courageous or proud enough. This experience is very fruitful for my notebook, a fact which would greatly disgust N. What do I feel?—Great peace, and no desire to destroy the things that belong or belonged to her. No, I don't feel bitter. I feel free—and am not waiting for a phone call.ᴳᴳ

1/2/45
[Mozart's] Jupiter Symphony, which one associates with one's seventeenth autumn, and the beginning of carnal love. To hear it now, after a dozen loves, after the end of the best, and to find it the same as ever. Yes, seventeen again, with the added pleasure of experience [and] wisdom, with the added pleasure in the

fact that seventeen was never so far away as it is at this moment. And still how good is this music! To know that there will come twenty-seven, thirty-seven, and fifty-seven, perhaps, and there will always be the Jupiter.

JANUARY 3, 1945
GNervous all day. I can't always know whether I'll be working well. Today it was the fact that B. Parsons would be coming for dinner. B. very serious when she arrived. And later our conversation grew so pleasant I didn't even want to eat. On reading my notebooks: "You really are a lonely person, aren't you, Pat? And you have learned this early on, that one is lonely all one's life."GG

JANUARY 4, 1945
GNothing from Natica. Each day brings more thoughts of her, more understanding, but not forgiveness. I don't like the cat. Her personality—she's inconsiderate towards me, jealous, always whining.GG

JANUARY 8, 1945
GCornell called, talked long, herself on the edge of suicide. God, what a sad world. Worked hard and rather well. I love her, and it will take time, time, time. And I'll always love her and honor her, because I had more with her than with any other person in my life.GG

1/8/45
To live one's life in the best way possible, one must live and move always with a sense of unreality, of drama in the smallest things, as though one lived a poem or a novel, attaching the greatest importance to the route one takes to a favorite restaurant, believing oneself while browsing in a bookshop, capable of being unmade or made, destroyed or reborn, by the choice of literature one makes. In one's room alone, one should be Dante, Robinson Crusoe, Luther, Jesus Christ, Baudelaire, and in short should be a poet at all times, regarding oneself objectively and the outer

world subjectively, compared to which state of mind the reality
of the sorrow of a lost love is destructively real and brutal.

JANUARY 9, 1945

ᴳI truly don't know where the day went. Got up rather early—
but for no reason. I couldn't write, think, read, and felt quite discouraged. In what was perhaps a moment of weakness, I phoned
N.'s house to say that I wanted her to call me. Now it is 2:00
A.M. and *silentium* in my chamber.ᴳᴳ

1/12/45

I wonder if any moment surpasses that of the second martini at
lunch, when the waiters are attentive, when all life, the future,
the world seems good and gilded (it matters not at all whom one
is with, male or female, yes or no).

1/15/45

Hangovers—Intimations of the tomb. Charming, and so much
more interesting physically and mentally than the evenings
before them. To be drunk and with the clarity of mind of tomorrow! That is the ideal.

1/16/45

Biographical note—11:50 A.M. I have done hardly any work
since breakfast at 10:50. A.M. Why? Because it is snowing in
big slow flakes outside my windows, and it has made a white-
bearded magic of a discarded but upright Christmas tree that
sits in a corner of the little lawn in my court. The chiaroscuro
of its branches half covered with snow suggest the pen lines of
an artist. The tree stands and seems to think by itself, awaiting something, but also being complete in itself. I am drunk on
three cups of coffee. I have a candle on my coffee table, candles
are so beautiful at midday, with the snow's gray glare and the
gloom of the room on the side away from the windows. Henry
James sits on a shelf, inviting me to forget my brief and unimportant day and stay with him in a slow moving, rarified world

which I know will leave me clean, belonging finally to no time and no place. The radio plays bassoon sonatas. The potential pleasure of this morning, this day, which I feel only in anticipation, is more intoxicating than any substance or any physical sight. Merely to exist is an ecstatic pleasure. How inadequate are all these words, when the physical sensation now makes me taut, wanting to shout, laugh, leap around my room, and at the same time be quiet and learn and feel all I can!

JANUARY 18, 1945

ᴳChambrun phoned: Lindley from [D.] Appleton [publishers] likes several chapters, dislikes others, and thinks the book will be too long. That's easy to see, he's right. Tonight, I am more determined than ever that the book shall never be published. Who knows or cares that G.B.S. [George Bernard Shaw] wrote three novels before his first play? One must never count the hours, the work, or the blood and sweat! I must finish this book without love, without courage, without—my love. Today at 3:30 P.M., N. called. Nothing out of the ordinary, but she said she tried to call me once. Yes, I can believe once, but what about the other days? But now it doesn't matter, and though I am trying to make myself believe I still love her, I know that under such conditions I can love no one. My friends tomorrow—God—it occurred to me today that of the eight, I've slept with six. My closest friends.ᴳᴳ

1/18/45

The specter of worthlessness, inferiority, inadequacy, haunts, and this is death in guise. Because when he beckons—I will go. But miserable most, not to love unloved, but to die not having drawn upon one's forces.

JANUARY 19, 1945

ᴳBIG—DECISION!!!

Made a big decision on my birthday—I won't finish the book. It's simple—it's not good, has no magic to it—it isn't me. Later more on this—now only the statement that if I felt it a duty (ending the book), I would end it. But this is not so. Today I will begin a new life, happier and more confident. Yes, with my new cup Natica gave to me.^{GG}

JANUARY 21, 1945

^GThinking of Cornell. But don't have time for it (i.e. no strong enough inclination) and really not even time for N. But as long as I love N., I will love her truly—there's no happiness otherwise. N. only calls rarely, but when she calls, she stays over. Have to renew my acquaintance with myself. I love Fétiche, and she loves me. At least—a cat!^{GG}

JANUARY 22, 1945

^GHappy just as I was at nineteen. My brain is a tabula rasa—and life excites me.^{GG}

JANUARY 24, 1945

^GChambrun is trying *The New Yorker* for "Mighty Nice Man."* Now or never.^{GG}

1/24/45

In lieu of a vacation: go someplace in the city by yourself, preferably a place where one has never been before. The Metropolitan Opera House will do. Ballets, after three martinis, dinner, with a friend or two, is not the same. Go alone and stand in the side aisle. Flirt with the young man who turns out, under the light, to be homosexual, or with the young woman with the pixielike hair, who encouraged by your attention, laughs too heartily to herself at Papageno's antics with the silver bells, and so spoils everything. Look at the golden brim of the orchestra's cup,

---

* "A Mighty Nice Man," written in 1940, is about a young girl who catches the eye of an older man, while her otherwise watchful mother remains oblivious to his intentions. It was originally published in the *Barnard Quarterly* (Spring 1940) and reprinted posthumously in *Nothing That Meets the Eye: The Uncollected Short Stories of Patricia Highsmith* (New York, 2002).

holding thousands of fascinating heads—most of them gray or
bald, however—and imagine yourself in Vienna, Paris, London,
with no attachments, tabula rasa. The world and its martinis
are mine! Incredibly enough, the sensation lasts even when one
arrives home and goes happily to bed.

JANUARY 26, 1945
ᴳI would like something more in my life—to love someone, of
course. N. doesn't want that, that's clear, that's all. What should
I say tomorrow? "Why didn't you call me?" "Why didn't you
write me?"—I don't want to ask these questions, but if I pretend
not to care, she will also be displeased. Read a lot this week—as
one should always do, but I haven't in four years. Reading is a
habit, said B. Z. [Goldberg], who knows everything.ᴳᴳ

1/26/45
Drawing—opens the heart, when too closely guarded and
guided by writing, makes the soul free and once more permits
the all essential freedom of association.

JANUARY 27, 1945
ᴳOne thing only—R. said that I am her best friend. This means
a lot, because I have earned it the hard way.ᴳᴳ

JANUARY 28, 1945
ᴳWork today—only work. Worked on everything, probably too
much. What I have lost in my art is confidence in myself. It is
hard to combine the two—confidence and a kind of humility
and modesty (an affectation, no doubt!) without which everything goes badly. Worked on comics, wood cut.ᴳᴳ

1/28/45
The long, indefinitely long period following a love affair that
logically, probably is ended, when the mind believes in the
end and the heart still refuses, this is the most difficult to bear
because of its dominating sense of futility. Some bestial instinct

of self-preservation leads one to seek another object. Then the heart is sickened, remembering how it was once, meeting and loving, without forethought and without warning. Oh, one must never be conscious of love in the mind!

JANUARY 30, 1945
    ᴳNothing but work and duties. Nothing—until 9:45 P.M. when Natica called. (Now she wants to try parachuting!)ᴳᴳ

1/31/45
    Nota bene: I must never write about myself or my attitudes toward anything, in a piece of prose. Poetry is another matter. Inspiration is another matter. But I mean as a policy of work, an overall policy.

FEBRUARY 4, 1945
    ᴳNot enough sleep yet. And no word from Natica. Didn't I once say that this book [this diary] shall be written about her alone? Yes, but this means I can only write that I have had "no word from N." Worked—much harder when I write comics. Worked for hours without the slightest satisfaction! But my life is attaining a form of dignity. Reading [Henry] James with great pleasure. Yes, another book N. gave me.ᴳᴳ

FEBRUARY 8, 1945
    ᴳOne of those days when I made dinner. And I will say here and now: it's not worth the trouble. Worked on my story (three hours) and was extremely happy at 2:30 PM. But from 2:30 PM until 2:30 AM I was busy with Cornell. We had a lot to drink, a too rich dinner, and didn't sufficiently discuss the things we had to say to each other.ᴳᴳ

2/8/45
    It is so simple why people drink—for the confirmation of the fact that they are the most important individuals in the world. It invests one with the light, clean fantasy of the novel, the isola-

tion of the poem. It is all, that the individual captivated, wants. (Drunkenness)

FEBRUARY 12, 1945

[G]Ernst came (at 5) and seems just like three years ago. He stays here for a month. The life of a war reporter does not seem attractive to me at all. He wants me to come back with him, or to go to Europe after the war. He kissed me long—and I don't know why I let him.[GG]

FEBRUARY 25, 1945

[G]A happy day—yes, I can call it "happy," a word I ordinarily only use for lovers. Robin* came at 8 o'clock. Conversing with her is a delight. She almost wants what I want—a real home, a house filled with familiar furniture, large desks, etc. We need money, and I probably need England—and she America or France, but we want the same things. I am very dissatisfied with my social life. It is hard—I love the gay crowd but I do not like bourgeois society, it bores me. Which to choose?[GG]

FEBRUARY 28, 1945

[G]I must confess that it pains me to read this diary—the pages on Natica! How short the time was in which I knew her! How sweet! How carefree!—and now she is like a wild animal, far away from me, but gazing at me as I look at her!!!—Why? And why not? Very agitated—and working nervously, but quickly. Am too tired—and a bit manic-depressive.[GG]

MARCH 3, 1945

[G]Last night I ended my second reading of the dictionary. I only think—that I found Natica during the J's. Made Catherwood's

---

* Pat notes in December 1944 that her friend Ann had changed her name to Robin. It is unclear, however, which Ann she means.

acquaintance during the P's—that the S's seemed almost unbearable and infinite when Natica and I broke up.^{GG}

$3/4/45$

Do you think I want sex? Do you think I am an animal, that I must have sex every month, every week? I want love, and if it is sex you want, don't come to me, woman. Sex I can have with any whore in any nightclub! Sex!—I flee it like I flee the devil! The curve of a head in a photograph is more fertile than a love experience. The same love as that of the painter for his brushstroke or the writer for his phrase, the composer for his melody. Love surrounds, embraces and permeates all things.

MARCH 5, 1945

^GFinished my story for Chambrun. Soon I will know what the world thinks of it. Tonight alone—quite lost, because I had finished my work and wanted to do nothing.^{GG}

$3/5/45$

It is the strangest feeling I have ever known, because the most unlike me as I know myself: I simply do not want to do anything. I have just finished correcting a story on which I have worked for six weeks, the evening is before me (by now, however, half over) and there are three other stories I have in mind to do eventually. There are a dozen chores around the house I might do. I might begin another story of the mechanical kind that earns my living. I simply cannot summon the urge that for the past ten years of my life has been present almost constantly—yes! even when with friends, when it should not have been present!

MARCH 7, 1945

^GVirginia's at 7 o'clock. I love her very much, and she loves me. This is friendship. But she could, I think, go further. I don't know. I realized today that without love, without a girl, I am quite lost, half asleep. That's what I thought until 11 o'clock

tonight—! And then I began to think that I lack only the right kind of work! I want to make a lot of money—but—more importantly, I want to write good stories.[GG]

MARCH 9, 1945

[G]Breakfast at the parents', where they read my story, "They," which Chambrun had just returned to me. He wants to send it out immediately—to *L.H.J.* [*Ladies' Home Journal*] and *G.H.* [*Good Housekeeping*]—expecting rejections, but convinced that the story will do something good for me, that he will finally sell it to *H.B.* [*Harper's Bazaar*] or *Charm* [*Magazine*]. Parents like it a lot—said I've improved. Tonight, I worked on a new story, which I don't yet have an ending for. It's about the Luzis of Taxco. I want to write stories like H. James. He is my God![GG]

MARCH 10, 1945

[G]Natica called around 2 in the morning—very drunk. She lectured me on how I should live my life. If I don't come down from my "ivory tower," I won't write about anything real. She screamed delightful words! "I'm calling all my fucking friends—"[GG]

3/10/45

I love every day in the week, but with a different kind of love for each. Sundays I love and fear. They can be heaven or hell. Mondays are exciting with promise. Wednesdays, though I am generally exhausted by Wednesday and have to declare this some sort of half-Sunday, are pleasant because they are the middle of the week which means Sunday comes soon, Sunday having vague childhood associations, more imagined than ever actual, of casual events and playing with anything that the mind hits on. Saturdays are one martini at lunch and art exhibits, and a nap from exhaustion at 5:30 P.M.

MARCH 12, 1945

[G]A wonderful evening at Jo P.'s. Food and drink, a fireplace, a Chesterfield, Bach's Chorale #140—what more could one want?

I need nothing else. Discussed the question of "ivory towers."
"Now you're worth something," she said. "Don't believe you're
in an ivory tower." Advised me to get a job with the Red Cross
for two months so I can observe all kinds of people and their
problems. I love Jo very much. She is a rare treasure.^{GG}

3/16/45

When I feel best physically and mentally, and feel unusually
optimistic and forward-searching, there is also present the
feeling I may in an instant become deathly ill, and quickly die.
Why this constant tug-of-war? I believe it is the old game of self-
preservation versus self-destruction.

MARCH 20, 1945

^GVery discouraged—as is normal when two people at once
throw my work back in my face! First Mr. Schiff from *Detective* [*Comics*], who said my stories were an "old hat." Next the
sketches for *Seventeen* [magazine], which weren't very good, to
be honest.

Rosalind and I discussed Natica—"devilishly attractive and
hopeless!"—R.C.

Germany is almost defeated.^{GG}

MARCH 21, 1945

^GBach's birthday two hundred and sixty years ago. More work
to do, but I'm tired. Read "Quiet Night"*—it's very good, I
think I can sell it. How lovely my writing was six years ago! At
least I could write economically—short! Now I always fear that
I've included too many details. I often think I don't have enough
to do with the world.^{GG}

---

* Presumably written in 1938–1939 in New York, "Quiet Night" tells the story of two sisters
trapped in a love-hate relationship with one another. It first appeared in *Barnard Quarterly*
(Fall 1939). A longer, revised version renamed "The Cries of Love," was published in
Women's Home Companion (January 1968) and in *The Snail-Watcher and Other Stories*,
Highsmith's first collection of short stories (New York, 1970).

3/26/45

To the twenty-three-year-old New Zealander I met tonight in a Sixth Avenue Penny Arcade. He walked me home and talked of American education. He did not ask to come upstairs. He kissed me with a clean mouth in the shadows of my court, and when I said he was an angel, he insisted that he had bad habits like all the rest. Tomorrow night he leaves for England. His last night tonight, and I did not invite him upstairs, for a cup of coffee, a long talk. Why not?—Remembering soldiers who were not like him, remembering my work tomorrow which is insignificant compared to war. When I am old and have seen almost everything, then I'll be sorry I did not ask him up his last night in America.

3/28/45

No joy on earth can compare with the artist's after he has done good work. No satisfaction or contentment can compare with it. God visits the artist personally, but people he merely watches.

4/11/45

"A woman is a sometime thing."*

APRIL 12, 1945

ᴳThe President is dead! I heard the first brief announcement on the radio at 5:40 P.M. Couldn't believe it at first—like all the others. He died of a brain aneurism suddenly, in Warm Springs, Ga. The whole world is astonished, and great preparations are being made for his memorial ceremony. The radio is playing only religious music tonight (which I like very much). Bach on four stations at the same time! God, if only Wallace were president now instead of Truman! Work is going quite well. But naturally—with F.D.R. dead, the world is quite different.ᴳᴳ

---

* A song from George Gershwin's opera *Porgy & Bess*.

4/15/45

At first glance, war would seem to be a machine greater than the individual who is caught up in it to behave as his character guides him. War is not like the overwhelming emotions of revenge, desire, hatred. War has nothing to do with the human soul, of individuals working upon individuals. It is in the most worldly sense unreal. It is the most artificial of any of man's creations, because it has least to do with the individual. Have this moment read in the letters of Richard Spruce,* a suggestion that war-riddled corpses be displayed in formaldehyde in museums, to keep down wars. I think it's a fine idea.

4/16/45

Someday there may be a community of nations, a world communal system, Japan producing artists and gadgets, Germany the scientists and doctors, America the entertainment and corn, France the liquor and the poetry, England the men's clothing and the literature. Seriously, it is one of the happiest of hopes to imagine suspicions forgot, the communal idea reborn in all nations, to imagine the utilization of the remarkable skills of some nations for the good of all the rest. An interdependence with no fear of starvation of a certain product through the suspicion or hatred of another. Distances have been abolished, language difficulties are next. Then racial pride and prejudice.

4/19/45

Conscience, dear conscience, I dedicate these lines to you. To you, who spoil everything from breakfast in bed, to sex—even in the head. From gorging myself on the most churchly music, to standing thirty seconds longer under a hot shower on a cold night. And should I have an evening free, by some quirk, you can conjure up some work. Dear conscience, you of the long and muscle-bound arms, why was I born with you? Why do I love you so?

---

* Richard Spruce (1817–1893), an English botanist and explorer.

4/21/45

Bach's heroic little piano concerto #5 in F Major was interrupted
by a special news bulletin from France, that the Russian and
Allied armies have met in the district of Dresden.* Germany
is split! The greatest fighting armies of the world have broken
through to each other and are embracing in the streets of Dresden! And immediately afterward, Bach's second movement continued, with perfect grace and with a terrible beauty! The tears
burst from my eyes, and I do not exactly know why. The emotion was like a spasm, its intensity gone before I could explain
it . . . Bach walked the streets of Dresden in knee breeches and
rather shabby shoes. He was greater, though, than Germany, as
Germany was less than God.

APRIL 28, 1945

GAfter an evening of false reports, the news just came that
Germany has capitulated. Through Himmler. I have nothing
to say—perhaps later. Sketched tonight, and am happy and
free as I only am when I paint or sketch. Would like to be an
artist.GG

APRIL 29, 1945

GQuite suddenly, I want, perhaps more than any other of my
heart's desires, to enjoy my life. I want to be like the Europeans—
freed from the dreadful struggle for money! That, in this country,
is the mistake of this century!GG

MAY 1, 1945

GHappy day in which I did too little, with not enough motivation. Hitler is dead, but no one knows how he died.GG

---

* In fact, Torgau in Saxony is considered the place where American and Soviet troops met,
on April 25, 1945, the so-called Elbe Day. Dresden itself was not captured by the Red Army
until May 8, 1945, while Eisenach, Bach's birthplace, was taken by the U.S. Army at the
beginning of April.

MAY 2, 1945

^GWork is much better since last night. Very happy and why—my God, why?! Because I am thinking of Allela—yes, I almost believe that we could still have one another! But these are foolish dreams, I know. She can't believe me. But this love gives me what I need so badly—security and hope, the belief that my life still lies before, rather than behind me, in misfortune. Saw films of the German atrocities with the parents. It is truly dreadful. The audience was silent, the images of the living and the dead terrible.^{GG}

MAY 3, 1945

^GHitler is dead—and did not die a hero's death, as was thought. He took his own life. With Goering. Mussolini died this week too,—the three—F.D.R., Mussolini, and Hitler—dead in two weeks! What does Cornell think about my letter? Is she too busy to call me? Read about the atrocities in Germany—(at Rosalind's). The country is flooded with German horrors! Photographs too!^{GG}

MAY 7, 1945

^GGood day: First Mrs. St. Cyr who talks way too much, hates the Jews, loves the Republicans (everything that disgusts me!). Finally free of her, I went with the parents to see the house in Hastings. And I think we found the house in which I (and they) will create so many wonderful things—but die there? I won't go so far.^{GG}

MAY 8, 1945

^GToday was "VE Day" but half of the city celebrated yesterday. It was a terrible mistake on Ed Kennedy's behalf, who thought he was doing "nothing wrong" by relaying the news.[*] He endangered the negotiations between Russia and America! (Or Russia and England and Germany.)^{GG}

---

* The American journalist Edward L. Kennedy (1905–1963) was the first Allied journalist to report on the German surrender despite a news embargo.

MAY 10, 1945

^GTried without success to break into S. & S. [Simon & Schuster]. One leafs quickly through my writing there, says: "We don't buy anything—at present—." Visited Timely. Dorothy Roubichek*— Jewish, very friendly, but dear God, how severe with the stories! Finally at mine—terrible evening. Mickey bored me, Alice T. disgusted me! Terrible. Saw *Kiss Them for Me*† from too close up, and still had to pay $3.00 for it. Judy probably good, but the fact I know her changes everything.^{GG}

MAY 11, 1945

^GCarefully prepared myself for lunch at the Colony‡ with Jacques [Chambrun] and Mr. Hall. Both of them very gracious. No news on the stories. They wanted to know, naturally, what I had in petto. "A play," I said, "but no specifics yet." They didn't seem very excited. (Three martinis—the first with mother. The bill must have been much higher than his commission for the story he sold!) We mostly discussed art. With Rolf Tietgens tonight, one of our strange and wonderful evenings. We talked about everything under the sun. More later.^{GG}

5/11/45

It does not matter what happened, but what you think of it.

MAY 12, 1945

^GNot so happy. Rosalind came by at 3:00, she doesn't like my story. Lately, I am depressed by my worthlessness: haven't written anything (good) in three years.

— Haven't been faithful to anyone. That hurts!!!
— Am not worthy of anything.

---

* Dorothy Roubichek, an editor at Timely, was one of very few women in those days to reach the upper echelons of the comic book industry.
† Judy Holliday's 1945 Broadway debut, which won her that year's Clarence Derwent Award for Most Promising Female.
‡ Colony was an elegant private club in New York.

(Now I am listening to [Bach's] "Bist Du bei mir." It penetrates my heart. But there it finds too much space!)^{GG}

MAY 17, 1945

^GThe comics are becoming harder to think up. And the cat— sometimes I wish it wasn't mine! Just now, late tonight, I began writing a story and have great hopes. No title.^{GG}

5/17/45

The beautiful wonderful sensations of working again, after cha- otic idleness that is anything but restful. To hell with the ship- getting-its-keel-back theory! This is literally being on top of the world. By dealing with three characters in a story, one somehow gets atop the entire world, understands all humanity (not in a moment, but in time) and above, beneath, through all, one has regained a momentum like that of the whirling earth and all the solar system, one has acquired a heartbeat.

MAY 20, 1945

^GA terrible argument—unpleasantness, really, between me and David (tonight). He wanted to kiss me when we sat around a table in a bar, seven of us. Teased me—said, I needed to get "—"—the most horrible language I've ever heard in mixed com- pany. Bob and I left as soon as possible.^{GG}

5/22/45

Thank God for animals! They never think themselves into jams. They are always right. They are an inspiration.

5/26/45

The month of May is manic with sunshine, greenness and Mozart divertimentos. Young greenness sits like jewels in the gray stone foil of the city. Now too sedate, I once fell in love in May. Too early then, now too late to start. The month of May is strangely sexless. Busy with building the inner man, and frames and bookshelves, puttering about the house, forgetting the bread and meat work. The month of May is mad energy spewed into a hundred channels, each proclaiming its beauty and success with a tiny candle-flame at its most extreme end, so that I am a coruscating pinwheel of delight. I want to burn myself out, never counting costs and losses. In June I must rest for the first time, Fatigue, having hovered just above me all this while.

MAY 30, 1945

ᴳCornell is not a quick talker, but when I mention a problem she's great. For example tonight, our old question: Man or no man, cook or no cook? The meals are the hardest, even though it seems strange. We need a man to govern our lives so we don't have to do anything outside our work, can have dinner with friends and then repair to our rooms. Where is this to be found?ᴳᴳ

MAY 31, 1945

ᴳHappy—still happy. Strolled through the city with mother, looking at furniture. We discussed the matter of marriage for a long time. She said (quite rightly) that Cornell and I are wasting a lot of time and energy by trying to have a friendship of some kind (instead of finding a man). Wrote tonight. I like the story.ᴳᴳ

JUNE 2, 1945

ᴳMet AC [Allela Cornell] at GC [Grand Central] at 8:35. The trip was long, but there were some beautiful moments. I wonder whether I will forget this trip like so many others. I have known AC for three years, and we have lived through so much together.ᴳᴳ

JUNE 4, 1945

ᴳIt rained all day. We read and sketched at home; I was very lazy! Tonight, when I tucked her into bed, I felt very close to her. I wanted to sleep with her, I felt as if I almost wanted her.

And we tried in the end—but it was quite impossible for me!
Decided to go to the A.S.L. [Art Students League] in New York
(this summer). It is my true calling, and yet—it is only my insane
power over myself which holds me back.GG

JUNE 6, 1945

GLong talk about my tension. Whether it is physical, sexual, or
mental. It is likely sexual, of course, and Cornell advised me
to have sex with someone, since love and sex are two different
things. I know this in theory, but I can't take my broken body
to a girl as if it were a broken watch. An impossible situation. I
can't say anything to Cornell, though I think every day that she
is the only one I could ever truly love.GG

JUNE 8, 1945

GTonight, after dinner, we took a walk through the fields, and
as we lay in the grass, we kissed—finally. Fate had never granted
us one this good before.GG

6/8/45

I hate arguments and really refuse to argue, because arguing
implies a fixed opinion of something. My most extreme arguments are the silent kind one has with some books. Even these
are evoked only when the author's position is insufferable,
untenable. The only fixed principles to have, the only truly ben-
eficial, advisable ones, are in the form of a recipe for happiness.
If one loses one's formula for happiness or a working amount of
optimism, then one is indeed lost.

JUNE 9, 1945

GMary drove us to the train station, and we took the 10:15
from Bath, looked out the window, and were very silent and
somewhat sad, each occupied with her own thoughts. These
train trips are pleasant, boring, happy and sad at the same
time.GG

JUNE 12, 1945

^GSchool at 9 o'clock [Art Students League]. The class isn't that great. The paintings I have seen seem to me dreadfully academic—though I know it is necessary, it still disgusts me.^{GG}

JUNE 16, 1945

^GRosalind said: "I'm much more excited about your drawings than about your writing, don't you agree?" Something like that—and asked me whether I might want to change careers. It's true. I want to be an artist but not become too serious, too mad about my art—that would be my downfall. I am so low (in my personal relationships) that I cannot write freely. It nonetheless seems that I can draw unreservedly. I know that I am less unhappy and tense when I paint or draw.^{GG}

JUNE 19, 1945

^GSo needed—yesterday, Joe Samstag* liked my painting very much. "Swell—exactly what I wanted—congratulations"—he said. And I was over the moon with happiness! Making progress in the class. I'm so happy I (sometimes) feel like a fool.^{GG}

6/20/45

T.S. said drunkenly tonight: "Never love an artist. When it comes time for them to work, they'll look at you as though they didn't know you, and kick you out in the cold."

6/20/45

Would I were greedy as now forever,
Not for fortune, nor yet knowledge, and for love—never,
A muscled horse obedient to ruthless master, art,
Exultantly racing till he break his heart.

---

* Gordon "Joe" Samstag, painter, muralist, and teacher.

JUNE 22, 1945

   ᴳFinally exhausted after these two weeks of insane strength and
energy. Am happy enough when I write (without much order
or discipline) but when I draw, I feel as I have never felt before:
happy like a girl who simply lives and learns and loves, who has
never known a dark thought, who has never thought about her
health or mental development. Am I in love? I don't know. I love
AC but I'm not in love with her. A situation that would no doubt
appeal to her if she knew.ᴳᴳ

7/1/45

   For future reference: In case of doldrums of mind or body or
both, sterility, depression, inertia, frustration, or the overwhelming sense of time passing and time past, read true detective stories, take suburban train rides, stand a while in Grand
Central—do anything that may give a sweeping view of individuals' lives, the ceaseless activity, the daedal ramifications, the
incredible knots of circumstance, the twists and turns in all their
lives, which no writer is gifted enough to conceive, sitting in the
closeness of his quiet room.

JULY 3, 1945

   ᴳWent to see Rolf this evening. It's a great pleasure to see his
house. It changes from visit to visit, like a museum. And Bobby*
also makes small pictures, paintings and things—very pleasant.
Rolf advised me to do only crazy things in my painting and drawing. "Do what no one else does."ᴳᴳ

7/8/45

   The actual time spent in creative work each day need be only
very little. The important thing is that all the rest of the day contribute to this strenuous time.

---

* Rolf's lover, the art dealer Robert (Bobby) Isaacson. Bobby would later date James Ingram
Merrill, winner of the 1977 Pulitzer Prize for Poetry.

7/18/45

Put all your fears into words, paint pictures of your enemies, prose poems of all apprehensions, doubts, hatreds, uneasinesses, to defeat them and stand upon them.

7/25/45

Write as a painter paints, with renewed awareness of the work of choosing and rejecting. Remember (and realize) that a sentence may be set into the middle of a previously written paragraph, without interfering with rhythm, that this sentence can be the iron bolt, or the germ cell, or the life itself, all added later, as the fleck of white at the end of a nose may quicken the entire portrait. Apply sentences like strokes of color. Survey the work as a whole from time to time and experience it as though it were a painting. This shift in itself provides a measure of poetry, the necessary untruth of art. Scenes are necessarily separate pictures, but the experience of the whole should be orgasmic, productive of the wordless joy and satisfaction one feels looking at van Gogh's *Night Café* or at Marsden Hartley's workman's shoes.

AUGUST 7, 1945

GVery happy. *Harper's Bazaar* arrived. My story ["The Heroine"] has no illustrations, and a stupid paragraph on P.H. at the end which should have been left out. Mailed it to grandma right away. Mother called. Very proud, she said, but hadn't seen the story yet. I wanted to say here that I felt nothing until I saw the magazine in the hands of a stranger this afternoon—I thought that he might read my story tonight—and then I felt something.GG

8/10/45

I here highly resolve to spend one hour per day in study, preferably eleven to midnight, devoting two months to each subject. At this time, I have been at it a week. God permitting, I shall study at least this amount the rest of my life.

AUGUST 11, 1945

^GBusy—as always. Got the OK for a synopsis from Famous,* my latest company. Saw girls in uniform in the museum at 3:00. Very nice. Excellent, and left much to the imagination. Possible homosexuality, without a doubt—and if the two will keep seeing other girls later, that's the question. Terrible soiree at Ann T.'s. A blue-stocking, an overaged Bea Lillie†—abound a dark, roofed-over table. That forced us close together. Everyone siting around, trying to be amusing. I drank way too much gin, was rather sick and left at 1:00 A.M. to go to Allela.^{GG}

AUGUST 12, 1945

^GAllela came at 11:30. Argued bitterly about the war. They are expecting peace with Japan, and A. is angry because I am not worked up. It is not enough for me that millions of men and women are waiting for freedom. It's not enough. Do you understand?^{GG}

AUGUST 14, 1945

^GShe is haranguing me because I don't share her feelings on the war! Nervous today and could barely work. Herb L. came at 6:30. Very handsome, out of his uniform for two months now. As bad luck would have it, the declaration of peace came at 7:00 PM! Of course (?) phone calls from Allela. Herb invited us out to dinner. Hotel Pierre, two bottles of champagne—and Allela, who takes everything and gives nothing, wanted to propose a toast to F.D.R., etc. It disgusted me so. Later I slept with Herb, just as I wanted, and immensely enjoyed it! Allela tried to call

---

* Famous Studios, the animation division of Paramount Pictures, had moved to New York City in 1943 and produced the Popeye the Sailor and Superman cartoons.

† A grand dame of the stage, Beatrice Gladys "Bea" Lillie (1894–1989) debuted on Broadway in 1924. During the war years, the Canadian actress went on tour to support the troops, traveling to the Caribbean, even Africa and the Middle East. Despite several long-term relationships with men, there were consistent rumors that Lillie was a lesbian.

several times and come up to the room, but we cut the doorbell wires.[GG]

AUGUST 20, 1945

[G]Arrived punctually at 12 at *Harper's Bazaar*. Saw C. Snow (whose temperature never rises above 30°) and accepted work, eight hours per day (!) $45 a week. Wasn't satisfied. I'll start Thursday or Monday. Lots to do. My small cabinet for records arrived, and I spent (sinfully!) 6 hours putting it together. But now my small collection is housed in it, and I am very happy.[GG]

8/21/45

The moral frame of reference. In five words the goal of all my past life & perhaps all my future! Where shall I ever find it? In England, in the Roman Catholic church, in a convent, within myself!? Oh, yes, to make one's own rigid code of laws in regard to society! Perhaps this is the only and final answer. Meanwhile, until our feet find this ladder, until our butterfly wings are fixed with pins and glue upon our labeled panel, then we flounder, drink, vaguely ponder, and flounder eternally some more.

8/21/45

An interview with my agents. It is three in the afternoon in a hot and half-sleeping New York, the month of August. One is in shirtsleeves, collar open, shiny with sweat, and lazily nervous and alert, as after a hangover. The other's impeccable dress is scarcely altered except that he wears no jacket. Both their pairs of hands are sleek, shiny, well cared for, with tiny points of knucklebones showing at the bend.

"If you could put a happy ending on this, Miss Highsmith, I think we could sell it. Just the ghost of a happy ending. That little concession to commercialism shouldn't ruin it. Just the merest touch."

"Like being a little bit pregnant," drawls the other agent.

Polite laughter. What can one say?

"Too bad you write like that, Miss Highsmith. It's sad to write and not be published."

It is not the least sad to write and not be published, but how can I explain this? I do not even begin it. I only sit there, alternately trying to smile, trying to control the leaping words in me. We do not speak the same language, I think as I go out into the sunshine.

AUGUST 22, 1945

^GEveryone is advising me to write a novel. I want to! I want to—!!!^{GG}

AUGUST 24, 1945

^GPhoned *Harper's Bazaar* to tell Ms. Snow I don't want the job. My excuse was the money. I don't like changing my mind about things, but it would be nonsense to have less time to work.^{GG}

AUGUST 27, 1945

^GAt war with *Harper's Bazaar.* Wish it had been a Blitzkrieg. There at 12 after a nervous morning. Couldn't wait for [Betty Parsons's] call because I had to take my tooth to the laboratory. I can clearly see that everything will go badly this week because I am too rushed. Ms. Snow kept me waiting for an hour. Sent me to various women. Finally, she offered me $75 a week, but it's still not enough. R. Portugal gave me an article to write on P. Mondrian. I don't know how much it will pay.^{GG}

AUGUST 31, 1945

^GVery frightened, brought my Mondrian article to *H. Bazaar* and—when Wheelock* was still there, R. Portugal pulled the poor thing out and read the first page. "Excellent beginning!" she said, and I breathed for the first time in five days.^{GG}

---

* Dorothy Wheelock Edson, features editor at *Harper's Bazaar.*

SEPTEMBER 3, 1945

ᴳThe last lovely day. I am suddenly wondering whether mother might not, in her despair, try to find happiness alone? Things are truly impossible with S. I think they haven't had sex—in months. It's quite easy to see.

My story—several hours of work. Made mother read the introduction to a book by H. Melville. She read the 50 pages but chastised Melville for neglecting his family.—There is something she will never truly understand: the life of an artist. No more than I can understand the life of a wife, a mother.ᴳᴳ

SEPTEMBER 5, 1945

ᴳHard work—too hard to be happy—(one needs time for happiness when one is happy enough already—time to play with one's cat, leaf through one's books. But I have no such thing).ᴳᴳ

9/8/45

Should like to determine the reason or the host of reasons why I avoid meeting people, encountering them on my walks, why I avoid greeting even the most pleasant acquaintances by crossing the street when I see them far ahead of me on the sidewalk. Perhaps it is, basically, the eternal hypocrisy in me, of which I've been aware since about thirteen. I may feel, therefore, that I am never quite myself with others, and hating deceit, constitutionally hating it, avoid its necessity. Then, too, I am sure I feel most contacts insignificant, because the polite phrases—there are layers and layers of polite, semi-polite, not quite natural phrases, which must be stripped away, used up, before one reaches the real person. And how rarely this happens! What troubles me somewhat is the superimposed problem of being in touch with humanity. Flatly, I do not want it.

SEPTEMBER 11, 1945

ᴳThe [prime minister of] Japan, Tojo, shot himself yesterday. Attempted suicide, but he's still alive, thanks to the blood of an American soldier. There will be a tribunal. In Germany too, for various war crimes. Worked hard until I was dog tired. This can't go on. First of all, the price is too high. But right now I have so many expenses—my tooth (which is still not finished!—now—once again—I look like a witch!)—my taxes, and, as always, the rent.^{GG}

SEPTEMBER 12, 1945

^GTake heed, future readers! This diary should be simultaneously compared to my notebooks, so that one will not have the impression I write only of worldly affairs! Worked. Prepared all kinds of things for my mother's birthday. Don't have enough presents. But I have a bottle of Champagne.^{GG}

SEPTEMBER 13, 1945

^GSometimes I feel as though I can't keep up with my work and social life. In ten years, perhaps, I will read this and laugh.^{GG}

9/16/45

Insane note with blushing face. Horror stories I adore, and I haven't even tried to write one since early college days, when I turned out one every six months at least. But I realized then that horror stories were my meat, that horror was, in a sense, my milieu, my *métier*. Should I not allow myself to try to write one horror story? (Chorus of yeses from the unseen, clamoring audience.) Suspense I adore, am excellent at creating because I don't worry about it at all. The accuracy of vision, the confidence unrealized as confidence, these are the sine qua non. Well then, a horror story. Tonight, in the country, the fluttering of a moth at my window screen is enough!

SEPTEMBER 18, 1945

^GInteresting—tried to buy something to "bring on menstruation" and was told that if he had such a thing, he would not be allowed to sell it, because it would be "against the law"! Imagine—against the law! My God! What a country! What a nation! If only I were in France or Russia! So—I called Doc-

tor Borak, and will see him tomorrow. I don't know whether I'm pregnant—what an ugly word! And as I write this, I feel as though I am not pregnant in the least! For months, my period has come two weeks late—and the last time very little—so perhaps it is starting to vanish again.[GG]

9/20/45

Again and again, for years now, in the most comfortable and happy moments of my life, I remember myself before the age of six, sitting in my beloved overalls before a gas stove in Gramma's living room, reading the evening *Press* or the morning *Star-Telegram*, reading the serials in them, now and again holding the paper close to my nose for it would still fragrant, almost warm, from the inky press. I recall the sound of the thin old door, wainscoted at the bottom, as my cousin Dan entered, chafing his hands. The house, though plain and ramshackle, showing a hint of poverty even here and there, could always make room for one more, could always provide food for one more mouth, and generously, and love for one more heart.

SEPTEMBER 21, 1945

[G]Tony Pastor's* almost incredibly boring, until I saw a girl—blond hair with a gray band, rather Russian. Really wanted to meet her. She's called Joan. She didn't tell me, but—we have a date, Sunday afternoon at 5 at the 1st Avenue Mayfair [Restaurant].[GG]

SEPTEMBER 23, 1945

[G]Was at the Mayfair at 5—she at 5:05. Very quiet—in everything! "But it's really rather fabulous we're having this date, right?" I had to smile. Over two drinks she admitted she's had "an experience" with a guy and a girl. She goes to Tony Pastor's

---

* Tony Pastor's Downtown, a club popular with lesbians at 130 West Third Street, was raided in 1944 on moral charges but survived—apparently backed by the mob.

too much, I think. She's really childlike, cute (German). And
she makes me laugh of happiness. Ate at Luigi's—Rocco. And
to Tony Pastor's for a moment. "I want a commission!," cried
May B., who introduced us. Later a Champagne Cocktail at that
quiet bar. A typical first night. In Wash. Park—I really just had
to embrace and kiss her—when six guys showed up—started
to hug us—especially Joan, who was shouting my name. What
could I do? I don't want my nose broken! Highly embarrassing.
Home late—not in love, but happy.GG

9/27/45

So little motivation, strength of purpose, is needed apparently
to turn a woman or a girl from her regular bourgeois world
into the road to homosexuality. Why do they choose this? I
must discover.

10/10/45

There is the unremitting instinct to find a focus for one's
ideas, all one's ideas. There is a need to find someone to
please, to make happy, simply to make understand. There is
a need for a person (or a thing) to criticize one or to praise.
There is a need, in brief, for another ego, much like one's own,
or with only interesting variations. Therefore one falls in love.
Yet if a substitute thing might be found for this, the destructive process of love, loving and being disappointed in the
person need not be suffered. Therefore, the quest for the substitute. Conceivably it might be God. Conceivably, given the
willingness, the necessary devotion and spirituality, it might
be a dead hero, a dead friend. Once, however, this alter ego
erects itself in whatever fetish of the individual, then the need
for love is precluded.

10/11/45

Loneliness is an emotion more interesting than love. And one
who is true to his loneliness is more faithful than any lover.

10/15/45

R.v.H.* told me tonight a most interesting situation. His two daughters, aged nine and fourteen are not, he says, developing into people. They read comic books avidly, and have not known the torture of crushes, the agony of self-consciousness and of imagined inferiority (the heroic sense, the desperate, world-ending sense of "I am not like the others"—mine), which to his European mind go on to make the character. How personally it affected me, for I agree with him absolutely! I felt sorry for him, for what he wishes is hopeless. He wishes to make unusual people out of two perfectly ordinary people. He wishes to expand consciousnesses that know better than to be expanded. All that remains for him is to take comfort in the knowledge that his daughters will never suffer as he has done, as I have done. Being European, he blamed this on America.

10/23/45

It is not conscience that prompts me to write, because I am a writer it is only dissatisfaction with this world.

OCTOBER 26, 1945

GLunch with Raimund von Hofmannsthal at Voisin.† He is the most suave, most charming man! Conversing with him is like taking a trip to Europe! He takes an interest in all of his friends' problems—especially Rosalind's and mine. Said he'd been anticipating this date for days, etc.—but no flattery. We discussed culture in America, my work, love, Rosalind.GG

---

* Raimund von Hofmannsthal (1906–1974), son of playwright and poet Hugo von Hofmannsthal. He married Ava Alice Muriel Astor in 1933, the only daughter of American tycoon John Jacob "Jack" Astor IV. In 1939, Raimund married his second wife, Lady Elizabeth Paget, an English aristocrat.
† French restaurant (1912–ca. 1969) and a New York city landmark. It is cited in both Ian Fleming's *Diamonds Are Forever* as well as in F. Scott Fitzgerald's short story "The Lost Decade" (published by *Esquire* in 1939).

10/26/45

Decision: never, never to expect a tranquil emotional life, above all never to count this a requisite for writing. Consequently, to hold emotional life apart from my writing, therefore from my life itself. "Emotional life"—the brick in the road that never can be laid smooth!

10/29/45

Fatigue + coffee = intoxication and elation.
Love + coffee = intoxication and ecstasy.

OCTOBER 30, 1945

ᴳThank God I'm not like B.Z.G.—dead when I am not in love. No, there are the pleasures of the mind. The difficulty is that one cannot enjoy them day in, day out—not all alone. I am leading an erratic life. It will be interesting to see how long I can keep it up.ᴳᴳ

10/30/45

Be content, be content, be content, be content.
Be continent. Be continental. And yet insular.

10/31/45

I am three months short of being twenty-five. Life presses upon me like a needle's point. I see things as though they were extremes of what they are. I feel too acutely a slightly pleasant or a slightly unpleasant happening. And all around me, melancholy amounting to real sadness becomes an atmosphere. The slightest tasks are done with great effort, and all life is without joy. Is this epic? Is this sensitivity? No, only the result of a distorted lens.

10/31/45

Whether to write a book about the unhealthy civilization of New York, and thereby rid myself of it; whether to jump clear of it all. At any rate, one must escape from it.

11/5/45

The process of culture—Suffering first of all, generally through love at the age of eighteen or seventeen or sixteen, but such humble and profound misery that one craves the richest medicaments. Therefore, one turns to poetry, music, books. Of course, some sensitivity is prerequisite. And perhaps the process begins long before, with this sensitivity which is present for always. So where has this analysis advanced me?

NOVEMBER 11, 1945

GI feel—no, I know—that when I am in love, and am loved, or at least feel hopeful of it, I can speak with others, say all the right things. And now, if only a desert or a wasteland were before me, I would say everything I do not want to say, be miserable and smoke.GG

11/15/45

Depression—Weltschmerz seizes one like a paralysis, in my case in attacks of two to three hours, generally in the broadest part of the day—between one and six in the afternoon. One cannot move, much less think of work. One cannot think even conclusively on one's own Weltschmerz, for to do this would be to reach some kind of goal, and against the reaching of goals, the entire mind is set.

Having come through the most ghastly war in history, the nations are again at one another's throats across the peace conference tables, while the governed classes nervously read their newspapers at home, realizing as thousands of generations have realized it after thousands of wars through the ages, that one more war has been fought in vain. Moreover, they have lost a son, a brother, a husband. Moreover, great Europe is broken and poor.

11/21/45

What's the matter with the world? Love is dying like flies.

NOVEMBER 25, 1945

GRaimund came here at midnight, and left me alone with the most troubling conclusions of our conversation: the difficulties and the drawbacks of being gay. That I feel more at ease when I wear men's clothing, that this is not an advantage, etc. It seems I cannot write down here how this conversation impressed me. But I will not forget it.GG

DECEMBER 4, 1945

GBad news—from *H.B.* [*Harper's Bazaar*], a letter from Mrs. Aswell with my story which she couldn't buy. "Your protagonist needs more charisma," she said. And that the topic is played-out. It's so much better than the story they published! But they want the story smooth. Learned from D.D. [David Diamond] that Cornell has been in the hospital for a week. Something with her stomach—and in critical condition for five days! God, and now she has so little will to live!GG

DECEMBER 5, 1945

GAm frightfully hungry for life—to see and learn, so decided to take a trip in January. I'll go alone, take the bus—perhaps to New Orleans, or Kentucky, Virginia, Tennessee. This hunger is the only—most natural and healthy feeling I've had in seven years! Thank God I'm dissatisfied with my small circle of gay friends! Phoned David Diamond for news on Allela. Yes, she attempted suicide—the Sunday after Thanksgiving. Nitric acid—half a bottle, quickly, on the roof, drunk at 6:30 AM after a fight with Annie, who was in her room then. Annie wanted to stay up and drink, Allela wanted to go to bed. And she is not allowed to see any of her loved ones. Later she'll be sent to her parents. How sad, and how unnecessary!GG

DECEMBER 6, 1945

GTired—but worked hard until 7 o'clock, when Natica arrived punctually. Always glad to have her at my house! Her face is beautiful, her hair even smoother, like fine gold. And tonight we didn't get drunk—didn't need it—but I discovered something I have known for a long time: I have loved no one else since Natica. She is the only woman who I have ever felt physical attraction for. Later lying on the bed, listening to music. We laughed a lot—this is new to me, perhaps because I'm so fat now—and our kisses were so lovely that she stayed in the end. Only once did I almost cry. No, I will never again cry over her.[GG]

12/9/45

The place is here, the time is now. These are the two principles of truth which the intellectual, who of all people professes to be aware of them, never puts into practice. Henry James based his life work on them, and awakened personally too late to them.

12/9/45

A satire—could be of indefinite length—on this twentieth century, which grows ever more like Huxley's *Brave New World*. Yet this would be more affecting because of its reality and instance: the half hour telephone calls to arrange finally a time when two people can see each other for five minutes, the article, in the biggest newspaper of the nation, on the subject of Washington officials' having insufficient time to think, the books in Brentano's and Scribner's entitled, "*How to Think about World Peace*," "*How to Read a Page*," all the Durant condensations, the classic abridgements, and et cetera too numerous to mention. Also, and not least, the practice of buying inferior goods with a view to discarding them when they wear out, in order to buy more with one's presumably then increased income. The fact that assistant professors' assistants are offered fifty cents an hour, sub-scrubwoman wages, that the young student when praised by his French teacher, told that he should teach, replies, "Is that all I'm fitted for?" In a word, the reverse of things as they should be. The Black Ages masquerading as the Age of Enlightenment, Racial Equality, Universal Democracy as the Universal Ideal, the

Age of the Atom, which is also the age of such Anti-christianity
that no man trusts his cousin in possession of it.

King Greed's Reign! No need to shout, "Long live!"

DECEMBER 10, 1945

^GAm happy like a fool. Life is opening up before me—and I am
an adventurer, a knight, a hero, a—Don Quixote, perhaps. All
because I saw N. today—only for a few minutes, but those minutes were worth more than five nights. God, how beautiful life is
when it is illuminated by a woman!^{GG}

DECEMBER 11, 1945

^GWorked—until I went to see Allela at 4:30 at St. Vincent's. She
is lying with a tube up her nose through which she must "eat."
She seems dark, thin, lifeless. Her mother was there at first, but
she left soon, as if we were lovers. I brought her my best and
newest book—Dostoyevsky's short stories. But she has a fever,
and can read little. God, how sad that so many people are worried about her, that she must rest for such a long time! She was
surprised that her friends are so caring. "Perhaps one learns,"
she said, "who one's friends are." She didn't know that I knew
about the suicide attempt. "It doesn't matter what you do, Pat—
I'll always love you." And she asked whether we could go to
Minot this winter. "How is your life? How is your love life?" I
told her that I had myself all to myself.^{GG}

DECEMBER 15, 1945

^GHave almost finished the fifth or sixth draft of my "Aaron"
story.[*] Shorter, but not short enough. Read a book on writing short stories, one of those books I usually hate, but I have
decided I must no longer write only for myself.^{GG}

---

[*] The story of Aaron Bentley, a newcomer in a small city who is rumored to have a taboo
relationship with a ten-year-old social outcast named Freya, was published posthumously
as "The Mightiest Mornings" in *Nothing That Meets the Eye: The Uncollected Stories of
Patricia Highsmith* (New York, 2002).

DECEMBER 20, 1945

ᴳI can't deny it, I am lonely because I have heard nothing from Natica! God, I must learn to live without hope, without goals, without love (of the ordinary kind) for Natica. Natica, the secret, the mystery, the fate, the happiness, the sadness of my life.ᴳᴳ

DECEMBER 22, 1945

ᴳOnce more I am typing up my "Aaron" story, which I must finish before beginning—or finishing—something new. Thinking of a novel based on my idea of two soul mates.* How is it possible that Natica can let Christmas go by without saying a word?ᴳᴳ

DECEMBER 28, 1945

ᴳRolf same as ever—my wonderful friend! He talks and talks and talks, until it's one thirty all of a sudden! About the country's economy, the difficulties of writing. We have some differences—he likes [William] Saroyan and finds Proust boring. Says that Geo. Davis found my stories immature. And also— that I have wonderful ideas but don't plumb them. They want magic—a little idea, brought to life with magic. Unfortunately, that's the style in which publishers think. And lately I want to tell stories, describe people, write at length. I love Rolf very much. He has become more relaxed. Also very fat, and worried about it. We promised to see each other more often.ᴳᴳ

12/28/45

For future pondering (no time now): Why does a person take inordinate pride in his appearance, in being dressed fresh and dapper? It affects sometimes the clever and the stupid, the rich and the poor.

---

* This will become her future novel *Strangers on a Train*.

Lovers Chart, which Patricia Highsmith drew up
in 1945 to rank and compare her lovers.
The initials of the women have been
removed to protect their privacy.

1946

Looking for Love, or:
"I can never be moderate in anything."

✕

LIFE GETS EVEN MORE hectic for Patricia Highsmith in 1946, both professionally and personally. She has a new agent, Margot Johnson, with whose help she gets two of her latest short stories, "Doorbell for Louisa" and "The World's Champion Ball Bouncer," published in the magazine *Woman's Home Companion*. Rather than develop the idea for *Strangers on a Train*, Pat spends her summer in Kennebunkport, Maine, working on a novel she'll later abandon called *The Dove Descending*.

The influential Catherwood family have a summerhouse in Kennebunkport; daughter Virginia, who goes by Ginnie, is Natica Waterbury's lover—that is, until Pat wins her over in June, thus ending Pat's relationship with Natica once and for all. Before Ginnie becomes Pat's new true love, however, Pat grapples with her feelings for Joan S., as the two visit New Orleans together. Joan is grounded and good, the embodiment of purity and stability—if a little boring. Amid the strife she will later encounter with Ginnie, Pat always wishes she could be satisfied by her "simple" love of Joan.

While Ginnie recovers from her latest jag at the family home, she and Pat discover a new hobby: collecting and breeding snails.

The wealthy heiress from Philadelphia, who was denied custody of her child following her divorce, will become (yet another) notoriously unfaithful, obsessive lover for the next year and a half. As in earlier relationships, Pat's life with Ginnie is marked by Pat's central conflict between writing (which requires retreat) and having a love life (which requires the opposite). Pat not only dedicates several short stories to Ginnie, she also uses her as inspiration for various female figures, from Carol in *The Price of Salt* to Lotte in *The Tremor of Forgery*.

In October, Joan S. is hospitalized following a failed suicide attempt. A few days later, Allela Cornell dies as a result of her suicide attempt the year before. Given the dramatic end to these recent love affairs, Pat considers therapy for the first time. There's also talk of her marrying Rolf Tietgens, to help him secure citizenship, and to start a family together. But in the end, her other loves prevail—the one she feels for Ginnie, and, not least, her love of freedom and independence.

❧

JANUARY 1, 1946

ᴳA happy day, like all my New Year days. Alive in body and spirit. Natica called me. I told her we were opening a bottle of champagne. So she arrived at 9 o'clock. Ate—then later a conversation with Rosalind, in which I was not much involved. She kissed Rosalind—and I didn't mind. I made a lot of sketches of them on the bed! N. and I left very early to get tattoos in Chinatown. Coffee at Rikers (after a lovely kiss on the steps of the L train!) and back home, where we drank, danced, kissed, and swore our undying love to each other. She wants to have a life with me "in the country." I think it would be better to move to a small city. The old problem—I don't know any. We're thinking of New Orleans, too. Am happy. Wish she'd stayed. She has her reasons. God—so many kisses tonight I'm still drunk!ᴳᴳ

JANUARY 2, 1946

^GWorked hard until 11:30 PM. Dog tired. Wrote another new opening for "The Magic Casements"*—simpler, sweeter. He needs the tender kisses of the woman he loves. He cannot deny it. The world (then) seems true—i. e. one sees it as it is.^{GG}

JANUARY 3, 1946

^G[Ernst] Hauser is here—we had dinner. He brought me three leather-bound books from Paris—one in Latin, the others French. And a few Gold Flake cigarettes, which I like a lot. If only Americans preferred milder cigarettes! Hauser's the same as ever. Disappointed I don't read his articles—but it doesn't matter. He's very loving. What will come of it, I wonder? I would have much rather seen Natica tonight! But she didn't call.^{GG}

JANUARY 7, 1946

^GWorked alone—(already) have a title for the story: "The Mightiest Mountains."† And paid a visit to Rolf tonight. God, how I love him! His room is so German, manly, clean! Robert Isaacson, Bobby's father, who looks very young, showed up at the same time. He's getting married in a week to a woman who's only twenty-four years old. Interesting to hear this practical, very ordinary Kansan speaking with Rolf. He doesn't worry much about his son; he joked with Rolf and me, and borrowed $10 before leaving.^{GG}

1/8/46

People unhappy in love never seem to remember others have known the same pain. The desolation one knows when so overcome with grief one cannot even fashion beauty of it and is thus deprived of this last consolation, has been experienced by seri-

---

* "Magic Casements" (working title: "The Feary Lands Forlorn") tells the story of a sad, solitary man who encounters a captivating woman at his regular bar one night. They agree to meet at a museum during the day, but the woman fails to keep their appointment, leaving the man all alone. The story was published posthumously in *Nothing That Meets the Eye: The Uncollected Stories of Patricia Highsmith* (New York, 2002).
† The story she refers to as "the Aaron story" in 1945, later renamed "The Mightiest Mornings."

ous, inconsolable young men since the beginning of time. Thus Schubert's *Die Winterreise*—the first verse being, "Frozen tears! How can my tears be so cold when they come from a heart so warm it could melt all winter's ice." The picture of the melancholy, energy-flagellated young man, roving the countryside, makes one's heart weep in sympathy.

JANUARY 9, 1946

^GWrote too little of the story until midnight. Then Natica phoned at 12:30 AM. She came over and we talked, kissed, drank tea until quarter to five! Time for love is not easily found, and shouldn't be taken lightly. We swore our love to each other once again—what does it count with such a neurotic? But I want to make it count as much as possible! I've promised myself! Saw Margot Johnson,* to whom I gave "The Mightiest Mornings."^{GG}

JANUARY 11, 1946

^G[Allela] Cornell's birthday. Went to see her at 1. She looks worse, though she said she was getting stronger. She weighs only 106, and has to have a tube put down her throat every week. It hurts terribly, she said. Surprised and curious that I'm seeing Natica again. No one knows when she will be discharged from the hospital. In about two months, perhaps. I loved [Natica] tonight as I have never loved before! I am enchanted with her! If I can't spend every night of my life with her, I don't want to live! I think (in these moments) that if she or I were to leave, my happiness and my reason to live would be over. And when she finally reciprocates my love (as she did tonight), I am almost sick with happiness and gratefulness.^{GG}

JANUARY 15, 1946

^GWoke up and almost cried because I'd slept until 2:30 PM instead of 8:30 AM! Too much work. Dinner with Natica, whom I met at Chop Suey on Lexington Ave. She had just seen [Vir-

---

* Margot Johnson, Pat's new agent.

ginia] Catherwood and was worried that she was following her.
But no. Natica has never looked as beautiful as she did tonight!
As I was sitting next to her in the movies, I had difficulty restrain-
ing myself. When she uses dirty words, she excites me!GG

JANUARY 19, 1946
GBusy all day with the party so I only had half an hour to myself
before the first guest arrived! Finally, only M. & A. & Natica
remained, and Natica, who was blind drunk, tried in every way
to devastate me: stubbing her cigarettes out on the floor, block-
ing the sink, necking with Maria until I was practically sick.
I stayed with A. in the kitchen, and heard everything taking
place on my bed. I was trembling like a dying man, and asked
A., "What are they doing?," as if we were in a bad play. Finally
Natica stormed out at 4:30, and I ran after her, not wanting us to
part on such bad terms (though she had kissed me upstairs and
said sweet things to me). "I love you and I'll call you tomorrow!"
she said when she got into the cab. She went, I hope, to Catherwood, because she was completely drunk, almost sick. Cleaned
the house, more depressed than I've ever been on my birthday.GG

JANUARY 21, 1946
GWhy am I still in love with N.? She's just the same as last year:
doesn't call me, hurts me and herself. And—it's raining. Rolf at
7:00—the best hours of my day. Why can't I have such a life for
myself? He's grown so much! He's an angel. No wonder Bobby
worships him!GG

JANUARY 22, 1946
GRosalind invited me to a cocktail party at her place on Saturday
night, but I can't bear to go; it's hell to see Natica kissing Maria.
My small, sour presence will not be missed.GG

1/30/46
And in childhood—the scenes we knew then, the specific
moments we remember, are preserved in some alcohol of mem-

ory, which to the individual's senses possesses a particular flavor and aroma as incommunicable to another fellow being as the description of a color to a blind man. Perhaps it is this, the sealed envelope of childhood each of us carries within him, which contributes to the sense of aloneness that is with us as long as we live.

FEBRUARY 4, 1946

^GWrote 5½ pages, my first children's book.* About Gracey. Am excited, calm, happy after my conversation with my most loyal friend, Rosalind, who is a constant source of support for me.^{GG}

FEBRUARY 6, 1946

^GWent to see Cornell, who's looking much better. Now she seems as if she wants to live! But only weighs around 99 pounds. Her hands look like a bird's. She wants to know about everything—so I told her funny stories about my party, that I had a suit made. "Oh, Pat, I hate to see you with them! You deserve so much better!" I loved her before I left.^{GG}

2/6/46

What does it matter if the months with you were few, the days of happiness so few they would hardly make a week? You made me happier than I had ever been before, so happy that more happiness might have been fatal. And now, reliving those moments with the precious instrument of memory, I recreate you, I recreate myself, and knowing I have attained such godly bliss, I am made finer, greater, humbled, prouder. A part of me will always live in that past, for better or for worse. A part of me will always worship you. (Alas, no. 4/27/50)

FEBRUARY 9, 1946

^GYesterday, I decided to buy a ticket for Natica, and give it to her for Valentine's day. We'll fly together on March 10.^{GG}

---

* Highsmith's first children's book is unfortunately not included in her literary estate.

FEBRUARY 11, 1946

 ^GNow is the time—God, when was it not the time?—in which I need understanding from N. She is not cool towards me, but shows no interest at all. Of course, I want her as much as ever. I give her the biggest presents I can—and only regret that they likely make her even more indifferent towards me.^{GG}

FEBRUARY 12, 1946

 ^GThe city is shut down. Worker's strike—towboat workers. No heat at home, etc. Restaurants and theaters are closed. At Rosalind's for lunch. Very pleasant. She obviously understood that I didn't want to see her friends (that evening). So, I had her the way I like—alone.^{GG}

FEBRUARY 14, 1946

 ^G1:45 A.M. Just spoke with N. She didn't mention the valentine. But I know she received it. What kind of a girl is she? I wonder what she thinks of the plane ticket? Neither of us wanted to mention it! What a situation!^{GG}

FEBRUARY 16, 1946

 ^GYesterday, she said, "I got your valentine. It's the sweetest thing I've ever seen," etc. Thank God she gave me so much! Will she come or not—? She will come. Went to see Marj. W. (at 9:15), one of my closest four friends: Rolf, [Ruth] Bernhard, Rosalind. How she soothes me when I am troubled! And even when I can tell her so little!^{GG}

FEBRUARY 27, 1946

 ^GHow lovely are days full of work. Lunch with S.W., who seems almost charming to me now. He has written a 244-page novel. The topic seemed somewhat nebulous to me, but perhaps it's only that I am not very interested in other people's work. I'm sorry for it, but I can't change it.^{GG}

MARCH 2, 1946
GCalled N. at 10:45 A.M. In bed. Asked about the article—"Yes, it's finished!" she shouted angrily. "And my skirt? Do you have it?" "You'll get it back! Today!" she shouted, and hung up. God, these impolite hang-ups are quite normal for her. Now I'm angry with her in earnest and am delighted that I will doubtlessly be in New Orleans alone.GG

MARCH 4, 1946
GAm planning my novel.* I have the plot. It's so simple I can hardly dare call it a plot. Am reading [Evelyn Waugh's] *Brideshead Revisited* with great pleasure. A serious novel written with humor. Waiting until tomorrow to call Natica.GG

MARCH 5, 1946
GVery happy as I was getting dressed to go see Joan [S.] We drank martinis in her room at the Barbizon† and played records. I wanted to embrace her and tell her of my troubles. She is so sweet and simple and honest. I invited her to come to New Orleans. "I'll have to think about it," she said. Until Thursday.GG

MARCH 9, 1946
GRelaxed—just after I told the news to [Richard E.] Hughes: that I'll write fewer comics from now on. "I've heard this so many times before I don't care," he answered. Joan called at four

---

* Pat begins her second attempt at a novel, *The Dove Descending*, a title she borrows from her favorite poet, T. S. Eliot. The manuscript, which she abandons after seventy-eight pages, follows a young orphan who travels to Mexico with her despotic aunt in search of a man they both secretly love, a sculptor as handsome as he is afflicted with alcoholism. Aunt and niece alike hope to save him and start a new life together, but he perishes in a storm off the coast of Acapulco.

† New York once had over a hundred residential hotels, but few were as glamorous as the Barbizon Hotel for Women on East Sixty-Third, named after the eponymous nineteenth century school of painters near Fontainebleau, France. It was geared toward a creative clientele, provided music rooms, a swimming pool, and free afternoon tea, and men were not allowed on the residential floors. Its famous onetime residents include Grace Kelly, Liza Minnelli, Sylvia Plath, and Nancy Reagan.

o'clock sharp—(what a delight to know a punctual girl!) and came at 6:30: martinis. I enjoyed introducing Joan to my mother. Of course, mother liked her a lot. When she'd left, mother said, "I like her more than any of the other girls you've gone out with."GG

3/11/46

One plus one is two's a measure
Just for arithmetic, not for pleasure.

3/12/46

New Orleans, the Vieux Carré—It is raining when we come out of Broussard's. It seems part of the fabulous scene, this rain that slides down gray cracked walls and makes the narrow streets glisten red and blue and yellow-orange with the reflections of neon bar signs. Coming out of the restaurant onto such a scene, one cannot speak for an instant—during which silence my escort says in sonorous monotone, "There's absolutely nothing to do. If it's raining—"

MARCH 16, 1946

GJoan's plane was two hours late! Naturally, I was as nervous as if I were waiting for a child to be born! Drank two cups of coffee, with cigarettes, and imagined how beautiful it would be to see the plane—small and delicate—emerge under the full moon against the clouds of the night sky.GG

MARCH 19, 1946

GA wonderful day. I love Joan more and more—she grows more and more beautiful—and it was a day which heralded the night. Took a boat trip down the Mississippi, sketching, laughing, and perhaps falling deeper in love. We didn't talk about it.GG

MARCH 22, 1946

GPerhaps I am lazy, but I feel like a king. There is nothing better in life than traveling the world with one's lover.GG

MARCH 26, 1946

ᴳLast night was the eleventh in a row that we have spent together. And Joan keeps saying, "God, how will I bear it tomorrow night when you're no longer here?" What sweet words to hear! Whether we can kiss one another at the airport—that was the problem!ᴳᴳ

APRIL 5, 1946

ᴳWe visited Cornell, who was in a somewhat better mood, but who is in grave danger. Four nurses. And her stomach, one said, is not even the size of an egg. If she gets a bad cough, she could die, the nurse said. "And it would be better if she could go quickly." God, how those words frighten me! It hadn't occurred to me that Allela might die. It's impossible.ᴳᴳ

APRIL 9, 1946

ᴳJoan's new feelings, which she tries to describe, are very precious to me. Almost every day she says, "Pat, I can't tell you how I feel—" Tonight, when we were in the kitchen, she said, "It's a shame you don't have a room I could sleep in while you work." It was the closest thing to saying that she'd like us to live together. I'd like that very much. We are so in love that one day without seeing one another is maddening—torture. God preserve it.ᴳᴳ

4/10/46

Painting is always so far ahead of writing. The images modern in literature are trite in painting. Goya foreshadowed Zola, Manet, Dos Passos, and de Chirico the loneliness and aloneness of Camus. What does Picasso foreshadow? Bombshells and bombast, masses without organization, a sterile anarchy of mind and heart.

APRIL 11, 1946

ᴳIt occurs to me that we will have difficulties if we are suddenly discovered. Her family's opinion, I think, could separate us like death itself! And the thought that something might separate us is unbearable to me. Tonight, we are both dreaming of tomorrow and the day after tomorrow.[GG]

APRIL 13, 1946

[G]This is heaven—working in my parents' house, sitting with them at the dinner table, and embracing Joan in my room! Tonight—my God, will we never sleep again? We see the sunrise every night![GG]

APRIL 14, 1946

[G]Dog tired at 7:15 A.M., when mother came into the bedroom with coffee and fruit juice. My—our—pajamas were in wild disarray, on the bed and the floor, and we were snuggled together in bed. "I don't mean to bother you, you look so cozy," mother said. "It got very hot last night," I remarked. "Yes, I bet," said mother.[GG]

4/21/46

A story about the tragedy of all my relationships with men (ships, and the *ineluctable* reef I strike!); the happy beginnings, the rapport of the likes & dislikes, the growing, glowing conversations, the good dinners he will (ominously) not let me pay for, the feeling of good will, power, brotherliness and Beethoven's "Ninth Symphony" (the negation of Rilke & Schopenhauer) and finally the impasse, the pass, made maudlin and tedious with liquor, until frustration, boredom makes one squirm in the car seat one has been in too long already. I am almost ready to cry with boredom, regret, the loss forever, the resurge of that deadly sense of impossibility! The tragedy of it!

4/23/46

Cities—none in the world—approaches New York, which is almost the site of the universal womb, or the simulacrum of the Wonderful Bed (physical comfort) from which the recluse, the cosmopolitan, the man of intellect, may stretch forth his hand to obtain whatever thing it be that he desires—food, art, or a character.

APRIL 24, 1946

We signed up for the sculpture class at the Jefferson School. $14.00 for two months. And visited Cornell. The meeting between Joan and Cornell touched me in a strange way. Joan was relaxed, laughing as usual, which made Cornell laugh too. I think A.C. likes her.^{GG}

APRIL 27, 1946

^GA month ago, how Joan feared N.—perhaps I did, too. But now, she is only what she is, a highly attractive, intelligent, dangerous woman. I can never feel towards Joan the way I feel towards her. And vice versa. There is a big difference, and this difference is entirely favorable to Joan.^{GG}

APRIL 28, 1946

^GWorked—and went to see Rolf Tietgens at 7. Every hour spent with him is like—a glimpse of the future? I don't know. I'm afraid to write down that I might have such a life with Joan. I'm afraid because I believe that I have no right, no power, to bind a person as free as her so tightly to me!^{GG}

MAY 10, 1946

^GIf someone were to ask me what the single most important thing in my life is right now, I'd answer, "Time to dream." It's only that relationships with others (Joan) bring to light so many of my inner foibles. Whether I should ignore the fact that Joan counts her pennies, has no cigarettes, doesn't bring enough money home—these are all trifles compared to her worthiness. But these things also disgust me! And I've been alone too long, alone for years. One can't change quickly, but I'm making great progress.^{GG}

5/10/46

Melancholy is directionlessness.

MAY 14, 1946

^GLong conversation (until 5!) with Joan about the circumstances of our love affair: firstly, that it doesn't "give her enough." It's too new, too unfamiliar for her, and I don't know whether she can endure it. Her strange, cruel philosophy (the philosophy of a butcher!) is that when something becomes too uncomfortable, too embarrassing, one must cut it off! So she might decide to cut me out of her life completely! It's dreadful! I want her—I need her, but I also need enough time for my work, which is my first great love. In this case, I am making great efforts and sacrifices to hold on to her!^GG

MAY 22, 1946

^GAlone after all—but only until 11 o'clock, when I went to see Joan at the Barbizon, dressed in Levis, which Joan liked a lot. "You look terrific (in Levis)!" she said, sounding like a schoolgirl with a new crush. But I like it a lot—her excitement! Of all the women I've known, only Joan completes me so perfectly! I need her as I've never needed anyone before.

Later—at 1:00 A.M.—I went to see Catherwood, where N. was, of course. They seemed very funny after J. Especially Ginnie, who made me laugh. Her stories! "Back to the point, Jeanie!," Natica screamed again and again. And Ginnie so polite and attentive, that one must like her despite oneself. They drove me home. "I want to see your room," Ginnie said. And we went upstairs. Very nice too, but didn't go to bed until 4:30 A.M.^GG

5/24/46

Let the artist surround himself with the bourgeois. (Thomas Mann was so right, this hankering for the bourgeois.) The artist is forever indelible, ineradicable in him. The artist needs all the bourgeois he can get.

6/1/46

To be alone is nearest that other heaven on earth, to love and be loved.

JUNE 7, 1946

ᴳJoan cried as we lay in bed, heavy and tired. "I'd like to die now!," J. whispered in tears. And I thought of a strange suspicion that I had two or three months ago: that one day—I don't know when—when we are in a small boat, on blue water, she will suddenly jump overboard without a word. Just because she's so happy.ᴳᴳ

JUNE 10, 1946

ᴳI am still occupied with various things, but my life is somehow heavy. And, strangely enough, I am getting tired of Joan.ᴳᴳ

JUNE 13, 1946

ᴳAt Virginia Catherwood's tonight with Joan and Natica. Ginnie was polite as always. I like her, if only because she's on a clear path. I don't think they like Joan very much. Joan is slow, calm, and not fun enough.ᴳᴳ

JUNE 14, 1946

ᴳIt hurts—that N. is so fake (towards Ginnie). "I don't like people like that," Ginnie said. "I like people like you."ᴳᴳ

JUNE 19, 1946

ᴳRead [Joseph] Conrad's "Youth." It warms the heart. He's a philosopher and poet, a true author! If only I could write with such gravity without employing quite so much blood and thunder! I have a stronger grip on my life than I've ever had before. The house is clean, everything is in order. I'm writing and making enough—just enough—money. I have friends, and—to top it off—a woman!ᴳᴳ

JUNE 20, 1946

ᴳDay of hellfire. Evening with Ginnie and Joan. A big salad, which nobody ate much of, and I was quite drunk, which always happens when I mix my own martinis and follow them with red wine, and soon it was midnight. Joan left. Ginnie pretended to leave but stayed—for about ten hours. The other person always has to make the first move for me. Then the kisses, wonderfully sweet, the embrace, dangerous, lovely, because one can feel the other body, the great pleasure and attraction that comes with something new. I've thought it over and realized that I can always reconcile such ugly deeds with my curiosity and "morality." And yet I'm quite ashamed of myself.[GG]

JUNE 25, 1946

[G]What do I feel? Sometimes I believe that I feel nothing. I love both of them in different ways. When I'm with Joan, I feel as though everything is all right. With Ginnie—it's only physical.[GG]

JUNE 27, 1946

[G]Could have spent tonight alone, but saw Ginnie. Last night, as I was falling asleep, J. said, "You don't seem to like sex all that much. You don't enjoy it." God, how can I deny it? Her body no longer entices me.[GG]

6/28/46

A sad aspect of one's growth—the gradual realization that the ways of the world are those even one's own mind and body are best fitted for. Orange marmalade, bitter in childhood, becomes the most palatable condiment at breakfast. Eight hours' sleep ensure the least concern with sleep—the morning hours prove themselves, despite our will, to be most profitable for production. Ideals wear away, and a mistress apart from home making wife becomes the most pleasant, salubrious, invigorating arrangement. The admission that one is no more different or idealistic than the next one is the beginning of mature wisdom.

(9/14/47 Alas, the above is false, from marmalade to mistress. And the higher wisdom always admits there is no higher than the spiritual. This paragraph was the threshold of a useless year.)

JUNE 29, 1946

^G[Joan] stayed at my place. After a week of Ginnie, I was almost dead of exhaustion. Couldn't fall asleep before 3:00. How sweet Joan is—she always helps me, is always kind and tender. I am the devil, unworthy and impossible.^{GG}

JUNE 30, 1946

^GWe both wanted to explain everything, Joan to end it all or at least understand it. It was hard. I didn't know what to say. One can't say that one is bored, that one wants to spend more time alone (to do what?). Finally, she walked down the street alone. And it was the saddest sight I've ever seen.^{GG}

7/1/46

The paramecia and I
Have this in common, that we ply
Our seas in search of friend or foe
Who'll kiss us once and let us go.
(Both of us but stipulate
That the kiss rejuvenate.)
What do we care if kisses please ya?
We are footloose paramecia!
We navigate by pseudopod
And give each passing form a nod,
Houseslipper-like steal up and thrill ya,
But linger on? What could be cilia!
(Both of us but stipulate
That the kiss rejuvenate.)
We figure, what's the use of fission
When a hump completes our mission?
Love is no saner or sweeter than this,
The unique first and final kiss.
(Both of us but stipulate
That the kiss rejuvenate.)
"Goodbye!" we shout, with mutual joy.
And skate on towards the next ahoy.

And who can say we are not clever?
Paramecia live forever.

JULY 9, 1946

^GThe story about the Texans is getting worse and worse. There's a mood that isn't right. I'll be happy when it's done! Today at 12:30 P.M. a visit from Natica, who said that Ginnie is still consistently drinking too much. About 12–15 drinks a day. She said Ginnie shakes in the morning before she has a drink. "G. is a sick woman," Natica said. "No one realizes it." I felt love for Natica. Sometimes she can be an angel, or at least a normal person who has all the virtues of a kind, understanding friend. And then all of a sudden, she's useless and horrible again!^{GG}

7/15/46

The sense of life is simply consciousness. There is no other thing. The rest is mere excitement.

JULY 18, 1946

^GG. drank a little every hour: watered-down Cutty Sark from a bottle of Listerine. Kissed her on a tree-lined path. God, I don't know why. Maybe I pity her. I wonder whether it will ruin everything with Joan. I think I need both of them.^{GG}

JULY 23, 1946

^GWhen Ginnie called me for the fortieth time to say goodbye, I said, "I'd like to see Boston." In half an hour, everything was set: at 4 o'clock I went with Ginnie to Boston, then to her house.^{GG}

JULY 25, 1946

[Kennebunkport, Maine.] ^GHow pleased G. and her mother are that someone is working in their house, making a living! God, it's hilarious! Her mother praises me to high heavens because I'm "forging my own path." Her children have nothing to do and do little. Ginnie is very proud of me. Every day, we love each other more.^{GG}

7/25/46

The constant need to retire into oneself—daily, if only for half an hour. It is only because reality bores one finally, becomes tragically, depressingly unsatisfying. To have thought of something fantastic in the midst of reality is not enough. It must be set down. And this is not vanity only. One fears that unless the nodes of growth are fixed, one will not grow higher in the next leap of growth.

JULY 26, 1946

^GSecond attempt on the opening of the book [*The Dove Descending*]. This one, I think, will work. I'm writing in a little room next to mine and Ginnie's. I write in the morning, before she wakes up, and at night between 11—12—1 o'clock. Ginnie needs nine hours of sleep.^{GG}

JULY 28, 1946

^GI am so happy now that life itself is a church, a religion. I ride the bike into Kennebunkport and come back to take a bath and write, and when Ginnie wakes up, I drink a cup of coffee with her. We collect snails and rocks at the beach and compare them to our geological books from the library. In short, we are living like kings.^{GG}

AUGUST 2, 1946

^GJoan came by yesterday evening. "Did you go to Maine with Ginnie?" she asked, looking straight into my eyes. "No, Ginnie took the car." Easy response. No, she doesn't suspect anything, I think. But if she did know that I love another woman—I can say "love," because that's how I feel—then everything would be over. It will have to happen, but I can't bear it.^{GG}

8/3/46

At the moment all things in the world are a delight to me—exhilarating to the senses, making the brain so happily drunk that it cannot form phrases. Not that I care now, about anything but loving. I wish only I could imprison this happiness forever in a dozen words, or a half dozen, or one which I might have to invent myself.

8/6/46

Homosexuals: their sexual emotion is their sorest, most vulnerable spot. The least difficulty—and they translate it into insecurity, Weltschmerz, inferiority, congenital bad luck—each of which may be devastating to their own personalities. Thus by yielding until they appear weak, whether they are or not, they defeat their main sexual purpose—to have and to hold. Since a partner, a potential partner, is not attracted by uncertainty or self-pity. Whatever their strength, they never can be strong.

AUGUST 7, 1946

ᴳVery peaceful, very happy. Am writing in the morning and evenings, working in the afternoons. But Joan S. came by unexpectedly at 7 o'clock. She was very cheerful at first and said that she had a lot to tell me. She said she was working "on her own initiative" to make money for the trip, and I finally had to confess that I didn't want to go away with her in the fall. It hurt, of course. And she cried.

This year, I have found a means of making a living. I am thoroughly changed, and why is it unlikely that my love should change too? Yes, these pages should be framed in gold. Have never been so happy. I am playing—playing—for days on end, playing what I want! Playing piano, writing, reading, thinking! I live, and God willing, I love!ᴳᴳ

8/7/46

Love: strangely enough, it's always you who say goodbye to the ones you love the most.

8/11/46

Man has no more soul than a garden snail. The point is, the garden snail has a soul, too.

8/15/46

To be strong and soft at the same time is the wisdom of saints.

AUGUST 16, 1946

^GYesterday evening when G. called—I began writing a new story: "The Man Who Got Off the Earth." I'm glad to have an escape, but for me it isn't an escape, it's a boon, a blessing. There is no other time in which I feel so alive. I'd like to tell [Ginnie] that if she doesn't start to drink less, I'll leave her. Yes, I'll tell her soon.^{GG}

AUGUST 31, 1946

^GIt takes a long time to describe Ginnie. She is so gentle, so soft, so sweet—and my God, how she loves me! "You have everything—you are everything I love," she always says. "And I am nothing."^{GG}

9/1/46

The gray, sooty white curtains at the window, looped around the heavier drape, the ends waving now and again, in the breeze. This is the color for ghosts. Gray, lived in, organic, not white. Soiled and unwashable.

SEPTEMBER 3, 1946

^GAt 5:45 P.M. news from Margot J. that I sold "Doorbell for Louisa"* to *Woman's Home Companion* for $800. M. excited, me too. God, news like this does wonders for my confidence.^{GG}

9/4/46

The tragic desperation the first drink represents—not the social drink but the one taken at three in the afternoon. For one seeks

---

* "Doorbell for Louisa," about a middle-aged woman whose job is her whole life, is not a story of frustration and disillusionment, but instead ends with the protagonist's employer inviting her to the Plaza Hotel. The story—according to Pat's records—appeared in *Woman's Home Companion* in 1948. It was also published in *Nothing That Meets the Eye: The Uncollected Stories of Patricia Highsmith* (New York, 2002).

peace of mind, and this drink is not the first resort, but the last. There is before it all the long chain of effort for silence, tranquility, love, faith that has somehow failed.

SEPTEMBER 6, 1946

[G]Went to see Cornell, who will die very soon, it seems. God, a new face full of fear, which had never been there before. Ginnie almost fainted before we said goodbye. Tonight I cried—I said she was two people. I'm jealous of the bottle. So, without saying it, I made it clear—it's the bottle or me. What does she want?[GG]

SEPTEMBER 15, 1946

[G]At 9:15 P.M. J. called. She said: "You love her more than me, don't you?" And I had to explain in words alone that I had stronger physical feelings for G. I knew that J. was crying, and before she hung up, someone knocked on her door.[GG]

SEPTEMBER 16, 1946

[G]At 6:30 P.M. Ann T. arrived, and later Ginnie. martinis. At 7 o'clock, a call from Sheila: "What does Joan S. mean to you?" "I can't answer that easily—" "She's at Payne Whitney hospital. I think she may have tried to kill herself."[GG]

SEPTEMBER 17, 1946

[G]Went to see Joan. Didn't know what to expect. She's unhurt except for a few small razor cuts on her right wrist. (Audrey said there was blood on a pair of pajamas in a corner of Joan's room.) Brought her white flowers. She asked me again if I wanted to leave. "I don't know why they're keeping me prisoner here. I haven't done anything." She was very nervous, downcast, thin. Later I discovered that I only got to see Joan by accident. The doctor doesn't want me to write nor visit her.[GG]

SEPTEMBER 18, 1946

[G]Every night I eat and sleep at Ginnie's. Went to Garden City to have lunch with Joan's mother. "Joan is in love with you, I don't know whether you know. That's what she told the doctor," Mrs. S. said. "Do you have influence over her?" she asked me. Once I almost had to cry. Everything was so hopeless. "Joan would like for you two to remain friends. But I'm afraid that won't be possible."[GG]

SEPTEMBER 22, 1946

[G]I don't look back. I'm working on the book, getting up every day at 8:15. And getting letters from publishers who want to publish my "novel."[GG]

SEPTEMBER 28, 1946

[G]Collecting snails. Have eleven (now).[GG]

OCTOBER 3, 1946

[G]Walked to Ginnie's. She spent the whole day with Natica. Terribly drunk. And when we were lying in bed, she told me that she had something to say to me—I knew: she had gone to bed with N. And I was right. "Only because she was nervous," Ginnie explained. Yes, I understand: there are no clear boundaries with Ginnie. It hurts. I cried a little. I didn't want to touch her.[GG]

OCTOBER 4, 1946

[G]Alone. Spent the night alone, thank God. Worked hard and was very tired at eleven. And at eleven o'clock, Allela died. These words—I am so sad. Could I have imagined such words three years ago? My dearest friend, what a hole you will leave behind. I cried for a few minutes, drank some Schnapps—and worked. I didn't know that this feeling of loss would only grow stronger later.[GG]

OCTOBER 6, 1946

[G]Sick, sad when going to bed. And it seemed as if Allela gently stepped into the room, smiling, in a white dress, and spread her arms—to show me that she was no longer suffering.[GG]

10/6/46

The farmer and the poet, providers of our physical and spiritual nourishment, are the least rewarded members of our society. At times it seems writing has only an amusement value. So be it, good enough. Then one is brought, by the death of a friend, at a funeral service, to the realization that these phrases of God's provision and refuge are not for rare occasions, as we hear them, but for all times and places.

10/6/46

Man has two enemies against which there is no weapon, from which there is no recourse: death and the bottle. Nothing, no person I have ever known has roused my jealousy except these immortal and mortal enemies. Yes, I am jealous of death, he takes my friends from me. I am jealous of alcohol, it takes my loves.

OCTOBER 13, 1946

GEvery night harder because I remember everything about AC. I have to reread all her letters. I must know what went wrong (with us), I must discover all I can. She threw out most of my letters. There are only the early ones, those from Mexico. I have about 25 from her.

Alone tonight.GG

10/14/46

What a void you leave, nothingness desiring nothingness. Having read all your letters I had strength for tonight, comparing them with my diary of the same dates, I see the impossibility then. We thought ourselves older and wiser than we were. We were not wise enough to cast off desires—and desire to you and me was always work, time, aloneness, the proper conditions for thinking and dreaming. Oh God, were any two people ever so alike! We clung to privacy and the cantankerous stove of art, that warmed us well when it chose to light. And I accused you of not loving enough, of loving yourself and your work more. And

you accused me of nothing, though these were my own failings I
flung in your face. And it was I who was least worthy. And I was
jealous of everything, stupidly jealous, being not great enough
to understand that you could love many, and that those you had
loved you always loved. What pained me tonight was to read
"There is so much time really, Pat—"

OCTOBER 20, 1946
ᴳI can't remember clearly. Only that I am working on my
book, making no money, and spending almost every night
with Ginnie.ᴳᴳ

10/23/46
Alone, one can feel as much after a glass and a half of wine as
two martinis with friends. And one can see much more.

OCTOBER 25, 1946
ᴳThis afternoon, J. called, and I told her what the doctor had
insisted, that my feelings towards her had changed. Joan was
somewhat disappointed, I think. Yes, I wrote her too many letters in which I hoped for something, promised her something.
Now I fear her sentiments, and perhaps even more the weakness
of my passion.ᴳᴳ

OCTOBER 26, 1946
ᴳIt's hard to say how I feel about Joan. I love her—she's very
attractive and physically desirable, just not like Ginnie. But Joan
is "better" for me. With her, I feel healthy, alive, honest, strong.
But it's not enough—I know that.ᴳᴳ

NOVEMBER 2, 1946
ᴳ[Her] Dr. warned me that Joan was "still the same girl," that I
had to make a decision (soon). Joan is dreamy, and wants only
to look at me and kiss me. Yes, I had to kiss her to discover how
things were. And they were the same as ever, just as exciting.
And then. "I love you so, Pat"—I brought her back at 10.

Suddenly alone, half drunk, more surprised, I walked home slowly.^{GG}

NOVEMBER 4, 1946

^GOh—something interesting: saw Rolf for dinner last week, and we discussed the possibility of getting married. I have no strong reason for doing so, but he would receive citizenship and be able to bring his mother over. (They have no shoes in Germany, for example!) And sometimes, I do want to have a child. But Ginnie said that I have no right to create a life if I don't want to feed it. Rolf and I are very shy together and laugh.^{GG}

11/4/46

I can never be moderate in anything—not sleeping, eating, working, loving. Who realizes this understands me (who wants to?) but still does not predict me.

11/4/46

In the midst of working, the thought of having to earn money, more money, arises—incongruous with life and love, paralyzing. One must not think of it. There is the steady and untarnished, untarnishable goal of what one should do.

11/5/46

To J.S. *that broke the crooked glass within myself.*
Earth has no flower finer than your love,
Which is but you yourself.
These lines I write in tears, before tomorrow
Brings me to you for the last time, our last goodbye.

11/5/46

When I visited Mrs. C. a month after A's [Allela's] death, she said she often felt A. "has just packed up and gone off on a trip to California. Then I have to wake up suddenly with a jolt. But so often I packed up her things for her after she'd gone . . ." Up until the coma, the last two days, A. thought that she would get well. And for ten days the doctors entered her room, came out marveling, shaking their heads, not knowing what kept her alive. "I want you to pose for me, and I'll never have to look for a model again," A. told one of the doctors two weeks before she died. "I'm going to be out of here in a month or so." When the doctor told her mother, he put his face in his hands and said, "I want to cry, Mrs. C."

11/5/46

The room with V.C. [Ginnie] and Virginia S. inside it. There is no whimsy here, neither is there reality. With a dazed and exhausted and tensely earnest expression, V.S. faces the mechanics of living, the lifting, smoothing, and setting down, V.C. prances about as though replacing a pair of worn pajamas in a closet were the most important function of her day.

Is the air too thin up there? For they have learned nothing, are able to do nothing. They have never heard of Virginia Woolf (I discovered when I told V.S. she resembled her). Nor have they read *Moby Dick*. Proudly they say their children will be financially independent, not realizing they will tie their hands, and worse tie their brains, and model them after their own empty selves.

V.C., I cannot tell you how sweet you are, and how inadequate. There are feelings which know more than the brain, are wiser than the intellect. All that lives really seeks the rightness.

NOVEMBER 6, 1946

"Visited Joan's doctor, who counseled me to break everything off or ensure Joan's happiness for the next five years. I have decided that we must part. So tomorrow I will go on this sad errand. Suddenly, everything seems pointless, sad, unreal, faded. Cornell, the difficult work on the novel, trouble with Ginnie—nothing serious, only nerves—Joan's unhappiness, the pain I've caused her—and now, breaking up with Joan for no reason. There comes a time when one must grasp one's love like a stick and break it.GG

NOVEMBER 7, 1946

^{G}Saw Joan—at two o'clock. Everything is unfair. But—I told her. We stood in someone's room, embracing; kissing, kissing for the last time, and it didn't matter that someone was looking at us from across the courtyard. "I hope I can bear it, Pat—I love you so much!" She didn't understand at first, and I had to explain to her that we can't phone or write letters. We were both crying when we parted. God, why? Why?! The only girl you've given me! Why? I want answers. And will go see a psychiatrist soon.^{GG}

NOVEMBER 8, 1946

^{G}The saddest of days. Brought the "Chas. Samuel" mug to Joan at two. Didn't see her, of course. I put a card in the mug thanking her for everything, that she is sealed within me so that I will never lose her. At 3:30 heard from Margot J. that I'd sold "World's Champion Ball Bouncer"* to *Companion* for $800. I had to tell Joan about it in my last letter, as well as how happy I was with her when I wrote that story.^{GG}

NOVEMBER 9, 1946

^{G}Went to Rolf's last night for his birthday. Excellent dinner, apartment very festive. Rolf cares for me very much, I think, because he went for a walk with me (later) to Ginnie's and spoke very quickly. "If you marry me, I won't permit such things," he said. And I feel hesitant: I want my freedom. I was awfully tired, but made love to Ginnie—God, sometimes I think that even if I were on death's door, I'd have to live just one more hour for her. Visited Rosalind and received Lola C. who came by at 5 o'clock. Briefly discussed some of the problems on my mind:

   1) I have wanted to torture myself for twelve years now.

---

* "The World's Champion Ball Bouncer" tells the story of a young Southern family that goes to New York in search of fame and fortune, but whose expectations are checked by a sobering first day in the city. The story is published in the April 1947 issue of *Woman's Home Companion.*

2) I don't want someone once I have her.
She'll make an appointment with a psychiatrist for me.*GG

NOVEMBER 11, 1946
GI'm half sick with the dreariness of the world, with the sadness, the deep sadness in myself. When I am alone (in the evenings, at night) I am strong. But after two martinis, at midnight, I'm a crying fool.GG

11/11/46
Pain sends one wandering into the dusk, the dusk of New York. It is all at once all sadness, all beauty, the soft blue gray of the air (and the gray will win), the yellow white red green lights that hang on the blue grayness like ornaments upon a Christmas tree. For it is near Christmas. Christmas, and the one we love! But she will not be with us. She has never been with us for Christmas and will never be. She is gone, she is dead, and all you have of her are the memories bound up in yourself that you carry on and on through the dusk. All at once this terrible sadness, inarticulate in the terrible beauty of dusk! Sadness so strange and beautiful and perfectly pure itself, it almost produces a kind of happiness. Where shall I not wander in the years to come? Through so many more dusks, beloved!

NOVEMBER 15, 1946
GNow I have two new holes with snail eggs! And thirty-three snails! Gave Ginnie 7. And [Babs] B. wants a pair! The striped African ones.GG

NOVEMBER 16, 1946
GAsked Ms. S. what she thought of me. Sturtevant: "I think you're pretty good." And she praised me, because I have been forcing myself to write for an hour a day for years. And

* Pat will try psychoanalysis briefly for the first time in March 1947, then again for longer from November 1948 onward.

that I don't need a psychiatrist, that I'm just an artist. She's right. W. S. Maugham said the same: an artist, a poet can never really fall in love, and women are quick to notice.^{GG}

DECEMBER 3, 1946

^GAn evening spent reading with Ginnie. Naturally, we had a long, delicious dinner, so we didn't begin our reading until 9:30. The snails are (almost) our greatest delight. From morning to night, we watch Bouncer and Mike, who can usually be found on the leaves of the plant. The little ones eat all day and grow, and we could spend all evening watching them.^{GG}

12/6/46

Dissatisfied with my day's work. Though actually eight pages typewritten, first draft material, is not bad production. And it reads well enough. What is it, underlying all, that creates dissatisfaction? The young person's fear that he is (basically) not on the right track, his own track, that all may have to be scrapped, the way retraced. Added to this as yet unsolvable problem (only time, age, will solve it) is the growing dissatisfaction, like the misery of a lover who has not satisfied his mistress, that inconsolable misery. My mistress, art, I love thee.

DECEMBER 7, 1946

^GSomething strange: I feel so little physical attraction for Ginnie, but great tenderness. And this troubles me.^{GG}

12/7/46

The Railroad Trip—the rhythmically swaying diner, the Romanesque women with fascinating though already crows-feet-marked eyes. Lesbians? Lesbians? The balding, pinched and wrinkled though well-fed men who enter, scouting places to sit. Journalists, newspapermen, writers of short stories of the *Saturday Evening Post* variety, hard bitten with the passion (whiskey and soda and cigarettes) of their craft.

12/8/46

10:30 A.M. in the artist's chambers. He sips at a half cup of tepid coffee, bites at a triangle of toast and marmalade, his second breakfast, brought up after the first. He stands on one leg, the foot of the other turned almost at right angles, to the one and catching a glimpse of his face in the mirror, he sees an expression he thinks first is of apprehension, sees finally is only the alertness of composition, imagination, self-abandonment, the very opposite of apprehension so far as personal danger is concerned. (If a lion should enter the room, he might stroke it, like St. Jerome. If an intruder knocks, however, it is another matter.) The air within the cube of his room is motionless and silent, a trifle smoky, almost stale, but he likes it: it is the increase of himself.

And why record these precious sentiments? Precisely because the artist of these times is so divorced from the people whom he creates from, who take a vain pride in not understanding, as though there were any thing to understand, only what they have forgotten since the age of five, plus a discipline a hundred times their own. So stood Mozart, Shakespeare, Henry James, Picasso, Thomas Mann. So will stand artists to the end of time alone in their rooms at 10:30 in the morning.

12/18/46

Sometimes writing is like being seen crying at a friend's funeral.

12/19/46

The rat-race: whether the speed of one's creative development (and production) can match the speed with which one's money and energy must be poured out into New York.

DECEMBER 23, 1946

ᴳGinnie didn't buy any presents at all this morning. Everything in the afternoon over the phone. How will she get in the Christmas spirit?ᴳᴳ

DECEMBER 24, 1946

^GBusy. It takes so much time to write a story! Four or five weeks, unless it's a "Doorbell for Louisa." Waited for Ginnie, really, from 2–4, while getting ready for Hastings.* Typical of her not to show in the end. I had to drink several brandies and told her that unless her behavior improved next year, I couldn't continue to love her.^GG

DECEMBER 25, 1946

^GFinally, I've grown up: Christmas is too much trouble for me. Mother is helping me wonderfully with my new story. She is truly my best critic.^GG

DECEMBER 26, 1946

^GI would like to reread the affair between myself, Joan and Ginnie again. I haven't done so yet, not a single page. I'm somewhat afraid to. And I would also like to write how my love has grown and changed. Now, as I said, I feel as though I'm married. And yet I haven't the slightest desire to physically enjoy her. But in fact, these past two weeks have been the best so far! These gentle feelings are extremely necessary as I grow to know her better and learn that I truly love her. Tonight, when I came to her, it was as though a veil separating us had been lifted: I felt her lips as never before and could barely control myself in bed. I love her madly.^GG

12/27/46

The Essence of manliness is gentleness; of womanliness, courage.

DECEMBER 31, 1946

^GGinnie and I never declare our love as vehemently as when we say goodbye to each other. At 3:00 P.M., when she left, we promised to think of one another, and kiss each other at midnight in our thoughts. I love her very much.^GG

---

* Hastings-on-Hudson, a suburb of New York where Pat's parents had lived since late 1945.

1947

Drafting *Strangers on a Train,* or: "One does not live forever, and one is young even a much shorter time."

🕊

PATRICIA HIGHSMITH reads voraciously this year and dives head-long into social life, her calendar so full she can no longer keep up with double-entry bookkeeping. Many of her diary entries, still primarily written in clumsy German, are recorded after the fact. There are times she can't even remember what she did the day before.

Virginia (Ginnie) Kent Catherwood serves as both the gas pedal and the brakes for this life in the fast lane. Pat continues to throw herself into the relationship, despite Ginnie's severe alcoholism and inexorable decline. She provides loving care after each of Ginnie's benders and subsequent emotional breakdowns, but the relationship peaks, and, just as Pat was always forced to share Ginnie, she now embarks on affairs of her own.

Pat's days are never long enough, and she even feels her creative development is lagging. The comic book contracts—which she aptly describes in her faulty German as "*Lebensmittel,*" which translates literally as the "means of living," but is actually the word for "groceries"—soon fall away entirely. Of the short stories she writes this year, only "The Still Point of the Turning World" sells, and the buyer isn't one of the literary magazines Pat would prefer.

When Pat finally begins drafting *Strangers on a Train,* her literary agent Margot Johnson offers the unfinished manuscript to Dodd, Mead & Co. The publisher enthusiastically accepts the book, but wants to pare down the text and pay Pat less than requested, citing the challenges facing the publishing industry after the war. On the second-to-last day of 1947, Pat completes the key scene of her novel.

JANUARY 1, 1947

^GPhoned Ginnie while I was drinking my first martini. And prepared something to eat at home. Ginnie in her gray trousers, the ones with the two green stripes, very happy, confident, looking comfortable as she walked about in the room talking about the big Dupont party. We called Rosalind, were invited over, and went by at 11. I was reminded of the evening when I brought Joan S. to her. I was drunk then too, and very excited for R. to meet my lover. Childish nonsense.^{GG}

JANUARY 2, 1947

^GPrepared a huge dinner for Chloe and Ginnie—a beefsteak from Gristedes—but Chloe didn't show. Ginnie and I quite content alone together. Jo P. and her friend Ellen Hill,* who ate half of my grandmother's fruitcake. Pigs! I like introducing Ginnie to my friends. Not for my sake, but for hers.^{GG}

JANUARY 6, 1947

^GStrange how it (alcohol) slowly creeps into the brain. Also nervous and troubled because I haven't had a quiet evening in a whole week! I have something like a hangover every morning. And though I'm losing sleep, I feel so much better when I've made love! Then I have the strength of angels!^{GG}

---

* Pat's first encounter with her future lover Ellen Hill.

JANUARY 8, 1947

GReading Kierkegaard. And Hannah Arendt on Existentialism. She suits my personality, I think. Want to study more Kierkegaard.GG

JANUARY 12, 1947

GYesterday, I sent flowers (white) to the Cornells because it was Allela's birthday, with a card that said: "Sincerely, Pat."

Very excited these days, but I am so in love with Ginnie. I truly love her. What does love need? Time to get to know each other. Now I feel very lonely when I spend a night home alone! This means I probably lose three hours (of time or sleep, and thus work and thought) every day. But she's worth it.

I revised the story, began to type it up. A walk at 7, visited R. for a few minutes. I like to pop in on her, chat with her briefly, discuss a story. R. is like a man, at least more of one than Ginnie!! But when I returned, she was worried; forty minutes! And she'd almost finished cooking dinner! What a dove. Ginnie my love is a dove!

Rosalind said that "Never Seek to Tell Thy Love" is an excellent story, that my writing has suddenly improved. I'm very happy about this, because I've been doubting myself with Ginnie. I thought it went better with Joan.GG

JANUARY 13, 1947

GGot up early and worked hard all morning. Days at Ginnie's are like an enchanted life in heaven, or a castle. The world cannot intrude, and the walls are thick.GG

JANUARY 19, 1947

GGinnie was the first one here tonight at 7:30, with flowers. For the first two hours, she kept telling me which guests seemed lonely. Sheila and Audrey, Jo P., Ellen H., Tex, Jan, Mel, Maria and Annette (who I finally kissed without much enthusiasm), Ann K., and Kirk and Rosalind (I was very happy to see them together. Thought they had reconciled, because they kissed

for a very long time in the bathroom, but apparently not) and
B.B. The house was very clean, with lots to eat, olives, cheese,
potato chips, shallots. I only had three drinks all evening. And
because I was surprised by Ginnie (kissing Sheila, etc.), I first
kissed Audrey (very sweet!) and Annette, who was very curious, which I enjoyed learning. Ginnie and everyone else amused
themselves greatly, I think. And I made a huge roast. Rosalind
was very sick after two of Ginnie's Cutty Sarks. (Ginnie kept
losing her drinks.)[GG]

JANUARY 23, 1947

[G]Rushing, rushing, Ginnie left at 2:35 P.M. So nervous I had to
have a Cutty Sark. Quick lunch at Le Valois which we couldn't
eat. At the station, Louise was waiting for us with the luggage.
Ginnie had a compartment, and we kissed as though we might
never see each other again! I gave her a letter, and that was it.
God, her sweet, serious face through the window as the train
was leaving. From Newark to Margot J. where I learned that
Companion rejected the N.O. [New Orleans] story. M.J. sent
it to *Good Housekeeping*. Rolf Tietgens for dinner, a surprise,
very pleasant. I told him without reservation how much I love
Ginnie. Now he knows that marriage is out of the question.[GG]

1/27/47

In cynicism, in constructive criticism, in a more vigorous
ignoring—how is the sterility of this age to be treated? The
prophet may become a poet, but none will follow. Jesus would
be crushed in the press of humanity, on Forty-Second Street,
any New Year's Eve in the Forties. This is the age of uncertainty, of the artist who vacillates between the devotion to art
and the desire for money, well upholstered furniture, the Dunhill lighter. He vacillates in his heart, though he determinedly
writes for the *New Masses* and the *Partisan Review*. It is
betrayed in his hectic, hit-or-miss style, hitting the one time in
ten, stimulated by benzedrine, brandy, cigarettes, by his own
exacerbated nerves on the eleventh floor of the hotel in the east

fifties, where he tries to write, out of which he will eventually jump.

JANUARY 27, 1947

ᴳThese days, which I am describing so fleetingly—were never more happy, more secure. My writing is so much better, my love is so much stronger; I see everything in the world with much greater passion, and owe this to Ginnie.ᴳᴳ

JANUARY 28, 1947

ᴳReady to work and suddenly mother came over—11—1:30, so I couldn't get anything done today. And I was feeling so creative! To annoy me further, she complained that I was impolite, etc. Had to have a drink. And then we both felt better. For the first time ever, I have no holes in my teeth. I am entering, the doctor said, a time in my life in which my teeth will not rot. Thank God!ᴳᴳ

JANUARY 29, 1947

ᴳWorked. Began to write "Flow Gently, Mrs. Afton."* I already feel rushed, so I won't find any leisure. Am trying to see many people while Ginnie is not in town. And who did I see? Can't remember. Am reading Dostoyevsky. He helps me a great deal— with his exclamation marks, his confusions! He makes me say what I want.ᴳᴳ

1/30/47

A probably healthy tendency in myself: to prefer reading science to fiction when writing a rather unusual story. And this increases, the more unusual the story is, and I take delight in observing plants and animals, the fat curve of a female goldfish's

---

* Like many of Pat's stories, "Mrs. Afton, Among Thy Green Braes," in which a Southern sophisticate hoodwinks her male psychiatrist, is only published in *Ellery Queen's Mystery Magazine* in the 1960s after she has already become a world-famous novelist. It later also appeared in her short story collection *The Snail-Watcher and Other Stories* (New York, 1970).

belly, for instance, her delicate armor gleaming like precious and hardly earthly metal, enclosing the little receptacle of her eggs, the most precious things in the world to her. When I feel like this, then I know the tempo of my life is adjusted to my own inner and constant tempo, and I am willy-nilly, regardless of anything else, happy.

JANUARY 31, 1947

 GCocktails with Margot J. When I talk to her, I feel as though I can make a living on fiction. Ginnie calls me every day. And I told the family all about my New York "social life." And I think they are quite jealous. It doesn't please me to write down this secret. And something else: I feel contempt for Stanley for not making more money. This contempt is quite separate from my true respect and love: but I know it is there. Wrote the ending to my story about Ms. Afton. Even after mother complained about me, she listened carefully to my story. And she gave me good advice. "Your writing is improving marvelously," she said, "but despite your life, not because of it."GG

1/31/47

A writer should not think himself a different kind of person from any other, since this is the way to the promontory. He has developed a certain part of himself which is contained in every man: the seeing, the setting down. Only in the realization of this humble and heroic fact can he become what he must be, a medium, a pane of glass between God on the one side and man on the other.

FEBRUARY 6, 1947

 GWork. Got up early to go to White Plains. Everything was easy. Now I am legally Mary Patricia Highsmith, and somehow feel stronger for it! Mother took me out to lunch. Discussed things I perhaps shouldn't have—the situation between us, the fact that she hasn't given me back my hundred. "She wants to keep you under her thumb," Rolf said, who thinks I'm in a dangerous

spot. Dreadful to think mother may not be a friend after all!
And hard to believe. But I know that they would be happy if I
had to live with them, that is, if I were unfortunate enough to
run out of money.^{GG}

FEBRUARY 12, 1947

^GLast night a visit from Jean C., who wanted to try out the
typewriter; she's starting a job with a typewriter soon. Did lots
of things around the house. How I enjoy having a woman in
the house! How happy and satisfied I am! And she looked at
me often: so serious and devoted and wanting me so much! A
(small) surprise around midnight, after we had leafed through
some art books. "What would you do if I kissed you?" And
I pulled her towards me. It was very sweet. And I feel a bit
guilty.^{GG}

FEBRUARY 18, 1947

^GWent with Jean C. to the movies to see *Well Digger's Daughter*
after dinner. She provides me with a kind of reality I find very
attractive. I have something quite different with Jean than I do
with Ginnie. Jean told me the story of her life during the war.
An unpleasant phone call with Ginnie, who was quite drunk,
and told me how different we were because she preferred lighter
fare and that I disdained her because she was not "intellectual"
enough. After 45 minutes I was so disgusted—though I know
that I encouraged the feeling so that it would seem quite right for
J.C. to spend the night.^{GG}

2/19/47

Your mistake that you did not ring my bell tonight at one fifteen in the morning. Years will come, but not these hours
again. Your mistake, I say. My mistake, you are saying in your
own apartment, for I was invited by you also. So tonight we lie
apart, whereas together we should have postponed the eight
hours or so [of] that terrible aloneness that surrounds and sat-
urates us beyond the saturating power of our own milieux:

For those who wish to be artists, for those artists who wish to contribute, saturation is necessary, be it good or evil, saturation from an environment. But the *faiblesse* of mind and spirit would ever seek to postpone this horror: a saturation with New York in 1947 is horror indeed.

The clock ticks, taxis draw up and slam their doors, footsteps sound in the courtyard, but they are not yours. Farewell, farewell! But I am denied even the beauty of watching you vanish upon a horizon. And because there is no horizon for your advent either, because your ring would startle me like a pistol shot, I never quite give up the possibility of your coming. Until at last, suffused with a beauty of my own creation, I decide that you give me as much away from me as with me. I settle myself in the last trench of the intellectual slave, a muddy, dark and unhealthily dampish trench. Here grows ringworm and eczema, body lice and cancer, here have human lips never felt a kiss.

2/22/47

A thought-conversation with Marjorie W. tonight. That there is no tragedy only pathos, in this age, because we have no fixed principles, as did the Greeks. Oedipus so knew he should be punished, he punished himself without hesitation. We have laws. Nothing in crime startles us. And even pathos can be questioned, is the recipient worthy? The closest to the Greek system of morals is the individual's private code. A subtle outrage to inner decency can produce Grecian reaction.

FEBRUARY 24, 1947

^GI went to Rosalind's tonight to give her my story. Later I went to Jean C.'s and, finally, I stayed for the night. I don't like this at all, I love Ginnie, but I do it (did it, and won't do it again) because I must see for myself how I feel after. I don't feel guilty, and strangely enough I am not sad that the affair with Ginnie is no longer as pure as it once was.^{GG}

FEBRUARY 25, 1947

^GAm writing Real Life Synopses for Standard.* At Angelica's at 7:30. Remarks made about Jean C. and me. It's not worth it to me, that is to say, Jean C. doesn't mean enough to me. So I decided I shouldn't see her anymore.^{GG}

MARCH 1, 1947

^GAm working on the story "The End Is Not in Sight." Mother read it by the fire yesterday—without stopping, which is a good sign. "It's interesting," she said. And later: "Do you think you'll always write about such strange situations?" I assured her that yes, this has been my path for the past two years.^{GG}

3/6/47

A momentous year of my life, this twenty-seventh, I know it. (Isn't every year more momentous after the crucial one of twenty-five? Until the greatest one of thirty—in suffering, not necessarily in action.) A greater happiness is mine, a greater ability to feel, and with it for the first time a greater concern with the problem of earning my living. The climax approaches. I see these two lives like those of a slowly narrowing V—the destiny line, with all the joys of creativity and its certainty, the line of the world, the Pandora misery of money, its earning, its keeping, its spending.

3/8/47

It is endurance that counts, in making love, in the writing of a story or a novel. Every theme must be made love to. This is the great secret of the universe!

MARCH 14, 1947

^GGave the Rollo story to M. [Margot] Johnson. "Why don't you go write a story for me that I can be sure to sell?" Was very sad

---

* One of the comic book publishers the Sangor Shop provides with artwork.

coming back, felt out of touch. The New Orleans story, which always reminds me of Joan S.—I have to make it better. Went to bed very late, with Dostoyevsky on my mind.[GG]

MARCH 16, 1947

[G]Breakfast in a diner close by (our cheapest restaurant) and a long discussion about the wealthy, about Jews and their customs with respect to current social mores. B. [Babs] B. is annoyed and angered by the rich. I am not. Or perhaps I simply do not admit it? I am happy—quite proud—that I have so many Jewish friends. It means that my affection for them has nothing fake about it.[GG]

3/17/47

At twenty-six, I still am not sure of the ingredients for happiness. Nearly ten years ago I realized that one goes to understanding "as an iron filing to a magnet." Now, to confuse one, there is the realization that different people understand one differently, and which is the true understanding? The truest? One is drawn both to the charitable and the brutally honest. Worse, one cannot decide between two loving people who are brutally honest in different ways. And what is the longing for an understanding? Not primarily for leniency, but for a perfection of self. There is that consolation. But there is no—no—no—decision, when the unreasonable heart refuses (unreasonably or reasonably?) to decide.

MARCH 19, 1947

[G]How nice (right now) it is to work for someone else! One sits at the typewriter without having to endure the torture of the damned! [Ernst] Hauser dictated an article about Europe's "Iron Curtain" to me in groups of three words. Against the U.S.S.R. of course, how Europe wants a planned economy and not democracy. We ate lots of chocolate, tea, etc. and finished at 3.[GG]

MARCH 20, 1947

^GMore work with Hauser. Working very hard at night too to finish the New Orleans story before Ginnie's return. And I am exhausted. Only three, four hours sleep. But as always, I enjoy the rush. I need it.^{GG}

MARCH 25, 1947

^GLots of little things. Today Ginnie was supposed to arrive—but she put it off again! After I almost killed myself with work! I was cursing her today!^{GG}

3/25/47

Love is a gentle, fluid, silvery thing, like the spring rain tonight, that makes a fantasia of my head, my room, my environs, my world. How I jump at the creak of furniture chilled by the open window! I think of Job in my foundering, grasping quest for solace. I think of everything in the world, perhaps, but my mother. Tonight I would turn all my eloquence to the cursing of myself. Whither have I strayed, God, from the path of happiness? Is it my desire? Is it my material desire and my greed? Shall I live yet more precariously and school myself to care not? Shall I take less thought of food and drink and raiment? Lord, lord, how I would believe! Then my heart would be swept clean, and the veils, the dusty glass before my eyes would break and I should not only see but participate with joyous clarity.

But tonight at twenty-six, alone and lonely and afraid in my room, I chew my nails and listen to my quickened heartbeat. Where is my love, I say? Where are my loves? How have I become so impure?

MARCH 28, 1947

^GStill rewriting the Rollo story—which now has a hero, "Bernard." This story, which three, four people have criticized! I'm changing the whole thing and—I don't know. It might be bet-

ter, yes, shorter, but all the philosophy, the ideas which made it relevant—thrown away!GG

MARCH 31, 1947

GWork. Chauncey Chirp.* Took care of the snails last night. They really do need daily care. I like giving them to Ginnie to hold. Ginnie will arrive on Tuesday at 12:55 P.M. And—we will delight one another, won't we? Yes—we won't leave the bed for three days! "Listen—bring everything from your house, you understand? I don't want you to have to go back!"GG

APRIL 1, 1947

GI practiced piano before going to Penn Station. Ginnie arrived at 2:15. "How are you, sweetie?" I kissed her cheek, I think. But could (barely) speak to her. A big kiss when we got to her room. I'd brought a few things for the icebox but was frustrated that I hadn't bought flowers! The only ones at Penn Station cost $7.50 for a dozen. Tonight, she suddenly wanted to see people—I was quite hurt—so we called R.C. and Jean C. Jean C. had nothing to say to me. I suspect that I should feel uncomfortable or nervous around her and Ginnie, but the affair was so quick and simply so meaningless—and I don't think Ginnie will ever find out. One of these days, I'd like to tell her about it. Tonight— when we finally threw Jean out of the house, it was wonderful, and in her embraces, I finally felt myself relax for the first time in months. I truly love her.GG

APRIL 6, 1947

GUp early, worked until Ginnie came in at 11:30. Lunch with Prentiss Kent†—we are very friendly and comfortable with each other now—at Valois, where G. often goes. Champagne, asparagus with hollandaise—we ate well.GG

---

* Reference to a Jingle Jangle comic strip featuring the bird Chauncey Chirp.
† Jonathan Prentiss Kent, Ginnie's brother.

APRIL 8, 1947

^GEven when I am exhausted at night, I must make love to Ginnie. Often more passionately because I'm so tired. Played piano. Am getting better at changing fingers. And—worked—on my new story about Vera Stratton, the angry woman of New York—which is already too long. Went to the movies.^{GG}

APRIL 12, 1947

^GReading Dostoyevsky's letters. Wonderful. Too bad I can't interest G. in them. I give her so much to read—and nothing comes of it. Tonight, she wanted to see "people." So after dinner at the restaurant, we took the car to see Texas E. Very pleasant time. Later we two went to Soho (a Bistro Night Club) where I was frightfully bored. And when we got home at 11:15, I cried. Suddenly it seemed like everything was impossible. The old story: I want to stay home and read, and she wants to go out. I want her to find someone else for her evenings. Ginnie said that these differences are always canceled out by men and women: that they somehow always go on being happy, etc. And though I can't recall her words exactly, I knew then that she was right. I am the serious fool. Read *P. [Paris] Review* until 12:30—about Kafka and people like me, until I felt strong and happy again.^{GG}

APRIL 12, 1947

^GWorked. And went for a walk with Ginnie in the park. She doesn't let me go to the park in trousers or in a raincoat. So I wore moccasins and my gray suit. I felt so stiff, but it was a nice day, and we watched the boats on the lake. Ate all sorts of things. Finished my story (about Mildred Stratton—no title, but G. suggested "New York, New York").^{GG}

APRIL 16, 1947

^GWorked and met mother at the library at 1 o'clock sharp. Talked and talked over lunch with martinis at Cortile. And bought black shoes, just like Ginnie's, I think. Tried to fix Ginnie's hallway door: Natica hit it with a chair! Used drywall.

Somewhat symbolic: I repair what N. destroys. That's what I hope for Ginnie. Her room was beautiful and yellow with the windows open. Shining like a summer palace.[GG]

4/17/47

Perhaps any sort of human association is stimulating to me. If the person is a bore, the mind is released like a sprung clay pigeon the instant it finds itself secluded from the bore. More and better thoughts come then than would have come, I think, during the combined time alone under so-called "ideal" conditions of solitude and quiet.

4/17/47

The essence of unreality in the modern world: (is not nightclubs, but) to look for work in the late afternoon, by appointment even, after having worked at one's own work all day. Now I know how A.C. [Allela Cornell] felt after a morning's painting when she called at a comics' outfit. The oppressive tedium and fatigue about it all—making one's effort at interest, readiness, simple alertness sour in the mouth. Beware these tireless slaves! How do they do it themselves? (Do you *really* want to know?) Where are their moments of reality—at the breakfast table, in bed with their wives? Gardening? Washing their cars? Or are they another species of animal that does not need reality?

APRIL 18, 1947

[G]Work. Saw a few Picassos, which I like more and more now. Why didn't I four years ago? His sketches are astounding! God— if an artist is so good that every movement, almost every breath is pure beauty—he must feel closer to God despite himself.[GG]

APRIL 21, 1947

[G]A perm at Ginnie's beauty salon, Park Ave. $17.50. "I'll pay for it," Ginnie said, but she forgot. It doesn't matter, this little I have! And at least I must look more presentable, I presume, which must please G. I am so very much in love with her—something so new to me—that whatever pleases her must please me. "You don't know," she said, "how often I think of you every day. You make me so happy—simply that you're true, that I can depend on you."[GG]

APRIL 22, 1947

[G]What a pleasure to wake up Ginnie! She has a pair of white pajamas that are just as soft as her skin! To embrace her in them! She smells so warm and sweet lying in bed in the morning! Finished the story for Margot "The Roaring Fire."[*] Tomorrow will be two weeks since I started it. Had lunch with B. Parsons, Strelsa Leeds,[†] Natasha H. and Sylvia—and Jane Bowles,[‡] who was very impressed with my O. Henry story[§] and really wanted me to call her after. I will. Margot joined us, too—and looked at me strangely during those ten minutes. Yes, she knows Natasha, etc. God, doesn't Margot know for certain that I'm gay?[GG]

APRIL 23, 1947

[G]My day off. What is it about a day off that makes one so sensitive! I made love to Ginnie passionately—we could barely restrain ourselves at lunch! We ate at Sea Fare (under my apartment) at 2:30—that's how long we took to get ready. We held hands under the table. Waitress was very understanding. We ate steamed clams, which G. loves. Finally went to see my family, where G. immediately suggested martinis. We changed (kissed) and took the car to a quiet road, where we—but we kept worrying that someone would come. Back home, we made love—between 7–7:45!—and went down calmly afterwards for a cocktail. Ginnie says so often how much she loves me, how happy I make her, how everyone says that she is a different per-

---

[*] This story has not survived.

[†] An actress and Broadway performer.

[‡] Jane Bowles (1917–1973) and her husband, Paul (1910–1999), were the epitome of bohemianism. Both writers, they shared a passion for alcohol, travel, and extramarital affairs—bisexual in both cases. For a while in the early forties, the couple lived at 7 Middagh Street under one roof with the likes of W. H. Auden, Carson McCullers, Richard Wright, Benjamin Britten, and Gypsy Rose Lee.

[§] Pat's story "The Heroine," in 1946 one of the O. Henry Prize Stories.

son since last spring—and that it's thanks to me. I like hearing this the most. Drank a lot, but it didn't show, thank God. Tonight, I truly felt at one with Ginnie.^{GG}

APRIL 27, 1947

^GJoan S. at 2:00, we took a walk and sketched in the park. God, when she is lying so close to me—asleep or awake—I can't help myself! I will always remember that night in Hastings when she was lying on the sofa, when I was writing "W.C. Ball-Bouncer." Something peaceful, something exciting, something good flows from her—God. And when I feel it, I don't know what to do—to stay with her or G. What a confession!^{GG}

(The most tragic error of my life—as Henry James might say. Joan was unique—in my world—October 27, 1947)

^GJoan drank her beer slowly and looked at me tenderly. She understands me in a different way than G. I can do more with this understanding than G.'s. In short, it's nothing more than the physical that makes a difference to me. Ginnie is older, yes, and I can learn more from her, but—sometimes, like now and over the next five days, I felt almost nothing for G. and so much for Joan. We ate at a Chinese restaurant. And in her room at the Barbizon she wanted me to kiss her goodbye. It counts more the second time. I love her in an uncertain way, and feel no guilt whatsoever when I kiss her. "I wish you could hold me close forever," she whispered. This is why the day seemed long, and very sad. G. was home when I came back with a piece of caramel cake the next day. "Hold me," she said—in the same hour that J.S. had said it.^{GG}

APRIL 30, 1947

^GWas invited by the editor of *The Writer* magazine to write an article about "writing for a living." I laughed. What do I know about making a living? But I'm very flattered, and would like to write something for him.* ^{GG}

---

* Twenty years later, Pat will write an insightful nonfiction work, *Plotting and Writing Suspense Fiction*, at the invitation of *The Writer*.

5/11/47

That an individual's faults are never quite without pardon, unforgivable—this is perhaps the only adult entry I have ever made in these bloody fifteen *cahiers.*

MAY 20, 1947

^GDinner with Jane Bowles. About 5 martinis—her idea—before dinner, which made me sick. I behaved stupidly—and will say no more about it. Both of us were too drunk. Good conversation only before the meal. "Ginnie is dreadful and dreadfully attractive," she said.^{GG}

MAY 22, 1947

^GWashed the windows so the summer sun could shine in. And—after two of Ginnie's APAC pills, with a swimming brain—worked with clarity on "Mrs. Afton." My hellish story! So—read, slept for 15 minutes, everything was wonderful! Met Ginnie at the bistro. She was very downcast, silent, complaining. And when we finally began discussing our relationship, I said (although we were both angry) that it was the first time we were actually discussing something. How can one understand women? And to ruin the evening, Sheila, Audrey, and Rolf showed up. Finally we left together for Ginnie's, Ginnie walking the whole way, generously buying Cutty Sark and bourbon. She marched through the streets like a majordomo, hitting the Spivy sign with her newspaper, etc. And at home, the dog, the radio, drinks. At 12:00 the house became suddenly quiet, when we were alone, and she turned to me slowly, somewhat sad.^{GG}

MAY 23, 1947

^GReady to leave and work when Ginnie came into the living room at 9:30 AM. She was nervous. After two drinks, she went to bed, where she couldn't stay calm. And suddenly—at 10 AM—she cried out for a doctor! "My nerves!" she cried over and over. I gave her a phenobarbital pill. I didn't really know what was wrong with her. "My fingers are cramping up!" she

cried, breathing heavily with fear. She wandered through the apartment completely naked, and I went after her with her bathrobe, shivering myself. "My speech!" And suddenly she couldn't speak anymore! Her lips were sunken in, her face fat and uncomprehending. It was awful and unforgettable. I gave her one more drink (she had to have it, wanted it). And during the whole affair, I called up Jacobson, Ellis, Terwilliger—the almighty doctors who couldn't help in the end. I quickly realized I would not only have to stay the day, but for days. "I'll buy you a new blouse," she whispered, glued to me. God! Later, she sat for several minutes on a chair in the bedroom, half-naked, realizing that she could move her fingers again and speak. Thank God, I said.

And during it all, I hoped that she was truly frightened, and that she won't forget today. It was 2 o'clock before the doctor came. "Alcoholic neurotic." We discussed it together, what she should do if she didn't want to die. And we came up with an excuse for her mother as to why she couldn't come to Philadelphia today. I hurried home to get my typewriter from 4–5. Mrs. Kent called me. I couldn't tell her about the fingers, but she certainly knew that this nerve sickness was caused by Cutty. And Mrs. K. was very happy that I was with her. Now Ginnie must sleep, have orange juice and milk and vegetables. And she is very serious about her new regimen.[GG]

MAY 28, 1947

[G]Thinking of my novel.[*] J. Bowles said: "Don't plan. It's always better first to write, then rework it." I just want a strong, clear idea. Was busy all day, started a new story, had to clean our room and finally went to see R.C. to retrieve "Mrs. Afton." Talked too much with Ginnie when we were lying in our two beds. Said that I felt unsure of her, that I didn't have enough in common with her. (Not to mention that I don't have enough of

---

[*] Pat begins to work in earnest on what will become her first published novel, *Strangers on a Train* (New York, 1950).

a sex life. Until she's healthy and lively again!) I had to say these things, had to learn if she truly loved me or if I was a mere comfort. I knew that I was tired, nervous, had too much to drink (good for work). And suddenly Ginnie was angry, hit me with her fists, and when I tried to protect myself and sat up in bed so she couldn't fight anymore, she called me a coward, of course.[GG]

MAY 31, 1947
[G]Drinking too much (lately). No more schnapps at home. Yesterday evening I spoke with Ginnie for a long time. I told her that I regretted my words. This was our worst fight because Ginnie has the strength of her sickness, the assurance of her mother's love and care and that of others. I promised I would come with her to Phil[adelphia] on Wednesday.[GG]

JUNE 2, 1947
[G]Parents. Stanley's birthday was yesterday or today. We bought him a jacket. If only I had gotten something that nice. Margot Johnson told me that *Today's Woman* may reprint "The Heroine." "Blue Ribbon Reprints." With Ms. [Marion] Chamberlain from Dodd, Mead Publishers. She talks too much—but is very nice, I think. It was an evening in which I felt myself to be all kinds of things—vain, for instance. Should I be more tender? But mostly it was interesting to observe her. Very satisfied, drunk when I got home at 11:30.[GG]

6/3/47
Telephone calls. I especially hate long distance calls, even when I don't have to pay for them. Distance is so exiting, so mysterious, so bounded by the size of the earth, after all, and by the limitation of aeronautics. I don't want it banished, for nothing, by a human voice.

JUNE 7, 1947
[G][Philadelphia.] Ginnie sleeps about 11 hours a day, her blood pressure is at 69 and that's why she believes she has no strength.

She is still in the corner room, and every evening at 11:30, she comes into my room to look at me silently and ask: "How long will you still be reading?" And later I go to her room. But sex? God no. And yet I'm with a woman who arouses me intensely![GG]

6/7/47

Again & again I am fooled by the egocentric pseudo-bliss of aloneness into thinking it makes me perfectly happy. I have to be blasted out of it. I should never be alone. It is a happiness without love or a woman, which (to my thinking, for me, now) can never constitute a real happiness. My intellect may be happy, it is. But I don't even function properly physically. Isn't this enough proof? Yet for ten years or more, my schizophrenic personality has tricked me. I revel in aloneness again and again, before I realize, again & again. The real trouble of course, as always with me, is in trying to find absolute and permanent values & advantages in experiences which are & should be only transitory.

6/7/47

The most important statement in this *cahier*: My life to date has been conditioned by strife, violence, bitter desperate effort and the absence of tranquility. It is impossible for me to produce now or in the near future a perfect work of art. All I produce (unless extremely short, produced in blissful madness) must be hectic, unsatisfied & therefore unsatis-fying, unless to the desperate few like myself who will read it. I long for tranquility, my worldly & spiritual goal since my fourteenth year, but consciously. Shall I provide my own insuperabilities when I effect it materially? The dearth of it, the great draught, has become so much a part of my psycho-logical make-up.

JUNE 18, 1947

[G]Changed the ending of "Mrs. Afton" a bit. The story must sell. Finished the two sketches (paintings) of Stanley and mother for the art room. I'll see Ginnie again Friday evening: our first anniversary together, and my first ever. God! It really is wonderful! I will bring her flowers and—we will drink champagne.ᴳᴳ

JUNE 23, 1947
ᴳBegan my novel. Difficult to start. I want a short first part, in which the two boys and the possibility of murder are introduced. After this prologue, the story will start slowly, pleasantly. Ginnie increasingly downcast.ᴳᴳ

7/1/47
Dinner with P.K. [Prentiss Kent] *et famille*—it may be phony but at least it has lightness. The house. At first barren. Then one invests it with one's own personality. This is attained only after three weeks or so. At first it is sad and barren, opulent and stark at once. The Louis Quinze chairs and the gilt frames, the Aubusson rugs contrasting with the sterile white bookless, eternally bookless walls and corners. The bathroom itself, incongruously modern with white cabinets and strip drawer pulls, three weeks later one goes into the same bathroom, and the white modern cabinets are invested with a familiarity. The veneer of self (ME!) over everything.) Self-assertion which is too aggressive, indicative of insecurity & inferiority, I realize. Yet tonight really it is tempered with love.

JULY 7, 1947
ᴳNot yet alone again. But—I am writing more now, I think, than if I were in N.Y. Here everything is so beautiful, and I can kiss my love all day long.ᴳᴳ

JULY 17, 1947
ᴳ[New York.] All alone. Ginnie calls every day. And I have learned from Rolf T. that Sheila is with her. What are they doing? I really don't know. "This stinks of an affair," R.C. said.ᴳᴳ

7/17/47

Mortal terror, the terror of the mortal mind: I shall go through life never finding for certain more than one-third the ingredients in that special formula of my own happiness. Solitude, tranquility of mind, excitement of the senses, people, loneliness, success, failure, advantage and handicap, gluttony and abstinence, memory and daydream, transfiguration and reality, love requited and unrequited, the faithful lover and the faithless, fidelity and experiment, curiosity and resignation, all these flow from my pen in less time by far than it takes to write them. But when and by how much of each shall I live? And what have I missed, what included that I do not need? Man must struggle according to his own tortured nature. At twenty-six I say perish the psychiatrists who would remold me. What I am blind to, that I shall remain blind to. Its vision would deprive me of that which I see.

7/19/47

Miraculous, coruscating conversation with R.T. [Rolf Tietgens], in which we concluded, it is the best of all possible worlds for artists. (Question at 3:15 A.M. Would not any conceivable world be the best of all possible worlds for artists? Would not the born artist find his irritating sand grain of unhappiness around which to form his pearl?)

JULY 22, 1947

^GRevised 93 pages. Excellent, first part—already done. I will be so happy to see it on white paper. Mother came very early—always when I begin to work. But she helped me a lot around the house. And finally we talked—she loves Ginnie very much—and drank many martinis. At 10:30 PM I went to Ginnie's, was cheerful and very happy to see N. [Natica] and her. Both were in trousers, tired after the trip back from Phil., and looking pretty. Later, alone (N. went home!), Ginnie was very cold and ugly to me: "No, you won't sleep with me!" I lay in bed for a few minutes, then quickly got dressed and left,

when Ginnie called down the stairs! Why should I tolerate
her coldness? Is this what being grown up means? No kiss, no
embrace! I don't understand it, but there's nothing to understand. We should separate, that's all. And in many ways, this
is very sad.^{GG}

JULY 25, 1947
^GAt parents'. Very busy, free, (thin!). Went with great expec-
tations for the weekend. A few long gins. Very pleasant. I'm
excited to show the parents my novel.^{GG}

JULY 26, 1947
^GI was just drinking martinis when Ginnie called. Can't deny it,
was very happy to hear her voice. "Do you love me?" "Yes, I do,"
I replied. These days are so strange. I love Ginnie. But I can't
bear the thought, can't forget that ever since I left, she's stayed in
West Hills with Sheila. If only Sheila had been good enough to
leave before I did—but no—she stays, and stays, and stays. Does
Ginnie even need me then? Why?^{GG}

AUGUST 3, 1947
^GWork was good. Am so happy whenever Bruno appears in the
novel! I love him!^{GG}

AUGUST 11, 1947
At 5 o'clock Owen Dodson arrived.* He is very agreeable, just
came from Yaddo with lots of news that pleased me. We would
have talked longer, but it wasn't possible.

8/20/47
Take nothing seriously and refuse to be sad.

---

* Owen Dodson, American poet and novelist, was a Yaddo resident in 1947. Yaddo had
started admitting Black artists a few years before, beginning with Langston Hughes in 1942.

484 Patricia Highsmith's Diaries and Notebooks

8/25/47

Eat heartily, drink heartily, except of martini cocktails, and open an advertising circular with passion, fling yourself into bed at night, exhausted, and with passion, and alone.

AUGUST 27, 1947

GYesterday Margot J. said that she likes the novel very much. "Both of the mothers are strong characters." (I doubt that.) And said I should show it immediately to [Marion] Chamberlain.

I'm still working on my story. No, only comics today. How capable I am now that I am alone! I washed the walls, cleaned this and that, did everything I had pushed off for so long. And I am not lonely at all. Walked to 84th St. and back, hungry and thirsty for life on the street! People, children, houses, shops, newspapers! God! I can feel my strength—if only I can maintain my good mood, my sense! Later a visit from Rolf, who was very boring for once. He doesn't want to go to New Mexico without Bobby. Still in love with him. Restless and lonely.GG

8/28/47

How I write these days: (or is anybody interested?) I do everything possible to avoid a sense of discipline. I write on my bed (bed made up, myself fully but not decently clothed), having once surrounded myself with ashtray, cigarettes, matches, a hot or warm cup of coffee, a stale part of a doughnut and saucer with sugar to dip it in after dunking. My position is as near the fetal as possible, still permitting writing. A womb of my own.

8/30/47

There is a way.

8/30/47

Wait for inspiration: mine come with the frequency of rodent orgasms.

SEPTEMBER 3, 1947

ᴳSpent the whole day typing the story. It's very good! Should I call the novel "Small Rain"? Called up Eleanor Stierham from *Today's Woman.* Burton Rascoe's stories begin in 1948, and mine will be in the first issue.* She wants to invite me for a drink next week. All alone. Too hot again. Yes, I miss Ginnie. Especially when I go to bed. And when I sometimes want to talk to her on the phone.ᴳᴳ

9/3/47

Advice to a young writer: approach the typewriter with respect and formality. (Is my hair combed? My lipstick on straight? Above all are my cuffs clean and properly shot?) The typewriter is quick to detect any nuance of irreverence and can retaliate in kind, in double measure, and effortlessly. The typewriter is above all alert, sensitive as you are, far more efficient in its tasks. After all, it slept better than you did last night, and just a little longer.

9/4/47

The first novel: rather the big messy thing than the little gem of art, an exercise to be reserved for crabbed old age.

SEPTEMBER 4, 1947

ᴳAlone. Worked. Sleeping less and less—about 3–4 hours. When I begin to fall asleep, I feel a kind of sudden excitation, awakening in my brain, or I think, probably, mostly, of Sheila with my Ginnie, and my heart is filled with murderous thoughts until I can no longer sleep.ᴳᴳ

9/7/47

This lump of Angst in my throat. The phlegm of twentieth century New York, the uncoughuppable.

---

* Probably *Today's Woman* has asked the editor and critic Arthur Burton Rascoe (1892–1957) to curate a selection of short stories. In any case, Pat's story "The Heroine" will appear in the *Today's Woman* March 1948 issue.

9/14/47

First nembutal*—I feel like I have taken strychnine as the capsule slides down. Ten minutes later: tingling in the nerves of the legs. I open my eyes. Do I feel "heaviness"? Not so trite. The legs. Socrates drank the hemlock. It rose from legs to heart. I am terribly alert. The ears begin to tingle. Tiredness tears at the rocks of me, a sea of lassitude tears at the rocks of me. And ebbs away, I turn over. I am awake, blinking brightly. Has it passed? Have I survived it? This is depressing. I could never take the second now, though I've been told it would not matter. The sea rises again. Second onslaught. Now I am afraid. The pill is relentless. It will have me. It has power to fight until it does, more power than I have. It will fight until it has me. Socrates drank the hemlock. What have I taken? What the hell do I know about nembutal? My ears tingle. Is the clock fainter? It is not. The sea rises, goes over my head, but it is not unpleasant, neither am I asleep. A sense of not caring wars with curiosity and fear, as when I am busy drinking the one excessive martini. I give up. I am lost. Socrates drank hemlock . . . Six hours later I awaken. I fancy I am fuzzier than usual, but it soon passes.

9/17/47

Why so like death? Why do the worms crawl? They crawl because I am two, three days dead. Man is all love, man can never die, he is reborn in each new love, he is alive always in the Love of God, his eternal spouse, but in the death of an earthly love each man dies too, and in two or three days, the worms have at him. O, do not think to bury yourself deep enough to escape them! There is no escape. I walk the streets and feel anointed. I walk the streets like the walking dead. I feel on the brink of physical death. I do not wish to die, by stoppage of heart or by being hit by a truck. I am with death, he knows I do

---

* Pentobarbital, sold under the trademarked name Nembutal, was prescribed for many years to treat insomnia. It was eventually discontinued as a sleep aid, following widespread abuse and the emergence of new treatments.

not fear him. But I am not ready for him yet. I have work to do: I
am the anointed.

9/20/47

Am I pledged to ill health? Pray God, no! I want to live a long
while. Sometimes I feel I cannot. Something drives me to the
destructive, which is a necessity for my seeing.

SEPTEMBER 21, 1947

ᴳWork. Very happy—the novel is going better. It lives in my
heart, at least. And it is the only thing that can make me happy
these days. I should say that this day should be written in red
ink, because Rosalind asked me if I would like to live with her in
a house in the country. It's an idea. We are both dissatisfied with
our lives in New York, where one is either lonely or exhausted,
it's impossible. What will happen? How much money will I have
in a year? Where will I be? With whom? And yet Rosalind (Tex
too) said, when I told her of my troubles, "Oh, in two months
you'll have someone new to get lost in." We'll see.ᴳᴳ

9/29/47

People say of artists that they live within themselves, but actually
they live more outside themselves than ordinary people. It is the
same world to which the artist goes when he is inspired or when
he works, but the actual actual world is different for him each
time he returns to it. (Thank God, or it would be boring to him
beyond endurance!) The artist only wonders that ordinary men
can tolerate what he knows to them is a constant and same world.

9/30/47

Do always, or almost always unless it interferes with a specific
desire to work, do always what you want to do.

10/3/47

Never fret over a character, it has to do with the mysteries of
birth. From the minutest beginning, a character is either alive

or not. And yet, as in real life, the sickly, fair-haired baby can become a dark brute, filled with vigor or the robust infant the object of its parent's hypochondriacal obsessions.

10/4/47

Dedication: to several women, without whom this (whatever it is) book could not have been written. God! (Not God save women!) I adore them! Without them I would and could do nothing! Every move I make on earth is in some way for women. I adore them! I need them as I need music, as I need drawings. I would give up anything visible to the eye for them, but this is not saying much. I would give up music for them: that is saying much.

OCTOBER 6, 1947

ᴳDon't feel very well. Am drinking rye now—more than ever. Mother at 10. Lunch. Dentist. I have no time. The curse! It's all too fast! I'm searching for adventure. Dinner with Babs B., who was quite drunk on bourbon, at Tomaldo's.* Beethoven there, the whole place very gay. Drank too much red wine to work. And at 12:45, when I was alone and in bed, the phone rang: Maria and Peggy,† who invited me out for a drink. I went over quickly, evening trousers and everything. Peggy had taken two sleeping pills, but we talked a lot. Four drunk women. What would mother have said! It was very strange!—And then the compliments they paid me, my trousers, etc. "They say you have a brain too, Pat."ᴳᴳ

OCTOBER 10, 1947

ᴳMy week was disrupted by the dentist. Had little time. Every visit about 1½ hours. And saw Lil [Picard]‡—to learn that she

---

* Italian restaurant at 812 Third Avenue, between Forty-Ninth and Fiftieth Streets.
† Presumably Peggy Fears.
‡ Lil Picard (1899–1994), a German-born, Jewish avant-garde artist more than twenty years Pat's senior, had already made a name for herself as a painter, sculptor, art critic, and photographer. She later served as Andy Warhol's muse and came to bear such honorifics as "the Gertrude Stein of the New York art scene" and "grandmother of the hippies." She was married to banker Hans Felix Jüdell.

could have dinner with me. She kissed me goodbye last night—
I'm a bit in love with you, I think, she said. Lots happening,
but no word from Margot on the book. Where is [Marion]
Chamberlain? And what does Dodd, Mead think?GG

10/13/47
Do not forget patience. Because I have it in such abundance,
I am inclined to take it for granted, yet in me it is not always
present.

10/15/47
On rereading a few of my notebooks: they are a mirror of a
rather bad mind floundering with incredible perseverance, inde-
fatigable curiosity, in all directions at once, never pursuing one
direction long enough to think any one subject through.

OCTOBER 17, 1947
GWork. Writing more slowly. 270 pages, roughly. And Ginnie
called several times—saying that I still love her, and that she
cares for me. "But don't you prefer Sheila?" Brought her flowers,
cleaned her shoes, and she was very impolite, didn't listen when
I spoke, etc., played records that she and Sheila had listened to
together, and couldn't bear it when I asked her, "Why are you
torturing yourself?" So—at 9:30 I went home to work. (Ginnie is
so sick, so weak, it was hell to take her out for a walk.)GG

OCTOBER 22, 1947
GBusy. And cocktails with Ms. Chamberlain at Michel. She
said that Dodd, Mead is not satisfied with the novel as it
stands. The 100 pages must be cut down to 60. So—I must
cut. Margot came later—but at first Chamberlain and I were
alone, and she impressed upon me how the publishing industry must be very careful now, etc. Margot was angry, because
D.M. [Dodd, Mead] has a lot of money. Am disappointed only
because I need the money, but it will be a better book once I've
made the cuts.GG

10/23/47

4:00 A.M. I cannot live alone in health. In the night, alone, awake after sleep, I am insane. I read Gertrude Stein. I eat like a Cyclopian giant, only my wine and my whiskey do not make me sleep. I do not desire anyone vaguely or specifically: I merely say, if I had so-and-so, I should not be insane now. I am without discretion, judgment, moral code. There is nothing I would not do, murder, destruction, vile sexual practices. I would also, however, read my Bible. My being is rent with frustration like the curtain before the false temple. Yes, I long to meet a beautiful woman at a tiny black table somewhere, and kiss her hand, and talk of things that would delight her. I long to pare myself as I long to pare my art of the extraneous that corrupts it. It must come first in my work. I drink whiskey to stupefy myself, and regret what it does to my body—fat cells, deterioration of the brain, above all indulgence in a dependence upon materiality when what keeps me awake is a spiritual intangible.

10/29/47

Life chose to play with you like a rubber ball, a soft rubber ball on a gravel field. You bear its scratches, its scars, but none can be said to be yours willingly. You were passive in the game. Your face is lined with life few poets have known, though they would. Your age has grown knowing with life that life painted in it stroke after painstaking stroke, but it is a flat eye on what was once a blank canvas. You pace your apartment alone in pajamas with your wise tortured face, like a bewildered captive of life, and even the alcohol that beclouds your brain is not you, is artificial, is one more cruel stroke of this life you yourself with your petty headstrong will deny, and the intoxication is the last insult to you. Even I, writing these lines at five thirty in the morning, sleepless, haunted by semi dream, semi nightmare, semi hallucination, know that I am touched by the same life, because I am insanely in love with you, yet I sought you and was not passive. When you die, you will die into its grasping hands

that are already closing about you. You will die with the same
plucked, confused expression on your small face grown wise to
overflowing with the life that was too much for your pusilla-
nimity to bear.

(*To V.K.C. [Virginia Kent Catherwood] at 3:30 A.M.
sleepless*)

OCTOBER 29, 1947
ᴳHaven't heard anything from Ginnie. Why? God, how my life
would have been different, better, more beautiful, and more
exceptional if I had always worn white collared shirts, gone to
church every Sunday, and lived with my parents. Lately, I am not
as orderly as usual, and it troubles my soul.ᴳᴳ

NOVEMBER 4, 1947
ᴳLast night was very nice—with Lil at Parsons Gallery Hedda
Sterne* exhibit. Wore my turtleneck sweater under my suit, and
felt so beautiful (with one of the roses that Joan sent me), that I
could have spoken to everyone.ᴳᴳ

NOVEMBER 4, 1947
ᴳDisgusting evening with H.S.† Everything was lovely at first—
dressing myself after work, making a martini—and later—his
boring words: "I don't understand you. Don't you love me?
Aren't you at all attracted to me?" God! Finally I told him
that I was in love with someone who didn't love me back. And
then I called mother in tears. Decided to go to Hastings. Am
too distressed and troubled here. And I'll bring along Lil. She
needs it too.ᴳᴳ

---

* Hedda Sterne (née Hedwig Lindenberg, 1910–2011) was an artist of Romanian-Jewish
descent. She was also part of Guggenheim's Exhibition by 31 Women and later gained some
notoriety for being the only woman in a photograph of the group the Irascible Eighteen. She
worked closely with Betty Parsons, who also gave her the exhibition Pat mentions here at
Wakefield Gallery, her first solo exhibition in the United States.
† A man she met on a trip to Charleston the year before.

11/4/47

Today life is so much concerned with unrealities, things done unwillingly, things done for no apparent purpose, without joy, without satisfaction, a little liquor is necessary to enable one to rediscover one's self. The self is a constructive and real being. The modern world is not.

NOVEMBER 12, 1947

GWork. But I'm not working fast enough. Why:

    a) Rewriting scenes which I wrote so happily the first time around!
    b) Regretting the time, since I wanted to be in Texas now.
    c) Very disappointed in Ginnie.
    d) Need money—first for the book—and yet I have to give so much of my time to Timely [Comics], who are getting harder and harder to please.

Also—I'm reading [André Gide's] *The Counterfeiters.*GG

11/13/47

I am troubled by a sense of being several people (nobody you know). Should not be at all surprised if I become a dangerous schizophrene in my middle years. I write this very seriously. There is an ever more acute difference—and an intolerableness—between my inner self which I know is the real me, and various faces of the outside world.

NOVEMBER 15, 1947

GStayed at Lil's last night. Discussed things until 3:00 AM as we lay in bed (two beds!). More later. She said I'm the most interesting person she's met in years. Worked on "Still Point of the Turning World"* this afternoon, and went with Lil to the Museum of M. Art to see "Potemkin." I very much enjoy being with Lil: she knows everything about me, but is not emotionally

---

* Published in *Nothing That Meets the Eye: The Uncollected Stories of Patricia Highsmith* (Norton: New York, 2002).

dependent. What is so unbearable? That I have so little money after so much work! Lately, I've often thought (too often) that if I weren't especially strong (or mad), I'd have lost my mind months ago.^{GG}

NOVEMBER 17, 1947

^GWorked on "Still Point T.W." and finished it! They wanted "smoother transitions"! Exactly what I didn't want! Burned leaves in the courtyard, which I enjoyed.^{GG}

NOVEMBER 26, 1947

^GBrought these 50 pages to Margot—up to page 183, for her flight to Boston today. Very happy to celebrate tonight after five straight days of work! Tonight Peggy, Lil (Rosalind?) for cocktails, and then Jeanne for dinner. Would like her to spend the night. Why not? We don't know each other. But it would do us good. So—why not? And soon after dinner when I was playing records, J. said: "I want to stay over . . . Why don't you invite me?" She's very passionate, and I like this about her. After Ginnie, who was so incredibly difficult, J. is a gift from heaven!! (Five times for her, she said.) And different interesting things: That Tex rarely went down on her. J. feels a bit selfconscious then. Naturally. "I never got such a bang out of it before," she said. Shortly my ego is 100 percent bigger! Breakfast, and then by car to see the family in Hastings. I felt delighted, and she too, as we drove up along the Hudson. Old fashioneds. And a wonderful turkey. I drank quite a lot and spoke like a fool. And came back from Jeanne (when she left at 6 o'clock) with lipstick on my chin. What did the parents think? They like Jeanne.^{GG}

11/26/47

Wisdom is to be gained in drunkenness and in the nightmares of the depths of tortured sleep, which are both contrary to God and to happiness, but not to nature. In the night I am myself, both self and a machine, an intuitively accurate one. In the night, I can work purely, by intuition. The night is no man's time but mine. In the night no one calls me. In the silence, I hear my own voices.

12/3/47

The impulse to drink is the same impulse that tends one (male or female, but especially female) to immerse oneself in the one person loved, to be lost, and relieved of identity.

DECEMBER 3, 1947

GNot a great day, since I had to write a synopsis. This ugly business of having to make a living! One day I will be free of it! Completely free! That I have Jeanne—and what "have" means, I do not know—saves me now. Yes, it saves me. We need each other terribly. I told her: "Don't try to love me." Lil is very interested in me and Jeanne. "But aren't you bored?" "No," I answered. Girls with whom I sleep are women to me, and I don't want an intellectual woman. I value warmth much more, I value true love much more. I value a smile full of love much more. Strange—that with Jeanne and Lil, with the drawing class, I have completely changed my circle of friends! And I like it. Most of all, I like seeing Jeanne happier. Every day she is happier, and shows it. She lost 8 pounds after Tex. Tonight she invited me up (for a glass of milk) and it was—right, lovely. It was an evening I would have enjoyed had I been a boy who wanted to marry her. And she was what I wanted—a lady, a real aristocrat.GG

DECEMBER 5, 1947

GMaking slower progress on the book. This week has been typical: Mon. and Tues. alone = 20 pages. Wednesday, Jeanne = 4 pages. Thursday, mother = 5 pages. Friday—disgust—and no pages—but today at 5 o'clock I began writing a short story, one about a girl and a chauffeur. I like the beginning a lot; like T. Capote, I need to rebuild my ego. Drawing class. Lots of men. My work is improving, and it's the greatest source of pleasure in my week. Sometimes I imagine what my life would be like if I were a painter. And yet—yesterday at the Dalí exhibit, I realized that painting is not developed or refined or clear enough (for me). Writing can do everything. Money is increasingly harder to make, I have no news on the novel or the story, and something in me doesn't want to end the book. I know this evil spirit within me already. I have waited for it. And it is here. I am fighting it. Alone. I don't want to bring Jeanne into it. I am so sick of soul that I cannot take in the happiness of a new, sweet love. And Jeanne likely—possibly—loves me. I could love her. She is a person like Joan S., who is good to me, someone for whom one can write poetry. (Strange, but one cannot write poetry about Ginnie or Natica. Mark my words if it isn't true!)[GG]

12/5/47

What do I feel with so much passion as my own angst? Do I feel love so? I pace my one room with fingers in my hair, shouting eloquently, and the one I love lies on my bed and listens—like a handkerchief for all my flying tears. Bitter years of my youth, and one does not live forever, and one is young even a much shorter time. What is it? That I have not yet made myself good enough to earn a comfortable living, to earn enough to be free. I have no angst for the possible constipation of my work either in writing or painting or whatever. I have no angst as to the limitations of my possibilities.

On the contrary it is mere frustration that my days are not long enough, that art is so long to learn, that I must give precious days to a game I do not care to play—the gamble of one's efforts for money. I am a coward, perhaps and perhaps not, not to chuck everything (which means friends, lovers, a home I like, entertainment which is recreation, alcohol and clothes, books and concerts) and work for myself so long as my money lasts. But I am so habituated that I cannot deprive myself of these things and be happy. Only in the arms of someone I love, who loves me, can I find temporary solace. These months, I believe, are the hardest of my life. From July until now. Much more I cannot stand. It is all emotional perhaps, not financial insecurity at all. A change must come swiftly. Or else. (But never suicide.)

DECEMBER 11, 1947

ᴳAll the news came today: sold "The Still Point of the Turning World" to *Today's Woman* for $800.* But Little, Brown doesn't want the novel right now. The novel has no conviction and no atmosphere, Lil said. She's right. And I'm constantly asking myself: Why not? The synopsis did, and the first chapter did. Back then I had Ginnie and a love. In the days immediately following, I wrote quickly, but it would have been better had I written everything out again slowly, by hand. I want to regain the warmth and the atmosphere of the first chapter, that feeling of comfort.ᴳᴳ

DECEMBER 12, 1947

ᴳJeanne was with me until noon. Even though I've sold a story and written a sellable story, I'm nervous! Very nervous—so I smoke too many cigarettes and want a drink! And I remember the words of my mother: "When you are very successful, you will have no happiness without love." Yes, and sexual, passionate love too. Made the great mistake of writing Ginnie a letter, in which I told her about my "Still Point" (whose kiss is hers).ᴳᴳ

DECEMBER 17, 1947

ᴳI wanted to write today, but how, when? Saw *Mourning Becomes Electra*—the best movie I've seen in America. Three hours of unrelenting tragedy, but one sees life, albeit in murders and suicides. That's what I want in my book.ᴳᴳ

DECEMBER 19, 1947

Worked alone. Alone tonight too. And happy. And satisfied. I am writing by hand again—and why did I believe that the typewriter would be "faster and clearer"? It's not true. Tucker† is moving quickly—towards murder.

---

* The story, retitled "The Envious One," about a dissatisfied housewife and mother observing another, happy mother with her lover on a bench in a New York playground, will appear in *Today's Woman*, but not until March 1949.
† Tucker will later be renamed Guy Haines.

12/25/47

In a novel, let mood motivate each paragraph, start each chapter. I think one is inclined to be oppressed by a sense of narration only—

DECEMBER 26, 1947

ᴳIt's snowing. 24 inches. The city seems like a different place. Nothing is stirring. But at 9 o'clock, a call from Joan S.! Was alone, writing, and so happy to hear from her. I made a drawing for her of my fireplace with baby Jesus and her stocking. And the face in the fireplace that she loves so much. Did a lot around the house. Very happy and satisfied. With friends and people like Jeanne, I feel strong and full!ᴳᴳ

DECEMBER 28, 1947

ᴳI'm alone. Writing again in the notebook in which Ginnie wrote on the first page "I love my love!" Five, six double pages a day. Tucker will commit murder tomorrow.ᴳᴳ

12/28/47

Note after writing my first insincere story:* it eats at my brain when I turn from it to write my book. I feel my thoughts are soiled and unclear. God forgive me for turning my talents to ugliness and to lies. God forgive me. I shall not do it again. Only this vow permits me to work any longer tonight at all. Best if I were punished by the story's being a complete fiasco. *Miserere mihi. Dirige me, Domine, sempiterne.*

DECEMBER 30, 1947

ᴳBig day today: wrote the murder, the raison d'être of the novel. Tucker fired his two shots. And Mr. Bruno is dead! I feel as though something has changed today. I am older, quite grown

---

* When Pat wrote her story "Where to, Madame?" about a girl and her chauffeur, she did so with the intention of making it "sellable." However, it still took some time until it was published by *Woman's Home Companion* in 1951.

up. Tucker's murder was a big, necessary job, a great step. I can almost see the wrinkles of age on my body. I returned home alone, quite pleased, quite content. I don't want to marry. I have my good friends (most of them European Jews) and girls?—I always have enough of them, have what I want, I think. Also— Valerie Adams, Kingsley, Lil, Jeanne, Joan, these people have shown me that I have already achieved some success in my work. This makes me feel concerned and careful.[GG]

12/31/47

2:30 A.M. My New Year's Toast: to all the devils, lusts, passions, greeds, envys, loves, hates, strange desires, enemies ghostly and real, the army of memories, with which I do battle—may they never give me peace.

1948

Yaddo Artist Colony, or: "If only I'd known how to write a book before I started!"

❧

PAT'S ACQUAINTANCE with author Jane Bowles and her associates brings her further into the fold of the New York arts scene. Composer Aaron Copland, choreographer Jerome Robbins, and actor John Gielgud are now in Pat's orbit, and over time she will become acquainted with Carson McCullers, Arthur Koestler, and W. H. Auden. Pat is part of the literati. Mid-January, she meets Truman Capote at one of Leo Lerman's Sunday evening salons. They're instantly intrigued by each other and begin spending time together.

When Pat expresses the need for peace and quiet to work, and relief from her acute pecuniary concerns, it is Capote who recommends for her to apply for a residency at the Yaddo artist colony. Thanks to letters of recommendation from Capote (who wrote his first novel, *Other Voices, Other Rooms* there the year before), her friend Rosalind Constable, and *Harper's Bazaar* fiction editor Mary Louise Aswell, Pat is invited for a two-month stay in May and June of 1948.

Founded in Saratoga Springs in 1900 by financier and industrialist Spencer Trask and his wife, Katrina, the artist colony boasts such twentieth-century creative titans as Leonard Bernstein, Hannah

Arendt, Milton Avery, Sylvia Plath, David Foster Wallace, and Jonathan Franzen. Pat will later name Yaddo the beneficiary of her estate and recipient of all future royalties.

Although her writing proceeds apace in the seclusion upstate, and despite Yaddo's strict work hours and lights-out policy, Pat cannot escape her old social habits: she drinks a lot, flirts a lot, and even sneaks off site to meet a girlfriend in the area. However, the discipline of the retreat does leave its mark on her: her bilingual (English and German) diary entries grow more concise, and within just six weeks, she finishes the first draft of *Strangers on a Train*.

Pat's fellow residents at Yaddo include crime novelist Chester Himes, Southern Gothic writer Flannery O'Connor, and English author Marc Brandel. Despite Pat's continued lesbian relationships (and an affair with another man), Marc becomes her on-again, off-again fiancé. In September, he rents a cottage in Provincetown, on Cape Cod, in the hopes that he and Pat might both finish their novels there (and get to know each other better). But the question of marriage for Pat constitutes a constant source of despair. In those years, she seems far more distraught about her sexuality than in her early twenties. While this might partly be due to her age, her personal development also mirrors that of society as a whole: The end of the war for the gay community has constituted a step backward compared to the relative freedom of the war years. Society's vigorous effort to return to "normalcy" will culminate in the persecution of homosexuals—the so-called Lavender Scare—in the McCarthy era, beginning in the late 1940s, and being suspected of being a homosexual is just as serious as being suspected of being a communist.

In a futile attempt to "cure" her homosexuality, she undergoes psychoanalysis. Ironically, it is this therapy that will indirectly lead to her writing a lesbian romance. To help finance her treatment, Pat finds seasonal work before Christmas in the toy department at Bloomingdale's, where she sells a doll to Mrs. E. R. Senn, the wife of a wealthy businessman from New Jersey. Pat is immediately smitten with the elegant blond woman in mink. She returns home that evening and, in a fever signaling a chickenpox infection, Pat begins to write . . .

❦

JANUARY 1, 1948

GMiserable, but why? I got up too late to enjoy much of the day. Why do I go out so much, when my family has a house in the country? I'm desperate and unhappy. Jeanne didn't make love to me. I don't even want to, but body and nerves are not the same.GG

JANUARY 2, 1948

GWork. Comics. Alone. Dinner at Sturtevant's. She hates women, admires men. She's not so wise.GG

JANUARY 6, 1948

GWatched *Crime and Punishment* with Jeanne. Really good: if only my murders occurred as early in my stories! Dostoyevsky!! My master! Saw Herb L. at 6 o'clock. Same as always—a little nicer, I thought. He writes six hours a day. Herb was quite drunk by 10:30. His own bottle, what could I do? Had half a mind to sleep with him, but he was utterly out of commission. Disgusted, I called Jeanne at 12:30 AM, and she politely invited me over. Wonderful to run there, find the door open, and stand by her bedside. I made love to her till 4:00 AM.GG

JANUARY 7, 1948

GAnd Herb still here at 9:30, rather confused when I returned. What a bore! And he'd written, "Where is Pat?—I love you" all over the house! A moron, and I never want to see him again.

JANUARY 8, 1948

GMaking progress. Drafted extensive notes on paper before starting to write. Jeanne likes Bruno's murder, but not the rest, I think. Alone in drawing class, and I'm reading [Jean-Paul]

Sartre's *What Is Literature?* with great pleasure—wonderful—
Sartre. I occasionally feel as though I hold art itself in my
hands!^{GG}

JANUARY 9, 1948

^GMother at 2:00 and no work done. I drink liquor because I'm so
miserable! Jeanne spent the night with me. We're growing happier and happier. It's wonderful but dangerous. I don't want to
hurt her. Sent Joan S.. photographs of Lil, Jeanne, and Peggy.^{GG}

JANUARY 12, 1948

^GJeanne's very quiet. Visited her Monday evening as well—10–
11—and she gives me so much strength—somehow—that I can
write till 2 in the morning afterwards! Anyway—she thinks she
needs to find a new circle of friends, and either work or get married. Yes, she needs someone—always. That's the difference.
So—I'm her last girl.^{GG}

JANUARY 14, 1948

^GSaw Rolf last night—although I would have preferred to
work. I get up late so I need to work late. But Rolf—I like
him, and know that woman's sense of obligation to appeal to a
man. Strange? But true. So to a beerhall. Very pleasant. I read
him Bruno's murder, which he liked a lot. We always discuss
our dream homes in New Mexico and New Orleans and the
unknown life of the future.^{GG}

JANUARY 18, 1948

^GWent to see Leo Lerman* with Rolf, Irv, and Jeanne. Rather
shy, with those three, but Leo was very polite. Spoke with Ruth

---

* Openly gay writer, critic, and editor Leo Lerman (1914–1994) wrote for the *New York
Herald Tribune*, *Harper's Bazaar*, *Dance* magazine, and *Vogue*. He was a fixture in New
York society who counted Marlene Dietrich, Maria Callas, and Truman Capote among his
close acquaintances, and his parties were legendary.

Yorck,* Schaffner (from G[ood] Housekeeping last year), and
Leo, who said "Send (your first chapter) to Mrs. Aswell this
week." Capote's book Other Voices, Other Rooms reviewed in
the Times and H[erald] Tribune today. Times wasn't so good,
but the Tribune was delightful! "Will become the greatest writer
of our time!" Williams praised him. He's only 23. Pure poetry, I
find.[GG]

JANUARY 19, 1948

[G]My birthday. Went to Hastings. Very nice with Old Fashioneds,
and lots of little gifts, but not what I wanted: a camera or pajamas. And fantastic food. Cutting the first chapter of the book so
Jeanne can work tomorrow. She wants to type for me. Beloved
girl. Mother wants to talk and talk. I always go to bed at 4
o'clock in Hastings and get up at 8 o'clock. Stanley works like
a dog. Late into the night. My sketches in the living room look
very good.[GG]

JANUARY 20, 1948

[G]Visited the Fearses, both of whom are sick. House of the dead!
Today a long letter came from Dodd, Mead, saying they prefer
Bruno to Tucker, and that I need to make it Bruno's novel. That
I'm "not ready" for a contract. Rita was reading it to me when
Jeanne arrived—and kissed me on the head—a disappointment
but—something to think about. Anyway—more work.[GG]

JANUARY 21, 1948

[G]Margot not at all discouraged, as usual—said that Pat C. at
Viking [Press] is interested in this kind of novel. So on Thursday,

---

* Ruth Landshoff Yorck, née Levy (1904–1966) was a well-known figure in the Weimar
Republic bohème before emigrating to the United States. Her Berlin friends included Bertolt
Brecht, Thomas Mann, and Albert Einstein; the publisher Samuel Fischer was her uncle and
Oskar Kokoschka painted her portrait. She appeared in the silent film Nosferatu (1922), but
once in New York she gave up acting and turned to writing instead, penning novels, poems,
and magazine columns.

I'll show her again. Have a lot to do. Thinking about Tucker a
lot and have been discussing him constantly with Lil. What else
today? I don't remember. Memory! One gets old.[GG]

JANUARY 23, 1948

[G]Mother. We went to Lil's for dinner. It was so cold, I spent the
night at Lil's. In such desperate need for a getaway that sleeping
over at hers was a great pleasure. Feel like a different person, a
European, when I sleep at Lil's. And am renewed by it.[GG]

JANUARY 25, 1948

[G]Went to Leo's—very pleasant. T. Capote.* Rainer.[†] And made
the acquaintance of Lewis Howard, a writer I liked. Really—
dreamed about what it would be like if we were married. Lil
enjoyed herself. She compared the evening to those she experienced in Berlin before Hitler: the intellectuals, free thinkers, etc.
And said we'd be the first to disappear. She's right. I'm reading
[Louis] Adamic on fascism in America.[GG]

JANUARY 29, 1948

[G]The trash can is full of white pages—everything thrown out.
And yet—is Tucker strong enough yet? What will Viking say?
I'll soon hear. Happy—back among people! Celebrating this
evening! Saw Wolfgang Heider and R[osalind] Constable with
two dogs that probably belong to Sylvia. Everyone cheery. Lil
drank martinis. And we discussed Truman Capote. R.C. says
he has nothing to say, that he's a whim created by Leo L[erman]
and *Harper's Bazaar* and *Vogue*, etc. Jeanne stayed over. I love
her more and more, but it's not enough for me. She loves me, she

---

* Truman Capote, former resident at Yaddo, wrote one of the five necessary letters of
recommendation for Pat. In a personal letter to the director of Yaddo, he stated: "She is
really enormously gifted, one story of hers shows a talent as fine as any I know. Moreover,
she is a charming, thoroughly civilized person, someone I'm quite certain you would like."
While Pat was at Yaddo, Capote used her apartment to finish his short story collection *Tree
of Night and Other Stories*.
† Luise Rainer (1910–2014), a German-born film actress who won two Academy Awards for
her roles in *The Great Ziegfeld* (1936) and in *The Good Earth* (1937).

said. "Do you want me to love you?" "No," I responded. "Do you love me?" "You know I do," she said.^{GG}

JANUARY 31, 1948

^GIt's terribly cold. About 10°. Vomiting, of course. Got up at 11:30 AM. (It was four by the time we fell asleep.) Called Margot—and visited her to see the editor of [Woman's Home] Companion. They want my last story, "Where to, Madam?," about the Rolls-Royce driver. But with changes, which I think I can make. And they're paying a thousand dollars. Then on to see Mr. Davis*—the strange man of 31 Rockefeller Plaza, editor of comic books and Ballet Theatre publications. He asked if I wanted work. My lucky day! And tonight with Kingsley. She told me what I already know about Tucker: he's weak, and the reader doesn't care what happens to him.^{GG}

FEBRUARY 1, 1948

^GI'm doing nothing. And feeling very happy. Took an impromptu trip to Hastings at 3 o'clock—how wonderful it is to have such a home!^{GG}

FEBRUARY 2, 1948

^GMy first truly free day in months! If only I had given myself more! I would have written much better!^{GG}

FEBRUARY 5, 1948

^GSaw A Streetcar Named Desire† with Jeanne yesterday, the best play of my life. I could have cried at the end, it was so accomplished. Jeanne said, "One should only see it with someone he loves." Later—went home, so happy and content, thinking of Jeanne. And wrote her a long, quick letter, in which I attempted

---

* Blevins Davis (1903–1971), American theatrical producer and a close personal friend of Harry S. Truman and his family. By 1949, he was president of the Ballet Theater of New York (now American Ballet Theater).
† Tennessee Williams's play opened on Broadway on December 3, 1947, directed by Elia Kazan with Marlon Brando in the lead role.

to give her some self-confidence. Said that if I were a man (so many of my fantasies begin that way: If I were a man—), I would venture to marry her. ("But you—never marry a writer!")[GG]

2/9/48

The East River in mid-winter. One comes upon it and stops with a sense of space, of broad and unstoppable, unstopping power that is a strange and frightening sensation to a man who has been imprisoned in the city for weeks and months. The fragments of filthy ice-floes that dot its surface seem the coldest, most miserable, most cruel, most destroyed objects to be found in New York. Some are so weighted with smut, so exhausted and honey-combed by the river, they float quite beneath the surface, and these are the most miserable and hideous of all. One's face must harden a little to look farther across the river. Seagulls that have found a perching place on a flat piece of ice yawp happily from the center of its surface triumphantly in mid-stream— strange and ghostly the sound from afar on the insubstantial river! The scene is gray. Concatenations of floes drift backward here & there confusedly in a divided current. Waste! Waste! And the heart does not dare raise a happier image, a private image, now that the physical eye beholds this physical statement.

My love, where are you now? You who were with me a block ago! In absolute silence a tug boat matted with soot-covered ice as thickly as with rope and truck tires, burrows through ice and water, thrusting on ahead a coal barge, or two, or three. The tiny girl in zippered leggings, who stands near me with her colored nurse, screams with sudden nervous delight at the passing tug. She holds a large doll up to see it! The doll has only empty black ovals for eyes. Beloved, where are you now, where a year hence, then, if you shall be with me again in a moment, when I turn away? A year hence you will not be in my bed—though we love each other now, though we have served each other and made sacrifices for each other, though I and you have given you and me gifts made with our own hands—you will not be with me, but the river, it will be here, if I come again.

And out the window near my desk, snow has found its bed between the close-set backs of apartment buildings. Not for a day was this snow permitted to lie in the white beauty that is its own nature. In its fifteen feet wide defile that extends the length of the block, it has been trampled and mauled by the feet of janitors, children and dogs in quest of food. Above this snow the clotheslines of a hundred Irish families crisscross and tangle. Even the beauty of its sweep extent is prevented by the choppings of fences, dividing one house's yard from the next. Between two slim cables of some sort, a handball is jammed for all time, by an incredible accident. The telegraph poles that support the clotheslines lean powerfully this way and that. Only the buildings are geometrically true. And their confused projecting mess of fire escapes. I must have a picture of this alley out my window. Like New York in minuscule, it works with the space above the ground, the ground being dilapidated cement merely.

2/13/48

The prevalence of "good" and "evil" characters in Dostoyevsky. This interests me, egocentrically, because of my similar tendency. Every true novel inspiration of mine has had these elements. Charles and Bernard in the first book.* Now Tucker and Bruno. I don't care about technicalities. Good and evil are present in a single individual in life, hence my themes, which are self-projections.

FEBRUARY 13, 1948

GI'm seeing more of Lewis Howard. Am inclined to see either Lil or Rosalind. Or, really, Jeanne, in rare moments of weakness. I'm reading Kafka—[Max] Brod and [Paul] Goodman.† I have this persistent suspicion that Lewis will become my husband.GG

---

* Her abandoned manuscript *The Click of the Shutting.*
† *Kafka's Prayer* by Paul Goodman (New York, 1947).

FEBRUARY 14, 1948

ᴳI spoke to my mother about my ignorance of birth control. (I feel very feminine tonight.) Mother said she had been afraid, because she'd tried to hurt me as a child!* "It's better you learned from the world, etc." Lewis strikes me as very young. "You should have our child!" he said.ᴳᴳ

2/15/48

The sympathetic pain (or sensation) centers of the body. Relieving the over-taxed bladder produces a pain-itch sensation in the teeth. If slightly intoxicated (as is often the case when the bladder is overtaxed) the connection seems demonical: the urination which centers about the genitals reacts in the teeth, that seat of earth bound infernal pain and inhuman torture, birth and death, ecstasy and agony, the base and treble of man's appercepions. The body itself, to me, takes on a transcendent and metaphysical meaning: surely this corporeal machine was devised for something beyond its physical functions, for something beyond and more perverse than beauty, something less pure in intent than a reflection of God, or an exemplar of Nature's most intelligent animal life. Then the sprawled hand becomes a wonderful, frightening and curious part, the hair an astounding phenomenon, the speech magical, the power to love the most blessed, most abstruse, most magnificent faculty of all, and in its beauty surpassing the brightest wing of the rarest butterfly, the pristine majesty of the farthest and highest mountain.

And I feel myself convinced as much as I can be convinced of anything that the body has a significance beyond any as yet ascribed to it, that as a house for man's spirit while he is on earth, it is an enigmatic structure to be surveyed insofar as we are able, as an entirely different structure in a foreign land might be surveyed by an industrious visiting architect. Then it seems, too, that the union of male and female, while so complex, is

---

* Presumably Pat's mother is referring to the fact that she (as she informed her daughter in an undated letter) had tried to abort Pat with turpentine at the beginning of her pregnancy.

almost universally accomplished in the most primitive way, that we therefore realize but five percent of our complexity, and the proportion known to ourselves is therefore even less than the proportion of an iceberg seen above the surface.

FEBRUARY 17, 1948

GHeard from Margot that Viking didn't like the premise of my novel enough. And the chaos creeps into me, widespread fear, the next war, and in me, downfall, failure—the situation with Jeanne is particularly bad, that we know we have to break things off soon.GG

2/17/48

Already the great dichotomy between the person I am at night, the person I am by day, even doing my own writing. The nocturnal person is far advanced in thought and imagination. The daytime person still lives and works too much with the world which is not mine. I must get them together, and toward the night.

FEBRUARY 18, 1948

GMiserable. Don't want to see anyone. [Woman's Home] Companion wants more work (on the story ["Where to, Madam?"]), and they're right.GG

FEBRUARY 20, 1948

GTook a walk with Lewis on Wednesday, had a coffee soda at Schrafft's. He makes me much cheerier, the sympathy of a man. And he's both strong and sweet. Something rare.GG

FEBRUARY 21, 1948

GHastings with Dell* and Lil. Miserable, despondent, depressed, because I want to work, because I don't really want Jeanne, because Lewis was bothering me. I want to change my sex. Is that possible? And then, Lewis is a Jew, which makes

---

* Lil's husband.

me feel all the more that I can't give myself to him. But we have so much in common. Drank too many Old Fashioneds and cried this evening.^{GG}

FEBRUARY 22, 1948

^GStill not happy. Reading Kafka and feeling afraid, because I'm so similar to him. And I'm afraid, because Kafka, wonderful as he was, never rose to the level of a great artist!* [Thomas] Mann is greater, because he could project his ideas!^{GG}

FEBRUARY 23, 1948

^GStayed in Hastings until I was finally feeling better. Telling myself I'm not at all disappointed with the book. But I want to have an idea of the whole rounded out in my mind before I start again. Margot said she wants a new synopsis for the novel before I leave for N[ew] O[rleans]. Further uncertainty—Jeanne—^{GG}

FEBRUARY 24, 1948

^G—is not going to N.O., I learned today. And there was reason to believe that we three—my mother, Jeanne and I—would drive there together. Joan called me Monday night. She married Chas. on Sunday (22). Am very happy to hear it!^{GG}

2/24/48

I am concerned at the moment with the biggest problems I have ever been concerned with. My foundations stir under me like huge slabs of stone. Unless they are steady, I can take no pleasure in the small achievements and satisfactions of every day existence—from which I and every normal human being derive greatest happiness.

---

* Only a few of Kafka's works were published in his lifetime. The earliest work to appear was *The Castle*, published posthumously in Germany in 1926 and in English translation in the UK and United States in 1930. A 1941 English edition with a homage by Thomas Mann spurred a surge in Kafka's popularity in English-speaking countries.

2/24/48

Comfort, my heart! With gentle comfort, soft as a woman's breast, I should be clothed as in armor!

2/25/48

Work at the bone. Which is to say, at the core of existence (life) after the rest is pared away. My difficulty is, what sort of person am I? Emotional, violent—these seem closer to my real nature than the refinements of Woolf and James, for instance! Perhaps the refinements I notice are merely part of my screen from life.

FEBRUARY 26, 1948

ᴳCrazier days than any I've ever known. And in the meantime—tried twice to sleep with Lewis. Only when I was so disgusted with myself for asking "So, do you want to go to bed?," and tired and bored, masochism set in. And of course I failed. Lewis, I must say, is an angel of patience. And I like him very much.ᴳᴳ

FEBRUARY 28, 1948

ᴳStarted the snail story.* I like it. But I'm tired. X-rays twice a week at J. Borak's.ᴳᴳ

2/29/48

The most discerning remark I can make about myself at this moment: that my emotions for the past six months (and before that, in endless succession!) have been so thwarted at every point, I can no longer even grasp tiny scenes in my writing with dramatic passion, can barely even express them! This at the psychic nadir of my twenty-seven years—February 29, 1948. Before today, I at least had a target for my centrifugal angst, at least an objective before me! Now I am incapable of the smallest deci-

---

* "The Snail-Watcher," a short story that Margot Johnson tried in vain to offer the periodicals, who reacted with rejection and disgust. It was only in 1964 that the story was purchased by Pat's friend Jack Matcha, then editor of the California-based magazine *Gamma*, which went bankrupt immediately after its publication.

sions, and cannot even envisage my future life, since I am undecided whether I can be happy alone, or whether I must spend it
with someone—in which latter case I shall have to make radical
adjustments, either to male or female.

A quandary? Hell.

FEBRUARY 29, 1948
GWhat? Social at Lewis's, so formal—and at Leo's, where I
found Truman Capote. Held my hand, apparently very devoted.
Wants to see my room.GG

MARCH 1, 1948
GTruman at 6. Likes the room. Ate at Louise [Aswell's]. I like
him a lot. Jeanne *au lit* though when we returned, which made
me mad.GG

MARCH 3, 1948
GHurried—for Hastings. Worked two days on the new synopsis
(of my novel), and this evening I'm bringing Kingsley with me (to
Hastings) to page through it.GG

MARCH 6, 1948
GVisited Dr. Rudolf Löwenstein, psychoanalyst, last week—
Monday. For the first time, I told a stranger that "I am homosexual." And he listened to the story of my life. And said that my
case will take about two years. A bit discouraging, but I felt better, just because I had told someone. Truman jokes: "When I was
14 years old, I told my parents that everyone was interested in
girls, but that I, T.C., was interested in boys!" And they let him
be. Don't want to go back to Löwenstein.GG

MARCH 8, 1948
GBack to N.Y.
Lil loves the snail story. I overflow with joy whenever someone loves something of mine! Trifles! My God! I think of Joan
often, of her husband, who now knows and loves the same

things in her that I loved and love and that captivated me. But Joan doesn't love him. Her letters make that clear.[GG]

MARCH 9, 1948

[G]Went for a walk with Lewis. And we ate (finally) and came back here. I worked for about two hours, while he slept. These past two days, I've written down the first chapter of the book with the new Tucker, Guy Haines. It seems appropriate that not a single line I wrote with Ginnie can remain! God—a sad thing, love. But working with Lewis—while he was here, the world was suddenly better. And he stayed a while—a little better in bed (the second time), but I don't want it, other than out of necessity, not for pleasure. I'm not even curious anymore.[GG]

MARCH 11, 1948

[G]Prepared dinner for Truman. Rolf and Mother here when he arrived. We had drinks, and Mother likes him a lot. "So quiet, unlike most N.Y. youngsters." And she praised his novel. Dinner was nice—but nothing remarkable for that gourmet, I don't think. Felt I should make the effort, though. Truman paid $180 to stay here [at my apartment] for two months. M[ary] L[ouise] Aswell, M[arguerite] Young,* etc. Very nice, and wore my dress pants, at Truman's insistence. Stayed out late—and later went for a drink at T. Trouville's. I like going out with little Truman: he is so considerate, and so famous! And so sweet.[GG]

MARCH 12, 1948

[G]Sent the letters [of recommendation] to Yaddo. Trying to apply for May-June. Mrs. Aswell, Young, and Truman recommending me. And Rosalind. Quite sick. I'm so depressed, my stomach isn't working. I'm still in love with [Jeanne]. That's the truth. I don't regret it, but it makes me sad. Worked a little while Lewis slept, and I suddenly felt so much better, I had the courage to try

---

* The novelist Marguerite Young, like Mary Louise Aswell, wrote a letter of recommendation for Pat's Yaddo residency.

sleeping with him again. I find it so terribly boring! No pleasure at all! God—how strange! The thing parents around the world forbid their children from doing, as ugly! I tried—really, until I was exhausted. It seems I am so small, and the man is so big. Meaning I have no interest in doing it.[GG]

MARCH 13, 1948

[G]Nevertheless, happier today. Prepared all day for Carl Hazel-wood* who arrived at 6:30. Carl very nice, we talked about him—he told me more, he said, than he ever told his wife or mother. And also said men are dirty. Carl has never enjoyed sexual intercourse. God! I play with the thought—that I could so easily marry Carl, that I prefer him to Lewis, that he would barely alter my life. I could "love" him, because he needs love so badly. And it would be an escape.[GG]

MARCH 14, 1948

[G]Work. Rosalind at 5:30. Martinis. She has a wonderful job now: just reading new books, seeing new actors, paintings, etc. and reporting on them.[†] Exactly what she would be doing if she didn't need to work. Visited Jeanne, because I was so drunk. And had no interest in staying the night, although I'd have been invited to. Hope that was the last time.[GG]

MARCH 15, 1948

[G]If only I'd known how to write a book before I started![GG]

MARCH 16, 1948

[G]Sketched the scene out the window, as I once sketched my house in Taxco before leaving forever. Have the feeling I won't come back here. Sent Bruno's murder to Yaddo, and a story.[GG]

---

* Carl Hazelwood is a young man Pat has recently met.
† According to Daniel Bell, publishing magnate Henry Luce named Rosalind Constable editor of an in-house newsletter—*Rosie's Bugle*—which informed all Luce editors of the cultural topics they should cover.

MARCH 26, 1948

My mother alarmed me by telling me she may give up the house,
come down here to live. What causes all this upset? Only a short-
age of money. And she says I do not give her the encouragement
I should. Behind this are many factors: 1) resentment of S. [Stan-
ley] who should be providing her more 2) stubborn attitude, that
since she stayed with him when I fought for a divorce, she should
take what he gives 3) childish attitude of the freelance artist, that
if he is not supported, he should at least not be compelled to pay
for the people who are steady salary earners 4) the conviction
that my parents' house is their bank, a bigger one by far than my
own, which my mother continually reminds me of, saying I am
"well off" 5) resentment at having lent her money without interest when it was inconvenient for me to lend it, that I am eternally
left holding the bag by creditors 6) resentment that my mother
says "You pay now. We'll settle later" and never does.

3/29/48

In Houston: even in a cheap beer saloon, frequented by fairies,
generally lower middle-class, clerks, knowing little of the arts,
for instance, there is still that terrifying glance of knowledge
exchanged across the room, from them by me, still that overwhelming sense of fraternity, bridging place, personality, interests. One realizes then that the sex life motivates & controls
all. (I am myself entirely a mass of tributaries from this great
river in me.)

MARCH 30, 1948

[Fort Worth.] Grandma & I leave at 4:15 P.M. I forgot my Proust
on the front porch, reading instead *The Atlantic*, which is most
stimulating. The train ride is pleasant, and I feel well dressed in
my gray suit, gray turtle neck, crown belt. I am attracted to the
quiet, intellectual girl across the aisle, who gets off in Dallas.
With clothes, with personal security, desire rises again. Tonight
in Ft. Worth, a letter from Margot, with "Where to, Madam,"
rejected by the *Companion*. Momentary chaos, despair, quickly

disappearing. Here in this sloppy house, incredibly more dilapidated than before, somewhere are those myriad hair-like roots which nourish my main root, formed in air and water.

MARCH 31, 1948
The days go by and I call no one.

APRIL 3, 1948
Have rented a typewriter, and begun, in good mood, another ending on the *Comp.* story. It flows. Yet each day that goes by—where is the writing I wish to do? I feel it in me. Shall I be like those people without number who feel a destiny to write magnificent works one day? Yet looking at them I know I am different, and I put my trust in my intensity—my enormous need—which I do not see at all in them. The fortune-teller's remark to my mother in N.O. haunts me: "You have one child—a son. No, a daughter. It should have been a boy, but it's a girl." All around me, the happy, light-hearted, happily living couples of the south. Courtship is so easy, the attainment so easy, their bodies so fortunate.

4/4/48
Venturing into the world again, among people, when a trip with two other people (are they people like me?) to a store becomes an adventure worthy of a hero, a voyage testing the skill and courage of a sea captain. The clay of myself, molded to a certain idiosyncratic shape by my hundred days of solitude, is pushed, poked, stabbed, smashed at a score of points at once, hammered into the mold of everyone else, beaten into a proportion just according to the laws of the world. My own work then is seen in proportion. And this is the precious gain: that works in progress are seen not to be the all of myself even, as I had thought, but microcosms in the universe of myself, in which float nebulously (I feel it now), thousands of other microcosms, scores of solar systems. Can a man express his all in a single work?

4/5/48

In the night, things exist naked; I am in perfect communication with them. (In the night, the concrete and the abstract are naked; one can make love to them.)

APRIL 10, 1948

My mother awakened me at 9 with a call that I have been admitted to Yaddo. I am thrilled and delighted. Such a relief, like a soldier, to have one's life planned for the next 10–12 weeks! My mother pleased too, and grandma impressed. Grandma read all about Yaddo in the pamphlet. How wide in range are her interests—how much grander a person is she than all her offspring. Constantly I think how the family since her children's generation has steadily married downward, with the exception of Claude. I read F. B. Simkins *The South Old & New, a History 1820–1947* with great enthusiasm every night until late. Am retyping my Mexican story. It is so good, so far as facts go. Maybe Margot can do something. What for a title?

4/24/48

[New Orleans.] Chicory coffee and over fatigue—How perfect these nightmarish moments—On awakening to close the green transom. Get a drink for medical purposes, there is that last brilliant cannon shot on the battleground of myself—(jolted, shocked, by shots of wisdom for which I would not trade a sound night's sleep at any time)—that because I deprived from her my alcoholic lover's first love alcohol, she was determined to deprive me of herself. O what in life is worth the wisdom of the heart? As I stand alone in my New Orleans hotel room at 3:15 A.M., my body subtly shakes, like Baudelaire's. I feel my intuitive powers, feel their end, too, for I am weak now, and the body which warreth against the spirit, does not last long under such treatment.

4/25/48

The homosexual is a higher type of man than other men. Inevitably he partakes less of the physical and the biologic forces for his passions, his intellectual powers. Is his sexual love not entirely within the highest faculty of humans, the imagination? And danger, uncertainty, incompleteness, an imposed and loathed philosophy of transience (with which his ideals are always at war) keeps him stimulated as if by drugs and mortal combat to the greatest effort of his mind and heart. It is this that makes him philosophically and artistically productive. Creative, I should say, not always productive. The homosexual's normal plane is that to which every ordinary artist must attain by chance or effort in order to align experiences for artistic value.

5/8/48

All the world is unreality, as the believers in Christ are the first to aver. Therefore, why do my parents assert that I live unreally? I live more purely, on more pure illusion, on more beautiful dream, than they, who live also on dream. Theirs happens to be the dream of the heterosexual world which lives undisturbed, untormented, buying and living in houses with the persons they love, as I cannot.

MAY 11–30, 1948

What to say of Yaddo? I shall never forget it. A singularly dull bunch, no big names—though Marc Brandel* is interesting. Bob White, Clifford Wright,† Irene Orgel, Gail Kubik,‡ Chester Himes,§ and Vivien K[och] MacLeod, W. S. Graham, a Scots poet, Harold Shapero¶ & wife, Stan[ley] Levine, painter, Flannery O'Connor.** Great desire to drink, after 3 days. The drunkest evening of my life after ten days. At the Maranese

---

* Marc Brandel (1919–1994), a British author and TV producer who wrote several titles in The Three Investigators book series.
† American painter Clifford C. Wright (1919–1999) went on to marry Elsa Gress, a famous feminist Danish writer.
‡ Gail Thompson Kubik (1914–1984), American composer.
§ Chester Himes (1909–1984), Black American crime novelist.
¶ Harold Shapero (1920–2013) was an American composer, his wife the abstract expressionist painter Esther Geller (1921–2015)
** Flannery O'Connor (1925–1964), short story writer and novelist from Savannah, Georgia.

Restaurant btw. here & Town, the place we took dinner when the kitchen moved from garage to mansion. None of us ate much. We trooped into the bar & drank as if we had never had cocktails before. Mixing was the order—for a thrill—Marc soon succumbed, with carrot hair in his carrot soup. I exchanged a revealing phrase with C. Wright, the solitary gay person here, which was carried no farther. We both know. So what? I must have had five martinis or six. Plus two Manhattans. A near blackout at Jimmy's with Bob & Cliff, who had passed out at the Maranese, & had to be carried by three of us into the cab. We propped him on a stool in Jimmy's, whence he fell like an egg. We seated him in the taxi, but when we came out he was gone! The taxi fare $7.50 for Bob & me by the time we finished looking at Bob's drawings in his studio. The driver drinking & looking too. When we refused, we were whisked back to town, passing Cliff on the way, staggering under the dark elms of Union Avenue on his 2-mile trek back home. This night has become legendary as "the Night Clifford Fell in the Lake."

^GChester tried (in his room) to kiss me. Did I mention it already? Doesn't matter.^{GG}

There are six artists here. We are all very different from one another, yet remarkably sociable, I think. What strikes me most forcibly, is our basic similarity, in fact. It occurred to me last night, if any of us saw a white note being slid under the crack of our door—with a sound like thunder in the silent depths of mid-morning—each of us would drop his work and spring for it. With what hope? Perhaps a friend, some sign of personal choice, of a singling out from the rest. And it followed—personal security, ego assurance, a lover. These every artist needs and wants. Even the married artist is constantly attuned to these needs. The mornings. Energy is too abundant at ten. The world is too rich to be eaten. One sits in a whirl at one's desk thinking of drawing, writing, walking in the woods. The overwhelming flood of experience rushing in from all sides. In the morning only do I ever desire a drink to reduce my energy from 115% to 100%.

5/15/48

Please try to notice if every artist isn't ruthless in some way. Even the sweetest of characters have done something, generally because of their creative life, that to the rest of the world is inhuman. Some cases are more obvious, others may be more concealed. I know mine exists, my cruelty. Though where, I cannot precisely say, for I try always to purge myself of evil. Generally it is selfishness in an artist. And because he subjects himself so cheerfully to all kinds of privations for his art, it is difficult for him to see wherein he has been guilty of selfishness. He sees it as selfishness for such an obviously worthy cause, too. Generally, in one form or another, it is a self-preservative selfishness, in regard to his not giving enough of himself to the world or another person.

[NO DATE]

After three weeks at Yaddo. The soul lusts for its own corruption—after only one week. Desperately, through alcohol, it tries to reestablish contact with the rest of humanity. One's eternal and individual loneliness is silhouetted sharply against dark green pine woods where it seems no human figure has ever walked or will ever walk. And too, there is the desire born of loneliness also, to mingle spiritually with all the rest of the world of this year 1948 which is now starving, fighting, writhing in agony of thirst and undressed wounds, whoring, cheating, scheming, developing private, secret fondnesses for the stinking gutter. We want that, for it is our destiny too, and Yaddo is depriving us. There is the moment of utter corruption, around eleven or eleven thirty in the morning. One goes to urinate, washes their hands and looks into the bathroom mirror. The clock in the workroom grows audible. One realizes the isolation and imprisonment of the body, one realizes the hell of the body (and not only here, everywhere and as long as one lives, one longs for another body, naked and loving, a man or a woman, as it may be). One mixes a drink of rye and water, sips half of it truculently at a window, looks at the sterile, made bed and contemplates masturbating and turns from it in fear and scorn. One stalks about the room like a criminal imprisoned, unregenerate, incorrigible. This is the moment delicious, nihilitive, supreme, all-answering, the moment of utter corruption.

JUNE 2, 1948

Happiness overwhelms me. Twenty-three days at Yaddo. My life is regular, pleasant, healthful on the obvious plane. (And how often and where in the past eight years, since I lived with my parents, have I been able to say this?) On the less obvious plane, it restoreth my dignity, my self-confidence, it enables me to complete what I have never completed, that child of my spirit, my novel, and give it birth.

JUNE 17, 1948

This persistent need to be forgiven. Romanticism? Mother complex? For it is always by a woman, one I must love. But how have I sinned? Tonight—depressed for the first time at Yaddo, due mainly to cumulative fatigue. Three days after Jeanne. I was with her Sunday afternoon to Tuesday morning. My book is nearing its close. I am no longer able to think about it logically or imaginatively, and feel I write like the blind. My contrary system will buck ferociously in the next days against the finish, but I shall conquer. (Which is I?)

If I cannot give birth in the supreme hospital of Yaddo, where can I ever? Here are no sexual or auditory distractions. Yet today so restless—melancholy—I asked myself whether I had bettered by seeing Jeanne or not, though she made me so happy. Incredible! Less than one year ago I hurried to my first anniversary with G[innie]. Now overwhelming fact and circumstances against my will have forced me to forget her. Yes, at last forget, the last step to annihilation! And no sooner is this done, than the emotional system begins to assimilate another, and to make her a part of it!

JUNE 23, 1948

ᴳAt 6:17 P.M., wrote "Finis" to my book. Feel tired, bored, and not excited. When I'm not tired, I suddenly see all the good spots in my book. Marc is very sweet, and treats me with increasing care. He's leaving Monday. And I'd like him to visit me in Hastings.[GG]

JUNE 26, 1948

A turning point. Went with Marc to the lake and discussed homosexuality quite a bit. Amazingly tolerant he is. And he convinced me I must abolish guilt for these impulses and feelings. (Can't I remember Gide? Must I always try to "improve" myself?) I returned with quite a different attitude. I think more highly of myself. I have opened myself a little to the world.

6/30/48

A certain calm is essential in order to live, relief from anxiety. I myself can never have this without belief in the power of God which is greater than man and all the power in the universe.

7/2/48

The attraction of bars: one can make of them what one wishes. As one can make of a woman what one wishes. A bar room is a laboratory to the artist, an opium chamber to the escapist, humanity to the lonely man. (And who is not lonely?)

JULY 5, 1948

I cannot uncoil myself—I have been a coiled spring so many weeks. For four days have tried to work leisurely. Now the tension is at the base of my neck in back. Psychosomatic, says Shapero. I long for the moon. Unshakable fatigue. I never want to go to bed. Aimlessly go to town with the crowds here, and long for something which alone will satisfy me, which I know I shall not find these evenings, the kiss of someone I love. Mrs. Ames* has classified me (included me) among the "hard drinkers"—Marc,

---

* Elizabeth Ames, director of Yaddo in 1948.

Bob, Chester, who are leaving. Marc sends me his book, *Rain Before Seven*. And declares again that he loves me. I long to go away with someone for a new life. Maybe N. of New Orleans, as Marc suggests. Yet won't this be further seclusion? Basically what torments me is a basic mistrust of men. Marc is exceedingly tolerant (and very affectionate) saying for instance, he considers me very feminine.

JULY 16, 1948

[Mother's] overconcern with me is our undoing. Tonight, walking to Hastings to see a movie, we discussed it over beer, and she almost wept. (Much sentiment intrudes also, beclouding.) I take her appetite & ability to work she says, through my curtness & lack of encouragement. Yet I shall not leave, though I offered to, for that would be worse. (Am now at Hastings since July 10, and shall be perhaps a month.)

JULY 20, 1948

^GConditions in Hastings unbearable, and I'm leaving. The most awful Sunday afternoon, when I reminded her of the anguish of my youth, and only S[tanley] understands a thing. Mother simply says: "You don't love me. I've failed." And—I can't bring myself to respond.^{GG}

JULY 21, 1948

^GWill probably work with Ace Magic, where Marty Smith works. Thank God! Herbert L. called. We had dinner and he spent the night. The best yet. God—maybe I'll learn to love men.^{GG}

JULY 22, 1948

^GToo many martinis—and another two at Leighton's. Kissed Jeanne like a lunatic in the car, and was too late getting to Hastings. Jeanne spent the night here—which I'd promised myself would never happen again. But I was so drunk—dangerous, like Yaddo.^{GG}

JULY 23, 1948

^G[Spent] the evening with Marc before he leaves for Kent, Con-n[ecticut]. He spent the night—(three nights, three people!) He held me and was so sweet. I hold him in very high regard.^{GG}

7/28/48

A coolly objective remark: in happiness, the artistic mind tends better to pare an idea to its essentials. Only the melancholic mind clutters and complicates. Once more, be damned to the people who think the artist well off when he suffers! Would my parents could read this, but they never will.

AUGUST 2, 1948

^GThese days, I've been speaking with Jeanne about the need for us to separate. Promised Marc I would. She was sad, but under-stands. Mostly she was jealous, I think. And later with Marc. I asked if he could spend the night with me. Said yes. He was very sweet, but nothing happened, and I was upset again.^{GG}

8/5/48

Persistently, I have the vision of a house in the country with the blond wife whom I adore, with the children whom I adore, on the land and with the trees I adore. I know this will never be, yet will be partially, that tantalizing measure (of a man) which leads me on. My God, and my beloved, it can never be! And yet I love, in flesh and bone and clothed in love, as all mankind. The pulse of love in me beats strongly in the winter as in the spring. Which is to say, I am no animal in season. I am God's man in all moments. Never will my strength fail. At night, alone, I walk the hilly roads of the country and the woods with feet that can if I wish run up hill and down, that balance perfectly, that keep their power in reserve. At night, I lie in moonlight on my pillow. My love is not with me. I am not with my love in flesh. Ah, yet my love is with me, purer than she ever was!

AUGUST 6–9, 1948

^GThese are important days, because I'm making the greatest effort with Marc. He wants to go to Louisiana in the spring, with me—to live and to work. Wants to marry me, too, but I prefer to wait. I don't want to hurt him. But I fear I will never love him. So disgusted with him on Saturday—he was drunk, ugly, not at all appealing. I lay there thinking, how beautiful and lovely and pure girls are! And I [was] terribly sad.^{GG}

AUGUST 14, 1948

^GI love Jeanne. I'm in love with her. It's because I've grown up, that it now takes on a different form. I'm slower, more serious and not more serious, but truly attentive. And today was hell. (2:30 P.M.) Had a tooth pulled.^{GG}

AUGUST 20, 1948

^GJeanne called me at 11:38 P.M. Made me very happy. J. and I were here again. But tomorrow I will seek her like I seek the sun. I want her. I only like women. Marc said last night, I want to spend my life with you, even if I have to sleep with whores, and you with women.^{GG}

SEPTEMBER 8, 1948

^GSaw Rosalind. And each time I see her I feel like she grows a little duller, a little smaller spiritually. Awful to see, to say. But true. I feel as though she envies me because I finished my book. Meanwhile, she's earning her 125 a week, running around with all her "chic ladies," but doesn't have a novel to show. She can't congratulate me, and was so short that she had to call later to say a proper goodbye. I've never felt so "free." It matters so little to me, how much money I have, what I'm doing, for instance, in December. If I have to work, I'll work. "Working!" What nonsense, to fear that! Was I not just working like a Hercules? As Thos. Wolfe said—aren't there a hundred thousand easier ways to earn a living?^{GG}

SEPTEMBER 10, 1948

Provincetown.* GMarc drunk when I arrived. Ann Smith†
visited us, I think probably to get a look at me. She interests
me—young, pretty, simple, and understanding. We wanted
to take a walk (a few days later), and Marc accompanied us.
Yes—I feel like I'm in prison. Always has to be like that—with
a man.GG

SEPTEMBER 26, 1948

GCan't stand it any longer. This boredom, loneliness. So I took
a walk to the train station to check the bus schedule. I'm leaving
tomorrow, I told Marc. And because of that, of course, I have
to sleep with him. And the fact that it's the last time is the only
thing that gives me the strength to endure it.GG

OCTOBER 5, 1948

GThese days pass quickly. Marc came back, and we ended
things while he was drunk. I said it was impossible physically, and he cursed, called me a liar, etc. and said the novel is
worthless, but I listened to everything and reminded myself:
this will help me.GG

11/23/48

Opening at Midtown of B.P.'s [Betty Parsons's] gallery. All
the ancient acquaintances, friends of my friends of my twenty-
first year. Age has sagged a chin line, silvered a golden head,
stamped its uniform signature of tiredness on a dozen faces.
I think of Proust, re-seeing the Guermantes clan in the last
chapter of *A La Recherche du Temps Perdu*. Apart from that,

---

* Provincetown on Cape Cod started to attract artists and bohemians around the turn of
the twentieth century, especially from New York's Greenwich Village community, for its
beautiful setting and light. By the 1940s, it was firmly on the map as a getaaway for artists
and the gay community. Pat returned several times over the years.
† The painter, designer, and ex–*Vogue* model Ann Smith was an acquaintance of Marc
Brandel's and vacationing nearby.

it becomes increasingly difficult as one's age and the complexities of this century's existence increase, to merge two personalities. How hopeless for real friendship, the savage crucible of an art gallery!

NOVEMBER 30, 1948

GFirst visit to psychiatrist: Eva Klein, M.D., recommended by D[avid] Diamond. I like her a lot—asked the most important questions first, and I asked: "You can't squeeze me in?" Need to take a Rorschach test. And of course need to find work to pay for all of this. Only $15 an hour, though. Following her questions, we first discussed the story of Ginnie—(just last Thursday I had one of my strange dreams about her) and that, and my work—that's all that concerns me. I left with a new happiness. What does the cost matter?GG

DECEMBER 3, 1948

GMore dumb work on a hopeless comic. And trying to get work. God, this struggle! But I'm happier than I have been in many months! I'm on my way out. I'm already half in love with Mrs. Klein.GG

DECEMBER 4, 1948

GThink about my analyst constantly. Back to the book this morning. But couldn't sleep last night, and was dull. Went to Stern's to find work. Too many there. So finally, after some hesitation, Bloomingdale's, where I immediately found work. Monday morning—8:45 God!

Am most tempted to call my parents and tell them to go to hell! I'm almost free of my neurosis—as from a cancerous tumor!GG

DECEMBER 6, 1948

GFirst day at Bloomingdale's. Training, and then toy department. Very pleased.GG

DECEMBER 7, 1948

ᴳHard work. Selling dolls, how ugly and expensive! And then—
at 5:00 P.M., someone stole my meat for dinner! What kind of
wolves one works with!ᴳᴳ

DECEMBER 8, 1948

ᴳWas this the day I saw Mrs. E. R. Senn?* How we looked at
each other—this intelligent looking woman! I want to send her a
Christmas card, and am planning what I'll write on it.ᴳᴳ

DECEMBER 15, 1948

ᴳLunch with Mother. Very pleasant, and I told her almost everything I've learned from Dr. Klein. She understands. They were
going to transfer me to "Lingerie," but I resigned. Am considering a novel about Bloomingdale's.ᴳᴳ

DECEMBER 17, 1948

ᴳI am very, very happy. So much happier than last December!
And—why should I not be in love with Mrs. Klein? Has she not
given me more than a mother?ᴳᴳ

DECEMBER 23, 1948

ᴳSick. 102° fever. Wrapped presents. An address book and par-
cel for Marc. Only wanted to see Mrs. Klein! She's the only person in the world who gives me the right answers! Was afraid,
because I was so sick, hot, and weak. Hence the fainting spell in
the subway. 58–125 St. She asked me what I was thinking about
then. "About death," I responded, "and that there's nothing to
hold on to in those moments."ᴳᴳ

DECEMBER 25, 1948

ᴳChristmas. Don't have enough presents for my parents. Or
enough strength to open mine. Poor Jeanne—I couldn't sleep

---

* After her brief encounter with Kathleen Senn—wife of Mr. E. R. Senn—Pat went straight
home and, as if in a fever dream, wrote the plot sketch for *The Price of Salt* in her notebook,
titling it "The Bloomingdale Story": "it flowed from my pen as from nowhere—beginning,
middle and end" in just two hours.

last night, so hard for her. Have fever, and so many more chick-enpox.^{GG}

DECEMBER 26, 1948

^GThe worst day. Had to call the doctor because my throat is unbearable. Fever of 104½ or higher.^{GG}

DECEMBER 27, 1948

^GA little better. My parents called me downstairs, to the fireplace, just to criticize me, to argue with me. Couldn't speak (sore throat) to defend myself. And wished I were alone upstairs again. God, what horrible people! ("You're disgusting, etc."!) Just see what we do for you!^{GG}

12/31/48

Really how the others live, the quality of their two-dimensional experience is really beyond me.

1949

A Book Deal and a Broken Engagement, or:
"I will not be imprisoned so."

※

PAT RETREATS to her parents' house in Hastings-on-Hudson in early January to recover from chickenpox. Rather than medicating her, Pat's mother embraces a Christian Science treatment, which is ineffective. Similarly futile is the psychoanalysis Pat resumes with Dr. Eva Klein upon returning to the city; although unable to help Pat reconcile her intention to marry with her aversion to sleeping with men, Dr. Klein does advise Pat not to rush into anything. In April, however, Pat officially becomes engaged with beau Marc Brandel. Following the news that Harper & Brothers wants to purchase her debut novel *Strangers on a Train*, she goes so far as to set a wedding date during the champagne-fueled celebration.

Between the failed psychoanalysis and ill-advised engagement, Pat's only remaining option is to flee, as fast and far as she can. In an impromptu decision, she buys a ticket on the *Queen Mary* with some of her comic book earnings and sets sail for England on June 4. She has long had many ties to Europe, from high school classmates to Greenwich Village emigrants and other friends who have invited her to visit the other side of the Atlantic.

In London, Pat falls in love with Kathryn Hamill Cohen, an American Ziegfeld girl turned psychiatrist married to Pat's London publisher, Dennis Cohen. Not much happens between them though before Pat leaves for Paris in late June. There, she spends her days sightseeing and touring the Louvre, then whiles away her nights in such haunts as Le Monocle in the Latin Quarter. Despite these diversions, she pines for other lovers. Pat travels next to Marseille, where she visits (and flirts with) the cartoonist Jean "Jeannot" David before continuing on to Cannes; there she encounters her ex-girlfriend, Natica Waterbury, and accompanies her to Saint-Tropez.

After Pat visits Rome, which she hates, she is eventually joined in Naples by Kathryn, with whom correspondence has grown increasingly tempestuous; together they tour the Amalfi Coast, and somewhere between Sicily and Capri, the two become lovers. By the time Kathryn is called back to London, though, Pat is also ready to go home.

Upon returning to New York, where she anxiously awaits word from Kathryn, Pat turns to her most reliable form of distraction: writing. She puts the finishing touches on *Strangers on a Train*, which will be published the following March. Having cashed in half her war bonds, Pat goes Christmas shopping and excitedly plans a trip to New Orleans with her friend Elizabeth Lyne, just like the two heroines of her work-in-progress, the lesbian romance *The Price of Salt*.

🜋

JANUARY 6, 1949
ᴳMarc at 9:30 P.M. One of our best evenings. Discussed my book, and he said that several pages made him quite envious, that many were absolutely wonderful. That was maybe the best thing I've heard in weeks.ᴳᴳ

JANUARY 16, 1949
ᴳMrs. Klein says that I'm far too young for twenty-eight. (Are married people that much happier?)ᴳᴳ

1/19/49

The writer projects, in projecting himself into his characters, his value of himself also. In an era noted for its unmemorable fiction heroes, the psychologists are quite right to diagnose a universal guilt complex.

JANUARY 27, 1949

GPage 195 of my novel. Marc says I'm working too hard. It's true. But I can't change it. [Dr.] Eva Klein—major progress today.GG

1/30/49

If I knew I should die tomorrow, with what eagerness I should visit an ordinary brownstone tenement in my block, look at all the children I have been mildly disapproving on the sidewalks all these years, admire the household's details, and love the expressions on the blunt Irish faces.

FEBRUARY 6, 1949

GMarc gave me an "Authors Guild" membership (as a second birthday gift). Since meeting Marc, I've had so much more to do. Want to improve "Mrs. Afton," (for instance). Marc liked the story a lot. Worked alone this evening, my novel should be done by next week.GG

FEBRUARY 27, 1949

GJeanne at 11 o'clock. [We] went to Nyack with Dione* to see Carson McCullers.† Jeanne bores me. I suddenly feel so free, without hard work, apart from dreaming, planning, etc. Carson was very hospitable, and we stayed about 4 hours. [Her husband] Reeves, her mother [Vera], Margarita Smith, her sister. Carson said repeatedly that I have "a very good figure." We drank Cokes and sherry. Books on the chairs and her and her

---

* Dione is a new love interest Pat has just met.
† Carson McCullers's family lived in Nyack, New York, half an hour by car from New York City.

mother were both wearing pants. I heard Reeves and her were drinking too much in Paris ^{GG}

2/28/49

Give me back the sensual pleasure of my aloneness. In these eighteen months, I have done a journey. I have listened to people shouting at me directions to get between rocks, over seas where I did not want to go, where I was tired of going. We shall lead you back to yourself, they cried, but I did not believe them for a moment. I only knew I must go. I knew very well they would lead me back to someone else, and cry triumphantly, "There you are!" but perhaps I should never get acquainted with that other person, and eventually kill us both. But I have back the sensual pleasure of my aloneness, that they will never touch, I know now. Like Ulysses, I am weary (but my wife has been faithful) and sitting about in the evening, I do not always know what to talk about at first. Yet the sea of words, the sea of my aloneness rocks me gently again, and after I rest a while, I shall know once more where to dip, where to drink, where to ignore the green current.

MARCH 3, 1949

24th Visit [with Dr. Eva Klein]. I hate and resent my mother to a very great extent, says Eva. Therefore my guilt drives me to girls, overcompensation. She declares I really hate women & love men, but renounced men, etc. For the first time, by these plain words, the muddled relationship with my mother begins to be clarified. I do not wish to see her now, feel contemptuous, sorry, ashamed of her, toward her. And now—for the past fortnight with Dione, Ann, Jeanne, I am "acting out" that with which my mother served me—the loving and leaving pattern, the basic heartlessness & lack of sympathy.

MARCH 4, 1949

There were three girls tonight, whom I might have called and passed the night with. I called one—a bit too late. But the point was, I didn't care which one I might have seen. I cannot work any longer in the evening when I have been working all day. Something different, but then, there is something different in my work lately too—more passion, which pays off even in the comics, even in the photographs in *LIFE* magazine, even in the shmoo.* No doubt Marc was especially annoyed because I was at Rosalind's. Because consciously or unconsciously, he knows she, in general, poisons my mind against him. "I doubt if he is good enough for you," she declares.

3/14/49

One's lover disappoints one, refuses to be seen, to be kind, to forgive, on a certain evening, and momentarily, one feels plunged in melancholy and grief. An hour later, or the next morning, the event seems less important, but this is illusion. Love itself has died in that instant of disappointment. Love always dies behind one's back. Later, weeks later, in the vacuum, one wonders at first what has happened? Why? When? Farther down on the vine, the stem has been broken.

MARCH 16, 1949

Eva minimizes the drinking thing, confident I am always repressed. This is not enough for me. No curse. Am 13 days late, though M. assures me I have no cause for concern.

MARCH 27, 1949

Analyst [Dr. Eva Klein]. Accuses me of being still the "nice" girl with her. Won't let my aggressiveness come out as I must. Pleasant evening cooking for Marc & a movie. He frets about money, has written to four colleges about a teaching job this fall. How wonderful if we could go to Tulane [University], since N.O. offers everything. But I still hesitate, have nightmarish dreams, of marriage.

---

* A comic figure from the strip *Li'l Abner.*

MARCH 28, 1949

No word this weekend from Marc until now, though nothing
was amiss. Oh, the unfairness of this sexual business to women!
My sleep is even disturbed by the fear I might be pregnant,
whereas Marc doesn't even know how I feel.

MARCH 29, 1949

With trepidation, wrong addresses got my alcohol-steeped specimen of urine to the bureaucratic laboratories of Garfield & Garner, 60 St. this noon. They clipped me $10 the first thing. (Who's
going to pay $10 later, for a simple no—or a terrifying yes?) My
head does not rest so easily tonight.

MARCH 30, 1949

A miserable morning trying to work. Got some beer for Ann [S.]
& me, drank it to celebrate the good news of my negative [preg-
nancy] test results. Amazing how good the world can look in one
moment! Though Marc who called later, said he was a bit disappointed, since we might have married sooner. Ann wants to go
to Europe with me this spring. I rather hope she doesn't, for I'd
like to be with Rosalind, or alone.

MARCH 31, 1949

Margot reports my alcoholic story needs drastic cutting. This
writing game is never ending! Oh to write a story or a book
which comes out properly the first time! And the doctors, the
doctors! Now the general practitioner, who has to fit me with
a diaphragm. The sign of the whore, to me, though I understand whores don't even wear them. I wrote to Rosalind. I eat
her Tiptree Scarlet Strawberry Preserves in the mornings, spar-
ingly, and dream of being with her. But now, I meant to do
more than dream. Babs & Bill quite absurd last evening with
their black & white communist outlook. Marc is so intelligent
about such things, can say in a short sentence the fault of their
thinking—which is that they do not think for themselves at all:
The remaining communists are a lot of fanatics. And actually it

seems to me, they serve Russian fascism, by breaking up the real liberals everywhere.

APRIL 4, 1949

Cocktails with Duchess, who has become a tequila addict, apparently. Vulgarity, coarseness, selfishness, materialism rampant—all this most hideous and depressing. The St. Regis waiters bow and scrape. Mentally I cringe with shame. So happy to come home alone and work. First evening free in 10 days.

APRIL 9, 1949

Trouble with Marc because I like to be alone—this evening intentions of seeing Ann or Dione, and decided on Dione. Marc called yesterday evening at 7:30, after Eva, and thank goodness we straightened out this slow warfare about my "time." I do not want to be absurd about it, but I cannot yet—bear to see him 6 nights per week, be dragged around here & there where I do not wish to go.

APRIL 10, 1949

The New Yorker, alas, does not like my alcoholic story. "Too unpleasant a subject—two people who become alcoholics," says Mrs. Richardson Wood. Talk, and puzzle working with Marc. Tonight we decided to be officially "engaged." Marc even wants to get me a ring!

APRIL 12, 1949

Evening with Ann, when I got woefully tight. (Why doesn't she serve canapes anyway?) Disgraced myself once more at the Brittany. Have only been there once sober. Continually reproaching myself about overdrinking. Terrific night with Ann.

APRIL 16, 1949

That I had to work seemed to make little impression on Dione. Marc for dinner tonight. Alas, I am weary from Dione, work, no rest, and he stayed the night. Disgusting business of diaphragm, which I trust eventually I shall get used to. We saw Liam O'Flaherty's *The Puritan* with J.-L. [Jean-Louis] Barrault. And Paul Monash.* When I am tired, as tonight, all becomes distorted, I lose all the ground I have gained. I want to be alone, I hate Marc, Paul, all people. I must discuss with Eva.

4/19/49
Will this longing never cease? Will this striving toward the unattainable never be discouraged? I have prayed and striven, too, for exhaustion, purification by pain, surcease for lack of fuel, but I come to think the fuel is life itself.

APRIL 23, 1949
How much I resent about Marc these days—his never doing anything but reading when he is here, while I attempt to play records, fix drinks, watch meat & canapes in the oven, simultaneously fix dinner, wash dishes, do the bed (and disgusting diaphragm) and in the morning, prepare breakfast. He hasn't the particular sensitivity to realize that a person in the bathroom does not wish another person sitting at the table just outside the door. These and a thousand things disturb my digestion, banish the gains made at other times. Eva suggests my illness Thursday morning was resentment.

APRIL 29, 1949
S. & S. [Simon & Schuster] rejected my book, though all have some praise for it, and all, like Margot, say I should have no difficulty finding a publisher. It now goes to Harper, though Knopf is very interested. Have rewritten a few pages. Margot so indifferent whether I put them in before sending it out; I so convinced they may make all the difference in the taste & style of the book.

---

* The Emmy Award–winning American author, screenwriter, and film producer Paul Monash (1917–2003), a new acquaintance of Pat's.

4/29/49

And anyway, is there any abnormality which is a bizarrer departure from "health" than art is from the normal living of the normal man?

MAY 1, 1949

Up after 4 hours' sleep to breakfast with Ann. Ann never looks more charming, or younger, than in her levis and big jacket. I dream fantastically of living with her, of having, for a time, the Bohemian life I have always been too constrained to take for myself.

5/1/49

Back of it all is a feeling that all this will change. A different life, different setting, something more permanent will evolve in the near future. (Homosexuals live more in the future even than most Americans.)

MAY 7, 1949

Very happy still, filled with expectation of Mme. Lyne's* party tonight. The party a fiasco, because dear Marc thought two boys were making passes at him. I got my coat and left. Wish I'd stayed on or told him off—one or the other, for I came home in a silent, pent fury.

MAY 8, 1949

In Connecticut with Ann. Very depressed from last night. "You'd better make up your mind whom you love," said Ann, "because you're wasting a hell of a lot of valuable time . . . irrevocable time." I feel she refers to my lack of achievement in my work, my age, etc. and it all overwhelmed me. Moreover, I feel literally deprived of something, now that I cannot fall in love with any-

---

* Elizabeth Lyne, fashion designer and painter from Great Britain who emigrated to the United States and designed collections for Hattie Carnegie.

one. However, it takes only a lunch with Dione (or even a good drawing) and laughter, to make me feel, and know I am, happier now, enjoying life more now, than ever before. Such a fact allows me to bear a great deal—even the thought of going away with Marc. Though actually, Saturday night dissuaded me from that. I will not be imprisoned so.

MAY 18, 1949

45th Visit [with Dr. Klein]—After the discussion with [Dr.] Gutheil, who has a shorter, stricter method of dealing with homosexuals. He strongly advises my not changing, of course. But he also prohibits alcoholic, homosexual, dope patients from "indulging" during treatment. Eva—flared up in typically Jewish way after I mentioned seeing Gutheil. In a spirit of honesty & scientific progress—I mentioned it. Deep analysis, the slow method (she is orthodox Freudian according to Gutheil, though Eva calls herself between Freud & Horney)* is the only one for me, and she suggests I consult with 20 analysts whose names she would provide, and unless they all concur with her my money back (!) We discuss progress in general. She says
    1) a basic maladjustment to people
    2) a basic maladjustment to sex.
From earliest anal-sadistic years.

MAY 18, 1949

Have a ticket on the *Queen Mary*, June 4th!

MAY 19, 1949

Europe crept up on me slowly, much a matter of friends, pressure, no doubt. Everyone so kind to me, and everyone to see there!

---

* Karen Horney (née Danielsen, 1885–1952) was a German psychoanalyst who practiced in New York from 1932. She is considered the founder of feminist psychology in response to Freud's theory of penis envy.

MAY 20, 1949

A gloomy, uneventful day, until Margot informed me that
Harper wants my book! Everything happens at once! After
all these months of plodding dullness, the book and Europe.
And—so I asked Marc to come over for dinner. He brought
champagne. And we decided to marry Christmas Day. Three
high points of my life—definitely! And to crown my good
fortune—the curse tonight also, for the first time in over four
months. I wonder if today is also Rosalind's birthday? It is mine
anyway!

MAY 23, 1949

My book's being taken does great things for my ego. No longer ashamed to face people, etc. Mother here, and Marc for
a drink. He thinks she is "weird," and can scarcely believe
she is my mother. "It may sound trite, but you have an air of
breeding that she just hasn't," said Marc, which surprised me
indeed.

MAY 24, 1949

47th ᴳvisitᴳᴳ [with Dr. Klein]. Last visit before sailing. I told her
of book & menstruation, but she showed little estimation of
either. General pep-talk and coaching about not getting emotionally involved with people (I am not so detached as she suggested, she says). And not expecting anything from them, so I
shall not be disappointed. (Bloody angry at having to pay this
bill before I leave.)

MAY 28, 1949

The fiasco party with Marc. Alas how dull all evenings that
should be social, because I cannot adjust to this hetero-social.
Rather stay home & play chess with him. On the other hand, I
view less dimly lately the idea of being married to him. Whether
this is because I have the immediate escape of travel, I don't
know.

JUNE 1, 1949

Nervous. Lunch with Joan Kahn* of Harper. All went well, and I believe we like each other. A very fine first novel, etc. and said it may (or may not) catch on extremely well. At luncheon, I decided "The Other" might be a good title, in fact, the best yet.

JUNE 2, 1949

Red tape. Renting the apartment. What results the N.Y. *Times* gets! People telephoning all day! With Rolf & Marc at Hastings with a load of stuff. Very nice, dull evening. Marc & I talked over beer. How I've got to be better (more affectionate) if we're to be married in Sept. Or December. We talk endlessly, mincing every point fine, then reminiscing!

JUNE 4, 1949

Because of Eva I go tourist instead of first class. Today I loathe her,—rather, am regretful of what I have spent, and do not intend to return. Rosalind, Marc, my mother saw me off. A short farewell, for the cabin is not attractive (D deck!) and the *Queen* sailed promptly. I could not see any of them from the deck. Who is with me most? Ann. I think of her thinking of me today. Everything a madhouse. One gets lost dozens of times a day. The meals are thrown at one, then snatched away. No one attractive in tourist class, and we are very effectively barred from fraternizing with the other two.

JUNE 6, 1949

A mad rush to the movies every night. There is not enough space for all of us anywhere. Especially at tea, where if one does not use a pig's tactic, one doesn't get anything. Began to write comics—very successfully. Six pages for Timely. My cabin is

---

* Harper & Brothers commissioned experienced editor Joan Kahn to supervise the Harper Novel of Suspense imprint. This was a period in which pulp publishers and publishers of "quality" books began to push into the others' respective territory.

horribly crowded with two Scotswomen (good eggs) and one snobbish woman from Illinois, whom we all dislike.

6/7/49

I am curious as to that part of the mind which psychology (which denies the soul) cannot find, or help, or assuage, much less banish—namely, the soul. I am curious as to the soul's dissatisfactions, that ever unsatisfied portion of man, which would ever be something else, not necessarily better, but something else, not necessarily richer, more comfortable, or even happier, but something else. It is this I want to write about next.

JUNE 9, 1949

Grand pre-preparations for landing at Cherbourg at 3 and Southampton at eleven tonight. Alas, I know the truth—I do not wish to change. I see marriage, babies, cooking, smiling when I don't mean to, don't mean it (and it is not being cheerful that I object to at all, but the falsity of all of it, the absence of love), the trips, the vacations together, the work, the movies, the sleeping together. The last repels me chiefly—and at times I feel I know it all, have been through it all somehow, and I say, not for me.

JUNE 11, 1949

A delightful first-class carriage ride from Southampton to London, where both Dennis [Cohen]* & [his wife] Kathryn met me at Waterloo Station. Dennis in a Rolls Royce. And a beautiful house to come home to—a Siamese cat, a superb lunch with Riesling. Kathryn is charming!

6/13/49

The warmth of brandy is very like that of mother's love.

---

* Pat's first encounter with her UK publisher, also a friend of Rosalind's, and his wife, Kathryn.

JUNE 17, 1949

With Kathryn to Stratford. Poor Kathryn—she unburdens her heart to me, I trust, about Dennis. She has money to play with, but passion—she cannot spend at the moment, and she has a treasure of that. A rushed bite of dinner at the Avon [Hotel], and to *Othello* with Diana Wynyard as Desdemona, John Slater as Iago, Geoffrey Tearle as Othello. What a beautiful performance, and a beautiful town. Visited Diana's dressing room afterwards. Then to her apartment in the Avon Hotel. She is charming, so sweet to us. A grand party also, and a walk home in pitch darkness. I felt well, thanks be to God, in my nice tan suit, which Diana adored.

JUNE 20, 1949

London. Increasingly I must be drugged to be creative. Whether this is a stage, whether it is wrong (it is momentarily wrong) is the great problem. The worst letter from Ann. She writes me almost daily. "Why do you write to me. If you loved me, we should live together & there would be no question. It has been almost a year . . . I cannot keep the light touch much longer." And from Marc, the first letter. Rather cool, otherwise all right. I feel so tenderly toward him. But which is I???? Extremely tired. I grow ever thinner.

6/20/49

There must be violence, to satisfy me, and therefore drama & suspense. These are my principles.

JUNE 22, 1949

Today at last a grand decision. It is impossible to think of marrying Marc—a sacrilege. I prefer Ann. But as yet, I cannot trust my emotions enough to believe I love her enough. Perhaps that will come—immediately—for her. But I know I would only hurt Marc and myself by marrying him. As Kathryn says, it is not enough.

6/23/49

How far I drift from sensuality. Away and away and away.

JUNE 25, 1949

Last evening. Tickets to the Monte Carlo ballet. And this morning climbed to the top of St. Paul's, a nightmarish venture. The highest thing in London! And this afternoon visited Westminster Abbey, Poet's Corner—where I found myself treading on the tombs of Charles Dickens & William Thackeray! And the beautiful Henry VIII chapel, the Catholic saints' names erased for the new Protestant faith. Kathryn so beautiful in her gray silk foulard and pink kid gloves. We had drinks between the acts, and loved the *Sleepwalker* ballet, both of us. Very new it is. A late supper—much talk afterward.

On saying goodnight to K. in my room, I asked her for a glass of milk. She ran down for it, tired as she was. And put her face up to be kissed. When I embraced her—it was with that sudden release as if we had been waiting long for it. I do not mean to read too much into those short minutes. I mean to read very carefully the small thing that is there. She let me kiss her twice on the lips. "I never thought I'd kiss you good night." "Why not?" she asked. "Because those things never come to be—And now I don't want to let you go." But of course we did let each other go, and there's the pity.

JUNE 26, 1949

Up early to catch the train *Golden Arrow* at Victoria [Station]. And Paris hell tonight. Mme Lyne gone, no message, no friend, no French money. Had to be lent 1500 francs by two women in the Pas de Calais [Hotel]. Made direct from the Gare du Nord to Rosalind's hotel Les Saints-Pères. But it was full. *Alors.* The Pas de Calais. A very small room, without water, without a window! But on the street I met Valerie A., dined with her. And rather pleasantly drunk, back to my dungeon at the top of the Pas de Calais.

[NO DATE]

Paris. Bold, sprawling, dirty, magnificent in a thousand places, indifferent, curious, amused, tragic, silent, laughing, awake, awake, awake always. The Seine—Breast and blood and dream of Paris, glassy surfaced, proud of herself, rippled by coal barges and the darts of fishing lines held by boys along the sloping rock banks.

[NO DATE]

How I miss the long talks with Kathryn. What things go through my head. What a charming woman is she. And the pity. The unjustness. The male form without context: Everywhere. Dennis incapable of loving her. How alive she still is. How worthy of adoration. What a beautiful instrument to play on! What songs could she sing! How proud could she make her lover! I come to Paris thinking of the strange kiss she gave me the night before I left, the way she held me close and would not let me go. And why? And why? And why was I not bolder? How many years since someone had kissed her—a modest kiss, but one with reality—as I did that night? I should have liked to hold her in my arms all night, to give her the feeling of being loved and desired, because the feeling is more important than the deed.

JULY 4, 1949

Five letters from American Express. What a lift for the morale! One from Marc, Ann, Mother, Margot. The world resumes again, I am attached again. But most of the time, it is like cotton wool in the head. No pleasant moments of clarity, none.

JULY 11, 1949

Day with Alan Tenysco, Eiffel Tower, Art (Modern) Museum, then white suit & called for Natica [Waterbury]. I like her instantly again—more candid, thoughtful, than before. Drinks, then to Nuit de Saint-Jacques for dinner of Chateaubriands béarnaise. (But I reproach myself for ordering Vin

Rosé d'Anjou.) To the Monocle—dull enough. Someone sat us down for champagne, but we got out. To the Rive Droite, Montparnasse, for the Fétiche, which was closed. Some other place on the Place Pigalle instead. Dancing, a party of girls, one (whore probably) in black dress, whose neck I kissed. Danced often with Natica. Out in broad daylight, 5 A.M. & a taxi ride (300 f.) to Quai Voltaire where we spent the remainder of the night. Natica—*Nike Samothrace*—

JULY 13, 1949

How miserable can one be? The French train was the acme of discomfort—soot, noise, heat, no water, no food—and I was overtired, dirty, hadn't even been to the john—In such condition, arrived at Marseille 8 P.M., and was met by Jeannot with orchid and mother's cover, framed. He took me home to very ordinary apt. 19, rue des Minimes. [His mother] Lily, *charmante*! I had a bath—washed off layers of Paris dirt and Midi soot! Everything is fascinating—Jeannot much as expected, chubbier, graying at temples, but real American esprit. We drove to nightclub—champagne & dancing—La Plage. I think of Natica in Cannes.

7/16/49

How like a child she slept.
The light of the Paris afternoon
Painted a tableau of our bed,
Gilded the hairs of her sprawled brown legs,
Silvered the tumbled white of her slip.
I kissed her naked feet.
How like a child she slept,
And how like a thief I crept
Beneath the tumbled white of her slip,

---

* One of the world's most famous sculptures, the *Nike of Samothrace* is housed by the Louvre. It depicts the Greek goddess Nike, who is said to bring victory as well as peace.

Between the tumbled golden legs
That clasped me faster and faster
For N.W. Like the arms of a little bear.

7/17/49

The French are very good for an English and or American writer
to live with for a time. They bring the Anglo-Saxon back to the
physical things, the body, to a certain practicality, obviousness
of human relation, which in the Anglo Saxon is decked in formality and reserve. Curious thought, watching the first French tender
from the deck of the *Queen Mary*, first glimpse, first hearing of
the French: They are like extremely intelligent, extremely shrewd
animals. Like a superiorly sharp intellect concerned with the animal aspects of existence. Somehow a frightening thought, and a
fascinating one.

JULY 18, 1949

I wrote to Marc—finally—severing everything, telling him I am
sure I cannot be to him what I should.

JULY 20, 1949

Cannes unusually comfortable the first few hours. Met Ruth
Yorck in the street. We had coffee—talked. How casual she is
about Europe—all Europe like her backyard, or her large old
house in the country. She went to Paris at 5 P.M. And I went
swimming, miserably, in my new tomato colored bathing suit.

JULY 21, 1949

Prolonged negotiations with Natica, quartered at La Bocca, to get
her to come to St. Tropez. At last we took off, 4 P.M. Swimming
in St. Raphaël before bus (the last one) left for St. Tropez. Everything ideal—absolutely ideal—A lonely town—LONELY &
LOVELY, 8 P.M. Natica on my hands—I simply yelled "Lyne!"
and she came down & welcomed us, found us a hotel room,
invited us for drinks and dinner in a place filled with ivy & leaves.

JULY 23, 1949

Stayed another day in St. Tropez. And evening—Discovering for the second time (as I did in Paris): There is only once to do everything. And one night that is the best, and that is the first.

7/29/49

Europe for the first time at twenty-eight: it widens one's interests again, makes one diverse as at seventeen. This closing up! I hate it. It grows on one slowly from nineteen onward, as S. [Samuel] Johnson said.

AUGUST 12, 1949

Still in Marseilles. And Thursday, the contract from England* arrived from Margot. I signed it—it looks very good—and sent it on to London. Jeannot much impressed also.

AUGUST 16, 1949

Very sad and rather frightened to set off into Italy. Gave Lily flowers, said a slow goodbye to everyone in the family— Difficult. Jeannot drove me to Nice, just in time for the bus and a brandy before. An Italian bus already. Night in Genoa. As usual painful experience with money, luggage, taxis and hotel. How I hate arriving at night, not knowing the language, being weighted with luggage!

AUGUST 17, 1949

Milan bustling and prosperous. Accosted after dinner tonight near cathedral by an Italian guy. (What forward young men, and old, they are, dear, dear!) He turned out very nice, engineer, blond. Tonio Ganosini, blue eyed. The rather tough but very intelligent & intellectual banker type. He was between the acts at a theater, & invited me to see the rest—a modern anticommunist play. Tonio invited me to lunch tomorrow.

---

* Presumably the contract for *Strangers on a Train* from Dennis Cohen, her British publisher at Cresset Press.

AUGUST 18, 1949

Very much happier with Tonio. We speak French. After lunch, he persuaded me to stay till this evening before going to Venice, so he can accompany me. We took off at 7:30—much fun, really, riding at night, arriving in V. [Venice] at 11:30, without hotel room. We checked everything, & took a taxi boat along Grand Canal to hotel near St. Mark's. Then dinner. Tonio most well behaved, never a pass, good hotel. Venice is spectacularly beautiful.

AUGUST 19, 1949

Venice—the Lido—I didn't want to swim, with all the museums to look at. St. Mark's a mosaical masterpiece. All gold, blue, and Moorish in style. Tonio & I to Bologna at 7:30, where we parted, he back to Milan. He invites me & Kathryn, too, to Sicily, Palermo, when he goes there next—7 Sept. Am very lonely suddenly to find myself on the train to Bologna, alone. I wonder would everybody be as lonely?

AUGUST 20, 1949

To Florence at noon. I do love Florence. Bought a handbag overnight, which will permit me to check stuff at station. Found, also, one of those Italian restaurants people are always talking about and never find—cheap, good, jolly, everybody in the family working, some conception of American needs in the W.C. such as a piece of newspaper.

AUGUST 21, 1949

Wanted to make the 1:30 train (noon) for Roma. My one regret—the fast trip through the Uffizi Gallerie. One astounding room after another, & I looking at my watch! Arrived in Rome 7:00 P.M. Miserable start, and miserable finish. Everything went wrong. Natalia* not at home. Finally in Hotel Bologna, where

---

* The journalist Natalia Danesi Murray, longtime partner of American author Janet Flanner. Her mother worked as an editor and later acquired *Strangers on a Train* for the Italian publisher Bompiani.

my acquaintance of the train (who said he would be there) was not. Dined alone. Town full of little alleys—Christ how old! When do they decide an alley gets too old and needs rebuilding? Never, apparently, in Roma. Small boys with the devil in their eyes, suddenly flying a bucket of crap at one's feet after a slow approach. I sat after dinner in a coffee shop—everyone takes coffee at a different place from where they dine, as the French sit on sidewalk cafeterias—My novel is here, all my mail, can hardly wait until tomorrow morning.

AUGUST 22, 1949

Letters from everyone except Marc. A check—$28(!) and $400 from my bank. This leaves a mere $154 in now. + $500 War Bonds. Alas, my ups and downs seem measured not by my own achievements, but by other people's estimation of me. I must learn to make a complete shift in my system of measurements. Wonderful letter also from Ethel Sturtevant, which I shall keep. A real writer's non-writer, is she! (or maybe she is writing something). She congratulates me on the book's publishers, on my new Bloomingdale thing especially,* and the way I feel about it, and thirdly on my breaking off with Marc. Says his book seemed very young for me, advises marriage to an older man less demanding (I'd like to be married to an 80 year old, maybe, very wealthy!) And my book, in Xray box of Kathryn's. Changed my hotel, unfortunately, stupidly. Hotel Roma, near the station, run by a fantastic old gourmand I should never forget. Ball bellied, half drunk, a hole of a room, no service, no hot water & bad light for £800 (lire) the day, an economy of 230 lire, to make me feel like an idiot![†]

AUGUST 23, 1949

Roma—a dirty town. All the men masturbating or something, staring with idiotic fixity at me. Wired K. [Kathryn Cohen]

---

* Pat's "Bloomingdale Story" will evolve into her novel *The Price of Salt* (New York, 1952).
† One U.S. dollar was worth approximately 600 lire in 1949.

last night & she telephoned at 6 last night. Wants to join me in Naples. Was so happy suddenly—a proper date with English speaking friend—and what a person—I bought cognac, wore my sweater from Florence. How lucky I am. Though suffering backache (?) and sore stomach, I feel like a god as I lie alone in my room, too sick, too frightened (physically) of what might happen in Rome, should I fall sick, to move out. Out finally to eat a beefsteak & nothing else. Had had nothing but 2 omelets for 2 days. Forgive food details, dear diary, but they become life details, perhaps. Kathryn will join me Friday. I spin out the days in Rome until then, therefore, hating it.

8/23/49
The emotional problems of men are universal, the negative and positive reactions to women, and the causes thereof. But a Latin man, being superior in his Latin country, can arrange his life, or arrange it so that he can believe, that he is superbly content. In America, the man having failed from the outset as a man, as the dominant sex, cannot do this, and is infinitely more miserable, he takes himself to the psychoanalyst. But they suffer the same malady.

AUGUST 24, 1949
A study in misery. So miserable yesterday, it became funny. Everything *"chiuso"* the only time one gets there. Shall leave having seen very few museums, etc. Took off for Napoli tonight—this P.M. 3. And very happy to be leaving Rome.

AUGUST 26, 1949
I love Naples—clean, orderly, interesting as a port. Thousands of American sailors in town. Spoke with Kathryn last night. She can't come before Tuesday. I was profoundly depressed about this, but shall bear up with the aid of work, I suppose. I have enough to do. Cannot sleep well these nights. No doubt because much on my mind—Kathryn, boat ticket, homesickness, etc., etc. I am up to the hilt in *turismo*, really had enough. Christ,

how happy I shall be to get home! I like Italy less than France—I really cannot stand the filth after a while, the sudden sight of a snotty nosed baby (or a baby's rear end, in mother's arms) when dining, which happens at the best of restaurants.

8/27/49

I shall have the best, in the long run. Not a home with children, not even a permanent thing (what is permanent in life or in art? Whatever is permanent except one's own heartbeat?), but the best will always be attracted to me. For this, I do, most sincerely, thank God.

AUGUST 29, 1949

Had meant to visit Pompei, but an abortive phone call from K. [Kathryn] kept me nervously (didn't sleep last night) glued to the phone—which never rang again. Tonight a cablegram, saying she is delayed until next Saturday! More than a whole month! But man's patience is infinitely extensible.

AUGUST 31, 1949

Great joy: Got passage SS *Exeter* 20 Sept. out of Naples! Now I cash checks. My story "The Great Cardhouse"* is coming nicely, I think, I dream—nothing more—of a book of short stories after my novel, of the snail story, the alcoholic, a few others. And this one. Perhaps, I have never been so happy as in these quiet, lonely days in Napoli. It is a profounder—though less exciting—happiness than Yaddo was. For the first time in my life, I like myself. I do not wish anything changed. What philosopher can make a greater statement than this? What poet a happier one?

Of course it is the foreignness all around me, which compresses myself within myself. But this leaves out the reason why I am content with myself. Perhaps it is merely because I am happy,

---

* "The Great Cardhouse" is a story about an art expert who collects forgeries and has his mystique of infallibility.

which in the truly good person, is always the best criterion. I
am happy. I feel how much longer I shall live. I accept and love
the burden of man's responsibility to himself and to humanity
during his lifetime. And of love I am sure, too. With these principles I cannot help but love. (And as my master Kierkegaard
says, one must love always, whether one is loved in return or not.
Thus one must be always, inevitably, truly happy.)

I have never felt so old before, so wise. It is not so. It is
merely that I live with myself now, as I might have done, had I
not been so confused, so undecided, since I was six years old. I
feel for the next five years, I shall look even older than I am. I
am in love, in love, in love! While in Marseille, I thought a little of how it would be, of how it would be possible to be Jeannot's wife, as he really seriously proposed. The reason I could
contemplate it must have been due to its foreign setting, the
external fascinations of the new language, country, relatives,
customs—the beautiful French Riviera. How strange, how
superficial am I at times.

SEPTEMBER 3, 1949

At last, the telephone call, and Kathryn downstairs in the lobby.
They'd told her I was no longer here. I went down to find her—
as she came up—and she approached me from behind—Some
poor Italian cognac, much talk in my room before lunch nearby.

SEPTEMBER 5, 1949

How wonderful to walk along the street with K. speaking
English, instead of being by myself, wandering, isolated, unhear-
ing and unheard, unnoticed and unwanted. Men stare one out
of countenance. This is a country of starers. Reading, writing,
working, has blissfully stopped. This is vacation at best, at last I
adore my company, and wish only to please Kathryn.

9/7/49

Between the pleasure of a single kiss, and the pleasure of the sexual act, is only a gradation. Between the pleasure of the single,

unexpected kiss of two girls, and the sexual act which results in a child, is only a gradation. Therefore the kiss is not to be minimized. It cannot be adjudged by any standard except the subjective. Does a man adjudge his pleasure on the terms of whether his actions produce a child or not? Does he consider them more pleasant, more important, if they do?

SEPTEMBER 8, 1949

I wanted to embrace and kiss Kathryn. Depression—for what? I am not in love with her, only afraid to show the least spontaneity in my emotions. Always afraid? Always afraid—not really of offending—but of being offended by someone else's rejection. With her, I can only think of my bad points, my untidy hair, bad teeth, my untidy shoes, perhaps. We leave tonight for Palermo. The boat is beautiful. Suddenly we both purr like kittens, responding to the cleanliness, the good service, above all the leaving of Naples, the change ahead. K. will stay with me until I go, then return to Rotterdam, finally to London where—everything hellish awaits her—

SEPTEMBER 12, 1949

Rest in bed, not even swimming. My stomach is upset, but am always hungry. I grow thin and ardent on pure feeling, which is too much for flesh to bear, too rich. There is so much, so much too much to digest and to absorb into myself. K. is a little bit in love with me. And I with her, only I know, to less extent. She is a delight. And I am flattered. A honeymoon must be like this. One exists in order to exist like a picture. The waiter where we get our 6 o'clock coffee smiles at us. The weather is kind, and the darkness. Before dinner, we walk along the sea road, palm trees, beach cabins, holding hands. Oh the newness is always so delicious!

SEPTEMBER 15, 1949

The train to Siracusa, and the loveliest day of all. Hotel des Etrangers on the sea front. Engaged a taxi driver to take us to

the catacombs—where a demented little friar showed us through
the early Xtian [Christian] hiding places, the tombs with bones,
the cloister. And K. and I embraced, kissed at every opportunity.

SEPTEMBER 20, 1949

The day I was supposed to sail. We go to Capri on the nine
o'clock boat—running. A lovely two-hour trip. K. very excited
and silent at the rail. I was too bored, too scared to swim past
the urchin laden waters. Disgraceful. My first trip to Capri, my
one day, & the water is too much for me! K. terribly sweet &
keeps me much company. For we are in love a little these days—
and such people always like to be with other people in those first
days. The visible—invisible!

SEPTEMBER 21, 1949

To the Grotta Azzurra with K. Very cluttered with rowboats,
so certainly 50% of the light was obscured. What a shame.
Caught the 4:10 bus back to Napoli. Then the parting. And the
rushing. Grapes. And a last dinner with K. I in my white suit,
which I'd wanted to wear the first evening with her. We dined—
indifferently—at the vine balcony restaurant of our first lunch.
K. often holds me, looks earnestly into my face, and kisses me
on the lips. What does she wish me to say further? (I have said
nothing.) She doesn't wish anything. But mightn't I? Plans—does
K. want them? I know it is I who do not want them. That K.
could more easily bear than I could say, I shall come to London
next year and we shall live together. No, I don't not know what
I want. With perfect equanimity, I can contemplate nothing but
brief affairs—promiscuous ones—in N.Y. And yet I hope for a
jolt (of time, in time) to crystallize my desires. I long to write,
and dream of its coming out easily as a spider's web. Now I know
why I keep a diary. I am not at peace until I continue the thread
into the present. I am interested in analyzing myself, in trying to
discover the reasons why I do such & such. I cannot do this without dropping dried peas behind me to help me retrace my course,
to point a straight line in the darkness.

9/24/49

Capri. From the Piazza, the piled up black & white domes of the church resemble one dimensional stage sets. Middle aged women sitting at the tiny tables, gazing straight before them with a dazed alertness, their bright, overfed, over-experienced eyes like shining jewels, so terrifying in their richness that one can scarcely meet them.

SEPTEMBER 24, 1949

Genoa. Morning spent in ascertaining stuff about the *Louisa C.* Departing at 5 P.M. The boat a bit cockroachy—but just a little bit. Much better than *Queen Mary* accommodations tourist class, & altogether a nicer bunch of people traveling on it. I am happy.

SEPTEMBER 25, 1949

The voyage may take 18 days. And we do not stop in Marseille. Probably touch Philadelphia first.

OCTOBER 1, 1949

The coast of Spain dry and mountainous, in sight all day yesterday and today, tho maybe it was islands yesterday. Rewrote & typed the last chapter of my book, condensing the tunnel explosion & rescue and results to two & ½ pages. Perhaps I am lazy, perhaps tired of it. Perhaps I shall decide it does not suffice. I hope not. I dread the first hectic weeks in N.Y. For this, one needs a wife. (For this, a wife needs a husband, strangely, just as imperatively.) We pass Gibraltar at 3:00 A.M. The whole ship will be up.

OCTOBER 2, 1949

Does K. think of me in this long silence? I know she does. We have a strange psychic communication, we two. I began my novel, *Argument of Tantalus.** Seven or eight pages that went along with

---

* Later *The Price of Salt*.

that ease and fluency (of vocabulary) that generally means, nothing much need be changed later. Naturally, I am very happy today. The happiest since leaving Kathryn.

OCTOBER 5, 1949

Page 28 of *Tantalus*. I have no clear detail of what happens once Therese meets Carol. But it goes romping along, much as I do. All is my own reaction, to things—with only at the extremes, some extensions to follow more closely the attitudes of my main character. The sea is rolling rather heavily tonight. Could not sleep until 2:00 A.M.

OCTOBER 9, 1949

Have never felt such outpouring of myself—in all forms of writing. A great gush. I want to get this book out of me in the shortest possible time, not even stopping to earn a bit of money. If I could bring out some short stories as well as *Tantalus* in the next six months! Three books in six months—that would mean something. Only disaster the breaking of the little glass from the Hotel des Etrangers, Siracusa, for which I would gladly have given several fingernails. And Kathryn—Kathryn—I am afraid to write her that I love her, that I should like us to live together in London—all of which I want to say.

10/10/49

Ship's rigging seen against the sky. Geometric complexities, rhomboids, parallels, triangles and intersections of vortices, all in swift and shuttling movement by day. By night, against a dark blue sky on a calm sea, there is nothing more static than the stump of a mast, supported and balanced so perfectly by the slanting ropes. One cannot believe then that the ship is moving. One thinks surely something has gone wrong.

10/11/49

On thinking early in the morning, before getting out of bed: one suddenly knows the why of everything, intuitively.

OCTOBER 15, 1949

Land at Philadelphia. Steaming up the Delaware since dawn. No one to meet me, of course. Very ecstatic to board a train at Phil. and arrive in New York at 7:00 P.M.

OCTOBER 19, 1949

Marc called yesterday, to my surprise. We had drinks and dinner tonight, says he still feels the same, still talks of marriage, "not in two years or even more, but you're still the person I want to spend the rest of my life with." Marc stayed the night, trying to please me, but being too self-effacing even.

10/21/49

On the insane: they are only trying to find a reality. It is very difficult, if not impossible, to find a reality in existence. The greatest philosophers have never found a satisfactory reality, or its explanation. Going under gas, for instance, the world is quite different, more overwhelmingly convincing than the so-called normal world, as to its reality. There is really no reality, perhaps, only writing a system of expedient behavior, action and reaction, by which people have come to live. That is, most people, who live like this for the same reason most peas fall into the center compartment when dropped from a central point above.

OCTOBER 22, 1949

Date with Marc. Went to dinner—bad at Le Moal's—and movie. He stayed. I was excessively tired, and then—(in fact, unless I am drunk) he is so much dead weight in my bed. Oh Christ, I want Kathryn in my bed! I trust her. I like the fact she is older than me. I think she is beautiful and intelligent. I had another letter from her. More affectionate, I would say, more half said, than the other.

10/24/49

In New York the ground is fertile for paradox—and nothing else. I realize the necessity for the tempering effects of common sense and practicality. I realize that these alone would operate in a climate in which I imagine I should be most content—say, a village in England, or a countryside in Italy. And yet, the choice seems really as inconsequential as a diet. One should live, perhaps, entirely on vegetables and cheese, fresh water and bread, yes. But it is not death to drink wine and to eat pâté de foie gras either.

OCTOBER 24, 1949

This day completely yielded to being in love with K. What happiness upon admitting it, believing it, fully. The future suddenly spreads wide, revealing a whole golden-pink horizon. I have not been so happy since Ginnie. Jeanne called in at 9. I kissed her finally, *chez elle*—(why else did she ask me up?) and though she is engaged, to a numbskull, I gather, aged 35, I am quite sure she will be available. The spirit of reconquest, of ego, (of evil) motivates me tonight and tomorrow.

OCTOBER 28, 1949

Dinner with Jeanne here. She is being very stubborn. So be it. Very little cause for sour grapes. And perhaps she really wants it so. She is very kind, generous, a good friend. I don't want to lose her, and really can't think of anything short of assault and burglary that would.

11/1/49

Aged 28. If I didn't know liquor, nor its social place, nor its usages, nor its ills, I should be utterly fascinated by it. (I should have tried it, as I try a pecan pie in the South.) I should have respected it as that gauge between a man's potentialities and his achievements. For every man has greater potentialities than his achievements. This is his blessing as a child of God, and his burden as a child of the Apes.

NOVEMBER 3, 1949

Last December, I went running to the psychoanalyst, asking to be made over, knowing very well I could not physically survive another debacle like Ginnie. I was not made over, but circumvented the problem by not falling in love any more. I began to feel better, with a gradual lessening of the barrier between myself and all kinds of people. In September this year, rather in October, I began to realize, I could fall in love again, even thought I *was*. Now (at this exact date) in the face of possible defeat, I quickly deny and flee. Should I meet disappointment in the next weeks, I shall, quite aware of it, try to stamp out any little flames in me that might have been said to be the beginnings of love. In short, I must be in the same conditions as last December, so far as courage goes. And yet, can one honestly speak of *courage* in such cases? Why speak of courage! I know what is unbearable. There are some tortures that are unbearable for the human being. There are certainly some tortures—perhaps only this one—that are unbearable to me any longer.

NOVEMBER 5, 1949

Time marches backward. Myron Sanft very amiable *chez lui*. Gore Vidal.* And an indifferent dinner at the Bistro. Party of neurotic people, where, typically, I did not get on swimmingly, being tired. I swear to make more effort next time.

NOVEMBER 6, 1949

Typed almost all my [story] "Instantly and Forever" today. All I can say is, I've seen such things printed. Marc came up with a title this morning. *Strangers on a Train*. I like it very much & hope they do. God bless him. He helps me so much. Am very grateful.

NOVEMBER 9, 1949

I feel vaguely guilty. And vaguely vague, I suppose. Should I write "Love Is a Terrible Thing"† or another horrid commercial

---

* Gore Vidal (1925–2012), openly bisexual American novelist. Almost forty years after this encounter, Pat and he will take up a correspondence, mostly on politics.
† Pat attempted to sell "Love Is a Terrible Thing," about a spurned lover longing for a letter, to *The New Yorker*, but the story ultimately only appeared as "The Birds Poised to Fly" in *Ellery Queen's Mystery Magazine* in 1968 and in her collection of stories *The Snail-Watcher and Other Stories* (New York, 1970).

story? Or should I go ahead on the novel? I must gather all my energies this winter, or rather now, for the great effort. There is no reason to wait, even one week. I have not the slightest desire for "social life" or for a girlfriend—who would take my time and my little money. And that last item will soon be a problem, too. I do not want to think of spreading the book over a period of time. I must fire it out, like a bullet, at one sitting. The painters come tomorrow AM to varnish the floors and then I'll have done with them. I so want tranquility—of living quarters. It always seems "only another week off." I have, strangely enough, a tranquility of mind (in the face of no income). And I make of Kathryn a religion.

NOVEMBER 11, 1949

Lunch with Harper. Joan Kahn & Mr. Sheehan, an editor, junior, who says he likes my book tremendously, thinks it's wonderful. (Later spoke with Mme Lyne, who said Sheehan dropped in, raved about the book, without knowing she knew me.) Kahn against short-story book, adamant. Will allow me to finish *Tantalus* without showing even a piece of it. And some money can be arranged, too. Wants McCullers, etc. to read *Strangers* and comment for jacket.

NOVEMBER 13, 1949

I finish my story at 6 PM & read it to the family, who pronounce it neurotic, all but degenerate. No sympathy whatever for my mind. Again they attack symptoms: "Pat, why are you preoccupied with such things? Don't be." (Just don't be!) The asses! When I told my mother, re Marc, that I had a nearly insuperable block against men: "Hm-m," with a frown. "Now, I wonder why, Pat. What could have brought that on?"(!)

NOVEMBER 14, 1949

Happy day. Bought Levi's. ($5.50 now.) And worked on story. Visited Rosalind at 9:30, Betty Parsons there. Betty and I are kindred souls.

NOVEMBER 15, 1949

Typed on yellow paper 20 pages "Love Is a Terrible Thing." I like it. But grew terribly restless 3 PM. The story is so much K. and myself. And surely my parents must have remarked it, too. This past weekend, I was too open about matters homosexual, in general. Must strike a medium. Why don't they ask me point-blank some time. "How do you feel about women?" my mother asked me. "I trust them much more. But you see, I have never lived with any. I am the remote type—forever."

NOVEMBER 19, 1949

Visited Rolf, who is still very much abed with jaundice. Poor fellow. Marc at seven. I remind him of his brother Aden. "Look like him?" "A little." I shall leave it to his psychoanalyst to tell him that he is attracted to me for homosexual reasons, which I have always known. Resented him so terribly, after this unaffectionate evening, when he asked to stay. When he touches me, anywhere, I cannot bear it.

NOVEMBER 23, 1949

Thanksgiving Morn: 2:45 AM. No letter from Kathryn. She doesn't love me. I had my chance, and I muffed it. (Will that be engraved upon my tombstone?) There is nothing in the world I want so much at this moment as a word from her. A new word. One cannot go on forever rereading the same letter. I am sick, and starving, from living on what one always lives on. Hope. The future that never comes, because one never makes it. That is, I don't. I must tell her that I love her. I want her. I am hers. I want only to be with her. I must ask her, does she want it, too.

11/23/49

Continually I toy with my "if—ifs." For instance, if my experience should be shut off now, sexually, emotionally (not intellectually), but mundanely, practically, I feel I should have enough. I have stretched an hour into eternity. It is all within me. I have but to draw upon it. I have not been to sea for many months, but neither have I been immured. And yet I know as I write this, that in a week, I shall condemn it as sterile, decadent, simply stupid. Thank God, I am not the single person, not even worshipping the Intellect and the Soul with single mind, like Melville! For Melville became insane, and I shall not. This afternoon in Hastings, I raked leaves, in the sun and the air and the smoke. And I loved my love with all my heart. Therefore, I felt and I knew that I was not entirely the priggish person I had been half an hour before, immersed in Melville's *Pierre* and following his vagaries of soul with the most personally involved fascination. Therefore, I know I shall not ever go mad. Which is one of the matters for which I give thanks this Thanksgiving Day.

NOVEMBER 26, 1949
Another letter from Kathryn. The first in two weeks, but well [worth] waiting for. It transforms everything. She misses me. It was a very intimate letter. I have never been so happy in my life. I must literally rest a while each day, lest I drop dead with the absurd ailment of Euphoria. Not that I am excited. I am calm, serene, my concentration is even good. But I am blessed, and I know it. All these years of repression, sacrifice, disillusionment, frustration, have come to be of value, for they help me to measure my extreme happiness now. Rosalind says: "You've always been happiest when you're alone, haven't you?" "Yes—physically perhaps." "Or do you consider yourself alone now?" "Yes."

NOVEMBER 26, 1949
Lyne informs me Sheehan of Harper was chiefly fascinated by my book's [*Strangers on a Train*] "homosexual theme" and presumably subject matter. I was astounded, a little disturbed. Felt wonderful this evening, going downtown after one martini here, my pinstripe suit. I prefer my hair straight. Frightfully, danger-

ously tired when I went to bed at 4 A.M. I am always afraid of dropping dead, of course.

11/29/49

However passionately one believes, and tries to live, and tries to write, how many days of passion can one net per week? About one. One's health must be perfect, and this is not even mentioned in the formula: food, sleep, exercise. The house must be clean, or passably so. There must be no social engagements to prey upon the mind. One must be emotionally secure, or have an emotional goal. (One is as hard of attainment as the other.)

DECEMBER 5, 1949

Delivered "Heloise"* [to Margot], & learned the *Companion* & *Today's Woman* rejected "Instantly and Forever." Which of course translated itself only as not seeing K. any ways soon. Gradually yielded to profoundest depression in months—mostly that interlude between projects, stories & the novel, in which I live suddenly, and realize the world around me. My world being most unsatisfactory, financially and emotionally at present.

DECEMBER 8, 1949

I read my notebooks all evening. A real thesaurus! I lay closer plans of *Tantalus*. I believe it will go well. I must not be too loose, that is all! I am happy tonight. And if I don't have a letter from K. tomorrow, the fourteenth day? I shall be disappointed, sorry, but not unhappy. For betrayal of faith and trust is the very theme of *Tantalus*, which tomorrow I hope to begin to write once more.

DECEMBER 10, 1949

Worked. And had a very pleasant date with Jeanne. A bad restaurant, she took me to, and to an English movie. This evening not so marvelous. I feel so detached from her, really, more

---

* "Heloise & Her Shadow": a short story that has not survived.

than usually, due to *Tantalus*. How well it all goes. How grateful I am at last not—as Lil says—to spoil my best thematic material by transposing it to a false male-female relationship! In Europe they would print "Love Is a Terrible Thing" as a story between two women, she says, and it would be excellent—wonderful!— like my "Heroine." But these shit-heels—!" says Lil. Lil is very fond of me. We are like our old selves again. I hope nothing ever happens to change it.

12/12/49

I don't think I trust anyone under the sun farther than the length of my arm. This—for the record—in a period of greater happiness and contentment than in the past three or four years.

12/12/49

I wonder if I reject Christianity—for the most part—because it is so obvious that the Christ ideal cannot be attained on earth? There is so much else in my own life that is obviously unattainable—the excellence I should like to see in my work, the straightening out of my emotional life, I mean some resolution of it. Therefore, I must have some religion more possible to attain. The bliss, of course, will always be higher than one can quite reach. That is quite to be desired.

DECEMBER 13, 1949

Mother here for breakfast. I talk quite freely to her about *Tantalus*, but not the love part.

R. [Rosalind] C. making an issue of the party, apparently seizing the opportunity to criticize my selection of guests. But I rebel against R.'s tyranny in the matter. *Tantalus* goes swimmingly.

DECEMBER 14, 1949

Lunch with Margot. She suggests I don't take an advance from Harper, so she can get better terms—but Christ! Today is my first real holiday. And moreover, Lyne & I talk of going to New Orleans together next week.

DECEMBER 15, 1949

Day of the party. I drank nothing. All went well after a sticky beginning. Lyne liked Tex best. R.C. accused Lyne & Lil of being of the same blood—meaning Middle European, which Lil took to mean Jewish. All too silly to recount. Sylvia wants to see me. I got many fine compliments. But I would not wish to see her again. "Totally base," I said. "Not quite," says R. and cites her money! Damn Rosalind for being a snob!

Yes—a wonderful letter from Kathryn this morning, which of course shed its light over the entire day and into the night. She makes me feel like a saint and an angel and a poet. It is no wonder people liked me tonight and that everyone had a good time.

DECEMBER 20, 1949

Took Marc his present yesterday. A little martini mixer. Alas, after New Orleans, I fear I may have to start back on the comics. I hope to be able to invite Lyne to Texas, and to put her up with Dan or Claude. Mother here. I am very excited by the trip. Unavoidably, since Therese does the same thing with Carol.* And I mean to keep my eyes, my heart open. I must feel everything, love everything, hear everything. Read Paul Bowles' *The Sheltering Sky* yesterday. Dreary with Sartre's dreariness.

DECEMBER 22, 1949

Too late a start after big social breakfast, and I am worried we shall not make it to Texas by Xmas. Manassas† campaign grounds, where my grandfather's two brothers were killed. Manassas, which means nothing to Lyne and so much to me.

---

* Therese and Carol are the protagonists of *Tantalus*, or *The Price of Salt*.

† Manassas, Virginia: Two important Civil War battles took place near the city, which were referred to as the First and Second Battles of Manassas, or Bull Run.

DECEMBER 23, 1949

Lyne surprised it is already Friday, and I think we shall make progress after this. To Knoxville to sleep tonight. I try to choose the best restaurants—something piquant—and thank God she loves to stop for coffees as well as I—but the South is not always good.

DECEMBER 24, 1949

We drive all night. The nightmarish café in Arkansas. We race for the Texas border. Lyne makes me feel wonderful, i.e. she makes me watch my manners. Always I am attracted to civilizers.

DECEMBER 25, 1949

Dangerously sleepy. Lyne singing songs to keep herself awake. We catnapped twice before getting into Dallas at 10:50 AM. Then to Ft. Worth. Claude & new wife welcomed us. New wife Doreen in a slip—to my great confusion. I dressed in Levi's, according to Dan's instructions. The hell with my tan suit. We met Claude, Ed, Grandma, wives, etc. at the Facette Apts. before trailing them out to Dan's. Much dinner, insufficient drinks, and dull, dull people sitting around. Where do they all come from? Women in glasses, sitting on couches, saying nothing, neither drinking nor smoking, waiting for the grand dinner to be served: turkey, cranberry sauce, potatoes, peas, gravy. Florine* did a heroic job. Dan in typical good form, charmed Lyne, I think, with Texas style table conversation: The disadvantages of a mustache, which gets wet and dirty. All the women screaming in horror & loving it. I had thought the family might speak more to Lyne. I had forgotten they were so self-absorbed. The asses. They really do not care to find out about things European. Whereas, Lyne is fascinated by the things Texan. We got too sleepy to stay for Dan's movies. Played football with Dannie. And rode Butter bareback.

---

* Florine Coates, the wife of Pat's cousin Dan.

DECEMBER 26, 1949

Luncheon with Lyne chez Grandma's. More turkey, eggnog. My
father came over. He wasn't bad, talking to Lyne about Grand
Mulet, Zermatt & the Matterhorn. At least he is interested in
a few general things. Lyne enjoys everything. She understands.
She tells me to take it easy—as yesterday, when I could not sit
still before arriving in Ft. Worth. And I know she is independent, that whatever happens cannot bother her in the least.

DECEMBER 27, 1949

These days go by like St. Tropez, proving it is the company, not
the scenery.

DECEMBER 29, 1949

We leave Ft. Worth after breakfast with Grandma. Very tired
tonight when we got into Houston at 9:30.

DECEMBER 30, 1949

The day very agreeable. We are in perfect coordination like a
single thing. We drove to Baton Rouge—a dull town. Lyne spoke
with a Cajun café proprietor near Opelousas. I couldn't understand him, but Lyne did very well. She hopes to find French in
New Orleans—we speed up as we get there—but I am not too
optimistic.

DECEMBER 31, 1949

Good start for N.O. [New Orleans]. We came in about 11:30
A.M. The town a roaring mess, because of the Oklahoma-
Tulane football game in the Sugar Bowl* Jan. 2. Lyne looks
everywhere with all her eyes. I feel so *en rapport* with her, so
much of the time. I got canape stuff for cocktails at 6. Before the
Grand New Year's Eve celebrations. The whole town is drunk
& I most of all. Too late for dinner at Tujaques, which I realize

---

* The Sugar Bowl is an American post-season college football game between top-ranked
teams played annually in New Orleans since January 1, 1935.

now (after France) is the only real Frenchy place in New Orleans. We went to Broussard's. Oysters Rockefeller & *pompano en papillote.* [F]Lyne is charming when she's tipsy.[FF] Got quite drunk, but perfectly under control, says Lyne, as we walked down the street, she holding my hand. She often teases me, or makes leading remarks, when I am drunk, though I never felter.

    Falter, alas!

1950–JANUARY 1951

Drafting *The Price of Salt,* or: "Writing, of course, is a substitute for the life I cannot live, am unable to live."

※

FOLLOWING HER TRIP over the holidays with Elizabeth Lyne, Pat returns to her apartment at 353 East Fifty-Sixth street in Manhattan and the manuscript of her second novel, *The Price of Salt.* Writing the book is an almost physically painful experience that defines the entire year for the author. "What is the life I choose?" is the question Pat asks herself, both in her personal life and in the book.

In the novel, characters Therese and Carol embark upon a trip across the United States to pursue their forbidden love. In an early version of the manuscript, the romance ends quickly and dramatically. Indeed, this is how same-sex love stories *must* end during the McCarthy era, if there is to be any hope of passing the censors and getting published. Until 1958, the U.S. Postal Service had the power to open any magazine or mail they determined to be "obscene, lewd, and/or lascivious." They also had the power to keep lists of people who received such publications. In her second draft, however, Pat allows her protagonists the prospect of a shared future, flouting sociopolitical norms by giving the novel a happy ending.

Regarding publication, Pat is faced with a critical decision: Wouldn't publishing a lesbian love story at this stage in her career risk her standing with her publisher and audience as a writer of psychological thrillers? She follows her agent's suggestion and decides to publish *The Price of Salt* under a pseudonym. There is no way for Pat to anticipate that the American paperback version alone will sell more than one million copies and that she will be inundated with fan mail by readers who, because of her, for the first time dare to hope for their own happy ending. It will be almost forty years before Pat will finally risk a professional coming out in 1990 and rerelease the novel under her real name and a new title: *Carol.*

"Prior to this book," Pat writes in the foreword to this new edition, "homosexuals male and female in American novels had had to pay for their deviation by cutting their wrists, drowning themselves in a swimming pool, or by switching to heterosexuality (so it was stated), or by collapsing—alone and miserable and shunned—into a depression equal to hell."

With the subject matter so close to her heart, it is no wonder there are many parallels between Pat's life and her novel. The character of Therese is the author's younger alter ego, and like Pat in 1949, she has a fiancé at the beginning of the story. Carol displays similarities to her current flame Kathryn Hamill Cohen, as well as her past lover Virginia Kent Catherwood. Mrs. E. R. Senn, the woman who inspired the novel, is also still on Pat's mind. To see her once more after their short encounter at Bloomingdale's, at one point, Pat goes so far as to seek out her home in New Jersey.

While Pat creates the life she would choose for herself in her novel, in real life lasting happiness eludes her. Her relationship with Kathryn currently consists of little more than exchanging letters and doesn't otherwise hold much promise—Kathryn has no intention of leaving her husband and comfortable life behind to start over with the considerably younger writer. Still, Pat plans to visit her as soon as possible in London.

There's very little standing in the way of attaining this dream, at least financially, after *Strangers on a Train* is finally published by Harper & Brothers on March 15. Pat's first novel is an overnight success with readers and reviewers alike, and the film rights sell immediately—to Alfred Hitchcock, no less! Pat calls off the engagement for the umpteenth time with her on-again, off-again

fiancé Marc, but on the very same day receives a breakup letter
from Kathryn. Hurt and humiliated, Pat moves upstate to Tarrytown, New York, and comes to occupy the world of her second
novel. She identifies so closely with her characters that she feels
happy for the time being, even without a partner. The love triangle
with Marc and Ann S. resumes briefly, which Marc will later fic-
tionalize in his novel *The Choice*. Back in New York, it's only once
she finishes *The Price of Salt* that Pat finally breaks up with him
for good. She stays in the city into the new year, then, just after her
thirtieth birthday, embarks for Europe a second time, no new novel
yet in mind.

JANUARY 1, 1950

Foul humor this morning. But after breakfast a perfectly lovely
day at Audubon Park, which reminded me again that one can
never be out of sorts in New Orleans. The animals were very
amusing, and we were both euphoric. I am very content to go
about with Lyne, trying to find funny bistros. Tonight more
cocktails at the St. Charles, and then to Tujaques. Polygamous
as I am, I imagine myself in love with her from time to time.
We bought some good wine for our dinner. Lyne very pleased.
Then Lafitte's* again. A couple of piano bars. Wasn't drunk this
evening.

JANUARY 8, 1950

Tedious trip to N.Y. I am very happy to come home, though it is
hideously cold. I had to walk a mile in the cold to fetch gas when
we ran out in Jersey. No home-cooked food at Lyne's as she had
expected, but she is so hospitable, buzzing around fixing things

---

* Café Lafitte, which opened in the 1940s in a Creole cottage-style building built in 1772,
became a popular gay venue in the early 1950s.

while I showered, drank martinis, and played our records. Life exceedingly pleasant with her. It is not the luxury I like but the manners that go with it. She even drove me home.

JANUARY 9, 1950

The galleys [of *Strangers on a Train*] are here. The entire book. I did half of them today, but intend to go over the whole thing twice. It will run about 330 pgs. it seems. My money is depressingly low. No letter from Kathryn. Dammit.

1/10/50

Loneliness. Not a mysterious visitation, not a disease. It depends what one has been doing last, what one will do next, whether it comes or not. This has nothing to do with "distraction" either. I mean loneliness has to do with the psyche's rhythm alone. Distraction never keeps loneliness [at bay], of course. I honor loneliness: it is austere, proud, untouchable, except by what it would be touched by. Melancholy on the other hand can quickly be touched by distraction. For it is a more logical thing. (And I can also see myself writing the very opposite of all this one day.)

1/10/50

A note on hearing "America."* From sea to shining sea. The many small towns I have driven through. The many lighted windows on the second floors of small homes, where young girls stand brushing their golden hair. The houses certain people call home. The rooms that are certain people's own rooms, unforgettable. And perhaps the rooms they will have all their lives. And the shaded window with the red cross over the sill, that I passed every morning on the way to high school in Ft. Worth. The bread they eat, and the boyfriends who call them, the cars they drive to hamburger stands in, the summer evenings when the boys are home from colleges, and the betrothals are made. The children that are born to lead the same simple lives

---

* "America the Beautiful," a patriotic song.

externally. And always, the loneliness, the unsatisfied striving that is below the surface, much or little below. The girl who is unsatisfied, and yet has not the energy or perhaps the courage to escape. She dreams of something better, something different, something that will challenge and use up the aspiration that she feels clamoring within her, that cannot be satisfied by the men she meets, the stores she buys her clothes at, the movies she dreams in, even the food she eats.

JANUARY 12, 1950

FLunch with Joan [Kahn] at Golden Horn. The famous seven martinis. One here, five during lunch. "One thing I must say. I always have fun with you," said Joan. I was almost drunk. Went to Harper's to deliver the galleys, then another drink. Joan is very beautiful.FF

JANUARY 13, 1950

FBad luck. I owe the government $122, which I won't pay. Margot says that I have to continue working for the comics industry for several months at least. Well, then I shall do that. At least I don't have a hangover this morning. Ann [S.] came to see me. She's not going to Europe this summer. Ann is too slim, not as attractive as before. My God, how many women do I want? Well, I don't get anything from Jeanne these days. How cold she is! Not the least bit of tenderness. I'm not a machine!FF

JANUARY 15, 1950

FDamn it, why do I drink so much? Actually I know very well why—that's why I allow myself to do it. I have nothing but my work. And now not even that. What's the point, God?FF

JANUARY 19, 1950

FMy birthday. 29. Work—I thought that the comics might be stimulating now. Unfortunately not. However, the checks will doubtless be. But the stories—! With the family tonight. martinis, good French wine, presents. And a check over $20 for a macintosh. Couldn't sleep tonight. I think of Lyne—who tickles my curiosity, that's all. Isn't that normal after three weeks together? And I was also thinking about my life. I should be writing now. I cannot possibly justify these two months I plan to work on comics. I don't get any younger.[FF]

1/25/50

Education. How we should love those years of formal education, especially in the university. To the reflective person, it is the last time he will remember that the world made sense, the world promised to continue to make sense. It is the only time when all he is filled and concerned with really concerns life. No wonder he is happy! No wonder each day is heroic adventure! No wonder he doesn't want to go to bed at night!

JANUARY 26, 1950

[F]I said goodbye to Marc. He looked very handsome and leaves for Los Angeles tomorrow. He asked: "Did you change your mind, Pat?" He wants to try again when he gets back. And I do, too. Only dead ends where women are concerned. And maybe, deep down, I want to try again with Marc because he complements my ego. And I admire him so much.[FF]

1/26/50

Insanity. When one has glimpses of it, it is not in the form of random irrational thoughts, but as the entire structure of one's information slipping. It is as if the crust of the entire world slips a bit, so that one easily imagines the north pole at the south pole one day.

1/29/50

And never forget (how can I) the energy remaining after frustration. The creative, demonic-angelic, bittersweet, and if the truth be told joyous energy remaining when one cannot leave home at midnight to go and meet her.

FEBRUARY 1, 1950

Thus, I go through life, subsisting on one drug or another.

2/2/50

I do indeed grow tired and depressed by realism in literature—especially à la O'Hara,* or even à la Steinbeck. I want a complete new world. Painters are doing it. Why not writers? I do not mean the pixie-like fantasy of Robert Nathan.† I mean a new world that is at once not real, and at once fascinating and full of message, that is art, too, as simply, timelessly, and unrealistically as the best of the cave dwellers' wall paintings.

2/2/50

I shall go and write a poem of silence.
I shall go and write a small black cube
Of silence, dedicated to you.
Through barred windows, I shall write
A poem about the view.
And of music as the deaf hear it.
And of your smile while I made love to you,
As seen reflected twice by mirrors.
For I am twice crazed and twofold mad,
Reflected in a mirror, too, flat, bloodless.
Reflected in a mirror, and twice removed.
And yet as full of life,
My head as bloody with love,
From dashing it into the mirror,
As any lover who ever plunged
With his lover down a cliff to the sea.

---

* Likely reference to John O'Hara (1905–1970), whose short stories began appearing in *The New Yorker* in 1928 and whose successful first novel, *Appointment in Samarra*, was applauded by Ernest Hemingway.
† Robert Nathan (1894–1985), favorite author of both F. Scott Fitzgerald's and Ray Bradbury's. His biggest success was his 1940 fantasy novel *Portrait of Jennie*.

FEBRUARY 9, 1950

Margot likes *Tantalus*. What more can I say? I am alive once more. I am in love with Kathryn. I am a writer, as I was on the Italian freighter. I am an angel, a devil, a genius. I must have nothing more to do with Lyne, who will not grant me her bed, as simply and partially as I should take it. (Idiot, she is!) I love Kathryn. My eyes are on the stars and beyond. My spirit wanders in the galaxies, and under the oceans. My breath is in the coming spring winds. My fertility is in the dry, living seeds as yet unplanted. My food is my love itself, better than any feast! The frame of my life is the frame of my work. *Gloria in Excelsis Deo!*

FEBRUARY 15, 1950

F Evening with Marc. He leaves for Plymouth Monday. For two months. Again—he still wants to marry me. He invited me to come to Europe with him in April or May. "I want to go there," I said—"But with me?," he asked. FF

2/27/50

The entire pattern of my life has been and is: She has rejected me. The only thing I can say for myself at the age of twenty-nine, that vast age, is that I can face it. I can meet it head on. I can survive. I can even combat it. It will not knock me down again, much less knock me out. In fact, I have learned to reject first. The important thing is to practice this. That my limping crutches are not trained to do. Ah, how insignificant it all is! And how significant! To one more love, goodbye. Adieu. But no—God will not be with you, not you. But fare thee well, all the same. God knows, I hold thee high.

MARCH 11, 1950

Worked. How hard the comics grow! Especially the dismal love story ones. I sit here, I stew here, goalless, getting sores on my gums, marking time in my career, imprisoning myself. A post-

card from Natica.(!) She is with Jane Bowles in Paris, going to
N. Africa next summer. Why don't I hop over, she asks. The
Duchess arrived blind drunk at 6:30 at my party, held forth
in praise of me for an embarrassing 3 minutes until her escort
arrived to take her to dinner. I shall ask her to the party, Friday.

MARCH 12, 1950

Frightfully difficult days—chiefly because I have no immediate
goal. No prospect of having enough money to go back to Europe
this summer (consequent guilt, self-reproach for stupidity). Situation with Kathryn still unclarified. Also due to my lack of
money and therefore power. It shouldn't be, I know with all my
heart, but I let it be. Whether I shall be with Marc—most likely
this summer, I shall be. But where? And married or not? Not too
happy a prospect either. My friendship with Rosalind continues
to degenerate. Do I torture myself also by trying continually to
return her coldness with my warmth, her duplicity with my sincerity? Lyne calls her a snob and a phony. And Christ—how I
admire G[raham] Greene's 19 Stories!

MARCH 17, 1950

The broadcast [of the interview] at 1:15. Very early, I was reading *The New Yorker* in an effort to be calm. Excellent review by
the way of *Strangers*, ending up "Highly recommended." And
calling Bruno [an] "oddly ingratiating young man who has about
all the complexes you ever heard of." The broadcast in a small
cozy room, not at all terrifying.

Helped Walter & Jeanne with the party preparations at
Lyne's.* Caviar, all kinds of liquor, almonds, pastry, gigot &
jambon.

The guests: Marjorie Thompson, Kingsley, Rosalind &
Claude, de la Voiseur, Dick Sheehan, Joan Kahn, Babcock of
the *Chi. Trib.* [*Chicago Tribune*] (drunk & very nice) Toni

---

* A party celebrating the publication of *Strangers on a Train* on March 15, 1950.

Robbins of *Holiday*, gay & very attractive, the Duchess—
but not H. Carnegie. Djuna Barnes called me at 9:30 AM.
She would have come, but was down with a sprained back.
Leo Lerman offended, I think, because I didn't send him an
advance copy of my book—didn't come. Everyone considered
the party a big success. Jeanne seemed irritable, so I was careful to help clean up. I also thought the butler was a guest—and
invited him for a drink.

MARCH 22, 1950

Margot reports a $4,000 movie bid, which she turned down.
Local. Hollywood hasn't had time yet. Margot doesn't hope for
more than $10,000 unless 2 companies start bidding. But any-
way, it will be soon, and it looks as if I can go to Europe this
summer, if I please.

MARCH 24, 1950

I don't like this upset state I live in—no inner peace, stability,
concentration of thought. I await word from Kathryn & from
Harper. Not to mention Hollywood, which will also alter my
life somewhat.

MARCH 28, 1950

Lyne told Marc all I need was a man to "make me feel like a
woman." Her usual, refreshing tack, and to hell with Freud,
and even past history. Pat's not queer, Lyne says. She's got this
wrong. Spent night with Marc. I am easier with him, but much
rebellion left, I can feel. And if Kathryn writes me favorably?
I envisage 2 months now with Marc, when I shall write my
book, followed by movie money, Europe, and I hope Kathryn.
If I were to do what I feel like doing, it would be Kathryn &
Europe, and not these 2 months (so far as pleasure goes) with
Marc even. Feel like a woman? He makes me feel like a male
pervert, a sailor in the Navy, a naughty little boy at school. He
has a knack of not knowing what I want.

4/2/50

A note after rereading all my notebooks—rather glancing through all of them, for who could possibly read them?—(and Kingsley, have some taste, have at least the taste I have in 1950 in weeding out what is already written, and recently written). *

Impressed only by the range of interest, the terrible striving in all directions. Depressed by the monotonous note of depression, and the affinity of melancholy. Impressed very rarely by cleverness, by poetry. But sometimes, I think, by an occasional good insight. A few usable things in literature.

Having made of my diaries exercise books in languages I do not know, the journals overflow with comfortable personal outgushings. I suffer too many hitches and delays, stagnations and frustrations, by self-consciousness, dwelling on melancholy. But this I must say: the sackcloth ashes age has past. The adolescent aloneness (reluctance to join with humanity) has past. So melancholy now, on the lonely gray seas, is tempered with sight of shore. I have my friends. More than that I have Life, and know how to repair to it at all times, under any conditions. Things which once were so bewildering and complex, marriage and sex, for example, are not so now. They have been torn down a bit. Become more lovable in fact.

I must get it all to flow. To let it dam up till it is an insufferable force, that has to be knocked out by liquor and dissipation to tire the body. In short—as I have ivy-towerishly preached since adolescence—I must learn to find life in my work, living there, with its dramas, hardships, pleasures and rewards. For I have yet another long road to go, before I can find in another person those compatible elements, which will enable all this to flow. I have merely learned, so far, to avoid those persons who would stop it.

---

* For a long time, Pat intended Gloria Kate Kingsley Skattebol to be her literary executor after her death.

APRIL 3, 1950

Margot sold my book to Hitchcock for $6000 + $1500 for Hollywood work or not at time of filming—6–9 months hence. Celebrated wildly with Lyne (broke date with Jeanne). Then called Ann at 3:00 AM. & was stupidly inveigled into inviting her here. Dismal, and I feel it's the last time.

APRIL 4, 1950

Very tired when went to Hastings at 6. Big gabfest, first visit in weeks. Family very proud of me & movie sale. I offered to pay off mortgages & interest-demanding debts. My mother refused loquaciously at first, then accepted a bit.

APRIL 7, 1950

Hysterical, because Lyne made me wait an hour for her. I have a cold & fever, but that's small excuse. The point is, the pattern resumes. The point is, I have a chance out of it now (a bit of money), and my imprisoned soul (in such bad shape that an ASPCA* would have guillotined me years ago, had they known, and God himself must be wishing, o profoundly wishing, he hadn't made such a creature or let such a creature be made). How about the insect in the country brook, born to live 30 seconds due to natural enemy living in the proximity? I think such a creature even would be considered happier. At any rate, drunk and sober tonight, I feel myself approaching the end of phoniness. I have lived as a phony too long. The honest money in my pocket is crying out against it. What do I cry? What is the cry of my soul? Kathryn. (Result of waiting for Lyne 45 minutes, plus 102 fever, plus lousy dinner in a nightclub, + 3½ martinis + a crying jag.)

APRIL 10, 1950

Excellent reviews last week sent by Joan Kahn. I copied them & sent them to Dennis, with news of movie sale. Didn't tell Kath-

---

* American Society for the Prevention of Cruelty to Animals.

ryn of Hitchcock yet. Jeanne for dinner here. I took pains—and
my pains were rewarded. We both were very, very happy.

APRIL 12, 1950

Am tired and terribly fed up with New York & this rat race I
keep leading socially. Visited Lil. She tells me (reminds me) I
care so little one way or the other about Marc, I shouldn't even
treat him this way, pretend to. Yes, a word from Kathryn, and I
should sail away.

APRIL 15, 1950

Rosalind & I went to Italian film at Museum [of] M.A. which
we walked out on (we both confessed preferring "brawls" to
polite parties) then to party at B. Parsons', and to the Village,
where the usual muck was stirring.

APRIL 17, 1950

I have borne heavier crosses than Kathryn. The letter came
today (written Thursday April 13) and it is not good, I suppose. She is incredibly burdened with all kinds of things just
now. "I have to learn to walk alone," she wrote, "before I'll
be of any use to myself or to anyone else." And that she would
like to see me whenever possible. Whatever remains but
friends? Marc got my negative letter today, too. Thus we both
get it in the neck the same day.

APRIL 19, 1950

Where have these five miserable months gone? Down the drain
with martinis, late coffees, naps in the daytime, a few comics,
and tears.

4/19/50

The one sane way of being successful in love—have the lowest
possible aspirations. What a season of vinegar this is!

APRIL 20, 1950

[Port Jefferson.]* One inconvenience after another. No gas. Parents left at noon, and I sat huddled by a fire the rest of the chill, rainy day, reading Greene's *The Man Within*. How brilliant it is. How like Kathryn is Elizabeth. And Andrews like me in my most cowardly, indecisive moments. (My cowardice, if any, lies in indecision alone.) I wept at the end. Real tears, à la *David Copperfield* when I was a child, tears now because I am grown up, and so are these people.

5/3/50

Herodotus says that certain Thracian tribes hold a weeping rite over every newborn babe, for the ills he will have to suffer in life. They bury a man with joyous laughter. This is ritual and nonsense to the modern man, who, however, could well do with a few of his emotional pipes opened up. Modern man goes about in a paralysis of fear, keeping ninety percent of his energies, his scope in general, repressed and hidden, even from himself. A man is unable to wave his arms, to leap with happiness, walking down a public street the first spring day.

Primitive man for all his rituals and his frightfully barbaric-seeming laws and customs, was freer. They lived closer to poetry, orally if they could not read it. Above all, they lived closer to their emotions. Education notwithstanding, a man got more out of himself in primitive ages than modern man. A man realized himself better, therefore was more godlike, more creative. What people am I talking about? I know few were educated, a mere handful, and that multitudes were slaves. I mean, however, the common men who were the farmers, the unbonded soldiers, the craftsmen, the bakers and the shoemakers. They might not have waved their arms, either, and they might have. They might have thought Jupiter sent the rain, and

---

* Pat leaves the city for some weeks, first for a cottage in Port Jefferson on Long Island, then a furnished room in a castle in Tarrytown in upstate New York.

not cold air striking warm, but if they did, so much the better for their emotions, and their emotional happiness. What were their fears? Only of the gods, really, even if they fell ill of a disease. The gods made them better social beings, too.

What are modern man's fears? He doesn't clearly even know. They are: Financial Insecurity—War—the Atom Bomb—his own old age—death (the physical)—cancer—tuberculosis—and the fact that the world, his world, might not exist in ten years—and the fact, a much more real one, that individually he can do nothing about it. For the first time in history, an individual man can do absolutely nothing about saving his own skin! He can't even run off to a desert and hide. The atom bomb will find him out there, too. And he made the atom bomb! What a basis for frustration!

People tell him to read books. His children go to public schools where they are told to read Shakespeare, Lamb, Wordsworth, Tolstoy, and told to keep reading them when they get out of school. That's the last thing they'll do. What should they be, recluses? They've got to mix in the world and add themselves to the inarticulate, paralyzed masses doing nothing about saving themselves or even preserving what they've got.

MAY 3, 1950

Ah, life can be beautiful. Chapter Nine done. P. 111. And the next chapter planned at the moment. Symbolism coming out fine. I've my sloppy shirt-paper notes pinned beside my desk. I might go all day without speaking to anyone here, except perhaps for my mail.

MAY 4, 1950

This is such a painful novel I am doing. I am recording my own birth. My 8-page stint is sometimes agony. So far, generally, I feel happy at night, however, after the pages are done.

5/4/50

To hell with the psychoanalyst's explanations of Dostoyevsky's gambling as sexual release. Dostoyevsky wanted to destroy himself, to experience his own destruction. Purge of the soul! Dosto-

yevsky knew. Touch bottom before you can thrust to the heights!
Touch bottom, indeed, merely for the sake of knowing bottom. I
know all this so well, I feel it, I enact it, too.

MAY 5, 1950
   A letter from Kathryn. A good one. Very good. She liked my
post cards, letters, congratulates me on the movie. "You are
neither an irrit[ation] or a distraction, but someone whom I feel
very close . . ." Excoriating letter from Marc, telling me I cling to
my disgusting, infantile sicknesses like as a little girl clings to a
doll, ending "and let's get married."

5/5/50
   To own a house is to stop in a way, in a way that I can't as yet.

5/6/50
   This won't come again (some things I know, as I knew when
I was twenty-three, and twenty-one, that the same sensations
cannot be reduplicated because of the very age element), the
sheeplike clouds on a pleasant evening in May, with the castle
nearby, all black and dark and huge, where I shall work alone.
And while my friends are leaving in the car. It is all pleasant, I
welcome it, and I am not afraid, and yet love goes with them,
the human voice, the touch of the flesh at all, and the possibility of something failing, some little thing, while the group goes
out to get into the car, while one or all of us look for a place
which sells newspapers after ten o'clock in the evening. No
this will not come again, I standing in the dark driveway, lighting a cigarette to comfort me, while the automobile purrs away
in the darkness. I staring to a different world and one which I
love better. Living life I do mistrust, but friends and lovers one
has always. One has always, at least, the remembrance of how
the lovers were, which indeed is no different from the way the
friends are. For I do project into friends the imaginative virtues, capabilities, which I project into lovers. Both are created.
And a man does love by an illusion.

5/7/50

It is freedom, which muddles a man up. I am not advocating totalitarianism. But a writer must learn how to impose his own totalitarianisms upon himself, himself being sole governor, knowing that he is free to change discipline and routine after due process of altering within himself his legislation.

MAY 8, 1950

Immensely happy tonight. Why shouldn't I be? This will be the finest book I have ever done, finest thing, I believe, better than "The Heroine." O to remove that curse one day!

MAY 10, 1950

This book I am cautious about, no headlong rushes as [in] the first. If I thought the ice had broken Monday, it is not quite so. The condensation and selection required in this book always demands effort. There are as many kinds of writers as people. Perhaps more.

MAY 12, 1950

Very pleasant. Worked, 7 usual pages. And read a bit to the family tonight. First chapters—tedious, full of extraneous matters, the characters weakly drawn. Other chapters—far superior, but I cannot read them to the family, since I balk at telling them T. falls in love with a woman! The family is interested, respectful, due to first book's success, but they cannot have real enthusiasm from this reading!

MAY 14, 1950

I began *Ulysses* but have little taste for fiction. I believe one can keep only one set of fictional characters, one family, in the head at once.

MAY 15, 1950

My happiest days are never spent with people. I wonder do I cherish only a dream of happiness, one day, with the person I love. I wonder do I want it as superficially as I want, sometimes, a house of my own. Oh, I am not willing to give up that dream of a person yet, though. I shall part with it most unwillingly. I am greedy to live so many lives, that is it. I shall be so many different persons before I die. And one has to be alone to be able to change so often. What would anyone make of it!

5/17/50

Writing, of course, is a substitute for the life I cannot live, am unable to live. All life, to me, is a search for the balanced diet, which does not exist. For me. Alas, I am twenty-nine, and I cannot stand more than five days of the life I have invented as the most ideal.

MAY 23, 1950

In a burst of confidence, I showed Ethel [Sturtevant] chapter six, in which Carol appears, picks up Therese. "But this is love!" Ethel exclaimed upon reading half of the first page. I admitted it was something like that but in later discussion, said T. had a schoolgirl crush, wanted back to the womb relationship, which Ethel said was borne out by the milk episode, but not in their meeting. "That's a sexual awakening. Your genius ran away with you here . . . Now this packs a wallop! This is an excellent piece of writing, Pat."

MAY 25, 1950

Decided to abandon the castle, so laboriously moved all my stuff out at noon. Stanley most helpful in taking me to Hastings, but no time to take me to New York. Stanley has to work constantly, and fast. I realize they have just about been making both ends meet the last few years. And they are not getting any younger. Something must happen soon. And now—now that I have $6000—mother says I have had it "too easy"—the old story. In fact, reminds me that most children help their parents, contribute to their upkeep. By George, not if they are both earners. And seldom, indeed, if the child is one afflicted with the fury of the arts. I do resent all this.

5/27/50

The happy fact for me at this date, May 27, 1950, is that the pleasant way of writing, the most entertaining and at the same time the most profound, is also the best writing for me. When I worry and rearrange, I always fail and always write badly.

5/28/50

I have just heard a remarkable popular song called "Let's go to church on Sunday" (we'll meet a friend on the way).* They will meet a friend on the way. Next Saturday night, the young man will hold up a candy store and the girl will sleep with the man who will necessitate an abortion. These two will marry in less than a year and produce five more Catholics. They will vote in the Catholic senators and boycott the best artists and writers. They will provide sons for the next war and dedicate the next superwar *mondial* to the unknown soldier. They will prevent people from parking on their block and they will turn the stomachs of the rest of us when they appear in bathing suits on public beaches. They will be honored because they carry on the race. But they will not be the people by whom this century will be known.

MAY 30, 1950

Worked well. A sunny day. Lil & Dell for dinner. A holiday today. They brought champagne—and we had a wonderful time. Later, went alone to the village, Pony Stable Inn. $3.00 in my pocket. I feel very self-confident these days, very cheerful, very secure in my book.

MAY 31, 1950

Went to Wanamaker's† on luxurious lady of leisure shopping tour, & picked up maps from RCA for Carol & Therese's trip. I live so

---

* In the song Pat refers to, "Let's Go to Church (Next Sunday Morning)" by Margaret Whiting, all that the singer envisages is going to church—and through life—with her love. Pat's dark imagination takes the story in a completely new direction.
† John Wanamaker Department Stores were one of the first department store chains in the United States.

completely with them now, I do not even think I can contemplate an amour (I am in love with Carol, too) and cannot read anything except Highsmith in the notebooks. Frightful egomania it must be!

JUNE 1, 1950

Intolerably dull writing today, for the simple reason I was too healthy. My Muse will not come at 9:00 AM after a healthy breakfast.

JUNE 4, 1950

Walked to hospital to see Lil—accompanied by the young man I met last night in the Irish bar, after seeing Marc. (Incidentally, Marc & I agreed to get married at the end of the summer.) Interesting—Sam (who is insufferably dull) said suddenly, "Oh, I was raised in Ridgefield N.J." as we walked in the park. My heart took a jump. "Do you know Murray Avenue?" I asked. I asked if he knew anyone named Senn. (Her name.) He said he'd take me there one afternoon. Alas, should I see her, my book would be spoiled! I should be inhibited!

6/6/50

Today I fell madly in love with my Carol. What finer thing can there be but to fling the sharpest point of my strength into her creation day after day? And at night, be exhausted. I want to spend all my time, all my evenings with her. I want to be faithful to her. How can I be otherwise?

JUNE 11, 1950

The book must come now to a swift and tragic close. Visited Hollis Alpert last week, now an editor of *The New Yorker*. He says they are immensely interested in my stuff. If I can get something short enough, perhaps it will go.

JUNE 12, 1950

I worked well, feeling even too well physically. On an impulse at 5 PM went to Hastings for this reason, I know: to steep myself in that which I hate, in that rejection, which is what I am about to describe in my book. My mother grows increasingly neurotic— my God! She never thinks, only opens her mouth and shouts! I drank too much Imperial, ate little. Told mother, Marc & I would marry. "I'm glad. I want a grandchild." "I haven't the courage." "I'd be ashamed. What's the matter with you?"

6/12/50

Suddenly the writing of novels has become a little game (even as I learn more and more that a single novel can absorb my last strength and tax my entire brain) that the main object is to please and to entertain and condense one's material, that the finished product is but a tiny fragment broken off of the great mass of material, and polished to the highest degree. It will be the same if at fifty I can look at a shelf with fifteen of my books on it.

JUNE 13, 1950

Unable to sleep last night. At 4 AM I thought out the ending—in action—of my book. What joy and relief!

JUNE 14, 1950

7:00 PM. Proposed sleeping with S.—most fluently. "Well, when?—Please." "Could be," says S. Jazzed around the Irish bar here. I am so elated yet tragically sad. I know I have written a good book, how good I don't yet know. And that is it.

JUNE 14, 1950

Carol has said no now. Oh God, how this story emerges from my own bones! The tragedy, the tears, the infinite grief which is unavailing! I saw Marc for a beer. Very detached, unreal feeling tonight.

JUNE 15, 1950

More work, and I draw very near the end, letting it come out— so it seems—in a wonderful natural way. It is all in action, no summing up, no philosophizing, no tying of ends. But I feel exhausted. My sleep is broken every night by stopped-up nose, and in the morning my thrashing brain is a blank until after strong coffee.

6/16/50

(One day before finishing my second novel.)

I have learned the trade of writing rather late. I am later still learning the art of life. I came home and only happened to look into Emily Dickinson, and was reminded afresh of that poor woman's (and rich poet's) fate of loving a man she saw so briefly—and of what she made of it, of what she gave the world and herself in beauty. I said, that's for me. I remembered my journal entries of my eighteenth year. I remembered that those things cannot be changed. Take a woman for what she is worth and no more. This is the art of life, or the most important rule of it.

JUNE 16, 1950

Showed R. [Rosalind] C. the letter of renunciation in my book, also the 4th chapter in which they meet. How odd that R.C. always exerts her dampening influence! And I think, how she would like to have written all that, though, and I know it is incontrollable jealousy. "This bit has your usual suspense . . . I don't think she sounds attractive here . . . The girl's rather dingy, isn't she? . . . It certainly needs a lot of work . . . Such an old cliché, I wouldn't be caught dead making a pass like that." How different from Lil!

I think I have suffered a minor relapse this week. I am profoundly and nervously exhausted, eager for the nepenthe of alcohol of an evening if I have a friend to share it with. Interesting concomitant: cynicism, caused only by nervous exhaustion. It is always so easy for me to see the world upside down.

JUNE 20, 1950

Summer begins. An era closes—this is Kathryn, my book, and many, many ideals.

JUNE 24, 1950

The doctor gave me some seconal. In order to relax enough to sleep. This exhaustion is like a solid thing within me, a disease over which I have no control. Now that I have money—why can't I go to a resort, pick up a girl, have a whirl, and drop her? Thus, one is free emotionally. I am ravenously hungry for a woman—It invades dream and waking hours. Yet so tired and pessimistic.

6/28/50

Thanks be to God. Glory be to God, I have finished another book today. In God is all my strength and my inspiration. In god and Jesus' name is all my courage and fortitude. I happen to have just come from a miserable party on South Fourth Avenue. Given by an impecunious and execrable painter. He said tonight, in his dirty white suit, with his dirty nails, dirty as his guests: "There are no absolutes in this world. If there were the world would stop." But I feel this in the marrow of my bones, and therefore would not readily utter it at a party. I feel a tremendous significance in the cross. Two opposite directions. In the instant of our revelation, the conjunction of the opposites will be manifest, and shown to be the sole and absolute truth.

JUNE 30, 1950

Today, feeling quite odd—like a murderer in a novel, I boarded the train for Ridgewood, New Jersey. It shook me physically, and left me limp. Had she [Mrs. E. R. Senn]* ever taken the same train? (I doubt it. She'd use a car.) Was compelled to drink two ryes before I took the 92 bus, the wrong one, toward Murray Ave. I asked the driver, and suddenly to my dismay and horror, I heard the entire bus shouting "Murray Avenue?"—and giving me directions! Murray Avenue is a comparatively small lane going into thickly wooded land, on one side of Godwin Avenue. There is a building on the left, a big, quiet, fine house on

---

* The real-life inspiration for the Carol character in *The Price of Salt*.

the right, where two cars stood, and women sat on the porch, talking. The number was 345—and I pushed on, seeing 39—on the next house, and thinking the numbers were going the wrong way, for hers is 315. Besides the street was so residential, there were no sidewalks, and I was a conspicuous figure. I dared not go any further up the avenue where the trees grew closer and closer, and hers might have been the only remaining house (I caught no glimpse of it!) and where she just might have been on the lawn or porch, and I might have betrayed myself with halting too abruptly. I walked on the opposite avenue, which was not even called Murray. (And felt safer because it was not hers.) And then as I came back to Godwin a pale aqua automobile was coming out of Murray Avenue, driven by a woman with dark glasses and short blonde hair, alone, and I think in a pale blue or aqua dress with short sleeves. Might she have glanced at me? O time, thou art strange! My heart leapt, but not very high. She had hair that blew wider about her head. O Christ, what can I remember from that encounter of two or three minutes a year-and-a-half ago. Ridgewood is so far away! When shall I ever see her in New York again? Shall I go to a party one evening and find her there? Pray, God, she never troubled to look up my name. (After the Xmas card.)* These things I shall never tell Mr. M.B. [Marc Brandel] of course!

7/1/50

I am interested in the murderer's psychology, and also in the opposing planes, drives of good and evil (constriction and destruction). How by a slight defection one can be made the other, and all the power of a strong mind and body be deflected to murder or destruction! It is simply fascinating!

And to do this primarily, again, as entertainment. How perhaps even love, by having its head persistently bruised, can become hate. For the curious thing yesterday I felt quite close

---

* Pat wrote Mrs. E. R. Senn a Christmas card following their short encounter in Bloomingdale's in 1948.

to murder, too, as I went to see the house of the woman who almost made me love her when I saw her a moment in December, 1948. Murder is a kind of making love, a kind of possessing. (Is it not, attention, for a moment, from the object of one's affections?) To arrest her suddenly, my hands up on her throat (which I should really like to kiss) as if I took a photograph, to make her in an instant cool and rigid as a statue. And yesterday, people stared at me curiously wherever I went, in the trains, the bus, on the sidewalk. I thought, does it show in my face? But I felt very calm and composed. And indeed, at a gesture from the woman I sought, I should have cringed and retreated.

JULY 6, 1950

Rosalind resents me thoroughly. Called me eccentric for living alone. R.C. and I shall never be the same again. I left in incontrollable tears. It is not this morning's outburst from her I hated but all the years past, all the horrible disillusionment—for I cling so to my gods and my loves.

JULY 12, 1950

Chez R.C. at 1:30 AM. I informed her quietly that I couldn't stand it any longer. The snobbery, her resentment against me in every way. With that she cut loose on a long array of insulting accusations, bitter, false observations, too long to recount. But I had shed my last tear. I took this calmly. When I took my leave, R.C. remarked I was surely going to the bar to pick up somebody else. Another whore. I went home and to bed, scarcely shaken by this cataclysmic, horrible end of a ten-year friendship.

7/17/50

Women came before men. Women are thousands of years older than men.

7/21/50

The night. I dream of earthquakes, the earth shaking and tipping out the window, while the house stands still! One half

awakens—more than half!—sits up in bed with the dream clinging heavily to the edges of one's brain, tipping the whole brain
like a house itself, caught in an earthquake. I call out someone's
name, because I don't know what bed I am in, or what house.
I see and hear myself doing it, knowing I am both asleep and
awake, and the limbo is horrible! I walk into the kitchen, thinking of getting some hot water and milk to drink, but my brain
grasps even this simple idea like the clumsy hands of a primitive
monster. And the primitive monster is myself. I chew voraciously
at a half-eaten chop which I really do not want, and put it down
again. The earth shakes, and I doubt even gravity. I am suddenly
somebody else, another creature I do not know. (I know, though,
that I lived a hundred million years ago.)

7/22/50

Because of a very simple combination of love & hate in myself
in regard to my parents, I am absorbed today in the ambiguities
throughout nature and philosophy. Out of this, I shall create,
discover, invent, prove, and reveal. Thus, life—thus all, all, all
of life is a fiction, based on something that might have been otherwise, yet which all is true! These things I shall do and discover,
they will all be true, too. (This, I sometimes speculate, will
finally drive me mad. I can feel its intimations, sometimes. But
then, I have always known the "insane" were not really insane.
And this transcends, my dear philosophers, solipsism and ide-
alism, existentialism, too! I am a walking perpetual example of
my contention: as I said brilliantly at the age of twelve, a boy in
a girl's body.)

8/11/50

Texas: I shall write about it as it has never been written about
before. The Levis, the second-hand cars, the oil millionaires, the
jukebox songs of women (redheaded, slatternly, in cotton housedresses) who must be loyal and true (my God, what are they
doing?). Always be mine, that we never will part—(the second-
hand car) but mostly the clean young dunces, the lean thighs,

the blond girls, the fresh food in the refrigerator, the sense of space just beyond the town limits, the rodeo next week, and the absolute certainty that the young men's bodies are in perfect condition, the legs spare and hard, and the spirit, too, clean. The women's voices southern but not dazingly southern, soft without being weak. They are clean like the bodies and minds of the young men. The jukebox songs, though whining and sentimental, are only whining because we have not yet developed our poetry. Texas—with the faith of the people who were born there, living there still. The beautiful, quiet, flat homes, the beautiful girls who inspire the men who drive bombers over Germany, Russia and Korea.

Infinite is the word for Texas. Infinite!

8/13/50

The secret of every art, of good art, is love. It is so pleasant to love, I wonder there are any bad artists. Yet I myself have been so guilty of not loving! O my Cornell!

AUGUST 17, 1950

Jolly good news—the chauffeur story sold for $1150! Margot & I very happy. ᶠSeriously—I must get to work immediately on my book. I dream of titles—"The Sun Gazer." "The Echo—" of some sort.ᶠᶠ I know what causes the apathy—the disillusionment today. It is that the first and second World War were fought in vain so far as the following peace machinery was concerned. Now the United Nations have failed to maintain peace. And it does seem horrible, ridiculous, that no one in South America, or France, or Turkey, no one but England and France, and they only a handful, have sent anything to stop the Reds in Korea.

SEPTEMBER 6, 1950

Subscribed to a British Clipping Service. My book comes out in October.* Marc came over at 8:30. He is bored with his wealthy

---

* The first UK edition of *Strangers on a Train* (London, 1950).

and very ideal girl, and wants to marry me—incredible
dictu!—again, now on flatly companionable basis. Like putting a thin, slack leash on me. He in fact no longer wants a
heterosexual marriage. His head is turned all the time, he says.
But they all love him, if taken on a lifetime basis. Some sense
there. We shall have something like Jane & Paul B. [Bowles].
For I think I may do it. It will not interfere at all with London
this winter—which I dream of—or anyone or anything else.
Hitchcock telegraphed me in P'town, but I didn't come back to
see him. He seems to be going tennis mad over my book,* and
apparently is already shooting at Forest Hills.

SEPTEMBER 22, 1950

I am tolerably happy. Yet not living yet, living only on the
thought life will be more, more pleasant, more rewarding, more
beautiful in the near future. Of course, it is all tied with emotional satisfaction. If Kathryn did not exist, I should contemplate
it in New York. But I know now, too, that no one affects me
more deeply, no one has roots in me as Kathryn has.

9/22/50

Of my book, in conclusion, two weeks before finishing the
rewrite: this is not a picture of the author sweating. The book-
stores at this moment happen to be glutted with tracts excusing
and apologizing for homosexuality, depicting their very rug-
ged male heroes writhing with heterosexual disgust as they try
to throw off the hideous coils that bind them, while in the last
scene, their beloved is without reason killed, lest somebody in
the Bible Belt despise the fact they may continue living together
in a cohabitation he has been hammered into countenancing, but
which may sour in his mind a week later. This is the story of a
woman weak because of social weaknesses in her society, having
nothing to do with perversion. And a girl starved for a mother,

---

* Hitchcock changed the character of Guy Haines in *Strangers on a Train* from an architect
to a star tennis player.

in whom the artificial upbringing of an orphanage's home, however scientific, has not sufficed as parental love. It is just a story that might have happened, with no ax to grind.

SEPTEMBER 26, 1950

Why do I work so hard on a book that will undoubtedly ruin me? Today I was at least concerned with the typewriter for twelve hours, and only with difficulty produced ten rewritten pages.

OCTOBER 12, 1950

In furious mood. Walked furiously up 2nd Avenue. And at 4:00 PM got the curse! First time since end of May or June. Because I finished my book today, too, perhaps. A nice writing streak, with the end in which Therese does not go back with Carol— but refuses her, and is alone at the last. Shall show M.J. both versions, and am sure she will prefer the "lift" ending in which T. & C. go back together. In the course of the evening got horribly blind drunk! Blackouts and everything else. Including spending all the money in my wallet. Lyne eventually poured me into a taxi at 3:00 AM.

OCTOBER 14, 1950

[Arthur] Koestler didn't know about movie sale of my book. "Then why do you need my patronage?" He wants to introduce me to *Partisan Review* crowd. He is tolerably respectful. But he won't be until I manage to hold my liquor a little better.

OCTOBER 16, 1950

Dinner with Koestler tonight. Semon's. He suggests I send novel to a typist immediately, get it back with a "new dignity" about it, and give him a copy to read. I don't really want him to, for he wouldn't like it. I go about vaguely depressed about my book, dreading publication day. Yet optimistic when I discuss it at length with someone. The newspapers are mentioning "my name" thrice weekly, about, so people tell me. Koestler came back here, we tried to go to bed. A miserable, joyless episode. Absurd and blush making to set down—he proposed that we lie together and do nothing, which of course he found impossible. There is a mood of self-torture in me—when it comes to men. Plus remembering the times I have lain in the same bed with women I adored and longed for, whom I loved so much I did not wish to annoy them, or jeopardize the pleasure of merely being with them later. And so hostility, masochism, self-hatred, self-abasement (making myself feel inadequate, out of step with the world, deficient in half myself) all these play their part in these scenes which leave me weeping at four AM and then alone at five. Koestler, efficient as always, decides to abandon the sexual with me. He did not know homosexuality was so deeply ingrained, he said.

OCTOBER 17, 1950

Day entirely devoted to errands, housecleaning, the doctor, dinners, and cocktails. Three gins in the Mayfair with Lyne, and we—I—told her miserably and weepingly about Koestler, and about my book—my feelings of having wasted my time writing something no one will want to read, etc. Perhaps the fact is, I cannot bear the thought of its appearing in print.

OCTOBER 18, 1950

Walter & I discussed my book. I told him I did not mind shelving it for five years. He suddenly agreed, and said Sheehan told him—"I'm glad Pat tackles a subject like this, because it's something she really knows about, but for her career I think it's very bad." To get a label. And I've already one as a mystery story writer!

OCTOBER 19, 1950

So that is the big news—I shall try to persuade Margot J. that the book should not be published now. And she will doubtless argue otherwise. Everyone will. But it is my career, my life.

10/20/50

Now, now, now, to fall in love with my book—this same day
I have decided not to publish it, not for an indefinite length of
time. But I shall continue to work on it for some weeks to come,
to polish and perfect it. I shall fall in love with it now, in a different way from the way I loved it before. This love is endless,
disinterested, unselfish, impersonal even.

OCTOBER 21, 1950

Margot reports [French publisher] Calmann-Lévy bought
Strangers in Paris. Koestler's publishers, & of course he claims
credit, though M.J. said she'd had requests before. $200 and 7%
on first 5000, I believe. Shall let the money sit there.

10/23/50

The whole trouble, of course, is caused by my present struggle
within myself, whether to follow my own nature, which I feel
maimed, or to borrow a few crutches from the world around
me, the rest of the people. As an artist, I can and should follow only my own nature. Yet I debate putting the crutches
under that, too, and wonder if it is possible. It is for this reason
only that I am egocentric at the moment. I should like to look
quickly and get the operation over quickly. But the process is
not a quick one. It is for this reason only, too, that I "live below
my mental level," as Koestler tells me, that I seek out the advice
of other people, feeling that because I have let other people control my emotional expression (the lack of it) I must take their
domination in my general mental operations also.

OCTOBER 27, 1950

With Lyne. Saw a Forain[*] exhibit, lunched late. And being tense
for some complicated psychological reasons, I drank 3 martinis, in good, calm spirits, at 6 PM and in the course of the

---

[*] Jean-Louis Forain (1852–1931) was a French painter and renowned caricaturist. He was a
close friend of the poets Arthur Rimbaud and Paul Verlaine.

evening—later Spivy's—drank too much. I fell apart at 3:00
AM when Lyne left me. Wanted secretly to go home with her—
and ended by making a vain call to her, to tell her rather sadly
I did not think I should see her again, because since I loved her
it was most difficult and hard on me, etc. A taxi home at 3:45.
I am ashamed of my self-indulgent and destructive behavior—
which I cannot seem to control. I can blame fatigue—but not
entirely. Such a deplorable waste of time and money.—And I
feel I sink as low morally as any of the Village wastrels of whom
I have heard, have known, all my life, without suspecting I
could ever be like them. I called Ann Smith at 4:10 AM and she
came up. I told her I was blind drunk. Actually, I went to bed
rather sober at 5:15—and suffered the minimum of hangover.

OCTOBER 29, 1950

Margot has finished my book. "I'm very pleased, Pat," but not
with too much enthusiasm, I thought. "What do you think of
getting it published under another name?" she asked. I don't
mind. Temporary, partial relief from shame. We must get the
opinions of several "independent readers." I was drunk again,
not so much from liquor as emotional relief and plain nervous
fatigue. But I think seriously these days of therapeutic measures
against alcoholism. Something must be done.

OCTOBER 30, 1950

Koestler called. He'd just finished his book. We went to the
Turkey Town House where I stood him drinks. Very pleasant.
4 martinis and more for me, and I was sober all the evening,
because of guilt. Hubris, I told Koestler. He has bought an island
in the Delaware River, invites me to come and work there next
week. He is very generous, impulsive, and we enjoy each other's company, I think. Stayed out until 4:15 with Koestler, who
continued to drink & bore up very well. Had been living on
benzedrine finishing last details of his novel. Wants Jim Putnam
[of G. P. Putnam's Sons, publishers] to read mine. Suspend judgment about homosexuality label until after he has seen it.

11/2/50

Random thoughts when too tired to work, lying on my couch with a beer and Koestler's *Dialogue with Death*. Some satisfaction and assuage of guilt (for laziness this past week, since finishing the second draft of a novel) in the thought that the short story I am lazily working on is not bad and may well sell. Outstanding characteristic of these past nine months for me: a turn away from religion, from my old introspection with mystical revelations. Not entirely explainable either by more social life and less solitude, but by world events, and a more personal participation in the world of people and events. This is an age of war & neurosis and conflict within conflict, and of Communism versus Capitalism.

NOVEMBER 14, 1950

These days are on the brink again. The least thing depresses me to the point of suicide. A completely tangled and stupid relationship with Lyne. I believe I am dedicated to madness. I know exactly what I should do, to "lead a happier life, etc." I cannot and will not do it, though the other way is death—preceded by unhappiness, frustration, depression and worst of all, inferiority.

11/14/50

In this past year: turning away from the mysticism that sheltered and glorified my youth, turning also from the Bible— especially in this period of crisis—as a sort of consolation & source of strength whatever. I am still subject to depression. A setback however small, in the midst of successes can nevertheless knock me down. Neurotic: the chief source of depression is emotional reversal or rejection. And—as a writer, a sense of chaos and decadence pervading my age. The greatest achievements in any age in writing will be made by the students of chaos. Lives fly off in every direction, and where they cross is no point of surety or security. Every man contains his own morals like an envelope, like a little world.

11/14/50

I am afraid there is no rest on earth for me, because I shall forever avoid it. The rope I am given everywhere lies slack around my feet and tangles me up.

DECEMBER 3, 1950

Saw Margot three successive nights. She reiterates most boringly, is very self-centered, but Christ, she has put up with my shortcomings, too, and she is a great girl. B.C. came in Monday—we sat on the sofa until late, drinking too much. Later, a terrific but slowly growing lust in me for Miss Bertha [C.]. I love her body. And quite by delicious & wonderful accident, she came into the dark room after me and joined me in bed. (Margot slept in the living room.) I had almost forgotten,—alas, I had almost forgotten that pleasure beyond all pleasures, that joy beyond all treasures, pleasures, findings, the pleasure of pleasing a woman. I did please Bertha. And her body, her head and hair in the darkness—as she lay by then with her head near the foot of the bed—was suddenly more than Europe, art, Renoir whom she resembled, one of his women. Bertha was mine then, a woman with terrific breasts and a figure like an hourglass, Margot says, but all women, the woman, a woman, woman, and I felt all the extraneous ones drop away from me, all the barriers dissolve. She is mysterious in a Russian-Jewish way, melancholic, devious by nature in her mind, witty as a fairy, however, and unfortunately now on the brink of a serious operation. That night was Tuesday. On Wednesday, she had a hemorrhage—not my fault—and she went to the hospital Saturday. Too bad I am going to Europe, for we can't plan a life.

12/17/50

Total mobilization over the world.* The edges of everything crumble, and the bottom drops out of the plans to spend next

---

* Reference to the national state of emergency declared by President Truman on December 16, 1950, following a crushing defeat by Chinese troops in Korea.

year in Europe. A day off in the midst of work, and a book at that, au contraire to all that the world is coming to today, and in the evening a somewhat broken somewhat engagement. Night falls. The radio plays Debussy's "Children's Corner." One has to have someone to love these days, I think tritely and immediately sound myself to see if I've still the necessary enthusiasm. I telephone my favorite friend—but not my love, who lies, potentially my love, in a hospital—but no one answers. I want to see a movie tonight. I work tomorrow, I am like a million other people, perhaps a little lonelier, a little more wistful, a little more violent, a little more enthusiastic, a little more despondent. O what will she [B.] say in one hour? O where shall I be in a month? And what will become of us? My darling, give me at least a sign to remember. Are all women nothing but images to look at and remember? Will I never get to know you? Never know whether you prefer roses to chrysanthemums? Or even take milk in your tea? Are all women nothing but symbols?

DECEMBER 19, 1950

Cooked steak for Margot last night, and this evening she wanted me to have dinner with her. She always overdrinks, undereats, and we end up sleeping at her apartment.

DECEMBER 20, 1950

Wrote to Marc last week, on his book, and for my $50 dollars. His book *The Choice* has me & him in excruciating funny bedroom scene, all literally me & my apartment. In general, I feel enormously more relaxed than before, like a different person. Less regimented—which of course is the anxious child's effort to build a stable existence around him—and I have that new surge of love for Bertha. How I wish I knew what will happen in advance. Do I really want her enough to go after her & demand her? For I think I could get her.

And how long will I be in Europe? K. [Kathryn] is impossible—alas. She will never give up what she has, or want to. Let's face it. On Europe—Margot wants this book [*The Price of*

Salt] definitely to be done anonymously. She said it may sell like hotcakes, however. Harper may accept it. But I believe Margot will wrest it from them and give it to Coward-McCann. In which case, I can then go to Europe & she'll handle the rest—as if I were dead—but not before Jan. 30, probably, can I get away. And of course these days I look for my Carol, Mrs. E. R. Senn, of Ridgewood, New Jersey. I look for her around Bloomingdale's, though I should think it more likely that she shops at Saks oftener.

DECEMBER 21, 1950

The War: We are losing again in Korea. The Chinese Communists are pouring down on us. The British want appeasement. The United Nations cannot afford to appease, recognize Communist China. HST [Harry S. Truman] proclaims state of emergency. Prices are frozen, and wages. D. D. Eisenhower leaves for Europe to head the European armies. I shall have to finagle to get to England under such conditions, for there may be restriction soon.

Everyone expects war immediately, the U.N. to get kicked out of Korea, and for Russia perhaps to sweep into Germany & France. I call often to see how Bertha is. I perhaps can visit her tomorrow, when I go also to pick up my new pale muskrat-lined coat—assembled for me by Lyne—and to cash in my remaining War Bonds with the dollar at .55 and going lower! Dennis [Cohen] will publish my book in January, suggested my being there for the appearance, but I can't. France has sent the contract [for *Strangers on a Train*] with Calmann-Lévy. Two bids from Italy, one from Denmark. My career—goes luckily, perhaps. But I must write another book immediately under my own name, I feel. And what shall I ever tell the family? That it is anonymous, first of all, and I have. And when it does appear next fall, I suppose I shall ignore it, not tell them. Say it's postponed. They have bought the trailer & sold the house. For $15,000. They leave Jan. 22. In time for Jan. 19—to see my 30th birthday in. I shall be delighted with it.

Yet withal, colossal depressive moments recently—as Sunday

night when I had a date broken by Margot, and I at last could see Bertha in the evening, at the hospital. And I thought—what will B. want when she comes out. If she even wants me, what good is it if I go away? And there is all this so close & heavy in the heart, plus the dismal atmosphere of war hanging over the whole world, because I had that unexpected and wonderful night with B. in my arms and my mouth against her breasts, and she as happy as I. So close—and yet so far—farther than ever. I feared like a soldier about to die, it might have been our first and our last night together. I wouldn't bet on it, says Margot cheerfully. Oh, Margot, thou sweetie! I told her if we did sleep together it would have to be at her house. I'd admire to let you both sleep there, she says. God bless her.

What shall I write about next, I think here in this diary where I think aloud. O more definitely than ever this 29th year, this third year and I always change on the thirds, has seen much metamorphosis. It will come to me. My love of life grows stronger every month. My powers of recuperation are wonderfully swift and elastic. I think of writing a startler, a real shocker in the psychological thriller line. I could do it adeptly.

DECEMBER 30, 1950

A bit tight after fine evening in the Village with Lyne, I called Marjorie from here at 3:30 AM and announced in a clear loud voice that I was in love with Bertha. I don't remember the ensuing conversation. Had meant to see Kay G. tonight for a moment, because I spent last evening with her, here, and it was stupendous, beautiful and all that, but I can't anymore. Besides, there is the guilt lest Margot should learn.

DECEMBER 31, 1950

Very tired. 2 PM date chez B.G. on 59th Street then to Margot's in fine mood, as Bertha was to be there. But got blind drunk. At first, tearful but excellent confab with B. in Margot's kitchen, telling her Europe didn't matter, the time I should spend away from her. She said, "Does it matter to you I'm going to share

an apartment with Marjorie? Because it doesn't to me." Slight
blackout delayed my arriving at Lyne's until 9:30 PM. Home at
8 & delighted to see bed. Emotionally—exhausted by B., tears,
frustration, desperation, and yet hope somehow.

JANUARY 6, 1951

I've been so busy on the book. Even now it must be reread by
me, and every 24 hours counts in my getting away to Europe at
the end of January. Oh, I write a book with a happy ending, but
what happens when I find the right person? When I return from
Europe—and I don't think I'll ever want to live there—I want a
house with a woman I love.

JANUARY 23, 1951

Margot reports from Harper Joan K. found the book perfectly
fascinating. More enthusiastic than usual. Wants to read it again
& make editorial comments for minor corrections.

JANUARY 25, 1951

Consultation with Margot, Red, E. Hume over a pseudonym
over drinks this afternoon. Claire Morgan, perhaps.* Hence, I
was late for Kay, who was waiting *en bas*—Disgraceful. Must
cut this with Kay. Not only can it have unpleasant—ghastly—
reverberations with Margot after I'm gone, but it is whorish on
my part. I don't care for her. Rather for Sheila! Wrote Lyne &
told her I shall fly. Air France.

JANUARY 27, 1951

Ann brought my book [the manuscript of *The Price of Salt*] back
with enthusiastic praise. So much better than the first. Even

---

* Claire Morgan did indeed end up being the pseudonym under which *The Price of Salt* was
first published. Only in 1990 was the novel finally released under Highsmith's own name.

minor characters come out, etc. And what a hell of a shame I can't have my name on this one instead of the first! Home alone tonight. Suspenseful: in seven days, I may be gone. Waiting, too, for the creative springs to fill up the well. And where, my God, will that mysterious and yet unknown impetus come from next? That meteor flung out of space that will strike my heart so invisibly and so violently?

OUTRO: 1951–1995

A Life Abroad

✒

PATRICIA HIGHSMITH'S SECOND TRIP to Europe lasts for more than two years. Unlike her first tour of the Continent, this time she has no set itinerary as she visits friends and work contacts. She's soon drawn to London to see Kathryn Hamill Cohen again—and is vexed by the latter's aloofness and, most of all, by her critical reception of the manuscript of *The Price of Salt* she in part inspired. Dismayed and mired in self-doubt, Pat makes a hasty departure for Paris, then travels on to Marseille and Rome.

In Munich, she encounters a woman who will be a lasting influence on her for the rest of her life: Ellen Blumenthal Hill, a sociologist six years her senior. The two women's relationship is a roller coaster of emotions, characterized by volleyed accusations, incongruous lifestyles, and fundamentally different needs. Life is hectic as the couple roves about Europe, alternating between Munich and France, Italy and Switzerland.

Pat cannot find the inner (or outer) calm and focus she needs to work, and the royalties from her books just barely keep her afloat. She starts writing travelogues, short stories, and radio dramas to sell to publishers, magazines, and broadcasters to finance her peripatetic existence. Even though Alfred Hitchcock's movie adaptation of *Strangers on a Train* is released in 1951 to great acclaim, when Highsmith returns to the United States in early 1953, she feels like a failure. Money remains a constant worry, and—officially—she has no second novel to show for herself. Her private life doesn't offer much stability; on the contrary, that summer Ellen attempts to kill herself in Pat's presence and nearly succeeds—decidedly the lowest point in their relationship, which, however, smolders on until 1955, when they break up for good.

As is her wont, Pat withdraws into writing. She immerses herself into the life of a protagonist who will secure her literary legacy and whom she will describe as her alter ego: *The Talented Mr. Ripley.* Over time, Pat will write no fewer than five psychological thrillers about this young American traveling in Europe, basking in the Mediterranean sun and in his talents, ready to kill for the achievement of his dreams.

As for herself, for the time being Pat remains in the United States. She makes a number of attempts to leave New York in order to achieve her own old dream of a settled life in the country with a woman she loves, yet repeatedly ends up back in the city, alone and disillusioned.

Still, for love Pat is prepared to go far—even if it means turning her back on New York and the United States. In 1963, after falling head over heels in love with a Canadian expat living in the UK, she packs up her cat, Spider, and takes a leap across the Atlantic to be closer to her. But Caroline (a pseudonym chosen by Highsmith's biographer Joan Schenkar) has a husband and a child, both of whom she hesitates to leave behind, condemning Pat to the life of a recluse in the country with her lover only joining her on weekends. Their final breakup leaves Pat disoriented and adrift—"the hardest time of my life," she laments.

Rather than returning to New York, Pat moves to France and settles in a solitary hamlet near Fontainebleau, whereto she will also relocate her hero Tom Ripley for her next novel and, so it seems, for company. Professionally speaking, Pat would have reason for optimism: although she no longer has a steady publisher in the United States, where she is labeled a mere genre writer, for the first time she enters a prolonged period of financial security, largely thanks to lucrative film deals in Europe, where she is revered as a best-selling literary star defying categorization.

Alone and lonely in the French countryside, however, contentment remains elusive. Pat considers a permanent return to the United States, where she also still sets most of her novels—but abandons the idea after a trip back in early 1970, during which her relationship with her mother reaches an all-time low: "My doctors say if you had stayed 3 more days I would be dead," Mary Highsmith writes to her daughter.

Pat's notebook and journal entries from the time are acerbic, at times hateful, revealing a deep loneliness and disorientation. Whenever she's not writing a book, she feels troubled and restless, distracting herself with gardening, painting, and woodworking: "Lately I have to live on a plane of reality. It never does for me" (2/24/80). She attaches herself to ever-younger partners. When a short-lived but intense affair with twenty-five-year-old avant-garde film star and costume designer Tabea Blumenschein from Berlin ends after only a few months in 1978, Pat is shattered. She finds some comfort in the arms of a young English teacher, Monique Buffet.

By this time, Pat's life in France is drawing to a close. She has long complained about the double taxation she is subject to as an American citizen living in Europe. When in 1980, the French fiscal authorities raid her house, she is outraged and decides to leave, even if this also means leaving behind Monique, her last love.

She moves to Switzerland, her literary home since 1967, where Daniel Keel, the founder of her German-language publishing house, Diogenes, acts as her international agent and is a longtime trusted friend; she will later also appoint him her literary executor and entrust him with the handover of her literary estate to the Swiss Literary Archives after her death.

Her book projects become fewer and farther between, not the least due to her failing health. In 1980, she has to undergo a leg bypass surgery in London; six years later, she is diagnosed with lung cancer. For the time being, the treatment is a success, and she can resume her life. With her twentieth novel, *Found in the Street*, she pens a late homage to the vibrant gender-fluid life in Greenwich Village the way she remembers it from her twenties and early thirties. And for the first time, she has a house built of her own: a bright U-shaped bungalow almost windowless to the street, but with big French windows opening on a sunny patio and a stunning view of the Southern Alps: la Casa Highsmith.

It is here that she spends her final years, a highly sought-after speaker at award ceremonies and book fairs. Thanks to her novel *Edith's Diary* (1977), in 1991, her name is even suggested for the Nobel Prize in Literature. Before Ripley returns one last time in *Ripley Under Water* in 1991, she, albeit reluctantly, agrees to a republication of her lesbian love story *The Price of Salt* under her own name—a literary coming out of sorts.

By then, her health is in sharp decline. In 1993, she tests positive for aplastic anemia and spends much of the year in treatment. In October that same year, she writes her last coherent notebook entry, stating that she'd rather death came as a surprise: "In this, death's more like life, unpredictable" (10/6/93). It marks the end of Patricia Highsmith's chronicle of her life. Her last notebook, titled "Book Thirty-Eight Tegna," remains empty. In 1994, she starts to require in-home care—working almost to the last on her final, happy-ending novel, *Small g: A Summer Idyll*. Six weeks before her death, she modifies her will, leaving her assets and any future royalties to Yaddo, the artist colony where she completed her first novel, *Strangers on a Train*. Patricia Highsmith dies from lung cancer and anemia on February 4, 1995.

Following her death, publisher Daniel Keel and editor Anna von Planta find her diaries and notebooks hidden in her linen closet. The great revelation: the early years. Whether one is familiar with the caustic, misanthropic image Patricia Highsmith presented to the public in later years or not, one cannot help being amazed and touched reading about the twenty-year-old, headstrong, brave young woman, so optimistically set on making it her own way. And on wanting everything from life: "To all the devils, lusts, passions, greeds, envies, loves, hates, strange desires, enemies ghostly and real, the army of memories, with which I do battle—may they never give me peace" (12/31/47).

These diaries and notebooks are now part of her formidable legacy comprising twenty-two novels and numerous short story collections: an incomparable account of the life of an exceptional person and the making of a great artist in New York in the 1940s.

commit suicide together, unbeknownst to the
others. But the man intends to kill the girl him=
self, and claim whatever proceeds may be. The
quiet boy falls in love with the girl, and the man
manipulates them so the young man will be
angry. Then to his surprise the young man mur=
ders the girl, and he is found at the unresp mo=
ment standing near the corpse. (i.e. her hus=
band.) Who has done it? And it might be the girl
killed herself to blame it on the husband. Know=
ing his schemes against her.

The husband would of course claim the girl
first killed herself, would confess their plot.
Actly, it would be true. Meanwhile, the boy
flees, and the police are after him, for it looks
like murder.

Texas: I shall write about it as it has never
been written about before. The Ferris, the second
hand cars, the oil millionaires, the jukebox
songs of women (red headed, slatternly, in
cotton housedresses) who must be loyal and
true (my God, what are they doing?)
Always be mine, that we never will part —
(the second hand cars) but mostly the clean
young unnicotined lungs, the lean thighs

the blond girls, the fresh food in the refrigerator, the sense of space just beyond the town limits, the rodeo next week, and the absolute certainty that the young men's bodies are in perfect condition, the legs spare and hard, and the spirit, too, clean. The women's voices southern but not cloyingly southern, soft without being weak. They are clear like the bodies and minds of the young men. The juke box songs, though whining and sentimental, are only whining because we have not yet developed our poetry.

Texas — Green fields, millionaires without thought, innocent still as they were in a horse showroom, in a brown desk. Texas — with the faith of the people who were born there, living those still the beautiful, quiet, flat homes, the beautiful girls who inspire the men who drive bombers over Germany, Russia and Korea. Infinite is the word for Texas. Infinite!

ACKNOWLEDGMENTS

I WAS LUCKY enough to have known Patricia Highsmith personally. Though her prickly facade featured more prominently, I was familiar with her softer side as well. Pat was a fascinating, complicated person and author who left us with eight thousand handwritten pages of diaries and notebooks that reveal things about her personal and creative development that she shared with only a chosen few during her lifetime—and even then, she never told the whole story.

This collection should not be read as an autobiography. By necessity, autobiographies are written retrospectively, often carefully edited to present events in a certain light, whereas Pat's diaries and notebooks provide a running account of a life in progress. They are, however, like two mirrors reflecting the interplay of her life and work from different vantage points.

How does one approach a body of work eight thousand pages in length and condense it to a single volume? During the coronavirus pandemic, no less, when work-from-home routines became the norm?

One certainly doesn't go it alone—to wit, this project represents the yearslong work of an truly exceptional team.

Thanks to Ina Lannert and Barbara Rohrer for their exacting transcriptions of Pat's handwritten diaries and notebooks, respectively. Gloria Kate Kingsley Skattebol, Pat's closest college friend, compared these transcripts against the originals, making corrections as needed, and annotated them extensively. As a lifelong confidante and contemporary of Pat's, Gloria Kate Kingsley Skattebol approached these annotations with unmatched insight and sensitivity.

"It takes two mirrors for the correct image of oneself" (Notebook 29, 2/23/68): Neither the diaries nor the notebooks could have been published as stand-alone works. I am most thankful to Daniel Keel, executor of the Highsmith estate, for his support in finding a suitable way to merge these two mirrors of Pat's being; and to his son and successor at the Diogenes helm, Philipp Keel, who not only trusted me but provided me with the time and means to complete this project. Corinne Chaponnière, Gerd Hallenberger, and Paul Ingendaay played central roles in the process as well: Corinne Chaponnière and I conducted the initial experiment of connecting diary and notebook, which gave way to a structural model I developed further with Gerd Hallenberger that took the characteristics of both into account while presenting Pat's life, loves, and work and the worlds in which they evolved. Paul Ingendaay and I compiled the thirty-volume collected works, one of my first exercises in looking back and reassessing the "work behind the works."

Philippa Burton, Lucienne Schwery, Stéphanie Cudré-Mauroux, Ulrich Weber, and Lukas Dettwiler at the Swiss Literary Archives provided expert guidance in navigating the Patricia Highsmith papers housed there. Ina Lannert's detailed time line of Pat's personal life and literary output, complete with quotations from the diaries and notebooks, was an indispensable resource, a map that allowed us to explore the Highsmith cosmos with a sense of direction.

Pat's early diaries are largely written in foreign languages. Credit and thanks to Elisabeth Lauffer (German), Sophie Duvernoy (German, French), and Noah Harley (Spanish) for their superb translations of these entries back into Pat's mother tongue—without them, the early diary years of Patricia Highsmith would have remained largely obscure.

Kati Hertzsch, Friederike Kohl, Marie Hesse, and Marion Hertle, my co-editors, were a dream team, astute, passionate, relentless, and giving their all. The introductory texts preceding each chapter were written by myself and Friederike Kohl and translated by Elisabeth Lauffer. The annotations, beyond those provided by Gloria Kate Kingsley Skattebol, were written by myself and Friederike Kohl, and translated by Elisabeth Lauffer and Sophie Duvernoy, who also translated the texts in the appendix. For the final sprint, Friederike Kohl was my most trusted co-driver.

Many thanks to Susanne Bauknecht, Claudia Reinert, Andrej Ruesch, and Karin Spielmann at Diogenes Verlag for ensuring clear communication with our publishing partners around the globe. Thanks to Charlotte Lamping for extensive preparatory work on this project. Susanne Bauknecht and Susanne von Ledebur advised on legal matters.

Last but not least, this book would not have been possible without editors Robert Weil and Gina Iaquinta at Liveright in New York, as well as copy editor Dave Cole, who masterfully edited the English version.

My sincere thanks to all,
Anna von Planta

A TIME LINE
OF HIGHSMITH'S LIFE AND
WORKS

⚓

1921 January 19: Mary Patricia Plangman is born in Fort Worth, Texas, to Jay Bernard Plangman and Mary Coates, who have recently divorced. Both parents are freelance graphic artists.

1924 Mary Coates marries Stanley Highsmith, another graphic artist, who becomes Patricia's stepfather.

1927 The family moves to New York, where Patricia attends school under the name Highsmith; however, her stepfather officially adopts her only in 1946. Pat spends her childhood alternately in New York and Fort Worth, largely in the care of her grandparents.

1934–1937 Pat attends Julia Richman High School in New York. She publishes her first short stories in *Bluebird*, the high school newspaper.

1938–1942 Pat attends Barnard College of Columbia University in New York and majors in English literature (with ancient Greek and zoology as secondary fields). Receives a bachelor of arts degree.

1942 onward Pat makes a living producing comic book scripts and writes in her spare time. She travels frequently, first to Mexico, later to Europe.

1948–1949 A stay at the Yaddo artist colony in Saratoga Springs, New York, allows Pat to finish her novel *Strangers on a Train*. She begins psychoanalysis to "cure" herself of her homosexuality, and agrees to get engaged to Marc Brandel, a colleague at Yaddo, but later breaks things off again.

1950 *Strangers on a Train*, Pat's first novel, is published. Alfred Hitchcock's film adaptation—the first of many film versions of her books by prominent directors such as René Clément (*Plein Soleil*, 1959), Claude Autant-Lara (*Enough Rope*, 1963), Anthony Minghella (*The Talented Mr. Ripley*, 1999), and Todd Haynes (*Carol*, 2015)—propels Pat to overnight fame.

1951–1953 Pat takes off on a two-year-long voyage across Europe (England, Italy, France, Spain, Switzerland, Germany, Austria). In 1952, her second book, *The Price of Salt* (later renamed *Carol*) is published under the pen name Claire Morgan. Since a lesbian love story with a happy end is a rare phenomenon at the time, it becomes an iconic book in the lesbian scene.

1955 *The Talented Mr. Ripley* is published. From now on, Highsmith will publish a new novel every two to three years, including four further *Ripley* novels. She must constantly find new publishers and is often forced to make significant revisions. In addition, many of her short stories are published, first in magazines and later in anthologies.

1964 After several longer stays in Europe, Pat moves to England to be near her lover Caroline. She lives in Earl Soham, Suffolk, in England, where she buys a house.

1967–1968 Pat moves to France, via Fontainebleau and Samois-sur-Seine to Montmachoux in the Île-de-France region, approximately fifty miles southeast of Paris.

1969 Highsmith's thirteenth novel *The Tremor of Forgery*, which draws upon a trip to Tunisia, is published. Graham Greene and literary critics praise it as her best work yet.

1970 Pat moves to Montcourt, near Montmachoux.

1980 Several surgeries due to blood circulation problems.

1982 After several run-ins with the French tax authorities, Highsmith moves to Aurigeno in Ticino, Switzerland.

1986 Lung cancer operation. Pat briefly gives up smoking.

1988 Pat moves into a house in Tegna, Ticino, which the architect Tobias Ammann designed according to her own specifications.

1995 February 4: Patricia Highsmith dies in the Locarno hospital, of cancer and a blood disease. She leaves her estate to the artist colony Yaddo, which had enabled her to complete her first novel, *Strangers on a Train*. The Swiss Literary Archives in Bern acquire her literary estate in 1996.

A SAMPLE OF HIGHSMITH'S FOREIGN-LANGUAGE NOTES

"Exercise books in languages I do not know."

🖋

Pat's original diary entries from the 1940s are written in English, French, German, and Spanish—and sometimes a mixture of all of them at once. She bends all of those languages grammatically, idiomatically, and syntactically toward her mother tongue, sometimes with unintentionally amusing results. Often, Pat jumps from one language to another even within a single sentence.

Habe Flohen. Tengo Pulges. I have many fleas, und eine purpurrote Besprecklung auf meinen Beinen. Ich bin elend!
(JANUARY 10, 1944)

Her foreign-language notes are intelligible—provided the reader has decent command of both English and the respective foreign language; after a quick mental translation back to English, most of it makes sense. That's because she usually simply translates her English word-for-word. "To phone" thus becomes *phoner* in French, a word that does simply not exist, and *phonieren* in German, where it does exist but does not mean "to phone" but "to phonate." In the same way, a turtleneck sweater becomes a *Schildkrötenhalssweater* in German, where this kind of pullover is much less graphically just described as having a "rolled-up collar." Wherever a term has various possible equivalents in her target language, Pat displays a bit of a knack for choosing the wrong one.

FRENCH

Of her foreign languages, French makes the most regular appearance in Pat's early diaries. Interestingly enough, she scarcely uses it during her years living in France, from 1967 to 1981. In the 1940s, it is often her language of choice when writing about romance, her frequent use of several "false friends" rendering her entries involuntarily amusing: Much like mid-century usage of "gay," for instance, the French word *gai* means "cheery or tipsy," but does not signify sexual orientation. The verb *baiser* means "to fuck," and not "to kiss," as Pat intends; on a related note, *dormir* means simply "to sleep," and not "to sleep with someone," which would instead be *coucher*.

> *Va. [Virginia] m'a phone à 7.30.h. Je l'ai rencontré chez Rocco-Restaurant à 9h. avec Jack un gai garçon—et Curtis et Jean—deux gaies filles. Sommes allés au Jumble Shop, etc. Des Bièrs et martinis et je suis ivre maintenant. Mais Va m'a baisé!! Je l'ai baisé—deux—trois—quatre—cinq fois dans le salon des femmes au Jumble—et aussi même sur le trottoir!! Le trottoir! Jack est très doux, et Va. voudrait dormir avec lui—mais d'abords elle voudrait faire un voyage avec moi quelque fin de semaine. Elle m'aime. Elle m'aimera toujours. Elle mè l'a dit, et ses actions le confirment.*
>
> (JANUARY 11, 1941)

GERMAN

Pat's "father tongue" is the second most common foreign language in her diaries. What she lacks in vocabulary, she makes up for in creativity, like when when she describes herself as *ein Ohnegeschlecht* ("one without sex, gender"); based on the context of the entry, what Pat presumably means is *ungeschlechtlich*, or "asexual." Again, she uses English syntax and translates idioms literally, at times calling attention to them: *Als wir in Englisch sagen, das Spiel ist nicht der Kerze würdig.*—"As we say in English, the game is not worth the candle" (December 30 1944).

Her German sounds especially odd in those regular instances when she borrows from antiquated sources such as Johann Wolfgang von Goethe, Friedrich Schiller, and Johann Sebastian Bach's chorales. For instance, Pat's *Seelenschafe* ("sheep of the soul," a coinage of hers) graze upon the *Seelenweide* ("meadow of the soul") of Bach's eponymous cantata BWV 497.

Ich bin ganz verrückt mit diesen Abenden ohne Ruhe, ohne Einsamkeit, worauf meine Seelenschafe weiden. Mein Herz ist so voll, es bricht in zwei, und die schöne Kleinodien und Phantasien sind wie Giftung in meinen Adern.
(OCTOBER 28, 1942)

SPANISH

Pat picks up some Spanish in anticipation of her 1944 trip to neighboring Mexico, her first time abroad, but her vocabulary remains paltry. While in Mexico, she evidently continues to learn by ear, because she has no grasp of the orthography, mixes in Hispanicized French words, and uses all three past tenses as well as the subjunctive, seemingly at random—or at least led by unreliable instinct. *Incapable*, for instance, is a false cognate that actually means "impossible to castrate," and *yo quite las cadenas* ("I remove the chains") is not a common metaphor in Spanish.

He trabajado muy duro, esta mañana, tarde, y hablabamos de mi novella esta noche. Goldberg dice que yo soy incapable de amar, que yo soy enamorido de mi misma. Es falsa. Mi grande problema es de escribir esta novella, así que yo quite las cadenas que me lian.
(MARCH 11, 1944)

BIBLIOGRAPHY

Primary Sources

A complete bibliography of Patricia Highsmith's work is beyond the scope of this book. The website for the Patricia Highsmith Papers at the Swiss Literary Archives in Bern, Switzerland (http://ead.nb.admin.ch/html/highsmith.html), will guide interested readers beyond the current Highsmith canon.

For the German-language *Werkausgabe der Romane und Stories*, the complete edition of Highsmith's novels and short stories, edited by Paul Ingendaay and myself (Zurich: Diogenes, 2002–2006), I had consulted not only her eighteen diaries (1940/41–1994) and her thirty-eight notebooks (1937–1994), but also many manuscripts of her unpublished works, among them more than a hundred hitherto-unknown short stories and essays (many of which had been published in various women's magazines and, later, in *Ellery Queen's Mystery Magazine*), and of course her letters to her friends and editors; all this material now could be brought to fruition again.

The following works are among the primary sources for this edition. They are listed here along with the details of their first publication in the United States.

NOVELS

Strangers on a Train (New York: Harper & Brothers, 1950).
The Price of Salt (as Claire Morgan; New York: Coward-McCann, 1952).
The Blunderer (New York: Coward-McCann, 1954).
The Talented Mr. Ripley (New York: Coward-McCann, 1955).
Deep Water (New York: Harper & Brothers, 1957).
A Game for the Living (New York: Harper & Brothers, 1958).
This Sweet Sickness (New York: Harper & Brothers, 1960).
The Cry of the Owl (New York: Harper & Row, 1962).
The Two Faces of January (New York: Doubleday, 1964).
The Glass Cell (New York: Doubleday, 1964).
The Story-Teller (UK title: *A Suspension of Mercy*; New York: Doubleday, 1965).
Those Who Walk Away (New York: Doubleday, 1967).
The Tremor of Forgery (New York: Doubleday, 1969).

Ripley Under Ground (New York: Doubleday, 1970).
A Dog's Ransom (New York: Knopf, 1972).
Ripley's Game (New York: Knopf, 1974).
Edith's Diary (New York: Simon & Schuster, 1977).
The Boy Who Followed Ripley (New York: Lippincott & Crowell, 1980).
People Who Knock on the Door (New York: Otto Penzler Books, 1985).
Found in the Street (New York: Atlantic Monthly Press, 1987).
Ripley Under Water (New York: Knopf, 1992).
Small g: A Summer Idyll (New York: W. W. Norton & Company, 2004).

SHORT STORY COLLECTIONS

The Snail-Watcher and Other Stories (UK title: *Eleven*; New York: Doubleday, 1970)
 [The Snail-Watcher—The Birds Poised to Fly—The Terrapin—When the
 Fleet Was In at Mobile—The Quest for Blank Claveringi—The Cries of
 Love—Mrs. Afton, Thy Green Braes—The Heroine—Another Bridge to
 Cross—The Barbarians—The Empty Birdhouse]

The Animal-Lover's Book of Beastly Murder (New York: Otto Penzler Books, 1986)
 [Chorus Girl's Absolutely Final Performance—Djemal's Revenge—There
 I Was, Stuck with Busby—Ming's Biggest Prey—In the Dead of the
 Truffle Season—The Bravest Rat in Venice—Engine Horse—The Day of
 Reckoning—Notes from a Respectable Cockroach—Eddie and the Monkey
 Robberies—Hamsters vs. Websters—Harry: A Ferret—Goat Ride]

Little Tales of Misogyny (New York: Otto Penzler Books, 1986)
 [The Hand—Oona, the Jolly Cave Woman—The Coquette—The
 Female Novelist—The Dancer—The Invalid, or, the Bedridden—The
 Artist—The Middle-Class Housewife—The Fully Licensed Whore, or,
 the Wife—The Breeder—The Mobile Bed-Object—The Perfect Little
 Lady—The Silent Mother-in-Law—The Prude—The Victim—The
 Evangelist—The Perfectionist]

Slowly, Slowly in the Wind (New York: Otto Penzler Books, 1979)
 [The Man Who Wrote Books in His Head—The Network—The Pond—
 Something You Have to Live With—Slowly, Slowly in the Wind—Those
 Awful Dawns—Woodrow Wilson's Necktie—One for the Islands—A
 Curious Suicide—The Baby Spoon—Broken Glass—Please Don't Shoot
 the Trees]

The Black House (New York: Otto Penzler Books, 1988)
[Something the Cat Dragged In—Not One of Us—The Terrors of Basket-Weaving—Under a Dark Angel's Eye—I Despise Your Life—The Dream of the Emma C—Old Folks at Home—The Adventuress (also as When in Rome)—Blow It—The Kite—The Black House]

Mermaids on the Golf Course (New York: Otto Penzler Books, 1988)
[Mermaids on the Golf Course—The Button—Where the Action Is—Chris' Last Party—A Shot from Nowhere—A Clock Ticks at Christmas—The Stuff of Madness—Not in This Life, Maybe the Next—I Am Not as Efficient as Other People—The Cruelest Month]

Tales of Natural and Unnatural Catastrophes (New York: Atlantic Monthly Press, 1987)
[The Mysterious Cemetery—Moby Dick II; or The Missile Whale—Operation Balsam; or Touch-Me-Not—Nabuti: Warm Welcome to a UN Committee—Sweet Freedom! And a Picnic on the White House Lawn—Trouble on the Jade Towers—Rent-a-Womb vs. the Mighty Right—No End in Sight—Sixtus VI, Pope of the Red Slipper—President Buck Jones Rallies and Waves the Flag]

The Selected Stories of Patricia Highsmith (New York: W. W. Norton & Company, 2001)
[contains all the short stories published in in the following volumes: *The Animal-Lover's Book of Beastly Murder—Little Tales of Misogyny—Slowly, Slowly in the Wind—The Black House—Mermaids on the Golf Course*]

Nothing That Meets the Eye: The Uncollected Stories of Patricia Highsmith (New York: W. W. Norton & Company, 2002)
[The Mightiest Mornings—Uncertain Treasure—Magic Casements—Miss Juste and the Green Rompers—Where the Door Is Always Open and the Welcome Mat Is Out—In the Plaza—The Hollow Oracle—The Great Cardhouse—The Car—The Still Point of the Turning World—The Pianos of the Steinachs—A Mighty Nice Man—Quiet Night—Doorbell for Louisa—A Bird in Hand—Music to Die By—Man's Best Friend—Born Failure—A Dangerous Hobby—The Returnees—Nothing That Meets the Eye—Two Disagreeable Pigeons—Variations on a Game—A Girl like Phyl—It's a Deal—Things Had Gone Badly—The Trouble with Mrs. Blynn, the Trouble with the World—The Second

Cigarette. Afterword by Paul Ingendaay—Notes on the Stories by Anna von Planta]

NONFICTION

Plotting and Writing Suspense Fiction (Boston: The Writer, 1966).

CHILDREN'S LITERATURE

Miranda the Panda Is on the Veranda (Doris Sanders, illustrations by Patricia Highsmith; New York: Coward-McCann, 1958).

Secondary Sources

REFERENCES AND FURTHER READING

All books are dated according to the edition used, not the date of first publication.

Abbott, Berenice. *Aperture Masters of Photography*. Introduction and commentary by Julia Van Haaften. New York: Aperture Foundation, 2015.
Baldwin, Nell. *Henry Ford and the Jews: The Mass Production of Hate*. New York: Public Affairs, 2003.
Barnes, Djuna. *Nightwood*. London: Faber and Faber (Faber Modern Classics), 2015.
Bedford, Sybille. *A Visit to Don Otavio: A Mexican Journey*. New York: New York Review of Books Classics, 2016.
Berg, A. Scott. *Lindbergh*. New York: G. P. Putnam's Sons, 1998.
Bérubé, Allan, *Coming Out Under Fire: The History of Gay Men and Women in World War II*. Chapel Hill: University of North Carolina Press, 2010.
Bradbury, Malcolm (ed.). *The Atlas of Literature*. London: De Agostini Editions,1996.
Brandel, Marc. *The Choice*. London: Eyre & Spottiswoode, 1952.
Broyard, Anatole. *Kafka Was the Rage. A Greenwich Village Memoir*. New York: Vintage, 1997.
Cavigelli, Franz, Fritz Senn, and Anna von Planta. *Patricia Highsmith: Leben und Werk*. Zurich: Diogenes, 1996.
Chabon, Michael. *The Amazing Adventures of Kavalier & Klay*. London: HarperCollins, New English Edition, 2008.

Dictionnaire des cultures Gays et Lesbiennes. Sous la direction de Didier Eribon. Paris: Larousse, 2003.

Dillon, Millicent. *A Little Original Sin: The Life & Work of Jane Bowles.* New York: Holt, Rinehart & Winston, 1981.

Dostoevsky, Fyodor. *Crime and Punishment.* Translated and edited by Michael R. Katz. New York: Liveright, 2019.

———. *Notes from Underground.* Translated and edited by Michael R. Katz. New York: W. W. Norton, 2000.

Faderman, Lillian. *The Gay Revolution: The Story of the Struggle.* New York: Simon & Schuster, 2015.

———. *Odd Girls and Twilight Lovers: A History of Lesbian Life in 20th-Century America.* New York: Columbia University Press, 1991.

Flanner, Janet. *Darlinghissima: Letters to a Friend.* Edited by Natalia Danesi Murray. New York: Random House, 1985.

Gide, André. *The Counterfeiters.* Translated by Dorothy Bussy. Penguin Books (Twentieth Century Classics), 1990.

Gronowicz, Antoni. *Garbo. Her Story.* London: Penguin Books, 1990.

Guggenheim, Peggy. *Out of This Century. Confessions of an Art Addict.* New York: André Deutsch, 2005.

Hall, Lee. *Betty Parsons. Artist, Dealer, Collector.* New York: Harry N. Abrams, 1991.

Harrison, Russell. *Patricia Highsmith* (United States Author Series). New York: Twayne, 1997.

Hughes, Dorothy B. *In a Lonely Place.* New York: Feminist Press, 2003.

James, Henry. *The Ambassadors.* Edited and with an introduction by Adrian Poole. London: Penguin (Penguin Classics), 2008.

Jones, Gerard. *Men of Tomorrow: Geeks, Gangsters, and the Birth of the Comic Book.* New York: Arrow, 2006.

Kafka, Franz. *In the Penal Colony.* Translation by Ian Johnston. https://www.kafka-online.info/in-the-penal-colony.html.

———. *The Metamorphosis.* Translated by Susan Bernofsky. New York: W. W. Norton, 2014.

Katz, Jonathan Ned. *The Invention of Heterosexuality.* Chicago: University of Chicago Press, 2007.

Köhn, Eckhardt. *Rolf Tietgens—Poet with a Camera.* Zell-Unterentersbach: Die Graue Edition, 2011.

Koestler, Arthur. *Darkness at Noon.* London: Vintage Classics, 1994.

Lerman, Leo. *The Grand Surprise: The Journals of Leo Lerman.* Edited by Stephen Pascal. New York: Alfred A. Knopf, 2007.

Maclaren-Ross, Julian. *Memoirs of the Forties.* London: Abacus, 1991.

Marcus, Eric. *Making History: The Struggle for Gay and Lesbian Equal Rights 1945–1990. An Oral History.* New York: HarperPerennial 1992.

Kaiser, Charles. *The Gay Metropolis. The Landmark History of Gay Life in America.* New York: Grove Press, 1997, 2019.

Meaker, Marijane. *Highsmith. A Romance of the 1950s.* San Francisco: Cleis, 2003.

Menninger, Karl. *The Human Mind.* New York, London: Alfred A. Knopf, 1930.

Newton, Esther. *Cherry Grove, Fire Island: Sixty Years in America's First Gay and Lesbian Town.* Durham, NC: Duke University Press, 2014.

Packer, Vin [Marijane Meaker]. *Intimate Victims.* New York: Manor Books, 1963.

Palmen, Connie. *Die Sünde der Frau: Über Marilyn Monroe, Marguerite Duras, Jane Bowles und Patricia Highsmith.* Zurich: Diogenes, 2018.

Plimpton, George. *Truman Capote: In Which Various Friends, Enemies, Acquaintances, and Detractors Recall His Turbulent Career.* New York: Nan A. Talese, 1997.

Poe, Edgar Allan. *Complete Stories and Poems.* New York: Viking, 2011.

Powell, Dawn. *The Locusts Have No King.* South Royalton, VT: Steerforth Press, 1998.

Schenkar, Joan M. *The Talented Miss Highsmith.* New York: St. Martin's Press / Picador, 2009.

Schulman, Robert. *Romany Marie, the Queen of Greenwich Village.* Louisville, KY: Butler Books, 2006.

Spark, Muriel. *A Far Cry from Kensington.* New York: New Directions, 1988.

Van Haaften, Julia. *Berenice Abbott. A Life in Photography.* New York: W. W. Norton, 2018.

Wetzsteon, Ross. *Republic of Dreams. Greenwich Village: The American Bohemia, 1910–1960.* New York: Simon & Schuster, 2002.

Wineapple, Brenda. *Genêt: A Biography of Janet Flanner.* Lincoln: University of Nebraska Press, 1992.

Wilson, Andrew. *Beautiful Shadow.* London: Bloomsbury, 2003.

Wolff, Charlotte, M.D. *Love Between Women.* London: Duckworth, 1971.

Yronwode, Catherine, and Trina Robbins. *Women and the Comics.* Forestville, CA: Eclipse Books, 1985.

FILMOGRAPHY

✣

- *Strangers on a Train*, Alfred Hitchcock, 1951
- *A Plein Soleil (Purple Noon*, after *The Talented Mr. Ripley)*, René Clément, 1960
- *Le meurtrier (Enough Rope*, after *The Blunderer)*, Claude Autant-Lara, 1963
- *Once You Kiss a Stranger (Strangers on a Train)*, Robert Sparr, 1969
- *Der amerikanische Freund (The American Friend*, after *Ripley's Game)*, Wim Wenders, 1977
- *Dites-lui que je l'aime* (This Sweet Sickness), Claude Miller, 1977
- *Die gläserne Zelle (The Glass Cell)*, Hans Geissendörfer, 1978
- *Armchair Thriller* (TV Series based on *A Dog's Ransom*, 6 episodes), 1978
- *Eaux profondes (Deep Water)*, Michel Deville, 1981
- *Ediths Tagebuch (Edith's Diary)*, Hans Werner Geissendörfer, 1983
- *Tiefe Wasser (Deep Water)*, Franz Peter Wirth, 1983
- *Die zwei Gesichter des Januars (The Two Faces of January)*, Wolfgang Storch, 1986
- *Le Cri du hibou (The Cry of the Owl)*, Claude Chabrol, 1987
- *Húkanie sovy (The Cry of the Owl)*, Vido Hornák 1988
- *Something You Have to Live With*, John Berry, 1989
- *La ferme du malheur (The Day of Reckoning)*, Samuel Fuller, 1989
- *Der Geschichtenerzähler* (after *A Suspension of Mercy)*, Rainer Boldt, 1989
- *Les Cadavres exquis de Patricia Highsmith (Chillers*, TV series)
  - *Pour le restant de leurs jours ("Old Folks at Home"),*
    Peter Kassovitz, 1990
  - *L'Épouvantail ("Slowly, Slowly in the Wind"), Maroun*
    Bagdadi, 1990
  - *Puzzle ("Blow It"), Maurice Dugowson, 1990*
  - *La ferme du Malheur ("The Day of Reckoning"),*
    Samuel Fuller, 1990
  - *A Curious Suicide, Robert Bierman, 1990*
  - *L'Amateur de Frissons ("The Thrill Seeker"), Roger*
    Andrieux, Mai Zetterling, 1990

- *Légitime défense ("Something You Have to Live With"),*
  John Berry, 1990
- *Époux en froid ("Sauce for the Goose"), Clare Peploe,*
  1991
- *La Proie du chat ("Something the Cat Dragged In"),*
  Nessa Hyams, 1992
- *Sincères condoléances ("Under a Dark Angel's Eye"),*
  Nick Lewin, 1992
- *Passions partagées ("A Bird Poised to Fly"), Damian*
  Harris, 1992
- *Le Jardin des disparus (after "The Stuff of Madness"),*
  Mai Zetterling, 1992
- *Trip nach Tunis* (after *The Tremor of Forgery*), Peter Goedel, 1993
- *Petits contes misògins (Little Tales of Misogyny)*, Pere Sagristà, 1995
- *Once You Meet a Stranger* (after *Strangers on a Train*), Tommy Lee
  Wallace, 1996
- *La rançon du chien (A Dog's Ransom)*, Peter Kassovitz, 1996
- *The Talented Mr. Ripley*, Anthony Minghella, 1999
- *The Terrapin*, Regis Trigano, 2001
- *Ripley's Game*, Liliana Cavani, 2002
- *Ripley Under Ground*, Roger Spottiswoode, 2005
- *The Cry of the Owl*, Jamie Thraves, 2009
- *A Mighty Nice Man*, Jonathan Dee, 2014
- *The Two Faces of January*, Hossein Amini, 2014
- *Carol (The Price of Salt)*, Todd Haynes, 2015
- *A Kind of Murder* (after *The Blunderer*), Andy Goddard, 2016
- *Deep Water*, Adrian Lyne, 2022

INDEX OF NAMES AND WORKS

"Aaron," *see* "Mightiest Mornings, The" (PH story)

Abbott, Berenice, xx, 5, 55–56, 145, 149, 156, 236

Abbott, Caroline, 161

Adamic, Louis, 504

Adams, Valerie, 213, 236, 498, 544

Alajalov, Constantin, 233

Albert, Gerald ("Jerry"), 299, 309, 317–18, 333, 338, 341, 345

Al Camy' (Cammarata, Al), 263, 275, 279, 281, 289, 306, 314–15, 321, 326–27, 333, 339–40, 342

"Alena" (lost PH story), 10

Alice T., 111, 172, 213, 408

Alpert, Hollis, 589

Amaya, Carmen, xx, 155, 238–39, 247, 253–54, 337–38

Ames, Elizabeth, 522

Ammons, Albert, 100

Amter, Israel, 221

Anderson, Sherwood, 149

Ann T., 321–29, 334, 345, 367, 415, 450

Arendt, Hannah, 5, 463, 499–500

Argument of Tantalus, The (working title), *see Price of Salt, The* (PH novel)

Arthur R., 7, 37, 47, 49, 64, 89–91, 94, 113, 239, 243, 248

Aswell, Mary Louise, xii, xxiv, 254, 385, 425, 499, 503, 512, 513

Auden, W. H., 194, 499
  Double Man, The, 194

Audrey, 450, 463–64, 477

Augustin, Johannes Jakob, 184, 192, 199, 205–6, 284

Augustine (St.), 325
  Confessions, 325

Augusto, 351, 353

Austen, Jane
  Pride and Prejudice, 103

Austin, Darrel, 262

Avery, Milton, 500

Babs B., 9–11, 17, 39, 47, 50, 59, 65, 143, 457, 470, 488, 535

Babs P., 92, 96–105, 110, 112–15, 118, 126, 144, 147, 148, 150–51, 158, 160, 193

Bach, Johann Sebastian, 14, 33, 88, 128–29, 185, 188, 212, 217, 222, 224, 228–29, 230, 253, 264, 267, 274, 346, 402–6, 409

Bacon, Francis (artist), 223

Bacon, Francis (philosopher), 105

Bailey, Helen, 7, 8, 15–16, 24, 26, 42

Barnes, Djuna, 137, 160, 579
  Nightwood, 137

Barney, Natalie Clifford, xxi, xxii

Barrault, Jean-Louis, 537

Barrera, 349, 351–53

Battlefield, Ken, 301

Baudelaire, Charles, 394, 517

Baur, Harry, 136

Beach, Sylvia, xxv, 355

Beaumont, Germaine, xxii

Bedford, Sybille, xxiii–xxiv
  Quicksands, xxiv

Beethoven, Ludwig van, 81, 218, 440

Bel Geddes, Norman, 227

Bemelmans, Ludwig, 10, 18, 28, 85, 169, 238, 240, 266
  Donkey Inside, A, 10
  My War with the U.S., 240

Bemelmans, Madeleine, 18, 22, 25, 28, 167, 239

Berch, Bettina, xxi

Berger, Jack, 116–19, 136–43, 152, 154, 157–60, 167, 168, 177, 179–86, 191, 193, 217–18, 235

Berman, Eugene, 342

Bernhard, Lucien, xx, 159

Bernhard, Ruth, xx, 52, 61–62, 65, 106, 121, 143–47, 150, 152, 155,

156, 158–62, 168, 172, 173, 176,
180–86, 190, 192–93, 195, 198,
215, 216, 218, 223–31, 235, 237,
239–43, 246–49, 252, 260, 264,
280, 283, 303, 313, 338, 342, 352,
383, 436
Bernstein, Leonard, 499
Bertha C., 603–6
Billie A., 82, 123–25, 142, 150, 156
Billie B., 26–36, 38–44, 48–54, 58, 60,
67, 80, 83, 92–93, 102, 113, 178,
213, 239
"Birds Poised to Fly, The" (PH story),
560–62, 565
Biryukov, Pavel, 158
Leo Tolstoy, 158
Blake, William, 150–52, 162, 191, 211,
227, 349
"Tyger, The" ("Tyger Tyger"), 150
Blechman, Marcus, 150, 168
Bloor, Ella Reeve, 8
Blumenschein, Tabea, 611
Blumenthal, Alfred Cleveland, xxv, 348
Blumenthal Hill, Ellen, *see* Hill, Ellen
Boas, Franz, 128
Mind of Primitive Man, The, 128
Boccherini, Luigi, 188, 274
Bohrmann, Horst, 277
Borak, J., 267, 419–20, 511
Boswell, James, 137
Life of Samuel Johnson, The, 137
Bowles, Jane, 387, 475, 477–78, 499,
578, 597
Bowles, Paul, 566, 597
Sheltering Sky, The, 566
Boyle, Kay, 213, 230, 235
Decision, 89
Monday Night, 331
Brand, Millen, 50
Brandel, Marc, 500, 518, 522–26, 528,
530, 532, 534–45, 547, 550, 558,
560–62, 566, 572, 575–79, 582,
585, 589–90, 593, 596, 604
Choice, The, 572, 604
Rain Before Seven, 523
Breton, André, 150
Brewster, William, 16
Brod, Max, 507
Brook, Clive, 170
Brooks, Louise, xxv

Browder, Earl, 9, 73
Browne, Thomas, 219, 225
Letter to a Friend, 225
Buck, Pearl S., 343
Dragon Seed, 343
Buffet, Monique, 611
Butler, Samuel, 16, 20–21

Cabell, James Branch, 35
Cream of the Jest, The, 35
Calas, Nicolas, 119, 246, 391
Camacho, Hernando, 351–52
Campbell (Miss), 248–49
Camus, Albert, 439
Capote, Truman, xii, 494, 499, 503–4,
512
Other Voices, Other Rooms, 499, 503
"Car, The" (PH story), 371
Carlyle, Thomas, 6, 89
Sartor Resartus, 6, 89
Carnegie, Hattie, 310, 579
Caroline (pseudonym), 610
Carol (retitled 1990 edition of *Price of
Salt, The*), xvii, 571
Carrington, Leonora, 216, 236
Carroll, Paul Vincent, 14
Shadow and Substance, 14
Strings, My Lord, Are False, The,
157
Carstairs, Jo, 20
Cather, Willa, 12, 128
Not Under Forty, 128
Sapphira and the Slave Girl, 12
Catherwood, Virginia Kent ("Ginnie"),
xxv, 355, 385–86, 390–91, 400–401,
430–31, 434, 442–47, 449–68,
471–85, 489–93, 495–97, 513, 527,
559, 571
Cecilia E., 25, 29–30, 267
Cervantes, Miguel de, 58
Don Quixote, 58
Cézanne, Paul, 61
Chagall, Marc, 150, 216, 339
Chamberlain, Marion, 479, 484, 489
Chambrun, Jacques, 355, 388, 396, 397,
401, 402, 408
Chandler S., 323, 334
Chaney, Stewart, 132
Chaplin, Charlie, 37
Great Dictator, The, 37

Chloe S., 251, 310–53, 354–59, 362–64,
    369–71, 462
Claudel, Paul, 42
    L'annonce faite à Marie, 42
Click of the Shutting, The (unfinished
    PH novel), xx, 38, 251, 260, 354,
    388, 392, 507
Coates, Claude (PH's uncle), 297, 324,
    517, 566–67
Coates, Dan ("Danny") Walton, 33, 567
Coates, Daniel (PH's grandfather), 124,
    129
Coates, Dan Oscar (PH's cousin), 282,
    285, 305, 326, 420, 566–67
Coates, Eric, 118
Coates, Florine (Dan Oscar's wife), 567
Coates, Grace, 9, 11, 70, 72–73, 79
Coates, John, 9, 11, 66, 70–78
Coates, Mary, *see* Highsmith, Mary
    Coates
Coates, Willie Mae (PH's grandmother),
    1–2, 10, 11, 15, 48, 51, 124, 158,
    159, 169, 170, 176, 224, 225, 244,
    296, 332, 333, 336–38, 342, 355,
    375, 414, 420, 462, 515, 517, 567,
    568
Cocteau, Jean, 119, 212
    Les enfants terribles, 212
Cohen, Dennis, 531, 542–43, 545, 581,
    605
Cohen, Kathryn Hamill, 530–31, 542–45,
    549–59, 561–66, 571–73, 577–79,
    581–83, 585, 591, 597, 604, 609
Colette, xxii, 204
    Indulgent Husband, The, 204
Conan Doyle, Arthur, 1
Connolly, Cyril, 89
    Horizon, 89
Conrad, Joseph, 2, 243, 443
    "Youth," 443
Constable, Rosalind, xxiii–xxv, 5, 66–91,
    93–98, 101–3, 106–8, 111–13,
    116–19, 122–23, 125–27, 129–32,
    135–46, 148–49, 153–68, 172–73,
    176–82, 185, 192–98, 200, 202–5,
    207–12, 215–16, 218–19, 222–24,
    241, 243–48, 252–54, 259–61,
    265–73, 275, 281, 288–90, 293–95,
    306–12, 319, 323, 327–32, 335, 338,
    341–45, 350, 363, 367, 375, 383–84,

386, 389–91, 398, 403, 407–8, 412,
    422, 431, 435–36, 456, 463, 468,
    472, 478, 481, 487, 493, 499, 504,
    507, 514, 525, 534–35, 540–41, 561,
    563, 565–66, 578, 582, 591, 594
    They Who Paddle, 86
Constant, George, 316
Cook, Paul, 366, 369–76
Copland, Aaron, 499
Cornell, Allela, 249, 251, 262, 267, 269–
    87, 289–93, 296–315, 317, 320–21,
    327, 337, 352, 356, 362–63, 383,
    393–94, 397, 399, 407, 410–11, 413,
    425, 431, 433, 435, 439, 441, 450,
    451–55, 463, 474, 596
Cornell, Katherine, 47
Coryl C., 17, 23, 33
Coward, Noël, 101
Cowley, Malcolm, 78
    After the Genteel Tradition, 78
Cralick, Jeva, 32, 42, 55, 87–88, 104, 116,
    143, 214
Crane, Stephen, 119
    Red Badge of Courage, The, 119
"Crime Begins" (PH story), 135
Crosby, Bing, 234
Crowninshield, Frank, 175
Curtis, 8, 24–27, 30, 38, 52

Dalí, Salvador, 61, 246, 266, 287, 300,
    494
    Secret Life of Salvador Dalí, The, 300
Daly, Maureen, 219
Danesi Murray, Natalia, xxii, 549
Dante Alighieri, 58, 78–79, 172, 176,
    178–79, 190, 394
    Divine Comedy, 78, 190
d'Arazien, Arthur, 182
Daves, Jessica, 161
David, Jean ("Jeannot"), 10, 12, 87, 137,
    176–77, 186, 234, 531, 546, 553
David, Lily, 546, 548
Davidman, Joy, 50
Davis, Benjamin, 221
Davis, Blevins, 505
de Acosta, Mercedes, xxii
Debbie B., 25, 103, 112, 158
Debussy, Claude, 246, 604
de Chirico, Giorgio, 61, 218, 307, 314,
    439

Defoe, Daniel, 394
  Robinson Crusoe, 394
Degas, Edgar, 54, 279
de Lanux, Eyre, 174
de la Voiseur, 578
Dell, *see* Jüdell, Hans Felix
Del P., 101, 118–19, 123, 156, 187, 219,
  261, 351
Desert Victory (documentary film), 280
Diamond, David, 425, 527
Dickens, Charles, 1, 188, 303, 544
Dickinson, Emily, 591
Dione, 532–33, 536, 539
Dobrow (Dr.), 65, 217, 221
Dodson, Owen, 483
Donne, John, 191, 314, 349
"Doorbell for Louisa" (PH story), 430,
  449, 460
Dos Passos, John, 439
Dostoevsky, Fyodor, 1, 136, 427, 465,
  470, 473, 501, 507, 584
  Brothers Karamazov, The, 136
  Crime and Punishment, 136
Dove Descending, The (unfinished PH
  novel), 430, 437, 447
Dubuffet, Jean, 145
Duchess, The, 374–76, 536, 578–79
Duchin, Eddy, 98
Dunham, Katherine, 337
Dunne, John William, 305
  Experiment With Time, 305

Earl (Helen's fiancé), 105, 107, 110, 112,
  151, 153
Eddy, 11, 38, 61, 97, 144
Eddy, Mary Baker, 17, 163
Edith's Diary (PH novel), 612
Edson, Dorothy Wheelock, 417
Einstein, Albert, 253
Eisenhower, Dwight D., 605
Eliot, T. S., 77, 97–98, 116, 119, 194, 279,
  302, 368
  Four Quartets, 279
Ellen B., 321, 324, 345
Ellis, Henry Havelock, 274
Elwyn, David, 6, 9
"End Is Not in Sight, The" (PH story),
  469
Engelhardt, Nina, *see* Duchess, The
Erdman, Jean, 215

Ernst, Max, 150, 216, 218, 244
Evergood, Philip, 213
Eyck, Götz van, 313, 323, 333–34, 346

Fauré, Gabriel, 245, 251
Fears, Peggy, xxv, 348, 488, 493, 502, 503
Feininger, Lyonel, 287
Fenton, Fleur, 284
Fielding, Henry, 112
  Tom Thumb the Great, 112
Finucane, Paddy, 178
Flanner, Janet (Genêt), xxii, 83
  "Letters from Paris," xxii
Flaubert, Gustave, 161
  La Tentation de Saint Antoine, 161
Flesch, Emil, 210, 214, 216, 219, 222
Flora W., 23, 32
Flynn, Elizabeth Gurley, 221
Forain, Jean-Louis, 600
Forster, E. M., 162
  Passage to India, A, 162
Found in the Street (PH novel), xiv–xv,
  611–12
Franzen, Jonathan, 500
Fraser (Mrs.), 148, 173, 228
Freud, Sigmund, 77, 102, 250, 282, 287,
  539, 579
  Moses and Monotheism, 282
Freund, Madeleine, *see* Bemelmans,
  Madeleine
"Friends" (lost PH story), 277
Fromm, Erich, 5

Ganosini, Tonio, 548–49
Garbo, Greta, 233
Garden, Mary, xxi
Genêt, *see* Flanner, Janet
Georgia S., 7, 15–16, 30
Gershwin, George, 404
  Porgy and Bess, 404
Gibbon, Edward, 137
  *History of the Decline and Fall of the
    Roman Empire, The*, 137
Gide, André, 102, 492, 522
  Counterfeiters, The, 102, 492
Gielgud, John, 499
Giorgione, 308
Goethe, Johann Wolfgang von, 162, 164,
  185, 200, 239, 243, 274
  Wilhelm Meisters Lehrjahre, 162

Goldberg, Ben-Zion, 171–83, 186, 190,
192, 195, 207–8, 210, 212–16, 219,
221–22, 225, 227, 235, 240, 258,
263, 308–9, 312, 333, 335, 363–64,
370–71, 398, 423
Goldfarb, Alex, 249, 317
Goodman, Paul, 507
Gordon, Dan, 306–7
Göring, Hermann, 85
Goya, Francisco de, 439
Graham, W. S., 518
Graham R., 31–32, 48, 53, 69, 96, 110
"Great Cardhouse, The" (PH story),
552
Green, Julien, 91, 228, 250, 254, 292, 295,
296, 299, 323, 334, 362
  Closed Garden, The, 334
  Dreamer, The, 91
  Varouna, 228, 254
Greene, Graham, 578, 583
  Man Within, The, 583
  19 Stories, 578
Grosz, George, 96
Guggenheim, Peggy, xxiii, xxiv, 156, 223,
244, 253
Gutheil, Emil, 539

Hall, Radclyffe, 351
  Well of Loneliness, The, 351
Hammer, Joseph, 263–67, 299, 333
Hamsun, Knut, 194, 206
  Mysteries, 194, 202, 206
Händel, Georg Friedrich, 115, 128
Hardy, Thomas, 116
  Dynasts, 116
Harwood, Gean, 40, 92
Hauser, Ernst, 10–13, 19, 23, 28, 43–44,
47–49, 52–53, 56, 59–60, 63, 90–91,
128, 130, 141, 164, 167, 174, 183,
320, 370, 400, 432, 470–71
Hawthorne, Nathaniel, 134
Hazelwood, Carl, 514
Heider, Wolfgang, 504
Heine, Heinrich, 77
  Lorelei, 77
Helen M., 6, 16, 19, 20, 22, 24–28, 31,
37, 41–42, 50, 90, 93–115, 118, 124,
125, 143, 147–48, 150–54, 157–58,
160–61, 175–76, 193, 195, 199, 204,
234, 247, 259, 261, 268

Hellman, Lillian, 85
"Heloise" (lost PH story), 564
Herbert (Herb) L., 33, 47, 268, 415, 501,
523
Herodotus, 583
"Heroine, The" (PH story), xxiv, 16,
89–90, 104, 225, 232, 384, 414, 475,
479, 565, 586
Highsmith, Mary Coates, 1–2, 5–11,
14–15, 17, 19, 25, 28–30, 34,
37–40, 44–46, 50–53, 56, 59, 65,
75, 76, 78, 82, 84, 86–90, 94, 95,
97, 102, 104–6, 112, 115, 119,
120, 122, 124–26, 129, 130, 133,
136, 138–46, 148, 149, 152, 154,
156, 158, 159, 163, 167, 168, 175,
177, 179, 180, 186, 189, 192, 194,
196–98, 203, 207–10, 212, 214,
215, 222–25, 229, 231–34, 237,
238, 240–43, 245, 246, 248, 250,
252, 255, 257, 261–63, 268–70,
277, 278, 283–86, 288, 290, 291,
294, 296–98, 301–3, 305, 307,
308, 314–21, 324, 326, 327, 331,
332, 334–38, 340–42, 344, 345,
355, 359, 360, 362, 364, 366, 370,
371, 375, 386, 388–90, 393, 402,
407, 408, 410, 414, 418, 419, 438,
440, 460, 465–67, 469, 471, 473,
479–83, 488, 491, 493, 494, 496,
502–4, 508, 510, 513, 515–18, 521,
523, 524, 527–30, 533, 540, 541,
545, 561, 562, 565, 566, 581, 583,
587, 590, 595, 611
Highsmith, Stanley, 1–2, 5–6, 9, 14, 15,
25, 30, 34, 38, 46, 50, 51, 53, 56, 58,
59, 84, 87, 89, 92, 95, 96, 106, 114,
118–20, 122, 126, 130, 133, 136, 139,
140, 142–45, 148, 152, 154, 156, 159,
163, 168, 175, 179, 192, 194, 210,
212, 229, 231, 233, 234, 240, 242,
245, 250, 252, 255, 257, 262, 263,
270, 277, 283, 284, 286, 290, 291,
296–98, 301–3, 305, 307, 308, 314,
316–18, 320, 324, 326, 327, 331, 335,
336, 338–42, 345, 371, 388–90, 393,
402, 407, 418, 440, 460, 466, 479–81,
483, 488, 491, 493, 503, 512, 515,
518, 521, 523, 524, 527–30, 562, 583,
587, 595

Hill, Ellen, 462–63, 609, 610
Himes, Chester, 500, 518–19, 523
Himmler, Heinrich, 406
Hirst, Gertrude, 13
Hitchcock, Alfred, 571, 581–82, 596,
    609–10
    Strangers on a Train (film), 596,
    609–10
Hitler, Adolf, 39, 43, 100, 407
Hoffman, Malvina, 176
Hofmannsthal, Raimund von, 422, 425
Hölderlin, Friedrich, 200, 284, 372
Holliday, Judy, *see* Tuvim, Judy
Homer, 28
"House on Morton St." (PH story), 7,
    21–22
Howard, Clare, 38, 91
Howard, Lewis, 504, 507–14
Hoyningen-Huene, Georg Freiherr von,
    277
Hughes, Richard E., 247–49, 253–55,
    260–61, 277, 285, 289, 292, 300–
    302, 333–35, 341, 361, 390, 437
Hughes, Toni, 101, 108–9, 132, 174
Huxley, Aldous, 209, 426
    Brave New World, 209, 426
Hyman, Stanley Edgar, 288

"Instantly and Forever" (lost PH story),
    560, 564
Irving, Washington, 108
    Tales of the Alhambra, 108
Isaacs, Leo, 315, 317–21, 324–31, 333,
    337, 341, 359
Isaacson, Bobby, 413, 434, 484
Isaacson, Robert (father), 432

Jackson, Shirley Hardie, 288
James, Henry, 134, 139, 150, 395, 399,
    426, 459, 476
    Ambassadors, The, 139
Jane O., 152, 208
Jean C., 467–69, 472
Jeanne, 493–98, 501–5, 507–10, 512–14,
    521, 523–25, 528, 532–33, 559, 564,
    574, 578–82
Jennings (Dr.), 49, 52
Joan S., 420, 430–31, 437–48, 450,
    453–56, 460, 462–63, 470, 476, 491,
    495–98, 502, 510, 512–13

Johnson, Buffie, xxi–xxiii, xxv, 5, 61–70,
    77, 79–80, 83–85, 90, 94, 96, 101–3,
    107–9, 118, 132, 150, 156, 158, 162,
    164–67, 173–74, 187, 189, 197–99,
    234, 236, 239–47, 252–53, 263, 290,
    310, 323, 364
Johnson, Crockett, 282
Johnson, Hewlett, 10
    Soviet Power, The, 10, 21, 35
Johnson, Margot, xxiv, 430, 433, 449,
    456, 462, 464, 466, 469, 475, 479,
    484, 489, 493, 503–5, 509–10, 515,
    517, 535, 537, 540, 545, 548, 564–
    66, 574, 577, 579–81, 596, 598–601,
    603–6, 607
Johnson, Samuel, 100, 548
Jo P., 110, 162–63, 166–67, 169, 173, 177,
    201, 208, 230, 235, 245, 251, 260,
    268–69, 402, 462–63
Joyce, James, 9, 236
    Finnegans Wake, 9
    Portrait of the Artist as a Young Man,
    A, 377
    Ulysses, 586
Jüdell, Hans Felix ("Dell"), 509, 588

Kafka, Franz, 212, 219, 250, 284–85, 473,
    507, 510
    Castle, The, 212, 272
Kahn, Joan, 541, 561, 574, 578, 581, 607
Kauffmann, Stanley, 260
Kay G., 605
Keel, Daniel, xiv, xv, 611, 612
Kennedy, Edward, 407
Kent, Arthur Atwater, 355
Kent, Jonathan Prentiss, 472, 481
Kierkegaard, Søren, 463, 553
Kiesler, Frederick John, xxiii, 223
Kingsley (later Skattebol), Gloria Kate,
    xiv, xv, 92–93, 99, 102–4, 112, 116,
    127, 130–31, 143, 148, 204, 211,
    213–14, 234, 236, 259, 268, 498,
    505, 512, 578–80
Kinstler, Everett Raymond, 259, 302
Kirkpatrick, Ralph, 266–68
Klee, Paul, 38, 162, 218, 287
Klein, (Dr.) Eva, 527–28, 530–34, 536–41
Koestler, Arthur, 132, 499, 598–602
    Dialogue with Death, 602
Koeves, Tibor, 123–24, 129

Krim, Seymour, 261, 272, 283, 288
Kubik, Gail, 518
Kuniyoshi (Mrs.), 90

La Guardia, Fiorello, 100
Lamb, Charles, 584
Lamy, Jacques, 216
Landowska, Wanda, 14
Landshoff-Yorck, Ruth, 503, 547
Larry H., 357, 359, 362
Latham, John, 197–99
Latham, Minor White, 9, 11, 13, 31,
    37–38, 47, 93–94, 98, 100, 103, 109,
    125, 133, 146, 157
La Touche (also Latouche), John, xxiii,
    174
Laurencin, Marie, 61, 236
Lawrence, D. H., 152
    Assorted Articles, 113
    Lady Chatterley's Lover, 75
Lechay, James, 343
LeDuc, Alma, 24
Lee, Stan, 250, 271
Leeds, Strelsa, 475
"Legend of the Convent of Saint
    Fotheringay, The" (PH story), 4–5,
    7, 27, 38
Léger, Fernand, xxiii, 132
Lenin, Vladimir, 8
Lerman, Leo, 499, 502–4, 511, 579
Levi, Julian, 174
Levine, Bertha, *see* Spivy (Bertha Levine)
Levine, Stanley, 518
Lévi-Strauss, Claude, 5
Levy, Julien, 310, 317, 319, 325, 342
Levy, Muriel, 317–19, 342
Lexy, 312–13, 315
Liebermann, Alexander, 301
Lillie, Beatrice, 415
Lindbergh, Charles, 39
Lola P. (later Lola C.), 66, 108–9, 118,
    123, 157, 187, 208, 219, 290, 294,
    391, 456
Lonergan, Patricia, 332
Lonergan, Wayne, 332–33
"Love Is a Terrible Thing" (PH story),
    see "Birds Poised to Fly, The" (PH
    story)
Löwenstein, Rudolf, 512
Luce, Henry, xxiii, 5

Luther, Martin, 394
Luzi, Alexander, 402
Luzi, Marguerite, 367, 371, 402
Lyne, Elizabeth, 531, 538, 544, 547, 561,
    563, 566–75, 577–81, 598–602,
    605–7

MacArthur, Douglas, 137
MacArthur, Mary, 240
MacLeod, Vivien Koch, 518
Maggie ("Texas," "Tex") E., 249, 251,
    262–77, 279–83, 285, 287, 293, 297,
    301, 304, 307–9, 329, 333, 362, 372,
    463, 473, 487, 493–94, 566
"Magic Casements, The" (PH story), 432
Mahler, Raphael, 244, 299, 353
Mallison, Clare, 301
Mandeville, Bernard, 109
Manet, Édouard, 439
Mann, Thomas, 64, 442, 459, 510
    Death in Venice, 64
Mannes, Marya, 391
Mansfield, Katherine, 16
Mantle, Robert Burns, 345
"Manuel" (lost PH story), 179–81, 183,
    190, 194–95, 201, 205, 227–28
"Man Who Got Off the Earth, The"
    (lost PH story), 449
Marcella, 17, 33, 54
Marcelle, 166
Marie T., 17
Marijann K., 10, 13, 16, 24, 98
Marlowe, Walter, 53, 67, 89, 123, 145,
    164, 177, 180, 190–91, 235
Marta (Countess), 75
Mary H., 11–13, 15, 17–19, 22, 120, 383
Mary R. (Billie's flatmate), 26–28, 59
Matisse, Henri, 145
Matta, Roberto, 145, 216
Maugham, William Somerset, xxiii,
    458
McCarthy, Joseph, 500, 570
McCausland, Elizabeth, xx
McCullers, Carson, 82, 373, 499, 532,
    561
    Reflections in a Golden Eye, 82
McCullers, Reeves, 532
McFadden (Miss), 232, 243
McGuire, Lorna, 26, 106
Melcarth, Edward, 109, 295

Melville, Herman, 418, 563
  Moby-Dick; or, The Whale, 455
  Pierre; or, The Ambiguities, 563
Menninger, Karl, 1
  Human Mind, The, 1
Mero, Bruhs, 40, 92
Mespoulet, Marguerite, 100, 259
Michelangelo Buonaroti, 288
Mifflin, John, 249
"Mightiest Mornings, The" (PH story),
  427, 432
"Mighty Nice Man" (PH story), 232, 397
Miller, Charles, 317, 320–21
Miller, Lew, 348
Miller, Ralph, 216
Milles, Carl, 69
Milton, John, 6, 58
Miró, Joan, 150, 218, 287
"Miss Juste and the Green Rompers"
  (PH story), 30, 44
Modigliani, Amedeo, 67
Monash, Paul, 537
Mondrian, Piet, 265, 266, 417
Monocole, Angelica de, 309–10, 329, 332
Montague, William, 93, 137
  Democracy at the Crossroads, 137
More, Thomas, 92
  Utopia, 92
Morgan, Claire (pseudonym of PH), 607
Morgenstern, Christian, 200
Morley, Christopher, 229
Moscow Strikes Back (film), 192
"Mountain Treasure" (PH story), 263
Mourning Becomes Electra (film), 496
"Movie Date" (PH story), 7
Mozart, Wolfgang Amadeus, 118, 132,
  185, 218, 274, 356, 393, 409
"Mr. Scott Is Not on Board" (lost PH
  story), 93–94
"Mrs. Afton, Among Thy Green Braes"
  (PH story), 465–66, 477, 480, 532
Muret, Charlotte, 103–4, 115
Mussolini, Benito, 407

Napoleon Buonaparte, 128
  Letters to Marie Louise, 128
Natasha H., 67, 82, 84, 100–102, 106–8,
  116, 118, 131, 139, 148, 156–57,
  167, 185–86, 193, 208, 309, 323,
  338, 343, 475

Nathan, Robert, 576
Nelson, George, 67, 88
Newton, Isaac, 253
Nietzsche, Friedrich, 124
Nijinsky, Vaslav, 274
Nina D., 20, 147
Nitsche, Erik, 291
Norris, Frank, 97

O'Connor, Flannery, 500, 518
O'Flaherty, Liam, 537
  Puritan, The, 537
O'Hara, John, 576
O'Keeffe, Georgia, 156
O'Neill, Eugene, 15
  Emperor Jones, The, 15
Orgel, Irene, 518
Orozco, José Clemente, 309, 363
Ossorio, Alfonso, 108
Ozenfant, Amédée, 150

Paige, Judith, 147
Pal Joey (musical play), 49
Palma, Florence, 97, 140
Parrish, Maxfield, 54
Parsons, Betty, xxiv–xxv, 5, 82–86, 91,
  100–102, 113, 119, 123, 128, 130,
  137, 144, 156, 173, 185, 193, 200,
  208, 216, 222, 224, 240, 246, 263,
  266, 329, 339–43, 349, 387, 417,
  526, 561
"Passing of Alphonse T. Browne, The"
  (lost PH story), 117, 119
Péguy, Charles, 277, 291–93
  Pensées, 277
Peirce, Waldo, 65
Pépé le Moko, 40
Perlman (Dr.), 342–43, 345
Peter (female college friend), 13, 24–28,
  41, 93, 96, 98, 105, 111–14, 158,
  160, 193, 234, 268, 323
Philadelphia Story, The, 21
Picabia, Francis, xxi
Picard, Lil, 488, 491–94, 496, 498, 502,
  504, 507–9, 512, 565–66, 582,
  588–89, 591
Picasso, Pablo, 66, 439, 459
Pinchot, Gifford, 319
Plangman, Jay Bernard, 1, 2, 19, 37, 78,
  205, 236, 237, 568

Plath, Sylvia, 500

Poe, Edgar Allan, 2, 22, 251

Portugal, R., 417

Posada, José Guadalupe, 309

Powys, John Cowper, 22, 70
  Meaning of Culture, The, 70
  Wolf Solent, 22

Preston, Kiki, 335–36, 339–40

Price of Salt, The (PH novel), xiii, xxv–
  xxvi, 431, 531, 550, 556–57, 560–
  61, 564–65, 570–72, 577, 604–5,
  607, 609, 612

Proust, Marcel, 14, 83, 182, 351, 360,
  372, 428, 515, 526
  À la recherche du temps perdu, 360

Prutman, Irving, 208

Pushkin, Alexander, 36
  Eugene Onegin, 36

Putnam, Jim, 600

Putzl, Howard, 208

"Quiet Night" (PH story), 403

Quirt, Walter, 150

Randolph, David, 321

Reichard, Gladys, 184–85

Renoir, Auguste, 61, 65, 603
  La Baigneuse, 128

Rice, Elmer, 20, 34
  Flight to the West, 34

Richardson, Dorothy Miller, 16, 219
  Pointed Roofs, 15

Rilke, Rainer Maria, 115, 440
  "Girl in Love," 115

Ringer, Norma, 164

Ripley Under Water (PH novel), 612

Rita G., 52–53

Rita R., 15, 17–18, 28, 31, 73–74, 90, 96

Rivera, Diego, 309, 363

"Roaring Fire, The" (lost PH story),
  475

Robbins, Jerome, 499

Robbins, Toni, 578–79

Robin, 400

Roger F., 6, 32, 36, 60, 78, 92, 94, 100,
  115, 119, 134, 164, 318, 359

Roger R., 12, 306

Rogers, Ginger, 82

Rogers, Roy, 326

Rommel, Erwin, 177

Roosevelt, Franklin Delano, 9, 73, 86,
  171, 404, 407, 415

Roosevelt, Sara Delano, 173

Rose M. (friend of Billie's), 52, 102

Rose M. (high school friend), 23, 65

Ross, Barney, 240–41, 246

Rossi, Gene, 348–49

Rostand, Edmond, 107
  Cyrano de Bergerac, 107, 112

Rouault, Georges, 38

Roubichek, Dorothy, 408

Ruth L. (Mary H.'s lover), 11–13, 16,
  19, 22

Ruth W., 59, 67

Saboteurs, The (lost PH play), 131, 135,
  142, 146, 160

Samstag, Gordon, 412

Sandburg, Carl, 156

Sanft, Myron, 560

Sangor, William, 241, 243–44, 260, 294,
  300–302

Santayana, George, 167, 377
  *Life of Reason; or, The Phases of
    Human Progress*, 167

Sarment, Jean, 23
  Le pêcheur d'ombres, 23

Saroyan, William, 12, 200, 428
  *Daring Young Man on the Flying
    Trapeze, The*, 142
  My Name Is Aram, 12

Sartre, Jean-Paul, 501–2
  What Is Literature?, 501–2

Schiff, Jack, 274, 403

Schiller, Friedrich, 164

Schopenhauer, Arthur, 440

Schubert, Franz, 243, 433

Schulberg, Budd, 45, 52
  What Makes Sammy Run?, 52

Senn, Kathleen (Mrs. E. R. Senn), 500,
  528, 571, 589, 592, 605

Shaftesbury (Anthony Ashley Cooper,
  Earl of S.), 105

Shakespeare, William, 9, 12–13, 24, 49,
  148, 156, 258, 383, 459, 584
  Hamlet, 41
  Julius Caesar, 43
  Macbeth, 101, 113, 117
  Measure for Measure, 43
  Much Ado About Nothing, 9

Othello, 543
Taming of the Shrew, 7
Tempest, The, 42
Shapero, Harold, 518, 522
Shaw, Artie, 10
Shaw, George Bernard, 14, 152, 396
  Apple Cart, The, 14
  Candida, 152
  Doctor's Dilemma, The, 47
Shaw, Irwin, 44
  Bury the Dead, 44
Shawn, William, 163, 165, 201, 210, 219,
  224–27
Sheehan, Dick, 561, 563, 578, 599
Sheila, 450–51, 463–64, 477, 481–83, 485,
  489, 607
Sheridan, Richard Brinsley, 95
  School for Scandal, The, 95
Shostakovich, Dmitri, 144
"Silver Horn of Plenty, The" (PH story),
  103–4, 107, 127, 132, 160, 194, 215,
  225–26, 232, 329
Simkins, Francis Butler, 517
  South Old & New, a History 1830-
  1947, The, 517
Simmons, Bill, 249
Sinclair, Upton, 97
Sitwell, Edith, 246
Skattebol, Gloria Kate Kingsley, *see*
  Kingsley (later Skattebol), Gloria
  Kate
Sloan, Pat, 16
  Russia without Illusions, 16
Small g: A Summer Idyll (PH novel),
  612
Smith, Ann, 526, 532, 535–38, 541–45,
  572, 574, 581, 601, 607
Smith, Gordon, 108
Smith, Margarita, 532
Smith, Marty, 301, 317–18, 523
"Snail-Watcher, The" (PH story), 511
Snow, Carmel White, 416–17
Snyder (college friend), 6
Socrates, 486
Song of Ceylon, The, 205
Spender, Stephen, 89
  Destructive Element, The, 89
Spider (PH's cat), 610
Spivy (Bertha Levine), 63, 68, 262
Spratling, William, 362

Spruce, Richard, 405
Stainer, John, 264
  Crucifixion, The, 264
Stalin, Josef, 7
  Foundations of Leninism, 7
Stauffer, Teddy, 348–51, 356
Steichen, Edward, 156
Stein, Gertrude, xxii, 84, 490
  Autobiography of Alice B. Toklas,
  The, 84
Steinbeck, John, 50, 126, 302, 576
  Forgotten Village, The, 306
  Grapes of Wrath, The, 50
Steinberg, Saul, 266
Stendhal, 78
  Le Rouge et le Noir, 78
Stern, James, 109, 227
Sterne, Hedda, 491
Stierham, Eleanor, 485
"Still Point of the Turning World, The"
  (PH story), 461, 493, 496
Strangers on a Train (PH novel), xiii,
  393, 428, 430, 461–62, 500, 530–
  31, 560, 563, 571–73, 578, 600,
  605, 612
Strauss, Johann, 380
Streicher, Henry, 152
Streng, Marion, 26
Sturtevant, Ethel, 3, 7, 10, 15, 38, 40,
  127, 133, 457, 501, 550, 587
Sullivan, Mary, xix–xx, 5, 26–27, 30,
  37–40, 42, 46, 52–56, 59–65, 80,
  83, 90, 94, 109, 118, 140, 152, 199,
  239, 312
Swedenborg, Emanuel, 185
Sylvia M., 102, 116, 118, 156, 240–41,
  475, 504, 566
Synge, John Millington, 157
  Riders to the Sea, 157

Takis, Nicholas, 316
Talented Mr. Ripley, The (PH novel),
  610–11
Tamayo, Rufino, 339, 349
Tamiris, Helen, 274
Tanguy, Yves, 203, 216, 246
Tantalus, see Price of Salt, The
Tchetilchew, Pavel, 150
Teller, Woolsey, 141
Tenysco, Alan, 545

Texas E., *see* Maggie ("Texas," "Tex")
E.
Thackeray, William Makepeace, 88,
544
History of Pendennis, The, 88
Themistocles, 253
"These Sad Pillars" (lost PH story), 201
Thomas, Mike, 52, 59
Thompson, Marjorie, 39, 87–88, 118,
125, 175, 223, 245, 290, 578
Thornbury, Ethel, 125–28, 150
"Three, The" (lost PH story), 328–29
Tietgens, Rolf, xx, 121, 185–86,
189–218, 222–23, 226, 231, 244,
264, 276–77, 280, 284–85, 300,
305–7, 310, 321, 331, 408, 413, 428,
431–34, 436, 441, 454, 456, 464,
466, 477, 481–82, 484, 502, 513,
541, 562
Tojo, Hideki, 418
Toklas, Alice B., xxii
Tolstoy, Leo, 584
Anna Karenina, 10
War and Peace, 44
Touche, *see* La Touche (also Latouche),
John
Toulouse-Lautrec, Henri de, 203
Trask, Katrina, 499
Trask, Spencer, 499
Tremor of Forgery, The (PH novel), 431
Triano, Antonio, 238
Truman, Harry S., 605
Tuvim, Judy, 2, 11, 19, 30, 39, 96–97,
142–45, 150, 267, 408

"Uncertain Treasure" (PH story), 231,
242–43, 251, 254,
328
Underhill, Evelyn, 212
Mysticism, 212

van Gogh, Vincent, 328, 414
van Paassen, Pierre, 58, 63
Days of Our Years, 58
Time Is Now, 63
Vidal, Gore, 560
Violet, 7
Virginia S. ("Va."), 8, 12, 19–20, 25,
27–30, 36, 38–44, 48, 61–64, 70, 81,
84, 115–16, 118, 143–45, 153, 168,
172–73, 229, 235, 253, 259, 292,
322, 327
Voltaire, 100

Wallace, David Foster, 500
Wallace, Henry A., 404
War and the Pettigrews (lost PH play),
44
Ward, Sheila, xxv
Waterbury, Natica, xxv, 311, 353, 355,
383–94, 397, 399–400, 403, 426,
428, 430–35, 437, 443, 446, 451,
473–74, 482, 495, 531, 545–47,
578
Waugh, Evelyn, 437
Brideshead Revisited, 437
Weber, Louis, 213, 215, 239
Weick (Miss), 181, 186, 193, 212, 221
Weidman, Charles, 147
Well Digger's Daughter, The, 467
Welles, Orson, 58
Citizen Kane, 58
Wells, H. G., 201
World Set Free, 201
Werfel, Franz, 194
Forty Days of Musa Dagh, The, 194
Werner, Tony, 343
"Where to, Madam?" (lost PH story),
505, 509, 515
White, Bob, 518, 523
White, T. H., 41
Sword in the Stone, The, 41
"White Monkey" (lost PH story), 96
Whitman, Walt, 124, 191, 203
Wilde, Oscar, 169
De Profundis, 169
Wilde, Percival, 32
Wilder, Thornton, 264
Skin of Our Teeth, The, 264, 303
Wilhelmina of the Netherlands, 183
Willey, Ruth, 98
Williams, Alice, 204–6, 210, 228, 300–
302, 503
Williams, Hope, 108
Williams, Tennessee
Streetcar Named Desire, A, 505
"Will the Lesbian's Soul Rest in Peace?"
(PH essay), xxiv–xxv
Wilson, Edmund, 94
Wound and the Bow, The, 94

Wolf, Marjorie, 58–59, 91, 116, 174, 213,
    228, 245, 249, 292, 321, 436, 468,
    606–7
Wolfe, Thomas, 18, 45, 56, 191, 211, 302,
    322, 525
Woolf, Virginia, 16, 67, 116, 183, 455
    Between the Acts, 116
Wordsworth, William, 584
Work of the Seventh Congress, 9
"World's Champion Ball-Bouncer, The"
    (PH story), 430, 456
Wright, Clifford, 518–19

Wynyard, Diana, 543
Wysbar, Frank, 200
    Fährmann Maria, 200

Yorck, Ruth, *see* Landshoff-Yorck, Ruth
Young, George Frederick, 305
    Medici, The, 305
Young, Marguerite, 513

Zavada, Margaret, 183
Zola, Émile, 79, 439
    Nana, 79